# THE BEGINNINGS OF CHRISTIANITY

## PART I
## THE ACTS OF THE APOSTLES, v. 5

EDITED BY

### F. J. FOAKES JACKSON, D.D.

AND

### KIRSOPP LAKE, D.D., D.Litt.

VOL. V

ADDITIONAL NOTES
TO THE COMMENTARY

EDITED BY

KIRSOPP LAKE, D.D., D.Litt.

AND

HENRY J. CADBURY, Ph.D.

BAKER BOOK HOUSE
Grand Rapids, Michigan

Reprinted 1966 by
Baker Book House Company

Reprinted under special arrangements with
Macmillan and Company, Ltd., London

Printed in the United States of America

# THE BEGINNINGS OF CHRISTIANITY

# THE BEGINNINGS
# OF CHRISTIANITY

## PART I
## THE ACTS OF THE APOSTLES

EDITED BY

### F. J. FOAKES JACKSON, D.D.

AND

### KIRSOPP LAKE, D.D., D.Litt.

VOLUME I.—PROLEGOMENA I.  THE JEWISH, GENTILE, AND CHRISTIAN BACKGROUNDS.

VOLUME II.—PROLEGOMENA II.  CRITICISM.

VOLUME III.—THE TEXT OF ACTS  By Professor J. H. ROPES.

VOLUME IV.—ENGLISH TRANSLATION AND COMMENTARY. By KIRSOPP LAKE, D.D., and HENRY J. CADBURY, Ph.D.

VOLUME V.—ADDITIONAL NOTES TO THE COMMENTARY. Edited by KIRSOPP LAKE, D.D., and HENRY J. CADBURY, Ph.D.

TO

FRANCIS CRAWFORD BURKITT

# PREFACE

MORE than twenty years have elapsed since Kirsopp Lake and I
agreed in a conversation in the University of Leiden that an
exhaustive study of the Acts of the Apostles was necessary in
order to prepare for a right understanding of the history of the
Christian Church. We had arrived at the conclusion that, despite
the noble labours of many generations of scholars, and the light
thrown on the book by antiquarians, the real problem of Acts
as an historical even more than a religious document had to
be faced. Impressed by the magnitude of the task, we resolved
to secure the aid of the most competent scholars we could
command. We were fortunate in securing the support of Messrs.
Macmillan and Co. as publishers, for whose generosity in producing these volumes without regard to anything but to the
excellence of the work we can never be sufficiently grateful.

Our undertaking began in Cambridge, where I was fortunate
enough to obtain the co-operation of Professor Burkitt, who
consented to preside at a Seminar, which was largely attended by
scholars of the most varied interests in the University, not only
theological, but historical, classical, mathematical, and Oriental.
Visitors were often present from Oxford, London, and different
parts of England ; and, as the minutes kept by me as Secretary
of the Seminar show, the United States and Canada were not
unrepresented. Lake paid frequent visits from Leiden, where he
held a professorial chair, to watch the progress of our deliberations. This preparatory work went on for a year or more, then
came the War ; and Lake and I, who had found spheres of work

in America, selected a body of coadjutors and began the task of compiling the first volume in Boston and New York.

The task before us had now become an international enterprise. In our group Great Britain, Holland, Canada, the United States and Germany co-operated. Jew and Gentile showed equal zeal in assisting us. To mention some of the names of the living friends who helped us might be invidious ; but in the course of twenty years it is inevitable that some should have already passed away. Among these we may mention one who never hesitated to place his vast fund of learning at our disposal, and spared no time nor pains in assistance and advice. To George Foot Moore, Professor in Harvard University, the Editors owe a debt which it is not possible to exaggerate, and the same may be said of Frederick Conybeare, Hon. Fellow of University College, Oxford. The other contributors to the first three volumes, who are now no longer with us, are C. W. Emmet, Fellow of the same University College, Oxford; Forbes Duckworth, Professor of Trinity College, Toronto, and Clifford H. Moore, Pope Professor of Latin in Harvard University, whose early deaths all who knew and appreciated them must deplore. Of those who attended the Seminar in Cambridge, two scholars, Israel Abrahams, the University Reader in Talmudic, and Arthur Charles Jennings of Jesus College, are no longer with us. Their advice and help whilst the scheme was in process of development was of the greatest value to the Editors.

To those who happily are still alive, I—and my colleague is in cordial sympathy with me—desire to express heartfelt gratitude, not only for the zeal and scholarship displayed in their contributions, but for their readiness to accept the suggestions necessary to reduce the whole work to a consistent whole.

The first and second volumes, which are introductory to the study of Acts, appeared respectively in 1920 and 1922. Volume I. provoked a certain amount of criticism, mainly on account of what appeared to some the detached attitude in which a book of Holy Scripture was approached in a thoroughly scientific spirit. Volume III., on the Text of Acts, was entrusted by the Editors to one man; and they were singularly fortunate in securing their friend James Hardy Ropes of Harvard University for the purpose. The Text of Acts, as every scholar knows, is one of the most interesting problems, not only in the New Testament, but in textual criticism generally, and it is not too much to say that, if this costly book can never appeal to the general public, no student of Greek MSS. can safely neglect it ; and that although it may be hereafter supplemented, it is not likely ever to be superseded. Volume III. appeared in 1926 and deservedly received the approval of the learned world.

There remained only the Commentary on Acts, the management of which Dr. Lake took entirely on his own shoulders, and he has, much to my satisfaction, received invaluable assistance from our mutual friend Dr. Henry Cadbury as co-editor. For this they were, in my judgement, admirably fitted; and it is a matter for sincere congratulation that they have brought their arduous task to a conclusion. Their two volumes mark the culmination of years of strenuous labour. Judged solely by the extent of the Commentary, and the variety of information contained therein, no book of the Bible has been subjected to so exhaustive a treatment in a single work ; and its Editors are worthy of the highest commendation for a splendid achievement I, as their friend and colleague, am delighted to add my congratulations.

F. J. FOAKES JACKSON

UNION THEOLOGICAL SEMINARY,
  NEW YORK,
   *September* 1932.

# CONTENTS

# ADDITIONAL NOTES

By KIRSOPP LAKE

THE difficulties in the Preface to Acts are a complex of literary, critical, *The Preface.* and textual problems which must be treated separately before being considered finally in relation to each other. Clearness therefore demands a summary before any detailed discussion.

The Preface certainly begins with a description of the contents of the 'first book'—the Gospel according to Luke—but as it stands at present it gives a very imperfect summary, and alludes to a period of forty days of which the Gospel gives no hint. Moreover, the text of the Preface has obviously suffered in transmission, and though some of the details remain obscure, in two or three of the efforts to improve it attempts can be recognized to deal with the difficulty of interpretation.

Whatever text and whatever interpretation be adopted the structure of the Preface offends against the canons of Greek writing. The μέν in vs. 1 is not balanced by a δέ-clause, nor by any adequate substitute for δέ, and there is no description of the subjects to be dealt with in the second book, as custom would have dictated and the opening of the Preface leads us to expect.

When these two problems have been discussed—they cannot be settled—the main question is the light, or possibly the darkness, which they throw on the composition of the whole book.

## 1. *The Text of the Preface and its Relation to the Gospel*

The Preface obviously is intended to give a description of the *The text.* first book. If ἤρξατο be not wholly otiose the first verse of Acts means 'I wrote the first book concerning all which Jesus did and taught from the beginning,' which is a fair description of the beginning of the Gospel, even though John the Baptist is omitted ; similarly the second verse describes the end of the Gospel 'until the day when, etc.' The problem is how much is covered by the 'etc.' and how far it really corresponds to the Gospel, and these questions are greatly complicated by doubt as to the original text.

The text of the Preface, according to B, followed by most editors, is *The neutral text.*

τὸν μὲν πρῶτον λόγον ἐποιησάμην περὶ πάντων, ὦ Θεόφιλε, ὧν ἤρξατο Ἰησοῦς ποιεῖν τε καὶ διδάσκειν ἄχρι ἧς ἡμέρας ἐντειλάμενος τοῖς

ἀποστόλοις διὰ πνεύματος ἁγίου οὓς ἐξελέξατο ἀνελήμφθη· οἷς καὶ
παρέστησεν ἑαυτὸν ζῶντα μετὰ τὸ παθεῖν αὐτὸν ἐν πολλοῖς τεκμηρίοις,
δι' ἡμερῶν μ' ὀπτανόμενος αὐτοῖς καὶ λέγων τὰ περὶ τῆς βασιλείας τοῦ
θεοῦ. καὶ συναλιζόμενος παρήγγειλεν αὐτοῖς ἀπὸ Ἱεροσολύμων μὴ
χωρίζεσθαι, ἀλλὰ περιμένειν τὴν ἐπαγγελίαν τοῦ πατρὸς ἣν ἠκούσατέ
μου· ὅτι Ἰωάννης μὲν ἐβάπτισεν ὕδατι, ὑμεῖς δὲ ἐν πνεύματι βαπτι-
σθήσεσθε ἁγίῳ οὐ μετὰ πολλὰς ταύτας ἡμέρας. The Western text,
partly reconstructed from the Latin, seems to have been τὸν μὲν πρῶτον
λόγον ἐποιησάμην περὶ πάντων, ὦ Θεόφιλε, ὧν ἤρξατο Ἰησοῦς ποιεῖν τε
καὶ διδάσκειν ἐν ἡμέρᾳ ᾗ [1] τοὺς ἀποστόλους ἐξελέξατο διὰ πνεύματος
ἁγίου καὶ ἐκέλευσε κηρύσσειν τὸ εὐαγγέλιον, οἷς καὶ παρέστησε κτλ.
. . . καὶ ὡς συναλιζόμενος μετ' αὐτῶν παρήγγειλεν κτλ. Ropes (see
Vol. III. pp. 2 and 256 ff.) accepts the major variants of the Western text
as representing the original.

The Western text.

The original text.

On such a complicated question disagreement is not unnatural
among even the closest allies, and this is one of relatively few places in
which I differ from Ropes, though the difference is small and unimportant for the theory of the history of the text. It has, however, a
more serious bearing on the exegesis of the passage. I cannot think
that ἐν ᾗ ἡμέρᾳ for ἄχρι ἧς ἡμέρας or the omission of οὓς after
ἀποστόλοις is original. ἐξελέξατο can, it seems to me, refer only to
Luke vi. 13 ff., and the Gospel neither began nor ended at that point.
Therefore οὓς must be retained before ἐξελέξατο. Similarly, in a
preface to the second book the important point to be noticed is that
which was reached at the end of the first, so that ἄχρι is essential to the
sense. On the other hand, Ropes is surely right in omitting from his
reconstruction of the original text the Neutral interpolation ἀνελήμφθη,
and in treating the Western καὶ ἐκέλευσε κηρύσσειν τὸ εὐαγγέλιον
as merely a paraphrase of ἐντειλάμενος. If so, the main verb in the sentence beginning ἄχρι ἧς ἡμέρας is παρήγγειλε in vs. 4. That this makes
a very bad sentence cannot be denied, but in one important point it is
apparently confirmed by Eusebius, Supplementa Quaestionum ad Marinum
xi. (Migne, P.G. xxii. col. 1005) ἔνθεν . . . ἐπιτηρεῖ λέγων ὡς ἄρα δι'
ἡμερῶν τεσσαράκοντα, ὀπτανόμενος αὐτοῖς καὶ συναυλιζόμενος, τὰ περὶ
τῆς βασιλείας τοῦ θεοῦ παρεδίδου μαθήματα, παρήνει τε ὁρμᾶν εἰς τὴν
Ἱερουσαλήμ, κἀκεῖ κηρύττειν Ἰουδαίοις πρώτοις τὸν λόγον μηδὲ πρότερον
ἀναχωρεῖν τῆς πόλεως κτλ. This certainly seems to prove that Eusebius
read ὀπτανόμενος and συναυλιζόμενος as linked together. But if so he
must have treated παρέστησε as the main verb to these participles, and
παρήγγειλε in vs. 4 as the main verb of ἐντειλάμενος, though of course
an element of doubt is brought in by the way in which he is paraphrasing.
His text may have run thus :

Eusebius.

Τὸν μὲν πρῶτον λόγον ἐποιησάμην περὶ πάντων, ὦ Θεόφιλε, ὧν
ἤρξατο Ἰησοῦς ποιεῖν τε καὶ διδάσκειν ἄχρι ἧς ἡμέρας, ἐντειλάμενος τοῖς
ἀποστόλοις, διὰ πνεύματος ἁγίου οὓς ἐξελέξατο, (οἷς καὶ παρέστησεν

---

[1] This, however, is not quite certain ; the evidence is only Latin, and there
is a bare possibility that the translator regarded ἄχρι as equivalent to 'in.'
Cf. xxvii. 33.

ἑαυτὸν ζῶντα μετὰ τὸ παθεῖν αὐτὸν ἐν πολλοῖς τεκμηρίοις, δι᾽ ἡμερῶν
τεσσεράκοντα ὀπτανόμενος αὐτοῖς καὶ λέγων τὰ περὶ τῆς βασιλείας τοῦ
θεοῦ καὶ συναυλιζόμενος αὐτοῖς), παρήγγειλεν ἀπὸ Ἱεροσολύμων μὴ
χωρίζεσθαι, κτλ.

No one who has read much of Eusebius will think that he would
have found this construction too complicated, as it is simplicity itself
compared to many passages in his own writings. It is hard to think
that it can be the finally revised text of any Greek writer, but on
objective grounds it seems to me to be the earliest form, which explains
the others. With it the summary goes down to vs. 5, but is obscure.
It was interpreted and emended in two ways :

(i.) The makers of the Neutral text, influenced by the Neutral text Early emendations.
of Luke xxiv. 51, or perhaps more probably by the interpretation
(probably correct) of διέστη as meaning ἀνεφέρετο, inserted ἀνελήμφθη in
vs. 2. They probably intended to make the description of the first book
end with vs. 2, thus avoiding the difficulty that the 'first book' says
nothing about the forty days, though it is still just possible to treat the
summary as extending to vs. 5.

(ii.) The Western text in the form found in Africa wished to make it
clear that the summary extended to vs. 5, but covered only the end of
the 'first book,' and therefore inserted a *quomodo* (= ὡς ?) before *con-
versatus est* (= συναλιζόμενος). But it also straightened out the obscurity
of the construction by omitting οὕς, paraphrasing ἐντειλάμενος into *et
praecepit praedicare evangelium*, and changing ἄχρι into *in die quo*. Thus
this commentator interpreted ἐντειλάμενος ἐξελέξατο as an allusion to
Luke xxiv. 47 f., a view which would be tolerable only if ἐποιησάμην
could mean *I ended.*

The other variants—and they are many—seem to be conflations of
these interpretations and texts, in which sometimes text and sometimes
interpretation takes the lead.

If the text suggested be right, the meaning is that the 'first book The original meaning.
described all that Jesus did and taught from the beginning up to the
day when he told the disciples not to leave Jerusalem. The narrative
begins again in vs. 6 with οἱ μὲν οὖν . . ., which is the real beginning
of the second book. This presents two difficulties : (*a*) It implies
that the 'forty days' is mentioned in the 'first book.' This difficulty
was probably perceived by the makers of the Neutral text, and influenced
the emendation which they made. There seems to be no solution to
this problem, for even if the Neutral text be right, the historical, even if
not the literary, difficulty remains. (*b*) It does not really cover the end
of the Gospel as we have it now. The question, however, may well be
raised whether the first book ended in quite the same way as the present
text of the Gospel. It is quite possible that when the first book was
separated from the second, and converted by Marcion into 'the Gospel,'
or by Catholics into 'the Gospel according to Luke,' it was felt necessary
to add a few words, bringing it to a more suitable end. Therefore Luke
xxiv. 50-53, summarizing Acts i. 6 ff., was added. It is true that there
is nothing un-Lucan in the language of Luke xxiv. 50-53, but it is not

hard to write in any given style for a few lines, and the suggestion made would bring the first book into closer though not complete accord with the author's statement of its contents.

## 2. *The Absence of a δέ-Clause*

*μέν solitarium.* The absence of a δέ-clause describing the contents of the second book has often been noted. But this in itself is not really the most serious point ; μέν solitarium is not unknown in Greek, and among those unaccustomed to literary composition it would obviously be as common an idiom in Greek as 'first' without a 'secondly' is in English. Examples in Acts of μέν solitarium can be found in (*a*) Acts iii. 13, for the δέ in vss. 14 and 15 are not correlatives to the μέν in vs. 13, the real answer to it coming only in vs. 18 ; (*b*) in iii. 20 f. καὶ ἀποστείλῃ τὸν προκεχειρισμένον ὑμῖν Χριστὸν Ἰησοῦν, ὃν δεῖ οὐρανὸν μὲν δέξασθαι ἄχρι χρόνων ἀποκαταστάσεως κτλ., and (*c*) in xxvii. 21. With these may be compared Rom. iii. 2 and 1 Thess. ii. 18. Thus the mere idiom of μέν solitarium does not necessarily prove that a δέ-clause has been omitted, or even that it was ever contemplated by the author. The important point is that the general usage of prefaces demands that after a μέν-clause giving the contents of the previous book there should be a δέ-clause giving a summary of what the second book is intended to contain. And this is lacking. Nevertheless the fact that this defect is not remedied in any of the ancient revisions of the text suggests that early Christian writers were not sensitive to it.

## 3. *The Composition of Acts*

*Norden and Loisy.* These two problems provide the starting-point of the school of commentators who suggest that an original work by Luke has been greatly mutilated and interpolated by a later editor. A very elaborate and thorough exposition of this school of thought is to be found in Norden's *Agnostos Theos*,[1] but it has been developed, and in some points improved, by A. Loisy in his *Les Actes des Apôtres*. The difficulty of giving a sympathetic hearing to their case is that they are obliged to attempt a reconstruction of a mutilated text, and in criticizing the details of the reconstruction we lose sight of the solid reasons for thinking that the text is mutilated. Norden thinks that a later editor cut out the original δέ-clause because Luke claimed to have been an eye-witness. Loisy thinks that the original document emphasized the importance of Paul, and spoke of him in the Preface in the δέ-clause which described the contents of the second book ; but the editor wished to emphasize the apostles rather than Paul, cut out the δέ-clause altogether, and added some rather clumsily constructed phrases about the appearances of Jesus· to the apostles.

*Loisy.* Of these two the theory of Loisy seems to me preferable. But I

---

[1] Earlier advocates of this view are Hilgenfeld, and especially A. Gercke (*Hermes* xxix. (1894) pp. 373 ff.).

cannot accept it, for it seems to me very improbable that a Greek editor would have allowed the Preface to go forth in its edited form without a δέ-clause if as a matter of fact it had originally had one. The absence of a δέ-clause is offensive to anyone who knows classical Greek. If the Preface ever had a δέ-clause, no one would have merely cut it out. Indeed, if the original text was at all the same as it is now, to add a δέ-clause is the first thing which would be expected of an editor. Therefore I incline to believe that the Preface—apart from textual variation—is preserved in its original form, and that it never had a δέ-clause. I should prefer the theory that the finishing touches (certainly including the description of the second book) were never given to Acts, rather than accept the view of large changes introduced by a later editor.

It requires so few words to state this opinion, and there is really so little evidence, that it is necessary to stress the extreme importance of the point. There is no doubt that the absence of a δέ-clause is very strange. It must be due to the original bad style of the author, or to deliberate excision. If it has actually been cut out, or, in other words, if we can really be sure that the μέν in verse 1 proves that there was once a δέ-clause, there is really a strong presumption in favour of Loisy's general theory that in Acts we must distinguish the original work of the author from that of an interpolating and mutilating editor. The difference between this theory and that adopted in Vol. II. pp. 130 ff. is important, but rather more subtle than appears at first.

According to the theory which I adopted in Vol. II. Acts is built up The theory of sources. out of earlier documents, Greek or Aramaic, fully worked over by the editor of Acts and moulded into his own reconstruction of the history of the Church. We can sometimes see that his sources told a rather different story, but there is very little question as to what he wished to say himself. The story as told is clear and intelligible ; our only reason for ever doubting it is that for Luke's first volume his main source—the Gospel of Mark—shows that he edited it so freely that the meaning was sometimes changed, and for his second volume the Pauline epistles indicate that the real course of events considerably differed from his account. The suggestion made is that a study of Luke's editorial methods shows that he was capable of modifying his sources, and that the Pauline epistles prove that his version of events is not wholly accurate. If, therefore, there are difficulties or inconsistencies in Acts in passages where neither Mark nor Paul supplies a ' control,' it is not irrational to ask if these may not be due to Luke's treatment of his source.

Loisy, on the other hand, thinks that Acts was once a much more consistent and better written book than it is now. Much of the text as it stands is interpolated, and the editor who made these changes was on important points at variance with the original author.

The difficulty of comparing and choosing between these theories is that again and again Loisy and I are in real agreement as to the actual facts. There is a fundamental difference between us as to the literary history of Acts but only, as it were, accidental differences as to the nature and history of the early Church. Moreover, if my suspicion be well founded that Acts was never quite finished, the difference between us as to the literary history resolves itself into the distinction between a book which has inequalities because it has been tampered with, and one which has inequalities because it has not been adequately revised.

The meaning of the author of Acts.

The argument which seems to me to weigh the balance down against Loisy is that apart from the Preface, which is the strongest argument in his favour, there seems so clear a line of development running through the earlier chapters that it is hard to ascribe any of them to an interpolator. As I read Acts the meaning of the author in chapters i.-v. is quite clear. The disciples, after witnessing the Ascension, were gathered together in Jerusalem under the leadership of the Twelve, of whom Peter was the chief. They completed the number of the Apostolic college by electing Matthias, and shortly after received the gift of the Holy Spirit. This enabled them to speak with tongues and prophesy, and many converts were added to their number. A little later Peter and John used the name of Jesus to perform a miracle of healing at the Beautiful gate of the Temple, and were summoned before the Sanhedrin on this charge, but dismissed with an injunction not to use the Name. They, however, refused to obey, and continued their work. Meanwhile the brethren, living in harmony, had solved the problem of poverty by the sale and distribution of property. Ananias and Sapphira, who tried to retain more than they admitted, were miraculously killed by Peter, and the community continued a career of miraculous healing, chiefly by Peter, whose very shadow was efficacious. Once more the priests intervened, and once more also the conclusive evidence in favour of the apostles led to their dismissal.

Almost all of this long narrative, except the miracle of healing at the Beautiful gate of the Temple, is regarded by Loisy as unhistorical, and due to the interpolator. To me it seems to contain nothing which contradicts any passage which can be held to reveal the point of view of the author, though in some places it seems not improbable that he has changed the meaning of his source. It gives an account of the Christians in Jerusalem which, judged by the standard of the time when it was written, is intelligible and probable. I partly agree with Loisy that some of it may be unhistorical, but I cannot see that it would have seemed so to anyone in the first century. It might just as well be the work of Luke as of a later editor.

Loisy's evidence.

The details of infelicity or inconsistency to which Loisy calls attention seem to fall into three classes : (i.) intrinsically improbable statements ; (ii.) inconsistencies, mostly of a minor order, with previous statements; (iii.) infelicities in language. I cannot see that any of these really justify Loisy.

Historical improbability is no evidence for or against either theory. Whatever we may ourselves think about the matter, there is nothing in these chapters which would have appeared improbable to an early Christian. The most serious point is not the miraculous Ascension, or the Pentecostal glossolalia, but the importance attached to the Twelve and to Peter. If it be really true, as Loisy thinks, that this is a late fiction, it would strengthen his case considerably. I am, however, inclined to think that, on the contrary, the 'Twelve' and Peter's early supremacy in Jerusalem are historically true (see Additional Note 6).

Inconsistencies of a minor order, though worth noting, prove nothing for or against either theory. No one ever can write quite consistently, or tell a story quite accurately. It is important to notice these discrepancies, and to decide if possible (which is but rarely) on which side the truth lies, but they scarcely ever prove anything as to authorship or composition, though if on other grounds a theory of composition be accepted, it may be a valuable point in its favour that it explains them. In the case of Acts, most of them seem to me to be accidental, and, if they mean anything, indicate that the book was not finally revised; the remainder is as explicable on a theory of sources as on Loisy's.

Infelicities of language point in the same direction. Many of them suggest mere lack of revision. They throw no light on the composition of the book except to suggest the possibility of translation from Aramaic sources, and here again the difficulty of distinguishing between a translation from a Semitic language, Semitic Greek, and unrevised translation-Greek seems to me insuperable. There is a fair, hardly a strong, case for the use of Aramaic sources, but it is not proved, is scarcely provable, and can be as easily adapted to a theory of sources as to Loisy's theory.

NOTE II. THE COMMAND NOT TO LEAVE JERUSALEM
AND THE 'GALILEAN TRADITION'

By KIRSOPP LAKE

The following note is essentially an *Auseinandersetzung* of differences and agreement with Professors Johannes Weiss and F. C. Burkitt, both of whom on a point of vital importance for the history of the early Church have adopted conclusions which differ from the view generally accepted and expressed in Vol. I. pp. 302 ff.

It has become almost a commonplace of writers on the narrative of the Gospels that there are two traditions as to the appearances of Jesus after the Resurrection—one placing them in Galilee, the other in Jerusalem. *The two traditions of the Resurrection.*

(i.) *The Galilean Tradition.*—According to Mark xiv. 27 f., after the end of the Last Supper Jesus said, "All ye shall be made to stumble, *The Galilean tradition.*

because it is written, I will smite the shepherd and the sheep shall be scattered, but when I have been raised up, I will go before you (προάξω ὑμᾶς) into Galilee." And according to Mark xvi. 7 the 'young man' at the tomb, with an apparent allusion to this saying, said to the women, "Go, tell his disciples and Peter that he goes before you (προάγει ὑμᾶς) into Galilee: there ye shall see him, as he told you."

The end of the gospel is missing, but the obvious suggestion of these verses is that Mark was leading up to an appearance of the risen Jesus in Galilee. More or less corrupted forms of such a tradition are to be found in Matt. xxviii. 16-20, in John xxi., and in the gospel of Peter.[1] They are, relatively speaking, unimportant; the theory of a 'Galilean tradition' really stands or falls with the interpretation of Mark xiv. 28 and xvi. 7. On this point Burkitt, Weiss and I are in complete agreement. Thus all that can be claimed is that Mark indicates that the risen Jesus was first seen in Galilee.

The Jerusalem tradition.

(ii.) *The Jerusalem Tradition.*—This is found in Luke xxiv. and John xx. in cognate but largely different forms. In each gospel the writer is obviously anxious to prove that the risen Lord was risen as a being of flesh, and not as a spirit, in apparent contradiction to the Pauline doctrine that there is no resurrection of the flesh but only of a 'spiritual body' (1 Cor. xv. 44), and possibly in opposition to early docetic teaching.

The general tendency of most writers for many years has been to accept the Galilean tradition, and to give two reasons for doing so. (*a*) Mark is the oldest and best source. (*b*) Seeing that the early Church was in Jerusalem, not in Galilee, it is easier to suppose that the Jerusalem tradition was the modification of the historical tradition of a previous generation by the ecclesiastical sentiment of the next. Indeed, the most convincing argument for the Galilean tradition has always been summed up in the question, 'If it be not true, why was it ever invented?'

Two writers, however—F. C. Burkitt and J. Weiss—in different ways have pointedly criticized this view, and though perhaps neither has quite done justice to the strength of the position which upholds the Galilean tradition, they have certainly shaken the confidence which I formerly felt. Their views are to be found in J. Weiss's *Urchristentum*, 1914, pp. 10 ff., and in F. C. Burkitt's *Christian Beginnings*, 1924, pp. 76 ff.

[1] For the purposes of this note it is unnecessary to discuss fully the details of the problem presented by the relation of these passages to the Marcan tradition; but it is perhaps not out of place to say that Matt. xxviii. 16-20 does not seem to me to be based on anything more than the incomplete or mutilated Mark which we possess. Matthew probably did not have more than we do, and Matt. xxviii. 16 ff. is comparable to Mark xvi. 9-20—the 'longer conclusion'—or to the variant found in LΨ *k*—the 'shorter conclusion'—rather than to the 'lost conclusion.' John xxi. may be a representative of the Galilean tradition, and the Gospel of Peter may quite conceivably—though not certainly—be based on the lost conclusion (see further my *Historical Evidence for the Resurrection of Jesus Christ*, pp. 161 ff.).

J. Weiss.

(i.) *Johannes Weiss.*—Johannes Weiss objects to the view that the disciples scattered and fled to Galilee immediately after the arrest of Jesus on the ground of a consideration of probabilities and the exact interpretation of special points.

The general background of the ordinary presentation of the Galilean theory is that the crucifixion was so great a shock to the disciples, who had expected the immediate coming of the Kingdom of God, that they momentarily lost all faith and fled. Why should they have done so ? asks Weiss. Jesus had foretold his death, and had warned his disciples that they would be persecuted. Why should they lose all faith, even momentarily, because their Master's words were fulfilled ? That they fled from the Garden at Gethsemane was natural, but not that they should go back at once to Galilee. Even if some of the details in the prophecy of persecution and death may be fairly taken as *post eventum* amplifications, the general fact —so Weiss argues—that these prophecies were made cannot be doubted.

Moreover, that the disciples actually did not leave Jerusalem is shown by Mark itself, for xvi. 7—" Go, tell his disciples and Peter that he goes before them into Galilee "—implies that the disciples were somewhere close at hand, where the message could be delivered—not in Galilee, and not in hopeless flight.

Mark xiv. 28.

Turning to the interpretation of Mark xiv. 28 Weiss argues that it does not mean that the disciples will leave Jerusalem, or take to final flight, but merely that they will leave Jesus at Gethsemane. This, he says, is the meaning which Matthew—the earliest commentary on Mark—attached to the phrase, as is shown by the addition ' *This night* ' [1] to the Marcan ' you shall all be offended.' Moreover he thinks that προάγειν ought to mean ' lead,' not ' precede,' and on this assumption builds up a new theory of the history of tradition on this point.

Jesus, he thinks, did actually foretell his rejection by the Jews at Jerusalem, and even his death at their hands. But he believed that his suffering would be the immediate preliminary to the coming of the Kingdom, after which he would lead back his followers in triumph to their own home—to Galilee. But the Kingdom did not come, so that the saying of Jesus remained an unfulfilled prediction. In the Lucan tradition it was ignored or changed to mean something else ; in Mark the ' Galilean episode ' was invented to account for it.

Mark's credibility.

The obvious objection to this theory is that it is so destructive of the whole critical edifice which Weiss himself did so much to build up on the basis of a belief in the trustworthiness of Mark. Few books ever did more than his *Die Predigt Jesu vom Reiche Gottes* (1892) to establish confidence in the accuracy of the Marcan presentation of the eschatological teaching of Jesus. Before his time the popular view was that the eschatological sections of the gospels could be discounted as the erroneous interpretation—if not interpolation—of Jewish disciples. The *Predigt Jesu* seemed to end this view. But if on so important a question as the appearance of Jesus to the disciples in Galilee the Marcan tradition is to be put aside, and " so gilt

[1] ' This night ' is not in the oldest authorities for Mark, though it is added in the later MSS. by harmonization with Matthew.

uns also die ' galiläische Überlieferung ' als ein Phantasieprodukt," what becomes of all our confidence in Mark ?

Nevertheless Johannes Weiss's criticism inevitably suggests a question which is probably insoluble but cannot be overlooked in any serious discussion either of the teaching of Jesus or of the beliefs of the early Church. Did Jesus foretell his resurrection or did he speak only of the coming of the Son of Man ? And if so, did he identify himself with that Son of Man ?

There can be no doubt that the gospel of Mark does in general represent Jesus as foretelling his death and resurrection, but few would deny the probability that the actual wording of this repeated prophecy (Mark viii. 31, ix. 31, x. 33 f.) is due to the influence of a knowledge of the facts as they actually happened. On the other hand, in the teaching of Jesus as represented by Q,[1] so far as we can trust critical judgement as to the contents of Q, there is probably nothing about the death and resurrection of Jesus. There is, however, a great deal about the coming of the Son of Man.

What is the meaning of this curious contrast ? I am inclined to think that Mark—as it says itself—represents the gospel about Jesus, which is surely the correct translation of εὐαγγέλιον Ἰησοῦ Χριστοῦ, and that Q, if we could reconstruct it, would prove to be based on reminiscences of the teaching of Jesus in Galilee, and probably does not go back to the circle of the Twelve. Both Matthew and Luke [2] are to some extent

[1] I use Q as a generally recognized symbol for the source or sources underlying matter common to Matthew and Luke but not derived from Mark.

Three cautions seem to me eminently necessary when this source is being discussed. (i.) There is no justification for assuming that Q is or is not a single source. (ii.) There is even less justification for thinking that it did not contain matter found in only one gospel, or that it contained everything found in Matthew and Luke, but not in Mark. (iii.) Least of all is there any justification for the belief that we can reconstruct it with any degree of verbal accuracy. The phrases about which we desire to know most, and need the greatest accuracy, are precisely those which were most likely to be emended either by Matthew or by Luke or by both. The inaccuracy attaching to any reconstruction of Q can be seen by considering how inaccurate would be our treatment of the relations between Matthew and Luke if Mark had not been preserved.

Still, giving full weight to these three cautions, it seems to me that three positive propositions may be tentatively put forward. (i.) Q was a Greek document, or, if Q was several documents, at least one was in Greek. The close similarity between the language of Matthew and Luke cannot otherwise be explained, unless we assume that Luke used Matthew, and though this theory is sometimes held, it seems to me rather improbable. (ii.) It contained, in comparison with Mark, a great deal about the teaching of Jesus, and very little narrative about his acts. (iii.) It did not contain any account of what happened to Jesus outside of Galilee. It did not relate his death or resurrection in Jerusalem, and it said nothing about his journey to Phoenicia. This conclusion would be profoundly modified if the Lucan account of the Passion could be attributed to Q, but this seems to me quite improbable.

[2] I cannot see any reason for thinking that Mark was influenced by Q.

conflations of these traditions, but Q in its absorbed form remains as a witness that the teaching of Jesus was ethical and eschatological rather than personal or Messianic. He announced the coming of the End and the beginning of the World to come, rather than prophesied his death and resurrection.

It is of course true that this teaching of Jesus did not ultimately survive except in connexion with the teaching about Jesus, but in the first century there must have been, at least in Galilee, a few who remembered it. Possibly the fact that they did so is the reason why there was never any Christian church in Galilee in the first century, for it must be remembered that whatever may be the case to-day, the Christianity which conquered the world was the teaching about Jesus, and that according to Acts the apostles in their missionary speeches had very little to say as to the teaching of Jesus. Nevertheless Q and the singular episode of Apollos, who seems to have known the teaching of Jesus as to the ' Way of the Lord,' but not to have understood that Jesus was the Messiah (see note on Acts xviii. 24-28), warn us that in the day of the apostles there may have been a few who adhered to the teaching of Jesus and prepared themselves for the coming of the New Age in ignorance of, or to the exclusion of, the message of the apostles as to the death and resurrection of Jesus.

Moreover, it is clear, even from Mark, that Jesus made no general and public prophecy of his death and resurrection ; but he did speak of the Coming of the Son of Man—who did not come. The apostles, on the other hand, naturally tended to emphasize the resurrection which—as they claimed—actually had taken place, and the prophecy of the Parousia became confused with the prophecy of the Resurrection, just as generally the Christian message that ' the Lord is risen' overshadowed, though it never wholly eclipsed, Jesus' announcement that 'the Kingdom of God is at hand.'

Similarly, it is extremely unlikely that the Galileans ever thought that Jesus himself was the ' Son of Man,' [1] but undoubtedly the contention that he was so formed a central part of Apostolic preaching.

The preceding paragraphs are intended to suggest problems, not to solve them, but they serve to show that there is some difficulty in taking the Marcan prophecies of the resurrection as a firm basis for the reconstruction of history.

Finally, the question may be asked whether Johannes Weiss was quite justified in so certainly regarding Mark xiv. 28 as the origin of xvi. 7. Could it not have been the other way ?   It is unquestionably true that vs. 28 does not fit very well into the context in which it is found, and many of the more radical critics of the gospels have regarded it as an editorial addition based entirely on the double belief that Jesus had been raised from the dead and had told his disciples that he would be. Professor Burkitt writes to me as follows :

" I am not really satisfied about Mark xiv. 28. It is absent from the

Mark xiv. 28 and xvi. 7.

---

[1] I doubt whether he did so himself (see Vol. I. pp. 377 ff.), but this problem is very obscure, and there are several possible views, though to discuss them is not germane to the present topic.

very ancient Fayyum Fragment in the Rainer Papyri.[1] This *may* mean one of two things : (*a*) the saying not genuine, but inserted later in view of Mark xvi. 7, or belief in the Galilean tradition generally ; or (*b*) the saying genuine, but the writer of the document saw its difficulty and dropped it. " I sometimes think that (*b*) is the truth. There are things in Mark's Passion-story that are really reminiscent, and only reminiscent. The Cry from the Cross—it has been *assimilated* to Ps. xxii. 1—must ultimately be reminiscent. The young man who left his blanket in the hands of the police is another reminiscence, nothing more. Gethsemane itself is only ' edifying ' to those who already believe : it was not put down in black and white to produce adherents to Christianity. It also is reminiscence. Did Jesus say ' Afterwards, I will go back first to Galilee, away from this Jerusalem ' ? Remember this is just before Gethsemane : He is not quite certain that He can stand the ordeal."

F. C. Bur-
kitt.

(ii.) *Professor F. C. Burkitt.*—Professor Burkitt's position is more subtle, and more acceptable. It is not open to the same criticism as the theory of Johannes Weiss. His chief argument—and its strength has certainly been overlooked by those of us who support the Galilean tradition —is that if the Risen Lord had been seen in Galilee the Church would have had its centre in Galilee, not in Jerusalem. It must be conceded that this might certainly have been expected ; but is it not at least a partial answer

[1] See *Papyrus Erzherzog Rainer*, vol. i. pp. 53 ff. The text of the fragment, which is generally ascribed to the third century, according to G. Bickell's transcription, is as follows :

    . . . ΦΑΓΕΙΝΩΣΕΞΗΓΟΝΠΑ
    . . . ΤΗΝΥΚΤΙΣΚΑΝΔΑΛΙΣ
    . . . ΤΟΓΡΑΦΕΝΠΑΤΑΞΩΤΟΝ
    . . . ΠΡΟΒΑΤΑΔΙΑΣΚΟΡΠΙΣΘΗΣ
    . . . ΥΠΕΤΚΑΙΕΙΠΑΝΤΕΣΟ
    . . . ΟΑΛΕΚΤΡΥΩΝΔΙΣΚΟΚ
        . . . ΠΑΡΝ

This he expands as follows :

    . . . [μετὰ δὲ τὸ] φαγεῖν, ὡς ἐξῆγον· πά[ντες ἐν ταύτῃ] τῇ νυκτὶ σκανδαλισ-
    [θήσεσθε κατὰ] τὸ γραφέν· πατάξω τὸν [ποιμένα καὶ τὰ] πρόβατα διασκορπισ-
    [θήσονται· εἰπόντος το]ῦ Πέτ(ρου)· καὶ εἰ πάντες, ο[ὐκ ἐγώ· προσθείς·] ὁ
    ἀλεκτρυὼν δὶς κοκ[κύξει καὶ σὺ πρῶτον τρὶς ἀ]παρν[ήσῃ με].

His reconstruction of the missing words is in the main doubtless correct in general, but some doubt has been expressed about φαγεῖν and ἐξηγον (see especially Wessely in the *Patrologia Orientalis*, iv. pp. 174 ff.). It is dangerous to judge from photographs, but to my own eyes it seems possible that ἐξῆγον might be read ἐξῆλθον, and the reconstruction—θησονται ειποντος το—seems too long. Moreover, in the photograph I cannot read φαγεῖν but seem to see -αγεν. It would be easy to suggest ἐξήγαγεν. It seems to me doubtful whether the letter before πετ- is a υ, and if it were possible to read ἔφη ὁ πέτρος I should prefer it ; in any case I cannot feel happy about πετ meaning Peter. Would it be easy to find examples in Greek MSS. of πετ being used for πέτρου ?

that the eschatological expectation (which the appearance of the Risen Lord surely confirmed) may have led the disciples back to Jerusalem ?

He also argues that, after all, we do not know that Mark really con- Peter's experience
tained the 'Galilean tradition.' "But what," he says on pp. 86 f. of *Christian Beginnings*, "if Peter saw the Lord on the way, before he had got far from the Holy City ?  Would it not make him retrace his steps ? Would he not take it first of all, in whatever form the vision may have been, as a sign that he ought not to leave Jerusalem ?  Where the Lord was seen, there He was, or somewhere near.  This, and not the old haunts, was the holy ground, Jerusalem, not Galilee.  If the experience of Peter— and it was Peter's experience, no doubt, that was decisive—took place at Jerusalem, then we understand why Peter is found at Jerusalem as soon as we hear of him again.  Otherwise it remains a riddle of which no reasonable explanation has ever been given.

"For these reasons I think the Lucan view, that Peter and the little nucleus of believers never got more than a day's journey from Jerusalem between the Crucifixion of Jesus and the Feast of Pentecost, is psychologically more probable than that which seems to be indicated in Mark and is actually set forth in Matthew, viz. that Peter and his companions did return to Galilee and there became convinced that their Lord had risen from the dead.

"I have said ' seems to be indicated in Mark,' for after all it is not quite certain what Mark went on to narrate.  It must continually be remembered that we have not only to deal with and explain the extant words of the Gospel, but also the fact of Peter's return to Jerusalem.  I do not wish to suggest that Peter did not intend to set out for Galilee ; very likely he did start on his way.  What I suggest is that he did not get very far.  If he saw his Lord alive again while he was still in the neighbourhood of the city it would not only make him stay, abandoning his projected journey, but he would regard it as a kindly and gracious change of purpose.  He who changed His settled and expressed practice for the sake of the Syrophenician woman might do so for Peter.

"I cannot help sometimes wondering whether the well-known story of *Domine quo vadis ?* where St. Peter flying from Rome meets Christ on the Appian Way and consequently turns back, may not have some historical foundation in what occurred on the first Easter Day near Jerusalem."

This is fascinatingly stated, and makes me waver in my opinion, though I do not see any loophole of escape from the argument that Mark's words imply the expectation of appearances in Galilee, not an appearance near Jerusalem before Galilee was reached.  If we can put this aside it is certainly much easier to accept the view that though the disciples believed that they were to go to Galilee, they actually saw Jesus before they went— or at least before they arrived—and that he seemed to them to reverse his instructions and to tell them to remain in Jerusalem.  Still, can we put it aside ?

One point, moreover, seems to me to be exaggerated by Professor Burkitt. The return to Jerusalem.
On pp. 85 f. of *Christian Beginnings* he says : "If we are to invent visions in Galilee to explain to ourselves the course of events we cannot rest with

mere visions, not even with visions accompanied by assurances, whether in the form of spoken words or intuitions, that the Lord Jesus was alive, and was or would be exalted soon to be with His Father in Heaven. We have to go on to invent a definite message to return to Jerusalem, something contrary to intuition, contrary to what was natural if Jesus had been seen in Galilee. It is not a question of believing an old tradition, but of inventing a new one, for the message to return is not included in the tradition. The documents that tell us of appearances in Galilee say nothing about returning to Jerusalem."

This seems scarcely fair. He has himself to 'invent' an episode to explain why the disciples did not go to Galilee, and the word 'invent' is really the wrong one; both he and the defenders of the 'Galilean hypothesis' are reconstructing a lost document. As a matter of fact, to reconstruct it as he does, by assuming that the disciples did not go to Galilee, but were intercepted by Jesus, is a more vigorous effort of imagination than to suggest that they did go to Galilee, as all the indications in Mark suggest, and then returned to Jerusalem, as the course of history proves that in this case they must have done.

Professor Burkitt therefore cannot claim that his theory is any less imaginative than the Galilean hypothesis, though he can claim that his view makes a less desperate cleavage between the Marcan and the Lucan traditions. If, in fact, the disciples did not actually go to Galilee, Luke has suppressed a less important episode than on the Galilean hypothesis is usually thought to be the case; but that is all.

Consequently I still hold to the remark made in Vol. I. p. 303, note: " This [the fact of the omission of the ' Galilean episode '] is the measure of the caution with which statements in the early part of Acts must be received, and the justification of a free criticism." Referring to this Professor Burkitt says (Christian Beginnings, p. 92): " Yes, indeed; if in recounting to Theophilus the things most certainly believed among Christians Luke has suppressed the sojourn of Peter and his companions in the north during which they became convinced that Christ was risen, and has substituted for it a tale of their remaining during this period at Jerusalem, then Acts ceases to deserve to be regarded as an historical document." This seems to me greatly exaggerated. Even if the Galilean theory be accepted, why should Acts be not regarded as an historical document ? The truth merely is that, in that case, Luke in choosing between two already divergent streams of tradition chose one which we think was wrong. He was not infallible, and he often omitted incidents which we should regard as important. No one can doubt this who studies Acts and the Pauline Epistles side by side. Even on Professor Burkitt's own hypothesis Luke omitted the command to go to Galilee, substituted a quite different message to the disciples from the angel at the tomb, and said nothing about the change of plan ordered by the Lord and resulting in a return to Jerusalem.

Thus, though Professor Burkitt's suggestion seems at least sufficiently attractive to make me waver in my allegiance to the Galilean hypothesis, I am not wholly convinced that he is right. If he be, I should be inclined to suggest a modification of his theory to the effect that the Galilean tradition may represent a belief widely current in Jerusalem. When the disciples disappeared it may have been generally assumed that they had gone back to Galilee, whereas they had really gone only a short distance. There is considerable reason to think that Mark is a Jerusalem document. The objection to this, just as to Professor Burkitt's theory as a whole, is the difficulty of explaining the Marcan tradition, which seems to leave no convenient room for this stay near Jerusalem and not in Galilee. Mark xiv. 28 and xvi. 7 are too explicit.

Supposing, however, that either this or Burkitt's theory be adopted, Bethany. where did the disciples stop ? If the hints given in Acts may be followed, probably they stopped just over the hill of Olivet, where Bethany was. The evidence is scanty, but it may be interesting to collect it.

(i.) The headquarters of Jesus and his disciples, during the week that they were in the neighbourhood of Jerusalem, was probably either Bethany or Bethphage. The suggestion of Mark xi. 1, 11, 12, 19, 27, xiv. 3, 16, 26, is quite clear that at no time did they sleep within the walls of the city. The general position is summarized correctly—with the possible exception of one detail—in Luke xxi. 37, " And during the days he was teaching in the Temple, but he went out and camped for the night on the mountain called Olive-orchard." The position of Bethphage and Bethany is doubtful (see Additional Note 35), but it probably was on the other side of Olivet. The most natural interpretation of the story in Mark, to anyone who has seen the exact spot, is that Jesus and his disciples reached the end of the long drag up from Jericho and were confronted by the final hills of Olivet and Scopus (really a single hill-complex) which rise sharply just before Jerusalem is reached and tower above it. The modern road goes round this mountain, but the ancient one went over it. At the bottom of this last and most fatiguing stage of the journey Jesus' strength gave out, and he sent his disciples into the village higher up on the hill to find an animal for him to ride on.

But if a village on the other side of Olivet was the headquarters of Jesus and the disciples, it would be thither that they probably went at the time of the arrest of Jesus. The situation is certainly made more intelligible if we suppose that Jerusalem was the home of Mark (as we know that it was) and of at least some of the women. They would not see the disciples, and might suppose that they had gone to Galilee. This would be in line with Professor Burkitt's view, and also with his belief that the gospel contains personal reminiscences of Mark himself.

(ii.) The same place may have continued to be the headquarters of the disciples in the period of forty days described in Acts i. 3. The strange word συναλιζόμενος or συναυλιζόμενος may well mean ' camping in the open.' (See note on the word in i. 4.)

Thus, *longo circuitu*, we reach the phrase in Acts i. 4, "he commanded them to abandon departing from Jerusalem." The note on the phrase μὴ χωρίζεσθαι shows that the true meaning of μή with the present infinitive is ' give up ' a course of action. μὴ κλέπτειν, for instance, does not mean ' not to steal ' (which would be μὴ κλέψαι) but ' give up being a thief.'

It is obvious that this meaning fits admirably with Professor Burkitt's view, or with the theory, expressed above, that the disciples originally lived in Bethany (or Bethphage). This, of course, may be true even if the Galilean theory be retained. The meaning of Acts i. 4 would then be that the disciples returned from Galilee to Bethany and lived there, as they and Jesus had done, but after forty days moved into Jerusalem, possibly to the house of the family of John Mark.

(iii.) A curious piece of evidence suggests that Bethany may have been frequented by the disciples even longer than the forty days. In Acts iii. 1 Peter and John are described as coming to the 'Beautiful Gate' of the Temple. It is unknown where this gate was, but tradition (though relatively worthless, see further in Additional Note 35) takes it to be one of the Eastern gates of the Temple, opposite Olivet. Why should anyone living in Jerusalem come in by this gate? The only possible answer is that he would not. The Mishna says that the Southern gate was the usual gate, and common sense suggests the same view. The Eastern gate is the natural approach to the Temple only for those who are coming from Scopus or Olivet; and if it be true that the 'Beautiful Gate' is the Eastern gate, it suggests that the disciples were living in Bethany or Bethphage rather than in Jerusalem.

## Note III. The Ascension

### By Kirsopp Lake

The belief in the Ascension is partly, at least, an attempt to define more clearly the relation between the living Jesus who died on the Cross and the risen Lord who appeared to the Apostles. The oldest tradition was that the Lord did not rise until the third day. This belief is probably a combination of two 'experiences': (i.) of the Apostles who saw the risen Jesus; (ii.) of the women who on the third day could not find his body. At first there was doubtless no attempt to discuss where the 'life' of Jesus was during the three days. Paul shows no consciousness of the question, and some of his incidental remarks might suggest that he thought of Jesus as passing straight from death on the Cross to life as a heavenly being. 1 Corinthians xv. 1 ff. is, however, clear evidence that he thought of the Lord, who is the Spirit, as a transmutation into spirit of the body which had been buried.

The soul after death. Sooner or later, however, the question was bound to arise, where had been the 'life' of Jesus during the interval of the three days? The answer to this question depended on the view taken as to the relation between soul and body. After death the body is buried, but where is the soul? The Jewish belief, older than any theory of a resurrection, said that the soul is in Sheol, and the story of Lazarus and Dives shows that in some circles it was thought that a preliminary judgement on men sent them immediately after death either to 'Abraham's bosom' or to a place of punishment. A similar view is implied by the words of Jesus to the penitent thief on the Cross, "To-day shalt thou be with me in Paradise," and by his last words, "Father, into thy hands I commend my spirit." [1] Possibly too ἀνάληψις was used of the departure of the soul to Paradise, and this may explain the curious use of the word in Luke ix. 51. It is quite possible that this was Luke's own view, and that he regarded the resurrection as the reuniting of soul and body. But in the main he is using older documents and does not elucidate this point.

A further problem, however, arose. The cessation of appearances of the risen body of Jesus had to be explained, and the story of a bodily ascension was an almost inevitable consequence. This was rendered the easier by the existence of a series of traditions as to the 'assumption' or 'translation' of living persons such as Elijah or Enoch, to which the Apocalyptists added Moses, Baruch, and Ezra. The common element in their stories is the taking up to heaven of a living person, and supplied a natural explanation for the passing of the risen Jesus from earth to heaven. *The tradition of 'translations.'*

Thus three positions emerge in the earliest Christian literature :

(a) According to the Pauline Epistles the resurrection of Christians will be a change from a σῶμα ψυχικόν to a σῶμα πνευματικόν, for flesh and blood cannot inherit the Kingdom of God (1 Cor. xv. 44 and 50). Inasmuch as Paul bases this anticipation of the resurrection or metamorphosis of Christians on the model of the resurrection of Jesus, who was the first-fruits (1 Cor. xv. 23), he must have held that the risen Lord had a 'spiritual' body, or, in other words, was a spirit (Rom. viii. 9 ff. and 2 Cor. iii. 17), for 'spirits' were held to have 'bodies,' [2] though not of flesh and blood. The home, if the word may be used, of the risen Lord was heaven, and his appearances were those of a heavenly being. [3] *The Pauline Epistles.*

(b) According to Luke and John the risen Lord had the same body as was buried, and it still consisted of flesh and blood (Luke xxiv. 39 ; John xx. 27 ff.). This view ultimately prevailed in the Church, and the Pauline view was forgotten. *Luke and John.*

(c) A third view is found in the Gospel of Peter, which seems sharply to separate the Ascension of the Divine Christ from that of the human Jesus. According to it the former 'ascended,' or was 'taken up' (ἀνελήμφθη—the word used in Acts) at the moment of his death, but the latter was raised in a state of glory on the third day. *Gospel of Peter.*

[1] It is very remarkable that Luke makes Jesus give this answer to the eschatological petition of the malefactor. The Manichaeans used this passage to prove that there is no resurrection of the body, but that the soul alone lives in Paradise. Some interesting remarks on this subject may be found in G. Bertram's 'Die Himmelfahrt Jesu vom Kreuz aus und der Glaube an seine Auferstehung,' in the *Festgabe für Adolf Deissmann*, 1927.

[2] Origen, *De principiis* i. 1 ff., shows that even in the third century the statement that God is πνεῦμα was taken to mean that God has a σῶμα, i.e. is 'material,' and Origen has to argue hard and subtly that it means that God is νοῦς, i.e. is 'immaterial.' Origen's success is shown by the extent to which in later Christian terminology 'spirit' and 'spiritual' are used as the equivalent of the Platonic νοῦς and νοητός. But in the beginning it was not so.

[3] See also K. Lake, *The Resurrection of Jesus Christ*, pp. 220 ff.

This is in some ways the clearest example we possess of the view discussed above that the soul of Jesus passed to Paradise at his death, and was afterwards reunited to his body.  It is doubtless very early, but it is mixed with a much later and fantastic picture of the resurrection of the body.  A similar view was held by Cerinthus,[1] but he identified that which was taken up with the Divine Christ as distinct from the human, or apparently human body of Jesus.

On the Pauline view, then, the Resurrection was the passage from earth to heaven, or was identical with the Ascension ; but on the Lucan and Johannine view which the Church adopted it was a temporary restoration of intercourse with the disciples on earth followed by the Ascension.  This raises the questions : (i.) What was the purpose of this renewed intercourse, and why did it cease ?  (ii.) How long did it last ?  (iii.) What was the place of the Ascension ?

**The purpose of the Lord's appearance.**    (i.) The first question can be answered shortly.  The purpose of the intercourse was threefold.  First, it was evidence of the Resurrection (Acts i. 2).  Secondly, it was for the purpose of further instruction (Acts i. 3).  Thirdly, both Acts and John indicate that Jesus left the disciples in order that they might receive the Holy Spirit (Acts ii. 33 ; John xvi. 7, and xx. 22 f.).

**Its duration.**    (ii.) The length of the intercourse is variously defined in different documents, and the variation indicates how relatively little influence Acts had in the formation of tradition in the earliest period, and how much it had later.

**Acts.**    (a) According to Acts the renewed intercourse lasted forty[2] days.  There is, however, no other reference in the New Testament to the period of forty days, and Paul seems to exclude it by regarding the Ascension as synonymous with the Resurrection.  Yet in the end it was

---

[1] Cf. Iren. *Adv. haer.* i. 21, ed. Harvey, or i. 26, ed. Massuet, and Hippolytus, *Refut.* vii. 33 ; and for a discussion of Cerinthus see especially the excursus in C. Schmidt's ' Gespräche Jesu ' etc. in the *Texte und Untersuchungen,* xliii., commonly quoted as the *Epistola Apostolorum.*  The Christology of Cerinthus seems to have been essentially a form of Adoptionism, securing the apotheosis of the human body, and is closely akin to the doctrine found in Hermas.

[2] The number 'forty' seems to be traditional in sacred history : Moses was forty days on Mt. Sinai (Exod. xxxiv. 28), Elijah travelled forty days and forty nights in the strength of the food given him by the angel (1 Kings xix. 8), and Ezra spent forty days in transcribing the Law before his exaltation to heaven (4 Ezra xiv. 23, 49), and Baruch waited forty days for his assumption (*Apoc. Baruch* lxxvi. 4).  The last two passages are in books that are scarcely independent of each other, but they are independent of Acts.  Their agreement with it in the detail of forty days before an ascension is a striking coincidence, if nothing more.  Many curious facts are collected by W. H. Roscher in ' Tesserakontaden ' in the *Berichte d. säch. Ges. d. Wiss.* (Leipzig) lxi. (1909) pp. 15 ff. on the number forty in legend and custom, but they bear only remotely on this passage.

universally accepted by the tradition of the Church, and is the reason for celebrating the feast of the Ascension on a Thursday.

(b) The Johannine tradition is not perfectly clear, but there are some John. indications that the writer thought that Jesus ascended after his appearance to Mary Magdalen. When Mary saw the risen Lord she went forward towards him (the narrative implies this even if the text does not state it), and Jesus said, "Touch me not, for I am not yet ascended to the Father" (John xx. 17). The form of 'touch me not' (μὴ ἅπτου, not μὴ ἅψῃ) shows that it almost means 'do not detain me.' Similarly in John xvi. 7 Jesus had said, "If I go not away the Paraclete will not come, but if I go I will send him to you," and in fulfilment of this on his reappearance to the disciples (John xx. 22 f.) he gave them the Spirit. It would thus appear that John's view was that Mary Magdalen saw Jesus just before the Ascension, of which he gives no description, and that the gift of the Holy Spirit followed after it. He seems to regard the risen Lord as remaining a being of flesh and blood even after the Ascension. This soon became the traditional belief, but was combined with the Lucan view that the Ascension took place forty days after the Resurrection. It is remarkable that John differs from Luke in that he does not conceive of the risen Lord as renewing his general intercourse with his disciples. The appearances after the Resurrection or Ascension are short and transitory, which is quite different from the picture given in Acts. It should be noted that the desire to harmonize John and Acts is the source of Chrysostom's explanation that δι' ἡμερῶν in i. 3 means appearances 'at intervals.' It is very doubtful whether δι' ἡμερῶν can mean this, and it is surely not the real meaning of Acts (see note ad loc.).

(c) In the Gospel of Peter the Ascension of the Christ takes place at Gospel of the death of the body on the Cross, and the resurrection of that body Peter. on the third day seems probably (though not necessarily) to imply that it also then ascended to heaven. (See H. B. Swete, Gospel of Peter, and K. Lake, The Resurrection of Jesus Christ, pp. 155 ff.)

(d) The Epistle of Barnabas xv. says, διὸ καὶ ἄγομεν τὴν ἡμέραν Barnabas. τὴν ὀγδόην (i.e. in distinction to the Jewish Sabbath) εἰς εὐφροσύνην, ἐν ᾗ καὶ ὁ Ἰησοῦς ἀνέστη ἐκ νεκρῶν καὶ φανερωθεὶς ἀνέβη εἰς οὐρανούς. This probably means that the writer placed the Ascension on the same day as the Resurrection, but may mean merely that he placed it on a Sunday. Neither view can be reconciled with the tradition of forty days. In this connexion, too, may be noted the view of Chrysostom (Hom. iii. 1) that the Ascension was on a Saturday; but this is merely his inference from the reference in Acts i. 12 to a 'sabbath day's journey.' It does not imply that he was ignorant of or rejected the forty days, but that he began to count them from the day after the Resurrection (Monday) and put the Ascension on the day after their completion.

(e) A tradition similar to Barnabas is in the Epistola Apostolorum Ep. Apost. (A.D. 150), which seems to place the Ascension on the third day, after Jesus had given to the disciples instruction and warning as to their future work. There is no suggestion that those instructions extended beyond the day of the Resurrection.   The *Epistola* ends :  "After he had said this, and had ended his speech with us, he said to us again, See on the third day at the third hour there comes he who sent me, that I may depart with him.   And as he spake there came thunder and lightning and earthquake, and Heaven opened, and there appeared a cloud of light, which took him up.   And there sounded the voices of many angels, who rejoiced and sang praises, and said, Gather us, O Priest, to the Light of glory.   And as he approached the sky we heard his voice, Go in peace."   (See C. Schmidt, *Epistola Apostolorum*, pp. 154 and 300 ff.)

*Valentinians.*    (*f*) The Valentinians, according to Irenaeus (*Adv. haer.* i. 3. 2, ed. Mass.), considered that the risen Jesus remained eighteen months with the disciples :  τοὺς λοιποὺς δεκαοκτὼ αἰῶνας φανεροῦσθαι, διὰ τοῦ μετὰ τὴν ἐκ νεκρῶν ἀνάστασιν δεκαοκτὼ μησὶ λέγειν διατετριφέναι αὐτὸν σὺν τοῖς μαθηταῖς.   This theory was also held by the Ophites, of whom Irenaeus (*Adv. haer.* i. 30. 14) says *remoratum autem eum post resurrectionem XVIII. mensibus et sensibilitate in eum descendente didicisse quod liquidum est ; et paucos ex discipulis suis, quos sciebat capaces tantorum mysteriorum, docuit haec et sic receptus est in caelum,* etc.   For the further explanation of this strange passage see Harvey's note in his *S. Irenaei . . . adversus Haereses*, tom. i. pp. 239 f.   The same tradition is also found in the Ethiopic *Ascension of Isaiah* (*Asc. Is.* ed. Dillmann, ix. 16) : "And when he has spoiled the angel of death he will rise on the third day, and will remain in that world five hundred and forty-five days ( = eighteen months)."   Cf. too Ephrem's Commentary in which he animadverted against this view (see Vol. III. p. 381).   Harnack thinks this period of eighteen months may represent a correct tradition as to the date of Paul's conversion, and the belief that the vision on the road to Damascus was really the last appearance of the risen Lord (see *SBA.*, 1912, pp. 677 f.).

*Pistis Sophia.*    (*g*) The *Pistis Sophia* and the *Book of Jeu* say that Jesus remained twelve years with the disciples.   The *Pistis Sophia* is the secret teaching which he gave in the twelfth year.

*The tendencies producing these traditions.*    All of these traditions show the growing tendency to look on the instruction given by Jesus on earth as superior in authority to all other, and two lines of development can be noted.   One of these lengthened the period of converse between Jesus and his disciples, in order to find room for much secret doctrine.   In the end it survived in the Catholic Church only in the very early form represented by Acts i. 3.   But the principle always remained that the words of Christ have an authority superior to that of the voice of God in living persons or institutions ; it was the basis of an 'Apostolic' canon [1] of the New Testament, and became dominant in Protestantism.   The other tendency was to emphasize the abiding

---

[1] The Church never said that the gift of prophecy had wholly ceased, but it was hard to convince it that individuals, such as Montanus, were inspired by the Holy Spirit ; and by putting 'Apostolic' authority above that of prophets it rendered it possible to close the canon of the New Testament.   It should, however, be remembered that this was the result, not the purpose, of the action of the Church.

presence of the Divine Christ in the Church and in men, as the 'sons of God.' This can be seen clearly in the Pauline literature, in which, however, it is sometimes obscured by the habit of the writer to speak indifferently of 'Christ,' the 'Spirit of Christ,' the 'Spirit of God,' and 'the Spirit' (cf. Rom. viii. 9 ff.). This principle was to some extent overshadowed by the other in official circles, but survived in all forms of mystical personal Christianity, and in the Catholic doctrine of the Church as an inspired institution, even though this was largely neutralized by the theory of 'apostolic' authority and of immutable tradition.

The difficulty of reconciling the two points of view—which represent the eternal conflict between institutional history and personal experience—was largely concealed by the rapid growth of a distinction between Christ, more and more used as the name of the heavenly Jesus, and the Spirit, regarded as the source of existing religious life.

Acts stands here, as so often, at the parting of the ways. The 'Lord' is the ever-present guide of Christians, and his commands are paramount ; but in some cases this guide of life is spoken of as the Spirit and already distinguished from the Lord, in contrast to Paul's 'the Lord is the Spirit.' For this reason the writer makes use of the Ascension as marking a difference of relationship, and limits the intercourse between the risen Jesus and his followers to forty days.

(iii.) The place of the Ascension.—Neither in the Gospel nor in Acts is this indicated so definitely as to be beyond question. *The place of the Ascension.*

The Gospel of Luke seems to place the Ascension at Bethany, for it says ἐξήγαγε δὲ αὐτοὺς ἕως πρὸς Βηθανίαν . . . καὶ . . . διέστη ἀπ' αὐτῶν (Luke xxiv. 50), and, even if (as is probable) the actual description of the Ascension ought to be omitted from this text, the event referred to as the separation of Jesus from the disciples (διέστη . . .) certainly is intended to be the final episode of his ministry, and is the same as the Ascension of Acts i. 6-11. It is, indeed, sometimes thought that ἕως πρὸς Βηθανίαν may mean 'until on the way to Bethany,' but this seems very harsh, for though πρός can mean 'towards' as well as 'to,' ἕως πρός can hardly do so. *Luke.*

In Acts the place of the Ascension is not named in i. 6-11, but in vs. 12 it is said that the disciples returned to Jerusalem, after the Ascension, from Olivet. The obvious implication is that the Ascension was on Olivet, i.e. 'the olive-yard,' *olivetum*, called 'Mount of Olives' in Matthew and Mark.[1] It is the long hill immediately to the east of Jerusalem, now called by the Moslems Jebel et Tur (the hill of the Mount), or by Christians Jebel ez-Zeitun (the hill of Olives). Tradition has accepted the view that the top of this hill was the site of the Ascension, and a church on the spot commemorates it. But tradition has also identified Bethany with El Azariyeh, 'the village of Lazarus,' *Acts.*

---

[1] The two places may have seemed to Luke to be almost the same. Following Mark xi. 1 he mentions them together in Luke xix. 29, and while the other gospels say that Jesus retired at nightfall from Jerusalem to Bethany (Mark xi. 11 f., cf. xiv. 3), Luke xxi. 37 says that Jesus spent his nights on Olivet.

almost at the bottom of the south-eastern slope of Olivet on the modern road to Jericho, and commentators have therefore endeavoured to explain ἀπὸ τοῦ Ἐλαιῶνος as 'returned by way of Olivet,' which is at least very unlikely Greek (see also Addit. Note 35).

The Messianic importance of Olivet.

It is not impossible that the emphasis on the Mount of Olives is due to its importance in Messianic expectation. The origin of this was Zech. xiv. 3 ff. : "Then shall the Lord go forth and fight against those nations, as when he fought in the day of battle. And his feet shall stand in that day upon the Mount of Olives, which is before Jerusalem on the east, and the Mount of Olives shall cleave in the midst thereof towards the east and towards the west, and there shall be a very great valley. . . . And the Lord my God shall come, and all the holy ones with thee." This appears to have been interpreted by the later Rabbis to mean that the Resurrection would take place through the cleft in the Mount of Olives, and that the righteous dead who had died outside of Palestine would be moved along underground, and so be able to come up in the proper place. It was also held that Messiah would frequent the mountain. Rabbi Janna also explained in a similar manner Ezekiel xi. 23 : "And the glory of the Lord went up from the midst of the city, and stood upon the mountain which is on the east side of the city." He said that the Shekinah stood three and a half years on Olivet, and preached saying, "Seek ye the Lord while he may be found ; call upon him while he is near," and when all was in vain returned to its own place.

## Note IV. The Death of Judas

### By Kirsopp Lake

There are three extant traditions of the death of Judas :

Matthew.

(1) Matt. xxvii. 3-10. Τότε ἰδὼν Ἰούδας ὁ παραδοὺς αὐτὸν ὅτι κατεκρίθη, μεταμεληθεὶς ἔστρεψεν τὰ τριάκοντα ἀργύρια τοῖς ἀρχιερεῦσι καὶ πρεσβυτέροις λέγων· ἥμαρτον παραδοὺς αἷμα ἀθῷον. οἱ δὲ εἶπαν· τί πρὸς ἡμᾶς ; σὺ ὄψῃ. καὶ ῥίψας τὰ ἀργύρια εἰς τὸν ναὸν ἀνεχώρησεν, καὶ ἀπελθὼν ἀπήγξατο. οἱ δὲ ἀρχιερεῖς λαβόντες τὰ ἀργύρια εἶπαν· οὐκ ἔξεστιν βαλεῖν αὐτὰ εἰς τὸν κορβανᾶν, ἐπεὶ τιμὴ αἵματός ἐστιν· συμβούλιον δὲ λαβόντες ἠγόρασαν ἐξ αὐτῶν τὸν ἀγρὸν τοῦ κεραμέως εἰς ταφὴν τοῖς ξένοις. διὸ ἐκλήθη ὁ ἀγρὸς ἐκεῖνος ἀγρὸς αἵματος ἕως τῆς σήμερον. τότε ἐπληρώθη τὸ ῥηθὲν διὰ Ἱερεμίου τοῦ προφήτου λέγοντος· καὶ ἔλαβον τὰ τριάκοντα ἀργύρια, τὴν τιμὴν τοῦ τετιμημένου ὃν ἐτιμήσαντο ἀπὸ υἱῶν Ἰσραήλ; καὶ ἔδωκαν αὐτὰ εἰς τὸν ἀγρὸν τοῦ κεραμέως, καθὰ συνέταξέν μοι Κύριος.

Acts.

(2) Acts i. 18-19. Οὗτος μὲν οὖν ἐκτήσατο χωρίον ἐκ μισθοῦ τῆς ἀδικίας, καὶ πρηνὴς γενόμενος ἐλάκησεν μέσος καὶ ἐξεχύθη πάντα τὰ σπλάγχνα αὐτοῦ· καὶ γνωστὸν ἐγένετο πᾶσι τοῖς κατοικοῦσιν Ἰερουσαλήμ, ὥστε κληθῆναι τὸ χωρίον ἐκεῖνο τῇ διαλέκτῳ αὐτῶν Ἀχελδαμάχ, τοῦτ' ἔστιν χωρίον αἵματος.

(3) A third tradition was represented by Papias in the fourth book Papias. of his Λογίων κυριακῶν ἐξηγήσεις. This book is no longer extant, but its evidence on this point was quoted by Apollinarius of Laodicea,[1] and has been preserved in various catenae. The best form is in Cramer's catena (Oxford, 1844), but there are two versions, one in the catena to Matthew and the other in the catena on Acts. Their texts [2] can readily be shown to be ultimately identical by printing the two forms side by side.

CRAMER: *Catena in Matt.* xxvii.

Ἀπολιναρίου · Ἰστέον ὅτι ὁ Ἰούδας οὐκ ἐναπέθανε τῇ ἀγχόνῃ, ἀλλ' ἐπεβίωκε κατενεχθεὶς πρὸ τοῦ ἀποπνιγῆναι, καὶ τοῦτο δηλοῦσιν αἱ τῶν Ἀποστόλων Πράξεις, ὅτι πρηνὴς γενόμενος, ἐλάκησε καὶ τὰ ἐξῆς · τοῦτο δὲ σαφέστερον ἱστορεῖ Παπίας, ὁ Ἰωάννου τοῦ ἀποστόλου μαθητής, λέγων · Μέγα ἀσεβείας ὑπόδειγμα ἐν τούτῳ τῷ κόσμῳ περιεπάτησεν ὁ Ἰούδας · πρησθεὶς γὰρ ἐπὶ τοσοῦτον τὴν σάρκα, ὥστε μὴ δύνασθαι διελθεῖν, ἁμάξης ῥαδίως διερχομένης, ὑπὸ τῆς ἁμάξης πταισθέντα τὰ ἔγκατα ἐγκενωθῆναι. τοῦ αὐτοῦ. Πρησθεὶς ἐπὶ τοσοῦτον τὴν σάρκα ὥστε οὐδὲ ὁπόθεν ἄμαξαν ῥαδίως διέρχεσθαι, ἐκεῖνον δύνασθαι διελθεῖν, ἀλλὰ μηδὲν αὐτὸν μόνον τὸν τῆς κεφαλῆς ὄγκον · τὰ μὲν γὰρ βλέφαρα αὐτοῦ τῶν ὀφθαλμῶν φασὶ τοσοῦτον ἐξοιδῆσαι, ὡς αὐτὸν μὲν καθόλου τὸ φῶς μὴ βλέπειν, τοὺς ὀφθαλμοὺς δὲ αὐτοῦ μηδὲ ὑπὸ ἰατρικῆς διόπτρας ὀφθη-

CRAMER : *Catena in Acta* i.

Ἀπο[λιναρίου]. Οὐκ ἐναπέθανε τῇ ἀγχόνῃ Ἰούδας, ἀλλ' ἐπεβίω καθαιρεθεὶς πρὸ τοῦ ἀποπνιγῆναι · καὶ τοῦτο δηλοῦσιν αἱ τῶν Ἀποστόλων Πράξεις, ὅτι πρηνὴς γενόμενος ἐλάκησε μέσος, καὶ ἐξεχύθη τὰ σπλάγχνα αὐτοῦ. τοῦτο δὲ σαφέστερον ἱστορεῖ Παπίας ὁ Ἰωάννου μαθητής, λέγων οὕτως, ἐν τῷ δ' τῆς ἐξηγήσεως τῶν Κυριακῶν λόγων · μεγὰ δὲ ἀσεβείας ὑπόδειγμα ἐν τούτῳ τῷ κόσμῳ περιεπάτησεν ὁ Ἰούδας · πρησθεὶς ἐπὶ τοσοῦτον τὴν σάρκα, ὥστε μηδὲ ὁπόθεν ἄμαξα διέρχεται ῥαδίως ἐκεῖνον δύνασθαι διελθεῖν · ἀλλὰ μηδὲ αὐτὸν μόνον τὸν τῆς κεφαλῆς ὄγκον αὐτοῦ · τὰ μὲν γὰρ βλέφαρα τῶν ὀφθαλμῶν αὐτοῦ φασὶ τοσοῦτον ἐξοιδῆσαι, ὡς αὐτὸν μὲν καθόλου τὸ φῶς μὴ βλέπειν · τοὺς ὀφθαλμοὺς δὲ αὐτοῦ μηδὲ ὑπὸ ἰατροῦ διόπτρας ὀφθῆναι δύνασθαι · τοσοῦ-

---

[1] Zahn has argued (*ThSK.*, 1866, pp. 683 ff.) that the Apollinarius quoted in the catenae is sometimes, and especially in this place, Claudius Apollinarius of Hierapolis who lived in the second half of the second century. It is not impossible that some of the passages attributed to Apollinarius may belong to this writer, and a critical investigation of catenae might be rewarded by results, but in this instance the probability is greatly in favour of Apollinarius of Laodicea, because we know that Claudius Apollinarius accepted the Matthaean version of the death of Judas without reserve. Cf. Eusebius, *H.E.* v. 16. 13, where Apollinarius says of Montanus and Maximilla : τούτους γὰρ ὑπὸ πνεύματος βλαψίφρονος ἑκατέρους ὑποκινήσαντος λόγος ἀναρτῆσαι ἑαυτούς, . . . καὶ οὕτω δὲ τελευτῆσαι καὶ τὸν βίον καταστρέψαι Ἰούδα προδότου δίκην.

[2] It is extremely likely that research in MSS. of the catenae would enable these texts to be greatly improved.

CRAMER : *Catena in Matt.* xxvii.

CRAMER : *Catena in Acta* i.

ναι δύνασθαι, τοσοῦτον βάθος εἶχον ἀπὸ τῆς ἔξωθεν ἐπιφανείας· τὸ δὲ αἰδοῖον αὐτοῦ πάσης μὲν αἰσχύνης ἀηδέστερον καὶ μεῖζον φαίνεσθαι, φέρεσθαι δὲ δι᾽ αὐτοῦ τοὺς ἐξ ἅπαντος τοῦ σώματος συρρέοντας ἰχῶρας, καὶ σκώληκας, εἰς ὕβριν δι᾽ αὐτῶν μόνον τῶν ἀναγκαίων. μετὰ δὲ πολλὰς βασάνους καὶ τιμωρίας ἐν ἰδίῳ φασὶ χωρίῳ τελευτήσαντος, ἀπὸ τῆς ὀσμῆς ἔρημόν τε καὶ ἄοικον τοῦτο τὸ χωρίον μέχρι τῆς νῦν γενέσθαι, ἀλλ᾽ οὐδὲ μέχρι σήμερον δύνασθαί τινα ἐκεῖνον τὸν τόπον παρελθεῖν, ἐὰν μὴ τὰς ῥῖνας ταῖς χερσὶν ἐπιφράξῃ.

τον βάθος εἶχον ἀπὸ τῆς ἔξωθεν ἐπιφανείας. τὸ δὲ αἰδοῖον αὐτοῦ πάσης μὲν ἀσχημοσύνης ἀηδέστερον καὶ μεῖζον φαίνεσθαι· φέρεσθαι δὲ δι᾽ αὐτοῦ ἐκ παντὸς τοῦ σώματος συρρέοντας ἰχῶρας τε καὶ σκώληκας εἰς ὕβριν δι᾽ αὐτῶν μόνον τῶν ἀναγκαίων· μετὰ πολλὰς δὲ βασάνους καὶ τιμωρίας, ἐν ἰδίῳ φασὶ χωρίῳ τελευτήσαντα· καὶ τοῦτο ἀπὸ τῆς ὁδοῦ [ἢ ὀδμῆς] ἔρημον καὶ ἀοίκητον τὸ χωρίον μέχρι τῆς νῦν γενέσθαι· ἀλλ᾽ οὐδὲ μέχρι τῆς σήμερον δύνασθαί τινα ἐκεῖνον τὸν τόπον παρελθεῖν, ἐὰν μὴ τὰς ῥῖνας ταῖς χερσὶν ἐπιφράξῃ· τοσαύτη διὰ τῆς σαρκὸς αὐτοῦ καὶ ἐπὶ γῆς κρίσις ἐχώρησεν.

The original form of the story in Papias.

It will be seen, however, that these versions differ in one very important point. In the catena on Acts the whole story is attributed to Papias ; but in the catena on Matthew the quotation from Apollinarius which contains the extract from Papias ends with the statement that Judas was crushed by a wagon, and a new extract from Apollinarius [1] then begins and gives a more elaborate and gruesome account of the swelling up and death of Judas. These two versions do not agree : in one the wagon is the cause of death, in the other it is part of the comparison and only mentioned to show the extent to which Judas was swollen. The question is whether the 'crushing by a wagon' or the longer version is really that of Papias.

The matter cannot be settled with certainty, but J. Rendel Harris has tried to bring the balance of probability to the side of the attribution of the longer version by pointing out in the *American Journal of Theology*, July 1900, p. 501, that Bar Salibi in his commentary on Acts quotes the passage about the σκώληκας, and definitely ascribes it to Papias. It is extremely improbable that Bar Salibi used the catena of Andreas, so that this is independent evidence that the passage was taken from Papias by Apollinarius.

If so, Papias described Judas as living after the betrayal, and dying from a disease so terrible that his estate remained unoccupied. Among the symptoms mentioned was extreme swelling, so that a place where a wagon could pass was too narrow for him. This comparison gave rise to a secondary form of the story which represented Judas as crushed by a

[1] E. Nestle, *Expos. Times*, xxiii., 1912, p. 331, refers to the *Acta Pilati*, Recension B (Tischendorf, *Evangelia Apocrypha*, 2nd ed. p. 290), where the text reads ἐλάκισεν, ἐπρίσθη (i.e. ἐπρήσθη). But this is very late. For the verb ἐπρήσθη cf. Num. v. 21, 22, 27.

wagon. This would justify the reconstruction of the fragment of Papias
by Hilgenfeld, *ZWTh.*, 1875, pp. 262 f., and printed by Preuschen in his
*Antilegomena*, ed. ii. pp. 97 f.

On the other hand, general probability would perhaps suggest that
the shorter version is likely to be original. If so, the gruesome details
and the changed form of the longer version is due to a desire to pile
up horrors and to make the death of Judas similar to that of other
notoriously evil men, such as Herod the Great or Nadan in the story
of Ahikar. To me this seems somewhat the more probable hypothesis.
Whichever view be taken, Papias clearly represents a tradition different
both from Matthew and from Acts.

It remains to consider ancient and modern attempts at harmoniza- Harmonization so far as they have any importance, and finally to discuss the possible tion.
origin of the three stories.

It was inevitable that ecclesiastical writers should endeavour to
reconcile the three traditions. The beginning of this can be seen already Apolli-
in Apollinarius, but he can scarcely be said to be harmonizing all the narius.
details. He is only anxious to maintain that ἀπήγξατο in Matthew
does not necessarily imply death, and quotes Acts and Papias to prove
his point. It is probable (though he does not say so) that he regarded
πρηνὴς γενόμενος and πρησθείς as giving respectively the reason why
Judas did not die—a man who tries to hang himself but πρηνὴς γίνεται
probably survives—and why permanent evil followed from the strangling,
ἐξεχύθη κτλ. being a shorter description of the disease described by
Papias. It is extremely improbable that this is what Matthew, Luke,
or Papias meant, but considering the conviction of ancient writers that
all scriptures agree, Apollinarius must have held some such view.

More extensive attempts at explanation and harmonization are to be
found collected by J. Rendel Harris in *AJTh.*, July 1900, pp. 490 ff.
The most interesting are (1) Theophylact. *in Matt.* 27 : Theophy-
lactus.

Τίνες δὲ λέγουσιν ὅτι ὁ Ἰούδας φιλάργυρος ὢν ὑπελάμβανεν ὅτι
αὐτός τε κερδήσει τὰ ἀργύρια προδοὺς Χριστόν, καὶ ὁ Χριστὸς οὐκ
ἀποκτανθήσεται ἀλλὰ διαφύγῃ τοὺς Ἰουδαίους, ὡς πολλάκις διέφυγε.
τότε δὲ ἰδὼν αὐτὸν κατακριθέντα, καὶ ἤδη καταδικασθέντα ἀποθανεῖν,
μεταμελήθη, ὡς τοῦ πράγματος ἀποβάντος παρ' ὅπερ ὑπελάμβανε. διὸ
καὶ ἀπήγξατο ἵνα προλάβῃ τὸν Ἰησοῦν ἐν τῷ ᾅδῃ καὶ ἱκετεύσας
σωτηρίας τεύξηται. πλὴν γίνωσκε ὅτι ἔθηκε μὲν τὸν τράχηλον αὐτοῦ
εἰς τὴν ἀγχόνην, ὑπὸ δένδρου τινὸς κρεμάσας ἑαυτόν· τοῦ δὲ δένδρου
κλιθέντος, ἐπέζησε, τοῦ θεοῦ θέλοντος αὐτὸν ἢ εἰς μετάνοιαν συντηρῆσαι
ἢ εἰς παραδειγματισμὸν καὶ αἰσχύνην. φασὶ γὰρ ὅτι νόσῳ ὑδερικῇ ὥστε
ἔνθα ἅμαξα ῥαδίως διέρχεται, αὐτὸν μὴ δύνασθαι διελθεῖν, εἶτα πρηνὴς
πεσὼν ἐλάκησεν, ἀντὶ τοῦ διερράγη, ὡς Λουκᾶς φησὶν ἐν ταῖς Πράξεσιν.

(2) A scholion, attributed to Eusebius, quoted by Matthaei, *Novum* Eusebius.
*Testamentum*, vol. v. p. 304 (Riga edition, 1782) :

ἐλάκησε] Εὐσεβίου. ἀπῆλθεν Ἰούδας καὶ ἀπήρτισεν ἑαυτὸν ἐν τῷ
σχοινίῳ, μετὰ τὸ ῥίψαι αὐτὸν τὰ ἀργύρια. τῆς δὲ σχοίνου κατ' οἰκονο-

μίαν θεοῦ ῥαγείσης, εἰς γῆν ἔπεσεν, οὐκ ἀπέθανε δὲ παρ᾽ εὐθύ, ἀλλὰ χυθέντων αὐτοῦ τῶν σπλάγχνων, ἐτέθη ἐν κραββάτῳ, δύο ἡμέρας ἡμίθνητος καὶ ἀπνευστιών [1] [forte ἄπνευστος ὤν] ἐκ δὲ τοῦ κραββάτου ἐκπεπτωκώς, ῥαγῆναι μέσον καὶ τότε ἀποθανεῖν, τελείως τῶν σπλάγχνων αὐτοῦ ἐξοχετευθέντων.

Armenian catena.

(3) A quotation in the Armenian catena, quoted by F. C. Conybeare in the *American Journal of Philology*, xvii. p. 150 :

"[Of Chrysostom [2] ?] Accordingly he (i.e. Peter) describes also the sentence which he suffered. ' *Being swollen up,*' he says, ' *he burst in the middle and all his bowels were poured out.*' He does well to relate, not the offence, but the punishment, in order to the comforting of those who were afraid of the Jews. But that he fell on the earth and burst and his bowels gushed out, is like this. For he shut the doors against himself before he strangled himself, and he remained there on the gibbet the Friday and the Saturday. When he had swollen up and grown heavy, the cord was cut by which he hung : he fell, burst asunder, and was poured out. But the stench of the putrifying heap and of his guts brought together the children of Jerusalem to come and view his infamous end, and the awful sign which was for him the precursor of hell-fire."

Isho'dad.

(4) The commentary of Isho'dad on the Acts,[3] published (for this passage) by J. Rendel Harris, *AJTh.*, July 1900, p. 496 :

"'He fell upon his face on the earth, and he burst asunder,' etc. They say that when Judas hanged himself either the halter was released and he escaped, or else someone saw him hanging and saved him ; and this happened by the providence of God, first that the disciples might not be accused of having hanged him, and then because it was fitting that he who had betrayed him openly should die openly. So he lived on and saw the resurrection of his Lord and heard that he had come to his disciples many times, and that he had ascended to heaven ; and then he came when many were gathered together, and fell on the ground in the midst of the city, and burst asunder, etc."

The African Latin.

More important for the study of Acts is the influence of this harmonizing process on the text of the Acts. This is found in the African Latin of Augustine *contra Felicem*, which reads—

*hic igitur possedit agrum de mercede iniustitiae suae, et collum sibi alligavit et deiectus in faciem diruptus est medius, et effusa sunt omnia viscera eius.*

Here it is clear that *collum sibi alligavit*, whatever Greek it may represent, is an attempt to harmonize Acts with Matthew. It is very remarkable

Jerome.

that Jerome seems to have been acquainted with this reading, though

---

[1] This is Matthaei's accentuation. Possibly the MS. reads ἀπνευστὶ ὤν.

[2] More probably Ephrem Syrus, see Vol. III. p. 391.

[3] Published in full by Mrs. Gibson in *Horae Semiticae*, x. 4, 1913.

in the shorter form of *suspensus* instead of *collum sibi alligavit*, but he apparently took it as a substitute—he can scarcely have thought that it was a translation—for πρηνὴς γενόμενος. He therefore reads in the Vulgate *suspensus crepuit medius et diffusa sunt omnia viscera eius*. Considering the relative dates of the authorities, this is a clear case of the well-known double process in textual history : first, a gloss is added to explain a difficult text ; secondly, the gloss takes the place of the difficulty, which is left out altogether.

An instance of exactly the same process, but dealing with the Papias The Armenian text. story of 'swelling' instead of with the Matthaean story of 'hanging,' is found in the history of the Armenian text. The Armenian Vulgate reads " Being swollen up he burst in the middle and all his bowels were poured out," representing apparently πρησθείς instead of πρηνὴς γενόμενος. This is clearly a harmonization of Acts with Papias, just as Jerome's Vulgate is a harmonization of Acts with Matthew. But just as Augustine shows an earlier text behind Jerome, which explained but did not omit πρηνὴς γενόμενος, so the Armenian catena suggests a similar text behind the Armenian Vulgate which read πρησθεὶς καὶ πρηνὴς γενόμενος, for the commentator (Ephrem ?) who is quoted in the catena is apparently aware not only of Matthew but also of a text of Acts which included both πρηνής and πρησθείς. The probability that this reading in the Armenian Vulgate goes back to an Old Syriac text of Acts is increased by the fact that it is also found in the Georgian version.

Modern writers have mostly abandoned the attempt to reconcile Dr. Chase. Matthew and Acts, but an important contribution by F. H. Chase in *JTS.*, Jan. 1912, pp. 278 ff., endeavoured to show that Papias was really dependent on the same tradition as Acts, and that πρηνὴς γενόμενος is an obscure medical term meaning the same as πρησθείς. This theory was accepted by A. von Harnack in *ThLZ.*, April 13, 1912, and by J. Rendel Harris, *AJTh.*, Jan. 1914, pp. 127 ff.

Unfortunately the only evidence from Greek sources in favour of this theory is derived from Zonaras, the compiler of a Byzantine dictionary, and Euthymius Zigabenus. Zonaras says πρηνὴς γενόμενος · ἤγουν πεπρησμένος, ἐξωγκομένος, and Euthymius Zigabenus (*Comment. in Matt.*) says εἶτα ἐν ἰδιάζοντι τόπῳ διέζησε καιρὸν ὀλίγον, καὶ πρηνὴς γενόμενος, εἴτ᾽ οὖν πεπρησμένος, ἐξωγκομένος, ἐλάκισε καὶ διερράγη μέσος. There is therefore no doubt that Euthymius and Zonaras thought that Judas swelled so that he died, but, as Harnack himself pointed out, the connexion with Papias and the desire to harmonize is very obvious.

The truth probably is that πρηνής is a word which became obsolete. πρηνής. It is not given in Sophocles' *Greek Lex. of the Byz. Period* (which means that Sophocles had nothing to add to the classical dictionaries), and it is instructive that in Wisdom iv. 19 the corrector of Codex Vaticanus added a note in the margin ἐπὶ πρόσωπον, showing that although he knew what it meant he thought that it might trouble the readers of the MS. which he was preparing.

Apart from these late and doubtful witnesses there is no Greek evidence which bears examination ; but some importance attaches to the fact that in Wisdom iv. 19 the Latin version translates ῥήξει αὐτοὺς ἀφώνους πρηνεῖς by *disrumpet illos inflatos sine voce*, and that the Armenian Version appears to have a similar translation.

This evidence is certainly susceptible of the interpretation that πρηνής was taken to mean 'swollen' by the Latin and Armenian translators. But four considerations show that this is inadequate to prove that πρηνής really has this meaning. (i.) Neither translator is known to us, and certainly the makers of the Old Latin were capable of quite extraordinary blunders : in the absence of further evidence the translation given in the Old Latin is quite inadequate proof of the meaning of a Greek word. (ii.) The Papias tradition, as has been seen in the case of the Armenian catena and Vulgate, is a *vera causa* for a glossing translation which in Acts interpreted πρηνής as 'swollen,' and this may have affected the translation of Wisdom. (iii.) In point of fact 'prostrate and silent' in Wisdom gives a far better meaning than 'blown up and silent'—which is, indeed, nonsense. So that even if it be conceded that the translator thought that πρηνεῖς meant *inflatos*, the context goes to show that he was wrong, and there is no need to spoil the meaning of Wisdom in order to find in Acts an ἅπαξ λεγόμενον, supposed to be of medical origin, and by so doing to harmonize the statement of Papias with a book which he quite possibly had never seen.

Apart from this there is no argument in favour of Dr. Chase's theory ; the other passages which he adduces are all merely repetitions of the Papias tradition, or can be preferably interpreted by giving πρηνής its ordinary sense. It is true that there are two verbs in Greek, πίμπρημι, to burn, and πρήθω, to swell (see Acts xxviii. 6), but πρηνής in the sense of 'prone' is not connected with either of them, and there is no instance of its use in Greek writers, medical or otherwise, in this sense. It is also true that the verb γίγνομαι is used by medical writers, but this is scarcely an unusual or strange idiom, and cannot be said to affect the meaning of πρηνής. In fact it seems as though Dr. Chase had forgotten that it is impossible to prove both that πρηνής is a medical term and also that it is a ἅπαξ λεγόμενον (*loc. cit.* p. 279).

The evidence of the Acts of Thomas is not cogent. It says that a dragon φυσηθεὶς ἐλάκησε καὶ ἀπέθανε καὶ ἐξεχύθη ὁ ἰὸς αὐτοῦ καὶ ἡ χολή. It may be admitted that ἐλάκησε is probably a reminiscence of Acts, but it no more proves that πρηνής meant φυσηθείς than it does that τὰ σπλάγχνα meant ὁ ἰὸς αὐτοῦ (see *Acta Thomae*, xxxiii.).

It is certainly not a legitimate inference from the comment of Apollinarius that he (or Papias) took πρηνής to mean a disease. He is busy showing that Judas did not die when he hung himself, and quotes Acts and Papias to prove his contention : if he implies anything it is that Judas was made prone by disease. It is entirely too rash a conjecture that he thought that πρηνής meant swollen by inflammation because he quotes Papias. It should be noted that it is inaccurate to say, as Harnack does, that Apollinarius quotes Papias to explain Acts : he quotes both Acts and Papias to prove his point that Judas continued to live, and it is to this—not to πρηνὴς γενόμενος—that τοῦτο refers.

The evidence of Athanasius in his account of the death of Arius points against rather than in favour of Dr. Chase's theory. Athanasius says ὁ δὲ ῎Αρειος . . . εἰσῆλθεν εἰς θᾶκος ὡς διὰ χρείαν τῆς γαστρός, καὶ ἐξαίφνης κατὰ τὸ γεγραμμένον · πρηνὴς γενόμενος ἐλάκησε μέσος καὶ πεσὼν εὐθὺς ἀπέψυξεν. The construction is a little complicated, because ἐλάκησε is part both of the sentence and of the quotation ; but it is surely clear that πεσών in the narrative answers to πρηνὴς γενόμενος in the quotation. In any case it is obscure why Dr. Chase thought that the nature of the disease "makes it reasonable to conclude" that Athanasius understood πρηνὴς γενόμενος as equivalent to πρησθείς, which he does not mention, rather than to πεσών, which he does (see Athanasius, *Epist. ad Serapionem de morte Arii*, Migne, *P.G.* xxv. 688).

It is therefore probable that Dr. Chase's theory must be abandoned. There is too much extant Greek literature for us lightly to accept a new meaning for a well-known word merely because Papias, Matthew, and Luke differ in their tradition as to the death of Judas.

Early narratives as to the death of men distinguished either for good or bad qualities are always liable to be coloured by the literary tradition as to similar persons. This fact certainly has its bearing on the story of the death of Judas. From the complete contradiction between the three narratives, which do not fully agree in any point and differ sharply on most, it is clear that we have not much real recollection of fact. The question is whether we can trace any of the literary sources of the traditions.

The account in Matthew is surely not independent of the LXX story of the death of Ahithophel, who betrayed David ; he also ἀπῆλθεν εἰς τὸν οἶκον αὐτοῦ . . . καὶ ἀπήγξατο. Of course, if the account in Matthew be taken for history, the coincidence in language is due to the perception of the parallel ; but if it be regarded as unhistorical, it is probably the LXX parallel which produced the story in Matthew (cf. 2 Sam. xvii. 23).

The account in Acts is clearly influenced by Wisdom iv. 17 ff. :

*Marginalia: Athanasius.*

*Marginalia: The tradition of the deaths of the wicked.*

*Marginalia: 2 Sam. xvii.*

*Marginalia: Wisdom iv.*

ὄψονται γὰρ τελευτὴν σοφοῦ
καὶ οὐ νοήσουσι τί ἐβουλεύσατο περὶ αὐτοῦ
καὶ εἰς τί ἠσφαλίσατο αὐτὸν ὁ Κύριος.
ὄψονται καὶ ἐξουθενήσουσιν
αὐτοὺς δὲ ὁ κύριος ἐκγελάσεται·
καὶ ἔσονται μετὰ τοῦτο εἰς πτῶμα ἄτιμον
καὶ εἰς ὕβριν ἐν νεκροῖς δι' αἰῶνος
ὅτι ῥήξει αὐτοὺς ἀφώνους πρηνεῖς
καὶ σαλεύσει αὐτοὺς ἐκ θεμελίων.
καὶ ἕως ἐσχάτου χερσωθήσονται·
καὶ ἔσονται ἐν ὀδύνῃ
καὶ ἡ μνήμη αὐτῶν ἀπολεῖται.

The whole passage is instructive, and attention may especially be called to ῥήξει . . . πρηνεῖς.

2 Macc. ix.     Finally, the account in Papias seems to be connected with the account in 2 Macc. ix. 7-18. The whole passage is too long to quote, but the following are the important parts :

σννέβη δὲ καὶ πεσεῖν αὐτὸν ἀπὸ τοῦ ἅρματος φερομένου ῥοίξῳ, καὶ δυσχερεῖ πτώματι περιπεσόντα πάντα τὰ μέλη τοῦ σώματος ἀποστρεβλοῦσθαι . . . ὥστε καὶ ἐκ τοῦ σώματος τοῦ δυσσεβοῦς σκώληκας ἀναζεῖν, καὶ ζῶντος ἐν ὀδύναις καὶ ἀλγηδόσιν τὰς σάρκας αὐτοῦ διαπίπτειν, ὑπὸ δὲ τῆς ὀσμῆς αὐτοῦ πᾶν τὸ στρατόπεδον βαρύνεσθαι τὴν σαπρίαν . . . 18 ἐπεληλύθει γὰρ ἐπ' αὐτὸν δικαία ἡ τοῦ θεοῦ κρίσις.

Ps. lxix.     It is also possible that the tradition was influenced by Ps. lxix. 23 σκοτισθήτωσαν οἱ ὀφθαλμοὶ αὐτῶν τοῦ μὴ βλέπειν, and the whole apparatus of the death suitable for a traitor may be studied by a comparison of the version of the death of Herod the Great in Josephus, *Antiq.* xvii. 6. 5, of the end of Catullus, the governor of Cyrene, in Jos. *B.J.* vii. 11. 4, and the story of the death of Nadan in Ahikar. (Cf. J. Rendel Harris, *AJTh.*, July 1900, 'Did Judas really commit suicide?') Finally, it is not impossible that the idea of traitors swelling up may be connected with Num. v. 21 ff., where swelling up (πρήθω in the LXX) is the fate which overtakes an unfaithful wife. But attempts to prove any conscious literary dependence of Matthew, Acts, or Papias on any one source, such as, for instance, the story of Ahikar, are to be deprecated. The truth probably is that there was a loose tradition of the way in which the death of a traitor ought to correspond to his offence. One writer put in one detail, the next added another, until finally nearly all had been incorporated.

From a mass of unimportant contributions the following stand out as of permanent value : Th. Zahn, 'Papias von Hierapolis' in *ThSK.*, 1866, pp. 680 ff. ; F. Overbeck, 'Über zwei neue Ansichten von Zeugnissen des Papias' in *ZWTh.*, 1867, pp. 39 ff. ; A. Hilgenfeld, 'Papias von Hierapolis,' *ZWTh.*, 1875, pp. 262 ff. These three form a complete *Auseinandersetzung*, and Hilgenfeld gives a full list of other writings on the subject. Zahn holds that Papias used Acts ; Overbeck and Hilgenfeld take the opposite opinion. Since then the only important treatments of the subject are those, noted above, by J. Rendel Harris, *AJTh.*, July 1900, and F. H. Chase, *JTS.*, Jan. 1912.


NOTE V. Μάρτυς

By ROBERT P. CASEY

In studying the history of the word μάρτυς, scholars have been principally interested in explaining how, in early Christian documents, it gradually lost its usual sense of a witness at a trial and came to mean one who testified to the truth of Christianity by sacrificing his life.[1]  In orienting investigation to this point, it has not been sufficiently recognized that the transition from ' witness ' to ' martyr ' represents only one development of meaning, and that several others, instead of contributing directly to what later became the standard usage, ran parallel courses which were briefer but which possess considerable independent interest for the history of early Christian thought.  All of these developments begin with a metaphorical application of the legal term, but all do not converge at the point where μάρτυς first clearly and unmistakably signifies a witness who died for Christianity.  It is the purpose here to indicate several early conceptions of the Christian μάρτυς which do not necessarily involve a witnessing with death, and to suggest in what way they may have contributed to the later idea of a Christian martyr.

In the New Testament μάρτυς often has the usual sense of a witness A witness at a trial, as, for example, when Jesus was examined before the high a trial. priest,[2] the testimony (μαρτυρία) offered by the Jews was so contradictory that even the prejudiced judge recognized its futility, but Jesus' own evidence made further witnesses unnecessary, τί ἔτι χρείαν ἔχομεν μαρτυρῶν; At Stephen's trial, also, witnesses were produced who later took part in the stoning (Acts vi. 13, vii. 58), and at Jerusalem Paul told the crowd that the high priest and elders would testify to his former zeal in persecuting the Christians, ὡς καὶ ὁ ἀρχιερεὺς μαρτυρεῖ μοι καὶ πᾶν τὸ πρεσβυτέριον, Acts xxxii. 5.  Without immediate application to a legal Metaphori- trial, but sustaining its force in metaphor, are instances like Paul's ' God cal exten- is my witness ' (Rom. i. 9, Phil. i. 8, 1 Thess. ii. 5), ' You are my witness and God ' (1 Thess. ii. 10),[3] and a more important group of passages in the gospels where the missionary work of the disciples involves testimony to the truth of the gospel or witness against its enemies.  An instance of the latter is Mk. vi. 11, where the disciples are to shake the dust from their feet when leaving an inhospitable house, εἰς μαρτύριον αὐτοῖς.  An example of the former is Mk. xiii. 9, where Jesus tells the disciples that they will be brought to trial and beaten, and will stand before governors and kings, εἰς μαρτύριον αὐτοῖς.  The following verses are also significant, where it is clear that they are to testify under the inspiration of the Holy Spirit, and that the subject of their testimony is the original ' good news ' of the imminent end of the world and coming of the kingdom of God.

The first specific mention of Christian μάρτυρες is in Lk. xxiv. 46-49, Lk. xxiv. where the risen Jesus says to his disciples, οὕτως γέγραπται παθεῖν τὸν

[1] There is a mass of literature of which the most important pieces are F. Kattenbusch, ' Der Märtyrertitel,' *ZNTW*. iv. (1903), pp. 111-127; K. Holl, *Gesammelte Aufsätze* (Berlin, 1928), pp. 68-115; R. Reitzenstein, ' Bemerkungen zur Märtyrienliteratur,' *Göttingen Nachrichten*, 1916, pp. 417-467; *Hermes*, lii. (1917), 442-452; G. Krüger, ' Zur Frage nach der Entstehung des Märtyrertitels,' *ZNTW*. xvii. (1916), pp. 264-269; H. Delehaye, *Sanctus* (*Subsidia Hagio-graphica*, 17), Brussels, 1927, pp. 74-121.

[2] Mark xiv. 59.

[3] Cf. Matt. xxiii. 29-32; Luke xi. 48; James v. 3.

Χριστὸν καὶ ἀναστῆναι ἐκ νεκρῶν τῇ τρίτῃ ἡμέρᾳ καὶ κηρυχθῆναι ἐπὶ τῷ ὀνόματι αὐτοῦ μετάνοιαν εἰς ἄφεσιν ἁμαρτιῶν εἰς πάντα τὰ ἔθνη, ἀρξάμενοι ἀπὸ Ἰερουσαλήμ· ὑμεῖς μάρτυρες τούτων. καὶ ἰδοὺ ἐξαποστέλλω τὴν ἐπαγγελίαν τοῦ πατρός μου ἐφ᾽ ὑμᾶς· ὑμεῖς δὲ καθίσατε ἐν τῇ πόλει ἕως οὗ ἐνδύσησθε ἐξ ὕψους δύναμιν. It is significant that there is no verb in the phrase ὑμεῖς μάρτυρες τούτων, and that even if ἔστε be supplied with some manuscripts, the context indicates that the testifying will be done in the future, after the disciples have been clothed with power from on high. In view of the close relation between Luke and Acts, and especially of the obvious connexion between Lk. xxiv. 47 ff. and Acts i. 8, there can be no doubt that this ' power ' is the Spirit and that the promise was fulfilled at Pentecost. Here, therefore, as in Mk. xiii. 9, the μάρτυρες are to testify under the inspiration of the Spirit, but in Mk. xiii. 9 the subject of their testimony is the end of the world and the coming kingdom of God, while in Lk. xxiv. 46 ff. it is the passion and resurrection of the Messiah and the universal opportunity for repentance, offered in his name to all nations.

Testimony to the Resurrection.

From this point on the emphasis is laid on the testimony about Jesus, and especially his resurrection. This is clear from Peter's speech on the necessity of filling Judas Iscariot's place among the apostles, Acts i. 21-22 δεῖ οὖν τῶν συνελθόντων ἡμῖν ἀνδρῶν ἐν παντὶ χρόνῳ ᾧ εἰσῆλθεν καὶ ἐξῆλθεν ἐφ᾽ ἡμᾶς ὁ κύριος Ἰησοῦς, ἀρξάμενος ἀπὸ τοῦ βαπτίσματος Ἰωάνου ἕως τῆς ἡμέρας ἧς ἀνελήμφθη ἀφ᾽ ἡμῶν, μάρτυρα τῆς ἀναστάσεως αὐτοῦ σὺν ἡμῖν γενέσθαι ἕνα τούτων. The Apostles then prayed and cast lots so that the new member should be, like them, not only an eye-witness to the risen Jesus, but also chosen by him to testify. This theory is re-stated in Acts x. 40-43, with the additional claim that the apostles, as witnesses, are successors to the prophets. Peter speaking of Jesus says, τοῦτον ὁ θεὸς ἤγειρεν τῇ τρίτῃ ἡμέρᾳ καὶ ἔδωκεν αὐτὸν ἐμφανῆ γενέσθαι, οὐ παντὶ τῷ λαῷ ἀλλὰ μάρτυσι τοῖς προκεχειροτονη-μένοις ὑπὸ τοῦ θεοῦ ἡμῖν, οἵτινες συνεφάγομεν καὶ συνεπίομεν αὐτῷ μετὰ τὸ ἀναστῆναι αὐτὸν ἐκ νεκρῶν· καὶ παρήγγειλεν ἡμῖν κηρύξαι τῷ λαῷ καὶ διαμαρτύρασθαι ὅτι οὗτός ἐστιν ὁ ὡρισμένος ὑπὸ τοῦ θεοῦ κριτὴς ζώντων καὶ νεκρῶν. τούτῳ πάντες οἱ προφῆται μαρτυροῦσιν, ἄφεσιν ἁμαρτιῶν λαβεῖν διὰ τοῦ ὀνόματος αὐτοῦ πάντα τὸν πιστεύοντα εἰς αὐτόν.

The qualification for a witness.

The qualification of a μάρτυς in Luke-Acts is that he should be one of those fore-ordained of God to see the risen Jesus, and so an eye-witness of the Resurrection: τοῖς προκεχειροτονημένοις ὑπὸ τοῦ θεοῦ ἡμῖν, οἵτινες συνεφάγομεν καὶ συνεπίομεν αὐτῷ μετὰ. τὸ ἀναστῆναι αὐτὸν ἐκ νεκρῶν. The reference here is evidently to Lk. xxiv. 33 ff., where the risen Jesus appears before a company consisting of Cleopas and his companion on the walk to Emmaus (Lk. xxiv. 13, 18, 33), the eleven apostles, and their friends (τοὺς ἕνδεκα καὶ τοὺς σὺν αὐτοῖς). Two others are also described in Acts as martyrs, Paul and Stephen, for the same reason as the others, viz. they had seen the risen Jesus.

Paul.

When Ananias explains to Paul the significance of his vision on the Damascus road, his words are directly parallel to Acts x. 41 ff., ὁ θεὸς τῶν πατέρων ἡμῶν προεχειρίσατό σε γνῶναι τὸ θέλημα αὐτοῦ καὶ ἰδεῖν τὸν δίκαιον καὶ ἀκοῦσαι φωνὴν ἐκ τοῦ στόματος αὐτοῦ, ὅτι ἔσῃ μάρτυς αὐτῷ πρὸς πάντας ἀνθρώπους ὧν ἑώρακας καὶ ἤκουσας (xxii. 14 ff.), and in a parallel account in Acts xxvi. 16 the risen Jesus says to Paul, εἰς τοῦτο γὰρ ὤφθη σοι, προχειρίσασθαί σε ὑπηρέτην καὶ μάρτυρα ὧν τε εἶδές με ὧν τε ὀφθήσομαί σοι.

The case of Stephen is similar. In Acts xxiii. Paul, having related *Stephen.* his own conversion and appointment as a witness (xxii. 14), tells how he went to Jerusalem where ἐν ἐκστάσει he saw Jesus, who told him to leave the city because the people would not receive his testimony (διότι οὐ παραδέξονταί σου μαρτυρίαν περὶ ἐμοῦ). Paul replies, "Lord, they know that I imprisoned and scourged in the synagogue those who believed in thee, and when the blood of Stephen, thy witness, was shed (καὶ ὅτε ἐξεχύννετο τὸ αἷμα Στεφάνου τοῦ μάρτυρός σου . . .), I also was standing by and consenting and keeping the garments of them that slew him." In what sense was Stephen a μάρτυς and how did he offer his testimony? The answer is clear in the account of his death in Acts vii. 54 ff., "And being filled with the Holy Spirit, gazing steadfastly into heaven, he saw the glory of God and Jesus standing on the right hand of God and said, 'Behold, I see the heavens opened and the Son of Man standing on the right hand of God.'" The subject of Stephen's testimony was his vision of the risen Jesus to which he bore immediate witness, and in doing so precipitated the violence of the crowd and met his death. There is nothing to suggest that his death was an essential part of his testimony. Stephen, like Paul, was an eye-witness to the risen Jesus, and the fact that he died in consequence of his testimony made him no more and no less a μάρτυς than Paul.

The view of Christian martyrs and their testimony which we have *Luke-Acts* been considering is characteristic of Luke-Acts, and is to some extent a *in contrast to other* development of the earlier conception found in Mark xiii. 9. In other *books.* writings of the New Testament somewhat different ideas are found. In the Epistles, Paul does not use the word μάρτυς in the technical sense which it bears in Acts, and his use of μαρτυρεῖν and its cognates shows that he had no conception of a closed group who on other grounds than possession of the Spirit could claim to be μάρτυρες κατ᾽ ἐξοχήν to Jesus. His conception of the content of Christian testimony is also much broader, *Paul.* and includes not only the Resurrection but the whole substance of the revelation dispensed by the Spirit.[1] In 1 Thess. ii. 11 f. he reminds his readers how he dealt with them as a father with his own children, exhorting them and encouraging and testifying (παρακαλοῦντες ὑμᾶς καὶ παραμυθούμενοι καὶ μαρτυρόμενοι) that they might walk worthily of God. Here μαρτυρόμενοι is the equivalent of 'preaching under inspiration,' and with Eph. iv. 17 τοῦτο οὖν λέγω καὶ μαρτύρομαι ἐν κυρίῳ μηκέτι ὑμᾶς περιπατεῖν καθὼς καὶ τὰ ἔθνη περιπατεῖ recalls the distinction in 1 Cor. vii. 25 between the authority of the Spirit and the judgement of common sense. In several passages, also, μαρτύριον stands for such inspired preaching (1 Thess. ii. 12, iv. 6; 2 Thess. i. 10; 1 Cor. i. 6, ii. 1). Nevertheless there is nothing in Paul's use of μαρτυρεῖν and

[1] Cf. Rom. iii. 21; 1 Cor. i. 6, xv. 15; 2 Thess. i. 10.

its cognates to indicate that he regarded it as having a technical significance. It is simply a convenient metaphor, sometimes employed in a way directly reminiscent of the Old Testament, more often to describe the impulsive character of moral or ecstatic experience.

John.    In the Johannine writings the word μάρτυς does not appear in either the Gospels or the Epistles, but μαρτυρεῖν and μαρτυρία are of more frequent occurrence than anywhere else in the New Testament. In a few cases the usage is conventional, but in a group of passages a characteristic meaning appears, a hint of which is given in the Johannine μαρτυρεῖν περί . . . instead of the more usual dative. In the first chapter of the Gospel the mission of John the Baptist is described as giving testimony. In i. 7-8 John came εἰς μαρτυρίαν, ἵνα μαρτυρήσῃ περὶ τοῦ φωτός, ἵνα πάντες πιστεύσωσιν δι' αὐτοῦ. οὐκ ἦν ἐκεῖνος τὸ φῶς, ἀλλ' ἵνα μαρτυρήσῃ περὶ τοῦ φωτός, and in i. 15 John μαρτυρεῖ περὶ αὐτοῦ καὶ κέκραγεν λέγων—οὗτος ἦν ὁ εἰπών—ὁ ὀπίσω μου ἐρχόμενος ἔμπροσθέν μου γέγονεν, ὅτι πρῶτός μου ἦν, where the antecedent of αὐτοῦ is the Logos. In i. 19 John testifies about himself that he is neither Christ nor Elias but 'the voice of one crying in the wilderness,' but in i. 32 he gives the μαρτυρία περὶ τοῦ φωτός when he tells of the descent of the Holy Spirit upon Jesus and concludes: κἀγὼ ἑώρακα καὶ μεμαρτύρηκα ὅτι οὗτός ἐστιν ὁ υἱὸς τοῦ θεοῦ. John's testimony is to a fact, the descent of the Spirit upon Jesus, but the real μαρτυρία is the consequence of that fact: that Jesus is the Logos, the Light, the Son of God. The contrast with the account in the Synoptics is interesting. There the Baptist does not testify to Jesus in particular but proclaims the coming of the Messiah, and knows nothing of the vision of the dove which appears as a sign to Jesus and not to him. When John is in prison he is still ignorant of Jesus' Messiahship, and Jesus testifies concerning him that he was greater than a prophet and the Elias that was to come. In the Synoptics Jesus appears as the fulfilment of John's prophecies; the Fourth Gospel recognizes Jesus as the Messiah, and the μαρτυρία of Jesus confirms the proclamation of John. In John iii. 26 ff., when the Jews come to the Baptist and tell him that Jesus to whom he had borne witness was now baptizing and attracting great crowds, John reminds them that he had testified that he himself was not the Christ, and that now Christ had come his work was done. "He who comes down from heaven is above all. He bears witness to what he has seen and heard and no one receives his testimony. He who does receive his testimony affirms that God is truthful." John's claim for Jesus' testimony is confirmed by Jesus himself, who says to the wondering Nicodemus, "We speak that we do know and testify to what we have seen, and you do not receive our testimony." In this chapter the testimony concerns baptism and the Spirit, but later it is the person of Jesus and his connexion with the Father that is the central point about which all other evidence is grouped. In v. 31 ff. Jesus compares the testimony which the Jews ask from John concerning him with the testimony which he has from the Father: "But I have testimony better than John's for the works which the Father has given me to do, these very works which I do testify of me that the Father has sent me, and the Father who has sent me has testified about me." This theme is repeated in viii. 18 f. and in x. 25 ff. The works which none other could do (xv. 24) are the miracles which are testimony both to himself and to the world of his prerogatives.

After Jesus' death the work of testifying is to go on under the direction of the Paraclete. " But when the Paraclete is come, whom I will send to you from the Father, the Spirit of Truth who proceeds from the Father, he shall bear witness of me, and you also are bearing witness because you have been with me from the beginning." [1] The testimony of the disciples and of the Spirit in the Christian life of future generations was undoubtedly in preaching, but the idea of the Spirit in the Fourth Gospel includes an influence on conduct as well as thought, and keeping the commandments (John xiv.-xv.) plays a similar rôle in the μαρτυρία of the disciples as miracles in that of Jesus, and the emphasis on keeping commandments in chapters xiv.-xv. shows that the μαρτυρία of the disciples also included works.

Nevertheless μαρτυρεῖν and μαρτυρία in the Fourth Gospel do not appear as technical terms, but as a natural and favourite metaphor of the author's to describe Jesus' knowledge of himself and his disciples' appreciation of his significance. There is no class of μάρτυρες as in Acts who having been with Jesus from his baptism are competent to speak of what they have seen and heard in his company. The κλητοί bear witness to supernatural truths to which the ordinary man has no access, and offer their evidence before a hostile world, but the case has been prejudged in heaven, and only in the court of last appeal will the truth prevail and the accusers stand accused.

The conception of Christian μάρτυς in the Apocalypse is directly con- The Apo-nected with that of the Fourth Gospel.[2] As in the latter, Jesus testifies calypse. to heavenly facts of which he is an eye-witness, and his followers testify both to his person and to his teaching by proclaiming Christian doctrine and in keeping the commandments. Christians are those who are in possession of Jesus' testimony, and when this is defined, Rev. xix. 10 ἡ γὰρ μαρτυρία Ἰησοῦ ἐστὶν τὸ πνεῦμα τῆς προφητείας, it means primarily that Christians advance the truth under the inspiration of the Spirit. It is evident that the Apocalypse was written at a time when the consequences of such testifying were dangerous, and often fatal. The author sees the Woman drunk with the blood of the saints and μάρτυρες,[3] and beneath the altar the souls of those who had been slain for the word of God and for the μαρτυρία which they had,[4] but it is quite clear that death and μαρτυρία are not equivalents. Some μάρτυρες have had to die for their testimony, but they died because they were μάρτυρες and did not become μάρτυρες because they died. It is often supposed that Antipas was a martyr in the later sense, because in ii. 13 he is called

---

[1] John xv. 26.
[2] Cf. Rev. i. 5, 9, iii. 14, vi. 9, xii. 11, 17, xvii. 6, xix. 10.
[3] Rev. xvii. 6.                [4] Rev. vi. 9.

'Αντίπας ὁ μάρτυς μου ὁ πιστός, ὃς ἀπεκτάνθη παρ' ὑμῖν, ὅπου ὁ Σατανᾶς κατοικεῖ, but it is more likely that here as in other cases death followed upon the testimony which, in this case, is presented in contrast to the later corruptions of the Nicolaitans.

The evolution of the word.

In the Johannine writings we have observed the transition from a testimony of words to a testimony of deeds. The miracles of Jesus and the virtuous conduct of the faithful are evidence of Christian truth. Nevertheless the element which became constitutive in the Christian conception of μάρτυς, viz. that the witness offers evidence not by living but by dying, is not yet present. It appears in two passages, one in the Epistle to the Hebrews, the other in 1 Timothy. The cloud of witnesses (Heb. xii. 1) who testify by their faith to the promise of immortality which awaits them are not missionaries but heroes. They have ventured much and suffered much, and their deeds are the evidence of things hoped for but not clearly perceived. The other passage is 1 Tim. ii. 5 ff., where the author explains that the death of Jesus was the evidence to that generation of the possibility of universal salvation, εἷς γὰρ θεός, εἷς καὶ μεσίτης θεοῦ καὶ ἀνθρώπων, ἄνθρωπος Χριστὸς Ἰησοῦς, ὁ δοὺς ἑαυτὸν ἀντίλυτρον ὑπὲρ πάντων, τὸ μαρτύριον καιροῖς ἰδίοις, εἰς ὃ ἐτέθην ἐγὼ κῆρυξ καὶ ἀπόστολος· ἀλήθειαν λέγω ἐν Χριστῷ οὐ ψεύδομαι, διδάσκαλος ἐθνῶν ἐν πίστει καὶ ἀληθείᾳ. This is the first case of martyrdom in the later sense. Here the death of Jesus is the testimony of which Paul is the herald and apostle, and Jesus offers the evidence by the sacrifice of his life.

We have shown that before the great persecutions, the general idea of Christian μάρτυρες as inspired witnesses to Christian truth played a considerable rôle, and that when the persecutions began and many witnesses must die for their testimony, they retained their title without altering its meaning. At the time of the Apocalypse, a μάρτυς is a witness whether he lived or died for the truth to which he testified, but shortly after this μαρτυρεῖν begins to have the sense of dying for the faith,[1] and the distinction between μάρτυς and ὁμολογήτης [2] indicates a growing tendency to reserve the former word for those who have given their lives. The reason for this specialization of meaning appears to be a natural development of the times.[3] From the beginning μάρτυς and μαρτυρεῖν were connected with the idea of Christian propaganda, but before the persecutions the usual methods of propaganda were public preaching and the realization of the Christian moral ideal, coupled with a zeal for Christian doctrine. The use of these words to describe these forms of activity persisted for some time, but during the persecutions external circumstances provided a new and sensational way of testifying to Christian truth, viz. admitting one's allegiance to Christ with the assurance that death would follow. This simple admission was more telling and, as we know from abundant evidence, produced a much greater impression upon pagans as testimony to Christianity than many hours of preaching or years of quiet conscientious living. The Christians,

[1] Cf. 1 Clem. v. 4.

[2] Delehaye, op. cit. pp. 85 ff.            Ibid. pp. 109 ff.

therefore, who died for their admission became witnesses *par excellence*, although the term was still occasionally applied to those who continued to witness in the old way.

NOTE VI. THE TWELVE AND THE APOSTLES

By KIRSOPP LAKE

### 1. *The Twelve*

The Twelve are mentioned in the Marcan narrative of the synoptic Gospels as having been appointed by Jesus, and they are referred to nine times as οἱ δώδεκα without the addition of the word ἀπόστολος (Mark iv. 10, vi. 7, ix. 35, x. 32, xi. 11, xiv. 10, 17, 20, 43). They are mentioned by this title in Matthew only in six places, all apparently taken from Mark, the same number of times in Luke, and four times in John (vi. 67, 70, 71, and xx. 24). They are, however, only mentioned once in Acts by this title (Acts vi. 2) and only once in the Pauline Epistles (1 Cor. xv. 5), where they appear as the witnesses of the Resurrection. In the non-Marcan parts of the synoptic Gospels the most significant passage is Mt. xix. 28 ( = Luke xxii. 30), where, though the phrase 'the Twelve' is not used, the promise is made to the disciples that they shall sit on twelve thrones judging the twelve tribes of Israel. (See Vol. I. pp. 295 ff.)

The choice of the Twelve is related in Mark iii. 14 ff. = Matt. x. 2 ff. **Mark.** = Luke vi. 13 ff.

The original meaning of the narrative, as given in Mark, is that the Twelve were the special lieutenants of Jesus, appointed by him to preach and to exorcise demons. In chap. vi. 7 Mark gives an account of a special mission in which the Twelve were sent out, by twos, in fulfilment of their function, with a few simple instructions for their conduct. The successful return of the Twelve to Jesus is not narrated until Mark vi. 30, the story being interrupted to make room for the long episode of the death of John the Baptist.

Matthew telescopes together Mark iii. 14 ff. and Mark vi. 7 ff., and **Matthew.** adds considerably to the address given by Jesus to the Twelve.

Luke takes over the Marcan account of the appointment of the **Luke.** Twelve in its proper place (so that Mark iii. 13-19 = Luke vi. 12-16), but significantly enough he omits the Marcan statement of the function of the Twelve—to preach and to cast out demons—and instead says that Jesus called them Apostles (which Mark does not say [1]), obviously in anticipation of his second book—Acts. Later on, when he comes to it, he also takes over from Mark the account of the mission of the Twelve

---

[1] There can be little doubt but that in Mark iii. 14 the addition οὓς καὶ ἀποστόλους ὠνόμασεν is a Western non-interpolation from Luke. It is found in ℵBCΔΘ and the Caesarean minuscules but not in the Old Latin or Old Syriac.

described in Mark vi. and the address given them by Jesus (so that Mark vi. 7-13 = Luke ix. 1-6), and once more he has considerably rewritten the rather simple sentences of Mark. Luke was also acquainted with some of the additional matter which Matthew added to the address of Jesus to the Twelve. But he put this into a separate context—the further mission of seventy apostles [1]—which is quite peculiar to him. Moreover, the sections which Luke took from Matthew's additional matter do not contain any of the significant paragraphs. On the other hand some of the paragraphs which are found both in Matthew and in Luke are considerably longer in Luke than in Matthew.

Matt. x. 5-8.    The significant verses, found in Matthew but not in Luke, are these : " Depart not into a way of Gentiles, but go rather to the lost sheep of the house of Israel. And as ye go make proclamation that the Kingdom of Heaven is at hand. Heal sick, raise dead, cleanse lepers, cast out demons ; freely ye received, freely give (x. 5-8). . . . And when they persecute you in this city flee to the next ; for verily I say to you, Ye shall not finish the cities of Israel before the Son of Man come (x. 23)."

The problem of these verses is dealt with in Vol. I. pp. 314 ff., and though a heavy stream of criticism has flowed under the bridges since its publication I do not see any necessity for change on any important point except one.[2] I then argued that the gospel of Matthew represented a conflation of the views of Jewish and Gentile Christians (cf. esp. Matt. xxiv. 14 (= Mark xiii. 10) and Matt. x. 5, 23). This still seems to me to be true, but whereas I then thought that the significant parts of Matt. x. were the propaganda of Jewish Christians, not the words of Jesus, I now incline to think [3] that they probably represent

---

[1] This may be a fragment of history which Mark has omitted, but unlike the Twelve the Seventy appear to have played no prominent part in the growth of the Church. Even their names are unknown to us, and the lists of pseudo-Dorotheos and others (conveniently published in Schermann's *Propheten- und Apostellegenden*) are obviously late and valueless compilations. It may be plausibly suggested that the Seventy are merely an echo of the Seventy Elders appointed by Moses in Numbers xi. 16 ff., but they are more probably connected with the belief (based on Gen. x.) that there are seventy nations of mankind.

[2] On which my opinion was changed by Burkitt's writings, public and private, and by his conversation.

[3] The hesitating nature of this phrase is not merely formal. No final judgement can be made, because it ought to be based on a previous investigation into Matthew's and Luke's methods of composition and of their relation to each other. Did Matthew ' collect ' the Sermon on the Mount, or did Luke ' separate ' its component parts ? Did either know the work of the other ? Who can really solve these puzzles ? The last half-century has really dealt very satisfactorily with the relation between Mark and the other synoptists, though the question of the original text of Mark as used by Matthew and Luke has been largely neglected, but the same cannot be said for the study of Matthew and Luke. Here almost everything remains to be done, and reconstructions of Q have been too often accepted as final, instead of as preliminary to the necessary study of details. (Cf. A. von Harnack, *Sayings of Jesus*, pp. x.-xiv.)

genuine words of Jesus which may have been known to Luke and excluded by him as too contradictory to the 'Mission to the Gentiles.'

In the Marcan narrative there is no suggestion that the Twelve were regarded as the foundation of a new organization. They are preachers who are sent out by Jesus in fulfilment of his own mission. If the verses quoted above from Matthew be taken as belonging to a primitive document they go even further. They mean that when the Twelve were sent out on their mission Jesus expected the parousia of the Son of Man before they finished their task. What was to be their position in the future, when the Son of Man did come? The answer of the document called Q is clear—they would be assessors at the Judgement. "Ye shall sit on twelve thrones, judging the twelve tribes of Israel" (Matt. xix. 28 = Luke xxii. 30). The main argument for thinking the Marcan-Matthaean concept of the work of the Twelve and their eschatological function to be primitive is that it was so soon falsified by the event that it can hardly be fiction. (See also below, p. 393.) Who would have invented it? *Cui bono?* The earlier view of the Twelve.

But in the early chapters of Acts, and in the later Christian literature, the Twelve have a different function and a different name. They are called 'Apostles'—a very strange word in Greek, though familiar in English—and their main function is to give the message about Jesus, rather than the message of Jesus, which is not mentioned in any of the missionary sermons quoted in Acts, or referred to in the Pauline Epistles. Moreover—and this is really the heart of the whole problem of Christian origins—the Twelve Apostles are no longer merely healers, exorcists, and the announcers of the End and of repentance opening the door to the New Age (as Mark vi. and Matt. x. make them), or even witnesses to Jesus, but in addition to all this are the inspired and miraculously powerful heads of a new society—the Church—endowed with the power to confer the gift of the Holy Spirit, which they had themselves received from the risen and glorified Jesus. The later view.

This Church is a prominent, probably the central feature of the general *Weltanschauung* of Acts. Its constituent elements are indicated by the variety of names used to describe its members (for a full discussion of which see Addit. Note 30); but perhaps the most significant description of them, at least for the present purpose, is the phrase σωζόμενοι— another of those remarkable words which did so much to make history by the varying connotation which they had for Greek or Jewish ears. The Church.

To the original Jewish Christians 'the saved' meant those who were 'safe' at the Judgement and would thus pass into the life of the World to Come; to unconverted Greeks it meant those whose nature had been changed from human and mortal to divine and immortal; to Greek Christians it had both connotations. At a later stage, visible in Acts and in the Epistles, teachers combined these with the idea of 'the Way,' and so added to Greek Christianity the typically Jewish concept of the value of conduct, and of salvation as partly conditional on a good life. Nevertheless, in spite of the variation produced by this and other connotations, the most important aspect of the Church, as it was destined to 'The saved.'

be throughout its history, is already clear in Acts.   It is the society of the 'saved,' who have attained salvation by the Holy Spirit[1] given by the risen Jesus to the Apostles, and afterwards by the Apostles to those who are worthy.

**The Twelve in Acts i.-v. and elsewhere.**   Thus the main feature of Catholic Christianity—the existence of an Apostolic Church—is clearly visible in the Acts and Epistles.   Between them, however, there is one significant difference.   In Acts i.-v. the Church is governed by the Twelve, and the Twelve are the 'Apostles.' So much importance is attached to the number that Matthias is elected to fill the place left empty by the defection of Judas the Traitor.   This theory that the Church was governed by the Twelve is perpetuated in the great mass of Didactic Literature, and became the dominant theory of Catholicism.   But in the Pauline Epistles, though the Church is as important and as supernaturally constituted under Apostolic leadership as in Acts i.-v., the Apostles are not the 'Twelve,' and there is no trace of any special limitation of the number of the Apostles.   Moreover, this is not because Paul is ignorant of the Twelve, but in spite of the fact that he knows them.   Similarly, in Acts, after the beginning of chapter vi. the Twelve are not mentioned.   The leaders of the Church are the 'Apostles,' but their head is James the brother of the Lord, not one of the 'Twelve.'   This agrees with the Pauline view, but not with Acts i.-v.   Here too, as in so many cases, Acts appears to be a combination of ideas and theories, as well as of sources and traditions.

**The historical nature of the Twelve.**   Influenced by this double usage of the word Apostle, some critics have argued that there is no historic foundation for the story of the appointment of the Twelve.   This theory seems unnecessary.   The historical fact is that the Apostles, in the narrower sense, are represented in Acts as preaching the resurrection of Jesus.   Apart from the limitation of number, which is for the moment unimportant, there can be no doubt but that this is probably true.   The resurrection of Jesus was by common consent the centre of the apostolic preaching.   If the synoptic Gospels had represented Jesus as choosing twelve disciples in order to preach his resurrection, there would be some reason for saying that this was an attempt to give the authority of the master to the preaching of the disciples.   But what are the facts?   That Mark represents Jesus as commissioning the Twelve, that they might be with him, and that he might send them out to preach and to have power to cast out devils.   To preach, that is to say, the message which he himself was announcing, the coming of the Kingdom and the necessity of repentance (Mk. iii. 14). Similarly, according to a narrative peculiar to Matthew but connected by him with the appointment of the Twelve (Mt. x. 5 ff.), it was specially enjoined on them to preach only in Israel, and their commission was to heal the sick, to raise the dead, to cleanse the lepers, to cast out devils. As they went they were to announce that the Kingdom of Heaven was at

---

[1] Is this quite as true of the earlier as it is of the later parts of Acts ?   Had Philip's converts in Samaria attained salvation before they received the Spirit ? (See further Additional Notes 9 and 11.)

hand.   They would raise opposition by this preaching, but before they had gone through .the cities of Israel the Son of Man would come. Could there be anything less like the course of history, or the message which they actually preached, as represented in Acts or by the Epistles of Paul ?   If Acts and the Epistles represent the actual preaching of the Apostles, Mark iii. 14 and Mt. x. 5 ff. cannot have been invented in order to give the authority of Jesus to the preaching of the Apostles.   It is of course possible that in the original form of the story the instructions of Jesus were given to all his disciples and not to a limited number, but why in that case should the story of the appointment of the Twelve have been so closely connected with it ?   Were it an invention it would surely be possible to see the reason for which it was put in.

## 2.  The Names of the Twelve

The question of the names of the Twelve stands on a different level. It is quite possible that the actual names were lost and that there is confusion in the tradition.   This can be seen in the first place from a double tradition of the names of the Apostles.

In Mt. x. 2, Mk. iii. 16, Lk. vi. 14, Acts i. 13, there are given The N.T. lists of the Twelve, with only the small differences which can be seen in tradition. the following table :

| MARK. | MATT. | LUKE. | ACTS. |
|---|---|---|---|
| Peter | Peter | Peter | Peter |
| James | Andrew | Andrew | John |
| John | James | James | James |
| Andrew | John | John | Andrew |
| Philip | Philip | Philip | Philip |
| Bartholomew | Bartholomew | Bartholomew | Thomas |
| Matthew | Thomas | Matthew | Bartholomew |
| Thomas | Matthew | Thomas | Matthew |
| James of Alphaeus | James of Alphaeus | James of Alphaeus | James of Alphaeus |
| Thaddaeus [1] | Thaddaeus | Simon the Zealot | Simon the Zealot |
| Simon the Kananean | Simon the Kananean | Judas of James | Judas of James |
| Judas Iscariot | Judas Iscariot | Judas Iscariot | Judas Iscariot |

The variations are only in the order of names, except that Thaddaeus is replaced in Luke and Acts by Judas of James.

A curiously different tradition seems preserved in two possibly The independent forms in the *Apostolic Church Orders* and in the *Epistola* tradition in *Apostolorum.* Apost. KO.

[1] Or possibly Lebbaeus : both in Mark and Matthew there is much early variation in the text.   But Thaddaeus seems the earlier reading, and Lebbaeus may be merely a Graecized form of Levi, in ignorance of, or in contradiction to, the theory which identified Levi with Matthew.

(i.) The *Apostolic Church Orders* (*Apostolische Kirchenordnung*) is a document of uncertain age. It is probably not later than 300 or earlier than 150. It is found in Greek in a manuscript at Vienna (*cod. Vindobon. hist. gr.* 7 [formerly 45]), and partially in manuscripts in Rome (*Ottobon. gr.* 408) and in Moscow (*Biblioth. synod.* 125). It is also preserved in the corpus of Church law found in Latin in the very ancient Verona palimpsest (Hauler, pp. 93-101) and in Syriac, Arabic, Bohairic, Sahidic, and Ethiopic. The first edition is that of J. W. Bickell, *Geschichte des Kirchenrechts*, 1843, pp. 107 ff. Later editions are by P. de Lagarde, *Reliquiae juris eccl. antiq. Graec.*, 1856, pp. 74 ff. (not to be confused with his edition in Bunsen's *Analecta Ante-Nicaena*, 1854, which is a retranslation into Greek from the Coptic) ; J. B. Pitra, *Juris eccl. Graecorum historia et monumenta*, 1864, vol. i. pp. 75 ff. (a text to be recommended, among other things, for the beauty of its printing) ; Hilgenfeld, *Novum Testamentum extra canonem receptum*, 1866 ; A. Harnack, 'Lehre der zwölf Apostel,' *TU.* ii. 1, 1884 ; and F. X. Funk, *Doctrina duodecim apostolorum*, 1887.

The relation of this document to the general body of pseudo-apostolic literature is obscure and complex. It appears to have been part of a collection containing the *Didascalia*, the *Apostolic Church Orders*, and the *Egyptian Church Orders*, of which the last was recently identified by Schwartz, and independently but a little later by Connolly, as the *Traditio Apostolica* of Hippolytus (see Connolly, ' The So-called Egyptian Church Orders ' in *Texts and Studies*, viii. 4). This collection became the foundation of the *Apostolic Constitutions* in the fourth century, and also is found in a somewhat different composition in which it was combined with the xvi *titloi* of John Scholasticus, and passed into the *Syriac Octateuch* of Clement and other oriental books of canonical law.

The *Apostolic Church Orders* was generally but not always included in these collections. Its history has been elucidated by Beneševic's treatise on the xvi *titloi*, unfortunately accessible only in Russian, and in Ed. Schwartz's very valuable *Über d. pseudo-apostol. Kirchenordnungen*, 1910. It is important to note that though the *Apostolic Church Orders* has been printed by most editors as a separate document, it is not so found in any manuscript or version. It is, however, sufficiently clear from its nature that it was originally independent. Its origin was discussed first by Krawutzcky in his ' Über das altkirchliche Unterrichtsbuch, die zwei Wege oder die Entscheidung des Petrus,' *Theol. Quartalschrift*, 1882, iii. pp. 359 ff., in which he indicated clearly the general characteristics of a document which lay behind the present one. One year later Bryennius published the *Didache*, which proved to be not exactly the document indicated by Krawutzcky, but an immediate descendant of it.

The list of Apostles in the *KO*. In the light of this discovery A. von Harnack wrote his magistral ' Lehre der zwölf Apostel ' in *TU.* ii. 1 in 1884, in which on pp. 193 ff. he dealt with the *Apostolic Church Orders*. For the present purpose it is unnecessary to pursue all the details of his analysis. The point which is important is that an early editor made use of a list of the apostles which ran :

John, Matthew, Peter, Andrew, Philip, Simon, James, Nathanael, Thomas, Cephas, Bartholomew, Jude of James.

The greater part of the *Didache*, rather freely edited, was distributed among these Apostles, with the exception of Judas of James, who was given nothing. Harnack and others therefore concluded that the redactor made use of an early uncanonical list of the Apostles containing only eleven names, Judas of James being a later interpolation, but no light was thrown on the identity of this source or on its affiliations until the discovery of another document.

(ii.) In 1895 there appeared in the *Proceedings of the Royal Prussian Academy* an account of 'Eine bisher unbekannte altchristliche Schrift in koptischer Sprache,'[1] by Carl Schmidt, at that time a scholar of the German Imperial Archaeological Institute in Egypt. Schmidt was helped in further research on this document by Pierre Lacau, the Egyptologist, but a full publication was delayed in the hope of wider knowledge, which came gradually. *The Epistola Apost.*

The first step was the discovery in Vienna by Dr. Bick, the librarian, of a palimpsest, originally from Bobbio, of a Latin version of the same document.[2] Schmidt then determined to publish the Coptic text, and in 1910 this had already been printed, when the present Provost of Eton, Dr. James, noticed an article by the Abbé Guerrier in the *Revue de l'Orient Chrétien*, entitled 'Un testament (éthiopien) de Notre Seigneur et Sauveur Jésu-Christ en Galilée.' He wrote to Schmidt, who in turn corresponded with Guerrier, and it was found that this Ethiopic document, which Dillmann had known but not thought worth publication, was identical with the Coptic apocryphon. Schmidt once more delayed his publication until Guerrier was ready, and it was not until 1913 that Guerrier published the text, with a French translation, in the *Patrologia Orientalis* of Graffin and Nau.[3]

Finally in 1919 Schmidt published in volume xliii. of the *Texte und Untersuchungen*[4] a parallel translation of the *Epistola* from Coptic and Ethiopic, with full discussions of all the questions connected with it.

Guerrier's publication had never attracted much attention, partly because it was unaccompanied by any introduction indicating its importance, but chiefly because its title was misleading and its contents composite. The title 'Testament of our Lord and Saviour Jesus Christ' implies some connexion with the *Testamentum Domini* of Rahmani[5]; but the opening chapters dissipate this notion, for they contain merely an

[1] *Sitzungsberichte der phil.-hist. Classe vom 20 Juni*, 1895.

[2] *Wiener Palimpseste*, I. Teil. Cod. Palat. Vindobonensis 16, olim Bobbiensis (*Sitzungsber. d. k. Akad. d. Wissensch. in Wien, phil.-hist. Klasse*, Band clix. 7 Abteil.), and Hauler, *Wiener Studien*, 1908, Bd. xxx. pp. 308 ff.

[3] Vol. ix. part 3, *Le Testament en Galilée de Notre Seigneur Jésus-Christ*.

[4] The title is *Gespräche Jesu mit seinen Jüngern nach der Auferstehung, ein katholisch-apostolisches Sendschreiben des 2ten Jahrhunderts*; but in the body of the book Schmidt always speaks of the document as the *Epistola Apostolorum*.

[5] *Testamentum domini nostri Jesu Christi*, 1899.

apocalypse, important mainly for its delineation of Antichrist. Guerrier seems to have been ignorant of Schmidt's preliminary notice in the Berlin *Sitzungsberichte*, and probably only the interest of M. R. James in the Antichrist led him to notice the book and read it through, and discover that in the middle its character suddenly changed. But Schmidt now showed beyond all doubt that the title 'Testament of the Lord' was taken from the ordinary book of that name, which was accidentally associated with the other document in the Ethiopic copy. He also shows —what is self-evident when it is pointed out—that the first eleven chapters of Guerrier's document have nothing in common with the remainder of it, which contains an *Epistola Apostolorum* identical with the Coptic document. The Coptic is an incomplete manuscript of a better text, while the Ethiopic is a complete manuscript of a worse text. Both are based, directly or indirectly, on a lost Greek original from which the Latin palimpsest, unfortunately only a small fragment, was also derived.

The date of this document is tolerably certain, and greatly enhances its value. It states that the second advent will take place in the year 120 after Christ, which from the context seems to mean 120 years after the Resurrection. This is the date given by the Coptic; the Ethiopic puts 150 instead of 120, which seems to be an attempt to give the date in terms of a chronology beginning from the birth of Christ, but even if the Ethiopic be the correct text, a document belonging to the year 180 in our reckoning is a sufficiently valuable discovery. In general there can be little doubt but that before 180 is the latest date to which the *Epistola* can be referred, and before 150 seems to me more probable.[1]

The provenance of the *Epistola* is doubtful, though Schmidt's view that it comes from Ephesus probably has the most arguments in its favour. The points on which discussion is always likely to turn are the references to Cerinthus, which indicate that Cerinthus and the *Epistola* belong to the same locality, and—unfortunately for the present purpose —the list of the Apostles.

Schmidt has a long excursus on Cerinthus and the Alogi, in which he controverts Eduard Schwartz, who in 1914 had argued that the tradition of Irenaeus linking Cerinthus with Ephesus was quite untrustworthy.[2]

[1] Can Papias have been referring to the *Epistola* when he expressed his famous preference for oral tradition to that which was written?

[2] *Zeitschrift für die neutestamentliche Wissenschaft*, 1914, pp. 210 ff. Schmidt endeavours to refute Schwartz and re-establish the old tradition, incidentally dealing at length with the question of the Alogi. In this he may be right, and it is perhaps more probable that Cerinthus belongs to Ephesus than elsewhere, but the whole question may well be re-opened. Whether, however, he is right in thinking that Cerinthus cannot have been a Judaist is more doubtful, and the whole question is still full of difficulties. Was it impossible for a man to be a Judaizer and a Docetist at the same time? Before this question can be answered we shall probably be brought back once more to the problem whether Ignatius in his epistles was attacking one party or two; but to discuss these points here would be to wander too far afield.

The connexion of Cerinthus with Ephesus and of the *Epistola* with Cerinthus is the main argument which Schmidt brings forward, but he also attaches great weight to the fact that the *Epistola* commands the celebration of the Passover in commemoration of the death of Christ, and connects this with the Quartodecimans of Asia.

The main argument against this reasoning is the generally supposed connexion of the *Apostolic Church Orders* with Egypt, and the similarity of the list of the Apostles in the *Epistola* and in the *Apost. KO*. Nevertheless the reasons for connecting the *Apost. KO*. with Egypt are very flimsy— there is in fact nothing in them which indicates their origin.

The *Epistola* enumerates the Apostles as follows :

John, Thomas, Peter, Andrew, James, Philip, Bartholomew, Matthew, Nathanael, Judas Zelotes, Kephas.

The list of the Apostles in the *Epistola*.

Schmidt argues that this is the source of the list in the *Apost. KO*. Certainly both lists have eleven names, thus implying that though recognizing the defection of Judas Iscariot, they knew nothing of the choice of a successor. Moreover, the only difference in the names is that Simon is replaced by Judas Zelotes, and that this is not an accident is suggested by the similar reading of the Old Latin codices *a b g h* in Matthew x. 3 which reads Judas Zelotes instead of Thaddaeus, who in Matthew seems to be substituted for Judas of James in Luke, and comes immediately before Simon the Zealot. Schmidt thinks that this list in the *Epist. Apost.* is the source of that in the *Apostolic Church Orders* in spite of the difference of order. Certainly it represents a cognate tradition. But the possibility of a common source seems to me not inconsiderable. (See Baumstark, ' Alte und neue Spuren eines ausserkanonischen Evangeliums [vielleicht des Ägypterevangeliums]' in the *ZNTW.*, 1913, and for a curious point of connexion with Hippolytus see the same writer's ' Hippolytus und die ausserkanonische Evangelienquelle' in *ZNTW.*, 1914, pp. 332 ff.)

Assuming, then, that the *Epist. Apost.* and the *Apost. KO*. at least represent a tradition either Ephesian or Egyptian in origin other than the canonical, it may be asked whether it has any claims to serious consideration. The decisive question is clearly the differentiation of Peter from Kephas.[1] This cannot be right, and seems to show that the list is inferior to the canonical. But the question may well be raised whether the absence of any allusion to Matthias as the successor of Judas Iscariot does not indicate that the story in Acts i. was either unknown to the compiler or was rejected by him.

It is obvious that both these traditions may contain some doublets. Doublets. This is certainly true of the second list if Kephas be really identical with Peter. It is possibly also true of the list in the Gospels, for Thomas can

---

[1] On the history of this differentiation see G. La Piana, *Harvard Theological Review*, vol. xiv. (1921), pp. 187 ff. It was often used to remove from Peter the stigma implied by Gal. ii. 11. It was not Peter but Kephas who was κατεγνωσμένος.

scarcely be a real name since it merely means 'twin,' and the old Syriac tradition says that he was Jude the Lord's brother. And if Lebbaeus be the right form of the text in Mark iii. 18 it probably is a Greek method of writing Levi, who is usually identified with Matthew. It is perhaps unprofitable to speculate far in the elucidation of the names in the lists of the Apostles, for certainty is unattainable ; but it is probably true that the confusions imply some very early loss of exact knowledge of the names.

### 3. The Word ᾽Απόστολος

In every language there is a word to describe a person who is sent by the king or by the magistrates to act as their authorized representative. The Aramaic word for such persons is שליחם. There is nothing unusual about it, and if Jesus sent out authorized representatives as Mark says that he did, this is the name which he would naturally have used. In the New Testament this is generally rendered into Greek by ἀπό-στολος, but this word, though etymologically correct, is not customary in non-Christian Greek.

᾽Απόστολος in classical Greek.

The word ἀπόστολος has had a curious history. The cognate word ἀποστολή was used in classical Greek to describe a mission, and the verb ἀποστέλλω was common in this sense. ᾽Απόστολος is found only once in the sense of a messenger, but is common as an adjective in the phrase ἐπόστολα πλοῖα, and so came to be used substantivally with the meaning of 'a fleet,' while ἀποστολεύς meant an admiral. In classical Greek of the later period ἀπόστολος has no other meaning than ' fleet,' though Hesychius says that it could mean an admiral, giving the definition ἀπόστολος, στρατηγὸς κατὰ πλοῦν πεμπόμενος.

For ἀπόστολος in the sense of 'envoy' there is in classical Greek only the example, referred to above, from Herodotus i. 21; cf. v. 38.

The LXX.

It is also found in this sense only once in the LXX (3 Kings xiv. 6) in reference to Ahijah, καὶ ἐγώ εἰμι ἀπόστολος (שלוח) πρός σε σκληρός. This is the more remarkable because the LXX uses ἀποστέλλω almost to the exclusion of πέμπω, and ἀπόστολος would have been expected as the correlative substantive, but ἄγγελος seems to have been consistently preferred.

Josephus.

᾽Απόστολος is equally rare in Josephus, but its one occurrence is important, for in Antiq. xvii. 11. 1 Josephus speaks of Varus, the head of a delegation of Jews, as ἀπόστολος αὐτῶν.

The N.T.

In the New Testament the word appears at first to be widely used, but analysis suggests that it is a Pauline-Lucan word, or at least one which owed its general use to Pauline-Lucan influence.

Mark.

In Mark it is once used in describing the Twelve, whom according to Mark iii. 14 Jesus had chosen ἵνα ἀποστέλλῃ αὐτοὺς κηρύσσειν καὶ ἔχειν ἐξουσίαν ἐκβάλλειν τὰ δαιμόνια. When they return from this mission they are described in vi. 30 as οἱ ἀπόστολοι. The word obviously refers to the mission which had been ended by their return, not to any future offices in the Church ; it may be a description rather than a title. Mark, indeed—and it is one of the most valuable indications of its early date and general trustworthiness—has no-. where any suggestion that Jesus contemplated the foundation of a 'Church.' The ministry of Jesus, according to Mark, was a campaign (i.) against demons and disease, (ii.) to induce men to repent, that they might be worthy of the Kingdom which would come so soon. The Twelve are not an official class in a new society, but emissaries sent out by Jesus to deliver his message.

In Matthew the word ἀπόστολος does not appear except in x. 2-5 in Matthew. the abbreviation of the Marcan account of the choice of the Twelve.

In Luke it is found five times (Luke ix. 10, xi. 49, xvii. 5, xxii. 14, Luke. xxiv. 10), and it is frequently used in Acts and in the Pauline Epistles (twenty-five times, not counting the Pastoral Epistles).

In John ἀπόστολος is only used once (John xiii. 16), where it is John. apparently a paraphrase of the saying given in Matt. x. 24.

In the Apocalypse ἀπόστολος is used three times. (i.) In ii. 2 of Apocalypse. 'those who call themselves apostles, and are not,' where the meaning clearly is 'Christian missionary' as it is in the *Didache.* (ii.) In xviii. 20, where apostles and prophets are joined together much as they are in the *Didache.* (iii.) In xxi. 14, where the 'twelve apostles' are the foundation-stones of the New Jerusalem, the Church.

Thus we have the extremely interesting linguistic fact that the The origin Pauline-Lucan branch of Christian literature seems to have popularized of the N.T. and given a technical meaning to a word which was otherwise scarcely usage. used, except in a different sense, in the whole course of previous Greek literature. At the same time, though the popularity of the word is doubtless due to Pauline-Lucan influence, Josephus, the Apocalypse, and perhaps the single example of the word in Mark, forbid the hypothesis that its original is Pauline-Lucan. The rarity of the word in John and in Matthew shows that it can hardly be quite primitive, but it is very early, and its place of origin is uncertain. What was the place of which the usage affected Paul, Luke, and the Apocalypse?

Possibly ἀπόστολος was used in this sense in the Koine Greek, and there was perhaps an underground stream of popular usage connecting Herodotus and Luke. This, however, seems unlikely, and I am inclined to think that the sudden emergence of the word is one of those happy accidents which happen so frequently in the history of language. Mark, I think, correctly represents the fact that the Twelve, in consequence of their mission of preaching in Galilee, were called שׁליחים ; they had been 'sent'[1] by Jesus, and they, or such of them as remained, held a position of prestige. How should that word be translated? ἄγγελος was the LXX rendering, and is probably used in the Apocalypse of those who in Pauline-Lucan phraseology would be termed the 'apostles' of the churches (see Rev. i. 20, etc.). But ἄγγελος was coming more and more to mean 'angel,' and so another word was desirable, but why did Mark hit upon ἀπόστολος as the right word?

[1] Professor Burkitt points out to me that it is worthy of note "that the best attested claim made about himself by Jesus is that he was one 'sent.' See Mark ix. 37, Luke iv. 18, Matt. xv. 24, John v. 38, etc."

Harnack's
theory.
It has been suggested, notably by Harnack in his *Mission und
Ausbreitung*, ed. 4, pp. 340 ff., that the word was first adopted by Jews,
but the evidence, though interesting, scarcely amounts to demonstration.
The facts are as follows :

The Jewish
Patriarch.
After the destruction of Jerusalem, and the extinction of the
high-priestly Sadducean families, the leadership of the Jews passed to
the rabbinical Pharisaic families, and one of them—that of Hillel,
to which Gamaliel belonged—was recognized by the Romans as the
official head of the Jews.   In Hebrew he was called 'Nāsi,' and in Greek
sometimes ἐθνάρχης, but oftener πατριάρχης.[1]   The exact date at which
this 'Patriarchate' was instituted is unknown, but it existed from the
second to the fourth century, when it was suppressed, and the leadership
of Judaism tended to pass more and more to the Exilarch of Babylon,
who was treated with great respect by the Persians.   (For the very
interesting details of the Exilarchate see S. Funk, *Die Juden in
Babylonien*.)

The *Codex
Theo-
dosianus*.
From the *Codex Theodosianus* it appears that the 'Patriarch' had official
representatives who were entrusted especially with the bringing back
of the *aurum coronarium* which the Romans sanctioned as a contribution
from the Jews outside Palestine.   These were called *apostoli* (*superstitionis
indignae est, ut archisynagogi sive presbyteri Iudaeorum vel quos ipsi apostolos
vocant*, etc., *Cod. Theod.* xvi. 8. 14 [April 11, A.D. 399]), and in the
twenty-fifth letter of Julian the Apostate (204 in the edition of Bidez
and Cumont, p. 281) the contribution collected is probably called
ἀποστολή, though it is possible that here, as in Epiphanius, the word
means 'the function of the Apostles.'   The text of the letter says ἐπὶ
πλέον δὲ ὑμᾶς εὐωχεῖσθαι βουλόμενος τὸν ἀδελφὸν Ἴουλον, τὸν αἰδεσι-
μώτατον πατριάρχην, παρήνεσα καὶ τὴν λεγομένην [εἶναι] παρ᾽ ὑμῖν
ἀποστολὴν κωλυθῆναι κτλ.   But it should be noted that the authenticity of this letter is disputed.   It is accepted by Juster, *Les Juifs
dans l'empire romain*, vol. i. p. 159, but rejected by Bidez and Cumont,
p. 279.

The Jewish
*Apostoli* in
Christian
literature.
Jerome.
The existence of these *apostoli* can be traced in the fourth century
in Jerome, Eusebius, and Epiphanius :

Jerome says in his commentary on Gal. i. 1 (Migne, *P.L.* xxvi. 311) :
" *Usque hodie a patriarchis Iudaeorum apostolos mitti, a quibus etiam tunc
reor Galatas depravatos Legem observare coepisse, vel certe alios de Iudaeis
credentibus in Christum perrexisse Galatiam, qui assererent Petrum quoque
apostolorum principem, et Jacobum fratrem Domini, Legis caeremonias
custodire.   Ad distinctionem itaque eorum qui mittuntur ab hominibus, et sui,
qui sit missus a Christo, tale sumpsit exordium* : '*Paulus apostolus, non
ab hominibus, neque per hominem.*'   *Apostolus autem, hoc est*, '*missus*,'
*Hebraeorum proprie vocabulum est, quod Silas* [v.l. *Silai*] *quoque sonat, cui
a mittendo* '*missi*' *nomen*[2] *impositum est.*"

---

[1] Cf. G. F. Moore, *Judaism*, vol. iii. note 5.

[2] Silas (or Silai) is apparently a bad transliteration of the Hebrew שלח, or
the Aramaic שלח with transposition of the vowels.

Eusebius, *In Esaiam* xviii. 1 (Migne, *P.G.* xxiv. 213), says Ἀποστόλους Eusebius.
δὲ εἰσέτι καὶ νῦν ἔθος ἐστὶν Ἰουδαίοις ὀνομάζειν τοὺς ἐγκύκλια γράμματα
παρὰ τῶν ἀρχόντων αὐτῶν ἐπικομιζομένους.

Epiphanius, *Panarion* xxx. 4, gives us fuller information, and shows Epiphanius.
that the *apostoli* were not merely collectors, but legates from the Patriarchs
with extensive powers.   The story is too long to quote in full, but it is
worth reading.   It concerns the adventures of one Joseph of Tiberias,
a Jew, who when an 'Apostle' of the Jewish Patriarch in the time of
Constantine had been a severe and unpopular disciplinarian.   In the
course of his travels he made friends with a bishop who lent him a copy
of the Gospels.   When the Jews discovered this they beat him and threw
him into the river.   He then became a Christian, and was given the
rank of *Comes* by Constantine, with the privilege of building churches
in Galilee.   Later on he was a vigorous opponent of the Arians, and—
according to his own account—when his wife died, married again, in
order to avoid ordination.

Joseph clearly made a great impression on Epiphanius, and his
statement about the *apostoli* is εἰσὶ δὲ οὗτοι μετὰ τὸν πατριάρχην ἀπόστολοι
καλούμενοι, προσεδρεύουσι δὲ τῷ πατριάρχῃ, καὶ σὺν αὐτῷ πολλάκις
καὶ ἐν νυκτὶ καὶ ἐν ἡμέρᾳ συνεχῶς διάγουσι διὰ τὸ συμβουλεύειν καὶ
ἀναφέρειν αὐτῷ τὰ κατὰ τὸν νόμον.

Thus in the fourth century the envoys of the Jewish Patriarch were
undoubtedly called ἀπόστολοι.   When and why did the custom begin of so
calling them?   Grätz (*Geschichte der Juden*, ed. 1, iv. pp. 345 ff.) thought
that it began after the calamities of the third century, in the Patriarchate
of Gamaliel IV. or of Judah III.   More recent scholars (Harnack,
Juster, and Monnier) think that it is far older, and goes back to the
fall of Jerusalem.[1]

Doubtless the institution of messengers is older than the fourth century,
and it would have been natural to call them שליח.   The question is
whether this word was translated into Greek as ἀπόστολος.   For this
there is no evidence.   All the testimony which we have is Christian,
and a Christian in the third century might naturally translate שליח
ἀπόστολος.

Still less is there evidence that similar envoys of the high priests The poll-tax.
were so called before 70.   At that time there was an authorized poll-
tax on all Jews of two drachmae.   The speech of Cicero *Pro Flacco* is the
classical evidence that in the first century, when there was a *senatus
consultum* against the exportation of gold, an exception was noted in
favour of the Jews.   This tax was not collected by representatives of the
high priests, but by delegates of the various settlements of the Diaspora.
The chief description of this tax and its dispatch to Jerusalem is Philo,
*De spec. leg.* i. 77 (Mang. ii. p. 224).   Even if the *aurum coronarium* be
taken as the legitimate successor of the 'didrachma' of the earlier period,
it is clear that it was collected in a different manner, and that the persons

---

[1] It is even argued that it may be traced to the Persian period.   See
'Apostle' in the *Jewish Encyclopaedia*, and F. Gavin's 'Shaliach and Apostolos'
in the *Anglican Theological Review*, January 1927.

'sent' with it came from the Diaspora, not from the high priests. Nor is there any evidence of the' use of the word ἀπόστολος. But it is noteworthy that ἀπόστολος seems to be used in a somewhat similar sense of Epaphroditus in Philipp. ii. 25.

Antiochian influence.

Thus there is no evidence that the word ἀπόστολος was borrowed from Jewish sources. More probably it was the Greek-speaking church of Antioch which hit on the idea of using the rare but natural word ἀπόστολος. If the word be Antiochian in origin the facts are easily explained. Paul—the earliest witness to its use—and Luke are certainly closely connected with Antioch, and the occasional and rare use of the word in Mark, Matthew, and the Apocalypse is natural ; for even if none of these documents came from Antioch, it was so influential a centre of Christian propaganda that its vocabulary was sure to influence writers from other places. It is indeed interesting how far all the earliest Greek terminology may point to Antioch. Certainly there is a fair case for the view that from Antioch came not only ἀπόστολος but also κύριος, ἐκκλησία, and Χριστιανός. But ἀπόστολος, unlike κύριος, which is important for its connotation in Greek religion, and ἐκκλησία, which is important for its connotation in Jewish religion, seems to have no history and no wide connotation. Of all the technical terms of the New Testament it is the most markedly and exclusively Christian.

The wider usage.

Paul.

Two usages can be distinguished. (i.) In the Pauline Epistles ἀπόστολος is used in the sense of a Christian missionary who has been commissioned to the service of the gospel. Paul himself claimed that his commission came from God and from Christ, but the form of expression used in Gal. i. 1 etc. suggests that he knew of apostles whose commission was from men. There is no implication that he regarded the Apostles as limited in number to twelve, and that he thought that an apostle need have seen the Lord is a rather rash conclusion[1] from 1 Cor. ix. 1. In the context of this passage St. Paul has been discussing the question of things offered to idols, and has said that he would rather never eat meat again than give offence to weaker brethren ; he then goes on, " Am I not free ? am I not an apostle ? have I not seen Jesus our Lord ? are not you my work in the Lord ? If I am no apostle for others, at least I am to you ; for you are in the Lord my seal of fellowship." It is customary to regard this passage as the answer to an attack on Paul's apostolate : indirectly it may be so, for the troubles in Corinth broke out soon afterwards ; but directly and principally it has to do with the question of things offered to idols. It is a mistake to think that all the qualifications mentioned in ix. 1 ff. are intended to prove that he was an apostle. The main point is the argument that he, in spite of his privileges, prefers not to use them lest he should give offence, and that the Corinthians ought in the same way to consider the feelings of others in relation to things offered to idols. Only incidentally does he put in a parenthesis defending his apostolate. If

[1] This conclusion is due to reading into the Epistles the view found in Acts x. 41, that an apostle was one who had been an eye-witness to the risen Lord.

this be so, the three clauses, "Am I not free? am I not an apostle? have I not seen Jesus our Lord?" are three separate claims to distinction, and it is an exaggeration to say that Paul only regarded as 'apostles' those who had seen Jesus.[1]

There are also traces of this use of the word ἀπόστολος in Acts.  In In Acts. xiv. 4 and 14 Barnabas and Paul are described as ἀπόστολοι, but it is unnecessary to suppose, as is sometimes done, that this apostolate is thought to begin with the commission described in xiii. 1. (See also note on iv. 36.)

As was stated above, this view of the apostolate is probably also In the preserved in the *Didache*, where ἀπόστολος seems to mean a Christian *Didache.* missionary and nothing more.  This is often stated as though it were certain, but to do so overlooks the fictitious nature of the *Didache* and the fact that it is not intended by the writer to be a description of his own time (a date more uncertain than most writings on the subject suggest[2]), but a picture of the days when the disciples of Jesus were still alive.  It is therefore intrinsically just possible that in *Didache* xi. 3 'apostle' means one of the original body of the Twelve.  The reason for doubting this is that, assuming, as we certainly ought, that the passage is intended as a picture of the first century, the writer thinks not merely that the Apostles may be unknown to those whom they visit, but even that they may be capable of bad conduct.  Could he have thought this if 'apostle' means 'one of the Twelve'?  It is therefore probable that the *Didache* really continues the Pauline tradition and uses ἀπόστολος in a general sense, not confining it to the Twelve.

(ii.) Over against this extended view is a more contracted one which The limits the Apostles to the Twelve.  This is plain from a comparison of narrower usage. Acts i. 2 ff., i. 17, i. 25 f., etc.  Even if it be not clear in every place that 'the Apostles' means the Twelve, probably no one will doubt that this is in the mind of the editor—as distinct from his sources—and that such a verse as Acts xiv. 14 represents the different usage of a source employed by the editor, not his own opinion.  The limitation of 'apostle' to the Twelve became general in the later Church, though Eusebius and others admit that the Seventy of Luke had a claim to the title of apostle, and explain the references to Barnabas and others as apostles by the hypothesis that they belonged to the Seventy.  (Cf. Eusebius, *Hist. Eccl.* i. 12.)

These facts suggest that originally Jesus chose twelve representatives Conclusion. who were naturally called 'Shaliach' and often referred to as 'the Twelve.'  Later on, perhaps before or perhaps after the Resurrection, other disciples were recognized as 'Shaliach' and in Greek were called 'Apostles.'  Still later this second stage was forgotten and the word

[1] I have ventured to reprint this passage from *The Earlier Epistles of St. Paul,* p. 229.

[2] See especially J. A. Robinson, *Barnabas, Hermas, and the Didache,* which shows very conclusively that it is—to say the least—extremely rash to date the *Didache* in the first century.  For myself, I think that the *Didache* in its present form is later than Hermas.

'apostle' was usually narrowed in meaning so as to be synonymous with 'the Twelve.'

#### 4. *The Apostles in Acts*

Apostles as witnesses.

According to the opening verses of Acts Jesus had chosen the Apostles during his ministry (in the Western text 'to preach the gospel'), and in his parting words before the Ascension commissioned them to be 'his witnesses' throughout the world.   This strikes one of the two primary notes found in Acts as to the function of the Apostles.

First, they were witnesses who were able to say 'what we have seen with our eyes,' and thus deliver authoritatively the 'message about Jesus.' The exercise of this function is illustrated in every speech of Peter in Acts.   Obviously the ability to give this witness was not necessarily limited to the 'Twelve,' but equally clearly the meaning of the writer is that only the Twelve received the commission, and probably that is why Paul's vision of the risen Jesus, and the commission which he received, are so emphasized at the beginning of the Pauline section of Acts.

As administrators.

Equally important for the historian is the second great function of the Apostles—to govern and administer the Church.   The Church at the beginning consisted of 120 persons (Acts i. 15), who were waiting in Jerusalem for the speedy coming of the End.   But as the End was delayed the problem of their common life became more and more important, and to regulate it was the work of the Twelve, of whom Peter is generally the leader and spokesman.   The exact nature and limits of this work are nowhere defined, but a reasonably clear picture of facts and of problems can be formed by considering the following passages.

Acts i.-v.

(i.) Acts i. 15 ff.   At the first meeting of the 'brethren' in Jerusalem after the Ascension Peter proposed that one of them should be elected to take the place of the traitor Judas.   The appointment was made by the community, but on the motion of Peter, and it obviously implies that being reckoned among the Twelve was a position of dignity and power. The exact extent to which the making of the appointment was divided between Peter and the community depends upon the text.   According to the Neutral text the community nominated two and then cast lots between them : according to the Western text Peter nominated two and the community either voted or cast lots between his two nominees. Which is the right text ?   It does not seem to be a case of accidental variation, and the Western text is remarkably like some forms of later ecclesiastical elections.   Did the Western text of Acts produce the ecclesiastical organization, or did the ecclesiastical organization modify the text ?   It is perhaps important to notice (*a*) that Peter and the Twelve took this position of leadership before the day of Pentecost, and therefore it was not due to the possession of the Spirit ; (*b*) that obviously the Twelve did not exhaust the number of those who were eligible to serve as 'witnesses' but had not been commissioned to serve by Jesus.

(ii.) Acts ii. 1 ff.   On the day of Pentecost, whether it was they only or the whole community which received the Spirit, it was in any case

Peter, acting as spokesman of the Twelve, who converted three thousand of the crowd who were listening.

(iii.) Acts ii. 41 ff., iv. 32 ff., vi. 1 ff. The Apostles appear in these verses as the recipients and distributors of charity, until the responsibility becomes more than they can manage without help. The result was that the Seven were appointed. By whom ? Is it an accident that once more there are textual variants at the critical point ? According to the Codex Vaticanus Peter said, " It is not good for us to leave the word of God to serve tables. Let *us* choose, brethren, seven men from among you. . . . But we ourselves will attend to prayer and the service of the Lord. And the proposal was accepted by all the congregation (singular) and they chose Stephen . . . and they stood them before the Apostles and they prayed and laid hands on them." The variation of ' we ' and ' you ' and ' they ' is extraordinarily ambiguous. It clearly means that the Seven were ordained by the Apostles. Does it mean that they were selected by the Apostles or by the community ? (See note *ad loc.*) The Western text has no doubt about the matter and rewrites the passage to make it clear that the Seven were selected by the congregation and ordained by the Apostles. Once more, what is the relation between the history of the text and the history of ecclesiastical institutions ?

In these three passages it is clear that the Apostles are the Twelve, that Peter is their head, and that the government of the Church is in their hands. There is no suggestion that they conferred the gift of the Spirit ; all that Peter says is that if others repent and are baptized in the name of Jesus Christ they will receive the same gift. It is quite possible (see Vol. I. pp. 339 f.) that the reference to baptism is editorial ; but in any case there is a remarkable absence of any reference to Apostolic mediation as necessary for the gift of the Spirit.  *Summary of Acts i.-v.*

(iv.) Acts viii. 5 ff. This is the story of Philip's work in Samaria : how he converted many by his preaching about ' the Kingdom of God and the name of Jesus Christ,' so that ' they were baptized, both men and women.' The narrative continues : " When the Apostles in Jerusalem heard that Samaria had accepted the word of God they sent to them Peter and John, who went down and prayed for them that they might receive Holy Spirit. For it had not yet fallen on any of them, but they had merely been baptized in the name of the Lord Jesus. Then they laid hands on them and they began to receive Holy Spirit." It seems clear from this passage that its writer believed that the Apostles and no one else had the power of conferring the Holy Spirit, and that they did so not by baptism but by the laying on of hands.[1] Simon Magus, the most prominent of Philip's converts, perceived that the Apostles had the power of conferring the Holy Spirit by the imposition of their hands and tried to bribe them to give him the same power that they had. The incident is very significant. Simon was not trying to purchase the gift of the Spirit, which the Apostles had apparently already given, but the  *Philip's work.*

[1] It would also follow that the author did not think that the gift of the Holy Spirit was necessary to salvation, for, if it had been, what would have been the point of the conversion and baptism of the Samaritans by Philip ?

power to confer it. Obviously, according to the author of this section, not everyone who had received the Spirit was able to impart it. It is to be noted that the story does not state that Peter could not confer the gift of imparting the Spirit, but only that he did not choose to do so in the case of Simon Magus. It is a pity that we cannot say with certainty whether this episode expounds the opinion of Luke, or of the source which he was using. (See Vol. I. pp. 338 ff.)

This passage belongs to the same class as the preceding so far as the identification of the Apostles with the Twelve is concerned, but it differs by the great emphasis it puts on the necessity of Apostolic mediation in addition to baptism for the gift of the Spirit.

**Paul's conversion.** (v.) Acts ix. 1 ff. The story of Paul's conversion is not so clear as might be wished, but it is obvious that the writer, like Paul himself, regards the vision on the road to Damascus as Paul's call to be an Apostle, and ix. 27 is probably intended as the recognition by the Apostles that Paul is one of their number.[1]

**Peter's speech in Caesarea.** (vi.) Acts x. 34 ff. Peter's speech in Caesarea. This is important because in verse 41 is the clearest explanation that the Apostles ($\dot{\eta}\mu\hat{\iota}\nu$) were the witnesses, chosen before of God, who ate and drank[2] with Jesus after the Resurrection.

**Antioch.** (vii.) Acts xi. 19 ff. The foundations of the Church at Antioch. This was the work of unknown followers of Stephen who had preached to Gentiles at Antioch. Just as Peter and John were sent to Samaria to investigate the work of Philip, Barnabas was sent to investigate the state of affairs in Antioch. He approved of what had been done and summoned Paul to help him. The interesting points in the narrative for the present purpose are : (a) Barnabas was not one of the Twelve ; but both here and elsewhere he is ranked as an Apostle. This is one of the clearest examples of the wider meaning of 'Apostle' making itself visible (see above, p. 402). (b) Paul is definitely put into a position of subordination to Barnabas, and comes to help him in territory which was not his own. Rom. xv. 20 is a curious commentary on this fact. Paul says, "I have striven to preach the gospel where Christ was not named, lest I should build on another man's foundation." Did he adopt this policy because his co-operation with Barnabas had proved unsatisfactory ? However this may be, it is clear that to the writer of Acts Barnabas' mission to Antioch represents apostolic control over a church founded by those who were not Apostles. Moreover, both here and in the story of Philip it is implied that in some sense the Christians in Jerusalem exercised an authoritative supervision over other communities.

**The Apostolic council.** (viii.) Acts xv. 1 ff. Although the story of Paul's journeys is reached in chap. xiii., the first important episode for the present purpose

---

[1] For the details of this episode and the parallel narratives in xxii. 3 ff. and xxvi. 9 ff. see Addit. Note 15.

[2] Obviously Paul did not really belong in this category, but he was a witness, the last (as he says himself), of the risen Lord. Does 'eating and drinking' belong to the original definition ? Paul would surely not have accepted it, and it is probably the anti-Docetic amplification of the editor of Acts.

is the meeting of the Church in Jerusalem, described in chap. xv., which seems to read as though Paul and Barnabas recognized the authority of that body. Once more the question of text enters into the problem. The Neutral text is very obscure, but it is plain in the Western text that representatives of the Church in Jerusalem came down to Antioch and summoned Paul and Barnabas, those dangerous innovators, to go up and answer for themselves before the Apostles. It is quite possible that here the Western text has at least correctly interpreted Luke's meaning (see note *ad loc.*). In the event it is true that Peter sides with Paul and Barnabas, and James the brother of the Lord sums up in their favour. But it is clear that the tribunal was composed of the Apostles and Elders, and Paul and Barnabas were to some extent on trial.

Who were the Elders, and what was the position of James is nowhere definitely stated, but the position of James [1] is clear not only in Acts xv., but also in Galatians i. and ii. and in Acts xxi. He is the leader of the Church in Jerusalem. Paul puts him before Peter and John (Gal. ii. 9), and represents Peter's backsliding in Antioch as due to the influence of James's representatives. In Acts he decides (ἐγὼ κρίνω, xv. 19) the question discussed at the Council, and when Paul comes to Jerusalem for the last time (xxi. 18) it is James who appears as the undoubted head of the Christian community.

Was he an 'Apostle'? According to Paul he certainly was, for the phrase in Gal. i. 19 (ἕτερον δὲ τῶν ἀποστόλων οὐκ εἶδον εἰ μὴ 'Ιάκωβον) can scarcely mean anything except that James was an Apostle. But he was not one according to Acts, which normally regards 'Apostle' as synonymous with 'the Twelve.'

K. Holl, in his brilliant *Der Kirchenbegriff des Paulus*,[2] has suggested K. Holl. that in 1 Cor. xv. 5 ff. may be found a solution of the difference between the Epistles and Acts. Paul here says that the risen Lord appeared to Peter, then to the Twelve, then to five hundred brethren, then to James, and then to all the Apostles. Holl thinks that the implication is that after he had seen the risen Lord James became an 'Apostle,' so that 'all the Apostles' means 'the Twelve and James,' and that it was by virtue of his relationship to Jesus that he was recognized as the head of the community. It is, however, obvious that this suggestive combination reads into Paul's words much more than is really stated. All that is certain is that Paul differentiates between the Twelve and the Apostles. He probably implies that James and the Twelve all belong to the larger group of Apostles, but not that 'the Twelve and James' form the whole of that larger group. Moreover, Holl's theory scarcely does justice to the description of Andronicus and Junias in Rom. xvi. 7 as ἐπίσημοι ἐν τοῖς

---

[1] The relationship of James to Jesus has been so fully discussed in Ropes' commentary on the Epistle of James, as well as in Lightfoot's commentary on Galatians, that it is unnecessary to deal with it here; and to consider the tradition as to his death preserved in Hegesippus-Eusebius belongs rather to a treatment of the Church in Jerusalem.

[2] *Gesammelte Aufsätze zur Kirchengeschichte*, ii. pp. 44 ff. (reprinted from the *Sitzungsberichte* of the Berlin Academy for 1921).

ἀποστόλοις, which most naturally implies that Andronicus and Junias were distinguished members of the Apostolic class, not that they were regarded as famous by the Apostles. But even if this be doubted it cannot be denied that in 1 Cor. ix. 5 f. Paul includes Barnabas and the Brethren of the Lord among the Apostles. He says : " Have I no right to take about a Christian wife like the other Apostles, the Brethren of the Lord, and Kephas ? Or have only Barnabas and myself no right to give up work ? " It is impossible to argue satisfactorily that the Brethren of the Lord are regarded as a class separate from the Apostles without admitting that Kephas also was not an Apostle, and to most minds this is a *reductio ad absurdum*.

Therefore Holl's theory, so far as it limits the meaning of 'Apostle' to 'the Twelve and James,' is probably wrong ; but it is certainly right in emphasizing James's position of primacy in Jerusalem and his rank as an Apostle.

The Presbyters.

The 'Presbyters' are a more difficult problem. The word obviously corresponds to the *zeqenim* of Judaism, a college of men who were at the head of the community. In the church at Jerusalem who can these have been except the Apostles ? In the absence of evidence it is only possible to guess, but it is an attractive hypothesis that as the function of the Apostles in Jerusalem gradually changed there was a tendency to call them the *zeqenim* rather than the *sheluchim*, and this resulted in their being called πρεσβύτεροι in Greek.

An alternative guess would be that the 'Presbyters' were what remained of the 'Seven.' Ecclesiastical tradition, it is true, calls them 'Deacons,' but Acts does not do so ; it merely says that they had the διακονία of administering charity. If, as may be the case, all the original apostles except James left Jerusalem and became missionaries, the 'Seven' would be the natural persons to be the *zeqenim* of the community. It is by no means improbable that the disturbance in the Church described in chapter vi. produced a more complete reorganization than Luke has thought fit to describe.

Moreover, it is not inconceivable that the Seven belonged to the circle of the Apostles—as distinct from the Twelve—and that (as is suggested above) πρεσβύτεροι merely indicates a tendency to describe the whole of this circle by their function in the Church. James had obviously become their president. Was he called the ἐπίσκοπος ? Possibly ; but there is considerable force in the contention that originally ἐπίσκοπος was synonymous with πρεσβύτερος. It would be going too far afield to discuss this difficult point, but perhaps attention may be drawn to the fact that the earliest suggestion that ἐπίσκοπος was a Christian title is found in Gal. ii. 4 where κατασκοπῆσαι is apparently a deliberate play of words on ἐπισκοπῆσαι, comparable to the use made in Philipp. iii. 2 ff. of κατατομή and περιτομή,[1] and the context shows that Paul held that in Jerusalem there was more than one of these κατάσκοποι-ἐπίσκοποι.

Paul in Ephesus.

(ix.) Acts xix. 1 ff. This is an important but disconcerting episode,

[1] See Holl, *op. cit.*

which, if taken in its natural sense, seems to contradict the implications
of the story in chap. viii.   Paul reached Ephesus from the East and
found a number of 'disciples,' that is, Christians.   He asked whether
they had received the Spirit after their conversion (again implying that
not all Christians had the Spirit, cf. above, p. 53, note), and when he
found that they had not done so he inquired into the nature of the baptism
which they had received.   If only the Apostles had the power to confer
the Holy Spirit, why is Paul surprised to find that the people in Ephesus
had not received it ?   Did he think at first, what we are not told, that it
was one of the Apostles who had baptized them ?   The implication of
the narrative is that it was Apollos, or some wholly anonymous missionary, and the fact that it turned out to have been only 'John's baptism' and
not a baptism in the name of the Lord Jesus makes it almost impossible
that it could have been done by one of the Apostles.   But if so, we are
forced to consider the possibility that Paul did not consider the conferring
of the Spirit as the exclusive prerogative of the Apostles (see further for
the bearing of this on Baptism, Addit. Note 11).

(x.) Acts xx. 18 ff.   In his speech to the πρεσβύτεροι [1] of Ephesus Paul's
Paul says that the Holy Spirit has made them ἐπίσκοποι to 'shepherd Miletus.
the church of God.'   Presumably he had appointed them himself, and
this identification of his own actions with those of the Holy Spirit is
entirely in keeping with the formula adopted at the council of Jerusalem
('it seemed good to the Holy Spirit and to us') which has since served
as the model of correct ecclesiastical idiom.   It is unfortunate that the
story gives no hint as to the theory of succession which is involved, or
the exact function of a πρεσβύτερος-ἐπίσκοπος, but it is clearly leading
up by inevitable sequence to the famous utterance of the Church of Rome
in the first epistle of Clement, written probably only a few years later
than Acts, which still remains a perfect commentary on the theory of
ecclesiastical government implied in Acts : "The Christ therefore is from
God and the Apostles from the Christ . . . they went forth filled with
the Holy Spirit, preaching the good news that the Kingdom of God was
about to come.   They preached from district to district and from city to
city, and appointed their first converts, testing them by the Spirit, to be
ἐπίσκοποι and διάκονοι of the future believers. . . . Our Apostles also
knew, through our Lord Jesus Christ, that there would be strife for the
name of the ἐπισκοπή.   For this cause therefore, since they had received
perfect foreknowledge, they appointed those who have already been
mentioned, and afterwards added the codicil that if they should fall asleep
other approved men should succeed to their ministry." [2]   An apostolic

---

[1] I have used the Greek for ἐπίσκοπος, πρεσβύτερος, and διάκονος to avoid the
necessity of choosing a rendering which must inevitably assume an answer to
one of the difficult questions—are these words descriptive of functions or the
titles of offices ?

[2] 1 Clement xlii. 2-4 and xliv. 1-2.   It should be noted that in the next
paragraph Clement refers to these ἐπίσκοποι and διάκονοι as πρεσβύτεροι.   If
these words were technical the vocabulary to which they belong was still
somewhat fluid.

ministry, sanctioned by the Holy Spirit, is almost as clearly the background of Acts as it is of Clement. The only difference, due to the single generation or less which intervenes between Luke and Clement, is that Acts emphasizes the divine prerogative of the Apostles, Clement of their successors.

**Paul and James in Jerusalem.**

(xi.) Acts xxi. 18 ff. The last episode in Acts which throws any light on the Apostles and the organization of the Church is Paul's return to Jerusalem in chap. xxi. The remarkable thing about the Apostles in this story is their absence. Paul is met by James and the πρεσβύτεροι: there is no mention of any Apostle in Jerusalem. Had they all gone to the mission field, or is it merely that Luke is using another name to describe them, partly because the custom—either in fact or in his source—had changed, partly because he was influenced by his theory that 'the Apostles' means 'the Twelve'?

**Summary.**

It is obvious that in these passages we have a series of glimpses into a complex of changing circumstances and rapidly developing terminology ; but in any attempt to trace the course of this evolution the one thing certain is that certainty cannot be attained. The following seems the most probable summary. The Twelve were appointed by Jesus in the way described in the gospel of Mark. At least some of the Twelve came to Jerusalem after the death of Jesus and preached that he was the Messiah, risen from the dead and destined to come again on the clouds of Heaven. They became leaders in the Church in Jerusalem, but in view of the evidence of the Pauline Epistles it seems probable that the Twelve were not a closed corporation governing the Church, as Luke (or the source which he uses in chapters i.-v.) would suggest, but that the chief position was held by a wider circle known as the Apostles. They were so called because they had been sent by Jesus, but in relation to the rapidly growing Christian community in Jerusalem they fulfilled the function of the Elders in the Jewish Council. It is therefore not strange if those of them who stayed in Jerusalem came to be called Elders rather than Apostles. At the beginning Peter was the chief of the Apostles in Jerusalem, but when he became more and more a travelling missionary his place was taken by James the brother of the Lord, so that in A.D. 45 (the approximate date of the Apostolic Council) James was the head of the Church in Jerusalem in spite of Peter's presence, and he is given the first place not only in Acts but also in the Epistle to the Galatians. How Peter's original supremacy, testified to not only by Acts i.-v. but also by Gal. i. 18, passed into the hands of James is, and will remain, an insoluble problem, because Luke has told us nothing about it.

**Spiritual and local rank.**

A further problem, which it is easier to state than to solve, is the relation of the spiritual supremacy of the Apostles to that of the local churches. There is much to be said for Holl's view that at the beginning Jerusalem claimed a certain power over all the other churches, and that Paul, for the moment at least, succeeded in asserting the supremacy of spiritual rank over the authority of any local centre. Whatever doubts may be entertained about the authenticity of the later epistles of Paul, it is certain that their emphasis on the Church as distinct from the churches is a natural and legitimate evolution of Pauline thought. The fall of Jerusalem and the influence of Paul combined to render the position of James of secondary importance in the history of the Church, and in ecclesiastical tradition it is Peter and Paul, the two great missionaries, not James, who are the chief of the Apostles. If in course of time Rome and Constantinople developed what seem to us local pretensions, more akin to the claims of James than of Paul, this was only because both the old Rome and the new Rome claimed to be more than 'localities'—they were 'the common superior of nations.'

## NOTE VII. THE HELLENISTS

### By HENRY J. CADBURY

The word Hellenist, like its derivatives or cognates, Hellenistic and Hellenism, is so familiar and well established that no question seems necessary about it. Nevertheless Ἑλληνιστής is not a common word in the Greek of the age that we call Hellenistic, and its first occurrences do not testify without ambiguity to the generally accepted definition: "A Hellenist is a Greek-speaking foreigner, specifically a Greek-speaking Jew."

*The word Hellenist.*

In post-Nicene times the word is used of heathen or pagans, in contrast mainly with Christians.[1] The passages listed by Sophocles in his Lexicon are Julian, ed. Spanheim 430 D ( = Letter 49, derived not from the MSS. of Julian but from Sozomen, *H.E.* v. 16; cf. Migne, *P.G.* lxvii. 1264 B) δίδασκε δὲ καὶ συνεισφέρειν τοὺς Ἑλληνιστὰς εἰς τὰς τοιαύτας λειτουργίας (i.e. such charitable support as the Jews and Galileans practise); Philostorgius, Migne, *P.G.* lxv. 537 B εἰς ἄρρητά τε καὶ ἀδιήγητα πάθη κατέστησε [sc. Ἰουλιανὸς] τοὺς Χριστιανούς, πανταχοῦ τῶν Ἑλληνιστῶν πάσας αἰκίας καὶ καινὰς βασάνους καὶ πικροτάτους θανάτους ἐπαγόντων αὐτοῖς ; *ibid.* 541 A τῶν Ἑλληνιστῶν τὰ ἀτοπώτατα κατὰ τῶν Χριστιανῶν πανταχοῦ παλαμωμένων κτλ.; Sozomen, *H.E.* iii. 17 (Migne, *P.G.* lxvii. 1093 B) ἡ θρησκεία (i.e. Christianity) . . . ἐθήρα καὶ πρὸς ἑαυτὴν μετῆγε τῆς Ἑλληνικῆς τερθρείας τοὺς Ἑλληνιστάς; *ibid.* vii. 15 (1456 A) λέγεται δὲ τῶν περὶ τούτων γραφέντων παρὰ βασιλέως εἰς τὸ κοινὸν ἀναγνωσθέντων μέγα ἀναβοῆσαι Χριστιανούς, καθότι εὐθὺς ἐκ προοιμίων ἐν αἰτίᾳ τοὺς Ἑλληνιστὰς ἐποιεῖτο. But before Julian, Philostorgius, and Sozomen, who use it thus of pagans or champions of Hellenic culture, I know of no instance of the word outside of the Book of Acts and

*In post-Nicene writers.*

*Julian.*

*Philostorgius.*

*Sozomen.*

---

[1] In the same era a still commoner term for pagan and heathen was Ἕλληνες. See A. D. Nock, *Sallustius concerning the Gods*, 1926, p. xlvii. note 43. To his examples many more could be added, including some in the very context of the instances of Ἑλληνισταί quoted here. The use of this word by Christians goes back to Jewish usage and perhaps ultimately to the anti-Hellenic prejudice of the Maccabean struggle.

passages dependent on it.[1]  So-called Hellenists like Philo of Alexandria, Paul of Tarsus, and Josephus do not use it.  We may therefore confine ourselves to a study of the two or three passages in Acts, trying to arrive at the meaning of ʽΕλληνιστής from its use in these passages, their context, their early translation and interpretation, as well as—or even, rather than—from the etymology of the word.

Etymology.  The word does not come from ʽΕλλην- directly by adding -ιστής but is rather to be derived from the verb ʽΕλληνίζω by the addition of the usual termination for the *nomen actoris*, -της.  Verbs in -ίζω based on racial or national names mean to ape the manners of, to be an enthusiast for the cause or culture of, like Περσίζω, Μηδίζω, Σικελίζω.  But I do not find that they always form nouns in -ιστης.  We have of course Ἀττικίζω and Ἀττικιστής.[2]  We have also nouns in -ιστής without corresponding verbs in -ίζω, but of similar meaning to our endings-phile, - maniac in Anglophile and Anglomaniac.  Etymologically ʽΕλληνιστής should therefore mean, like ʽΕλληνίζω, anyone who practises Greek ways—whether a Greek himself or a foreigner.[3]  That such endings are not always causative is quite evident from their usage.  Nor are they limited to outsiders.  Finally we should observe that they have no special reference to language.  The adverbial ending -ιστί does refer to language, e.g. ʽΕλληνιστί, ʻin Greek,ʼ but it is independent of -ιστής, though of course popular etymology might come to connect the two.  With this brief etymological preface we may now turn to the New Testament instances of ʽΕλληνιστής.

Acts vi. 1.  The facts about these instances are familiar to students of Acts.  The first is in vi. 1 : ἐν δὲ ταῖς ἡμέραις ταύταις πληθυνόντων τῶν μαθητῶν ἐγένετο γογγυσμὸς τῶν ʽΕλληνιστῶν πρὸς τοὺς ʽΕβραίους, ὅτι παρεθεωροῦντο ἐν τῇ διακονίᾳ τῇ καθημερινῇ αἱ χῆραι αὐτῶν.

This passage is the foundation of the belief that the word Hellenist means a Greek-speaking Jew.  The scene is the early church in Jerusalem. Both parties are of course Christians.  The author does not say this, but it is obvious from the context.  Further, both are commonly regarded as also Jewish ; but the author does not say this, and it is not so evident from the context.  The word ʽΕβραίοι used here only in Acts is thought to mean ʻ Semitic-speaking Jews,ʼ and ʽΕλληνισταί therefore ʻ Greek-speaking Jews.ʼ  While the inclusive word for Jews is Ἰουδαῖοι, used elsewhere in contrast with Gentiles who may be called Ἕλληνες as well as ἔθνη, this passage seems to divide the Ἰουδαῖοι into two linguistic subdivisions : ʻ Hebrews,ʼ who spoke Aramaic, and ʻ Grecians,ʼ as the A.V. translated

---

[1]  A Jewish schismatic sect is called by Justin, *Dial.* 80. 4, ʽΕλληνιανοί, a unique word.  The ending is not irregular, however.  Cf. Christian, etc., and see p. 130.  In the same passage are named other sects in -ιστής, γενισταί, μερισταί.

[2]  Ἰουδαιστής, Judaizer, from Ἰουδαΐζω (Paul, Josephus, LXX), occurs in Adamantius 1784 B.  Of course the participle of the verb took the place of the noun as Ἰωάννης ὁ βαπτίζων alternates in Mark with Ἰωάννης ὁ βαπτιστής. The forms in -ισμός also often occur more frequently than those in -ιστής. Cf. Ἰουδαισμός in 2 Macc., Paul, Ignatius, and ʽΕλληνισμός in 2 Macc.

[3]  For the proper etymological use of ʽΕλληνισταί see Zahn, *Introduction to the New Testament*, § 2. note 21.

'Ελληνισταί, who spoke Greek. Such at least has been the universal explanation.

There is at first sight much to commend this interpretation. (i.) The author of Acts is elsewhere sensitive to the matter of language.[1] At the beginning of the book his narrative of Pentecost is a striking instance ; he emphasizes the fact that Paul did not catch the Lycaonian vernacular of his sudden admirers at Lystra [2] (xiv. 11), that he was not to be confused with an Egyptian who could not speak in Greek ('Ελληνιστί xxi. 37) to the military tribune Claudius Lysias, that at Jerusalem he spoke to the mob at the castle of Antonia τῇ 'Εβραΐδι διαλέκτῳ (i.e. in Aramaic xxii. 2), and that even the same language explains the Semitic form ' Saoul ' by which the divine voice called him at his conversion near Damascus (xxvi. 14). The writer also omits, or translates into Greek, the Roman or Semitic words that appear in his sources, or else apologizes for the foreign word if he retains it.[3] It would be natural that such a historian should realize the existence of two linguistic groups in Jewry and the early emergence of a Greek-speaking Christianity even in Jerusalem.

(ii.) Furthermore, the position of the passage in Acts is usually thought to forbid the view that these converts to the gospel were purely Gentile. It is thought that the innovation of taking Gentiles into the church would be marked more explicitly, as it is later at Caesarea and Antioch. The complaining party were Jews—Jews of the diaspora, who, though they were not few in Jerusalem and in the church of Jerusalem, were over-shadowed by the Palestinian party to which the Twelve as Galileans naturally belonged. The committee of Seven chosen, as the sequel tells us, to remedy the difficulty all bear Greek names. One of them is called a proselyte of Antioch ; another is at once involved in fatal controversy with Jews of the Synagogue of the Libertines. It is natural to suppose that all the Seven were ' Hellenists ' and that Stephen's opponents were of the same class.

*Luke and language.*

*The exegesis of Acts vi. 1 ff.*

---

[1] It should be observed, however, that in none of its three occurrences does the context of 'Ελληνισταί suggest any difference or difficulty of language.

[2] The present editors have increasingly come to suspect that elsewhere in Acts geographical names like Lycaonia (xiv. 6, cf. 11) and the much discussed Φρυγία and Γαλατικὴ χώρα indicate linguistic rather than political areas. Surely the traveller more readily observes the frontiers of language than those of race or government. For the perseverance of local languages in Asia Minor see Additional Note 18.

[3] See my *Style and Literary Method of Luke*, pp. 154 ff. In the evidence for Luke's interest in languages we can scarcely include the words about the inscription on the cross in Luke xxiii. 38 γράμμασιν ἑλληνικοῖς (καὶ) ῥωμαικοῖς (καὶ) ἑβραικοῖς. They are omitted by a few good and ancient textual authorities and are under suspicion of being a harmonizing scribal addition based on John xix. 20. And it is Matthew xxvi. 73 who changes the taunt to Peter in Mark xiv. 70 from Γαλιλαῖος εἶ to ἡ λαλιά σου δῆλόν σε ποιεῖ. One may doubt, however, whether λαλιά means ' the Galilean accent,' as Zahn, *Introd. to N.T.* § 1 note 13, and others have held. Cf. John viii. 43.

Objections. Nevertheless to this common understanding of the passage and of the term Hellenist some weighty objections can be raised.

The names of the Seven. (i.) The Greek names of the Seven do not limit the bearers to Jews of the diaspora. They could have been borne, on the one hand by Palestinian Jews,[1] who must often have been partly bilingual,[2] or on the other hand by non-Jews.

Historical difficulties. (ii.) It is not clear how the choice of seven members of one party would satisfactorily provide for the poor widows of both parties, nor why men chosen to allow the Twelve to preach rather than to ' serve tables ' appear later only as preachers and evangelists. The connexion beween the choice of the Seven and the controversy of Stephen is not close, and it is not stated that the foreigners at the synagogue of the Libertini should be called Hellenists. The loose connexions of an obscure passage are pressed too hard when all these deductions are drawn from them.[3]

The use of Ἑβραῖοι. (iii.) The word Ἑβραῖοι is not commonly used elsewhere in a strictly linguistic sense. It means ' Jewish,' and when contrasted, as it often is, with Gentiles it may, of course, include a difference of language. I know no evidence of its use to describe a part or subdivision of Judaism. Paul calls himself 'a Hebrew' (2 Cor. xi. 22) or a Hebrew from Hebrews (Ἑβραῖος ἐξ Ἑβραίων Phil. iii. 5), and the fact that he also calls himself in one passage an Israelite of the seed of Abraham, and in the other of the stock of Israel, has been forcibly explained in the light of the passage in Acts as implying that he was giving a narrower and linguistic description of his Jewish prerogatives by emphasizing that he and even his ancestors were not really of the Greek-speaking type so often found in the Dispersion, but were brought up in the Semitic speech of the Palestinian Jews and primitive Christians.[4]

---

[1] See notes on Acts i. 23 and vi. 5.

[2] J. Weiss, *Urchristentum*, pp. 119 f., believes that not only Galilee but a large part of Jerusalem also was bilingual in New Testament times. On Galilee see G. Dalman, *Jesus-Jeshua*, Eng. Trans., 1929, pp. 5 f.

[3] The assumptions are illustrated in W. L. Knox, *St. Paul and the Church of Jerusalem*. Those who accept the theory of ' panel markers ' (see Addit. Note 31 and Vol. II. p. 176) may be reminded that one of them occurs at vi. 7 dividing the choice of the Seven from the dispute of Stephen.

[4] A somewhat different suggestion is that Ἑβραῖοι is geographical, of Jews born in Palestine. This may possibly be implied by Jerome, *Commentary on Philemon*, vs. 23, where Paul's birth at Gischala rather than at Tarsus is brought into connexion with his claim to be Ἑβραῖος. One can see that birth in Palestine might be a less unintelligible ground for boasting than the ability to use Aramaic. The tribe of Benjamin apparently claimed as a reason for prestige that their ancestor alone among the twelve patriarchs was born in Palestine. Jews of the dispersion, whether at Rome, Corinth, Tarsus, or even at Jerusalem, might distinguish from members of the older dispersion the more recent Jewish emigrants from Palestine, including those whose exile dated from the Roman conquests of Pompey (cf. note on Acts xxii. 28), or of Vespasian. This view of a difference between Aramaic- and Greek-speaking Jews *within the dispersion* is now espoused by Deissmann in a note in Nik. Müller's posthumous work, *Die Inschriften der jüdischen Katakombe am Monteverde zu Rom*, 1919,

But in the light of its general currency this special meaning for Ἑβραῖοι
is improbable and less likely than one more nearly synonymous with Jew
or Israelite.

Outside the New Testament there is little evidence of Ἑβραῖος meaning
a Jew speaking Ἑβραϊστί.[1] Philo uses it of Hebrew proper names in
contrast to their Greek interpretation.[2] Josephus uses it of the Jews in
general, and so do many Gentile writers of his time.[3] The name occurs in

---

p. 24; in *Licht vom Osten*[4], 1923, pp. 12 f. note (Eng. Trans.[2], 1927, p. 16 note);
*Paulus*[2], 1925, p. 71 note 7 (Eng. Trans.[2], 1926, p. 90 note 5). Contrast his
earlier editions, German and English, of these works.

[1] This adverb, like Ἑλληνιστί and others in -ιστί, is linguistic. The word
does not usually distinguish Aramaic from Hebrew, but we may assume it
always means Aramaic in New Testament times. The argument of the present
note is not concerned to distinguish the earlier from the later Semitic speech of
the Jews, but is directed against the inference that the word is used of either
Semitic language as the distinguishing mark of a part of the Jewish or Jewish-
Christian community.

[2] The instances of Ἑβραῖος, as listed by Leisegang, *Index Philonis*, mostly
refer to the Hebrews in the time of Moses as contrasted with the Egyptians
or other peoples. Moses' own name is described as Egyptian rather than
according to the language of the Hebrews. In giving other proper names
from the Old Testament, Philo contrasts their LXX spelling as the way in
which the Ἑβραῖοι name them with the Greek force of the original meaning.
Once (*De confus. ling.* 26, § 129, M. p. 424) he substitutes for his usual Ἑβραῖοι
. . . Ἕλληνες the contrast Ἑβραῖοι . . . ἡμεῖς. This seems at first sight to
confirm the view that Ἑβραῖοι in Philo are contrasted with Jews who speak
Greek. I think rather Philo identifies himself with all modern speakers in
Greek, and by Ἑβραῖοι means the Old Testament Hebrews. It is after all
ancient Hebrew, not Aramaic, to which Philo is referring. The translators of
the Septuagint under Ptolemy Philopator he describes as Ἑβραῖοι who in
addition to their own culture are educated with the Hellenic παιδεία Ἑλληνική
(*De vita Mosis*, ii. 6, § 32, M. p. 139). Cf. Chrysostom quoted below, p. 424,
who says of the Hellenists of Acts, Ἑλληνιστί ἐφθέγγοντο Ἑβραῖοι ὄντες. Philo
himself was thoroughly Greek in language. Yet Eusebius, *H.E.* ii. 4. 2, calls
him Ἑβραῖος, and Photius seems to contrast him with the Hellenists when he
says, *Bibl. Cod.* 105, that his power of discourse inspired τοῖς Ἑλληνισταῖς with
admiration. Photius is here following the Greek translation of Jerome, *De
vir. ill.* xi. which reads *apud Graecos*. Suidas in the parallel reads παρ' Ἕλλησι,
the so-called Sophronius τῶν Ἑλληνικῶν (see *Texte und Untersuchungen* xiv.
1b, 14 ff.). But for these writers Ἑβραῖος meant Jews in general and Ἑλληνισταί
Gentiles. For Christian uses of Ἑβραῖος as possibly linguistic see *Acta Philippi*
116 (ed. Bonnet, p. 47), ἐγὼ Ἑβραία εἰμί, θυγάτηρ Ἑβραίων. λάλησον μετ' ἐμοῦ
ἐν τῇ διαλέκτῳ τῶν πατέρων μου. Cf. *Acta Thomae* 8.

[3] Interesting, though of uncertain date and origin, is the adjuration of the
Great Magical Papyrus of Paris (line 3019), which begins ὁρκίζω σε κατὰ τοῦ θεοῦ
τῶν Ἑβραίων Ἰησοῦ. On the use of Ἑβραῖοι and Ἰουδαῖοι by Greek and Roman
writers see Juster, *Les Juifs dans l'Empire romain*, i. 173 note.

Mr. Nock has called to my attention a passage—the only one known to me
that uses together, as does Acts vi. 1, Ἑβραῖοι and Ἑλληνισταί—in the *Testament*

inscriptions of the early imperial period describing ' synagogues of Hebrews'
—at Corinth,[1] and at Rome,[2] and at Philadelphia in Lydia [3]—but there is
no reason to suppose that we have in these names references to separate
language-groups or that the synagogue in Jerusalem mentioned a little
later in Acts vi., called "of the Libertines, and of the Cyrenians and of the
Alexandrians, and of them of Cilicia and Asia," [4] would be called a synagogue of the Hellenists and not a synagogue of Hebrews. There are other
instances of the word in the Jewish catacombs in Rome.[5]

---

*of Solomon*, vi. 8 (p. 27* McCown) : καλεῖται δὲ παρ' Ἑβραίοις Πατικῇ, ὁ ἀφ' ὕψους
κατελθών· ἔστι δὲ τῶν Ἑλληνιστῶν Ἐμμανουήλ, οὗ δέδοικα τρέμων.   But this is
the reading only of recension A ; two other recensions read παρὰ δὲ Ἕλληνας
or Ἕλλησιν.

[1] [συνα]γωγὴ Ἐβρ[αίων].   See Deissmann, *Licht vom Osten*[4], pp. 12 f.
(second English translation, p. 16); *Corinth*, vol. viii. part i. 'Greek Inscriptions,' ed. by Benj. D. Meritt, pp. 78 f.   On Jews in Corinth see the
article by F. J. M. de Waele, *Studia Catholica*, iv., 1928, pp. 163 ff.   For the
opposite view see most recently the long argument of Zahn on Acts xviii. 4,
*Kommentar zum N.T.* vol. v. pp. 638-646, ' Ἑβραῖοι—Ἰουδαῖοι,' and the note
of Windisch on 2 Cor. xi. 22 (Meyer, *Kritisch-exegetischer Kommentar über das
Neue Testament*, vol. vi., 9th ed., 1924, pp. 350 f.).

[2] *CIG*. 9909 Σαλω[μη] θυγατηρ Γαδια πατρος συναγωγης Αιβρεων.   Cf. Schürer,
*Die Gemeindeverfassung der Juden in Rom*, 1879, p. 35; *GJV*.[4] iii. p. 83 ; Juster,
*Les Juifs dans l'Empire romain*, i. 415, note *f*.

[3] τ]ῇ ἁγιοτ[άτῃ σ]υναγωγῇ τῶν Ἑβραίων.   Keil and von Premerstein, 'Bericht
über eine dritte Reise in Lydien,' *Denkschriften der Akademie der Wissenschaften in Wien*, lvii., 1914, pp. 32 ff., No. 42.

[4] Possibly more than one synagogue is intended, see note *ad loc.*

[5] See N. Müller, *Die jüdische Katakombe am Monteverde zu Rom*, 1912,
pp. 104 f., 109 f. ; Kaibel, *Inscr. Graecae Ital. et Sicil.* 945 πατρὸς τῶν Ἑβρέων
Γαδία (in Portus); N. Müller and N. Bees, *Die Inschriften der jüd. Katakombe
am Monteverde zu Rom*, 1919, Nos. 50, 109, 110, 111, 118, and see Index, s.v.
Ἑβραῖος.   The word is used of individual Jews, including one known to be a
Palestinian Jew (No. 118 Μακεδόνις ὁ Αἴβρεος Κεσαρεὺς τῆς Παλεστίνης).   In
this early cemetery one of the few inscriptions to use Semitic translation is
to the daughter ἀρχ(οντος) Ἑβρέων (No. 50, 2nd to 3rd cent. A.D.).   The
Semitic is Aramaic, not Hebrew.   The fact that another synagogue Βερνα-
κλησίων or Βερνακλώρω or Βερνάκλων is mentioned (Nos. 109, 110, 111) might
seem to imply a language classification, but the word *Vernaculi*, *Vernaclenses*
doubtless means Jewish imperial slaves born in the household, and is to be
compared rather with the other Roman synagogue titles *Augustenses*, and
perhaps with the Synagogue of the Libertines in Acts vi. 9, and Caesar's
household in Phil. iv. 22.   The synagogue groups need not be expected all to
follow the same basis of nomenclature any more than do modern churches.
G. La Piana, 'Foreign Groups in Rome,' in *The Harvard Theological Review*,
xx., 1927, p. 356, note 26, after discussing other theories proposes that the
synagogue 'of the Hebrews' was the oldest of all, and when newer ones were
added it kept the name, and perhaps certain conservative customs and ancient
pride.   It is obvious how uncertain the real force of Ἑβραῖος is both in the
New Testament and on the inscriptions.

'Hebrews' as used in the O.T.,[1] Apocrypha, and New Testament implies a contrast of Jews with foreigners. It is not the word used of the Hebrews speaking of themselves to others of their nation, but often is specially employed when a Jew is represented as speaking to a foreigner or being spoken of by foreigners.[2] Similarly in Acts vi. 'Hebrews' would seem to mean simply Jews spoken of from a Jewish standpoint and with a view to contrast, and 'Hellenists' would mean those who were not Jews at all but outsiders, Gentiles (as at its later occurrences), or, in other words, it is a synonym of ἔθνη or Ἕλληνες.

But, it will be objected, would the author of Acts introduce a reference to Gentile Christians so early in his story and so casually? He pays so much attention to Cornelius the centurion a few chapters later, and seems so clearly to imply that his case was an innovation (xv. 14), that it is usually assumed that he regards it as the great turning-point in the missionary history of the Church. My own impression is that the author of Acts, for all his attention to lines of development—an attention not expected in an ancient writer as it is in the days influenced by the evolutionary understanding of history—has nevertheless not attempted to portray a consistent picture of an originally Jewish and Judean Christianity systematically expanding to other lands and groups by definite intervening steps, but rather to emphasize the acceptance of the Gospel by non-Jews as a repeated phenomenon, which gradually broke down all opposition, not as one event which had one single beginning. It was the divine plan from the beginning, though its clear understanding came later and gradually. The preaching of Paul of course shows this process in city after city. "Lo, we turn to the Gentiles, . . . the Gentiles will also hear," are Paul's first and last words in Acts from Pisidian Antioch to Rome.

*Acts and the evolution of Christianity.*

[1] The title to the Epistle to the Hebrews is πρὸς Ἑβραίους. This is probably not original, and the intention of those who used it is not clear. See J. Moffatt, 'Hebrews,' in *International Critical Commentary*, p. xv. It may have been a deduction from the apparent polemic against Judaism in the letter. Or it may be an inference made after the letter was attributed to Paul that since his other letters were addressed to Gentiles this different letter was addressed to Jews. In either case it implies nothing as to the Semitic language of the readers. If, however, the title came in still later when the difference of style between this and the other Pauline letters was urged by some against Pauline authorship, and was explained by others as due to the fact of translation into Greek (by Luke) from another language, then the Εβραῖοι may be supposed to mean Aramaic-speaking Jews. An allegorical use of the name is claimed by F. M. Schiele in his article on the Epistle to the Hebrews in the *American Journal of Theology*, ix. (1905), pp. 290 ff. Compare also the *Gospel according to the Hebrews* as a title. It is said to have been written in Aramaic.

[2] Both Ἑβραῖοι and Ἰσραήλ occur appropriately distributed in Judith. The author of Acts shows in other cases a like regard for the different terms suitable for different speakers or situations, e.g. ἔθνος vs. λαός. See Addit. Note 32 and *The Making of Luke-Acts*, p. 228.

But even earlier in the book emphasis is laid on the successive and, one might almost say, repeated beginnings of Gentile Christianity. This can be seen most clearly by reviewing some passages in reverse order.

Acts xiii. f.      (a) The missionary journey of Paul and Barnabas (xiii., xiv.) is regarded as an innovation in spite of the episode of Cornelius. Its scale and scope were of course impressive, but it is reported to various audiences as the opening of a door of faith to the Gentiles (xiv. 27 ; xv. 3, 4, 12).[1]

Antioch.      (b) A little earlier at Antioch (xi. 19, 20), in spite of textual problems, the sense requires that while at first others preached the Gospel exclusively to the Jews, it was ultimately preached to non-Jews by certain men of Cyprus and Cyrene.   But it is not explicitly said that Gentiles were first converted at Antioch, though the name ' Christian ' was used there for the first time.   The whole movement received the endorsement of Barnabas as a representative of the Church of Jerusalem, just as Philip's work in Samaria was investigated and completed by Peter and John.   But I believe that the innovation both in Samaria and at Antioch was regarded as geographical rather than racial, as in the plan outlined in Acts i. 8 : " both in Jerusalem and in all Judaea and Samaria, and unto the uttermost part of the earth."

Cornelius.      (c) The story of Cornelius (x. 1-xi. 18) precedes that of Antioch. The visions, the repetitions, etc., indicate how important it was considered. It is later recalled as a precedent (xv. 7). It was a notable instance of Gentile conversion, and it raised questions of divine authentication, of apostolic approval, and of the intercourse between Jewish and Gentile converts which find their echoes and their parallels elsewhere.

Philip
and the
Ethiopian.      (d) Still earlier in Acts comes Philip's conversion of the eunuch, treasurer to the Ethiopian queen (viii. 26-40). The author's interest in him is partly, of course, his high rank, but he is certainly a representative of ' the ends of the earth.' Nothing is said as to whether he was a Jew or Gentile. That he was at least a proselyte is suggested by the two facts that he had come to Jerusalem to worship and that he was reading the Book of Isaiah.   Whether in point of fact a eunuch could have become a proselyte or been admitted to the service of the Temple is a query which probably did not interest Luke.[2] Probably he could have done both. But, on the other hand, Greeks who were not necessarily converts to Judaism

---

[1] The reports to Jerusalem follow also the episode of Cornelius (xi. 1-3, 18), and recur as late in the book as xxi. 19 f. These passages, like the ' monotonous ' turning to the Gentiles, show that the author did not regard the conversion of Gentiles as a single new departure.

[2] Strack's *Kommentar* fails us at this point. Professor G. F. Moore has kindly replied to an inquiry as follows : " The question turns upon the interpretation of the phrase ' the congregation of the Lord ' in Deut. xxiii. 2 (E.V. xxiii. 1). The Jewish interpretation of these words in that and the following verses (3-9) is that the classes of persons thus denied admission to the congregation may not marry a Jewish woman of pure race. It is so in the codes : Maimonides, Issurè Bi'ah 16, 1 ff. ; Caro, Shulḥan 'Aruk, Eben ha-'Ezer 5, 1 ff. ; in the Talmud in various places, e.g. Yebamot 76 b. The

went up to the temple to worship (John xii. 20 ἦσαν δὲ ῞Ελληνές τινες ἐκ
τῶν ἀναβαινόντων ἵνα προσκυνήσωσιν ἐν τῇ ἑορτῇ), and there was a court
of the Gentiles to which they were admitted.[1]   The eunuch may have
been offering gifts on behalf of his queen.   Such Gentile presents were not
unusual at the temple.   And that Gentiles read the Jewish scriptures
in Greek is not improbable.[2]   It is therefore possible that Luke regarded
the eunuch as a Gentile, and ranked him as a notable convert from
heathenism.[3]

(e) Last in the list is the story of Pentecost (ii. 1-42).   It is for the Pentecost.
author an epoch-making event, as his emphasis on it shows.   With the
usually accepted text in ii. 5 (ἦσαν δὲ ἐν ᾽Ιερουσαλὴμ κατοικοῦντες
᾽Ιουδαῖοι, ἄνδρες εὐλαβεῖς ἀπὸ παντὸς ἔθνους τῶν ὑπὸ τὸν οὐρανόν) the
audience is all Jews, and the Parthians, Medes, Elamites, etc., must be

Jewish mediaeval commentators on Deut. (Rashi, Ibn Ezra) give the same
interpretation, which is found also in the Jerusalem Targum. It goes as
far back as we can trace the interpretation at all, namely, to Sifrè on Deut.
xxiii. 2 (cf. Midrash Tannaim, ed. Hoffmann, p. 144), that is to the juristic
authorities of the middle of our second century or earlier, who state it as an
unquestioned tradition.   There is no reason to think that it was otherwise
understood before the destruction of the temple.

"Kahal is for them not the whole ' congregation of Israel,' as it is probably
meant in the law, but is used of each one of four or five distinct classes, who
worshipped together in the temple and synagogue, but in matters of marriage
and succession are subject to different rules (Sifrè Deut. 247, Judah ben Ila'i)
—priests, levites, (lay) Israelites, proselytes.   Some counted only three, others
five (Kiddushin 72b-73a).

"There is on the part of the Rabbis no suspicion that Jews of illegitimate
birth (ממזרים) or proselytes from the different peoples named in the following
verses were excluded from the temple worship; it is solely a question of when,
if ever, their descendants may marry Israelites pur sang." Cf. D. Hoffmann,
Das Buch Deuteronomium, part ii. ad loc. The point is not what the original
intention of the law in Deuteronomy was, but how it was understood and
applied in the times in which the story is laid.   About that there can be no
doubt.   Not only the passage in Acts but Wisd. iii. 14 (following Isaiah lvi. 5)
and Tos. Megillah 2, 7, dealing with the religious obligations of eunuchs (Jewish
and proselyte), might be cited as indicating that the authors knew of no
exclusion of eunuchs as such from the temple worship.

[1] Cf. Schürer, GJV.[4] ii. pp. 357-363.
[2] Cf. xv. 21 and see Harnack, Bible Reading in the Early Church, pp. 57
and 76 f.
[3] Cf. Karl Pieper, ' Wer war der Erstling der Heiden ? ' in Zeitschrift für
Missionswissenschaft, vol. v., 1915, pp. 124 ff. Eusebius, H.E. ii. 1. 13, calls
the Ethiopian the first Gentile convert. Origen, Hom. ad Num. xi. 3, p. 306,
speaks of Cornelius as the first-fruits not only of the church of Caesarea,
but perhaps of all Gentiles, for he was the first to believe from the Gentiles
and the first filled with the Holy Spirit. Irenaeus, Adv. haer. iii. 18. 1,
evidently regarded the converts at Pentecost as the first-fruits of all the
nations.

Jews of the diaspora or at least proselytes.[1] But, as is argued on p. 113, it is probable on the ground partly of textual evidence but still more of internal evidence that Ἰουδαῖοι should be omitted in vs. 5, but retained in vs. 10. The writer probably regarded the event as the first and immediate fulfilment of the combined promise and command ,in i. 8. The ' men of every nation under heaven ' in ii. 5 correspond to ' the ends of the earth ' in i. 8. Of course the complete fulfilment came only when the disciples travelled to remote districts, but it began when they spoke to those who had come from these regions.

The preaching to these strangers was successful, and many of them believed, ' and there were added in that day about three thousand souls ' (ii. 41). Therefore we need not be surprised if in chapter vi. the author refers casually to Gentile Christians already in Jerusalem.[2] Certainly as far as language is concerned, the story of Pentecost shows that the author regarded the varieties in Jerusalem, even among converts to the Church, as numbering not two but many.

Conclusions.    The result of the preceding paragraphs is to suggest from a review of Acts that the author did not represent the Church as taking a series of systematic logical steps, which would imply the evolution of a changing policy towards the problem of missionary work among the Gentiles. He recognized of course that the process of conversion proceeded by degrees, but the divine plan was present from the beginning ; Luke's real interest is not the evolution of an institution, but the gradual attainment of God's predestined purpose. Such gradations of difference as, beginning with orthodox Jews at one end of the scale, and ending with Greeks at the other,

---

[1] We might argue that, even if we omit Ἰουδαῖοι at vs. 5, an audience called εὐλαβεῖς (vs. 5, see note) and addressed as Jews and dwellers in Jerusalem (vs. 14, see note) or Israelites (vs. 22) may have consisted of Jews, of full proselytes (who were treated as Jews and admitted as such into the Christian Church without controversy), and of looser adherents to Judaism (see Additional Note 8). But why are Jews and proselytes named in vs. 10 as though only part of the groups listed ? Evidently the account of Pentecost is confused in more ways than one. For Luke's carelessness see Harnack, *Luke the Physician*, p. 112. It is instructive to see with what circumspection Harnack has to use all these items in Acts in giving his account of ' The Transition from the Jewish to the Gentile Mission ' (*Mission*, book i. chap. v.). Gardner in *Cambridge Biblical Essays*, 1909, p. 391, throws out to defenders of Luke's inerrancy the challenge : " If anyone thinks him accurate in the report of fact, let such an advocate try to determine, out of Acts, when and where Gentiles were first admitted as members of the Christian Church."

[2] In like manner after mentioning the conversion of Ἑλληνιστάς at Antioch in Acts xi. 20 f. the author assumes in xv. 1 that there were uncircumcised Christians there. The omission of Ἰουδαῖοι in Acts ii. 5 and the consequent interpretation of the assembly at Pentecost as Gentiles was urged by Blass, *Neue kirchliche Zeitschrift*, iii., 1892, pp. 826 ff. The objections of Zahn, *Introduction to the New Testament*, § 2, note 8, are weighty, unless, as I believe, the present account in Acts is a confusion on this question.

cover Jews of the Dispersion, Greek-speaking Jews, Samaritans, Proselytes, and perhaps God-fearers—all these were doubtless well known to Luke, and he regarded them all as coming under Christian influence. But that influence did not pass through those gradations by a steady evolution, so dear to our modern minds. On the contrary, all were represented at the Day of Pentecost.

There is therefore no difficulty in supposing that Acts vi. 1 may have introduced a story (perhaps from a new source, as is often supposed [1]) in which Gentiles and Jews already formed the two national divisions of the Jerusalem church. Whether this description is historically true is another question. The scribes who added Ἰουδαῖοι in ii. 5 obviously thought that it was not. But it must be remembered that Jerusalem, then as now, was not inhabited only by Jews. The existence of foreigners in it presents no special difficulty, and Acts says nothing of the crucial question whether the converts were circumcised. The whole problem is intimately bound up with that of syncretistic types of religion—partly Jewish, partly heathen. All recent inquiry suggests that more of these existed in Syria than used to be thought (see especially the second edition of W. Bauer's *Commentary on John* in Lietzmann's *Handbuch*).

Moreover, the possibility cannot be ignored that to some extent Luke read back into the story of the beginning of the Church facts which were and had long been a reality when he wrote. It should be remembered that his material for this part of his work must have been fragmentary and miscellaneous, and not easily conformed to such an evolutionary arrangement as modern scholars would like to trace through it. The absence of reliable information about the chronological order of the different episodes would make precarious for him and for us any claim that the events mark a logical and chronological progression.[2] Even if the scene at Pentecost was not understood by him as indicating the conversion of Gentiles to Christianity, a reference at vi. 1 to Gentiles and their widows would really be no more abrupt than the sudden and unexplained introduction of two linguistic groups among the Christians. The author is perhaps here for the first and nearly the only time distinguishing within the Church those who were formerly Jews and those who were formerly Gentiles. For neither of these categories has he a fixed terminology. Indeed there is scarcely a terminology even to distinguish Christians from non-Christians, Jews who were Christians from those who were not, etc. We have such loose terms as οἱ ἐκ περιτομῆς πιστοί (x. 45), οἱ ἐκ περιτομῆς (xi. 2), τινες τῶν ἀπὸ τῆς αἱρέσεως τῶν Φαρισαίων πεπιστευκότες (xv. 5), γυναικὸς Ἰουδαίας πιστῆς (xvi. 1), ἐν τοῖς Ἰουδαίοις τῶν πεπιστευκότων (xxi. 20), and τοῖς

[1] See note on Acts vi. 1 ff. and Vol. II. pp. 128, 147 f. Harnack, *Acts*, p. 219, lists among cases of difficulty the abrupt introduction at vi. 1 of Hellenists and Hebrews. But οἱ μαθηταί also appears here for the first time in Acts (cf. p. 109).

[2] Even if he wished to give Gentile Christianity a methodical development, the facts did not permit him to do so. He lets us see in spite of himself that there were other communities or converts at Ephesus, Damascus, and Alexandria. Cf. D. W. Riddle, *Jesus and the Pharisees*, 1928, pp. 57 ff.

ἀπὸ τῶν ἐθνῶν ἐπιστρέφουσιν ἐπὶ τὸν θεόν (xv. 19), τοῖς ἀδελφοῖς τοῖς ἐξ ἐθνῶν (xv. 23), τῶν πεπιστευκότων ἐθνῶν (xxi. 25). It would not be surprising, then, if in speaking of Jewish and Gentile groups in the Church he should use at vi. 1 ʿΕβραῖοι and ʿΕλληνισταί without repeating the former at all and without using the latter later in quite the same sense of Gentile Christians.[1]

Of the other two passages in Acts one provides no obstacle to the view that ʻ Hellenists ʼ really means Gentiles, and the other confirms it, though in each case the evidence is not quite decisive.

Acts ix.        (i.) The first is Acts ix. 29 where we read of the newly converted Paul that at Jerusalem ʻ he spake and disputed against the Hellenists.ʼ The context has nothing in it to indicate who are meant. But there is no reason why the author may not be supposed to have introduced here a prompt fulfilment of the prediction made at Paul's conversion that he would be a missionary to Gentiles.

Acts xi.        (ii.) The other passage is Acts xi. 19 f. already referred to : οἱ μὲν οὖν διασπαρέντες ἀπὸ τῆς θλείψεως τῆς γενομένης ἐπὶ Στεφάνῳ διῆλθον ἕως Φοινείκης καὶ Κύπρου καὶ Ἀντιοχείας, μηδενὶ λαλοῦντες τὸν λόγον εἰ μὴ μόνον Ἰουδαίοις. ἦσαν δέ τινες ἐξ αὐτῶν ἄνδρες Κύπριοι καὶ Κυρηναῖοι, οἵτινες ἐλθόντες εἰς Ἀντιόχειαν ἐλάλουν καὶ πρὸς τοὺς

---

[1] If Hellenists is a party name it may have originated not in Judaism but in Christianity itself, used not so much of those whose race or language was Jewish, but of those who, unlike many Christians (cf. Ἰουδαίζειν Gal. ii. 14), did not keep the Jewish way of life. Such a cleft existed already in Jerusalem. So, as I understand him, argued G. P : son Wetter in Archiv für Religionswissenschaft, xxi., 1922, pp. 410 ff. He accepts the word neither at xi. 20 nor at ix. 29 (which would put Paul among the Judaizers!).

My friend A. D. Nock is also inclined to regard ʿΕλληνισταί as a Christian party name. He writes me : " The curious thing is the matter-of-fact way in which the word is used in vi. 1. Any Greek reader outside the Christian circles would have been puzzled, I think. Now the two certain examples are vi. 1 and ix. 29, both relating to Jerusalem. Have we here a Schlagwort, whose meaning was familiar at the time but which disappeared from use ? Supposing the ecclesiastical literature of the nineteenth century were reduced to the slender bulk of early Christian writings, Tractarian might present very serious difficulties. ʿΕλληνιστής does seem to me to mean something quite definite."

By a somewhat different route Walter Bauer (ʻ Jesus der Galiläer ʼ in Festgabe für Adolf Jülicher, 1927, pp. 32 f.) comes to the conclusion that ʿΕλληνισταί is not a term for Greek-speaking Jews but is used of members of the Christian community whether Jews or Gentiles " who had no positive relation to the Law, and in any case did not allow themselves to be subjected to its tyranny. In the main they probably originated from Galilee and the adjacent heathen districts." Bauer derives the word from ἑλληνίζειν as meaning, in antithesis to ἰουδαΐζειν, ʻ to conduct one's life in the manner of the heathen.ʼ He adds in a note : " What the word means in ix. 29 I don't know. In any case there they are not believers as at vi. 1. Ἑλλ. occurs beside at xi. 20 as a variant, but only to strengthen the impression that the meaning of the word was early lost to Christian usage."

'Ελληνιστάς, εὐαγγελιζόμενοι τὸν κύριον 'Ιησοῦν. The reading of the best manuscript evidence is certainly in favour of 'Ελληνιστάς, though ADℵᶜ read "Ελληνας. But the latter is the commoner word and is more likely to have been substituted, especially since its usual correlative 'Ιουδαίοις occurs in the preceding verse. But if 'Ελληνιστάς is the right reading,[1] the same 'Ιουδαίοις and indeed the whole context show that it cannot mean Jews—not even Greek-speaking ones—it must mean Gentiles and be synonymous with "Ελληνας. We may feel assured that, if interpreters of the word 'Ελληνισταί had taken their point of departure from this third instance rather than from the first, they would have quickly concluded that it meant not Jews but Gentiles.

The objection may perhaps be raised that the word thus loses any distinction from "Ελληνες, and that in vi. 1 'Εβραῖοι is likewise made to mean much the same as 'Ιουδαῖοι. Would the author use two words in the same sense for the same persons ? I believe that he would, and that his variation between "Ελληνες and 'Ελληνισταί is parallel to his variation for other words. It is worth noticing that while in the latter part of the book of Acts "Ελληνες is frequent, only 'Ελληνισταί is used in the first twelve chapters. Possibly 'Ελληνισταί emphasizes more than the usual "Ελληνες the alien character of these persons in a mainly Jewish atmosphere. The author of Acts is sensitive to make his words accord with the feeling of the context. It is a matter of common knowledge that his variation between the Greek and the Semitic spelling of Jerusalem ('Ιεροσόλυμα and 'Ιερουσαλήμ) is best explained by the variation between the more or less Hellenic standpoint of the context. With Paul and Barnabas travelling forth from the Levant into the lands of Asia Minor the author makes two other changes. The name Paul replaces Saul, and for the Jewish phrase God-reverer (φοβούμενοι) he substitutes God-worshippers (σεβόμενοι). My conjecture is that at about the same point he quietly and unconsciously drops 'Ελληνισταί and uses "Ελληνες.[2] In like manner 'Εβραῖοι, though it occurs only once to about 82 instances of 'Ιουδαῖοι, also occurs suitably

Conclusion.

[1] On the reading see among others F. J. A. Hort in *Notes on Selected Readings*, pp. 93 f.; B. B. Warfield, 'The Readings "Ελληνας and 'Ελληνιστάς, Acts xi. 20,' *Journal of the Society of Biblical Literature and Exegesis*, [iii.], 1883, pp. 113-127; J. H. Ropes, *Beginnings of Christianity*, vol. iii., 1926, on Acts ix. 29 and xi. 20. On behalf of "Ελληνας see F. H. A. Scrivener, *A Plain Introduction to the Criticism of the New Testament*, 4th ed., 1894, vol. ii. pp. 370 f. The reading of ℵ* (εὐαγγελιστάς), due to confusion with the following εὐαγγελιζόμενοι, apparently supports by its termination the reading of B, and that A in ix. 29 shows the same tendency to alter 'Ελληνιστάς into "Ελληνας.

[2] For other examples of such changes see my *Making of Luke-Acts*, pp. 225 ff. With the variation discussed in this note compare the limitation of the word 'Ισραήλ to the songs and speeches of Luke and Acts except in the familiar LXX phrase in the narrative of Acts v. 21 γερουσία τῶν υἱῶν 'Ισραήλ. In the Sermon on the Mount Matthew twice uses οἱ ἐθνικοί for Gentiles (v. 47, vi. 7) and once τὰ ἔθνη (vi. 32; Luke xii. 30 τὰ ἔθνη τοῦ κόσμου), but it is difficult to see any difference of meaning between them.

in this older narrative. There is reason to believe that other writers also use it in an archaizing sense.[1] Possibly a source suggested to Luke this isolated occurrence. The use of two words for the same thing is not unlike this author's habits. Elsewhere it would seem that he likes to substitute a long word for a like-sounding shorter one. It is not merely that he likes prepositional compounds, but that, for example, he uses in his preface ἐπειδήπερ for ἐπειδή and πληροφορέω for πληρόω. Probably other examples exist in his writings.[2] Ἑλληνισταί both by its length and by its implication of contrast is thus a more emphatic synonym for Ἕλληνες.

The evidence of the early versions and commentators is not adverse to this interpretation. The Latin, Sahidic, Bohairic versions and the Syriac Peshitto render Ἑλληνισταί as they do Ἕλληνες. It may be argued that they could not easily find one word to fit the meaning 'Greek-speaking Jews,' but to translate it simply 'Greeks' was misleading if they understood it really of Jews.[3] A paraphrase would have been possible if not a single word, and the Peshitto once does use the expression 'those who knew Greek.' Strangely enough this is not at vi. 1 but at ix. 29. But the Peshitto is later than Chrysostom, and was made in circles which were affected by Antiochian influences.[4]

It may be that the word was not familiar to translators. I have spoken of its infrequent occurrence in the writings known to us. Chrysostom, *Hom.* xiv. on vi. 1, says Ἑλληνιστὰς δὲ οἶμαι καλεῖν (sc. Λουκᾶν) τοὺς Ἑλληνιστὶ φθεγγομένους· οὗτοι γὰρ Ἑλληνιστὶ διελέγοντο Ἑβραῖοι ὄντες.[5] It is evident that Chrysostom is guessing, though he is usually sure enough of his Greek. He uses the expressions οἶμαι and ἴσως, and

---

[1] See Windisch on 2 Cor. xi. 22: "in allen späteren Schriften in archaistischem oder in gehobenem Stil."

[2] See Vol. II. p. 496; E. von Dobschütz, *Vom Auslegen des Neuen Testaments*, 1927, p. 12, note 23. I may venture here to suggest a few cases of possible sesquipedalian substitution in the Book of Acts: ii. 46 ἀφελότητι καρδίας for the usual ἀπλότητι καρδίας (see note *ad loc.*); xiii. 18 (from LXX Deut. i. 31) τροποφορέω or τροφοφορέω for τρέφω; xvii. 4 προσεκληρώθησαν, cf. v. 36 προσεκλίθη with *v.l.* προσεκολλήθη; xvi. 37, xxii. 25 ἀκατάκριτος for the usual ἄκριτος; xviii. 28 διακατηλέγχετο, cf. xvii. 17, xviii. 4, etc., διελέγετο; xx. 24 τελειώσω (v.l. -ῶσαι) τὸν δρόμον, cf. xiii. 25, 2 Tim. iv. 7; xx. 32 κληρονομίαν ἐν τοῖς ἡγιασμένοις, cf. xxvi. 18 κλῆρον ἐν τοῖς ἡγιασμένοις, Col. i. 12 κλῆρον τῶν ἁγίων; xxv. 7 αἰτιώματα καταφέροντες, cf. 18 αἰτίαν ἔφερον.

[3] Those who believe that these chapters of Acts are the rendering of an Aramaic original will be equally puzzled to know what Semitic term can lie behind Ἑλληνισταί if the one Greek word means explicitly Greek-speaking Jews.

[4] Eb. Nestle, *ZNTW.* iii., 1902, pp. 248 f., in noting two other agreements in Acts between Chrysostom and the Peshitto (i. 12 ἀπέχον στάδια ἑπτά; xviii. 3 σκυτοτόμος) suggests the reverse relation, that Chrysostom worked from the Syriac.

[5] Cf. *Hom.* xxv. on xi. 21 ἴσως διὰ τὸ μὴ εἰδέναι Ἑβραιστί, Ἕλληνας (sic) αὐτοὺς ἐκάλουν. Evidently Chrysostom's text and commentary originally read Ἑλληνιστάς here. A like note, but of contrary nature, occurs in the Armenian

he is making inferences from the likeness of Ἑλληνισταί to the adverb Ἑλληνιστί. Since his day commentators have followed him except in his admission of doubt, so that it is worth while to remind ourselves how little we really know of the word Hellenists and how much can be said on behalf of regarding it as much more nearly a synonym for ' Greek ' or ' Gentile.' Certainly it must mean non-Jews rather than Jews at xi. 20, where our only escape is to adopt what is textually the inferior reading Ἕλληνας, probably an emendation rendered necessary by accepting Chrysostom's exegesis of vi. 1.

It is, of course, not the intention of this note to suggest that there were no Greek-speaking Jews. In the diaspora they were abundant. The inscriptions in the Jewish catacombs at Rome are with slight exception not in Hebrew or Aramaic,[1] nor does Egypt under the Ptolemies or the Caesars yield many Semitic papyri from the many Jews there.[2] In the former place they used Greek or Latin, in the latter Greek or Demotic. In Palestine also, where Luke mentions the Hellenists, doubtless many Jews spoke Greek, not only in Galilee near the Decapolis but also in Jerusalem. If we retain for Hellenist its supposed meaning of those who could speak Greek, there were doubtless Hellenists there, including some of the many Jews who had returned from abroad. Like Paul, many if not most of them could also speak Aramaic. The surprise expressed in Acts xxii. 2 was not that a Jew of the dispersion could speak Aramaic, but that a stranger not recognized as a Jew at all but perhaps an Egyptian (xxi. 38) or one of some other nationality should prove able to speak in Aramaic.

How many Jews knew Greek only, whether in Palestine or abroad, we do not know. Nor do we know by what name they were distinguished. Evidently not commonly by ' Hellenists ' or the word would occur more frequently. The rabbinic sources also fail to show a definite designation for Greek-speaking Jews. In Palestine neither the various vernaculars nor the language of the learned appear to have had any simple classification of Jews in accordance with their use or non-use of the Aramaic or Greek

catena (Vol. III. p. 437) on the difficult passage xviii. 17, where Codex Bezae and the Antiochian text describe those who beat Sosthenes as Ἕλληνες: " By Greeks here he means those Jews who spoke in the Greek language." The preceding words are from Chrysostom, the succeeding ones from Ephrem. Either the commentator read Ἑλληνισταί or he felt that Ἕλληνες had the same force as was usually given to that word. I may add, if only to increase our confusion, that it seems to some students of John quite possible that Ἕλληνες in that gospel (vii. 35, xii. 20) means precisely the diaspora or Greek-speaking Jews.

[1] Schürer, *GJV*. iii.⁴ pp. 140 f. Even Scriptural personal names are quite scarce in the Jewish sepulchral inscriptions at Rome.

[2] L. Fuchs, *Die Juden Ägyptens in ptolemäischer und römischer Zeit*, 1924, pp. 114 ff. L. Blau, *Papyri und Talmud in gegenseitiger Beleuchtung*, 1913, p. 10, writing of Egypt emphatically declares "there can be no doubt that there was in the Hellenistic world an Aramaic diaspora beside the Greek diaspora." His evidence is, however, slight. See also A. Causse, *Les Dispersés d'Israël*, 1929.

language, though there are many references to the Jews abroad living among the Gentiles, οἱ κατὰ τὰ ἔθνη Ἰουδαῖοι (Acts xxi. 21). Possibly within Judaism they did not form as distinct, self-conscious, and well labelled a group as we have commonly supposed.[1] They were much more aware of their difference from Gentiles. The frequent bilingualism of the first century doubtless made less conspicuous and significant the relatively few Jews who spoke exclusively either Greek or Aramaic. Using the terms in their generally accepted meaning, J. H. Moulton says : "There were clearly senses in which it was possible to be both Hebrew and Hellenist— Hebrew in that the tie to the mother country was never broken and Aramaic was retained as the language of the family circle, Hellenist in that foreign residence demanded perpetual use of Greek from childhood." [2]

On the other hand the difference between Jews (or Hebrews) and Gentiles (or Greeks) was not insignificant. The Book of Acts is aware of it and never obliterates it in its story of Christianity, though Paul gives an impression of the relation between them more hostile in fact and more united in theory than does the Book of Acts. The three occurrences of Ἑλληνισταί in it are perhaps to be understood as indicating in two cases the missionary approach of Jewish Christians like Paul and the men of Cyprus and Cyrene to non-Jews, in the other as an early case of friction between the two elements within the Church.

## Note VIII. Proselytes and God-fearers

### By Kirsopp Lake

The Jewish Mission.    The existence of the Diaspora of the Jews produced what is sometimes called the Jewish mission. But this phrase is liable to be misunderstood. There is no evidence at all that missionaries were ever sent out in the modern

---

[1] Cf. *supra*, pp. 69 ff. As time went on sub-classification of this sort did not increase either in Christianity or in Judaism, and was less needed as Greek-speaking Jews and Aramaic-speaking Christians became negligible. Only three groups emerged needing sharp distinction—the Jews, the Gentiles, and the Christians. See Harnack, *Mission und Ausbreitung*, vol. i., Exkurs. 'Die Beurteilung der Christen als drittes Geschlecht.'

It is evident that much of the neatly pigeon-holed picture of the early church and its rivals to which we are accustomed goes further than our sources warrant. Beside the doubts expressed here about the Hellenists and Hebrews, the new historian of the apostolic age will have to consider the questions simultaneously raised by D. W. Riddle in the *Anglican Theological Review*, xii., 1929, pp. 15 ff., 'The So-called Jewish Christians,' and by J. H. Ropes in his 'Singular Problem of the Epistle to the Galatians,' 1929. Without 'Hellenists' in Acts, or 'Judaizers' behind Galatians, or 'Jewish Christians' anywhere, such a book as Hort's *Judaistic Christianity* would require re-writing.

[2] *Cambridge Biblical Essays*, 1909, p. 481. Both Philo (note 2, p. 63) and Chrysostom (see p. 72) still seem to call such Greek-speaking Jews Ἑβραῖοι.

or Christian sense.  But wherever Jews settled, they established a synagogue which, by its peculiar practices, attracted the attention of non-Jews who were not wholly satisfied with heathenism.

The facts have been so excellently stated by my friend, Professor G. F. Moore, that I venture to put in his words what I could not express equally well in my own.  Even, he says,[1] " if some of the methods of Jewish apologetic and polemic provoked prejudice rather than produced conviction, the belief in the future universality of the true religion, the coming of an age when ' the Lord shall be king over all the earth,' when ' the Lord shall be one and his name One,' led to efforts to convert the Gentiles to the worship of the one true God and to faith and obedience according to the revelation he had given, and made Judaism the first great missionary religion of the Mediterranean world.  When it is called a missionary religion, the phrase must, however, be understood with a difference.  The Jews did not send out missionaries [2] into the *partes infidelium* expressly to proselyte among the heathen.  They were themselves settled by thousands in all the great centres and in innumerable smaller cities ; they had appropriated the language and much of the civilization of their surroundings ; they were engaged in the ordinary occupations, and entered into the industrial and commercial life of the community and frequently into its political life. Their religious influence was exerted chiefly through the synagogues, which they set up for themselves, but which were open to all whom interest or curiosity drew to their services.   To Gentiles, in whose mind these services, consisting essentially of reading from the Scriptures and a discourse more or less loosely connected with it, lacked all the distinctive features of cultus, the synagogue, as has been observed above, resembled a school of some foreign philosophy.   That it claimed the authority of inspiration for its sacred text and of immemorial tradition for its interpretation, and that the reading was prefaced by invocations of the deity and hymns in his praise, was in that age quite consistent with this character.   That the followers of this philosophy had many peculiar rules about food and dress and multiplied purifications was also natural enough in that time.

" The philosophy itself, whose fundamental doctrines seemed to be monotheism, divine providence guided by justice and benevolence, and reasonable morality, had little about it that was unfamiliar.   Even what they sometimes heard about retribution after death, or a coming conflagration which should end the present order of things, was not novel.   But at the bottom Judaism was something wholly different from a philosophy which a man was free to accept in whole or in part as far as it carried the assent of his intelligence.   It might be a reasonable religion, but it was in an eminent degree a religion of authority ; a revealed religion, which did

---

[1] *Judaism*, i. pp. 323 f.  See also A. Bertholet, *Die Stellung der Israeliten und der Juden zu den Fremden*, 1896, and J. Juster, *Les Juifs dans l'empire romain*, 1914, i. pp. 253 ff.

[2] It is perhaps curious that Moore does not refer to Matt. xxiii. 15, which speaks of the Jews compassing sea and land to make one proselyte, but apparently there is nothing in Rabbinic writings to suggest that this means missionary enterprise in the modern sense.

not ask man's approval but demanded obedience to the whole and every part, reason and inclination to the contrary notwithstanding ; an exclusive religion which tolerated no divided allegiance ; a religion which made a man's eternal destiny depend on his submission of his whole life to its law, or his rejection of God who gave the law.  Such, at least, was the rigour of the doctrine when it was completely and logically presented.

**Judaism in the Diaspora.**      " It is certain that it was not always preached so uncompromisingly. Especially in the Hellenistic world, polytheism and idolatry was so decisively the characteristic difference between Gentile and Jew that the rejection of these might almost seem to be the renunciation of heathenism and the adoption of Judaism ; and if accompanied by the observance of the sabbath and conformity to the rudimentary rules of clean and unclean which were necessary conditions of social intercourse, it might seem to be a respectable degree of conversion.   Nor are utterances of this tenor lacking in Palestinian sources ; e.g. The rejection of idolatry is the acknowledgement of the whole law.[1]

**The religious heathen.**     " Such converts were called religious persons (' those who worship, or revere, God '),[2] and although in a strict sense outside the pale of Judaism, undoubtedly expected to share with Jews by birth the favour of the God they had adopted, and were encouraged in this hope by their Jewish teachers.   It was not uncommon for the next generation to seek incorporation into the Jewish people by circumcision.[3] . . .

" However numerous such ' religious persons ' were, and with whatever complaisance the Hellenistic synagogue, especially, regarded these results of its propaganda, whatever hopes they may have held out to such as thus confided in the uncovenanted mercies of God, they were only clinging to the skirt of the Jew (Zech. viii. 23) ; they were like those Gentile converts to Christianity who are reminded in the Epistle to the Ephesians that in their former state, when they were called uncircumcised by the so-called circumcision, they were aliens to the Israelite commonwealth, foreigners without right in the covenanted promises." [4]

**Proselytes of the Gate.**      In the eighteenth century the erroneous custom arose [5] of saying that these ' religious persons ' were regarded by the Jews as a special kind of proselyte—proselytes of the Gate.   That is now recognized as a mistake, but the evil result has remained, so that even in books such as Strack-Billerbeck's magnificent commentary on the New Testament, the name of ' half-proselyte ' is given to this class of non-Jew who was interested in Judaism.   Yet this name is surely unjustifiable.   A proselyte is within the covenant, a non-Jew is without it, and fractional proselytes are impossible.

[1] Sifrè Num. § 111 ; Deut. § 54 ; *Ḥullin* 5a, and parallels.  One who renounces idolatry is called in Scripture a Jew.  *Megillah* 13a, top.

[2] φοβούμενοι τὸν θεόν, σεβόμενοι τὸν θεόν, or abbreviated, σεβόμενοι.  In Hebrew, יראי שמים.

[3] Juvenal, *Sat.* xiv. 96 ff.

[4] ἀπηλλοτριωμένοι τῆς πολιτείας τοῦ Ἰσραὴλ καὶ ξένοι τῶν διαθηκῶν τῆς ἐπαγγελίας, Ephesians ii. 12.  Proselytes, on the contrary, have come over to καινῇ καὶ φιλοθέῳ πολιτείᾳ, Philo, *De monarchia*, c. 7 § 51 (M. ii. p. 219).

[5] See below, p. 81.

After abandoning the view that this non-Jew interested in Judaism was God-fearers. called a proselyte of the Gate, scholars adopted the theory, first made popular by Jacob Bernays, that in Acts these non-Jews were called ' God-fearers,' φοβούμενοι or σεβόμενοι τὸν θεόν, and that the same phrase in the LXX also applies to them. This is doubtless correct, though the technical nature of the phrase has been exaggerated. (For the discussion of this point see pp. 82 ff.)

Thus it is clear that the synagogues in the large cities of the Roman Empire were surrounded by a fringe of non-Jew worshippers, some of whom ultimately became proselytes, some of whom did not. It is also probable that some of the non-Jew worshippers may have thought that a combination of the best points of Judaism with the best points of heathenism would be a more satisfactory religion than either. (For the evidence that this actually happened see pp. 88 ff.)

Obviously this fringe of non-Jews, not satisfied with heathenism, and hesitating whether to become proselytes or to start some new method of worshipping God, provided the Christian missionaries with the best possible opportunity for making converts. Almost certainly a majority of the first Greek Christians came from this class, and this illumines two of their characteristics which are otherwise difficult to explain. On the one hand they were not Jews—the existence of any large body of Jews converted to Christianity is doubtful and improbable [1]—but on the other hand they were all acquainted with the LXX.

This note is therefore devoted to discussing three topics belonging to the general subject of Jewish missionary practice and terminology :

    (i.) The requirements made from converts to Judaism.
    (ii.) The words used to describe proselytes, and those who were in varying degrees interested in Judaism.
    (iii.) The evidence for separate syncretistic cults organized by those who, starting with an interest in Judaism, ended by establishing societies distinct from, though analogous to, the Synagogue or the Church.

### (i.) *The Requirements made from Converts who wished to become full Members of the Synagogue*

The requirements which the Jews laid down for accepting a convert into the People were :

(a) Some kind of instruction. The nature of this instruction was Jewish probably left to individual rabbis in the earliest period and afterwards instruction. became standardized, but no written record exists. It has been argued, notably by Taylor, Seeberg, and Klein, that the Christian *Didache* is based upon a Jewish book of instructions for converts which was called *The Two Ways*. This is possible, but the evidence adduced does not amount to demonstration. It should, however, be noted that it is quite inconceivable

---

[1] See especially J. H. Ropes, 'The Singular Problem of the Epistle to the Galatians,' in the *Harvard Theological Studies*, xiv. (1929).

that this process of instruction did not exist.   Jews and Gentiles were both intelligent groups and neither would wish to make converts or to be converted without some understanding of the questions involved.   So that in any district where the Jewish mission was at all successful there must have been a group of Gentiles interested in Judaism but not yet fully converted.

Circum-
cision.

(b) The one essential for reception into the People was circumcision. This is so universally acknowledged that it is unnecessary to accumulate evidence.   But it is very interesting to notice that there is in Judaism a curious controversy between the school of Shammai and the school of Hillel as to the validity of circumcision *ex opere operato*.   If a man who belonged to an Arab tribe which practised circumcision was converted to Judaism, was this non-Jewish or heretical circumcision to be regarded as valid ?   The school of Shammai said ' no ' ;   the school of Hillel said ' yes.' Obviously Cyprian would have felt quite at home in this discussion.

Baptism.

(c) *Baptism.*—In Judaism washing the body was one of the ways by which an Israelite who had become unclean through leprosy or through ceremonial accident could recover his cleanliness.   Similarly a convert was washed or baptized when he was taken in to the People.   It was true that a heathen, inasmuch as he was not under the Law, could not be unclean in the sense of the Law, but from the point of view of the Jew he was as a heathen essentially unclean. (Cf. John xviii. 28 and Acts x. 28.)   It would appear that as time went on this baptism became more and more important. The earliest evidence of it seems to be contained in the story of a dispute between the school of Shammai and the school of Hillel.   According to the school of Shammai, if a proselyte was circumcised on the day before the Passover he was baptized and then could eat the Passover, but the school of Hillel said that the circumcised are like those who have been defiled by the grave (that is, by touching a corpse or a grave), and there-fore could not be baptized for seven days.   Whether this baptism was on a level with other ceremonial washings or had a different nature is open to argument.   (For the evidence about this controversy see Strack, vol. i. pp. 102 f. ; G. F. Moore, *Judaism*, vol. iii. note 103.)

This baptism gradually became more and more important.   In the case of women it was the only act of initiation, and it is not difficult to see that this would tend to make it more and more important for men also.   The classical illustration of this fact is a discussion between Rabbi Eliezer ben Hyrcanus and Rabbi Joshua ben Hananiah.   Eliezer (representing the school of Shammai) maintained that the convert is a proselyte, i.e. an adopted member of the People, as soon as he has been circumcised, and independently of baptism, while Rabbi Joshua went so far as to claim that a man was a proselyte if he were baptized even though he were not circum-cised.   But the opinion of Rabbi Joshua appears to have been in the nature of a paradox which no one else accepted.   The story is given in a baraita (Yebamot 46a).   " Of a proselyte who is circumcised but not baptized," said Rabbi Eliezer b. Hyrkanus, " behold, that man is a proselyte, for we find it so among our fathers (the Israelites who came out of Egypt) because they were circumcised but not baptized (before the entrance into the covenant of Sinai)." If he was baptized and had not been circumcised, so said Joshua b. Hananiah, " behold he is a proselyte, for we find it so among our mothers (the Israelitish women who came out of Egypt) that they were baptized but not circumcised (at their entrance into the covenant of Sinai). But the learned (that is the contemporaries of Rabbi Eliezer and Rabbi Joshua) said, If he has been baptized, but has not been circumcised, or if he has been circumcised but has not been baptized, he is no proselyte until he is circumcised and has been baptized."

The suggestion that baptism without circumcision was valid is startling and contrary to everything which we know of Judaism, but two things must be remembered. In the first place, much of the controversy attributed to distinguished rabbis in the Talmud is merely staged in order to clear up a position by more or less fictitious opposition. In the second place, the question has been raised whether behind this argument there is not a certain sense that belief, circumcision, and baptism form a connected whole. The first step—belief—implies an obligation to the other two, and so also circumcision and baptism each implies an obligation to the other. Undoubtedly this would be accepted as a fair statement by any learned Jew. The question was at what stage in this threefold process did the convert enter upon the full possession of the privileges given to him. The old answer was when he was circumcised ; the later answer was when he had been circumcised and baptized, and the passages dealing with the subject in the Talmud are intended to emphasize the importance of baptism, not to minimize that of circumcision. Thus, for instance, according to Yebamot 46a, Rabbi Ḥiyya bar Abba, who lived about A.D. 280, declared that the children of a Jewish mother and of a proselyte who had been circumcised but not baptized were illegitimate, and according to the Abodah Zarah 57a, Rabbi Simi ben Ḥiyya said that slaves bought from the heathen, who had been circumcised but not baptized, defiled by their footprints on the street.

(d) A fourth requirement in theory was that the proselyte should offer Sacrifice. sacrifice in the temple. Clearly this could not be carried out because the temple had been destroyed, and it remained in a condition of suspense.

It is obvious that to the Christian scholar the most important part of Christian these conditions for the acceptance of a proselyte are the two which were parallels. taken over by the Christian church—instruction and baptism. Originally, as in Judaism, instruction preceded baptism, though the position was reversed when child baptism was introduced, just as it was reversed in Judaism where, with children born into the covenant, circumcision preceded instruction. Unfortunately we have no examples of the formulation of Jewish instruction contemporary with the New Testament ; it may have influenced Christian instruction, but here again our knowledge does not begin to be full until much later. Roughly speaking, we have four main sources of information : (i.) the *Didache*, (ii.) the *Didascalia*, (iii.) the *Epistola Apostolorum*, and (iv.) the *Epideixis* of Irenaeus. Except in the *Didache*, there would seem to be little trace of Jewish influence, but much anti-Jewish argument. In the *Didache* there is perhaps evidence that an early document was used—'The Two Ways'—and that this was based on an original Jewish book of instruction. Such, at least, is the opinion of Klein [1] and others who have special knowledge of the Jewish sources. It is also probable that the instructions for worship which follow 'The Two Ways' are influenced by Jewish practice, though largely by way of contrast. Thus the Eucharistic and other prayers are constructed on Jewish lines, but the Lord's Prayer is substituted for the Tefillah, and the fast days, Wednesday and Friday, are chosen in contrast to Monday and Thursday.

### (ii.) The Names used for Converts

*Ger.*

HEBREW.    (i.) *Ger* (גֵּר).—Two views have been held about the meaning of this word.    (a) Throughout the Old Testament it means a non-Israelite living in Israelite territory.  This is the older view, at least in modern books, and is accepted without discussion in Strack ii. pp. 715 ff.    (b) It has this meaning in the more primitive parts of the Law, including Deuteronomy, but in the later parts, and in the later books generally, it means a convert to the religion of Israel.  This view is adopted by Moore in *Judaism*, i. pp. 328 ff.,[2] and seems to have the weight of evidence in its favour.

In rabbinical writings the word *ger* has the second meaning and is used to describe a Gentile who has become a Jew by the methods discussed on pp. 77 ff.

*The two meanings of ger.*

Owing to this change in meaning, it was necessary to distinguish between *ger* in the original sense and *ger* in the later.  Thus Kohut's '*Aruch Completum* says, "There is a *ger* who is a foreigner residing in Israel who has promised not to serve other Gods.  He is a *ger toshab*.  There is also a *ger* who has become a convert in all respects and has become a Jew.  This is the *ger zedek*."  That the rabbis fully recognized that the *ger* in the primitive sense was, to say the least, frequently not a convert, can be shown by such passages as the commentary on Exodus xx. 10 in the *Mekilta* of Rabbi Simeon ben Yoḥai : "If this had referred to a *ger zedek* (that is, a convert), it would repeat what had been said already where it is said that there shall be one law to you and to the *ger*. . . . 'Thy *ger*' refers to the *ger toshab* who is your hired man, and the command prevents Israelites from forcing him to work on the Sabbath ; but he may work if he himself will."

Human nature being what it is, it is obvious that conversion is often due to mixed motives, and the rabbis distinguished these motives by the various adjectives which they used to describe different types of *ger*. A convert actuated by worthy motives was a *ger sedek* or *ger emet*, a proselyte from righteous motives or for the sake of the truth ; and similarly the convert actuated by unworthy motives was described as a *ger zeker*, a proselyte of fraud.  Most of these phrases are self-explanatory, but there is one which calls for explanation as a curiosity of literary allusion.  This is the 'lion proselyte,' which means a convert through fear of consequences, and the reference is to the story in 2 Kings xvii. 24-33 which described

---

[1] G. Klein, *Der älteste christliche Katechismus.*
[2] See also Robertson Smith, *O.T.J.C.* 2nd ed. p. 342 note 1.

how the aliens introduced into the region of Samaria by the Assyrians after the captivity of the Northern Kingdom were attacked by lions and accepted the worship of Jehovah on the theory that the lions came from him.

Thus *ger* completely changed its meaning; instead of being a foreigner living among Israelites but *not* converted to their religion, the *ger* came to be the name of a foreigner who was converted.

(ii.) *Toshab.*—Another name used in the Old Testament to describe *Toshab.* these strangers living in the land of Israel was *toshab* (תושב), and this word and *ger* were frequently combined with a copula (*ger we-toshab*). The phrase is generally represented in the English version by 'stranger and sojourner' and in the LXX by προσήλυτος ἢ πάροικος. Without the copula between the words it is found in the Old Testament only in Lev. xxv. 47, and inasmuch as in this passage the Samaritan and the ancient versions insert the copula the reading of the Massoretic text may be accidental. Nevertheless it is apparently the origin of rabbinic use; for to express the original meaning of *ger* the rabbis took over the phrase *ger toshab* and used it in the sense of an unconverted foreigner who lived in the land of Israel. It was especially used to explain *ger* in the Old Testament, where it obviously could not mean a convert (cf. the quotation given above from the *Mekilta* of Rabbi Simeon ben Yoḥai). It will be seen, however, that the phrase had little more than archaeological or exegetical importance, as in the days when it was used Israel possessed no territory of its own.

The rabbis laid down various rules for governing intercourse between *Noachian* Jews and the *ger toshab*. These rules naturally enough are all put in the *rules.* form of regulations implying the possession of Palestine by the Jews. The *ger toshab* was required to keep the seven commandments known as 'Noachian,' that is to say traditionally given by Noah to his sons. These seven commandments are directed against blasphemy, idolatry, fornication, the shedding of blood, robbery, the use of meat containing blood [1] (lit. from a living animal), and disobedience to the legal authorities. It is possible that they represent a real tradition as to the practice of Israel in Palestine, but it is very curious that they do not include the observation of the Sabbath. It has been suggested that in practice these regulations were used in the time of the rabbis to control the conduct of those who were meditating conversion or for other reasons wished to be on friendly terms with the Jews, but the evidence that this was the case is lacking and the theory merely depends on general probability. For the possible relations between the Noachian commandments and the apostolic decrees in Acts xv. see Addit. Note 16.

(iii.) *Ger sha'ar.*—At quite a late period the mediaeval rabbis possibly *Proselytes* but not certainly used the phrase *ger sha'ar*, generally translated in modern *of the gate.* books 'proselyte of the gate.' This expression is said to have been used as a synonym for a *ger toshab* in allusion to the Old Testament phrase 'the stranger within your gates,' for which it is an abbreviation, but

---

[1] This was the additional command given to Noah; the remainder were given to Adam.

according to Strack, vol. ii. p. 723, it was first used by Rabbi Bechai in the thirteenth century.[1] Unfortunately the phrase caught the eye of Deyling in the eighteenth century, and in his *Observationes Sacrae* (1720), vol. ii. pp. 462-469, he devoted part of his essay *De σεβομένοις τὸν θεόν* to arguing that the σεβόμενοι τὸν θεόν are the proselytes of the gate. This identification was generally accepted, so that it figured in all books on the New Testament up to and including the second edition of Schürer's *Geschichte des jüdischen Volkes*. But in his third edition Schürer showed that Deyling's view was unsound. However, owing partly to the fact that the English translation of Schürer was made from the second German edition, it is still quite frequently met with.

Fearers of<br>Heaven.   (iv.) *Jere Shamaim.*—Another phrase important in this problem is *jere shamaim* (שמים ירא), 'fearers of Heaven,' which was used to describe a Gentile who had accepted the truth of the Jewish religion but had not joined it by being circumcised. This use can be traced back as far as the Midrash *Rabbah* on Deuteronomy (cf. *Mekilta* on Exod. xxii. 20) in connexion with a story referred to the time of Gamaliel III. (*circa* A.D. 90). There does not appear to be any clear evidence of this use in earlier literature, but in the later Midrashim it is fairly often used, and the writers explain that the phrase *jere adonai* (for which *jere shamaim* is of course merely a substitute with the usual *shamaim* by metonymy for *adonai*), which is so common in the Old Testament, has this peculiar meaning, which modern writers generally represent by the very dubious phrase 'half-proselyte.' It is, however, extremely doubtful whether there is really any passage in the Old Testament where the phrase has this meaning, and in an overwhelming majority of instances it is merely used to indicate the exemplary nature of the Israelite to whom it refers. It is perhaps desirable to point out that eisegesis has often been substituted for exegesis in treating the phrase in the Old Testament. For instance, 2 Chron. v. 6 is sometimes quoted as an example of a reference to 'half-proselytes' as *jere shamaim* or φοβούμενοι τὸν θεόν, but, apart from the fact that there is nothing in the Hebrew to represent οἱ φοβούμενοι τὸν θεόν, it is tolerably clear that the real meaning is 'the whole house of Israel'—the pious and the proselytes.

Greek ren-<br>derings of<br>*ger.*   THE GREEK. (i.) προσήλυτος and πάροικος.—In the LXX *ger* is rendered sometimes by προσήλυτος, sometimes by πάροικος, and in two passages (Exod. xii. 19 ; Is. xiv. 1) by γειώρας, which is a transliteration of the Aramaic for *ger*. (Cf. Simon ben Giora in the Jewish war.)

It has often been held that προσήλυτος in the LXX is a synonym of πάροικος and that both words correctly render the meaning of *ger* = a foreigner, not a convert. This view was maintained by Geiger, *Urschrift und Übersetzungen der Bibel*, pp. 353 ff., and is adopted with little or no discussion by Schürer and Strack.

The evidence of Josephus and Philo is interesting in its implication

[1] G. F. Moore, *Judaism*, i. p. 341, knows of no occurrence earlier than R. Moses ben Naḥman (d. 1270).

rather than its direct statements.  Josephus [1] apparently does not use the
word προσήλυτος, and Philo uses it only three times.  In each case it is
with reference to a passage in the Old Testament, and he explains the word
almost apologetically.  Apparently the word did not seem to cultivated
Greek-speaking Jews to be a satisfactory phrase to be used in educated
Greek, as indeed might be guessed from its absence from Greek literature
in general.  Nevertheless a passage from *De monarchia* makes it plain that
Philo interpreted the word προσήλυτος as meaning a convert.  In the
*De monarchia*, 7, § 51, M. ii. p. 219, he says : καὶ πάντας τοὺς ὁμοιοτρόπους
εἴτ᾽ οὖν φύντας ἐξ ἀρχῆς εἴτε καὶ ἐκ τοῦ μεταβάλλεσθαι πρὸς τὴν
ἀμείνω τάξιν κρείττους γεγονότας ἀποδέχεται, τοὺς μὲν ὅτι τὴν εὐγένειαν
οὐ κατέλυσαν, τοὺς δ᾽ ὅτι πρὸς εὐσέβειαν ἠξίωσαν μεθορμίσασθαι—
τούτους δὲ καλεῖ προσηλύτους ἀπὸ τοῦ προσεληλυθέναι καινῇ καὶ
φιλοθέῳ πολιτείᾳ,—οἳ μυθικῶν μὲν ἀλογοῦσι πλασμάτων, περιέχονται
δὲ ἀκραιφνοῦς ἀληθείας.  Obviously this interpretation is connected with
the change in the meaning of *ger*, which in turn reflects the gradual
development of Israel from a nation with resident aliens to a church with
converts, and corroborative evidence can be found in *De sacrificantibus*,
10, § 308 f. (M. ii. p. 258); *De iustitia* 6, § 176 ff. (M. ii. p. 365); *De humani-
tate*, 12, § 102 ff. (M. ii. p. 392) ; *De poenitentia*, 1, § 175 ff. (M. ii. p. 405).

Thus beyond doubt the development of the word προσήλυτος was the
same in Greek as that of *ger* in Hebrew.   The question is whether the
change was made before or after the translation of the Old Testament into
Greek.   In other words, should we always translate προσήλυτος in the
LXX by ' sojourner,' or did it in the intention of the translator mean
' convert ' ?

There is no doubt but that πάροικος means a resident foreigner—*ger*
in the older sense—but προσήλυτος is a more doubtful question, for it is
certain that in the New Testament and in Patristic Greek it regularly means
a convert.  But Geiger and his successors were influenced by the view that
*ger* in the Old Testament always means a resident foreigner, and thought
that the change of meaning both in *ger* and in προσήλυτος was not made
until the first century A.D.

An article by W. C. Allen (*Expositor*, October 1894, pp. 264 ff.), which
seems to have been strangely overlooked, gives a full analysis of the question
and suggests that the matter is not so simple as it is usually represented.
He points out that although it is true that in biblical Hebrew the *ger* is
a foreigner, and only in rabbinical writings is regularly used to mean a
convert, still the priestly code in the Pentateuch shows that the word
was fast developing into the later sense, and he goes on to argue that
by the time of the LXX the word had already acquired its later meaning.
The translators were aware of the change, used πάροικος in passages
where *ger* obviously can only mean ' foreigner,' and substituted προσήλυτος
where the word might conceivably be used for ' convert.'   That is to say,
in Allen's words, " in the great majority of cases where *ger* occurs in the
Hebrew text the Greek translators have not simply translated into the

---

[1] Josephus, *Antiq.* xviii. 3. 5, § 82, almost presupposes the word by using
the perf. part. προσεληλυθυῖαν.

exact Greek equivalent but have read into the word the later meaning which it has in the Mishna." Allen goes on to give a list of passages in which *ger* is translated by πάροικος, and in all of them the sense of 'convert' is excluded by the context. He then gives a list of 69 passages in which προσήλυτος renders *ger* and may have been interpreted as 'convert,' though this was not the real meaning of the original Hebrew. Furthermore, he argues that just as the LXX distinguishes the sense in which it interprets *ger* by using sometimes πάροικος and sometimes προσήλυτος, so it distinguishes it in the cognate words which have to be rendered by verbs, sometimes using παροικεῖν but changing to προσέρχεσθαι when the sense of convert appears possible. He is, however, obliged to force the meaning a little in some instances, especially those in which *ger* is used of the Israelites in Egypt. They were certainly not 'converts' but quite definitely 'sojourners'; nevertheless in these passages *ger* is sometimes rendered by προσήλυτος and not by πάροικος (Exod. xxii. 20, xxiii. 9; Lev. xix. 34; Deut. x. 19).

Thus, though Allen's paper certainly shows that the question is not quite so simple as it is often represented to be, he seems somewhat to overstate his case. It is true that πάροικος is used eleven times, and that in these cases the sense 'convert' is inadmissible; and it is also true that in the much larger number of passages where προσήλυτος is used it is often possible to suppose that the translator meant 'convert,' that is to say, was interpreting *ger* in the later rabbinic sense. But even so he has to admit that in certain passages προσήλυτος cannot mean 'convert,' and in a good many more passages it seems that his interpretation is somewhat strained. On the whole it seems probable that the translators of the LXX knew that *ger* did not always mean 'convert,' and sometimes —when they were specially careful—used πάροικος to render it, but it had already acquired its later meaning for which Greek-speaking Jews used προσήλυτος, so that the tendency of the translators was regularly to use προσήλυτος to render *ger*, and to do so too often.

In any case it is certain that *ger* changed its meaning. It began by meaning 'foreigner' and ended by meaning 'convert.' Similarly προσήλυτος probably once meant 'foreigner' and afterwards 'convert.' The evolution of the two words is exactly the same. The only doubtful point is the date at which the change was made; but at any rate it was before the Christian era.

Fearing God.    (ii.) φοβούμενοι τὸν θεόν and σεβόμενοι τὸν θεόν.—A somewhat similar situation arises with regard to the phrase φοβούμενοι τὸν θεόν or σεβόμενοι τὸν θεόν. This has been the centre of a long and complicated discussion [1] of which the outcome is not clear as yet and perhaps never will be.

The point at issue is to what extent φοβούμενοι τὸν θεόν is a technical description of the non-Jewish fringe attending the Synagogue, or is merely an honourable epithet applicable to Jew, Gentile, or Proselyte, as the context may decide.

[1] See especially E. Schürer, *GJV*. iii.[4] p. 174, note 70, and Strack, ii. pp. 716 ff.

*The LXX.*—The phrase φοβούμενος or σεβόμενος τὸν θεόν is the usual LXX. rendering of *jere adonai*, which, as shown above (p. 82), is a common description of good Israelites. But since the practically identical phrase *jere shamaim* was used in the Rabbinical literature to describe the ' pious Gentiles ' who came to the Synagogue, it is obviously possible that the same meaning may have been earlier attached both to *jere adonai* and to its Greek equivalent. Many scholars are quite certain that this is so, and, by interpreting φοβούμενοι τὸν θεόν whenever it occurs in the Psalms or elsewhere as a reference to the pious Gentiles, obtain much information as to the presence of a large class of this kind, not only in the Synagogues of the Diaspora but also in the Temple at Jerusalem. It is possible that there was such a class ; but this cannot be proved by reading a special meaning into φοβούμενος τὸν θεόν and then treating that meaning as evidence.

*Josephus.*—Use has been made in this connexion of *contra Apion*. Josephus. ii. 10 and ii. 39, but nevertheless these two passages, though they indicate the growth of proselytism among the Jews, do not make use of the phrase in question, and the only important one is *Antiq*. xiv. 7. 2 θαυμάσῃ δὲ μηδείς, εἰ τοσοῦτος ἦν πλοῦτος ἐν τῷ ἡμετέρῳ ἱερῷ πάντων τῶν κατὰ τὴν οἰκουμένην Ἰουδαίων καὶ σεβομένων τὸν θεόν, ἔτι δὲ καὶ τῶν ἀπὸ τῆς Ἀσίας καὶ τῆς Εὐρώπης εἰς αὐτὸ συμφερόντων ἐκ πολλῶν πάνυ χρόνων. But unfortunately the technical meaning which has been seen in this passage is based on a wrong translation. Jacob Bernays, followed by Emil Schürer, says that Josephus appeals not only to the rich offerings of Jews throughout the world but also to those of the God-fearers, but the Greek surely makes it plain that σεβομένων τὸν θεόν is a further description of those who are called Ἰουδαίων, and καί connects it with κατὰ τὴν οἰκουμένην, so that the meaning of the whole phrase is ' all the Jews worshipping God throughout the world.' Bernays' interpretation would require a τῶν before σεβομένων. It is of course true that Josephus cannot be trusted to be conventional on small points of Greek grammar, but in this case the supposition that he is observing its rules gives a perfectly good sense. He is not distinguishing between Jews and God-fearers any more than he is distinguishing between τῶν κατὰ τὴν οἰκουμένην and those from Asia and Europe.

*In Acts.*—The following passages contain the phrases under discussion : Acts.

(a) x. 1 f. ἀνὴρ δέ τις ἐν Καισαρείᾳ ὀνόματι Κορνήλιος, ἑκατον-τάρχης ἐκ σπείρας τῆς καλουμένης Ἰταλικῆς, εὐσεβὴς καὶ φοβούμενος τὸν θεὸν σὺν παντὶ τῷ οἴκῳ αὐτοῦ.

(b) x. 22 ἀνὴρ δίκαιος καὶ φοβούμενος τὸν θεόν.

(c) x. 35 ἀλλ' ἐν παντὶ ἔθνει ὁ φοβούμενος αὐτὸν καὶ ἐργαζόμενος δικαιοσύνην δεκτὸς αὐτῷ ἐστιν.

(d) xiii. 16 ἄνδρες Ἰσραηλεῖται καὶ οἱ φοβούμενοι τὸν θεόν, ἀκούσατε.

(e) xiii. 26 ἄνδρες ἀδελφοί, υἱοὶ γένους Ἀβραάμ, οἱ ἐν ὑμῖν φοβού-μενοι τὸν θεόν, ἡμῖν ὁ λόγος τῆς σωτηρίας ταύτης ἐξαπεστάλη.

(f) xiii. 43 λυθείσης δὲ τῆς συναγωγῆς ἠκολούθησαν πολλοὶ τῶν Ἰουδαίων καὶ τῶν σεβομένων προσηλύτων τῷ Παύλῳ καὶ τῷ Βαρνάβᾳ, οἵτινες προσλαλοῦντες αὐτοῖς ἔπειθον αὐτοὺς προσμένειν τῇ χάριτι τοῦ θεοῦ.

(g) xiii. 50 οἱ δὲ Ἰουδαῖοι παρώτρυναν τὰς σεβομένας γυναῖκας τὰς εὐσχήμονας καὶ τοὺς πρώτους τῆς πόλεως καὶ ἐπήγειραν διωγμὸν ἐπὶ τὸν Παῦλον καὶ Βαρνάβαν, καὶ ἐξέβαλον αὐτοὺς ἀπὸ τῶν ὁρίων.

(h) xvi. 14 καί τις γυνὴ ὀνόματι Λυδία, πορφυρόπωλις πόλεως Θυατείρων σεβομένη τὸν θεόν, ἤκουεν.

(i) xvii. 4 καί τινες ἐξ αὐτῶν ἐπείσθησαν καὶ προσεκληρώθησαν τῷ Παύλῳ καὶ Σείλᾳ, τῶν τε σεβομένων Ἑλλήνων πλῆθος πολὺ γυναικῶν τε τῶν πρώτων οὐκ ὀλίγαι.

(k) xvii. 17 διελέγετο μὲν οὖν ἐν τῇ συναγωγῇ τοῖς Ἰουδαίοις καὶ τοῖς σεβομένοις καὶ ἐν τῇ ἀγορᾷ κατὰ πᾶσαν ἡμέραν πρὸς τοὺς παρατυγχάνοντας.

(l) xviii. 7 καὶ μεταβὰς ἐκεῖθεν ἦλθεν εἰς οἰκίαν τινὸς ὀνόματι Τιτίου Ἰούστου σεβομένου τὸν θεόν.

It is strange that φοβούμενοι τὸν θεόν is characteristic of the first half of Acts, and σεβόμενοι (τὸν θεόν) of the second. Is this connected with the sources of Acts ? (See H. J. Cadbury, *Making of Luke-Acts*, p. 225, for other possibilities.)

God-fearers, or God-fearing.

On the basis of these passages the theory has been erected that in Acts φοβούμενος τὸν θεόν should be translated ' God-fearer,' as though it meant that the person so described belonged to a recognized separate class in the Synagogue. It has been a serious question whether to adopt this in the translation in Vol. IV., but in the end I decided not to do so, because it seems to me that though in some cases an excellent meaning is obtained in this way, in others it probably reads into the text more than the writer intended. That Gentiles came to the Synagogues is undoubted, and that they were called ' God-fearing ' persons is natural, but they were not a clearly defined group parallel to Jews and proselytes.

The first of the two strongest instances in support of the theory mentioned is the group of passages in chapter x. referring to Cornelius, who was certainly neither a Jew nor a proselyte but is described as φοβούμενος τὸν θεόν. Does this mean that he belonged to a special class of persons who are designated as God-fearers, or merely that he was a pious man who worshipped the true God ? Similarly, in chapter xiii. the phrase ' Men of Israel and those who fear God ' may mean Israelites and non-Israelites who fear God, but the passage gives almost as good a sense and is quite as accurately rendered if Israelites and God-fearers be regarded as two adjectives applied to the same persons. The scene is the synagogue in Pisidian Antioch. Paul is speaking at the request of the rulers of the synagogue, and the introductory phrase may well be merely a reference to the Jews and proselytes who are present. It should be noted in passing that a proselyte is in Jewish thought quite as much an Israelite as a born Jew. Verse 26 is a somewhat stronger example : " Men and brethren, sons of the race of Abraham, and those among you who fear God." It is obviously possible that ' those who fear God ' are treated as part of those of the race of Abraham—" and I appeal especially to those among you who are most interested in religion." But the ' among you ' rather suggests that ' those

who fear God ' is contrasted with the sons of Abraham—' you ' is the whole
congregation, ' sons of Abraham ' are the Jews, ' those who fear God ' are
Greeks who worship in the Synagogue but are not proselytes.  The probability seems on this side, but the passage is not enough to prove that
φοβούμενοι τὸν θεόν would have meant this if the context had not
suggested it.

The same applies to xvi. 14 καί τις γυνὴ ὀνόματι Λυδία, πορφυρόπωλις
πόλεως Θυατείρων σεβομένη τὸν θεόν, ἤκουεν, which would naturally be
rendered " a certain woman named Lydia, a purple-seller of the city of
Thyatira, attending the service, listened."  σεβομένη τὸν θεόν is a perfectly
natural phrase to describe Lydia's presence in the synagogue, or προσευχή,
though of course if it were proved that it was the name of a special class it
could be interpreted in that way.  In the same way in xvii. 4 obviously
τῶν σεβομένων Ἑλλήνων can quite naturally be rendered ' the Greeks who
were worshipping.'  It is of course quite possible, and indeed probable, that
the word ' Greeks ' implies the presence of those who were neither Jews nor
proselytes but taking part in the worship of the synagogue.  But the point
is that it is quite unnecessary to regard σεβόμενοι as a technical term for
this class.  xvii. 17 is a stronger example, and in any case illustrates how
easily οἱ σεβόμενοι might have become technical.  The phrase might be
rendered ' he argued in the synagogue with the Jews and the worshippers,'
and by implication some at least of the worshippers were not Jews ; but
it is clear that this meaning is given to οἱ σεβόμενοι by the context.
It may be illustrated by asking a question.  Supposing that the Greek ran
διελέγετο ἐν τῇ συναγωγῇ τοῖς σεβομένοις, should we be justified in
saying that τοῖς σεβομένοις is a technical term for non-Jewish worshippers,
or could we translate ' he argued with the worshippers,' without differentiating between Jews and Greeks ?  Formerly I thought that the first view
was right, but I now incline to the second.

Finally, xviii. 7 gives the other piece of evidence for the technical
use of the phrase, comparable in force to those in the story of the centurion
Cornelius.  Justus is referred to as σεβόμενος τὸν θεόν, which seems to
mean an attendant at the synagogue.  If this is not a technical use
implying that he is neither a heathen nor a proselyte, it comes very
near it.  The question is not so much what the phrase actually means in
this context as what it might have meant in a different one.  Could Luke
have referred to Jews frequenting the synagogue at Corinth as σεβόμενοι
τὸν θεόν ?  Or had the phrase become so stereotyped that it could only
be used of non-Jewish worshippers ?  I cannot see that there is sufficient
evidence in Acts itself to justify a confident answer to the question.  It
should be remembered that the question affects the use of words rather than
the facts of history.  There is no reason whatever to doubt that there were
non-Jews who went to the synagogue.  It is so intrinsically probable that
the *onus probandi* would be on those who maintained the opposite.  The
question is merely whether φοβούμενος τὸν θεόν and σεβόμενος τὸν θεόν
were technical terms to describe this class and whether it had a recognized status in Judaism.  In favour of such a theory is the fact that the
words are applied at least most often to this class in Acts.  Against it is

the fact that they are perfectly well-known Old Testament phrases which do not bear any technical meaning.

Conclusions      These passages show that φοβούμενοι τὸν θεόν and σεβόμενοι τὸν θεόν were used as appropriate phrases to describe those who though non-Jews believed in the monotheistic God of the Jews and possibly attended the synagogue. Such non-Jews are often spoken of by modern Jewish theologians as ' the pious Gentiles,' and it is held that they will inherit the Life of the World to come though they will not share in the glories of the Messianic time. But the reason why these words were used was because they were appropriate to a vague class, not because they were the recognized title limited to a specific group with a definite place in organized Judaism. The epithets by themselves could have been given to a pious Jew, and it is only when they are applied to a non-Jew that the context gives them a peculiar meaning. It must always be a question whether φοβεῖσθαι or σέβεσθαι τὸν θεόν means that a Gentile was inclined to accept Jewish theology or whether it should be translated more generally. For instance, I think that in Acts xviii. 7 σεβόμενος τὸν θεόν is certainly intended to imply that Justus was an attendant at the Synagogue, but that in xvii. 4 τῶν σεβομένων Ἑλλήνων means the Greeks who were actually worshipping on the occasion when Paul was speaking in the Synagogue.

That σεβόμενος need not always refer to a non-Jew is shown by xiii. 43. The writer says λυθείσης δὲ τῆς συναγωγῆς ἠκολούθησαν πολλοὶ τῶν Ἰουδαίων καὶ τῶν σεβομένων προσηλύτων τῷ Παύλῳ καὶ τῷ Βαρνάβᾳ. The phrase οἱ σεβόμενοι προσήλυτοι has naturally been a difficulty to those who regard οἱ σεβόμενοι as meaning a class who were not proselytes, and it has been contended that proselytes is an interpolation, but in reality the difficulty is entirely due to following a fixed idea rather than the meaning of the Greek, which is ' many of the Jews and the proselytes who were worshipping.' There is no suggestion that the word has a technical sense.

(iii.) *Evidence for the Existence of Syncretistic Cults on a Basis of Judaism*

Bernays.      In a paper [1] printed in a volume published in honour of Theodor Mommsen's 60th birthday in 1877, Jacob Bernays wrote an article on ' Die Gottesfürchtigen bei Juvenal ' (republished in Usener's edition of *Gesammelte Abhandlungen von Jacob Bernays*, vol. ii. pp. 71 ff.). In this he began with a discussion of a famous passage in Juvenal xiv. 96 ff. :

> quidam sortiti metuentem sabbatapatrem
> nil praeter nubes et coeli numen adorant,
> nec distare putant humana carne suillam
> qua pater abstinuit ; mox et praeputia ponunt.
> Romanas autem soliti contemnere leges
> Iudaicum ediscunt et servant ac metuunt ius
> tradidit arcano quodcumque volumine Moyses.

[1] This paper might equally well have been dealt with in the last section, but it is so closely connected with the further development of research in another direction that the present arrangement seemed better.

The general meaning is plain : the father observes the Sabbath and abstains from pork, and does not otherwise observe the Law, but the son becomes a full proselyte. Most commentators saw nothing more in the passage, but Bernays fastened on a suggestion of John Selden (*De iure naturali et gentium*, iii. c. 18, g. A) that *metuentes* means Judaizing Romans. Of course it is clear that this is the meaning of the passage in Juvenal, but Bernays amplified the suggestion that *metuentem* is an odd word to use with *sabbata* in line 96 or with *ius* in line 101. He thinks that it must be used technically and in the same way in which the rabbis used *jere shamaim*. To support this conclusion he quoted the following inscription from *CIL*. v. 1, no. 88, p. 18 :

AVR. SOTER. ET · AVR.

STEPHANUS · AVR.

SOTERIAE · MATRI · PIEN

TISSIMAE · RELIGIONI

IUDEICAE · METVENTI

F. P.

The translation of this is clearly " Aurelius Soter and Aurelius Stephanus, her sons, erected this to Aurelia Soteria their mother, a most pious fearer of the Jewish religion." Bernays thought it plain that Soteria was a Jewess, and here he is doubtless right, but if so, *metuens* does not here mean a half-proselyte.

In the *Gesammelte Abhandlungen* of Bernays, the editor, H. Usener, added another inscription from the *Ephemeris Epigraphica*, iv., 1881, p. 291, no. 838 :

AEMILIO · VA(L)

ENTI · EQ. RO

MANO METV(E)

NTI · Q. AN. XV

MES. III · DIE XXIII.

He thinks that *metuenti* must here also be taken as meaning a semi-proselyte to Judaism, but adds that another inscription in the *CIL*. vi. 1, no. 390, p. 73, *domini metuens I(ovi) O(ptimo) M(aximo) l(ibens) m(erito) sacr(um)*, cannot be so explained. Twenty years later Emil Schürer read to the Berlin Academy (*SAB.*, 1897, pp. 200 ff.) a paper entitled 'Die Juden im bosporanischen Reiche und die Genossenschaften der σεβόμενοι θεὸν ὕψιστον ebendaselbst.' He accepted Bernays' position, though Usener's additional evidence ought surely to have made him hesitate. How does he know that Aemilius Valens was interested in Judaism ? Simply because he is already convinced that *metuens* implies Judaism. It surely somewhat resembles arguing in a circle. And so far from its being true that the second inscription cannot be used, it is really an extremely important piece of evidence which shows that *metuens* does not necessarily mean an adherent or semi-adherent of the Jewish religion, which is completely ruled out of court by the reference to Jupiter. The obvious meaning of the word is 'religious' or 'God-fearing' in the sense in which that word might be used of pious members of any religion. The same thing may be said of further inscriptions which Schürer quotes, namely—Larciae Quadrati[llae natione] Romanae metue[nti] (*CIL.* vi. 29759); Dis Manib. Maianiae homerididae (l. deum ?) maetuenti (*CIL.* vi. 29760); [De]um metuens (*CIL.* vi. 29763); [fidel]is metu[ens] (*CIL.* viii. 4321).

It is clear that there is nothing in these to prove that they refer to the Jews exclusively, and the reference to *Dis manibus* indicates heathen rather than Jewish divinities.[1] The general impression formed on my mind by going through the evidence and reading the inscriptions quoted is that there is no reason whatever to think that *metuentes* means more than 'religious.' In this sense it is clearly used, but the specific religion must in each case be determined from the context. In the first inscription which Bernays quotes, it obviously is Jewish. In the one which refers to *Iupiter Optimus Maximus* it clearly is not. In all the other cases the context is ambiguous and the person referred to may be either Jew or Gentile.

**Latyschev's inscriptions.** Schürer then discussed the inscriptions from the kingdom of Bosporus north of the Black Sea which had been published by Latyschev in *Inscriptiones antiquae orae septentrionalis Ponti Euxini graecae et latinae,* vol. ii. (*Inscriptiones regni Bosporani*), Petropoli, 1890. These inscriptions are so important, and owing to their connexion at the beginning of Schürer's article with the σεβόμενοι of Acts have so often been interpreted in a manner which goes beyond what Schürer himself says, that it is desirable to give their texts in full, especially since neither the *Proceedings of the Berlin Academy* nor Latyschev's *Inscriptiones* are easily accessible, except in large libraries.

(i.) [Latyschev, vol. ii. no. 52 ( =*CIG.* vol. ii. p. 1005, Addenda no. 2114^bb), from Pantikapaeum, dated A.D. 81.]

βασιλεύοντος βασιλέως Τιβερίου Ἰουλίου Ῥησκουπόριδος φιλοκαίσαρος καὶ φιλορωμαίου, εὐσεβοῦς, ἔτους ζοτ' μηνὸς Περει[τί]-
ου ιβ' Χρηστὴ γυνὴ πρότε-
ρον Δρούσου ἀφείημι ἐπὶ τῆς [προ]-
σευχῆς θρεπτόν μου Ἡρακλᾶν
ἐλεύθερον καθάπαξ κατὰ εὐχή[ν]
μου ἀνεπίληπτον καὶ ἀπα[ρ]ενό-
χλητον ἀπὸ παντὸς κληρονόμ[ου]
[τ]ρέπεσται αὐτὸν ὅπου ἂν βού-

[1] Though there is some evidence for the use of Dis Manibus or D.M.S. in Jewish and Christian inscriptions (cf. *CIL.* vi. 29760, viii. 7530). But this is part of the later survival of heathen language (cf. Deo Optimo Maximo). Would it have been customary in the first century ?

λ[ητ]αι ἀνεπικωλύτως καθὼς ε[ὐ]-
ξάμην, χωρὶς ἱς τ[ὴ]ν προ[σ]ευ-
χὴν θωπείας τε καὶ προσκα[ρτε]-
[ρ]ήσεω[ς], συνεπινευσάντων δὲ
                sic
καὶ τῶν κληρνόμων μου Ἡρα-
κλεί[δο]υ καὶ Ἑλικωνιάδος,
συνε[πιτ]ροπεούσης δὲ καὶ τῆ[ς]
συναγωγῆ[ς] τῶν Ἰουδαίων.

(ii.) [Latyschev, vol. ii. n. 53 ( = *Corp. Inscr. Graec.* vol. ii., Addenda
no. 2114ᵇ), from Pantikapaeum.]

[χωρὶς]
[εἰς τὴν] προσευχὴν θωπεί[α]ς [τε καὶ προσ-]
[καρτ]ερήσεος συν[ε]πιτροπε[νούσης]
[δὲ κα]ὶ τῆς συναγωγ[ῆς] τῶ[ν]
Ἰουδαί[ων].

(iii.) [Latyschev, vol. ii. no. 400, from Gorgippia (the present Anapa),
dated A.D. 41.]

θεῶι ὑψίστωι παντο-
κράτορι εὐλογητῷ, βα-
σιλεύοντος βασιλέ-
ως [Πολέμωνος] φιλο-
γερμα[νί]κου καὶ φιλοπάτ-
ριδος, ἔτους ηλτʹ, μη-
νὸς Δείου, Πόθος Στ-
[ρά]τωνος ἀνέθηκεν
τῆι [προσ]ευχῆι κατʼ εὐχ[ὴ]-
ν θ[ρ]επτὴν ἑαυτοῦ ᾗ ὄνο-
μα Χ[ρ]ύσα, ἐφʼ ᾧ ᾗ ἀνέπα-
φος καὶ ἀνεπηρέαστο[ς]
ἀπὸ παντὸς κληρον[όμ]-
ου ὑπὸ Δία, Γῆν, Ἥλιο[ν].

(iv.) [Latyschev, vol. ii. no. 401, from Gorgippia (Anapa).]

[θεῷ ὑψ]ίσ[τῳ παν]-
[τοκράτ]ορι εὐλο[γη]-

[τ]ῷ· βασιλεύοντ[ος]
βασιλέως Τιβερίου Ἰω-  sic
ουλίου λιου Σαυρομά-  sic
του, φιλοκαίσαρος καὶ φι-
λορωμαίου, εὐσεβοῦς,
Τειμόθεος Νυμφα-
γόρου Μακαρίου σὺν
ἀδελφῆς Ἥλιδος γυ-
ναικὸς Νανοβαλα-
μύρου κατὰ εὐχὴν
πατρὸς ἡμῶν Νυμ-
φαγόρου Μακαρίου
ἀφείομεν τὴν θρεπ-
[τὴν ἡμῶν Δ]ωρέαν

[The rest is lacking.]

(v.) [Latyschev, vol. ii. no. 449, from Tanais.]

θεῶι [ὑψίστωι]
βασιλεύοντος β[ασιλέως Τιβερίου]
Ἰουλίου Ῥησκουπό[ριδος φιλοκαί]-
σαρος καὶ φιλορωμ[αίου, εὐσεβοῦς],
ἰσποιητοὶ ἀδελφο[ὶ σεβόμενοι]
[θεὸ]ν ὕψιστον ἀν[έστησαν τὸν]
τελαμῶνα ἐνγ[ράψαντες ἑαυτῶν]
τὰ ὀνόματα.

An illegible list of names follows.

(vi.) [Latyschev, vol. ii. no. 452, from Tanais, dated A.D. 228.]

[Ἀγαθῇ]ι    τύχῃ
θε[ῷ    ὑ]ψίστῳ    εὐ[χή].
βασιλεύοντ[ος]    βασιλέ[ως    Τιβερίου]
[Ἰ]ουλίου [Κό]τυος φιλοκα[ίσαρος] καὶ φι-
[λορωμαίο]υ    εὐσεβοῦς,    εἰσποιητοὶ
ἀδ[ελφοὶ    σ]εβόμενοι    θεὸν    ὕψιστον,

ἐνγρ[άψαντ]ες      ἑαυτῶν      [τ]ὰ      ὀνόματα

[π]ερὶ      πρεσβύτερον      Μ[. . . . . . . ]  'Η-

ρακ[λείδ]ου  καὶ  'Αρίστωνα  [Μ]ενεστράτου καὶ Καλλι-

γ[ένη]ν Μύ[ρω]νος, 'Αλεξίωνα Πατρόκλου, Εὐτυχιανός.

[A list of names follows ; at the end is the date.]

'Εν τῷ εκφ' ἔτει, Γορπιαίου α'.

These inscriptions prove several things :

(i.) That in the kingdom of Bosporus the custom of manumitting a Conclusions. slave by handing him over to a temple had been extended to the Jewish synagogue just as it was transferred later on to the church.  (See especially Mitteis, *Reichsrecht und Volksrecht in den östlichen Provinzen des römischen Kaiserreichs*, pp. 374 ff.)

(ii.) The phrase θεὸς ὕψιστος was commonly used in this country, but the association of the word in the sentence in the third inscription with Zeus, Ge, and Helios shows that the phrase was not used exclusively by Jews.  This of course was at once seen by Schürer, and he therefore made the suggestion that in the kingdom of Bosporus there was a syncretistic cult of the Most High God which had been produced by the influence of Jewish missionaries.  The population had accepted part of their preaching but not all of it, and produced a sect which was neither completely Jewish nor completely heathen.

(iii.) The word σεβόμενοι is used in connexion with the title θεὸς ὕψιστος to describe the worshippers in this cult.

Rather unfortunately, however, Schürer went on to connect σεβόμενος in these passages with the σεβόμενος in the Jewish Synagogues referred to in Acts.  Of course the verb is the same in both places and means ' worship,' but that does not justify the assumption that the persons referred to were worshipping in the same way.  Nor does the fact that this sect in Bosporus had originally been inspired by the teaching of the Synagogue prove that they had necessarily continued to be on good terms with the Jews who had first taught them.  The history of Christianity is a proof to the contrary.

After Schürer's article, but during the same year, F. Cumont published Cumont. in the *Supplément à la Revue de l'Instruction publique en Belgique*, 1897, an illuminating article on ' Hypsistos ' which was also issued separately.  It is very hard to obtain, but the contents are given in the article on ' Hypsistos ' in Pauly-Wissowa.  This article brings together the chief evidence for the use of ἁ ὕψιστος as the Greek name of Jahweh, not only by Jews themselves, but also by Gentiles who worshipped him but did not accept Judaism.

In classical Greek ὕψιστος is one of the less frequent epithets of Zeus, ὕψιστος. but in the Semitic world it was used to render the name of the God Eliun, עליון, well known in the Old Testament as the God of Melchizedek (God Most High).  He was the God of the vault of heaven, whose relation in Phoenician mythology to Baal Shammim—the Balsamem of Plautus (*Poen.* 1027)—is not quite clear.  Eliun survived in Judaism as a title for his former rival Jahweh,[1] and later on, in non-Israelite Semitic theology, under the influence of astrology and Mazdaism he became the Supreme God, who lives in the highest sphere of heaven, whence he governs the stars, and through them rules the events of earth. In Greek he was called ὁ ὕψιστος.

Among the Jews of the Diaspora ὁ ὕψιστος became a favourite method of referring to Jahweh, and was used by Gentiles in speaking of the God of the Jews (cf. Philo, *Leg. ad Gaium*, 23, 40, M. ii. p. 569, 592, and *In Flaccum* 7, M. ii. p. 524). It was so used by Celsus, and when Julian in the fourth century gave the Jews permission to build a temple in Jerusalem, he spoke of it as for τὸν ὕψιστον. (See also above, p. 193.)

Thus two streams of religious thought tended to use the name ὁ ὕψιστος to describe a monotheistic God—Judaism, and a Semitic variant of the current astralism. These two might easily be confused in popular thought. Similarly this ' highest God ' might easily be identified with the chief god of any locality. Thus it is not surprising that in Palmyra there are many inscriptions to Zeus ὕψιστος, μέγιστος καὶ ἐπήκοος—a formula which finds an echo in Semitic inscriptions as " The God whose name be praised for ever, the Good, the Compassionate," and still lives on in the formula of Islam. ὕψιστος is also found in Syria to denote Attis.

In the mixed theology of these monotheistic cults the supreme God, ὁ ὕψιστος θεός, is ἀγένητος, he is the Creator and Governor of the Universe, but he has many ministers of his power, the Sun, Mithras, and a host of angels, and Hermes conducts to him the souls of the pure (Diogenes Laertius viii. 1. 31).

The Bosporus inscriptions clearly represent a cult of this nature—that much is demonstrated by Schürer and Cumont. The references to Jews and to a προσευχή show that Judaism was a strong element, and the ὕψιστος θεός so often mentioned is doubtless Jahweh. But the mention of Zeus, Ge, and Helios shows that it was not a purely Jewish Synagogue. Moreover, it does not necessarily follow that all these inscriptions should be grouped together. The first two, which refer to a συναγωγή of the Jews, but not to the θεὸς ὕψιστος, may well belong to a purely Jewish Synagogue, the third clearly belongs to a syncretistic cult; and as this inscription is the first to speak of the θεὸς ὕψιστος there is a presumption that inscriptions v. and vi., which do the same, belong to the same cult.

The bearing of these inscriptions on Acts.    But what is the bearing of this on the meaning of σέβεσθαι in Acts ? In the inscriptions σεβόμενος is used in Nos. v. and vi. (the reconstruction of v. is rendered certain by vi.), but it is not a technical term for a Gentile who was attending a Jewish Synagogue and thinking seriously about becoming a proselyte, nor does it in the least suggest the tendency, which Juvenal deplores, for Romans to become strict members of the Synagogue. I imagine that εἰσποιητοὶ ἀδελφοὶ σεβόμενοι θεὸν ὕψιστον means 'initiated brethren, worshippers of God Most High.' There is nothing technical here about

[1] The Maccabees, perhaps taking the title from Melchizedek, call themselves on their coins ' priests of God most high,' and R. H. Charles thinks that ' most high God ' became a popular usage in the second century B.C. among the admirers of the Maccabees (cf. Jubilees) and was avoided by their opponents (cf. Enoch 37-70 and Pss. Solom.).

σέβεσθαι, and even if the inscription had referred to a real Synagogue, all that could have been said is that εἰσποιητοί means ' proselytes,' and a proselyte was by definition not a Gentile still thinking about proselytism. In this case, too, σέβεσθαι cannot be a technical term.

The most important contribution of these inscriptions and of Cumont's Acts xvi. 17. work for the understanding of Acts is really in another direction. In Acts xvi. 17 the slave who had a ' python-spirit ' said that the Apostles were the servants of the θεὸς ὕψιστος. Does that mean the God of the Jews, or is it not more likely that it refers to the θεὸς ὕψιστος of a syncretistic cult ? It would be a very natural conclusion for anyone who recognized that the Apostles were preaching the God of the Jews and the morality of the Jews but not the Jewish Law or customs.[1]

The survival of these syncretistic cults having their origin in Gentile Survivals of syncretistic cults. attendants at the Synagogue can be traced down to the fifth century.

Gregory Nazianzenus[2] and Gregory of Nyssa[3] both refer to worshippers of Hypsistos, though one (the Nazianzene) calls them ὑψιστάριοι and the other ὑψιστιανοί. They recognized only one God, rejected images and sacrifices, but revered Fire and Light ; refused circumcision, but observed the Sabbath and part of the food-law.

Similarly Cyril of Alexandria[4] speaks of a similar sect in Egypt called θεοσεβεῖς, and finally the Codex Theodosianus[5] mentions the suppression of a cult of *Coelicolae* in Africa in A.D. 408–409. Theodosius merely knew that they ought to be suppressed, *qui nescio cuius dogmatis novi conventus habent*, but they may have been an old sect similar to the Hypsistarii of Cappadocia. Schürer, Cumont, and Krüger take this view. But it seems doubtful to me, for Augustine in *Epist.* 44 (*al.* 163). 13, says *Miseramus ad maiorem Coelicolarum quem audieramus novi apud eos baptismi institutorem exstitisse et multos illo sacrilegio seduxisse*, etc. This at least suggests that their baptism was a new thing, though Augustine does not say that the sect was. After all, no century is immune from new cults.

The *Coelicolae* are peculiarly interesting to the textual critic because in two places (Acts xiii. 50 and xvii. 4) Codex Bezae renders σεβόμενος by *caelicolae*. Is this a hint of the African affinities of the Latin of this manuscript ? It seems an interesting indication of judgement on the part of the translator as to the meaning of σεβόμενος, and the nature of the *caelicolae*.

Whether the *Massaliani* of Epiphanius[6] is another example of the same kind is more doubtful.

---

[1] A similar cult with another name has been pointed out by Cumont in his ' Les Mystères de Sabazius et le Judaïsme ' in *Comptes Rendus* of the *Académie des Inscriptions*, 1906, pp. 63 ff., and ' A propos de Sabazius et du Judaïsme in the *Musée Belge*, xiv. (1910) pp. 56 ff. He shows that there was a θίασος σεβασιανός which was a combination of the Thracian cult of Sebazios with that of Jahweh Sabaoth.

[2] *Or.* xviii. 5; *P.G.* xxxv. 990 ff.

[3] *Contra Eunomium*, ii. ; *P.G.* xlv. 484.

[4] *De adoratione in spiritu et veritate*, iii. ; *P.G.* lxviii. 282.

[5] xvi. 5. 43 (408) and xvi. 8. 19 (409).

[6] *Haer.* lxxx. 2.

Conclusions.

The results of this investigation may be summarized thus :

(i.) In the Diaspora there was a rather wide circle of Gentiles who were interested in the teaching and practice of the Synagogue. To distinguish them from other Gentiles they were called " (the Gentiles) who fear or worship God." But 'those who fear God' was not a title exclusively appropriated to this type of Gentile. It could also have been used of pious Israelites, and 'those who worship' (οἱ σεβόμενοι), while an appropriate description for these Gentiles, could also be used in a perfectly simple sense of anyone, Jew or Gentile, who was in point of fact worshipping in the Synagogue.

(ii.) These Gentiles tended to go in one of three ways :

(a) Some of them became proselytes and were absorbed into the Synagogue.

(b) Some of them developed an eclectic monotheism of their own. A common form of this was called the worship of the ' Most High ' (ὁ ὕψιστος θεός). Some of them, at least, took over many Jewish customs, but rejected circumcision. Communities of this kind survived until the fifth century.

(c) Some of them became Christians.

## Note IX. The Holy Spirit

### By Kirsopp Lake

The evolution of the meaning of Spirit.

A necessary preliminary to any discussion of the meaning of the Holy Spirit in Acts is a brief statement of the evolution of thought by which ' Spirit' reached the meaning which it had at the time that Acts was written. It is clearly impossible to treat this question fully in this place. To do so would require a volume. On the other hand it seems undesirable to leave the matter wholly undiscussed in this note. The subject at first sight obviously falls into two divisions—Jewish and Greek—and each of these into the two subdivisions of educated and uneducated thought. But speaking generally the extremes meet. The most educated Jewish thought is much nearer educated Greek thought than it is to uneducated thought in its own nation, and there is a noticeable similarity between uneducated Jewish and uneducated Greek thought ; so that it is impossible to organize any statement so as to fall within these divisions without suggesting a sharpness of distinction which the facts do not justify.

The O.T.

*The Spirit in the Old Testament.*—The Hebrew word most generally rendered by πνεῦμα in the LXX is ' ruach ' (רוח). Another word is ' neshama ' (נשמה), but even if this were not originally a synonym for ' ruach ' it must have been so for the makers of the LXX, and it is to be remembered that to the student of the New Testament it is πνεῦμα in the LXX, not ' ruach ' in the Hebrew, which is important.

'Ruach' is primarily ' breath.' The opposite to it is 'flesh.' Spirit and flesh are both related to life, but in different ways. ' Flesh ' is alive, but not of itself. Its life is given to it by ' Spirit,' which is $\zeta\omega o\pi o\iota o\hat{v}\nu$. A corpse has Flesh, but not Spirit; therefore it is dead, not alive. On the other hand there are beings which are alive, but have only Spirit without Flesh. Such are angels and demons. And to those who, like the Israelites, thought of the gods as essentially anthropomorphic, it was naturally obvious that a god had ' ruach' or breath.

The origin of Spirit or Breath in men and animals is not often discussed in the Old Testament. But the one outstanding exception to this rule is important in the history of both Jewish and Christian thought. In the portions of Genesis ascribed by critics to J, the Breath of the Lord is the special source of human life. " The Lord God formed man of the dust of the ground and $\dot{\epsilon}\nu\epsilon\phi\acute{v}\sigma\eta\sigma\epsilon\nu$ $\epsilon\dot{\iota}s$ $\tau\grave{o}$ $\pi\rho\acute{o}\sigma\omega\pi o\nu$ $a\dot{v}\tau o\hat{v}$ $\pi\nu o\grave{\eta}\nu$ $\zeta\omega\hat{\eta}s,$ $\kappa a\grave{\iota}$ $\dot{\epsilon}\gamma\acute{\epsilon}\nu\epsilon\tau o$ $\dot{o}$ $\dot{a}\nu\theta\rho\omega\pi os$ $\epsilon\dot{\iota}s$ $\psi\upsilon\chi\grave{\eta}\nu$ $\zeta\hat{\omega}\sigma a\nu$ " (Gen. ii. 7). Thus human life is akin to divine life; both God and man have the same ' breath.' The comment of Philo (see pp. 100 f.) is proof that to Hellenistic Jews $\pi\nu o\acute{\eta}\nu$ was synonymous with $\pi\nu\epsilon\hat{v}\mu a$.

The Spirit or the Breath of God was regarded in ancient times as the The Judges. instrument by which God worked. Through it God influenced and controlled the heroic figures of the Old Testament. It was, for instance, when the Spirit of the Lord came upon Jephthah that he attacked the children of Ammon (Judges xi. 29), and it was when the Spirit of the Lord came upon Samson that he slew a thousand men with the jawbone of an ass (Judges xv. 14 ff.).

An alternative figure was to speak of the ' Arm of the Lord.' But The Arm of<br/>the Lord. whereas ' Arm of the Lord' is only rarely distinguished from the Lord himself (see, however, Is. lxiii. 5), the ' Spirit of the Lord' was frequently distinguished so completely from God that it was almost if not quite regarded as an angelic being. In this respect it is interesting to note that the reverse process can be seen in the history of the phrase ' Angel of the Lord.' Originally the Angel of the Lord was doubtless a celestial messenger, distinct from Jahveh, but later on, perhaps under the influence of monotheistic thought and of the dislike of the direct mention of God, ' the Angel of the Lord ' was used as a synonym for God himself (see Judges vi. 11 ff.).

But the age of the Judges or Heroes belonged to a distant past. In Prophets. later times the Spirit of the Lord worked through Prophets rather than through Judges, and the prophetic gift was so closely identified with the Spirit that it overshadowed everything else. It was during this period, represented by the historical books, that the personification of ' Spirit,' mentioned above, was at its height. The classical example of this anthropomorphic visualization is 1 Kings xxii. 5 ff., in which the prophets speak before Ahab and Jehoshaphat, and Micaiah explains that it is due to the influence of a Spirit sent by the Lord to deceive the prophets. Inasmuch as the Spirit in question is represented as discussing with God the way in which he can deceive Ahab, it is clear that Spirit is here almost equivalent to an angel. Nevertheless the change is not complete, for the lying Spirit is regarded as inspiring all the prophets simultaneously, not merely speaking to them.

**Holy Spirit in O.T.** It should be noted that in the Old Testament the phrase 'Holy Spirit' is very rare. It is found only in Psalm li. 11 ; Is. lxiii. 10 f. ; Sirach xlviii. 12 (in Cod. A) ; Susanna 45 (Theod.) ; Wisdom i. 5, ix. 17. It is somewhat more frequent in the pseudepigraphic literature, for instance Jubilees i. 21 and i. 23, xxv. 14 ; and in the Ascension of Isaiah v. 14. This, however, is a relatively unimportant point. The fact that the Old Testament speaks of the Spirit of God while the New Testament and the later literature use another phrase does not reflect change in doctrine, but merely illustrates the tendency to avoid using the word God.

Moreover, in the rather vague metaphysics of the Old Testament it is difficult to draw any sharp line between angels and such phrases as a 'Spirit of jealousy' or a 'Spirit of wisdom.' Did the writers of the Old Testament regard a 'Spirit of jealousy' as a 'demon,' or were they consciously personifying an abstract quality of disposition ? This question has often been raised and answered, but never satisfactorily, for—as Constantine said of another controversy—the discussion depends on improper answers to questions which ought never to have been put. That generation did not distinguish clearly between persons and personifications, and to introduce distinctions which were not perceived is as bad exegesis as to leave them out when they were.

**Judaism.** *Jewish Thought.*—In the period beginning after the close of the Old Testament, that is in the second century before Christ, the difference between educated and uneducated thought becomes clearly marked. This is not only because the influence of Greek thought affected the educated so much more than the uneducated classes, but also because the written sources at our disposal cover much more diverse types than are to be found —at least in such extremes—in the Old Testament. Roughly speaking, we have at our disposal for educated thought, though of very different types, the Rabbinic literature, Josephus and Philo ; and for uneducated thought, the Apocalyptic literature and the Synoptic Gospels.

**The Spirit and angels.** In the centuries which elapsed between the period of the Exile and the Christian era, the requirements of monotheism modified the forms of thought. To that generation an angel might be never so exalted, but it was wholly distinct from God, and no part of God was actually an angel. Thus a heavenly visitor who brought a message to men was an angel, and the inspiration of a prophet was the 'Breath of God,' yet the 'Breath of God' was not an angel. But during this period the prophets ceased to exist. The communication of God with men was still carried on by his Breath or Spirit, but through Scripture, through the learning of scholars, and through the Voice from Heaven (*Bat Qol*), not through a 'Succession' of inspired prophets. A further change in terminology can also be noted. The phrase 'Spirit of God' or 'Spirit of Jahveh' became less general, if not obsolete, and the Rabbis from the first century onwards spoke of the 'Holy Spirit' or 'Spirit of holiness' when they referred to Scripture, and of the 'Spirit of prophecy' when they were alluding to the prophets.

**Inspiration of Rabbis.** The evidence of Rabbinical literature is generally clear, but not always. The Spirit spoke through the Prophets, not through the Rabbis. It now speaks only through the Scripture which is its written word. There are indeed a few exceptions to this rule, and some Rabbis, notably Akiba, are said to have received the Spirit. But against this view appears another tradition which merely says that these Rabbis were worthy of the Spirit, but their generation was not, so that they did not receive it. (See Strack, i. pp. 216 and 557, and Büchsel, *Der Geist Gottes*, p. 124.) Jewish authorities are not clear which is the sounder view. Nor is there agreement among scholars whether the ' laying on of hands ' at the ordination conveyed a ' charisma ' of the Spirit, or merely recognized a function. The most reliable information on the teaching of the Rabbis can be found in Strack, ii. pp. 126 ff. and iv. pp. 435 ff. " Die Inspiration der heiligen Schrift," and in Moore, *Judaism*, i. pp. 421 f.

The parallel of later Christianity is instructive. After the second century the Church insisted as firmly as did the Rabbis that the prophetic διαδοχή was closed. But did it deny the presence of the Holy Spirit, or disclaim infallibility ? The facts are much clearer than the logic.

With the Rabbinical literature Josephus may fairly be reckoned as representing educated, though not theologically educated, opinion. Josephus was an historian and a politician, not a philosopher or a theologian, and his writings may be taken as typical of the views of an educated layman ; they ought not to be too closely compared or contrasted with the views of the professional theologians reported in the Talmud. *Josephus.*

His opinion about the Spirit world may be summed up thus : he believed that the world is full of invisible beings who like men are good and bad. This is because they are the souls (ψυχαί) or spirits (πνεύματα) of dead men.[1] The wicked become devils (δαιμόνια) ; the good become ' genii ' (δαίμονες) or heroes (ἥρωες).[2] The ' stuff,' as it were, of which these supernatural beings were made was the same that makes human beings, and Josephus calls it πνεῦμα and ψυχή, between which he apparently made no clear distinction. It is essentially, or in its origin, a part of God.[3]

He clearly agreed that the Prophets as a διαδοχή had come to an end. Nevertheless he regarded John Hyrcanus as a prophet (*Antiq.* xiii. 10. 7 and *B.J.* i. 2. 8). He explains that Hyrcanus was visited by a Spirit (δαιμόνιον), so that he knew all that was to happen (μηδὲν τῶν μελλόντων ἀγνοεῖν), and he describes this as προφητεία. The δαιμόνιον is clearly ' the Spirit,' and Josephus is completely hypostatizing it—in fact, we may fairly say that he regards it as an angel. He also claimed to foretell to Vespasian that he would be Emperor (*B.J.* iii. 8. 3, 9, and iv. 10. 7).

*The Wisdom Literature and Philo.*—The Rabbis and Josephus must certainly be reckoned as educated opinion, but the Rabbis were not only not influenced by Greek thought, but were opposed to it. Josephus was not so strongly opposed, but in theological matters he had learnt little from the Greeks. The situation is different when examination is made of the Wisdom literature, especially of course those parts which are only in Greek, and of the writings of Philo, which are in so many ways the cul- *The Wisdom literature.*

---

[1] *B.J.* vii. 6. 3.    [2] *B.J.* vi. 1. 5.    [3] *B.J.* iii. 8. 5.

mination of the Wisdom literature. ' The Spirit ' gradually merged more
and more completely in the concept of Wisdom. Wisdom, says Solomon, is a
φιλάνθρωπον πνεῦμα (i. 6), it makes men prophets,[1] and gave Solomon all
his knowledge, which in Jewish thought was certainly due to the ' Holy
Spirit '—otherwise the writings of Solomon would not have been in the
Canon of Scripture. Elsewhere he slightly modifies his phraseology, and
speaks of Wisdom as possessing a ' Spirit.' Ὅσα τέ ἐστι κρυπτά, he says
in vii. 21 ff., καὶ ἐμφανῆ ἔγνων, ἡ γὰρ πάντων τεχνῖτις ἐδίδαξέ με
σοφία, ἔστι γὰρ ἐν αὐτῇ πνεῦμα νοερόν, ἅγιον, μονογενὲς . . . μία δὲ
οὖσα πάντα δύναται καὶ μένουσα ἐν αὐτῇ τὰ πάντα καινίζει, καὶ
κατὰ γενεὰς εἰς ψυχὰς ὁσίας μεταβαίνουσα φίλους θεοῦ καὶ προφήτας
κατασκευάζει.

A similar view of Wisdom is found in Proverbs, and in Sirach in the
description of the learned scribe (xxxix.), where among the rewards to
those who spend their lives in the study of the Law of the Most High is
ἐὰν κύριος ὁ μέγας θελήσῃ πνεύματι συνέσεως ἐμπλησθήσεται. It is
therefore not peculiar to Greek as distinct from Hebrew writings.

Thus for these writers inspiration is 'Wisdom.' Moreover, the description of Wisdom (especially in Wisdom vii.) is strongly reminiscent of Stoic
philosophy. The Jewish writers tremble on the verge of identifying
Wisdom with the ethereal and penetrating—but still material—substance
which the Stoics called πνεῦμα. (See below, p. 103.) It would probably
be a mistake to assume that these writers were students of Stoic philosophy
at first hand, but they lived in a world which was permeated by it, just
as the modern world is by evolutionary philosophy—even those who disagree with it constantly use its language, though, on the other hand,
many who think they agree with it constantly abuse its terminology.
Probably it is not wrong to say that the concept of Wisdom as Spirit, as an
energizing substance, belongs to the Greek environment of the writers.
The apparent—and quite occasional—suggestions of an hypostatizing of
Wisdom or of the Spirit are largely only verbal, partly metaphorical, and
partly an inheritance from an earlier world which was far more anthropomorphic, and thought of spirits—good or evil—as creatures rather
than substances.

Philo.     To this class of Hellenistic Jews permeated with Stoic metaphysics
belonged Philo, though in his case there is also a strongly-marked Platonic
element. He explains [2] that man is made up of earthly matter and divine
πνεῦμα. The 'Mind' (διάνοια) is essentially a piece of the divine substance
—πνεῦμα. Elsewhere [3] he explains that πνεῦμα was one of the seven
entities of the first creation—the ' ideal ' world of Platonism—described in
Genesis i. The seven entities are Heaven, Earth, Space, Air, Water,

[1] What is the relation between this identification of the Spirit of the
Prophets with Wisdom and its attribution to Solomon and the parallel story of
his power over demons in Josephus, *Ant.* viii. 2. 5 ? Was there a conscious
effort on the part of the Wisdom literature to minimize the exorcistic power
of Solomon ? Both elements — learning and exorcism — are combined in
Josephus's account.

[2] *Opif. mundi*, 134 f.                    [3] *Ibid.* 28 f.

πνεῦμα, and Light. The πνεῦμα is 'God's' Spirit, and is the source of life.

The details of his doctrine of Spirit are complicated, difficult, and not always clearly consistent, but their discussion would go beyond the present purpose. For this it is sufficient to note that for Philo as for the Wisdom literature πνεῦμα is the divine substance which energizes the universe.

*The Apocalyptic Literature.*—For the development of uneducated thought among the Jews, this is almost our only source : it may indeed be objected that it was not the work of uneducated writers, but ' uneducated ' is a relative term, and means " below the normal standard of education at the time referred to," judged by the opinion of that age, not by that of ours. It is doubtful whether either the Rabbis or Philo would have regarded the book of Enoch as the product of educated men, or Johanan ben Zakkai would have accepted 4 Ezra. But in any case, whether the Apocalyptic literature be educated or uneducated, it has a perfectly clear theory, according to which evil spirits are the ghosts of the giants who were the offspring of angels and women. They had been drowned in the Noachian flood, but their spirits remained and endeavoured to return to the pleasures of flesh and blood by obsessing some human being.[1] *The Apocalypses.*

It should be noted at this point that this general view of a world infected by evil spirits is also that of the Synoptic gospels. In Mark especially there is great emphasis on the power of Jesus, given also by him to his disciples, to cast out demons. It is true that the origin of the demons is not described, but no one who studies the parallels collected in the introduction to R. H. Charles's *Book of Enoch* can doubt that, at least so far as demons are concerned, the ' Weltanschauung ' of Mark is the same as that of Enoch. *Mark.*

The Apocalyptic literature speaks frequently of 'Spirits,' and in Enoch God is especially the ' Lord of Spirits.' If these spirits are not angels, it is hard to say what they are. But the same book speaks constantly of the ' Spirit of Righteousness,' the ' Spirit of Wisdom,' etc., and in at least one place (lxii. 2) the Spirit of Righteousness inspires God himself. Similarly the *Testaments of the Twelve Patriarchs* are full of ' Spirits ' both good and evil, and it is difficult to say whether they are Angels and Demons or personified feelings. But it is hard not to think that both Enoch and the writer of the *Testaments* lived in a world which was full of Spirits and that they explained the facts of human nature, its passions, its achievements, and its sins, as due to obsession. This is as typical of the Apocalyptic literature as the identification of Spirit with divine substance is of the Hellenistic literature. Just as the Wisdom literature is clearly influenced by Greek thought, the Apocalyptic literature was influenced by Persian. *Enoch.* *The Test. xii. Patr.*

There is unfortunately less in the Apocalyptic books or in the Synoptics about the spirits who were good than about those who were evil. But *Good and evil Spirits.*

---

[1] Cf. Enoch xv. 1 ff., Jubil. x., and Justin Martyr 1 *Apol.* v. In Justin, however, and in later writers, this view is eclipsed in importance by the identification of the demons (or some of them) with the heathen gods and heroes.

a parallelism can be noted between their natures. At the baptism of Jesus 'the Spirit' descends on him like a dove, and he hears a *bat qol* announcing that he is God's beloved son.[1] Immediately after this the Spirit drives Jesus into the desert, where he stays for forty days. When he returns he manifests irresistible power over demons and explains in Mark iii. 29 that he has this power through the Holy Spirit. As Gunkel pointed out, it is of primary importance that the Rabbis of Galilee held that he was a demoniac and that his family said that he was mad—which amounts to the same thing. Jesus' reply is not that he is a normal man, but that he is obsessed—that is true—by the Holy Spirit, not by a demon.[2] But there is relatively little about the Holy Spirit in Mark. The same is true of Matthew. In Luke there are more references, but there is no passage which really settles the central problem, namely—do the Synoptic Gospels, and did the circle of Jewish thought which they represent, think that there were many bad but only one good spirit, or did they think that there were many of both, and that both obsessed mankind?

Angels and demons.

If this question is confined to the actual fact of the existence or non-existence of many good spirits, there can be but one answer. There were many. The Apocalyptic literature and the Gospels have many references to 'angels,' and 'angels' are good spirits just as 'demons' are bad spirits.

But this simple answer is not enough. An ἄγγελος is, of course, merely a messenger. God and the Devil have each their own messengers. But by custom ἄγγελος was used for God's messengers, and πνεῦμα ἀκάθαρτον or δαιμόνιον was used for the Devil's messengers. Ἄγγελος became so far limited that (except perhaps in Revelation) there was a sentiment against using it of men, and ἀπόστολος was coined for the purpose (see Additional Note 6). Perhaps evil spirits were so much more frequent and obvious than good ones that if it were said that a man 'had a spirit' the natural assumption was that he was obsessed by a demon, and this tended to produce the Christian use of 'Holy' Spirit.

Moreover, though there are innumerable examples of men possessed by evil spirits being described as 'demoniacs'—δαιμονιζόμενοι—there is no corresponding word based on πνεῦμα to describe men possessed by good spirits; πνευματικός is the word which corresponds to δαιμονιζόμενοι in the Epistles, but πνευματικός is not found in the Synoptic Gospels, and δαιμονισθείς is not found in the Epistles.

These facts partly reflect peculiarities of language, but that is scarcely the whole explanation. It would seem as though any demon might be expected to obsess anyone whom he could, but that angels confined themselves to carrying out God's commission to do or to say what he ordered. The Spirit with which God obsessed prophets or others was not personified;

---

[1] Does 'like a dove' imply—as Luke carefully explains—that the Spirit was actually in the form of a dove, or is it merely a metaphor? Cf. the curious fact that according to the MSS. when Polycarp died the Spirit was seen to escape in the form of a dove: "Blood came out and a dove." It is unfortunate that in Lightfoot's *editio minor* this is emended out by changing περιστεράν to περὶ στύρακα.

[2] Cf. Gunkel, *Wirkungen des heiligen Geistes*, p. 35.

if a definition had been given—but it was not—perhaps it would have been said that the Spirit which (rather than ' whom ') God sent was that of which angels consisted—they were πνεύματα, but τὸ πνεῦμα was not necessarily an angel. Was Paul the first to go further and identify the Spirit with the Lord ?

*Greek Thought.*—In the first century ' Spirit ' was the name given to the finest form of matter in the Stoic physical philosophy which was pre-dominant among educated men. The gods consisted of Spirit, and human minds were thought to consist of the same material. Whether Spirit was regarded as a fifth element or was a combination of fire and air is not perfectly clear. Nor does the point matter much for the present purpose, for it is tolerably clear that in the language of educated men who were not professional philosophers Spirit was at least equivalent to a fifth element, and was naturally destined to be the point of union between pure Stoicism which recognized no reality that was not material, and Platonism with its doctrine of immaterial reality. Stoic ideas of Spirit.

Plutarch is probably our safest [1] guide in trying to form some idea of educated opinion. He doubtless held to the metaphysical doctrines of Plato, at least in part, but his ' physics ' were mainly Stoic, and his use of πνεῦμα belongs to his ' physics ' rather than his ' metaphysics.' In this respect he is an interesting parallel to Philo. For our purposes his exposi-tion of inspiration, especially in his *De Pythiae oraculis, De genio Socratis,* and *De defectu oraculorum,* is the most important evidence which we possess. His theory is this. The soul of man is a δαιμόνιον which has the extra-ordinary power of remembering the past and foreseeing the future. But it can foresee the future only when it can struggle free of the present by Dreams or Ecstasy. He recognizes that Ecstasy is a physical condition, and says that it is produced by πνεῦμα which comes from the earth in certain places. Is it the soul which foresees the future, or the πνεῦμα ? He presents the parallel question—which gives sight, light or the eye ? Just as the eyes ' see,' but not unless ' light ' is present, so the ' soul ' foretells, but only if πνεῦμα is present. The Spirit comes from the sun or from the earth, and they are the true gods. The δαιμόνια may take part in the process of inspiration—that is Plutarch's concession to orthodoxy—but essentially inspiration is the natural effect of a natural substance of which the name is πνεῦμα. Plutarch.

In uneducated Greek thought πνεῦμα seems to mean especially ' breath,' and then by a natural extension of the term ' the principle which makes things alive.' In this respect it is almost the same as ' ruach ' in Semitic thought. In post-Christian times πνεῦμα, especially in the plural, means ' daemons,' good or bad, but there is not sufficient evidence that this usage obtained in purely heathen circles in the first century. In interpreting obscure allusions it is hard to avoid making them mean what we believe they ought to mean. Uneducated Greek thought.

Great importance would of course attach to the position of inspiration

---

[1] All the better because, somewhat like Josephus, he was not a professional philosopher.

and to the use of the word πνεῦμα in the 'mystery' or 'sacramental' cults and in magical papyri if the facts were clear, but unfortunately only very little can be stated. The 'sacramental' cults were acquainted with the phenomenon of ecstasy. Plutarch, Apuleius, Euripides, and Livy leave no doubt on that point. But where is the evidence that this ecstasy was described as due to πνεῦμα ? In some of the cults there were 'prophets,' and Livy (xxxix. 8) speaks of the leader of the Dionysiacs in Italy as a *vates*. But surely the popular theory was merely that the God spoke through or to his representative who then became his προφήτης. The explanation that inspiration was due to πνεῦμα is later and due to more or less sophisticated theories as to physical phenomena. Plutarch doubtless would have explained the facts in this way, but did the average initiate or ordinary priest do so ? There is no evidence that πνεῦμα was used by them for this purpose.

It is sometimes forgotten that the only sacramental religion of the first three centuries of which we have anything approaching complete knowledge is Christianity. Investigation into the other sacramental cults is very unlikely seriously to change our interpretation of Christian documents. If the context does not make the central ideas and the characteristic phraseology intelligible, very rarely will the difficulty be cleared up by the study of magical papyri or of other cults. The importance of such study is in the main in another direction. It teaches us not what was, but how little we know about what was the background against which we ought to place our picture of Christianity.[1]

It is of course true that in such documents as the Paris and Berlin magical papyri, and in the 'Mithras liturgy'—which is now said to have nothing to do with Mithras—there are many references to πνεῦμα, and, among other things, in connexion with ecstasy and the attainment of immortality. But who knows what is the date of these documents ? They may all be as late as the third century after Christ.

My own impression is that the early Christians—including the apostles —explained the fact of the inspiration which they experienced as due to the working of the Spirit, but did not define exactly what they meant. That they should do so was the natural result of the fact that they were Jews and used the terminology of the Old Testament. When they spoke Greek, influenced by the LXX, they said that this was a χάρισμα of the πνεῦμα and they claimed to be πνευματικοί. Any educated or half-educated Greek might naturally have interpreted this language in the light of Stoic phraseology. But the Epistles are rather to be interpreted as in the main materials on which Greek thought worked than as the results of Greek speculation.

[1] The most interesting though not often the easiest treatment of the subject is that of Reitzenstein's *Hellenistische Mysterienreligionen*. He has contributed enormously to our understanding, but probably has overstated the case for the use of πνεῦμα in the Graeco-oriental sacramental cults. As a corrective to Reitzenstein, especially his later books, see the article by H. H. Schaeder, 'Reitzenstein, die Vorgeschichte der christlichen Taufe' in *Gnomon* v., 1929, pp. 353 ff.

The whole matter can be seen most plainly if we do not try to read into Acts or similar books of early Christian literature metaphysical definitions of which the writers were probably quite unconscious. The study of Plato, or even Philo, gives little help to understanding the conception of the Spirit which dominated Acts, nor can more be found from the study of Zeno or Cleanthes.

*The New Testament.*—The varying position given to the Spirit in different books of the New Testament is a reflection of the main question of New Testament exegesis, and this in turn reflects the chief problem of early Christian history. It is extraordinarily important, and it is not difficult to define. The Spirit in the N.T.

The easiest and clearest method is to begin with the latest books of the New Testament—the Johannine. In these clear and indisputable expression is given to the thesis which has ever since remained central in Catholic theology : " Except a man be born again of water and the Spirit, he cannot enter into the Kingdom of God." [1] This is, of course, the foundation of the Catholic doctrine of baptismal regeneration. Similarly, in the prologue it is written that to as many as received the λόγος ' power ' was given to ' become ' children of God—a view which is reflected in the Baptismal Service by the statement that baptism gives those who are baptized a gift which by nature they cannot have.[2] The Johannine and Catholic theory.

This characteristically Johannine and Catholic doctrine calls for no long discussion. Its existence is not open to argument.

If, however, we turn to the Synoptic gospels, there is no trace of this doctrine. Not merely is there no evidence, except Matt. xxviii. 19 (which very few students would accept as historical), that Jesus regarded baptism The Synoptic view.

---

[1] John iii. 3 and 5.

[2] The doctrine of the Spirit in the Johannine writings is in some ways parallel, in others complementary, to those of Luke and Paul. The identification of baptism with the gift of the Spirit and the necessity of both for immortality is clearly expressed in Jo. iii. 5-6. The importance of inspiration by the Spirit in Christian worship is sanctioned by Jesus' declaration in Jo. iv. 24 that the time has now come when the Father must be worshipped ἐν πνεύματι καὶ ἀληθείᾳ. The statement in the same verse, πνεῦμα ὁ θεός, is probably the repetition of a Stoic commonplace which beyond this appears to have exercised no considerable influence on the thought of the writer. With regard to receiving the Spirit, John holds two mutually inconsistent views. One is similar to that of Luke's, that the Spirit is first given after the Resurrection (Jo. vii. 39), the other that it is inherent in the teaching of Jesus and is assimilated in the acceptance of that teaching (Jo. vi. 63). It is characteristic of the author's somewhat cloudy mysticism that he sees no inconsistency in maintaining that the Spirit is both a present possession and a future acquirement (Jo. xiv. 17, 26). The latter view is similar to that of Luke, and the scene in Jo. xx. 22-23 is parallel to that in Luke xxiv. 49 with this difference—that instead of a promise to be fulfilled at Pentecost, Jesus conveys the Spirit himself. John's conception of the function of the Spirit is much more similar to that of Paul than to that of Luke-Acts. The Spirit will be a constant helper, and will replace the influence of Jesus and his words as well as convey immortality.

as necessary to salvation, but there is no evidence that he even thought or said that the gift of the Holy Spirit was needed. The Spirit enabled him and others to work miracles and to utter prophecies ; but salvation was not the prerogative of prophets or of workers of miracles. Nor, finally, was the Spirit, or sacramental grace, thought of as necessary for men to become sons of God or to obtain forgiveness of their sins. Jesus is represented in the Synoptic Gospels as regarding all men as children of God. Whether their end in the world to come would be salvation or damnation depended not on sacraments, but on themselves. The Prodigal is not saved by anything except his own repentance.

Moreover, there is another great difference between the Synoptic and the Johannine attitude toward the Spirit world. In the Synoptic gospels nothing is more prominent than the fact of demoniacal possession. The background of thought is exactly that of the Apocalypses discussed above (see p. 101). The work of Jesus and of his disciples is to drive out demons, and thus to heal disease. Jesus is represented as inspired by the Holy Spirit, and at least in one passage in Matthew this inspiration is the source of his power over demons. But there is no suggestion that anyone, even the disciples, is given the Holy Spirit, still less that such a gift is necessary for salvation. The contrast with the Johannine picture is complete. In the latter we have not only the insistence on the necessity of re-birth by the Spirit, spoken of above, but there is no mention of demoniacal possession. There is indeed much mention of a devil—a single being—who is ' the ruler of this world,' but there is an immense difference between the Apocalyptic-Synoptic picture of Jesus and his followers exorcising demons, and the grandiose Johannine picture of a cosmological struggle between the Son and the Devil.

These two extremes are clearly marked. It is equally clear that they represent the contrast between Jewish and Greek thought. Repentance, completely and entirely sufficient for salvation, is a Jewish doctrine ; and sacramental regeneration by the Spirit is Greek. There is no doubt about these two extremes. The problem comes when we try to trace the passage of Christian thinking from the one to the other. Here the evidence is contained in the Epistles of Paul and in the Acts of the Apostles.

The Pauline epistles.

In the Pauline epistles the idea of the Spirit receives a much wider application than in the Synoptic gospels, and interest in a theological formulation begins to appear. The Spirit is the possession of all Christians, it supplies the ' enthusiastic ' features of Christian worship, expresses itself in prophecy and glossolalia, and through ecstasy provides special revelations. Paul's own contribution to the doctrine of the Spirit consisted of three main points : (i.) he identified the Lord, i.e. Christ, with the Spirit ; (ii.) he regarded the Spirit as the source of Christian virtue and the foundation of Christian moral life ; (iii.) he held that possession of the Spirit was necessary for immortality. Possibly, too, he established a necessary connexion between the gift of the Spirit and Baptism, but this is less certain.

The result of the first point was to interpret the relation of Christ and the believer in terms of ' possession,' the normal way in which a spirit

influenced human individuals. In this experience it is notoriously difficult
both in theory and in practice to maintain the distinction between the
personality possessed and the personality possessing. This difficulty is
responsible for the obscurity of what is often called Paul's 'mysticism.' The
essence of this obscurity is the impossibility of always keeping distinct
Christ, the Spirit, and the personality of the ' spiritual ' Christian.[1] The
other two points are really corollaries of the first. From one point of view
the process of salvation consisted in the sacrifice of Christ and the acquirement of the Spirit, and the former paved the way for the latter, but the
identification of the Lord with the Spirit intimately connected the effect
with the cause. From another point of view salvation consisted in gaining
the necessary moral power for the realization of the Christian ethical ideal
and in securing immortality. The natural man, of whom Adam was the
prototype, is mortal and morally impotent ; the man endowed with the
Spirit, of whom Christ, the second Adam, was the prototype, is immortal
and capable of exemplifying those lists of virtues which Paul so often indicates to be the spontaneous expression of a Christian character. It is possible for the Christian to sin, for he always retains a sufficient amount of his
old individuality to escape from the influence of the Spirit, but it is unnecessary and unnatural for him to do so. Moreover, though it is doubtful
whether Paul fixed baptism as the moment at which the believer received
the Spirit and its accompanying privileges, it is quite certain that his
followers in the next generation did so, and thus resolved a theological
ambiguity the potential embarrassments of which for church organization and discipline are patent in Acts. A positive significance was thus
attached to baptism which there is no evidence to show that it previously
possessed ; and for the loose connexion between the gift of the Spirit
and baptism suggested by some passages in Acts, a fixed relation was
substituted which was of constitutive significance for later history.

So much is reasonably clear. Paul is on the way to the Johannine
position, but he has not reached it, and the Epistles present a most
puzzling problem which can merely be stated in this note without any
attempt to discuss it fully.

Did Paul think that the gift of the Spirit—whether imparted by The Spirit
baptism or not—was either the necessary cause or the inevitable result of and Salva-
being a Christian ?                                                        tion.

This question is, of course, closely associated with that of Paul's view
of baptism, but it is not identical with it. He may have held that the gift
of the Spirit came through faith, not through baptism. But did he think
that a man could be a Christian, and ' safe ' at the day of judgement, who
was not πνευματικός ? It is very doubtful. Did he think that ' faith ' was
a gift of the Spirit ? He seems to say so, but it is perhaps improper to
build too much on a single phrase. Perhaps it is probable that he held
that all Christians are πνευματικοί, but had varying χαρίσματα. But
whether he thought that Christians were saved because they had the Spirit,
or had the Spirit because they were saved, is more than the evidence allows
us to decide. We may suspect—there is no means of knowing certainly—

[1] See also pp. 129 ff.

that Paul himself held that men were saved by the decree of God, who willed their salvation, and therefore gave them faith and filled them with his Spirit.[1] But it is extremely probable that many of Paul's Greek converts thought that salvation depended on their own volition in accepting the sacrament (or mystery) of baptism, which changed their nature by giving them the Spirit.

Acts.     Where does Acts stand ? The whole background of the book is the guidance of the Holy Spirit, and the consequent actions of the Apostles, just as the background of Mark is the war against the evil spirits. It is indeed very remarkable that there is hardly any reference to demons in Acts.[2]

This is characteristic. To Mark the important thing was to drive out demons and heal disease ; apart from demons and disease (which are not really separate) men are in no need of change. Repentance is a change of conduct, not of nature. But to Luke the gift of the Spirit is the all-important fact ; possibly he did not think it necessary to salvation, but a Christian who did not have the Spirit was a very imperfect Christian.

The promise of the Spirit.     In the opening verses [3] the promise is made that the Apostles will shortly receive the Spirit. In the second chapter this promise is fulfilled,[4] and under the influence of the Spirit Peter made a speech which converted three thousand of his hearers.[5] After the healing of the lame man at the Beautiful Gate by the Name of Jesus, when Peter was arrested, he was filled with the Holy Spirit [6] to make his defence to the Sanhedrin, as Jesus had foretold.[7] When Peter was released and returned to the brethren, they were all filled with the Holy Spirit, and the place in which they were gathered was shaken.[8]

Ananias.     In chapter v. the deceit of Ananias is regarded as a ' lie to the Holy Spirit,' apparently because it was a lie to the Apostles.[9]

The Seven.     In chapter vi. the Seven are chosen as men full of the Holy Spirit,[10] and at the end of his speech before his death Stephen is " filled with the Holy Spirit and saw the Glory of God." [11]

Philip.     In chapter viii. 5-25 the absence of the Holy Spirit from the converts of Philip is supplied by the laying on of Peter's hands.[12] This passage may be grouped with that in chapter vi. as suggesting a permanent gift of the Spirit, rather than the intermittent gift in the other passages. It is also noticeable that here we have a return to the ' war against demons ' which Philip drove out in Samaria.[13] Philip could not give the Spirit, but Peter could do so. Clearly in the source from which this story was taken the gift of the Spirit could be conferred by the Apostles, but not by the Seven. It would also appear that it was a *donum superadditum*. It was neither the

---

[1] I cannot understand Rom. ix.-xi. on any other hypothesis.

[2] The exceptions are that in Samaria Philip (viii. 7) and at Ephesus Paul (xix. 12) drove out evil spirits. Possibly also the story of the woman with a Python (xvi. 16 ff.) should be reckoned in this category.

[3] i. 5.      [4] ii. 1 ff.      [5] ii. 41.      [6] iv. 8.

[7] Luke xii. 12; Matt. x. 20, cf. Mark xiii. 11, contrast Luke xxi. 15.

[8] iv. 31.      [9] v. 3.      [10] vi. 3, 5.

[11] vii. 55 f.      [12] viii. 17.      [13] viii. 7.

cause nor the necessary result of salvation. Acts is in this respect far removed from the Pauline position.

In the following episode the references to divine intervention are curiously phrased. In viii. 26 the ' angel of the Lord ' sent Philip to the Gaza road ; when he meets the Eunuch ' the Spirit ' speaks to him ; and after he baptized the Eunuch, " Spirit of the Lord seized Philip and the Eunuch saw him no more," or if the Western text be followed, " Holy Spirit fell on the Eunuch, and an angel of the Lord seized Philip." What is the difference between the angel and the Spirit who speak to Philip ? Probably it is only a characteristically Lucan change of phrase, though it is hard to prove this. If so, does $\pi\nu\epsilon\hat{\upsilon}\mu\alpha$ mean the same in vs. 29 and in vs. 39 ? It will be noticed that in this story there is no question of obsession or inspiration, unless the Western text be followed in vs. 39,—it is throughout external command given by the Spirit to Philip.

In the conversion of Paul (chapter ix.) it is implied, though not stated, that Paul received the Spirit through his baptism by Ananias. This is the more interesting because it differs from Paul's own assertion that he owed nothing to men, but received his apostleship directly from God (see Additional Note 15), and also differs from chapter viii. by the implication that the Spirit could be given by others than members of ' the Twelve,' and that it was the result of baptism. *Paul's conversion.*

In the $\dot{\alpha}\rho\iota\sigma\tau\epsilon\acuteia$ of Peter (chapters ix. 30-xii. 17) the whole point of the story of Cornelius is that he miraculously received the gift of the Spirit without human intervention, which seems to imply the same theory of the power of the Apostles as does chapter viii. *Cornelius.*

This chapter may be taken, for some purposes at least, as the end of the first part of Acts. The preceding analysis shows that it is characterized by a vivid belief in the Spirit as a special gift conferred on at least some Christians. In some passages this gift, which was given to the Apostles of Jesus, can be handed on only by them, and is independent of baptism. But other passages suggest that it was expected by all Christians. These passages are nearer to the Pauline and Catholic view, but even in them there is no suggestion of regeneration by the Spirit, or of the view that salvation depends on it. In general, the gift of the Spirit in these chapters is sudden and drives preachers such as Philip or Peter to unpremeditated words or actions, and produces sudden outbreaks of glossolalia and prophecy.

There is a marked difference between this and the second part of Acts. In this the Spirit sometimes acts suddenly and unexpectedly, as in the first part, as for instance in xvi. 6 f. when the Spirit (once described as the Holy Spirit, once with a characteristically Lucan change of phrase as the Spirit of Jesus) intervenes to change Paul's plans. But there are good reasons for regarding this passage as editorial (see Additional Note 18). In general however the number of references to the Spirit is remarkably smaller than in the first part of Acts. In xx. 22 Paul says that he is ' bound by the Spirit ' ; in xxi. 11 Agabus, the prophet, is inspired by the Spirit ; and in xxvii. 23 the Angel who appeared in the night might be regarded as ' the Spirit,' described in words more suited to the heathen whom Paul is addressing. *The second part of Acts.*

It is the paucity of these references in contrast to the first part of Acts rather than their character which is remarkable, and it is perhaps noteworthy that they come in speeches, not in the direct narrative.

There are, however, two other references of great importance. (i.) In xix. 1 ff. Paul is surprised that the Ephesians had not received the Spirit, and attributes this to some defect in their baptism. (ii.) In xx. 28 the pastoral administration of the community is regarded as due to the Holy Spirit. The second point is entirely Pauline, and is extremely important for the history of the doctrine of the Episcopate. The first is not only Pauline in the expectation that the Christians should have the Spirit, but is markedly different from the earlier part of Acts in that it connects the Spirit with a correct baptism. In Acts viii. 15 ff. a correct baptism is supplemented by the laying on of Apostolic hands, and this, not the baptism of Philip, conferred the Spirit. Here Paul expects that a correct baptism would confer the Spirit, and this baptism includes the ' laying on of hands.' But it is essentially Baptism, not 'Apostolicity,' which is effective. (See also p. 137.)

Summary.    To summarize this complicated enumeration of complex phenomena, the evolution of thought seems to have been this : (i.) In Mark Jesus himself is inspired by the Holy Spirit, and he promises that his disciples will have the same gift in times of stress, but there is no suggestion that this gift will be common, or is in any way connected with salvation. The other Synoptic gospels do not noticeably differ from this point of view.

(ii.) In the early part of Acts the gift of the Spirit is general. It is conferred on the Apostles by the risen Jesus, and by the Apostles on other Christians. But it is an eschatological phenomenon, not the means of salvation. In the later part of Acts it is portrayed in much the same way, but is connected with baptism.

(iii.) In the Pauline epistles the Spirit is identified with the risen Jesus, and the Christian is ' obsessed ' by him in a manner parallel to that in which a demoniac is obsessed by a demon. This ' obsession,' which sometimes leads to a complete identification of the Christian with the Christ, is the state of salvation obtained by believers. But it is not stated by Paul that it is obtained sacramentally ; it is rather the free gift of God.

(iv.) In the Johannine literature the Spirit is the cause (as well as in some sense the result) of sacramental regeneration which in baptism changes the nature of the man baptized and makes him a child of God.

The basis of belief in Spirits.    The basis of the whole belief is the experience of certain men that their words and acts seemed at times, both to themselves and to others, to be due to an irresistible power which made them do or say things which they had never previously contemplated.

That experience is not peculiar to the early Church. It can be traced in every generation. Both its source and its value are difficult and important questions.

Its source.    It may produce conduct of the worst and most irrational type. Persons who suffer in this way used to be called demoniacs and are now called either criminals or insane. It is generally agreed that their conduct is not due to obsession by any malevolent spirit, but to some defect of constitution, natural or acquired.

Similarly there are, and always have been, leaders of men, reformers, teachers, poets, and prophets who seem to themselves to have spoken and acted as they did because some higher power controlled their words and deeds. Their own generation has often stoned them, but their true memorial is not in their tombs but in the history of the race. It used to be said that they were inspired by God : it is now thought that, like the demoniacs, they can be explained as the result of some unusual development of mind or nature,

There can be no doubt that the demoniac type is a menace of evil Its value. and that the best of the prophetic type are often the direct cause of progress. But just as the ancient world hesitated in which class certain persons should be placed, so to-day it is often impossible to say whether a man is a psychopathic subject or a great leader. As the writer of Deuteronomy perceived, only the future can settle the question. "When a prophet speaketh in the name of the Lord, if the thing follow not nor come to pass that is the thing which the Lord hath not spoken."

It is therefore not surprising that the Jews emphasized obedience to the Law rather than to the voice of Prophets, and that the Church *mutatis mutandis* ultimately did the same. Nevertheless, 'inspiration,' whatever its source may be, is the motive power of life, while reason is its guide; and the problem of sane existence is not a choice between Reason and Inspiration or between the Law and Prophecy, but how to maintain them both in that relation of unstable equilibrium which in the spiritual as well as in the physical world is the condition of life in contrast with death.

## Note X. The Gift of the Spirit on the Day of Pentecost

### By Kirsopp Lake

The problem involved by this episode is twofold. First, what did the writer himself think was the importance of the event described ? Secondly, what is the relation between the editor, the sources, and the actual facts ?

### 1. *The Opinion of the Writer*

1. The writer of Acts regarded the Day of Pentecost as the moment The Lucan when the gift of inspiration was conferred on the disciples and they began theory. the ministry of Evangelization. The apostles had not possessed this power before. It had not been given them at their appointment by Jesus, described in Luke vi., though it had been foretold in his parting words on the day of the Ascension. But from the moment of Pentecost they had been inspired by the same gift of the Holy Spirit of God which had filled their master during his ministry on earth, by which also he had himself chosen them (Acts i. 2). Henceforward all they did or said was inspired

by the Spirit, and the Church of which they were the leaders was the society of those who acquired the Spirit (see Vol. I. pp. 322 ff.). Three points, however, are doubtful.

Obscurities.    (a) It is not clear whether the writer thought that at Pentecost the Spirit was given to the apostles or to all the Christians, of whom he says (Acts i. 15) that there were 120. The question depends on the meaning of ' all ' in ii. 1 and 4, which is unfortunately obscure (see note *ad loc.*).

(b) It is also not clear whether the writer thought that the Spirit received at Pentecost was to be transmitted by baptism or by the laying on of hands. Certainly some of his sources thought that it was conferred by baptism, but in other places it seems that it came through the laying on of hands by the apostles, and that baptism itself was not sufficient to confer the gift (see Vol. I. pp. 332 ff.).

(c) Finally, it is not clear whether the writer thought that the preaching to the crowd which had assembled in surprise, immediately after the gift of the Spirit, was the beginning of preaching to the Gentiles or merely to Jews of the Diaspora. If Ropes's view be adopted, the word Ἰουδαῖοι in ii. 5 should be omitted; if so, the intention of the writer is to depict the crowd as representing the Gentiles—possibly God-fearers, but not Jews,—but if Ἰουδαῖοι be retained, he means that they were Jews of the Diaspora. This question is discussed further on p. 113 f.

Tongues.    2. The writer believed that the immediate effect of the gift of the Spirit was that the recipient spoke with other tongues. From the context it is clear that he interpreted ' other tongues ' to be ' other languages,' so that some, but not all, of the foreigners who were listening were able to understand what was said. Thus there was a miracle of hearing as well as a miracle of speech. But the details of the situation are obscure. Did he think that all the Christians present were speaking, or only the Twelve ? Did he think that each of the Twelve spoke in a different language ? If so, but not otherwise, there is much force in Harnack's suggestion that the original text of the list of nations mentioned twelve. These questions can be raised, indeed must be, but there is no evidence in the narrative to answer them.

Prophecy.    3. A further point of less doubt is that he clearly identified glossolalia with prophecy. In 1 Corinthians Paul clearly distinguishes glossolalia from prophecy, regarding the one as intelligible, the other as unintelligible. But according to the speech of Peter the speaking with tongues at Jerusalem was a fulfilment of the prophecy of Joel ii. 28-32, that in the last days the Spirit should descend on Israel conveying to their sons and daughters the gift of prophecy, and into the text of this quotation he perhaps inserts ' and they shall prophesy.' These words, if genuine, are central in his argument, though they are not in the original text of Joel; all the more, therefore, do they represent his own opinion, and he must have thought that ' speaking with tongues ' was ' prophecy.' It is unfortunate that a textual problem is again involved in this question (see notes *ad loc.*), but even if the words be omitted the meaning of the quotation remains the same.

4. From the emphasis laid on the point in the speech of Peter it is The Spirit clear that the writer regarded the gift of the Spirit as eschatological. But logical. once more a textual question is involved. The eschatological meaning of Pentecost is emphasized by a change which he makes in the quotation from Joel. Joel said, "After these things I will pour out my spirit," and this is the reading of B and of a papyrus fragment of Acts, but other MSS. substitute 'in the last days,' bringing out the eschatological meaning. It is hardly safe to hold a decided opinion on the text, for the external evidence is not sufficient, though the powerful internal evidence seems convincing.

Nevertheless, here the question of reading is secondary. The end of the quotation amply proves the eschatological meaning attached to the gift of the Spirit. This perpetuates the tradition, found in the Synoptic Gospels and attributed to John the Baptist, which connected the gift of the Spirit with the purification which would take place in the last day (see H. Windisch, *Taufe und Sünde*, pp. 34 ff., and Vol. I. p. 324), and though this view is not explicitly found in Acts, it is unlikely that it was not shared by the writer of the book. Perhaps the eschatological cleansing of the nation was being replaced in his mind by a cleansing of the individual, but it would be difficult to prove this, probable though it may appear.

5. Did the writer also regard Pentecost as beginning the preaching of Pentecost the Gospel to the Gentiles, or, in other words, did he think of the crowd, and Gentiles. which assembled when they heard the apostles speaking with tongues, as Jewish or Gentile ? The question is partly one of textual criticism, partly of general consideration.

The text of ii. 5 in the Textus Receptus is ἦσαν δὲ ἐν Ἰερουσαλὴμ The Text. κατοικοῦντες Ἰουδαῖοι, ἄνδρες εὐλαβεῖς ἀπὸ παντὸς ἔθνους τῶν ὑπὸ τὸν οὐρανόν. This text is found in B, but in the other old uncials of the Neutral group (אAC) there is considerable variation of order ; א omits Ἰουδαῖοι, and C puts Ἰουδαῖοι between ἄνδρες and εὐλαβεῖς, and κατοικοῦντες before ἐν Ἰερουσαλήμ. Such confused evidence raises a strong suspicion that κατοικοῦντες and Ἰουδαῖοι may be additions to the text, derived probably from the opening words of Peter's speech in ii. 14 (ἄνδρες Ἰουδαῖοι καὶ οἱ κατοικοῦντες Ἰερουσαλήμ).

The case for omitting κατοικοῦντες is much the less strong, and for the present purpose at least much the less important. Apart from the external evidence, in which the variations of order suggest, but do not prove, that κατοικοῦντες is not original, the word seems to contradict vs. 9. The same people can scarcely have been κατοικοῦντες both in Jerusalem and also in Mesopotamia. But this point cannot be pressed, as in ii. 14 κατοικοῦντες is used in a different sense, apparently synonymous with the ἐπιδημοῦντες of vs. 10, and it is very doubtful whether there was clear difference in the mind of the editor between κατοικοῦντες and ἐπιδημοῦντες. It is his custom to vary his phrase without changing his meaning.

But the omission of Ἰουδαῖοι is very strongly supported by internal evidence. In vs. 10 'Jews and proselytes' are treated as one of the component parts of the crowd. If so, obviously the rest of the crowd was not composed of Jews. Probably Ἰουδαῖοι in vs. 5 was originally a mistaken gloss on εὐλαβεῖς, and later, as so often happens, the gloss and the original reading were conflated. The gloss without the text is found in the African Latin, which reads *Iudaei* instead of translating εὐλαβεῖς. (See also Vol. III. p. 12.)

The suggestion that Ἰουδαῖοί τε καὶ προσήλυτοι in vs. 10 does not mean a separate group, but is a definition of οἱ ἐπιδημοῦντες Ῥωμαῖοι, can hardly be sustained, as the same τε καί construction is used twice previously in the list (τὴν Μεσοποταμίαν, Ἰουδαίαν τε καὶ Καππαδοκίαν and Ἀσίαν, Φρυγίαν τε καὶ Παμφυλίαν), and in neither case can the τε καί phrase be taken as modifying the previous word.

If the word Ἰουδαῖοι be omitted from vs. 5 it is impossible to resist the plain statement of the text that the multitude at Pentecost represented the whole world, heathen and Jewish alike, and, if so, the writer of Acts must have regarded the preaching at Pentecost as the beginning of the world-wide mission given to the apostles in i. 8. It is, perhaps, to be noted as characteristic of the style of Acts, which so frequently changes a phrase while repeating its meaning, that ἕως ἐσχάτου τῆς γῆς in i. 8 is represented by παντὸς ἔθνους τῶν ὑπὸ τὸν οὐρανόν. The desire of the writer was not to describe the development of doctrine or the evolution of the Church, both of which are ideas foreign to his age, but to show that from the beginning the Gentiles heard and the Jews refused the testimony of the Spirit.

Biblical and Jewish parallels.

6. Three Old Testament and Jewish parallels are so obvious that although they are not actually pointed out by the writer it is difficult to think that they were not present to his mind.

(i) Babel.

The first is that of the Tower of Babel, where the phenomena were the reverse of those of Pentecost. The men of ' the beginning ' had but one speech, intelligible not only to all men but even to all animals. Cf. Philo, *De confus. ling.* 3, p. 405 M. : "And there is also another story akin to this, related by the devisers of fables, concerning the sameness of language existing among animals : for they say that formerly, all the animals in the world, whether land animals, or aquatic ones, or winged ones, had but one language, and that, just as among men Greeks speak the same language as Greeks, and the present race of barbarians speak the same language as barbarians, exactly in the same manner every animal was able to converse with every other animal with which it might meet, and with which it did anything, or from which it suffered anything." [1]  And cf. also Josephus, *Antiq.* i. 1. 4: "Now God commanded Adam and his wife to eat of all the other plants, but to abstain from the tree of knowledge, and foretold them, that if they touched it, it would prove their destruction. But as all living creatures had one language at that time, the serpent, who then lived together with Adam and his wife, was envious of their happiness, for he thought they would be happy if they obeyed the commands of God, and that if they

---

[1] ἕτερος δέ τις συγγενὴς τούτῳ περὶ τῆς τῶν ζῴων ὁμοφωνίας πρὸς μυθοπλαστῶν ἀναγράφεται · λέγεται γάρ, ὡς ἄρα πάνθ᾽ ὅσα ζῷα χερσαῖα καὶ ἔνυδρα καὶ πτηνὰ τὸ παλαιὸν ὁμόφωνα ἦν, καὶ ὅνπερ τρόπον ἀνθρώπων Ἕλληνες μὲν Ἕλλησι, βαρβάροις δὲ βάρβαροι νῦν οἱ ὁμόγλωττοι διαλέγονται, τοῦτον τὸν τρόπον καὶ πάντα πᾶσι περὶ ὧν ἢ δρᾶν ἢ πάσχειν τι συνέβαινεν ὡμίλει.

disobeyed them, they would fall into calamities.

So he persuaded the woman, out of malicious intent, to taste of the tree of knowledge, telling her that in that tree was the knowledge of good and evil; which knowledge whoso should obtain would lead a happy life; nay, a life not inferior to that of a god."[1] Owing to their sin this primitive language was 'confounded': that of animals at the fall, that of men at the Tower of Babel, but at 'the End' the redeemed will again have but one speech. Cf. *Test. XII. Patr., Jud.* 25. 3, καὶ ἔσεσθε εἰς λαὸν κυρίου καὶ γλῶσσα μία καὶ οὐκ ἔσται ἐκεῖ πνεῦμα πλάνης τοῦ Βελίαρ, and Plutarch, *De Iside*, c. 47, ἕνα βίον καὶ μίαν πολιτείαν ἀνθρώπων μακαρίων καὶ ὁμογλώσσων πάντων γενέσθαι. Considering the eschatological nature of the story of Pentecost, especially Peter's speech, this evidence is significant.

The second passage of importance is Isaiah xxviii. 11 f., which is quoted by Paul in 1 Cor. xiv. 21: "For with stammering lips and another tongue will he speak to this people . . . yet they would not hear." This parallel is much more striking if we accept the text omitting 'Jews' at the beginning of the story and think that the writer regarded the preaching at Pentecost as the beginning of the mission to the Gentiles; the foreigners understood what was said, each man hearing the Apostles speak in his own language, but it was unintelligible to the Jews who thought that the speakers were full of new wine. {(ii.) Is. xxviii.}

The third parallel—from Jewish literature, not the Old Testament—is that traditionally the Day of Pentecost was that on which the Law was given, and was marked by phenomena similar to those described in Acts. {(iii.) Pentecost and Sinai.} The tradition as to the date is found in the Talmud (Pesahim 68b), but not in Philo or Josephus, and therefore cannot be proved to be as early as Acts. But the following quotations from Philo describing the phenomena which attended the giving of the Law show a marked similarity to those which accompanied the gift of the Spirit to the disciples. "For God is not like a man, in need of a mouth, and of a tongue, and of a windpipe, but as it seems to me, he at that time wrought a most conspicuous and evidently holy miracle, commanding an invisible sound to be created in the air, more marvellous than all the instruments that ever existed, attuned to perfect harmonies; and that not an inanimate one, nor yet, on the other hand, one that at all resembled any nature composed of soul and body; but rather it was a rational soul filled with clearness and distinctness, which fashioned the air and stretched it out and changed it into a kind of flaming fire, and so sounded forth so loud and articulate a voice like a breath passing through a trumpet, so that those who were at a great distance

---

[1] ὁ δὴ τοίνυν θεὸς τὸν Ἄδαμον καὶ τὴν γυναῖκα τῶν μὲν ἄλλων φυτῶν ἐκέλευε γεύεσθαι, τοῦ δὲ τῆς φρονήσεως ἀπέχεσθαι, προειπὼν ἀψαμένοις ἀπ' αὐτοῦ ὄλεθρον γενησόμενον. ὁμοφωνούντων δὲ κατ' ἐκεῖνο καιροῦ τῶν ζῴων ἁπάντων ὄφις συνδιαιτώμενος τῷ τε Ἀδάμῳ καὶ τῇ γυναικὶ φθονερῶς μὲν εἶχεν ἐφ' οἷς αὐτοὺς εὐδαιμονήσειν ᾤετο πεπεισμένους τοῖς τοῦ θεοῦ παραγγέλμασιν, οἰόμενος δὲ συμφορᾷ περιπεσεῖσθαι παρακούσαντας ἀναπείθει κακοήθως τὴν γυναῖκα γεύσασθαι τοῦ φυτοῦ τῆς φρονήσεως ἐν αὐτῷ λέγων εἶναι τήν τε τἀγαθοῦ καὶ τοῦ κακοῦ διάγνωσιν, ἧς γενομένης αὐτοῖς μακάριον καὶ μηδὲν ἀπολείποντα τοῦ θείου διάξειν βίον.

appeared to hear equally with those who were nearest to it " (*De Dec.* 9).[1] "And a voice sounded forth from out of the midst of the fire which had flowed from heaven, a most marvellous and awful voice, the flame being endowed with articulate speech in a language familiar to the hearers, which expressed its words with such clearness and distinctness that the people seemed rather to be seeing than hearing it " (*De Dec.* 11).[2]

These quotations speak for themselves. Even more remarkable are some of the statements in the Rabbinic literature, conveniently collected by Spitta (*Apg.* pp. 27 f.), though none of them can be proved to be as early as Acts. The most striking is in Midrash Tanhuma 26c : "Although the ten Commandments were promulgated with a single sound, it says, ' All people heard the voices ' ; it follows then that when the voice went forth it was divided into seven voices and then went into seventy tongues, and every people received the law in their own language." It will be noted that this parallel is much more striking if it be accepted that those who understood the glossolalia of the apostles were Gentiles as well as Jews.

## 2. *The Facts, the Source of Acts, and the Editor*

Paul and glossolalia.

1. *Paul's Description of Glossolalia.*—The view to be taken of the relation between the historical facts, the source of Acts, and the editor depends largely on the description given of glossolalia in 1 Corinthians. In 1 Cor. xii. 10, Paul says that there " are given to one diverse kinds of tongues and to another the interpretation of tongues." Then in chap. xiv., distinguishing between ' glossolalia ' and ' prophecy,' he writes as follows :

"For he that speaks in a tongue speaks not unto men, but unto God; for no man hears ; but in the spirit he speaks mysteries. But he that prophesies speaks to men,—edification, and comfort, and consolation. He that speaks in a tongue edifies himself ; but he that prophesies edifies the church. Now I wish you all to speak with tongues, but rather that you should prophesy : and he that prophesies is greater than he that speaks with tongues, except he interpret, that the church may receive edifying. But now, brethren, if I come to you speaking with tongues, what shall I profit you, unless I speak to you either by way of revelation, or of knowledge, or of prophesying, or of teaching ? Similarly inanimate things making a sound, whether pipe or harp, if they give not a distinction in the notes, how shall it be known what is piped or harped ? For if the trumpet

---

[1] οὐ γὰρ ὡς ἄνθρωπος ὁ θεός, στόματος καὶ γλώττης καὶ ἀρτηριῶν δεόμενος. ἀλλά γέ μοι δοκεῖ κατ' ἐκεῖνον τὸν χρόνον ἱεροπρεπέστατόν τι θαυματουργῆσαι κελεύσας ἦχον ἀόρατον ἐν ἀέρι δημιουργηθῆναι πάντων ὀργάνων θαυμασιώτερον ἁρμονίαις τελείαις ἡρμοσμένον, οὐκ ἄψυχον ἀλλ' οὐδ' ἐκ σώματος καὶ ψυχῆς τρόπον ζῴου συνεστηκότα, ἀλλὰ ψυχὴν λογικὴν ἀνάπλεω σαφηνείας καὶ τρανότητος, ἢ τὸν ἀέρα σχηματίσασα καὶ ἐπιτείνασα καὶ πρὸς πῦρ φλογοειδὲς μεταβαλοῦσα καθάπερ πνεῦμα διὰ σάλπιγγος φωνὴν τοσαύτην ἔναρθρον ἐξήχησεν ὡς τοῖς ἔγγιστα τοὺς πορρωτάτα κατ' ἴσον ἀκροᾶσθαι δοκεῖν.

[2] φωνὴ δ' ἐκ μέσου τοῦ ῥυέντος ἀπ' οὐρανοῦ πυρὸς ἐξήχει καταπληκτικωτάτη, τῆς φλογὸς εἰς διάλεκτον ἀρθρουμένης τὴν συνήθη τοῖς ἀκρωμένοις, ᾗ τὰ λεγόμενα οὕτως ἐναργῶς ἐτρανοῦντο ὡς ὁρᾶν αὐτὰ μᾶλλον ἢ ἀκούειν δοκεῖν.

give an uncertain voice, who shall prepare himself for war ?  So also you, unless you utter by the tongue intelligible speech, how shall it be known what is spoken ? for ye will be speaking into the air.  There are a given number, whatever it may be, of kinds of sound in the world, and nothing is without sound.  If then I know not the meaning of the sound, I shall be to him that speaketh a foreigner, and he that speaketh will be a foreigner to me.  So also you, since you are zealous of spiritual gifts, seek that you may have many of them to the edifying of the church.  Wherefore let him that speaks in a tongue pray that he may interpret.  For if I pray in a tongue, my spirit prays, but my understanding is barren.  What is to be done then ?  I will pray with the spirit, and I will pray with the understanding also : I will sing with the spirit, and I will sing with the understanding also.  Else if you bless with the spirit, how shall he that occupies the place of the unlearned say ' Amen ' to your giving of thanks, seeing he does not know what you are saying ?  For it is true that you are giving thanks well, but the other is not being edified.  Thank God, I speak with tongues more than you all ; but in church my wish is to speak five words with my understanding, that I may instruct others also, than ten thousand words in a tongue.

"Brethren, be not children in mind.  Yet in malice be babes, but in mind be grown up.  In the Law it is written, By men of strange tongues and by the lips of strangers will I speak unto this people ; and not even thus will they hear me, saith the Lord.  Wherefore tongues are for a sign, not to them that believe, but to the unbelieving : but prophesying is for a sign, not to the unbelieving, but to them that believe.  If therefore the whole church be assembled together, and all speak with tongues, and there come in men unlearned or unbelieving, will they not say that you are mad ?  But if all prophesy, and there come in one unbelieving or unlearned, he is reproved by all, he is examined by all ; the secrets of his heart are made manifest ; and so he will fall down on his face and worship God, declaring that God is indeed among you."

From this passage it is clear that to the mind of Paul glossolalia was speech becoming more and more ecstatic until at last it was entirely unintelligible, so that if any stranger came into the church while a Christian was speaking, he was likely to say that the Christian was mad.  Turning to Acts, only just below the surface of the account of Pentecost, can be seen phenomena of just the same nature as Paul describes.  It is true that as it stands the narrative suggests speech of unusual intelligibility ; but the opinion of some of the bystanders was that the apostles were drunk, and Peter in his speech does not say that this was an absurd accusation ; indeed, he rather accepts it as natural, and merely says that it cannot be true because it is too early in the day.  It is scarcely necessary to add that this kind of glossolalia is very common in history, and is merely the removal of inhibitions under the stress of great emotion.  (See K. Lake, *Earlier Epistles of St. Paul*, p. 241, and E. Mosiman, *Das Zungenreden*.)

2. *The Theory of a ' Source ' for Acts ii.*—The facts given in the previous Source-section have often suggested the theory that Luke was dealing with a criticism. written source which did not say anything about speaking in unknown

languages, but gave an ordinary description of glossolalia, such as Paul describes. He himself had not been present at scenes where glossolalia was to be observed, but he knew that it had been a common experience of the early church. Influenced by a natural but wrong etymology and by the Old Testament and Jewish parallels discussed above, he explained glossolalia as speaking with foreign languages and re-wrote the story so as to bring out his own interpretation. Nevertheless, the accusation of drunkenness and Peter's speech remain to show that this is editorial and not historical.

This hypothesis can be supported on two grounds : (a) Inconsistency with the Pauline description of glossolalia, and (b) Inconsistencies in the narrative itself.

Paul and Acts.

(a) *Inconsistency with the Pauline Description.*—This is obvious, but it can be easily exaggerated. It is often overlooked that Paul speaks not merely of glossolalia but also of a corresponding gift of the Spirit which enabled men to understand glossolalia. Translating his words into terms of modern experience, what he says is that in early Christian communities brethren were sometimes seized with an attack of ecstatic speech which was entirely unintelligible to most of the congregation. This was glossolalia. But there were sometimes a few in the congregation who believed that they did understand, and they interpreted to the rest what they had heard. To them at least glossolalia was not unintelligible ; they were hearing in it the ' wonderful works of God.' The rest of the crowd heard nothing but confused babble, and unless they were Christians thought that the speakers were mad.

In the same way Luke may mean that on the Day of Pentecost, when the Christians were gifted with glossolalia, some of the pious visitors were also gifted with the power of interpreting the speech which they identified with their own dialects, while the rest were not so inspired and, therefore, needed Peter's speech in order to explain the situation. Interpreted on these lines there is nothing in the narrative essentially inconsistent with Paul's statements. It may have been written either by Luke or by some earlier writer.

It should be noted that the importance of these remarks is not necessarily to discredit the hypothesis of a Lucan redaction of an earlier account, though of course they can be used in that sense. That hypothesis ultimately stands or falls according to the weight attached to the arguments in the next section. But it seems to me that it is intrinsically improbable that Luke, whether he was a companion of Paul, or belonged to a younger generation, should have written anything in unredeemed contradiction to Pauline teaching. Even if—as is probable—he had never read 1 Corinthians, he can hardly have been ignorant of Paul's teaching, and it is important to note that the story as it stands can well be a redaction of an earlier document, made by a member of the Pauline school, who did not fully understand it, but was imbued with the Pauline distrust of unintelligible glossolalia.

It therefore remains a problem of literary rather than historical criticism, whether we suppose that Acts ii., as we have it now, is a recension of an early source, or is the composition of the writer of the book.

(b) *Inconsistences in the Narrative itself.*—None of these are obtrusively
evident, for Luke was an extremely good editor who often concealed admirably his editorial changes. This can be seen by a comparison of Mark and
Luke, which often shows that Luke has edited his sources without leaving
any trace, so that if Mark was not extant it would never be guessed that
he had done so. Nevertheless, it is strange that there is no word in the
speech of Peter about the miracle of interpretation by the ' pious '—merely
a refutation of the criticism by the ' others ' who said that the apostles
' were full of sweet wine.' Moreover, vs. 7 seems to be a doublet [1] of vs. 12,
and though τὸ πλῆθος in vs. 6, with its present context, apparently means
' the whole company ' of the εὐλαβεῖς just mentioned, it would more naturally mean 'the populace' (see note on iv. 32). The facts would be adequately
covered if it were supposed that the original source ran " and they were
all filled with the Holy Spirit and began to speak with tongues, as the
Spirit gave them utterance, and when this voice arose the populace came
together, and they were all astonished and perplexed, one saying to another.
' What does this mean ? ' But others jeered and said, ' They are full of
sweet wine.' "

This would lead up perfectly to Peter's speech, and it is not inconceivable that Luke believed that glossolalia was speaking in languages
which some pious people could understand though ordinary men could
not, and therefore inserted ' other ' before tongues, and added the story
of the ' pious ' visitors. In this way he produced the double statement
of their astonishment in vss. 7 and 12, and forgot to insert any reference
to this story into the speech of Peter.

If this suggestion be accepted, the next question is whether there are
any signs that the source was in Aramaic rather than Greek. There is
certainly no reason for thinking that it was Aramaic. The only sign of
the kind in this section is οὐχ ἰδού in vs. 7, which is certainly curious Greek,
and may be a translation from the Aramaic, but may be an imitation of the
LXX (see note *ad loc.*). Moreover, it unfortunately comes in one of the
verses most likely to be editorial.

Thus, returning to the main question, it seems that there is not enough
evidence to make the hypothesis certain, though it is not impossible or
even improbable. Incidentally it may be noted that if it be true it indicates that the speech of Peter was in Luke's source, and was not composed
by him ; for had he composed it, he would surely have dealt with the
story of the pious Jews who understood the apostles.

A final judgement must be based on the accumulated evidence of all
the passages in which Luke certainly or conceivably is editing sources. It
depends far more on a study of the gospel than of Acts, for in the gospel
the source is extant, and the method of editing is visible. Speaking generally, it would seem that Luke, like other ancient writers, took sections from
his sources and more or less remodelled the language, sometimes changing
the meaning, but did not make a mosaic out of several narratives. If he
had two narratives he was more likely to use both consecutively than to

---

[1] ἐξίσταντο δὲ καὶ ἐθαύμαζον λέγοντες (vs. 7), ἐξίσταντο δὲ πάντες καὶ διηποροῦντο
ἄλλος πρὸς ἄλλον λέγοντες (vs. 12).

attempt a combination.  Sometimes, however, he certainly inserted one narrative into the middle of another.  Thus in Luke v. 1 ff. he inserts the story of the 'miraculous draught' into the story of the 'call of Peter.' The parallel narratives of Mark i. 16 ff. and John xxi. 1 ff. is the proof that the stories existed separately.  The only question is whether the combination was made by Luke, or found by him in a source.  This is exactly the same question as confronts us in Acts ii., but in neither place is there enough evidence to justify an unqualified decision.

The facts.        3. *The Historical Value of the Narrative.*—In any consideration of this question, in the end we appeal to probability and to preconceived ideas as to what may or may not have happened.  This much must be conceded, but it does not necessarily follow that such preconceived ideas are wrong. Taking, then, the general standard of probability as a guide, there are certain features in the account of the day of Pentecost which do not seem to be historical.

(a) It is unlikely that any body of men witnessing the phenomena described ever made a speech in which they gave a complete catalogue of the nations from which they had been taken.

(b) It is unlikely that men who were not members of the Christian community thought that they were capable of understanding Christians who were speaking with tongues.  The same emotional circumstances which lead one man in any given congregation to speak with tongues may conceivably lead another in the same congregation to think that he understands him, but this would not apply to those outside the group.

(c) Just as it is extremely likely that the Day of Pentecost was marked by the first instance of glossolalia in the Christian community, it is extremely unlikely that this took the form of speaking in foreign languages.  The tradition of the foreign languages is the attempt to explain the glossolalia by a friendly author, separated by time from the actual event, just as the charge of drunkenness was the attempt of unfriendly observers, separated by lack of sympathy.  Quite possibly the form of the Lucan narrative was partly brought about by the desire to refute damaging accusations.  The presence of the foreigners may be merely complementary to that of the miracle of languages, and designed to support it.  This would be by no means a unique instance of an improbable imaginary incident being supported by an equally imaginary but slightly less improbable collection of witnesses.  But this view is not necessary, and it is by no means impossible that the first notable increase in the numbers of the Christian community was really the result of the inspired preaching of the Day of Pentecost, and was due to the effect of the glossolalia on those who listened.

After allowing to these points as much or as little weight as may seem necessary, one positive conclusion stands out clearly.  At the beginning of its history the apostolic circle in Jerusalem underwent a deeply moving psychological experience.  It was of the nature which to that and many later generations was known as 'inspiration.'  They had made no claim to inspiration during Christ's life, but did so almost immediately afterwards.

There were apparently two traditions as to the exact moment—the Lucan, which said that it was fifty days after the Resurrection, and the Johannine, which said that it was when Jesus breathed on them and said "Receive ye the Holy Spirit" (John xx. 22). Both traditions connect the gift with the risen Lord, but in Acts it is primarily an eschatological phenomenon, in John it is the basis of the power to forgive sins—a function of the permanent Church, not a sign of the last days.

To that generation it appeared clear that the phenomenon of 'inspiration' was the result of obsession by 'spirit'; to us it appears rather as a problem of psychology; but whatever may be its explanation, the phenomenon itself is one which constantly recurs in the history of religion.

It has also often been suggested that in some circles the experience of the apostles of Pentecost may have been regarded as a Christophany rather than as the gift of the spirit (see for instance E. von Dobschütz, *Ostern und Pfingsten*). All such hypotheses have too little definite evidence in their support ever to become more than interesting possibilities. There is however nothing intrinsically improbable in the suggestion, especially in view of Paul's statement that the Lord is the Spirit. If it be accepted, it is not difficult to take the next step and say that the event described by Luke as the outpouring of the Spirit may be the same as that described by Paul in 1 Cor. xv. 6, as the appearance of the risen Lord to about five hundred brethren at once. *[marginal note: Pentecost as a Christophany.]*

[On the whole subject see especially H. Gunkel, *Die Wirkungen des heiligen Geistes*; K. Lake, *Earlier Epistles of St. Paul*, pp. 241 ff.; J. Weiss, *Der erste Korintherbrief*, pp. 335-339; E. Mosiman, *Das Zungenreden*; Feine's article on *Zungenreden* in the *Realencyklopädie für prot. Theologie*, ed. 3; Reitzenstein, *Poimandres* (especially pp. 55 ff.); and O. Pfister, *Jahrbuch der Psycho-analyse*, iii. (1911) pp. 427 ff.]

NOTE XI. THE NAME, BAPTISM, AND THE LAYING ON OF HANDS

By SILVA NEW

The belief that a name is a powerful instrument in dealing with many phases of daily life is primitive and very widely spread. Like various other practices now termed superstitious it is one of those fundamental human reactions which are found in similar forms throughout the world, but it would be a fallacy to attempt to link them more immediately than by the fact that they are instinctive responses to similar phenomena. *[marginal note: The magical use of names.]*

In even the most casual study of anthropological sources instances of the use of names are readily found. In some tribes each member still entrusts his real name to some material object such as a stick or a stone and then hides this container, lest by knowledge of his name his enemies be enabled to do him harm. The complement of this is the theory which is implied by giving an enemy's name to a doll, a waxen image, or some other representative of the person named and then injuring or destroying the image, in the belief that the enemy himself will thus be injured or destroyed. Others have the custom of taking a new name in old age in order to ensure a new lease of life.[1] Moreover, not only the names of human individuals have been considered of magical importance. Frequently the true name of a god was concealed and only the initiates could use it to compel him to do their will. In one story Osiris died because Set learned his real name and was thereby enabled to do him harm. Roman liturgies enumerate all the known names and epithets for each of the gods addressed, to avoid the possibility of omitting just the one which will be potent,—nor are the Roman liturgies alone in this characteristic. Even cities were felt to be involved with their names, so that the name of a city or of its protecting deity was carefully guarded, lest enemies might use the latter to entice away the guardian power or the former to break down the defences.

All of these varied practices are in some sense parallels, at least in that there may be supposed to be some human instinct which is in the last resort the origin of each one of them. Behind each is the identification of the name used with the person or thing to which that name refers. To enumerate a list, as above, partially states the problem but it does not solve it. Why was this identification so constantly made? Probably because many people think in pictures, and to them the name of a person and a mental picture of the person named are fused. Thus, at an uncritical and unselfconscious stage, the man and his name were the same thing, and the next step was easy and natural : the use of a person's name controlled his actions and his very existence as effectively as did a man who battled with and overcame him. A corollary to this belief was that the qualities and powers of a man or a deity were also inherent in his name. The elaborations of these beliefs were in some cases as little thought out as the original primitive association of the person and his name, and in some, as in the Roman liturgies, were purely mechanical attempts at consistency. Even to the present day, when the beliefs formulated above would certainly be rejected by educated people, there are many parallels to this instinctive association of name and person. Why do children so often bear the names of parents or more remote ancestors? Why do most men dread to die without descendants who will carry on the family name? How many people hope that they will be remembered by name, long after they themselves are dead, for something which they have said or done ? And yet an attempt to explain these desires reasonably and coldly sounds quite as unconvincing as an anthropologist's discourse on why a savage expects certain definite magical results from the utterance of a name.

Further discussion of why a name became a powerful instrument of

---

[1] Mk. iii. 16 f. can hardly be claimed as an example of an attempt to induce certain qualities magically, by giving men names which suggest them. It is far more probable that by 'Peter' and 'Sons of Thunder' Jesus was describing qualities which he had discerned in Simon and the sons of Zebedee, —whether Luke ix. 54 f. be accepted as true, and a probable reason for calling the latter Boanerges or not.

magic is probably futile, and for the present purpose unnecessary, since it is certain that it did so. In the world into which Jesus was born [1] it was so implicitly accepted that he and his contemporaries wasted no more time in discussion of it than a later generation does in querying the effectiveness of antiseptics. It is this assumption of the power of a name which must be emphasized at the beginning of any intelligible treatment of its place in the theory and practice of early Christianity, since in the modern world it has been so far outgrown that the formulae which embody it can only be repeated if no question be asked as to what the words actually mean. [2]

*The Gospel of Mark.*—The clearest example of the use of the Name in Mark is in ix. 38 ff.: ἔφη αὐτῷ ὁ Ἰωάννης, Διδάσκαλε, εἴδαμέν τινα ἐν τῷ ὀνόματί σου ἐκβάλλοντα δαιμόνια, καὶ ἐκωλύομεν αὐτόν, ὅτι οὐκ ἠκολούθει ἡμῖν. ὁ δὲ Ἰησοῦς εἶπεν, Μὴ κωλύετε αὐτόν, οὐδεὶς γὰρ ἔστιν ὃς ποιήσει δύναμιν ἐπὶ τῷ ὀνόματί μου καὶ δυνήσεται ταχὺ κακολογῆσαί με. ὃς γὰρ οὐκ ἔστι καθ᾽ ἡμῶν ὑπὲρ ἡμῶν ἐστιν. There is no doubt as to the meaning. The disciples saw a stranger who cast out devils by commanding them in the Name of Jesus. They objected because he was not a disciple, but Jesus pointed out that the man who worked miracles by the use of his Name could not very well then turn about and become his enemy. Here it is not any power, consciously conveyed to the miracle-worker by Jesus, which commands the devils ; it is simply the use of his Name by a completely unauthorized person. [3] To

[1] Compare the account of Eleazar in Josephus, *Ant.* viii. 2. 5. This man used to heal demoniacs by drawing the devil out through their noses, using a ring with an herb in it recommended by Solomon, and Solomon's name—Σολομῶνος μεμνημένος.

[2] However helpful to the interpretation of the New Testament a clear perception of historical perspective may be, it was not the atmosphere in which the early Christian moved. It is easier to understand a 'superstition' if parallel or causal phenomena are studied also. The danger is in forgetting that those for whom this superstition was a living thing were unaware of any parallels or any of those facts which seem to the historian the ultimate explanation of the belief. It was simply a reaction to some part of the world as it was then seen. Nor is it legitimate to condemn as inconsistent beliefs about two different things which had no connexion in the minds of those who formulated the beliefs.

[3] Much recent discussion has been expended on the nice problem of whether there is not a slight variation of meaning between the phrases ἐν τῷ ὀνόματι, ἐπὶ τῷ ὀνόματι, and εἰς τὸ ὄνομα, but a negative answer would seem to be offered by the usage of the New Testament itself. Paul, the earliest of the writers, rarely uses the phrase ' in the name of,' but on the three occasions on which he mentions it in connexion with baptism it is twice εἰς τὸ ὄνομα and once ἐν τῷ ὀνόματι. In the passage from Mark quoted above ἐπί is found in some manuscripts in verse 38 and ἐν in some in verse 39. In verse 38 τῷ ὀνόματι without a preposition also occurs. Is there any difference of meaning in the expressions ? According to the text preferred by the editors the disciples say

cast out a devil by commanding him in the Name of Jesus to go was so fully in accord with the beliefs of the time that it raised no comment. The disciples were not surprised at the success of the measure ; they objected to it as unauthorized. Jesus himself had the power to cast out devils, and therefore his Name carried the same power, no matter who pronounced it.[1]  This belief persisted for centuries.  In the second century

---

ἐν τῷ ὀνόματι and Jesus ἐπὶ τῷ ὀνόματι in referring to the same occurrence, but in the Lucan parallel it is the disciples who use ἐπί and not Jesus.  It is thus difficult to suppose that the phrases are not synonymous.  The opinion, also, of the scribes who wrote the extant manuscripts of the New Testament seems clearly to have been that there was no distinction between the various ways of expressing ' in the name,' and translators have usually rendered the Greek on this assumption.  This is natural in a language which was already using εἰς and ἐν interchangeably in all connexions, the first step toward that modern Greek in which εἰς serves for both and ἐν is lost to the spoken language.

The question is only one aspect of the larger problem of the character of the language used by the writers of the New Testament and of its relation to Aramaic and to the Koine Greek of the period.  The point of chief importance is that Greek is the language in which the New Testament, as we have it, was written, whatever its sources may have been.  This Greek was not the language of careful scholars : it was the current speech of the period and locality.  Christianity had its beginnings in a society in which at least a fair proportion of the population spoke both Aramaic and Greek.  Many converts had been familiar from childhood with the language of the Septuagint, a document which had been translated in great part from Hebrew.  Undoubtedly Semitic idiom had to some extent influenced their speech, from one source or another, but the language they spoke was Greek, not Aramaic, or even translated Aramaic.  A modern parallel is the English spoken by the negroes in the south of the United States.  In accent, intonation, and idiom it is very different from English as it is spoken by any other people, but it is English and not an African dialect.

Moreover, subtle shades of meaning, achieved by slightly varying an expression, are not the ordinary language of every day, nor are they so understood by ordinary people.  A convert knew perfectly well that when he said that he had been baptized in the name of Jesus he meant that someone had said ' I baptize you in the name of Jesus ' or something similar, and that in consequence he had attained the way of Salvation; but it is very hard to believe that he would have distinguished between εἰς τὸ ὄνομα to express the aim of baptism and ἐν τῷ ὀνόματι to imply the words of the formula which had been used.

[1] Running parallel with this belief in the power of Jesus' Name there is also apparent in the Gospel of Mark that belief in the power of Faith which persisted and grew stronger, while the other died.  In v. 34, ix. 23 f. and other places the belief of the sick person (or in one case of the demoniac's father) was at least partially responsible for the cure and necessary for it.  In vi. 4 ff. Jesus was actively hindered by the unbelief of the Galileans, καὶ οὐκ ἐδύνατο ἐκεῖ ποιῆσαι οὐδεμίαν δύναμιν, although he was able to heal a few individuals who presumably did believe in him.  In xi. 23 ff. it is again πίστις which is asserted to be the power by which mountains may be moved.

xvi. 16 ff. gives the later, developed theory, in which the man who believes

the synagogue forbade the use of the Name of Jesus to exorcise or to heal : it was effective, but it was wrong.

The theory is the same as that found in various Hebrew documents, some of which long antedate and some of which are contemporary with Jesus. The names of angels had magical power. The name of God himself was much too sacred for this purpose, and it was blasphemy to utter it, but its power if pronounced or written was not doubted. By it God had created heaven. Inscribed on Moses' staff it divided the waters of the Red Sea. Spoken by him it killed the Egyptian. Isaiah, threatened by Manasseh, used it to raise about him a cedar—though the sequel was curious, for Manasseh sawed through the cedar and thus killed Isaiah.

So far there is no difficulty. Jesus had the power to heal and to exorcise. This was also incorporated in his Name. But whence did his power come ? What name did he use ? None. He expels devils and commands men to be healed ; or he lays his hands on them and they are healed. The priests and the scribes queried this : ἐν ποίᾳ ἐξουσίᾳ [1] ταῦτα ποιεῖς ; ἢ τίς σοι ἔδωκεν τὴν ἐξουσίαν ταύτην ἵνα ταῦτα ποιῇς; (Mk. xi. 28.) καὶ ἐθαμβήθησαν ἅπαντες, ὥστε συνζητεῖν αὐτοὺς λέγοντας Τί ἐστιν τοῦτο; διδαχὴ καινή· κατ᾽ ἐξουσίαν καὶ τοῖς πνεύμασι τοῖς ἀκαθάρτοις ἐπιτάσσει, καὶ ὑπακούουσιν αὐτῷ. (Mk. i. 27.) He acted with 'authority,' that is of his own power, not by the use of the name of any other being.[2]

Nowhere does Mark tell of the disciples exorcising or healing in the Name of Jesus, but in iii. 14 f. Jesus ἐποίησεν δώδεκα . . . ἵνα ἀποστέλλῃ αὐτοὺς κηρύσσειν καὶ ἔχειν ἐξουσίαν ἐκβάλλειν τὰ δαιμόνια,

and is baptized can cast out devils in the Name of Jesus and heal the sick by laying his hands on them. Mark, however, had not achieved this fusion and a general view of his account must bring out inconsistencies. It is probable that in the beginning the dominant belief was that anyone could do the things which Jesus did by uttering his Name, but that the current of thought which emphasized the power of Faith was already widely diffused. In Mark the two run side by side and unreconciled : perhaps heritages from two different sources, but equally possibly merely the reflection on a not too critical mind of different beliefs in the contemporary world.

[1] This is not the place to discuss the character of this ἐξουσία, or whether it was thought of as πνεῦμα, but it is worth remembering in this connexion that when the woman in Mark v. 25 was cured merely by touching Jesus' garment he knew of it immediately, not because he saw or felt her touch but because ἐπιγνοὺς ἐν ἑαυτῷ τὴν ἐξ αὐτοῦ δύναμιν ἐξελθοῦσαν. This is clearly a loss of strength of some sort, parallel to the loss of strength which would come from lifting a burden.

[2] What did Jesus himself think of as the source of or reason for this power ? Did he believe it was due to his prayers ? Cf. Mk. ix. 29 and xi. 24. Or was it because at the Baptism he had been specially appointed by God as his Son ? Mark apparently not only held the latter view, but also thought that Jesus did so. The gift of the Spirit made Jesus Son of God, and enabled him to triumph over demons.

and in vi. 7 it is said καὶ ἐδίδου αὐτοῖς ἐξουσίαν τῶν πνευμάτων τῶν ἀκαθάρτων, in consequence of which in vi. 12 f. the apostles went out and ἐκήρυξαν ἵνα μετανοῶσι καὶ δαιμόνια πολλὰ ἐξέβαλλον, καὶ ἤλειφον ἐλαίῳ[1] πολλοὺς ἀρρώστους καὶ ἐθεράπευον. According to Mark, then, the disciples were authorized by Jesus to do just the things which he was doing—preach, exorcise, and heal. Although it is not said that they did these things in the Name of Jesus, they at least received from him the authority to do them, and they were able to work the miracles which Jesus performed as they had previously been unable to do. Either Mark thought of them as having received from Jesus the power which he had by some such direct transference as the laying on of his hands, or as doing their works in his Name in the same manner in which the unauthorized man in Mk. ix. did. The latter is the more probable view when the various stories in Acts, where healing is done in the Name of Jesus, are compared with the statements in Mark.

Exorcism and Eisorcism.

Since healing and the casting out of devils are so constantly linked the question arises whether they were not considered as in reality the same thing. Was all illness due to the presence of evil spirits ? Or was it perhaps necessary in some cases to give to the person who was ill a good spirit—eisorcism—rather than to exorcise an evil spirit ? If this be so it may solve the question raised above as to why Jesus felt power depart from him when he inadvertently healed the woman. It was not that she had an evil spirit which must be driven out, but a good spirit entered into her to perform the cure. What, also, is the relation of sinfulness to illness and to evil spirits ? Jesus himself asks his critics whether it is easier to say to the man sick of the palsy "Thy sins be forgiven thee," or to say "Arise, take up thy bed and walk." The question is merely a verbal "score" if there be no connexion between sin and disease.

Other uses of the Name.

Somewhat different from the other uses of the Name are the references to persecutions which will be inflicted on Jesus' followers ' for my name's sake ' and to those who are received or benefited ' in my name.' The Greek phrases, like the English, do not differ from those used in speaking of the use of the Name for exorcism or baptism, but it is improbable that here they have any magical significance. ' Persecuted for my name's sake ' means that Jesus thought that those who were known to be his followers would on that account be persecuted. It is even possible that by the time when Mark was writing the term ' Christian ' was already in use and influenced the phrasing of such passages. Heitmüller believes that James ii. 7 οὐκ αὐτοὶ βλασφημοῦσι τὸ καλὸν ὄνομα τὸ ἐπικληθὲν ἐφ' ὑμᾶς is a specific reference to those who have had the name ' Jesus ' pronounced over them in baptism, but it seems unnecessary to assume that it means more than that Christians were already called Χριστιανοί. No reference to baptism need be seen beyond that contained in the assumption that people who were called Christians had for the most part been baptized.

[1] Cf. James v. 14 ἀσθενεῖ τις ἐν ὑμῖν ; προσκαλεσάσθω τοὺς πρεσβυτέρους τῆς ἐκκλησίας, καὶ προσευξάσθωσαν ἐπ' αὐτόν, ἀλείψαντες αὐτὸν ἐν τῷ ὀνόματι τοῦ Κυρίου.

The exact meaning intended in the passages dealing with men who are received by others ' in my name ' is clarified by the parallel in Mt. x. 41-42 : ὁ δεχόμενος προφήτην εἰς ὄνομα προφήτου μισθὸν προφήτου λήμψεται καὶ ὁ δεχόμενος δίκαιον εἰς ὄνομα δικαίου μισθὸν δικαίου λήμψεται. καὶ ὃς ἂν ποτίσῃ ἕνα τῶν μικρῶν τούτων ποτήριον ψυχροῦ μόνον εἰς ὄνομα μαθητοῦ, ἀμὴν λέγω ὑμῖν οὐ μὴ ἀπολέσῃ τὸν μισθὸν αὐτοῦ. This is only an elaborate way of saying " he that receiveth a prophet because he is a prophet," or " he that receiveth a prophet because he honours a prophet." In the same way Mk. ix. 37 and similar passages means : " Whosoever shall receive one of such children for love (or honour) of me." So also the cry at the triumphal entry : εὐλογημένος ὁ ἐρχόμενος ἐν ὀνόματι κυρίου.

*The Gospel of Matthew.*—Matthew reflects the same views as does Mark in regard to the power inherent in the Name of Jesus. He omits the story of the man who was working miracles by it without authority, but makes the same assumptions in vii. 20 ff. : ἄραγε ἀπὸ τῶν καρπῶν αὐτῶν ἐπιγνώσεσθε αὐτούς. οὐ πᾶς ὁ λέγων μοι Κύριε κύριε εἰσελεύσεται εἰς τὴν βασιλείαν τῶν οὐρανῶν, ἀλλ' ὁ ποιῶν τὸ θέλημα τοῦ πατρός μου τοῦ ἐν τοῖς οὐρανοῖς. πολλοὶ ἐροῦσίν μοι ἐν ἐκείνῃ τῇ ἡμέρᾳ Κύριε κύριε, οὐ τῷ σῷ ὀνόματι ἐπροφητεύσαμεν, καὶ τῷ σῷ ὀνόματι δαιμόνια ἐξεβάλομεν καὶ τῷ σῷ ὀνόματι δυνάμεις πολλὰς ἐποιήσαμεν; καὶ τότε ὁμολογήσω αὐτοῖς ὅτι οὐδέποτε ἔγνων ὑμᾶς· ἀποχωρεῖτε ἀπ' ἐμοῦ οἱ ἐργαζόμενοι τὴν ἀνομίαν.[1] It is again clear, as in Mark, that there is no question of the efficacy of the use of Jesus' name ; but it is also clear that its successful use does not necessarily mean that the user will be worthy to enter the kingdom of heaven.

On the other hand, the theory of the power which Jesus himself possessed is more fully elaborated. He makes the claim (xi. 27) πάντα μοι παρεδόθη ὑπὸ τοῦ πατρός μου : for Matthew the primary fact was that he was Son of God, and to that fact his power was directly due.[2] Mark tells the story of the descent of the Spirit at the Baptism and it can be inferred that he regarded this possession of the Spirit as the source of Jesus' power. Matthew more definitely states this in the discussion in xii. 18-28 : ἰδοὺ ὁ παῖς μου ὃν ᾑρέτισα· ὁ ἀγαπητός μου ὃν εὐδόκησεν ἡ ψυχή μου. θήσω τὸ πνεῦμά μου ἐπ' αὐτόν, καὶ κρίσιν τοῖς ἔθνεσιν ἀπαγγελεῖ . . . εἰ δὲ ἐν πνεύματι θεοῦ ἐγὼ ἐκβάλλω τὰ δαιμόνια, ἄρα ἔφθασεν ἐφ' ὑμᾶς ἡ βασιλεία τοῦ θεοῦ.[3]

This power he is represented as delegating to his disciples on two

---

[1] There is no parallel to this passage in Luke, and it is therefore doubtful whether it is taken from Q. Perhaps it reflects the troubles caused in the Church by false prophets. Cf. 1 John ii. 18, iv. 4.

[2] That God is the ' Father ' of men—not only, but especially, of Jesus— is characteristic of Matthew, see Vol. I. pp. 401 ff.

[3] The υἱοὶ ὑμῶν in vs. 27 may refer to Jesus' followers and the reasoning be that if Jesus casts out devils through the Devil his followers are possessed of Satan, but if he casts them out through the spirit of God which is in him, he has passed that spirit on to his disciples and the Kingdom of God is therefore among them.

different occasions.[1]   The first is the parallel to the Marcan story, when during his own ministry he sends out the Apostles.   Here he gives them the power to cast out devils and to heal, and sends them forth to do these things and to preach that the Kingdom of Heaven is at hand. The second is the command laid on the Twelve by the risen Jesus to go forth and make disciples, and is found in the last three verses of the gospel, the trustworthiness of which is very doubtful.   But whoever wrote them meant to make it plain that it was because all power in heaven and in earth had been given to Jesus that he could pass on to the disciples the authorization to go forth and teach the nations and baptize them.

The Name<br>in Luke. *The Gospel of Luke.*—Luke holds the same views in regard to the power of Jesus' Name as do the other synoptic gospels, but adds one important point.   He clearly states what has been assumed in the stories told in the others, that when Jesus sends forth his disciples the power which he gives them is exercised through the use of his Name.   In x. 1 ff. he tells of the sending forth of seventy, as well as twelve, and the seventy return saying with joy, Κύριε, καὶ τὰ δαιμόνια ὑποτάσσεται ἡμῖν ἐν τῷ ὀνόματί σου.

One of the points which are very difficult to understand, both in Luke and in Mark, is how the power given to the disciples by Jesus differed from that possessed by the man who used his Name without having any authorization to do so.   Or was there no difference in that respect ?   Was it only the command to spread the teaching of Jesus which was the important part of the mission, both to Jesus himself and to the man who told the story ?   This is one of those tantalizing questions, an answer to which would be so valuable for an understanding of the period when the gospels were written, but dealing with a subject so obvious to the writers that it was never raised to the level of discussion or explanation, so that it will probably never be answered.

Up to this point the evidence for the beliefs held about the Name of Jesus and the uses to which it was put is fairly simple and consistent, and does not in kind go beyond those expressed in earlier or contemporary Hebrew documents.   But with the Pauline Epistles and Acts there is a change.   This may be due to currents of thought which began to influence Christianity when it spread into the cosmopolitan world of the great cities of Asia Minor, Egypt, and Greece, where the Jews were only one foreign element in a mixed population which had many varying traditions behind it [2] ; or the change may be due to Paul himself and to his development of the ideas prevalent among the Christians of his day.   This raises a problem which constantly confronts the student of the New Testament : Should the Pauline Epistles, which were certainly written first and contain

[1] The " succession " is as clear as when Clement of Rome says that Jesus depends from God and the apostles from Jesus.

[2] The sources of the Synoptic Gospels, or at least the events which are their theme, are earlier than the writing of the Pauline Epistles.   This accounts for their more primitive ideas in regard to the Name, and also for the difference in the theories reflected in the Gospel of Luke and in Acts.

ideas that must to some extent have been familiar to the writer of Acts, be considered first ?  Or should Acts, which portrays a period of Christian development before the conversion of Paul, which is in some ways more primitive than that reflected in the Epistles of Paul ?  In this case it seems better to begin with the Epistles.  It is very probable that Paul's beliefs were already spreading over the Christian world, or perhaps that the ideas which influenced Paul had also to some extent shaped the beliefs of the majority of Greek-speaking Christians.  In either case it seems more useful to study what little Paul has to say on the subject before going on to consider the mass of evidence in the Acts—evidence greater in quantity and more specific than all that has gone before.

*The Pauline Epistles.*—These introduce us into a different world from that of the Synoptics.  This is due in part to the different purpose for which they were intended, and mere omission must not be regarded in the same light as in an historical writing.  But when all allowance has been made for this, it remains clear that Paul had a different *Weltanschauung* from Mark. The Pauline Epistles.

The Epistles constantly refer to the believer as united to Christ, and it is this sense of the identity of the Christ and the Christian and its importance as the basis of a changed life which is often called Paul's mysticism.  This is a correct statement if it be correctly understood.  The central point in all ' mystical ' experience is that it gives those who enjoy it a sense of unity, whereas almost all sensuous experience heightens the perception of difference and individuality.  But this experience, like all others, is criticized and explained by the intellect, and always in terms of the theories as to Man, God, the Universe, and Reality which it happens to hold.  Mysticism is an experience common to the race, though not to all members of it ; it is always a sense of freedom, of lifted barriers and achieved unity ; but it has been explained in many different and even contradictory ways.  To Paul it seemed due to the relation between himself and the risen Lord—the Spirit—but it is necessary to distinguish between the reality of Paul's mystical experience and the truth of the intellectual explanation which he accepted.  The former is doubtless the more important, but its discussion lies outside the present note.  Similarly, Paul's intellectual explanation must be judged as part of his general *Weltanschauung*, and a criticism of this cannot now be undertaken.  For the present all that is intended is a statement of Paul's beliefs, not a criticism of them. Mysticism.

The general view which seems to underlie Paul's theory of his own mystical experience—and he himself at least certainly did not distinguish this theory from the experience itself—is much more closely associated with the Jewish doctrine of spirits and their power of 'obsessing' human beings than it is with any Greek philosophy, which latter seems to have affected the language of the Epistles only slightly and the thought not at all.  Just as the Spirit of the Lord possessed a prophet, or an evil spirit possessed a demoniac, so the Lord—who is the Spirit—possessed Paul and other Christians, and in such a way that henceforth everything they did and the whole course of their lives was dominated and controlled by the Mysticism and obsession in Paul's theory.

Lord, not by themselves. "I live no longer," says Paul, "but Christ in me." To obtain this possession by the Lord or by the Spirit and so become a 'new creature' was the most important thing. It was accomplished by faith and by baptism. It was the reverse of exorcism, but just as miraculous, and might perhaps be called 'eisorcism.'

It is natural to expect that the Name of the Lord should play a considerable part in Paul's writings. Investigation confirms the expectation, though perhaps not so much as might have been anticipated. There is no mention anywhere of exorcism or of cures in the Name of Jesus. This does not mean necessarily that Paul disbelieved in them or did not practise them, but that they were not points which he felt it necessary to impress on the people whom he was addressing. It is quite possible that this is simply an indication that they were taken for granted and were not, at that time, a subject of controversy. But though exorcism is not mentioned the Name often appears.

The Name in the Epistles. In Philippians ii. 9-11 it is said that God has given Jesus τὸ ὄνομα τὸ ὑπὲρ πᾶν ὄνομα, ἵνα ἐν τῷ ὀνόματι Ἰησοῦ πᾶν γόνυ κάμψῃ ἐπουρανίων καὶ ἐπιγείων καὶ καταχθονίων, καὶ πᾶσα γλῶσσα ἐξομολογήσηται ὅτι κύριος Ἰησοῦς Χριστὸς εἰς δόξαν θεοῦ πατρός. The name given to Jesus is obviously Κύριος,[1] 'Lord,' which was 'above every name,' because in the LXX it was the Greek equivalent of 'Jahveh.' The meaning is that God gave his own name to Jesus.

In Rom. x. 9, he says: "If you confess the word[2] with your mouth " (referring to Deut. xxx. 14) "that Jesus is Lord, and believe in your heart that God raised him from the dead, you will be saved." The phrase 'the name' is not actually mentioned, but it is surely implied by the 'confess with your mouth,' and ῥῆμα is used here owing to the influence of the LXX instead of the ὄνομα of Philippians.

The most significant point in these two passages is that they ascribe power to the Name of Jesus without mentioning baptism. Possibly, though very far from certainly, Paul is thinking of baptism and its relation to the phrase 'Lord Jesus,' but in any case it is clear that the Name is not limited in its efficacy to its use in baptism.

The Mystery cults. What was the origin of the idea involved? Salvation by identification with Jesus, whether through baptism or through faith, is in a different category from anything found in the synoptic gospels. A popular solution is to say that it was probably taken over from the mystery religions which were so widely spread at that period. Generally speaking, however, it is easier in the present state of knowledge to use the accurate information which we have about some phases of early Christianity to explain the few remaining accounts of the mysteries than to bring any knowledge of the mysteries to bear on the interpretation of Christianity. It is known, however, that in Egyptian burials there was a re-enactment of the burial of Osiris, and that each corpse bore his name and was thus identified with him, was in point of fact an Osiris and supposed to live, as he does, in the Lower World. It is not justifiable to assume that this influenced Paul's develop-

---

[1] Cf. Mt. xxiv. 5, and Luke xxi. 8, where 'my name' means 'Χριστός.'
[2] B Clem[Al] read τὸ ῥῆμα . . . ὅτι Κύριος Ἰησοῦς.

ment of Christian theology; but he certainly lived in a world in which many similar beliefs were common, so that combined with the already widespread opinion that the utterance of the Name of Jesus would accomplish the miracles of healing and exorcism which he himself had performed, they may have led Paul to the conclusion that not only did the other powers which Jesus possessed pass to those men who used his Name, but that his power over death was also conveyed to them.

Moreover the further conviction was perhaps held by Paul, certainly by the Catholic Church, that not only was the pronouncing of the Name of Jesus capable of saving men, but that quite especially to have it pronounced over them in baptism did so. There are only four passages in the Pauline Epistles which can be cited as definite evidence for Paul's views on baptism—and of these one is the obscure reference to baptism for the dead in 1 Cor. xv. 29. In spite of this, however, it is possible to reconstruct some part of his beliefs. *Paul and baptism.*

In 1 Cor. i. 11 ff. it is assumed that those who were baptized in the Name of Jesus belonged to Him—were Christians. Paul's concern is the denial that he had baptized in his own name—that is, made 'Paulines.' If the disciples were using the Name of Jesus in baptism to distinguish themselves from the followers of John, this is the sort of accusation which enemies might have brought,—that they were splitting into futile little groups headed by individual leaders. There is no need to perceive in this discussion a belief in 'sacramental' baptism, although there is nothing to contradict it. Nor need a reference to a definite formula be understood, although the parallelism 'Paul'—'Christ' and then 'in my own name' is surely significant. Paul's curiously slighting disclaimer of a mission to baptize, a few verses below, gives the impression that in any case he did not at this time consider baptism as of great importance.

In 1 Cor. vi. 11 washing ἐν τῷ ὀνόματι τοῦ Κυρίου Ἰησοῦ Χριστοῦ must refer to baptism. Perhaps this is the baptismal formula and the next phrase, ἐν τῷ πνεύματι τοῦ θεοῦ ἡμῶν,[1] refers to the gift of the Spirit which is the result of baptism and is the sanctification.

Finally, in Rom. vi. 3 ff., baptism is the means of uniting the Christian with Jesus Christ in his death and in his resurrection.[2]

Such a baptism is definitely sacramental. That of John was a baptism unto repentance, and did not assume that it at all changed the nature of the penitent or had any direct connexion with salvation. Jesus himself probably did not baptize, but after his death his disciples may have done so and used his Name in order to distinguish their converts or penitents from those of John and his disciples. Of this stage, however, there is no evidence, and it is a long step from it to sacramental baptism. It is a step which might well have been made by a man who connected the

[1] It is just possible that this is a unique reference to a double baptismal formula, but I think it very improbable.

[2] A reference to the baptismal formula has also been seen in Rom. x. 9. If so, it is again the simple 'in the Name of the Lord Jesus' (cf. Acts ii. 21). Paul was certainly not acquainted with the Trinitarian form.

outward ceremony of baptism and the consequent sloughing off of his own sinfulness with the inward experience of unity with Jesus; but if so, it is another instance of how often in the history of religion similarity of phrase bridges a deep diversity of thought.

Acts.

*The Acts.*—In the early chapters of this book, and particularly in those usually ascribed to the Jerusalem source A, the story is told of a great struggle between the Disciples and the Jewish authorities, which centred in the use of the Name of Jesus.[1] The account begins with the story of the lame man at the Beautiful Gate whom Peter cured ἐν τῷ ὀνόματι Ἰησοῦ Χριστοῦ τοῦ Ναζωραίου (iii. 6), and his explanation to the marvelling crowd that it was not his own power but that of the Name of Jesus which had worked the miracle.[2]

Acts iii.-iv.

The excitement which followed was made the pretext for the arrest of Peter and John and an inquiry into the source of their power, but the true reason was that the authorities were disturbed because they taught the people, and preached through Jesus the resurrection from the dead. Doubtless it was this which provoked Peter's rather lengthy answer, not only that they had healed the man in the Name of Jesus Christ of Nazareth, but that οὐκ ἔστιν ἐν ἄλλῳ οὐδενὶ ἡ σωτηρία, οὐδὲ γὰρ ὄνομά ἐστιν ἕτερον ὑπὸ τὸν οὐρανὸν τὸ δεδομένον ἐν ἀνθρώποις ἐν ᾧ δεῖ σωθῆναι ἡμᾶς. This may refer to the cure of the lame man who ἐσώθη, it may mean eschatological safety, or it may imply salvation by regeneration. There is nothing in the context to suggest the last, but the other two are probable, and the transition from one to the other is bridged by ambiguous phrases (σωτηρία, σωθῆναι) in a manner which is characteristically Lucan. The Sanhedrin could not fight the logic of facts so far as to punish the Apostles, but illogically enough issued a command to them to abandon the use of the Name. The Apostles took no heed and they were again brought before the council, to receive the same injunction, "and they departed from the presence of the council, rejoicing that they were counted worthy to suffer shame for his name. And daily in the temple, and in every house, they ceased not to teach and preach Jesus Christ" (v. 41 f.).

This is the last heard of this conflict, except for a possible reference to it in the story of Ananias, who protests to the Lord that he has heard much of Paul's evil treatment of Christians "and here he hath authority from the chief priests to bind all that call on thy name" (ix. 14). But if there is no more about the struggle over the use of the Name, stories of cures by it are scattered throughout the book. The

[1] The probability that this picture is true to history is shown in the stories in the Talmud, which indicate that the controversy persisted to a much later date. (See Vol. I. pp. 319 and 426.)

[2] The part played in this cure by 'faith' is very obscure, and in iii. 16 it is certainly not clear whether Peter or the lame man was possessed of the 'faith in his name' referred to. The lame man does not seem to have been aware of what might befall him when he approached Peter. In any case, the Name of Jesus was the agency by which the cure was effected.

disciples heal and exorcise in the Name of Jesus,[1] but the most important and curious passage is the story of the sons of Scaeva.[2]  They were Acts xix. exorcists [3] who took it upon themselves to drive out evil spirits in ' the name of Jesus whom Paul preacheth.'  The demons recognized the names both of Jesus and of Paul, but not the right of these exorcists to use them, and they therefore fell upon the sons of Scaeva, injured them, and drove them away.  That is, in this case the unauthorized use of the Name of Jesus did not succeed.  This is remarkable and rare.  In the history of the magical use of names authorization is seldom an element.  Usually the Name works *ex opere operato.*  It would appear that, contrary to Jesus' example, the Christian community of this period resented the use of his Name by any but themselves, and did not believe in its efficacy unless supported by Christian faith.

But, although Luke narrates these cures and exorcisms in the Name The Name and salvation. of Jesus, its connexion with salvation and its connexion with baptism interest him far more deeply.  Yet it is no easier to find a simple answer to the question of what Luke regarded as the means of salvation than to that of what he meant by salvation.  In iv. 16 f. and in ii. 21 (a quotation) it is, however, achieved through the Name of Jesus or ' the Lord.'

---

[1] ix. 33 f., xvi. 16 ff.  Cf. also xiv. 8 f. and xxviii. 7 ff.  In the former the faith of the man healed is the effective instrument—but is this not faith in Paul's power ?   In xxviii. 7 ff. Paul cures Publius's father by praying and laying his hands on him, just as Jesus did in some cases.          [2] xix. 13 ff.

[3] Whether they were Jewish or not, whether they were seven or less in number, and whether or not Scaeva was a high priest, are points immaterial to the present purpose.  See also Addit. Note 23.  But the Western text here differs from the Neutral on one point important for this discussion.  D reads ἐπικαλεῖσθαι τὸ ὄνομα, and the simplicity of the formula is in contrast to the tendency to expansion in Codex Bezae.  It may be noted, however, that the Western text does not use ὄνομα in any essentially different manner from the Neutral or Ecclesiastical texts.  The following points are of interest :

(i.) In ii. 38 ἐν τῷ ὀνόματι Ἰησοῦ Χριστοῦ becomes ἐν τῷ ὀνόματι τοῦ κυρίου Ἰησοῦ Χριστοῦ in D Cyprian but ἐν τῷ ὀνόματι Ἰησοῦ in Irenaeus, which may be original.  (Cf. the textual facts in Mark i. 1.)

(ii.) In vi. 8, in describing the miraculous activities of Stephen, D and Syr-hl[mg] add that he did these miracles διὰ τοῦ ὀνόματος κυρίου Ἰησοῦ Χριστοῦ, and the African Latin (h) has the simpler *in nomine Iesu Christi.*

(iii.) In ix. 17 the Neutral text reads καὶ ἐπιθεὶς ἐπ' αὐτὸν τὰς χεῖρας εἶπε κτλ., but h (D is missing) reads *et inposuit ei manum in nomine Iesu Christi.*

(iv.) In ix. 40 Syr-hl[mg] Cyp add *in nomine domini nostri Iesu Christi* to Τάβιθα ἀνάστηθι.

(v.) In x. 48 D reads ἐν τῷ ὀνόματι τοῦ κυρίου Ἰησοῦ Χριστοῦ.

(vi.) In xiv. 10 the Western reading adds σοὶ λέγω ἐν τῷ ὀνόματι Ἰησοῦ Χριστοῦ before ἀνάστηθι.

(vii.) In xviii. 8 (D) Syr-hl[mg] etc. add διὰ τοῦ ὀνόματος τοῦ κυρίου ἡμῶν Ἰησοῦ Χριστοῦ after or before καὶ ἐβαπτίζοντο.

(viii.) In xix. 5 D Syr-hl[mg] read εἰς τὸ ὄνομα κυρίου Ἰησοῦ Χριστοῦ εἰς ἄφεσιν ἁμαρτιῶν.

After the gift of the Spirit was given on the Day of Pentecost, Peter explained to the crowd that the glossolalia was the fulfilment of the well-known eschatological prophecy of Joel which ends " whosoever shall call on the name of the Lord shall be saved." ' The Lord,' in the intention of Joel, is of course Jahveh, the god of Israel; but it is at least open to doubt whether Luke was not influenced by the growing custom of calling Jesus ' the Lord ' and referring to him all passages in the LXX which allude to κύριος. Moreover, in the sequel, when the audience ask Peter what they must do he says, " Repent, and be baptized each one of you in the name of Jesus Christ for the remission of your sins, and you will receive the gift of the Holy Spirit." It is possible that the reference to baptism is editorial (see Vol. I. pp. 339 ff.), but if so it is all the more important as illustrating Luke's own opinion. We are clearly confronted with an evolution of thought in which eschatological salvation, baptism ' in the name,' and the gift of the Spirit are concerned. The final step, which makes baptism effect a sacramental change of nature as in Catholic Christianity, is not taken, but it is imminent. Similarly, it is not actually stated that baptism confers the Spirit, but a close connexion between the two is implied and baptism is at least a pre-requisite.

At Philippi when the jailor came to Paul and Silas [1] to ask what he must do to be saved, they answered, " Believe on the Lord Jesus Christ and thou shalt be saved and thy house." This is the second of the requisites for salvation which Paul quotes in Rom. x. 8 ff., and it may well be that Luke also believed that both faith and calling on the Lord were necessary, but he does not mention them together. It is, however, true that the jailor and his family were baptized as soon as Paul had preached to them, so that salvation is in practice, if not verbally, equated with baptism.

Similarly in chap. xv., in Peter's speech to the Church at the Apostolic Council, it is said that " not through the Law of Moses but by the grace of the Lord Jesus shall they be saved." Here too there is no reference to baptism. It is of course possible that Luke and Paul mean that for baptism (which gives salvation) faith is a necessary preliminary. This would have been the Catholic position at a later time, but it is significant that neither Acts nor the genuine Epistles [2] ever state clearly that salvation is achieved through baptism : belief in Jesus, or calling on his Name, are the requisites.

Baptism.     Thus we come to the central problem of baptism in the Name of Jesus, as referred to in Acts. What powers or privileges did it confer ? The evidence is definite but curiously inconsistent. Belief in Jesus (or in his Name), baptism, the remission of sins, the laying on of Apostolic hands, and the reception of the Spirit seem to have formed a single complex of associated ideas, any one of which might in any single narrative be either omitted or emphasized.

Earlier evidence for Christian baptism is almost non-existent. The only reference to it in the Synoptics is at the end of the first gospel, and if these verses were written by Matthew it is evidence that at that

[1] xvi. 30 f.          [2] Contrast Titus iii. 5.

period in the early history of the Church it was already believed to be an institution which had been founded by Jesus himself. But since they are almost certainly one of the latest parts of the Gospel of Matthew, it becomes necessary to explain the silence of the gospels on the subject of this most important of the uses made of the Name of Jesus. Jesus himself, of his own power, did the other things which the disciples later did in his Name, but there is no record of his ever having baptized anyone. Why then does baptism appear so early and in so important a way? Did Jesus himself baptize his followers or others, in spite of the silence of the gospels, or must the origins of the practice be looked for not in him but in other currents in the contemporary world?

In the opening verses of Acts it is explained that the followers of Jesus did not need the water-baptism of John, but were to receive the spirit-baptism of his successor, as John himself had prophesied. After 'holy spirit' had come upon them they would receive 'power' and would then be witnesses to Jesus throughout the earth. All this Jesus is represented as telling them before the Ascension; there is no hint of baptism in his Name. Then comes Pentecost, and each is touched with a tongue of fire and receives the Holy Spirit. The Christians, at least according to Peter (ii. 33), received this spirit directly from Jesus, who in turn had it from the Father. Thus far there is complete agreement with the gospels—a continuation and fulfil-ment of their story. But immediately comes a new note. Peter had been explaining these things to an audience which had seen but not shared the events of Pentecost, and aroused by his words they ask him and the other apostles what they are to do. " Then Peter said unto them, Repent, and be baptized every one of you in the name of Jesus Christ for the remission of sins, and you shall receive the gift of the Holy Spirit. For the promise is unto you and to your children, and to all that are distant, whomsoever the Lord our God shall call."

What is the explanation of this apparent contradiction? It is so strik-ing that it seems hardly possible that even Luke could have ignored it. Probably it did not strike him as a contradiction,—which may have been because the crowd Paul was addressing was primarily non-Jewish.[1] Luke may have assumed the necessity of water-baptism only as a preliminary for Gentile converts, not for Jews such as those who shared the gift of the Spirit at Pentecost.[2] 'The promise' obviously refers to the gift of the Spirit which was to come after baptism—and baptism merely served to put the Gentiles in the same position for its reception as Jews. This view has much in its favour. Baptism of converts as a ceremonial preliminary was a Jewish custom. It had no sacramental efficacy, but neither had the baptism which Peter advocates. This, like John's baptism, was for the remission of sins. The pronouncing of the Name of Jesus may merely

---

[1] See Addit. Notes 7 and 10.

[2] There are no references to baptism in that part of Acts credited to the Jerusalem source A, but it is full of the controversy over the use of the Name of Jesus in other connexions. Those things which were direct con-tinuations of Jesus' practice, cures and exorcisms, were the source of the trouble.

indicate the sect of Judaism—for Christianity has not yet become another religion—or may be the effective magical formula.

The rest of the book to some extent supports the view that Gentiles were to be baptized with water in the Name of Jesus. In ii. 38 ff. there is the double probability that those addressed were not Jews, and that the reference to baptism is editorial (see Vol. I. pp. 239 ff. and Additional Notes 7 and 10). In chapter viii. the Samaritans and the Ethiopian eunuch [1] are baptized by Philip. In chapter x. it was to baptize Gentiles that Peter called for water, pointing out to the Jews that he could not very well avoid baptizing them (i.e. indicating ceremonially that they were proselytes), since the Holy Spirit had already been given to them as well as to the circumcised. And in chapter xix. the Ephesians were baptized by Paul.

There remains the story of Paul's baptism by Ananias. This is mentioned in two accounts of the conversion (ix. 18, xxii. 16) but not in the third. Paul of course was not a Gentile, and that he was baptized at all is part of the general difficulty of the episode of Ananias of Damascus (see Addit. Note 15).

Baptism and the Spirit.

In most of the accounts baptism and the gift of the Spirit are closely, though not necessarily causally, connected. "Then Peter said unto them, repent and be baptized every one of you in the name of Jesus Christ for the remission of sins, and ye shall receive the gift of the Holy Ghost." This is the norm from which the other accounts vary in one detail or another, but the broad lines of which they all follow. If this is editorial it is Luke's own belief and the variations are due to the stories told by his sources. But the variation is, after all, not very great. In x. 43 it is the Name, and belief in Jesus, not baptism, which give remission of sins. In the story of the conversion of the Samaritans the gift of the Spirit followed, not on baptism by Philip in the Name of the Lord Jesus, but on the laying on of the hands of Peter and John. "And when Simon saw that through the laying on of the Apostles' hands the Holy Spirit was given he offered them money." In ix. 14 f. the sequence is not clear, but Ananias lays his hands on Paul and announces that he will receive his sight and be filled with the Holy Spirit. Paul's sight returns and immediately he arises and is baptized. In x. 44 ff. the Gentiles first receive the Spirit while Peter is speaking and are then baptized, for "can any man forbid water, that these should not be baptized, which have received the Holy Spirit as well as we ? " [2]

In these stories a stage preliminary to the sacramental baptism of the Church may be discerned. Jesus had the Holy Spirit—the use of his Name enables it to be conveyed; but Acts still makes the distinction : baptism in the Name of Jesus is the preliminary to the recognition of a proselyte ; the gift of the Spirit (usually given by the laying on of hands) is a separate thing. The two, however, are so closely associated that they are often merely two parts of one ceremony.

If at the beginning of the Apostolic age Jewish converts to Christianity

[1] It is, of course, possible that he may already have been a Jewish proselyte. Cf. pp. 418 f.

[2] Cf. xi. 15 ff. and xv. 8 f.

had no water-baptism, what had been their preparation for the gift of the
Spirit ? Probably the original requirement was simply belief in Jesus :
" and by him all that believe are justified from all things, from which you
could not be justified through the law of Moses." But already with the
baptism of Paul, if he was baptized, the precedent of baptism for everyone
was being established. Insistence on baptism in the Name of Jesus as the
source of the gift of the Spirit, not the preliminary to it, completes the cycle.

Acts xix. 1-6 shows that the point of view of Luke when he wrote the
second part of Acts, or possibly of the source which he followed, was ap-
proximating more closely to that of the Catholic Church. The story tells
how Paul found in Ephesus disciples—which must mean Christians—who,
to his surprise, had not received the Holy Spirit. His question, " To
what then were you baptized ? " shows that he associated baptism and
the gift of the Spirit. The reply of the Ephesians was that they had been
baptized with John's baptism. Paul then explained that this was in-
sufficient, baptized them in the Name of the Lord Jesus, and " when
Paul laid his hands on them " they received the Holy Spirit. The story
is tantalizingly obscure. There are three factors in it : baptism in the
Name of the Lord Jesus, the laying on of the hands of an apostle, and the
gift of the Spirit. The actual form of the preceding verses giving Paul's
inquiry about the Spirit and baptism suggests the later Johannine and
Catholic view, but the reference to the laying on of apostolic hands is
reminiscent of the story of Peter and the Samaritan converts.

The ' laying on of hands ' is not only a well-known Jewish custom, The laying
but frequent in all ages and in all countries. It implies the passage of on of hands
power by the contact of one person with another. It is therefore common
as a means of healing,[1] and by a natural transition of thought passed on to
the imparting of special functions, or finally of supernatural power. Thus
it was the gesture used in blessing, and especially at the ordination of a
Rabbi (the Seminkha). It is this last which has often been regarded as an
analogue of Christian baptism and ordination. There are apparently a
few passages in Rabbinic literature which suggest that the Seminkha conferred the gift of inspiration, but, though this highly controversial question
can only be discussed properly by those who have special knowledge of
Rabbinic literature, it seems probable that the Rabbis did not claim the
gift of inspiration, and cannot have claimed to transmit it.

In the Synoptic Gospels the laying on of hands is described as a means
of healing employed by Jesus in Mark i. 40 ff., v. 23, vi. 5, viii. 22 ff.[2] and
in parallel passages, and also in the Lucan summary in Luke iv. 40. It also
appears in Mark x. 13-16 and Luke xxiv. 50 as an act of blessing.

In Acts ix. 17 Ananias cures Paul of blindness by putting his hands on
him, and in xxviii. 8 Paul heals the father of Publius by the same means.
This apostolic use of the ' laying on of hands ' as a means of healing is
reflected in the spurious conclusion of Mark (xvi. 18), where Jesus is made

[1] Its effectiveness is doubtless due to the strong suggestion of well-being
made by contact with a healthy and highly vitalized person.

[2] Mk. i. 31 may also be an example.

to promise the Eleven that " they shall lay their hands on the sick and they shall recover."

In two places in Acts the laying on of hands is the gesture of ordination to a special function—of the Seven in vi. 6 and of Paul and Barnabas in xiii. 1. The development of this custom can be seen in the Pastoral epistles (1 Tim. iv. 14 and 2 Tim. i. 6) and in the Catholic sacrament of Ordination. Cf. Heb. vi. 2.

Most important of all, in viii. 16 f. the laying on of the hands of the Apostles is regarded as the cause of the gift of the Spirit to the Samaritans, and in xix. 1 ff. is apparently the direct cause of the reception of the Spirit by the Ephesian Christians, but here it is closely related to instead of being distinguished from baptism in the Name of the Lord Jesus. The direct descendant of the practice indicated by these passages is obviously the Catholic association of Baptism and Confirmation, so closely combined yet never quite identified, and the difficulty of interpreting Acts finds its analogue in the difficulty which the Church historian finds in distinguishing between the gift of the Spirit in Baptism and in Confirmation.

The Johannine theory.

It will be seen that Acts and the Pauline Epistles both bring us to the verge, if not over the verge, of the fully developed system of practice and belief which is essential to Catholicism. This system appears in the New Testament in the Gospel of John. To discuss it in detail is outside the scope of this note, but attention may be drawn to the following points.

The Johannine theory is stated at the beginning and end of the Gospel : " But as many as received him, to them gave he power to become the sons of God, even to them that believe on his name " (i. 12). " But these are written, that ye might believe that Jesus is the Christ, the Son of God, and that believing ye might have life through his name " (xx. 31). These are the classical expressions of John's theology, in which immortality is the goal and Jesus' Name the means. Their importance cannot be over-emphasized. The Church which formulated them was no longer a body of preachers exhorting men to repent in expectation of the coming Kingdom of God, but a supernaturally endowed society which could give salvation through the power of the Name of Jesus.[1] Within this society petitions to God are answered, if made in the Name of Jesus, and the essential and sole means of entry to this society is Baptism, which conveys the Spirit and effects a miraculous change in the nature of those who undergo it.

The discovery that historical evidence is not always consistent makes the task of its analysis more difficult, but is entirely to be expected.

[1] It is interesting to note that the Gospel of John has moved away from the Markan tradition which represents Jesus as surprising everyone by working miracles by 'authority' and not by means of anyone else's 'name.' In John Jesus works miracles in 'his Father's name' (cf. John x. 25), and emphasizes that requests made in his Name will be granted both by him and his Father. Cf. God's concern for his own name, e.g. 1 Sam. x., xii. 22 ; Jeremiah xiv. 20 f. ; Ezekiel xx. 9 and 14.

Christian usage was the direct result of the currents of belief prevalent in the world in which it was born, but their assimilation and application was not a deliberate and self-conscious one. The great difficulty in approaching a problem of this kind by a study which places it in its historical perspective is that it is so easy to forget how completely this perspective was lacking in the people whose ideas are being studied. They were not aware of the causes which lay behind their beliefs or of the parallels to them which existed. They reacted to the world in which they found themselves in the idiom and with the interpretative ideas to which they were accustomed : the value of historical perspective is the recovery of a point of view which has disappeared from the world and its interpretation against the background from which it grew.

The formulae which embody the beliefs held in the early centuries of Christianity about the importance and power of the Name of Jesus are still uttered in Christian services. " Our Father which art in Heaven, hallowed be thy Name," and petitions which conclude " and this we ask in the Name of Jesus Christ our Lord " are constantly being repeated, but those who use them do so as a rule because of habit engendered by a long tradition, not because they attach to them any clear meaning or pronounce them with any passion of affirmation.[1] The theory is dead : the practice remains. It is somewhat difficult to break through the resulting casualness and to realize completely that the writer of Acts and his contemporaries in no way shared it. Theirs was a world full of spirits, both good and bad, and they were convinced of the value of using the Name of Jesus in their attempts to deal with these spirits.

[For the most useful literature on this subject see W. Heitmüller, *Taufe und Abendmahl bei Paulus*; H. Windisch, *Taufe und Sunde im ältesten Christentum*; J. V. Bartlet and K. Lake in Hastings, *Encyclopaedia of Religion and Ethics*, ii. pp. 375-390; A. Seeberg, *Der Taufe im N.T.*[3], 1913; G. Kittel, ' Die Wirkungen der christliche Wassertaufe nach den N.T.,' in *Studien und Kritiken* (1914), pp. 25 ff.; W. Heitmüller, *Im Namen Jesu*; R. Hirzel, *Der Name (Abhandlungen der sächsische Gesellschaft der Wissenschaften*, xxxvi. 2), 1918; E. C. Achelis in *Zeitschrift für*

---

[1] The fossilized expressions of that once vivid belief are found in many of the services of the church. All the ceremonies of blessing and consecrating are in general both exorcism and eisorcism—sometimes in the Name of Jesus, sometimes of the Trinity. Benediction is actually the complement of exorcism —it prevents devils entering in.

The third grade in the minor orders of the clergy, below those of acolyte and reader, gives the right to exorcise devils ceremonially. Aside from the ancient rite of exorcism in connexion with Baptism, which is still retained in the Roman ritual, a form of service for the exorcising of possessed persons may be found. The exorcist asks the devil his name, then laying his right hand on the head of the demoniac he says : "I exorcise thee, unclean spirit, in the name of Jesus Christ; tremble, O Satan, thou enemy of the faith, thou foe of mankind, who hast brought death into the world, who hast deprived men of life and hast rebelled against justice, thou seducer of mankind, thou root of evil, thou source of avarice, discord and envy."

*Pastoraltheologie* (1889), pp. 58 ff., 441 ff., 481 ff., 525 ff.; J. Behm, *Die Handauflegung im Urchristenthum*; A.J. Maclean in Hastings, *Dictionary of the Apostolic Church*, ii. pp. 115 ff.; I. Abrahams, *Studies in Pharisaism and the Gospels*, i. pp. 36 ff.; Strack-Billerbeck, *Kommentar zum N.T.* i. pp. 110 ff. and ii. pp. 647 ff.; R. Reitzenstein, *Die Vorgeschichte der christliche Taufe*, 1929 (but cf. the admirable review of H. H. Schaeder in *Gnomon*, v. pp. 353 ff.).]

### Note XII. The Communism of Acts II. and IV.-VI. and the Appointment of the Seven

#### By Kirsopp Lake

Three questions must be clearly distinguished; unfortunately only the first can be answered with any certainty :

(i.) What was the view of the editor of Acts ?

(ii.) How far was he using different sources, and what is the relation of these to the two 'summaries'?

(iii.) What were the actual facts of history ?

Ananias and the Seven.

(i.) The stories of Ananias and of the Seven are the best information as to the mind of the editor. Whatever the facts implied in the summaries in Acts ii. and iv. may really have been, he cannot have intended them to contradict his interpretation of the plain meaning of these stories. But the narrative is not written quite so well as some in Acts, and it may be doubted whether it has not suffered in transmission. Three points stand out. (*a*) That Ananias died suddenly, under circumstances which led the Church to see in his death the punishment for some offence, is almost certainly historical. (*b*) The words attributed to Peter are quite likely to be an exegesis of the events by Luke, to suit his view of the administration of the early Church. They are all the more important for the reconstruction of Luke's view. The narrative itself does not make clear what was the offence of Ananias ; but this is elucidated by the conversation between Peter and Sapphira, which is intended to explain the condensed statement ἐνοσφίσατο ἀπὸ τῆς τιμῆς, and shows that the offence was a false statement as to the amount obtained by the sale (see note on ἐνοσφίσατο in v. 2). (*c*) The Seven were appointed to administer the 'dole' given to 'widows,' because this task interfered too much with the main work of the Twelve.

The Lucan picture.

The picture of the early Church presented by Luke then becomes plain. He thought that all the Christians were living together. But this scarcely means that they were all still in the Upper Room. It is true that ἐπὶ τὸ αὐτό, in ii. 44 and 47, might be interpreted to mean actually living together ; but it is almost impossible to believe that after saying there were 3000 converts the writer can have thought that they were all in one house. The expenses of life were covered by the periodic sale of property, and by the use of all possessions to help the needy. The imperfects ἐπίπρασκον, διεμέριζον ought to be pressed. The central feature of the system implied is the creation of a fund by the periodic sale of property, which was disposed of, not all at once, but as occasion arose. The reason for describing this system as communism is because the Christians deemed all things 'common,' and did not recognize any exclusive right in private property. But in view of the recent use of the word to describe a different and wholly modern economic system, 'communism' is a doubtful phrase. Luke is not thinking of 'communism' of production, or of possession, for though no one claimed an exclusive right over his own property, it was still regarded as in some sense his own. Moreover, the fund can scarcely be called 'communistic' in the modern sense, for it was created by sales, used for the poor, and administered by the apostles. It may be added with some probability that Luke saw in this picture of life devoid of poverty the fulfilment of Deut. xv. 4 (" save when there shall be no poor among you "), which so emphatically states that there shall be no poverty among the people of God.

But after a short time the 'communistic' experiment broke down for two reasons. First, owing to dissension which arose between the Hellenists and Hebrews about the doles received by the widows in the 'daily ministration,' so that seven administrators had to be appointed to relieve the Apostles; secondly, because these administrators were killed or driven out of Jerusalem by the Jews. This much is clear, though it is far from certain what the author meant by Hellenists and Hebrews. (See also Vol. I. pp. 306 ff.) The failure of the experiment.

This question has been discussed in Additional Note 7. It is usually taken to mean Greek-speaking and Aramaic Jews. But all the linguistic evidence shows that Ἑλληνιστής merely means a Greek, and that Ἑβραῖος means a Jew, so that the writer may have meant Greeks and Jews, and thought that there were Greeks in the Church from the day of Pentecost. This is contrary to exegetical tradition, which has unanimously followed Chrysostom, who however admitted that he was doubtful, but is more in accord with the general usage of the words, and probably the intention of the writer. Hellenists and Hebrews.

The appointment of the Seven presents no such hard problem, so far as the author's meaning is concerned. He regards them as selected either by the Apostles or by the whole Church (see note on vi. 3) in order to look after the administration of the dole to the widows. It is not impossible that he had in mind the parallel appointment of the Elders to assist Moses (Exod. xviii. 13 ff.). It is also obvious that he thought that the dole had been raised by the communistic methods described in ii. 41-47 and iv. 32-35. The Seven.

(ii.) Can we discriminate the sources in the complex of narratives which begins with ii. 1 and ends with vi. 6 ? The Sources.

A. von Harnack [1] has argued that in Acts ii.-v. Luke used two forms of the tradition of Jerusalem, J[a] and J[b]. J[a] supplied iii. 1-iv. 31, and J[b] supplied ii. 1 - 41 and v. 17 - 42, each giving accounts, in slightly

---

[1] See Vol. II. pp. 126 ff. and 139 ff.

differing arrangements of order and expression, of the same series of incidents—a miraculous episode, a speech by Peter, interference by the Jewish authorities, and the outpouring of the Spirit on the disciples.

This much seems probable : is it possible to assign to either of these sources or to the editor the two summaries (ii. 41-47 and iv. 32-35), the story of Barnabas (iv. 36-37), the story of Ananias (v. 1-10), and the story of the appointment of the Seven in consequence of dissatisfaction among the recipients of charity ?

It is tempting at first sight to assign the first summary (ii. 41-47) to J[b], and the second (iv. 32-35) to J[a]. I did this in Vol. II. pp. 145 ff. But the investigation of H. J. Cadbury (see Additional Note 31) shows that Luke was in the habit either of repeating the summaries of his own composition, or of repeating, though with considerable variation, part or all of a summary which he found in one of his sources. Thus there is considerable probability that the two summaries in ii. and iv. are doublets, representing only one original document. Was this source J[a] or J[b], or was it Luke's own manufacture, and which is the more original form ? The point cannot be clearly decided. In favour of the form in ii. 43 ff. is that ἐπὶ τὸ αὐτό in vs. 47 is one of Torrey's strongest arguments for an Aramaic original (see Vol. II. pp. 55 and 143 f.). If this argument be conceded, ii. 41 ff. must come from a source, and is more original than iv. 32 ff. But the Aramaic problem is still unsolved. It must be left an open question whether the possible explanation of ἐπὶ τὸ αὐτό as an Aramaism is evidence against the editorial nature of the summary, or the editorial nature of the summary is evidence against the theory of Aramaism (see note *ad loc.*). On the other hand, the reference to fear in ii. 43 does not suit this context nearly so well as that of v. 5 and 11 where it recurs. Also, as is shown in Addit. Note 31, when a summary is used in two places there is a slight balance of probability that the second place is the original one.

However this may be, the improbability that J[a] supplied the summary in iv. 32 ff. is shown by the fact that v. 12 ff. are logically the continuation of iv. 29 - 31, and iv. 32 - v. 11 completely destroy this logical continuity. This can be seen by reading iv. 29-31 and v. 12 ff. continuously :

"'And now, Lord, look upon their threatenings : and grant unto thy servants to speak thy word with all boldness, while thou stretchest forth thy hand to heal ; and that signs and wonders may be done through the name of thy holy servant Jesus.' And when they had prayed, the place was shaken wherein they were gathered together ; and they were all filled with the Holy Ghost, and they spake the word of God with boldness. And by the hands of the apostles were many signs and wonders wrought among the people ; and they were all with one accord in Solomon's porch. But of the rest durst no man join himself to them : howbeit the people magnified them ; and believers were the more added to the Lord, multitudes both of men and women ; insomuch that they even carried out the sick into the streets, and laid them on beds and couches, that, as Peter came by, at the least his shadow might

overshadow some one of them. And there also came together the multitude from the cities round about Jerusalem, bringing sick folk, and
them that were vexed with unclean spirits : and they were healed
every one."

Thus it is probable that v. 12-16, or at least the beginning of it (see
note on p. 52), belongs to the same source as iv. 29-31, that is to J$^a$. This
view is confirmed by the fact that J$^a$ is specifically a 'Peter and John'
source, and J$^b$ is an 'Apostles' source. Consequently the intervening
sections, the story of Barnabas and of Ananias and the summary in
iv. 32 ff., do not belong to J$^a$, but to another source. Was this J$^b$, or
yet another ? (a) In favour of J$^b$ is that, as was shown above, the
reference to fear in ii. 43 is far more suitable to v. 11 (the end of the
story of Ananias). It is therefore an attractive guess that J$^b$ originally
contained the stories of Barnabas and Ananias immediately after the end
of Peter's speech, and then was concluded by the summary. Read thus
it presents not the slightest break : "And with many other words did he
testify and exhort, saying, Save yourselves from this untoward generation.
Then they that gladly received his word were baptized : and the same
day there were added unto them about three thousand souls. And they
continued steadfastly in the apostles' doctrine and fellowship, and in
breaking of bread, and in prayers. And Joses, who by the apostles was
surnamed Barnabas (which is, being interpreted, the son of consolation),
a Levite, and of the country of Cyprus, having land, sold it, and brought
the money, and laid it at the apostles' feet. But a certain man named
Ananias, with Sapphira, his wife, sold a possession, . . . and, carrying
her forth, buried her by her husband. And great fear came upon
all the church, and upon as many as heard these things. And all that
believed were together, and had all things common." (Notice that
ii. 43a is a doublet of v. 11.) In this case the summary in iv. 32 ff. is
an editorial repetition of ii. 44 ff. to lead up to what follows.

(b) The alternative is that the stories of Barnabas and Ananias were
in general circulation, together with iv. 32 ff., which is an admirable introduction to them, and were not included either in J$^a$ or J$^b$. Luke inserted
them, somewhat violently, into J$^a$, separating iv. 29-31 from its proper
conclusion, v. 12-16. A somewhat similar readjustment of material,
chiefly in order to find a place for new stories, can be seen by comparing
Mark i. 16-33 with the complex of passages, Luke iv. 16-v. 11, where
it is clear that Luke disarranged the order of Mark, and partially rewrote
its language, in order to make room for two new stories—the Sermon
at Nazareth and the Miraculous Draught of Fishes.

Between these two possibilities no decision can be made. Both explain
the facts, and each has its attractive features ; but I incline to the
second, because it is more in accordance with Luke's methods.

It is now possible to return to the summaries.

As is stated in the note on ii. 41 the summary begins, in the The
intention of the writer, with vs. 41 rather than vs. 42, though vs. 41 is Summaries.
really the legitimate end of the preceding narrative. But apart from
this it seems to be made up out of phrases recurring elsewhere. In general

the best context may be assumed to be the original. The evidence can be most clearly perceived when arranged thus [1] :

(1)     ii. 41.

οἱ μὲν οὖν ἀποδεξάμενοι τὸν λόγον αὐτοῦ ἐβαπτί-σθησαν, καὶ προσετέθησαν ἐν τῇ ἡμέρᾳ ἐκείνῃ ψυχαὶ ὡσεὶ τρισχείλιαι.

| (2)   ii. 42. | i. 14. | ii. 46 |
|---|---|---|
| ἦσαν δὲ προσκαρτεροῦντες τῇ διδαχῇ τῶν ἀποστόλων καὶ τῇ κοινωνίᾳ, τῇ κλάσει τοῦ ἄρτου καὶ ταῖς προσ-ευχαῖς· | οὗτοι πάντες ἦσαν προσ-καρτεροῦντες ὁμοθυμαδὸν τῇ προσευχῇ σὺν γυναιξὶν καὶ Μαριὰμ τῇ μητρὶ Ἰησοῦ καὶ σὺν τοῖς ἀδελφοῖς αὐτοῦ. | καθ' ἡμέραν τε προσ-καρτεροῦντες ὁμοθυμαδὸν ἐν τῷ ἱερῷ, κλῶντές τε κατ' οἶκον ἄρτον, μετε-λάμβανον τροφῆς ἐν ἀγαλ-λιάσει καὶ ἀφελότητι καρδίας. |
| (3)   ii. 43a. | v. 11. | v. 5b. |
| ἐγείνετο δὲ πάσῃ ψυχῇ φόβος. | καὶ ἐγένετο φόβος μέγας ἐφ' ὅλην τὴν ἐκκλησίαν καὶ ἐπὶ πάντας τοὺς ἀκού-οντας ταῦτα. | καὶ ἐγένετο φόβος μέγας ἐπὶ πάντας τοὺς ἀκούοντας. |
| (4)   ii. 43b. | v. 12a. | |
| πολλὰ δὲ τέρατα καὶ ση-μεῖα διὰ τῶν ἀποστόλων ἐγείνετο. | διά τε τῶν χειρῶν τῶν ἀποστόλων ἐγείνετο σημεῖα καὶ τέρατα πολλὰ ἐν τῷ λαῷ. | |
| (5)   ii. 44-45. | iv. 32, 34-35. | |
| πάντες δὲ οἱ πιστεύσαντες ἐπὶ τὸ αὐτὸ εἶχον ἅπαντα κοινά, καὶ τὰ κτήματα καὶ τὰς ὑπάρξεις ἐπίπρασκον καὶ διεμέριζον αὐτὰ πᾶσιν καθότι ἄν τις χρείαν εἶχεν· | τοῦ δὲ πλήθους τῶν πισ-τευσάντων ἦν καρδία καὶ ψυχὴ μία, καὶ οὐδὲ εἷς τι τῶν ὑπαρχόντων αὐτῷ ἔλε-γον ἴδιον εἶναι, ἀλλ' ἦν αὐτοῖς πάντα κοινά . . . οὐδὲ γὰρ ἐνδεὴς ἦν τις ἐν αὐτοῖς· ὅσοι γὰρ κτήτορες χωρίων ἢ οἰκιῶν ὑπῆρχον, πωλοῦντες ἔφερον τὰς τει-μὰς τῶν πιπρασκομένων καὶ ἐτίθουν παρὰ τοὺς πόδας τῶν ἀποστόλων· διε-δίδετο δὲ ἑκάστῳ καθότι ἄν τις χρείαν εἶχεν. | |
| (6)   ii. 46a. | v. 12b. | i. 14a. |
| καθ' ἡμέραν τε προσκαρ-τεροῦντες ὁμοθυμαδὸν ἐν τῷ ἱερῷ, | καὶ ἦσαν ὁμοθυμαδὸν πάντες ἐν τῇ Στοᾷ Σολομῶνος. | οὗτοι πάντες ἦσαν προσ-καρτεροῦντες ὁμοθυμαδὸν τῇ προσευχῇ. |

[1] It has seemed best to print here as well as in Addit. Note 31 this tabular arrangement of the text, as the arguments can scarcely be followed in either place without it.

(7)    ii. 46b.

κλῶντές τε κατ' οἶκον
ἄρτον, μετελάμβανον τρο-
φῆς ἐν ἀγαλλιάσει καὶ
ἀφελότητι καρδίας,

ii. 42.

ἦσαν δὲ προσκαρτεροῦντες
τῇ διδαχῇ τῶν ἀποστόλων
καὶ τῇ κοινωνίᾳ, τῇ κλάσει
τοῦ ἄρτου καὶ ταῖς προσ-
ευχαῖς.

(8)    ii. 47a.

αἰνοῦντες τὸν θεὸν καὶ
ἔχοντες χάριν πρὸς ὅλον
τὸν λαόν.

iv. 33b.

χάρις τε μεγάλη ἦν ἐπὶ
πάντας αὐτούς.

v. 13b.

ἀλλ' ἐμεγάλυνεν αὐτοὺς ὁ
λαός.

(9)    ii. 47b.

ὁ δὲ κύριος προσετίθει
τοὺς σωζομένους καθ'
ἡμέραν ἐπὶ τὸ αὐτό.

v. 14.

μᾶλλον δὲ προσετίθεντο
πιστεύοντες τῷ κυρίῳ
πλήθη ἀνδρῶν τε καὶ γυ-
ναικῶν.

In these passages the repeated and cumulative similarity certainly
indicates community of origin ; but in no case does probability suggest
that the context in ii. 42 ff. is preferable to that of the parallels, and in
(3), (4), and (5) it indicates that the parallels give the better sense.
There is thus considerable reason for thinking that iv. 32 ff. was originally
the appropriate introduction to the stories of Barnabas and Ananias.    It
had been used previously by Luke in ii. 42 ff. in combination with
fragments from other sources.    One of these other sources is the end of the
story of Ananias, v. 11, which supplied the 'fear' passage.    Another was
possibly Jᵃ, which may have contained v. 12.

Therefore ii. 42 ff. is almost certainly editorial and borrowed from
the source (Jᵇ or another) which provided iv. 32.ff. ; iv. 32 ff. and
v. 12 ff. may be derived from sources.

Thus the final—though quite tentative—conclusions to the small but Conclusions.
complicated problem of analysing the 'narrative' and 'summary' material
in this section are probably these :

(a) ii. 1-40, narrative, from Jᵇ.

(b) ii. 41-47, summary, an editorial duplication of iv. 32-35, but
possibly nearer the original form of the text.

(c) iii. 1-iv. 31, narrative, from Jᵃ.

(d) iv. 32-35, summary, possibly from Jᵇ but more probably from
the original introduction to the stories of Barnabas and
Ananias, and almost certainly considerably revised by the
editor of Acts.

(e) iv. 36-v. 11, narrative, the stories of Barnabas and of Ananias,
possibly from Jᵇ but more probably a separate tradition.

(f) v. 12-16, summary, possibly composed by the editor, but it
probably contains the end of the Jᵃ source.

(g) v. 17-41, narrative, the end of the Jᵇ source.

The remaining section which has to be discussed in this note is vi. vi. 1-6.
1-6.    It is necessarily connected—at least for a commentator—with the
preceding narratives by the reference to the daily administration of alms,

and it is impossible that this connexion was not also made by the editor of Acts, to whom the appointment of the Seven is not only the beginning of the persecution of Stephen with its far-reaching consequences, but also is the end of the communistic experiment described in the earlier chapters. But here the connexion ends. Few points in the *Quellen-kritik* of Acts are so generally recognized to be certain as that with chapter vi. Luke begins to use a new source, or more probably complex of sources, which can only very doubtfully be identified with any of those used in the earlier chapters. The exact analysis of Acts vi.-xv. is doubtless impossible, though some tentative suggestions may be advanced.[1] For the present purpose the important point is that vi. 1-6 is differentiated from the ' communistic ' account of J[b] in two ways. (*a*) Instead of the picture of peace and contentment offered by the summaries in chapters ii. and iv., in which everyone is contented with a distribution ' according to his needs,' there is a less pleasant if more probable picture of dissatisfaction among the poor and inability to stand the pressure of the situation among the apostles. (*b*) The Christians are called μαθηταί (see note on vi. 1 and Addit. Note 30)—a designation which though common in the rest of Acts is not found in i.-v. or in the Pauline Epistles.

Nevertheless, though clearly there is as good a case for distinguishing the source of this section from J[a] or J[b] as there is for separating these two from each other, Luke's opinion is clear—he wishes it to be understood that the ' communist ' experiment broke down owing to the increase of members in the Church. The Seven were specially appointed by the church as administrative officers. Persecution drove them out, and this paved the way for a description of the ἀριστεία of Stephen and Philip.

How far is it probable that vi. 1 ff. should be classed with the ' summaries ' rather than with the continuous narrative ? The possibility cannot be excluded, and obviously vi. 1 may be an editorial addition intended, as the summaries generally are, to connect what has gone before with what is to come.

Harnack thinks that it may belong to the Antiochian source (A) which was certainly used in chapter xi. and elsewhere. But the whole background of the story of Stephen is in Jerusalem. There are, in fact, three tenable views about the whole story :

(*a*) It is taken from the Antiochian source and preserves the tradition of his followers who fled to that city.

(*b*) It is a genuine piece of the reminiscences of the church in Jerusalem, though not part of J[a] or J[b].

(*c*) It is Luke's compressed edition of pieces of tradition from more than one source, not perhaps always quite consistent with each other (see Vol. II. pp. 148 ff. and the note on vii. 57, and for the speech in chap. vii. see Addit. Note 32).

On the whole the third of these possibilities seems to me somewhat the most probable, but no certain judgement can be made.

[1] See Vol. II. pp. 147 ff., the notes in the commentary on vi. 1-xv. 35 (p. 63), vii. 2-53, vii. 57, xi. 19 ff., and Addit. Note 16.

(iii.) What were the actual facts? In other words, how far can we trust Luke to have interpreted correctly the facts described in his sources, and how far is it likely that he modified their statements in accordance with his own opinion? The answer to this question depends mainly on our general judgement on Luke's methods and reliability. Opinions range from Ramsay, who in his later writings scarcely admits the possibility of error in Acts on any point, to Loisy who scarcely accepts anything in the earlier chapters as correct or even as the writing of the original author. Any discussion is obviously very subjective and largely depends on the cumulative effect of details which cannot be repeated in writing but which are always present in thought.

My own personal opinion is that Luke always produces an intelligible story, which is very rarely open to decisive criticism, but that this superficial intelligibility breaks down rather badly when we are able to compare Luke's narrative with other contemporary documents, such as Mark and the Pauline Epistles. Moreover, the points where it breaks down are often such that without the parallel documents no one would have the faintest suspicion that the narrative is not impeccable.

For these reasons I feel doubtful about the complete accuracy of Luke's account of the communistic experiment and the appointment of the Seven, but even more doubtful whether it is possible to go behind his narrative and reconstruct a more accurate picture of what really happened. All that can be done is to indicate points which may modify the general view which we derive from Acts or throw light on special details in the narrative.

Two opposite possibilities have often been suggested. Neither can be demonstrated: neither can be disproved.

(a) In favour of the 'communistic' view of the summaries repre- senting all things as held in common, so that no one was in want, it may be argued that this would be the logical result of the teaching of Jesus.[1] Certainly he enjoined on the rich that they should sell their property and give it to the poor, and offered rewards in the future to those who sacrificed riches for his sake. He had undoubtedly blessed the poor, and there is no similar beatitude extant on those who have wealth. He did not say that the door of the Kingdom would be closed to the rich, but the opportunity afforded to them was compared to a camel trying to go through the eye of a needle.

It might well be argued that such teaching would naturally produce the 'communism' of Acts, which represents not so much an economic theory as a 'horror of wealth'—Tertullian's *fastidium opulentiae*. But the weak spot in such an argument is that in point of fact this 'communism' does not reappear in Acts, and is not mentioned in the Pauline Epistles. It may have been tried for a few months, but if so it died an early death.

---

[1] In addition to the usual commentaries, or even to such books as Troeltsch's *Soziallehren der christl. Kirchen*, it is well to read R. v. Pöhlmann, *Geschichte der sozialen Frage in der antiken Welt*, vol. ii. (2nd ed.) pp. 587 ff.

Organized
charity.
(*b*) On the other hand it may be argued that nothing really existed in Jerusalem except an organized charity which was quite consistent with Jewish practice.

The picture of communism is only found in one of Luke's sources. It is not mentioned or implied in the Antiochian source, or in J[a]; it may belong to J[b], but more probably was found by Luke in the introduction to the stories of Barnabas and Ananias. Is it more than an idyllic generalization from these two stories?

Professor Cadbury's note on the Summaries (Addit. Note 31) suggests that they are often generalizations from special cases. Taken by itself the story of Barnabas and his gift is typical of the good man who honestly contributed to the charitable funds of the church, and Ananias is typical of the bad man who did so dishonestly. Both types are common in all periods; rich men constantly contribute to charity, and their motives are not always single. The question is whether the summary is correct in saying, or at least implying, that all rich men in the Christian community sold their property and gave it to the apostles.

The reason for doubting its accuracy is the very significant passage in Peter's speech to Ananias. "While it (the property) remained did it not remain yours? And when it was sold, was it not in your power?" This must mean that the offence was his dishonest pretence, not his failure to sell property for the good of the poor. But this is not the communistic picture suggested by the summary, and we have reasonable ground for saying that though Luke thought that the practice of the church was communism, his source originally implied only wide and generous charity, so organized that the apostles were its immediate recipients and its distributors to the poor.

The
*Kuppah.*
Moreover this system of organized charity is almost the same as that which prevailed in Judaism in the second century and probably in the first.[1] According to the Rabbinic accounts Jewish practice discouraged charity given directly to needy persons, but in each municipality there were two collectors who every Friday went around to the market and to private houses to collect contributions either in money or in kind. On Fridays there was also a distribution to those in want, in accordance with their needs,[2] by a committee of two or more. The poor who actually belonged to the town were given a weekly dole sufficient for fourteen meals. The fund from which this dole was made was called the *Kuppah* (קופה) or 'basket.' No one could claim support from it who had a week's food in his house.

The *Tamḥui.*
Besides the *Kuppah* there was also another collection of food called the *Tamḥui* (תמחוי) or 'tray.' This was made daily, instead of weekly,

---

[1] There is no direct evidence for the first century; but that is because the Talmud is the only document we have which deals with the subject. The evidence is all collected by Strack, vol. ii. pp. 641-647, and by G. F. Moore, *Judaism*, ii. pp. 162-179, especially pp. 176 ff.

[2] Needs appear to have been liberally interpreted, and a man of good position who had fallen on evil days was helped with due regard to his former state (see Strack *l.c.*).

from house to house, for those who were in actual need of food for the coming day.[1]

It is obvious that these facts throw a flood of light on the 'daily ministration' of Acts vi. 1, and the natural explanation of the story is that the Christians formed a separate community in so far as they collected and distributed a 'basket' and a 'tray' independently of the rest of the Jewish population.

Apparently it is not known whether the distribution of charity in Jerusalem was carried out by the synagogues in the various wards of the city, by the Temple authorities, or by both. The last view would seem the most probable, but of course our information is derived from sources which are later than the destruction of the Temple, and, though they probably represent in general a system which was in use far earlier, the exact relation between Temple and synagogue authorities is just one of the points where we do well not to be too certain. If, however, we may make the double assumption—both parts of which are extremely probable—that at least some charity was managed by the synagogues, and that the Christians regarded themselves as and were organized as a 'synagogue of the Nazarenes' (see note on v. 11), it is clear that the organized charity implied in Acts vi. is exactly similar to that described in Rabbinical writings. The stories of Barnabas and Ananias are merely a presentation of extreme cases.

The collection and distribution of the Christian 'basket' and 'tray' were at first managed by the apostles, but the work became too much for them.[2] They then appointed the Seven to take over their work. The number seven has many associations in Jewish thought, but far the most probable in this case is supported by the fact that Jerusalem was divided into seven wards.

Further than this it is hard to go. The questions are inevitably raised, The Seven. Who were the Seven, personally and apart from their administrative functions, and why were they chosen? Unfortunately neither question can be answered, and it is only possible to indicate certain lines of thought along which critics have worked.

It has been shown on pp. 37 ff. that though the Twelve were probably a group of distinction and influence, the apostles—a wider circle —were the leading factor in the life of the church. Barnabas, for instance, was an apostle, but not one of the Twelve. It is therefore possible that the Seven were themselves apostles before they were appointed as 'Charity Commissioners.' The implication of Luke's words is much rather that the Seven were not apostles, but it cannot be doubted that he —as distinct from his sources—was inclined to identify the Twelve with the apostles, as the later church did. The question thus remains open,

---

[1] Is there a reference to this in the obscure ἐπιούσιον ἄρτον in the Lord's Prayer? Does it mean 'keep us from the necessity of accepting the charity of the tray'? Or is it a prayer for the continuance of the 'tray' as Mark vi. 8 μὴ ἄρτον rather suggests?

[2] Moore quotes an interesting parallel: Rabbi Jose ben Halafta prayed that his lot might be among the collectors rather than the distributors.

though it must be admitted that the problem of the two Philips—the Apostle and the Evangelist—would be greatly simplified if they were really one person.

It is in any case clear that the Seven—or at least Stephen and Philip—did not owe the whole of their importance in the church to their position as charity commissioners. It has often been pointed out that they never appear again in the exercise of their administrative functions, but as preachers, controversialists, and missionaries. What, then, is the exact meaning of their ordination by the Apostles?

*Their ordination.* Ordination by the laying on of hands is a Jewish practice (see p. 137), and is one of the many examples in which this method was used to pass on from one person to another some power or responsibility or function. The meaning of Acts is that the apostles 'ordained' the Seven to administer charity. It does not necessarily mean more.

*The Seven as Hellenists.* Nevertheless, a long line of critics, of whom Harnack is the most famous representative, have been struck by the fact that the Seven all have Greek names, and were appointed to satisfy the grumbling of the 'Hellenists' (whatever that means) against the Hebrews. It has therefore been suggested that the Seven were really the leaders of the 'Hellenistic' Christians, and the Twelve of the Jewish Christians. The Lucan story of the Seventy[1] is, on this theory, perhaps another form of this tradition, intended to give the Hellenistic leaders the same sanction of appointment by Jesus as was enjoyed by the Twelve. This theory which, for lack of evidence, can neither be confirmed nor confuted, suggests two opposite considerations:

(a) There is nothing improbable in the theory that Luke exaggerated the degree to which all Christian missionaries were subject to the Twelve. This exaggeration can be seen in his treatment of Paul, for, though the details may be uncertain, it is hard to doubt that the picture in Acts represents him as more complacent towards the authority of the apostles than is consistent with the epistles. Moreover in the *Epistola Apostolorum* we can see the growth of this desire to paint in vivid colours the importance of the Twelve. A curve of increasing emphasis can be traced from the Pauline Epistles, the earliest documents, where it is at the lowest point, through the position of Acts, to that of the *Epistola*, where it reaches its maximum.

(b) On the other hand there is historically nothing in favour of the view that the Twelve represent the Hebrews. They may represent a mission to the Jews of the Diaspora; but so far as the facts go—and it is not far—everything indicates that the Twelve, the Seven, Barnabas and Paul, were all equally missionaries to the world outside Judaea. None of them was the leader of the 'Hebrews in Jerusalem.' That was the position of James. Parity of reasoning suggests that just as Luke and later writers exalt the Twelve, and bring Paul into subjection to them, they may have minimized the importance of James. The exception to this rule, representing indeed the opposite tendency to exalt James, is found in the *Clementine Homilies* and *Recognitions.*

[1] Luke x. 1. Perhaps 'Seventy-two' is the correct number.

Further than this—and it is perhaps already too far—it seems impossible to analyse and undesirable to speculate as to the organization of charity in the Apostolic church in Jerusalem and the appointment of the Seven. The way in which the tradition of the later church connected the Diaconate with the Seven is outside the purpose of this note.

## NOTE XIII. SIMON MAGUS

### By ROBERT P. CASEY

In Christian tradition Simon Magus has enjoyed the reputation of being the first heretic, and historians must regard him as at least the first well-known and widely successful teacher of an exotic form of Christian thought. Accounts of his life and teachings are found in the canonical Acts of the Apostles, in most of the heresiologists, and in a long series of apocryphal acts and romances beginning with the Acts of Paul and extending through the Middle Ages.[1]

Of his early career we have only the account in Acts viii. 9 ff.[2] that he was a magician in Samaria, where his sensational feats attracted many followers who acknowledged him to be ' the power of God which is called great,' ἡ δύναμις τοῦ θεοῦ ἡ καλουμένη μεγάλη. The preaching of Philip in these regions drew away many of his adherents, and he ultimately followed them and was baptized. Later, when Peter came up from Jerusalem, introducing the gift of the Spirit by the laying on of hands,[3] Simon's professional instinct appears to have been reawakened. The remarkable cures and exorcisms of Philip and the gift of the Spirit by Peter's laying on of hands must have appeared to him as a new magic art, and he suggested that he might pay to acquire it. The offer was rejected by Peter with a

*Simon in Acts.*

---

[1] Acts viii. 9 ff.; Justin, *Apol.* i. 26, 56; *Dial. c. Tryph.* 120; Irenaeus, *Adv. haer.* i. 16 (H.), i. 20 (G.); Tertullian, *De anima*, 34, *Adv. omn. haer.* 1; Clemens Alex. *Strom.* ii. 52. 2, vii. 107. 1 (Stählin iii. p. 75, Sylburg p. 325); Hippolytus, *Ref.* vi. 7. 20, x. 12; Philastrius, *Div. haer. liber*, 29; Epiphanius, *Panarion*, *haer.* 21; Theodoret, *Haer. fabl.* i. 1; Ps.-Augustine, *De haeresibus*, 1; Cyril of Jerusalem, *Catechesis*, vi. 13 (*P.G.* xxxiii. 561); *Acta Pauli* 7 (Schmidt, pp. 73-75); *Acta Petri cum Simone*, 4 ff. (and allied documents, cf. M. R. James, *The Apocryphal New Testament*, Oxford, 1924, pp. 471-472); *Epistola Apostolorum*, 1 (Schmidt, pp. 25, 33); *Clementine Recognitions* and *Homilies, passim*; *Apost. Const.* vi. 8-9. On Oriental sources cf. F. Haase, *Altchristliche Kirchengeschichte nach orientalischen Quellen*, Leipzig, 1925, pp. 322-327; *Apostel und Evangelisten in den orientalischen Überlieferungen*, Münster, 1922, *passim*. After a varied career in medieval romantic literature Simon emerges in the figure of Goethe's Faust.

[2] On the possible identity of Simon Magus with another magician of the same name mentioned by Josephus, *Antiq.* xx. 7. 2, cf. H. Waitz, 'Simon Magus in der altchristlichen Literatur,' *Zeitschrift für neutestamentliche Wissenschaft*, v. (1904) pp. 127 ff.

[3] Vol. I. pp. 337 ff.

sharp rebuke, and Simon, apparently taking his rebuff in good part, begged Peter to pray that he might not be punished for his presumption. Of his later history we have no details, but it is evident from the existence and character of the Simonian sect known in the second century that he later set up a religion of his own, in which he borrowed some elements from Christianity.

Simon the Samaritan.

The supposition that Simon was a member of the Samaritan sect has no support in Acts and has been largely read into the later evidence.[1] Justin, whose home was in Neapolis [2] and whose testimony is therefore of great value, calls Simon a Σαμαρεύς, but uses the word in a strictly geographical sense to signify the inhabitants of the district of Samaria.[3] The account of Simon's early history in the Clementines clearly does not imply it.[4] Simon operated either in Sebaste, the capital of Samaria, a Hellenistic town of mixed culture which was never a centre of the Samaritan religion, or an unnamed city in the province.[5] Nothing in the Simonians' theology suggests a connexion with the worship at Gerizim, while their secret cultus before pagan statues,[6] their depreciation of the Law, and their antinomian ethics all point in an opposite direction.

[1] Vol. II. p. 58.

[2] *Apol.* i. 1. Neapolis is the ancient Shechem, the modern Nablus, which has always been the home of the Samaritan sect.

[3] καὶ σχεδὸν πάντες μὲν Σαμαρεῖς, ὀλίγοι δὲ καὶ ἐν ἄλλοις ἔθνεσιν, ὡς τὸν πρῶτον θεὸν ἐκεῖνον ὁμολογοῦντες, ἐκεῖνον καὶ προσκυνοῦσι, *Apol.* i. 26; Σίμωνα μὲν καὶ Μένανδρον ἀπὸ Σαμαρείας, *idem* 56; οὐδὲ γὰρ ἀπὸ τοῦ γένους τοῦ ἐμοῦ, λέγω δὲ τῶν Σαμαρέων, τινὸς φροντίδα ποιούμενος, ἐγγράφως Καίσαρι προσομιλῶν, εἶπον πλανᾶσθαι αὐτοὺς πειθομένους τῷ ἐν τῷ γένει αὐτῶν μάγῳ Σίμωνι, ὃν θεὸν ὑπεράνω πάσης ἀρχῆς καὶ ἐξουσίας καὶ δυνάμεως εἶναι λέγουσι, *Dial. cum Tryph.* 120, cf. *Apol.* ii. 15. It is clear that in these passages the Σαμαρεῖς are, like Justin, inhabitants of the district of Samaria and not Samaritans in a sectarian sense as in *Apol.* i. 53.

[4] *Hom.* ii. 19 ff., *Rec.* ii. 7 ff., where he is described as Σαμαρεὺς τὸ ἔθνος, *gente Samareus*, with a pagan education, οὗτος ἐν᾽ Ἀλεξανδρείᾳ τῇ πρὸς Αἴγυπτον γεγονώς, ἑλληνικῇ παιδείᾳ πάνυ ἐξασκήσας ἑαυτόν, καὶ μαγείᾳ πολὺ δυνηθείς, *ante magus, Graecis tamen literis liberalibus adprime eruditus.*

[5] See note on Acts viii. 5.

[6] At the time of Antiochus Epiphanes, the temple on Gerizim, like that at Jerusalem, was desecrated by association with the worship of Zeus (2 Macc. vi. 1, cf. the spurious correspondence in Josephus, *Antiq.* xii. 257 ff.; Niese iii. pp. 116-117), but a real syncretism appears to have been effected as little in one place as the other (cf. M. Gaster, *The Samaritans : their History, Doctrines, and Literature*, Schweich Lectures (1923), London (1925), pp. 35, 40 ff.). The statement of the philosopher Marinus quoted by Photius, *Bibl.* 345 b 18 (*P.G.* 103, 1284)—ὅτι ὁ διάδοχος Πρόκλου, φησίν, ὁ Μαρῖνος, γένος ἦν ἀπὸ τῆς ἐν Παλαιστίνῃ Νέας πόλεως, πρὸς ὄρει κατῳκισμένης τῷ ᾽Αργαρίζῳ καλουμένῳ. εἶτα βλασφημῶν ὁ δυσσεβής, φησιν ὁ συγγραφεύς, ἐν ᾧ Διὸς ὑψίστου ἁγιώτατον ἱερόν, ᾧ καθιέρωτο ῞Αβραμος ὁ τῶν πάλαι ῾Εβραίων πρόγονος, ὡς αὐτὸς ἔλεγεν ὁ Μαρῖνος. Σαμαρείτης οὖν τὸ ἀπ᾽ ἀρχῆς ὁ Μαρῖνος γεγονώς, ἀπετάξατο μὲν πρὸς τὴν ἐκείνων δόξαν, ἅτε εἰς καινοτομίαν ἀπὸ τῆς ᾽Αβράμου θρησκείας ἀπορρυεῖσαν, τὰ δὲ ῾Ελλήνων ἠγάπησεν— is probably no more than the affectation of a recent convert to Hellenism in

The title by which Simon was known in Samaria is a curious one, and The 'Great Power.' Acts gives no clue to its original meaning. Various possibilities of confusion in the text have been suggested. Klostermann [1] supposed that μεγάλη was a transliteration of מגלא or מגלי‎, participial forms of the verb ' to lay open ' or ' reveal,' and that Simon was originally known as ' the Power of God which is called the Revealer,' but it does not seem likely that the author of Acts would have left so misleading a transliteration unexplained. Torrey,[2] on the assumption that Acts viii. is based on an Aramaic source, translates viii. 10 b into Aramaic דין חילה די אלהא די מתקרא רב and maintains that the adjective רב, ' great,' which may be taken grammatically either with אלהא, ' God,' or חילה, ' power,' was intended by the Aramaic author to go with the former but was misunderstood by his translator to modify חילה. The correct rendering, on this hypothesis, would have been ἡ δύναμις τοῦ θεοῦ τοῦ καλουμένου μεγάλου. It is always assumed that the god whose ' power '[3] Simon was held to be was Jehovah, but it is evident both from later Simonian theology and from the fact that Simon

---

calling his native deity by a Greek name. Cumont's statement (' Hypsistos,' Pauly-Wissowa's *Realencyklopädie der classischen Altertumswissenschaft*), " In Samaria soll ein Tempel zu Zeus H. (Διὸς ὑψίστου ἁγιώτατον ἱερόν) von Abraham gegründet worden sein (Marin. Vit. Isid. bei Phot. *Bibl.* 345 b 18. Die Überlieferung geht auf Alexander Polyhistor zurück, vgl. Euseb. *Praep. Ev.* ix. 17. 4; Movers *Phönizier*, i. 557; Dussaud, *Notes de myth. syrienne*, 5)" goes too far, for Alexander Polyhistor, who at this point is apparently drawing on an anonymous Samaritan historian (cf. Freudenthal, *Hellenistische Studien* i.-ii., Breslau, 1875, pp. 82 ff.) says : πρεσβέων δὲ παραγενομένων πρὸς αὐτὸν ὅπως χρήματα λαβὼν ἀπολυτρώσῃ ταῦτα, μὴ προελέσθαι τοῖς δυστυχοῦσιν ἐπεμβαίνειν, ἀλλὰ τὰς τροφὰς λαβόντα τῶν νεανίσκων ἀποδοῦναι τὰ αἰχμάλωτα, ξενισθῆναί τε αὐτὸν ὑπὸ πόλεως ἱερὸν Ἀργαριζίν, ὃ εἶναι μεερμηνευόμενον ὄρος ὑψίστου, παρὰ δὲ τοῦ Μελχισεδὲκ ἱερέως ὄντος τοῦ θεοῦ καὶ βασιλεύοντος λαβεῖν δῶρα. Eusebius, *Praep. Ev.* ix. 17, p. 419 a. ὃ εἶναι μεθερμηνευόμενον ὄρος ὑψίστου is obviously wrong and may be a gloss (cf., however, Freudenthal, *op. cit.* p. 89 n.), but there can be no doubt that ὕψιστος is merely a conventional description of Jehovah. Cf. p. 446.

[1] A. Klostermann, *Probleme im Aposteltexte*, Gotha, 1883, p. 18.

[2] 'The Composition and Date of Acts' (*Harvard Theological Studies*, i., Cambridge, 1916), pp. 18-20. Cf. Vol. II. pp. 147-148.

[3] It is characteristic of the two religions that Christianity claimed Jesus to be the λόγος τοῦ θεοῦ and Simonianism conceived Simon as the δύναμις τοῦ θεοῦ. On the theological conception of δύναμις in and about this period cf. the charm published from an Egyptian papyrus of the fourth century by Wessely, *Griechische Zauberpapyrus von Paris und London* (*Denkschrift der Akademie der Wissenschaften zu Wien*, Phil.-hist. Classe, 36, 1888), pp. 76-77, ll. 1275 ff.: ἀρκτικὴ πάντα ποιοῦσα · λόγος· ἐπικαλοῦμαί σε τὴν μεγίστην δύναμιν τὴν ἐν τῷ οὐρανῷ (ἄλλοι· τὴν ἐν τῇ ἄρκτῳ) ὑπὸ κυρίου θεοῦ τεταγμένην ἐπὶ τῷ στρέφειν κραταιᾷ χειρὶ τὸν ἱερὸν πόλον, νικαροπλῆξ ἐπάκουσόν μοι, Ἥλιε Φρη, τὸν ἱερόν, ὁ τὰ ὅλα συνέχων καὶ ζωογονῶν τὸν σύμπαντα κόσμον ; A. Deissmann, *Bible Studies*, 2nd edition, London, 1903, p. 336; and the valuable collection of material by A. D. Nock, ' Studies in the Graeco-Roman Beliefs of the Empire,' *Journal of Hellenic Studies*, xlv. (1925) pp. 84 ff.

was worshipped before statues of Zeus that the Simonian conception of God was a mixture of Zeus and Jehovah.[1]

**Justin.**

The first to add new material to the story in Acts is Justin Martyr (1 *Apol.* 26, 56, *Dial. cum Tryphone* 120), who describes Simon as a magician, a native of Gitta in Samaria, who came to Rome in the reign of Claudius. He was accompanied by a Phoenician woman named Helen, who had abandoned the career of a professional prostitute to live with him, and his followers, who comprised most of his fellow-countrymen and some others, worshipped him as the supreme God and regarded Helen as the ' primary notion' emanating from him.   At Rome a statue was erected in his honour on the Tiber between two bridges and bore the inscription, SIMONI DEO SANCTO.   Justin adds that another Samarian magician, Menander of Capparetia, became Simon's disciple and by his magic deceived many at Antioch, persuading them that by following him they would gain immortality.

Justin's account is brief but clear.   He does not refer to the story in Acts, and all his information appears to have been derived from other sources.   The birthplace of Simon, the account of Helen and the place she occupied in his theology, his presence in Rome under Claudius, his disciple Menander : all this is fresh material and is not even suggested by Acts.   Justin himself was a native of Neapolis and had visited Rome.

**The alleged statue of Simon.**

His account of the statue is probably inexact, for a monument with the inscription SEMONI SANCO DEO FIDIO SACRUM SEX(TUS) POMPEIUS SP(URII) F(ILIUS) COL(LINA TRIBU) MUSSIANUS QUINQUENNALIS DECUR(IAE) BIDEN-TALIS DONUM DEDIT [2] was unearthed in the sixteenth century.   This is generally held to be that to which Justin referred.   Semo was an ancient Italian deity often identified with Jupiter and Ζεὺς ὅρκιος or πίστιος.[3] Besnier and others assert that the connexion with Simon is simply a mis-understanding of Justin's.   That the statue had originally no connexion with Simon is evident, but it is not impossible that Simonians at Rome used it for their own worship.   The cultus of Simon was regularly performed before statues of Zeus, and the similarity of the names Semoni and Simoni may have proved an added attraction to such persistent allegorizers.   The fact that the monument was used by others for a different worship need also have been no hindrance in so cosmopolitan an age.   Examples of temples and images used by different sects for their own religion are attested in the *De dea Syra* [4] and were probably not uncommon.

Furthermore a simple misunderstanding of the inscription does not

---

[1] For similar combinations cf. E. Schürer, ' Die Juden im bosporanischen Reiche und die Genossenschaft der σεβόμενοι θεὸν ὕψιστον,' *SBA.*, 1897, i. pp. 200 ff. ; F. Cumont, ' Hypsistos,' in Pauly-Wissowa.   See also pp. 88 ff.

[2] *C.I.L.* vi. 567, now at the Vatican.   Cf. M. Besnier, ' L'île tibérine dans l'antiquité ' (*Bibliothèque des Écoles Françaises d'Athènes et de Rome*, 87), Paris, 1902, p. 273.

[3] G. Wissowa, *Religion und Kultus der Römer*, 2. Aufl., München, 1912, pp. 130 ff. ; Besnier, *op. cit.* pp. 286 ff.   Besnier gives reasons why the identification of Semo and Jupiter is particularly likely at this sanctuary.

[4] Ps.-Lucian, *De dea Syra*, 11 ff.

dispose of the statement that Simon was in Rome under Claudius. This information may be wrong ; but it should not be discounted merely because it is associated with the reference to the statue. It is inherently no more improbable that Simon made a journey to Rome than that Justin or Peter did. It seems extremely unlikely, however, that Justin, who knew of Simon's activities in Samaria, would have invented his presence in Rome and confirmed it with an imaginary date simply from having misread *Semoni Sanco Deo*. The existence of Simonians in Rome at the time of Hippolytus is tolerably certain, and it is not unlikely that they were the descendants of Simon's personal followers there.[1]

The historic character of Helen has also been questioned. Waitz supposed her to be the Phoenician moon-goddess with whose worship Simonianism became entangled at the close of the first century. " Werden wir nämlich mit der Helenageschichte von Samarien auf einmal nach Tyrus versetzt, so können wir uns diese Entwickelung nicht anders vorstellen, als dass sich die samaritanische Verehrung Simons als des obersten Gottes mit der phönizischen, speziell tyrischen Verehrung des Sonnengottes (Sem, Schemesch, Herakles, Melkart, Baal) und der Mondgöttin (Helena, Selene, Luna, Astarte) verbunden hat."[2] Of such a development of Simonianism, however, Justin is entirely ignorant, and none of the fragments or accounts of Simonian sources suggest it. Only the Clementines, in a curious passage on the origins of a sect supposed to have been founded by John the Baptist, could be offered as evidence in this connexion : Ἰωάννης τις ἐγένετο ἡμερο-βαπτιστής, ὃς καὶ τοῦ κυρίου ἡμῶν Ἰησοῦ κατὰ τὸν τῆς συζυγίας λόγον ἐγένετο πρόοδος. καὶ ὥσπερ τῷ κυρίῳ γεγόνασιν δώδεκα ἀπόστολοι, τῶν τοῦ ἡλίου δώδεκα μηνῶν φέροντες τὸν ἀριθμόν, ὡσαύτως καὶ αὐτῷ ἔξαρχοι ἄνδρες γεγόνασιν τριάκοντα, τὸν μηναῖον τῆς σελήνης ἀποπλη-ροῦντες λόγον. ἐν ᾧ ἀριθμῷ μία τις ἦν γυνή, λεγομένη Ἑλένη, ἵνα μηδὲ τοῦτο ἀνοικονόμητον ᾖ. ἥμισυ γὰρ ἀνδρὸς οὖσα γυνή, ἀτελῆ τὸν τῆς τρια-κοντάδος τέθεικεν ἀριθμόν, ὥσπερ καὶ τῆς σελήνης, ἧς ἡ πορεία τοῦ μηνὸς οὐ τέλειον ποιεῖται τὸν δρόμον. τούτων δὲ τῶν τριάκοντα, τῷ Ἰωάννῃ πρῶτος καὶ δοκιμώτατος ἦν ὁ Σίμων· ὃς καὶ τοῦ μὴ ἄρξαι αὐτὸν μετὰ τὴν τελευτὴν τοῦ Ἰωάννου, αἰτίαν ἔσχεν ταύτην, *Hom.* ii. 23 ; cf. *Rec.* ii. 8. This account is suspicious from every point of view ; but the astrological theory contained in it is evidently its own and not a Simonian feature. The Simonians themselves identified Helen with Athena,[3] and for an obvious reason. Just as the Homeric Helen assisted in the explanation of this Phoenician's too romantic career, so the story of Athena's birth from the head of Zeus could be used as an allegory for the emergence of Helen as the primeval notion from the divine mind of Simon.[4]

*Helen as moon-goddess.*

---

[1] *Ref.* vi. 19. 7. The passage appears to indicate that Hippolytus was acquainted with Simonians. It is no more than a natural assumption that they were at Rome.

[2] Waitz, *op. cit.* p. 134.

[3] Iren. i. 16. 3 (H.) ; Hippolytus, *Ref.* vi. 20 ; Epiphanius, *Haer.* 21. 4.

[4] Iren. i. 16. 2 (H.) "hic Helenam quandam, quam ipse a Tyro civitate Phoenices quaestuariam cum redemisset, secum circumducebat dicens hanc esse primam mentis eius conceptionem, matrem omnium, per quam in initio

Another piece of Simonian exegesis also militates strongly against the view that Helen was a moon-goddess, and that is in the parable of the lost sheep.[1] The explanation given in the sources is that Simon came to earth to rescue from the power of the angels his Ἔννοια, incarnate in Helen, just as the Good Shepherd sought the lost sheep. Once having found her it is natural that he should not wish to lose her, and hence their companionship was explained. This ingenious, if not entirely ingenuous, explanation of an awkward situation is surely too good not to have been invented à propos, and it is, besides, entirely consistent with the rest of Simonian theology. There is, however, no obvious connexion between it and mythology of the sun and moon. There seems to be no reason, therefore, for rejecting the view of all the ancient writers that Helen was a historical character. It may well be that Simon deceived himself as well as others about the supernatural importance of his mistress, but apart from their theology, which was, if nothing else, their stock-in-trade, a liaison between a magician of Samaria and a Tyrian prostitute is neither improbable nor remarkable.

Irenaeus.    Irenaeus (i. 16 H.) relates that Simon held the supreme God to be an exalted Power (*sublimissimam virtutem*) which manifested itself in three individuals, the Father, the Son, and the Holy Spirit.[2] From this Power the Father produced a Notion (*ennoia*) who following her Father's will descended to a lower sphere and created angels and powers (*angelos et potestates*). These subordinate beings fashioned the visible world, but were so desirous that they should not be thought the children of another that they kept the ' Notion ' a prisoner, preventing her from returning to the Father, of whose existence they were unaware, and subjecting her to all manner of humiliations, for while under their control she was obliged to assume one human body after another. Thus she appeared in history as Helen of Troy, and later as that Helen of Phoenician Tyre who was Simon's companion.[3]

mente concepit angelos facere et archangelos. Hanc enim Ennoian exsilientem ex eo, cognoscentem quae vult pater eius, degredi ad inferiora, et generare angelos et potestates, a quibus et mundum hunc factum dixit."

[1] Iren. i. 16. 2 (H.) " et hanc esse perditam ovem "; cf. Hippolytus, *Ref.* vi. 19. 4; Epiphanius, *Haer.* 21. 3. 5 διὸ πάλιν ἔλεγεν, ὡς προεῖπον, ὑποφαίνων ἐκείνην τὴν μετ᾽ αὐτοῦ γυναῖκα τὴν ἀπὸ Τύρου ληφθεῖσαν αὐτῷ τὴν ὁμώνυμον τῆς παλαιᾶς Ἑλένης, τὰ πάντα ταύτην καλῶν καὶ Ἔννοιαν καὶ Ἀθηνᾶν καὶ Ἑλένην καὶ τὰ ἄλλα " καὶ διὰ ταύτην," φησί, " καταβέβηκα· τοῦτο γάρ ἐστι τὸ γεγραμμένον ἐν τῷ εὐαγγελίῳ τὸ πρόβατον τὸ πεπλανημένον."

[2] Iren. i. 16. 1 (H.) " hic igitur a multis quasi Deus glorificatus est, et docuit semetipsum esse qui inter Iudaeos quidem quasi Filius apparuerit, in Samaria autem quasi Pater descenderit, in reliquis vero gentibus quasi Spiritus sanctus adventaverit "; Ps.-Augustine, *De haeresibus*, 1, and Cyril of Jerusalem, *Cat.* vi. 13, P.G. xxxv. 561, must be garbled versions of this passage.

[3] Iren. i. 16. 2 (H.) " posteaquam autem generavit eos, haec detenta est ab ipsis propter invidiam, quoniam nollent progenies alterius cuiusdam putari esse ; ipsum enim se in totum ignoratum ab ipsis : Ennoian autem eius detentam ab iis, quae ab ea emissae essent potestates, et angeli ; et omnem contumeliam ab iis passam uti non occurreret sursum ad suum patrem, usque adeo ut et in

She is referred to in the New Testament as the lost sheep of the parable. At length the supreme God took pity on her and the world in which she was imprisoned and descended to rescue her, bringing salvation to mankind and relief to a world suffering from the mismanagement of the angels whose counsels were divided by jealous rivalries. Taking a form like those of the angels and 'powers,' he appeared in Judaea, seeming to be a man and apparently enduring pain, though in fact he was not human or passible. Those whom he has saved and who place their hope in Simon and Helen are secured once for all by his favour and need acquire no further merit from good works. They are not bound by the precepts of the Law, which was delivered by the angels who made the world, but may act according to their own desires, since conduct is not absolutely but only relatively good.[1] Irenaeus concludes his account by saying that Simon's followers lived licentiously, practised magic, and worshipped Simon and Helen before statues of Zeus and Athena.

Closely connected with this description is the Simonian source Epiphanius. employed by Epiphanius, *Haer.* 21. 2 ff. In the passages quoted Simon speaks in the first person, and it is likely that the work was a dogmatic apocalypse in which developed sectarian doctrine is put into the mouth of the founder as was done in Christianity in the Fourth Gospel. The structure of the myth is the same as in Irenaeus, but some details are clarified and others added. Simon's descent to rescue Helen is thus described : ἐν ἑκάστῳ δὲ οὐρανῷ μετεμορφούμην, φησίν, κατὰ τὴν μορφὴν τῶν ἐν ἑκάστῳ οὐρανῷ, ἵνα λάθω τὰς ἀγγελικάς μου δυνάμεις καὶ κατέλθω ἐπὶ τὴν Ἔννοιαν, ἥτις ἐστὶν αὕτη ἡ καὶ Προύνικος καὶ πνεῦμα ἅγιον καλουμένη, δι' ἧς τοὺς ἀγγέλους ἔκτισα, οἱ δὲ ἄγγελοι τὸν κόσμον ἔκτισαν καὶ τοὺς ἀνθρώπους. This passage explains the obscure sentence

---

corpore humano includeretur, et per saecula veluti de vase in vas transmigraret in altera muliebria corpora. Fuisse autem eam et in illa Helena, propter quam Troianum contractum est bellum ; quapropter et Stesichorum per carmina maledicentem eam, orbatum oculis : post deinde poenitentem et scribentem eas, quae vocantur palinodias, in quibus hymnizavit eam, rursus vidisse. Transmigrantem autem eam de corpore in corpus, ex eo et semper contumeliam sustinentem, in novissimis etiam in fornice prostitisse."

[1] " Quapropter et ipsum venisse, uti eam assumeret primam et liberaret eam a vinculis, hominibus autem salutem praestaret per suam agnitionem; cum enim male moderarentur angeli mundum, quoniam unusquisque eorum concupisceret principatum, ad emendationem venisse rerum, et descendisse eum transfiguratum, et assimilatum virtutibus et potestatibus et angelis, ut et in hominibus homo appareret ipse, cum non esset homo ; et passum autem in Iudaea putatum, cum non esset passus; prophetas autem a mundi fabricatoribus angelis inspiratos dixisse prophetias : quapropter nec ulterius curarent eos hi qui in eum et in Helenam eius spem habeant, et ut liberos agere quae velint : secundum enim ipsius gratiam salvari homines, sed non secundum operas iustas, nec enim esse naturaliter operationes iustas, sed ex accidenti quemadmodum posuerunt qui mundum fecerunt angeli, per huiusmodi praecepta in servitutem deducentes homines, quapropter et solvi mundum, et liberari eos qui sunt eius ab imperio eorum qui mundum fecerunt, repromisit." Iren. i. 16. 3 (H.).

in Irenaeus (i. 16. 1 H.): "hic igitur a multis quasi Deus glorificatus est, et docuit semetipsum esse qui inter Iudaeos quidem quasi Filius apparuerit, in Samaria autem quasi Pater descenderit, in reliquis gentibus quasi Sanctus Spiritus adventaverit." The Simonian trinity evidently consisted of the Father = Simon, the Son = Jesus, the Holy Spirit = Helen, but in a sense Simon was all three. His appearance in Samaria was that of the Father in person ("in Samaria autem quasi Pater descenderit"), but he was also identical with the Godhead manifested in Jesus ("inter Iudaeos quidem quasi Filius apparuerit"), and his was the mind from which the Notion Helen emanated.

The doctrine of the angels who created this world is also explained more fully than in Irenaeus. They all bear outlandish names and have their own celestial domain, and to be saved it is necessary to know their names and to sacrifice to the Father of all through them. This last feature is very peculiar in view of the hostility implicit in the whole system between the régime of the angelic beings and that of the supreme god. This age is one of evil like its creators, and the flesh of man which they fashioned is contemptible, only his soul being capable of salvation through the gnosis imparted by Simon, the supreme god. The Old Testament is not the work of the good god but is a composite production inspired in its several parts by different demons, all of them emanating from the 'left power' who stands outside the pleroma. This doctrine no less than the account of Simon's descent through the spheres is obviously connected with Valentinian teaching.

Epiphanius gives more fully than Irenaeus examples of Simonian exegesis, both of Homer and of the New Testament. The transmigrations of Helen and her redemption by Simon are described in a quotation from his source, where Simon declares "ἦν δὲ αὕτη τότε ἡ ἐπὶ τοῖς Ἕλλησί τε καὶ Τρωσὶ καὶ ἀνωτάτω πρὶν ἢ τὸν κόσμον γενέσθαι καὶ μετὰ τὸν κόσμον διὰ τῶν ἀοράτων δυνάμεων τὰ ἰσότυπα πεποιηκυῖα. αὕτη δέ ἐστιν ἡ νῦν σὺν ἐμοὶ καὶ διὰ ταύτην κατελήλυθα. καὶ αὕτη δὲ προσεδόκα τὴν ἐμὴν παρουσίαν· αὕτη γάρ ἐστιν ἡ Ἔννοια, ἡ παρὰ Ὁμήρῳ Ἑλένη καλουμένη. καὶ τούτου ἕνεκεν ἀναγκάζεται αὐτὴν διαγράφειν Ὅμηρος ἐπὶ πύργου ἑστηκέναι καὶ διὰ λαμπάδος ὑποφαίνειν τοῖς Ἕλλησι τὴν κατὰ τῶν Φρυγῶν ἐπιβουλήν. ἐχαρακτήριζε δὲ διὰ τῆς λαμπηδόνος, ὡς ἔφην, τὴν τοῦ ἄνωθεν φωτὸς ἔνδειξιν." διὸ καὶ τὸν παρὰ τῷ Ὁμήρῳ δούρειον ἵππον μεμηχανημένον, ὃν νομίζουσιν Ἕλληνες ἐπίτηδες γεγενῆσθαι, ἔλεγε πάλιν ὁ γόης ὅτι ἄγνοιά ἐστι τῶν ἐθνῶν· καὶ "ὡς οἱ Φρύγες ἕλκοντες αὐτὸν ἀγνοίᾳ τὸν ἴδιον ὄλεθρον ἐπεσπάσαντο, οὕτω [γὰρ] καὶ τὰ ἔθνη τουτέστιν οἱ ἄνθρωποι οἱ ἐκτὸς τῆς ἐμῆς γνώσεως, διὰ τῆς ἀγνοίας ἕλκουσιν ἑαυτοῖς τὴν ἀπώλειαν" (Haer. 21. 3).

The identification of Helen with Athena and with the 'lost sheep' also appears in Epiphanius: ἀλλὰ καὶ Ἀθηνᾶν πάλιν τὴν αὐτὴν ἔλεγε τὴν παρ' αὐτῷ Ἔννοιαν καλουμένην, χρώμενος δῆθεν ὁ πλάνος ταῖς τοῦ ἁγίου ἀποστόλου Παύλου φωναῖς, μεταποιῶν τε τὴν ἀλήθειαν εἰς τὸ αὐτοῦ ψεῦδος, τὸ "ἐνδύσασθε τὸν θώρακα τῆς πίστεως καὶ τὴν περικεφαλαίαν τοῦ σωτηρίου καὶ κνημῖδας καὶ μάχαιραν καὶ θυρεόν," πάντα ταῦτα ἐπὶ τῆς τοῦ Φιλιστίωνος μιμολογίας ὁ ἀπατεὼν τὰ ὑπὸ τοῦ ἀποστόλου εἰρημένα διὰ στερεὸν λογισμὸν καὶ πίστιν ἀγνῆς ἀναστροφῆς καὶ δύναμιν θείου λόγου καὶ ἐπουρανίου εἰς χλεύην λοιπὸν καὶ οὐδὲν ἕτερον μεταστρέφων. "τί γάρ;" φησί, "ταῦτα πάντα εἰς Ἀθηνᾶς τύπους μυστηριωδῶς ἐσχημάτιζε" . . . "καὶ διὰ ταύτην," φησί, "καταβέβηκα. τοῦτο γάρ ἐστι τὸ γεγραμμένον ἐν τῷ εὐαγγελίῳ τὸ πρόβατον τὸ πεπλανημένον" (Haer. 21. 3. 4-5).

Hippolytus's account of the Simonians repeats in part details familiar from Irenaeus, but adds long extracts from a Simonian source entitled Ἡ Μεγάλη Ἀπόφασις. This document, which has marked affinities with Valentinianism, teaches that the first principle of the universe is fire,[1] which is sometimes called the great or infinite power.[2] It has a double aspect, one hidden, the other visible, and of these the latter represents the phenomenal world, the former its underlying reason.[3] The universe came into being from fire, and the whole cosmic history is conditioned by the activity of fire. The first step in the process was the emergence from the fire of six 'roots' and is thus described: γέγονεν οὖν ὁ κόσμος ὁ γεννητὸς ἀπὸ τοῦ ἀγεννήτου πυρός. ἤρξατο δέ, φησί, γενέσθαι τοῦτον τὸν τρόπον, ἐξ ῥίζας τὰς πρώτας τῆς ἀρχῆς τῆς γεννήσεως λαβὼν ὁ γεννητὸς ἀπὸ τῆς ἀρχῆς τοῦ πυρὸς ἐκείνου, γεγονέναι δὲ τὰς ῥίζας φησὶ κατὰ συζυγίας ἀπὸ τοῦ πυρός, ἅστινας ῥίζας καλεῖ, νοῦν καὶ ἐπίνοιαν, φωνὴν καὶ ὄνομα, λογισμὸν καὶ ἐνθύμησιν· εἶναι δὲ ἐν ταῖς ἓξ ῥίζαις ταύταις πᾶσαν ὅμου τὴν ἀπέραντον δύναμιν δυνάμει, οὐκ ἐνεργείᾳ (Ref. 6. 12. 1-2). The six roots are equated with parts of the universe thus: νοῦς καὶ ἐπίνοια = οὐρανὸς καὶ γῆ, φωνὴ καὶ ὄνομα = ἥλιος καὶ σελήνη, λογισμὸς καὶ ἐνθύμησις = ἀὴρ καὶ ὕδωρ, but the Seventh Power is immanent in them all. The visible world is the offspring of νοῦς and ἐπίνοια, and its only value lies in the realization of the rational element in it.[4] Man is a dichotomy,

The μεγάλη ἀπόφασις.

---

[1] Μωσέως γὰρ λέγοντος, "ὅτι ὁ θεὸς πῦρ φλέγον ἐστὶ καὶ καταναλίσκον" δεξάμενος τὸ λεχθὲν ὑπὸ Μωσέως οὐκ ὀρθῶς, πῦρ εἶναι τῶν ὅλων λέγει τὴν ἀρχήν . . . Ref. vi. 9. 3.

[2] ἀπέραντον δὲ εἶναι δύναμιν ὁ Σίμων προσαγορεύει τῶν ὅλων τὴν ἀρχήν . . ., Ref. vi. 9. 4. It is also called ῥίζα τῶν ὅλων, Ref. vi. 9. 4-5.

[3] ἔστι δὲ ἡ ἀπέραντος δύναμις, τὸ πῦρ, κατὰ τὸν Σίμωνα οὐδὲν ἁπλοῦν, καθάπερ οἱ πολλοὶ ἁπλᾶ λέγοντες εἶναι τὰ τέσσαρα στοιχεῖα καὶ τὸ πῦρ ἁπλοῦν εἶναι νενομίκασιν, ἀλλὰ γὰρ εἶναι [τὴν] τοῦ πυρὸς διπλῆν τινα τὴν φύσιν, καὶ τῆς διπλῆς ταύτης καλεῖ τὸ μέν τι κρυπτόν, τὸ δέ τι φανερόν· κεκρύφθαι δὲ τὰ κρυπτὰ ἐν τοῖς φανεροῖς τοῦ πυρός, καὶ τὰ φανερὰ τοῦ πυρὸς ὑπὸ τῶν κρυπτῶν γεγονέναι. Ref. vi. 9. 5-6.

[4] τῶν δὲ ἓξ δυνάμεων τούτων καὶ τῆς ἑβδόμης τῆς μετὰ τῶν ἓξ καλεῖ τὴν πρώτην συζυγίαν νοῦν καὶ ἐπίνοιαν, οὐρανὸν καὶ γῆν· καὶ τὸν μὲν ἄρσενα ἄνωθεν ἐπιβλέπειν καὶ προνοεῖν τῆς συζύγου, τὴν δὲ γῆν ὑποδέχεσθαι κάτω τοὺς ἀπὸ τοῦ οὐρανοῦ νοερούς καταφερομένους τῇ γῇ συγγενεῖς καρπούς. διὰ τοῦτο, φησίν, ἀποβλέπων πολλάκις ὁ λόγος πρὸς τὰ ἐκ νοὸς καὶ ἐπινοίας γεγεννημένα, τουτέστιν ἐξ οὐρανοῦ καὶ γῆς λέγει· "ἄκουε, οὐρανέ, καὶ ἐνωτίζου, γῆ ὅτι κύριος ἐλάλησεν· υἱοὺς ἐγέννησα καὶ ὕψωσα, αὐτοὶ δέ με ἠθέτησαν." ὁ δὲ λέγων ταῦτα, φησίν, ἡ ἑβδόμη δύναμίς ἐστιν ⟨ὁ⟩ ἑστώς, στάς, στησόμενος· αὐτὸς ἃ αἴτιος τούτων τῶν καλῶν, ὧν ἐπήνεσε Μωσῆς καὶ εἶπε καλὰ λίαν. ἡ δὲ φωνὴ καὶ τὸ ὄνομα ἥλιος καὶ σελήνη, ὁ δὲ λογισμὸς καὶ ἡ ἐνθύμησις ἀὴρ καὶ ὕδωρ. ἐν δὲ τούτοις ἅπασιν ἐμμέμικται καὶ κέκραται, ὡς ἔφην, ἡ μεγάλη δύναμις ἡ ἀπέραντος, ὁ ἑστώς. Ref. vi. 13.

created κατ᾽ ϝἰκόνα καὶ καθ᾽ ὁμοίωσιν τοῦ θεοῦ,[1] and his goal is perfectly to image the divine principle in his nature. The universe is the rationally developed character of men.[2] The process of salvation, however, has more than a human significance, for in realizing his own best nature man releases the Seventh Power from the prison of potentiality, so that in becoming actual it is united with the ultimate divine principle of the universe from which it was originally derived.[3]

The 'Απόφασις and Stoic thought.

This outline of the ideas underlying the system of the Apophasis is sufficient to show its affinity with Stoic ontology and cosmology. The dynamic materialism, the doctrine of elements which maintains that fire, though not itself a simple substance, was the primary element to which all others could be reduced,[4] the dissolution of the world in fire, the identification of πνεῦμα and πῦρ,[5] the doctrine of immanence, and the idea that man achieves perfection in the exemplification of the divine latent in him—all these are unmistakable evidences of Stoic influence and show that the author of the Apophasis was profoundly steeped in Stoic philosophy. But this was only one aspect of his thought. He was more a theologian than a philosopher, and much of his interest lay in the invention of elaborate metaphors and the adaptation of a variety of mythology and tradition to his philosophic ideas. His method is the same as that of Philo and Cornutus, but his ingenuity if anything more perverse than theirs.

The affinities between the Apophasis and the Simonianism described

---

[1] "ἔπλασε," φησίν, "ὁ Θεὸς τὸν ἄνθρωπον χοῦν ἀπὸ τῆς γῆς" λαβών· ἔπλασε δὲ οὐχ ἁπλοῦν, ἀλλὰ διπλοῦν "κατ᾽ εἰκόνα καὶ καθ᾽ ὁμοίωσιν." εἰκὼν δέ ἐστι τὸ πνεῦμα τὸ ἐπιφερόμενον ἐπάνω τοῦ ὕδατος (Gen. i. 2, cf. Ref. vi. 14. 4). ὃ ἐὰν μὴ ἐξεικονισθῇ, μετὰ τοῦ κόσμου ἀπολεῖται, δυνάμει μεῖναν μόνον καὶ μὴ ἐνεργείᾳ γενόμενον—τοῦτό ἐστι, φησί, τὸ εἰρημένον· "ἵνα μὴ σὺν τῷ κόσμῳ κατακριθῶμεν" (1 Cor. xi. 32). Ref. vi. 14. 5-6.

[2] καθόλου δὲ ἔστιν εἰπεῖν, πάντων τῶν ὄντων αἰσθητῶν τε καὶ νοητῶν, ὧν ἐκεῖνος κρυφίων καὶ φανερῶν προσαγορεύει, ἔστι θησαυρὸς τὸ πῦρ τὸ ὑπερουράνιον, οἱονεὶ δένδρον μέγα ὡς ⟨τὸ⟩ δι᾽ ὀνείρου βλεπόμενον τῷ Ναβουχοδονόσορ, ἐξ οὗ πᾶσα σὰρξ τρέφεται. καὶ τὸ μὲν φανερὸν εἶναι τοῦ πυρὸς νομίζει τὸ πρέμνον, τοὺς κλάδους, τὰ φύλλα, τὸν ἔξωθεν αὐτῷ περικείμενον φλοιόν. ἅπαντα, φησί, ταῦτα τοῦ μεγάλου δένδρου ἀναφθέντα ὑπὸ τῆς παμφάγου τοῦ πυρὸς ἀφανίζεται φλογός. ὁ δὲ καρπὸς τοῦ δένδρου ἐὰν ἐξεικονισθῇ καὶ τὴν ἑαυτοῦ μορφὴν ἀπολάβῃ, εἰς ἀποθήκην τίθεται, οὐκ εἰς τὸ πῦρ. γέγονε μὲν γάρ, φησίν, ὁ καρπός, ἵνα εἰς τὴν ἀποθήκην τεθῇ, τὸ δὲ ἄχυρον, ἵνα παραδοθῇ τῷ πυρί, ὅπερ ἐστὶ πρέμνον, οὐκ αὐτοῦ χάριν ἀλλὰ τοῦ καρποῦ γεγενημένον. Ref. vi. 9. 8-10. The passage is an ingenious combination of Dan. iv. 7-9 and Matt. iii. 12 as an allegory for the Stoic doctrine of the final conflagration. Cf. Ref. vi. 16. 5-6. The term καρπός in a similar connexion appears in some Valentinian systems.

[3] Ref. vi. 12. 2-4, 14. 6. An elaborate mixture of physiology and allegory explains this process further in Ref. vi. 14. 7-17. 7.

[4] ἔστι δὲ ἡ ἀπέραντος δύναμις, τὸ πῦρ, κατὰ τὸν Σίμωνα οὐδὲν ἁπλοῦν, . . . ἀλλὰ γὰρ εἶναι [τὴν] τοῦ πυρὸς διπλῆν τινα τὴν φύσιν, καὶ τῆς διπλῆς ταύτης καλεῖ τὸ μέν τι κρυπτόν, τὸ δέ τι φανερόν. Ref. vi. 9. 5.

[5] Cf. Ref. vi. 14. 5-6.

by Irenaeus are few and slight.[1]  Irenaeus presents a frankly mythological The 'Aπό-<br>φασις and<br>Irenaeus.
scheme, operating with distinct individualities, and the doctrine of the
incarnation exemplified in Simon and Helen gave to it a picturesque realism.
The theology of the Apophasis is fundamentally philosophic, and the collection of myths and metaphors which express it are of secondary importance, serving principally to illustrate the cosmopolitan religious taste of
its author.  Furthermore the cosmologies of the two systems are not only
notably different but irreconcilably contradictory.  In Irenaeus the world
was created by angels, and the need for its redemption was due to their
mismanagement while its redemption was effected by a personal saviour.
The Old Testament was held to be inspired by the creating angels and to
have no importance for the redeemed.  In the Apophasis the Old Testament is accepted but allegorized.  The very idea of creation is inapplicable
to a world evolved out of fire and dissolved into it again, and the angels are
replaced by the abstract ῥίζαι.  There is no room for a personal saviour,
and Helen is completely eliminated.

The figure of Simon is a favourite one in early Christian imaginative Simon in<br>early<br>Christian<br>fiction.
literature, and the encounter between Peter and Simon (Acts viii. 18-24)
especially supplied a dramatic theme which was developed with some skill
and variety in the apocryphal acts and romances.  The most elaborate as
well as the most familiar of these stories is found in the Clementine literature,
a misreading of which supplied the Tübingen school of three generations
ago with the principal support for their theory of early Christian history.
In both the *Recognitions* and *Homilies* Simon and Helen are placed in a
group of thirty disciples of John the Baptist.[2]  After the death of the
master Dositheus attempts to assume the lead, but is overcome by Simon
who convinces him that he is really ὁ ἑστώς.[3]  He adopts Helen as his
companion, and explains that she is a fallen power for whose salvation he
has appeared.  In a series of debates with Peter he maintains the existence
of two gods (*Hom.* iii. 2, *Rec.* ii. 38 ff., *Hom.* xix. 2 ff.) and declares that
he is the representative of a higher divinity of whose existence Jehovah
the Lawgiver was unaware.  This higher god even Jesus announced, though
he was a messenger of Jehovah and did not rightly understand his own
prophetic utterances (*Hom.* xviii. 11).  The myth of the angels is told by
Peter to the crowd, and Simon is enraged at having his mysteries made
public.  Peter's words are unfortunately deeply corrupted in the Greek
text, which runs thus : ἡμεῖς, ὦ Σίμων, ἐκ τῆς μεγάλης δυνάμεως, ἔτι τε
καὶ τῆς κυρίας λεγομένης, οὐ λέγομεν δύο ἀπεστάλθαι ἀγγέλους, τὸν
μὲν ἐπὶ τῷ κτίσαι κόσμον, τὸν δὲ ἐπὶ τῷ θέσθαι τὸν νόμον· οὐδὲ ὅτι
ἑαυτὸν ἕκαστος ἐλθών, ἐφ᾽ οἷς ἐποίησεν, ὡς αὐτὸς ὢν αὐθέντης αὐτὸν
ἤγγειλεν. οὐδὲ ὁ ἑστώς, στησόμενος, ἀντικείμενος (*Hom.* xviii. 12).
This obviously defies all attempts to construe it, though its general
meaning may be guessed.

The Clementine account of Simon's activities and teaching appears to

---

[1] It has, however, some resemblance to the system of Saturninus.  Cf.
Iren. i. 18 (H.), i. 22 (Gr.).

[2] *Rec.* ii. 7 ff., *Hom.* ii. 22 ff.

[3] *Rec.* ii. 11, *Hom.* ii. 24.  Cf. Hippolytus, *Ref.* vi. 17. 1-2.

be a composite of materials familiar from the heresiologists with a liberal addition of fiction, but the obviously distinctive features caution against oversimplifying the problem.[1]  The figure of ὁ ἑστώς recalls the *Apophasis megale*, but the discussion of Scriptural texts, especially in proof of the existence of two gods,[2] is not found in the extracts in Hippolytus, and is not likely to have been invented by the author of the Clementine *Grundschrift*. It seems more probable that this author had independent access to the *Apophasis* or to some kindred document, extracts from which he adapted to his exposition of Simon's teaching.

The Simonian mysteries.

The Simonian mysteries had a bad name among early Christian writers. The priests, Irenaeus says, lived licentiously and devoted themselves to the study and practice of magic.[3]  Hippolytus is more precise : οἱ δὲ αὖθις μιμηταὶ τοῦ πλάνου καὶ Σίμωνος μάγου γινόμενοι τὰ ὅμοια δρῶσιν· ἀλογίστως φάσκοντες δεῖν μίγνυσθαι, λέγοντες, "πᾶσα γῆ γῆ, καὶ οὐ διαφέρει ποῦ τις σπείρει, πλὴν ἵνα σπείρῃ." ἀλλὰ καὶ μακαρίζουσιν ἑαυτοὺς ἐπὶ τῇ ξένῃ μίξει, ταύτην εἶναι λέγοντες τὴν τελείαν ἀγάπην, καὶ τὸ ἅγιος ἁγίων [ἐπά]λλη[λ]ος ἁγιασθήσεται· οὐ γὰρ μὴ κρατεῖσθαι αὐτοὺς ἔτι τινὶ νομιζομένῳ κακῷ, λελύτρωνται γάρ.[4]  Of the ritual we know only that it was secret and that Simon and Helen were worshipped before statues of Zeus and Athena.  In the liturgy they were addressed as κύριε and κυρία and never by their proper names, so that an intruder who violated this custom could be recognized and ejected.[5]

Simon's death.

The death of Simon, like that of Judas Iscariot, was variously described. In the Acts of Peter, Simon attempts a feat of levitation at Rome, but the spell is broken by Peter and the magician crashes to earth so badly damaged that he must be carried to the house of a colleague, Castor, at Tarracina,

[1] Schmidt's statement is obviously an oversimplification of the problem: " Die gnostischen Lehren der Simon Magus und die Figur der Helena haben für den Verfasser der Clementinen ebensowenig Bedeutung wie für den Autor der Petrusakten.  Beide schöpfen ihre Nachrichten höchtestwahrscheinlich aus Justins Syntagma, das wieder eine Quelle für Irenaeus gewesen sein muss, denn die Anspielung an die Helena im Trojanischen Kriege findet sich wörtlich bei Iren. *Adv. haer.* i. 23. 2, ein sicheres Zeichen für eine benutzte schriftliche Quelle," *Studien zu Pseudo-Clementinen* (*T.U.* 46. 1, Leipzig, 1929), p. 51.  But the accounts in Iren. i. 26. 2, *Rec.* ii. 12, *Hom.* ii. 25 are not in *literal* agreement, though all represent the same Simonian allegory of the Homeric figure, and it is obvious that the Simonian system in the Clementines is either a genuine one, but somewhat different in detail from those given in other sources, or a patchwork of the author, materials for which have been drawn from several sources.

[2] *Rec.* ii. 38 ff., *Hom.* xvi. 5 ff.  Was Simon's claim to have been born of a virgin (*Rec.* ii. 14) an invention of the Clementine author or a Simonian doctrine ?

[3] i. 16. 3 (H.).                              [4] *Ref.* vi. 19. 5.

[5] *Ref.* vi. 20. 1-2.  The appearance of tongues of fire over the baptismal water referred to in Ps.-Cyprian, *De rebaptismate*, 16, is usually ascribed to the Simonian rite, but this is not necessarily the meaning of the passage.

where he dies.[1] Hippolytus relates that Simon, seeing his end was near, announced that if he were buried alive he would rise again on the third day. Hippolytus concludes: οἱ μὲν οὖν τὸ προσταχθὲν ἐποίησαν, ὁ δὲ ἀπέμεινεν ἕως νῦν. οὐ γὰρ ἦν ὁ Χριστός.[2] This account may well represent some Christian's conception of poetic justice to a daring and persistent competitor of Christianity, but it is not impossible that it tells the truth. Simon was not merely a heretic but a rival of Christianity, and an attempt at the end to reproduce the miracle of the Resurrection is entirely in character. His failure need have been no more of a blow to his followers than the crucifixion of Jesus to the disciples, and could no doubt have been satisfactorily explained so as to constitute no obstacle to the growth of the sect.

Of the history of Simonianism, apart from its theology and a few details of its worship, there is little knowledge, but there is no reason to suppose that it was ever a religion of the magnitude or influence of Marcionism and Valentinianism. It is certain from Justin's remarks that there were Simonians in Samaria in his time, and it is at least probable that there were also some in Rome. Celsus mentions them in his attack on Christianity, and Origen writing against him from Palestine circa A.D. 244–249 remarks that only a handful of them remained.[3] This is fair evidence that they were at least not flourishing in the East at this time, and the absence of fresh information in Western sources after Hippolytus encourages the supposition that the sect came to an end late in the third or early in the fourth century.

*The later Simonians.*

[1] *Vercelli Acts*, 32.
[2] *Ref.* vi. 20. 3.
[3] *Contra Celsum*, i. 57 ἠθέλησε δὲ καὶ Σίμων ὁ Σαμαρεὺς μάγος τῇ μαγείᾳ ὑφελέσθαι τινάς. καὶ τότε μὲν ἠπάτησε, νυνὶ δὲ τοὺς πάντας ἐν τῇ οἰκουμένῃ οὐκ ἔστι Σιμωνιανοὺς εὑρεῖν τὸν ἀριθμὸν οἶμαι τριάκοντα, καὶ τάχα πλείονας εἶπον τῶν ὄντων. εἰσὶ δὲ περὶ τὴν Παλαιστίνην σφόδρα ἐλάχιστοι· τῆς δὲ λοιπῆς οἰκουμένης οὐδαμοῦ τὸ ὄνομα αὐτοῦ, καθ' ἣν ἠθέλησε δόξαν περὶ ἑαυτοῦ διασκεδάσαι. Cf. *idem* vi. 11 οὐδαμοῦ γὰρ τῆς οἰκουμένης Σιμωνιανοί. Cotelier (*Patres Apostolici*, i. p. 512 n. 2) suggests that the number thirty here is a reminiscence of the thirty disciples of John the Baptist (*Rec.* ii. 8, *Hom.* ii. 23) as the Dositheans are credited with the same number of survivors, *Contra Celsum* vi. 11 οἱ δὲ Δοσιθηνοὶ οὐδὲ πρότερον ἤκμασαν· νῦν δὴ παντελῶς ἐπιλελοίπασιν, ὥστε τὸν ὅλον αὐτῶν ἱστορεῖσθαι ἀριθμὸν οὐκ εἶναι ἐν τοῖς τριάκοντα. It is significant that in both passages Dositheus and Simon are associated.

## Note XIV. Paul and the Magus

### By Arthur Darby Nock [1]

#### Summary

1. Magi to the time of Alexander the Great: early derogatory use of name by Greeks and derived sense of 'quack': later revision of this estimate: survival of derived use.
2. How far was the connexion of the Magi and magic justified? difference of ancient and modern ideas of religion and magic: the Magi in origin dignified priesthood, but ultimate explanation of the use of words derived from them to describe magic probably lies in their strange foreign rites.
3. (i.) Development of Magus concept in Hellenistic period and its extension beyond racial boundaries.
   (ii.) Canonization of the association with magic through the book ascribed to Ostanes and similar works.
4. Summary on meaning of μάγος.
5. Jews as magicians and as religious confidants.
6. The story type—(1) faith produced by a miracle, (2) the conflict of representatives of rival religions.
7. Its place in Acts.

In considering the story told in Acts xiii. 6-12 we have first to ask ourselves what the word μάγος means in a text of this period. We shall see that it can mean one of two things: (1) a Persian fire-priest; (2) a magician or quack; and in order to put this double meaning in its right setting we must survey a long process of development. The subject is in fact a chapter in the history of the interaction of East and West.

The Persian tribe of Magi.

1. μάγος is a loanword in Greek, borrowed from Persian to describe the priestly Median tribe. Members of this tribe performed the daily worship of fire,[2] and one of them had to be present at every sacrifice and sing a chant narrating the birth of the gods.[3] The name Magus occurs once only in the Avesta, from which fact Moulton has inferred that it was originally a name given to the tribe by outsiders [4];

---

[1] I am indebted to Professors F. C. Burkitt, R. P. Casey, F. N. Robinson, H. J. Rose, M. Rostovtzeff, G. A. S. Snyder, for help of various kinds.

[2] Strabo xv. 3. 15, p. 733.

[3] Herodotus i. 132.

[4] *Early Zoroastrianism*, pp. 428 ff. Cf. Chr. Bartholomae, *Altiranisches Wörterbuch*; H. Güntert, *Der arische Weltkönig und Heiland*, pp. 108 f., on its etymology. G. connects it with *magha*, 'might,' 'power.' On Persian religion in general cf. now C. Clemen, Pauly-Wissowa, Supp. v. 679 ff.

but its use in the Behistun inscription shows that it was an official title in the sixth century B.C., and it remained such in Sassanid times.[1] The caste has continued till our times, though the course of time has brought changes.

The Magi are therefore a dignified priestly tribe like that of Levi in Israel. An admirable illustration of one and his assistant in their religious duties is afforded by a bas-relief of the fifth century B.C. found at Dascylium and made by an artist who was either a Greek or dominated by Greek art.[2] Their functions are ritual, and they are also credited with skill in interpreting dreams.[3]

It is therefore with some surprise that we find μάγος used in the fifth century B.C. to mean ' quack.' So it is uttered in anger by Oedipus of Tiresias in Sophocles, *O.T.* 387 (Tiresias is a diviner, not a magician). In Euripides, *Orestes* 1497, Helen's disappearance is explained ἤτοι φαρμάκοισιν ἢ μάγων τέχναισιν ἢ θεῶν κλοπαῖς, and μάγοι is employed of magicians in general. A significant example of this sense is given by Hippocrates, *On the Sacred Disease*, a work assigned to the end of the fifth century B.C. The author is arguing against the view that epilepsy is a divine disease and says, ch. 2, " The men who first sanctified this disease must, I think, have been of the type of our present-day magi and purifiers and mendicants and humbugs. They actually pretend to be very pious and to have special knowledge." He uses the verb μαγεύω in this sense, mentioning the claims of such men to bring down the moon and to darken the sun and to make storm or calm, which are the ordinary claims of a Greek magician.[4] The derivative noun μαγεία appears, so far as I know, first in the *Helena* of Gorgias, now commonly accepted as genuine of the same period. Gorgias is discussing four possible explanations of Helen's going to Troy—divine compulsion, human force, persuasion by word, and the passion of love. *A propos* of the third hypothesis he speaks of inspired ἐπῳδαί or charms, able to give pleasure or to remove pain, and explains this by γοητεία, continuing γοητείας δὲ καὶ μαγείας δισσαὶ τέχναι εὔρηνται, αἳ εἰσι ψυχῆς ὁρμήματα καὶ δόξης ἀπατήματα.[5]

*(margin note: μάγος =quack.)*

---

[1] E. Herzfeld, *Paikuli*, i. 80, 82, magus of magi, 121, 213.

[2] Macridy Bey, *Bull. Corr. Hell.* xxxvii. pp. 348 ff. pl. viii. ; F. Cumont, *Les Religions orientales dans le paganisme romain*[4], p. 135, Fig. 10, 275, note 29.

[3] Moulton, pp. 182 ff.; C. Clemen, *Die griechischen und lateinischen Nachrichten über die persische Religion*, pp. 205 ff. Achmes in his *Oneirocriticon* gives what profess to be Indian, Persian, and Egyptian explanations. I do not know whether they have any relation to their supposed origins.

[4] Ch. 3 ὅστις οἷός τε περικαθαίρων ἐστὶ καὶ μαγεύων ἀπάγειν τοιοῦτον πάθος : 4 εἰ γὰρ ἄνθρωπος μαγεύων καὶ θύων σελήνην καθαιρήσει καὶ ἥλιον ἀφανιεῖ καὶ χειμῶνα καὶ εὐδίαν ποιήσει. In Plato, *Rep.* p. 572 E, μάγοι=clever deceivers.

[5] Something seems to be lacking from the text : the *two arts* are probably, as Immisch suggests, prose and verse.

This passage is very important, for the matter-of-fact way in which Gorgias uses μαγεία as an amplificatory synonym for γοητεία indicates that, whether the abstract noun was or was not already common in this sense, he could depend on his hearers so understanding it. When Plato, *Alcib. I.* p. 122 A, says μαγείαν . . . τὴν Ζωροάστρου τοῦ Ὠρομάζου—ἔστι δὲ τοῦτο θεῶν θεραπεία he has to explain his meaning.[1] Aristotle and Dinon protested against the common view, Aristotle saying τὴν δὲ γοητικὴν μαγείαν οὐδ᾽ ἔγνωσαν to avoid the ordinary assumption,[2] but the use in question of μάγος remained general in Greece, μάγος being a more colourful word than γόης, and gave its sense to *magus.* That this linguistic practice became universal appears from the use of *magicus* in Roman law.[3] How denuded of special and ethnic significance μάγος became is shown by the statement of Vettius Valens, writing in the second or third century, that a particular stellar conjuncture makes magi, cheats, sacrificers, doctors, astrologers, and members of other kindred trades[4] : again in the *Confessio Sancti Cypriani* the saint studies in Egypt and Chaldaea but not with the Magi, although he says of himself (ch. 7) ὀνομαστὸς ἤμην μάγος φιλόσοφος,[5] and in the cognate Ὁμολογία edited by Radermacher is Κυπριανὸς ὁ μάγος, busied with μαγεῖαι, and possessed of μαγικαὶ γραφαί.[6] Further, Pausanias v. 27. 3 speaking of the bronze horse dedicated by Phormis at Olympia says δῆλα δὲ καὶ ἄλλως ἔστιν ἀνδρὸς μάγου σοφίᾳ γενέσθαι τὰ συμβαίνοντα τῷ ἵππῳ and passes on to say that he has seen another wonder in Lydia, μάγων μέντοι σοφίας οὐδὲ αὐτὸ ἀπηλλαγμένον. This other wonder is the kindling of the wood by a Magus at Hierocaesarea and Hypaepa. Clearly to Pausanias μάγος connotes *in primis* simply ʻ magician.'

[1] A similar matter-of-fact use in Theophrastus, *Historia Plantarum,* ix. 15. 7, *à propos* of *moly*: χρῆσθαι δὲ αὐτῷ πρός τε τὰ ἀλεξιφάρμακα καὶ τὰς μαγείας (A. Hort translates ʻ against spells and magic arts,' but the meaning is probably ʻfor antidotes and magic arts'); a definition in Apuleius, *Apol.* 26. So also Porphyry and Pseudo-Chrysostom ; cf. Cumont, *Textes et monuments figurés relatifs aux mystères de Mithra,* i. 36₂.

[2] Cited by Diogenes Laertius in his proem. Aristotle's statement is important in view of his and his school's interest in Persian thought. A work called Μαγικός was ascribed by some to him, by others to Antisthenes.

[3] Mommsen, *Römisches Strafrecht,* pp. 639 ff., and p. 173 *infra.*

[4] *Anthologiae,* p. 74. 17 Kroll, ποιεῖ γὰρ μάγους πλάνους θύτας ἰατροὺς ἀστρολόγους ὀχλαγωγοὺς καὶ τραπεζίτας παραχαράκτας ὁμοιογράφους διά τε πανουργίας καὶ ἐπιθέσεως καὶ δόλου τὰς πράξεις διοικοῦντας. Clem. Al. *Strom.* vi. 3. 31, says τοὺς ἐν Κλεωναῖς μάγους of the local hail-watchers.

[5] In the *Cyprian* of Baluzius and in *A.SS.* Sept. vii. 204 ff. So Herodotus and Dinon *ap.* Cic. *De divin.* i. 46.

[6] *Griechische Quellen zur Faustsage (Sitzungsber. Ak. Wiss. in Wien,* 206 iv.), pp. 84, 16, 104.

2. Can we explain this applied use of μάγος as resting on true observation of the magical practices of Persian Magi, as in fact such a generalization as that by which astrologers in general were designated as *Chaldaei* ? This is a question very hard to answer, for of the character of the Magi in pre-Sassanian times we know hardly anything except what Greek writers tell us. Now there is nothing to suggest that any of them were familiar with the Persian language, and it must always be remembered that the Greek was seldom a good observer of strange religions, prone as he was to hasty conclusions and identifications and to a contempt or to a veneration which were equally uncritical. In any case all that is asserted by Greeks professing to describe the Magi is that they interpreted dreams,[1] and that by their charms they caused a violent wind on the Strymon to stop.[2] The second statement may well mean no more than that they invoked good spirits or used apotropaic rites to avert evil spirits.[3] It is probably in the order of prayers for rain or the celebration of the Mass for special purposes, which an alien might describe as ἐπῳδαί.[4] The observations made by those Greeks who had studied the Magi of any particular place are in striking contrast to the generalizations of those Greeks who talked vaguely. It is well worthy of note that among the various charges brought by St. Basil against the μαγουσαῖοι who inherited their tradition magic does not appear.[5]

If we turn to our Persian sources we read of what is in them called by words corresponding to magic as something on the side of evil in the continual cosmic struggle. The Zoroastrian confession

---

[1] *Yasna* 30. 3 refers in one translation to a dream vision, but is hardly relevant to oneiromancy as a practice.

[2] Herodotus vii. 191. Cf. N. Terzaghi, *Arch. f. Relig.* xi. pp. 145 ff., for the scourging of the Hellespont; Cumont, *Comptes rendus de l'Acad. des Inscr.*, 1917, 278₂, on the throwing of chains into it. Both are what we should call sympathetic magic.

[3] So Rapp, *Zeitschrift der Deutschen Morgenländischen Gesellschaft*, xx. p. 77. Of course the control of weather is commonly ascribed to θεῖοι ἄνδρες like Empedocles (Diels, *Fragm. d. Vorsokratiker*[4], i. 201. 5).

[4] I am not speaking of the abuses discussed by G. L. Kittredge, *Witchcraft in Old and New England*, pp. 147, 466 f. ; they are instructive as an example of the possibility of decline later suggested for the Magi.

[5] *Ep.* 258 (Migne xxxii. 952 f.) : so also Epiphanius, *Adv. Haereses*, iii. 13. Strabo, xv. 2. 39, p. 762, in a list of prophets honoured by various peoples includes οἱ μάγοι καὶ νεκυομάντεις καὶ ἔτι οἱ λεγόμενοι λεκανομάντεις καὶ ὑδρομάντεις. Here the practice is associated with Persia (cf. Boehm, Pauly-Wissowa ix. 79 f.) but not certainly ascribed to the Magi. (A similar list, Brahmans, Magi, Ἑλλήνων οἱ θεολογικώτατοι, is given by Proclus, *Comm. in Timaeum*, vol. i. p. 208 Diehl ; here they are adduced as sages whose example supports the practice of prayer.)

of faith includes a renunciation of " the Daevas and all possessed
by them, the sorcerers and their devices, and every existing being
of the sort," [1] and the legends of Zoroaster tell how sorcerers and
enchanters endeavoured to destroy him when young,[2] and how he
struggled against superstition, sorcery, and devil-worship.[3] These
traditions give us the conscious orientation of Zoroastrianism, though
it is indeed the purified and canonized Zoroastrianism of the Sassanian
period.

Modern students looking in Persian tradition for an explanation
of the Greek use of $\mu\acute{a}\gamma os$ and $\mu a\gamma\epsilon\acute{\iota}a$ as typical words have drawn
attention to a talisman given by Zoroaster,[4] to his possession of a
feather of the bird Varengana credited with the power of giving
protection and glory,[5] and to his use of water from the sacred river
Dāityā mixed with consecrated hōm-juice as an elixir.[6] But surely
these things are in the world of folktale, not of serious magic. Emphasis has been laid also on the Persian use of spells for medicinal
and other apotropaic purposes.[7] This was no doubt common, and
may be due in part to Babylonian analogies,[8] but it should be noted
first that the use of these proceedings is world-wide and was familiar
in Greece, secondly that medical magic is not associated with the
Magi in particular.[9] The Magi are not specialists in this side of life,
though their presence in such an act might be thought useful. So

---

[1] *Yasna* 12. 5 (transl. by L. H. Mills, *Sacred Books of the East*, xxxi. p. 249);
cf. Cumont, *Textes et monuments*, i. 141, for parallels.

[2] A. V. W. Jackson, *Zoroaster*, pp. 10 ff.

[3] *Id., Zoroastrian Studies*, pp. 27, 103, 280. This picture of Zoroaster survives in Manichee times (if we accept Le Coq's identification, *Sitzungsber. Preuss.
Akad.*, 1908, 398).

[4] *Zoroastrian Studies*, p. 255.

[5] *Yast* 14. 35 ; cf. Geiger, *Ostiranische Kultur im Altertum*, p. 332.

[6] *Zoroastrian Studies*, pp. 280 f.   For miracles later ascribed to him by Shara-
stānī, etc., cf. R. J. H. Gottheil, *Studies in Honour of Henry Drisler*, p. 50. Like
the subjugation of the *daevas* by Jamshid (Firdausi, *Shanama*, i. p. 33) they are
not relevant. Late tradition makes Zoroaster an arch-magician. Jackson cites,
*op. cit.* p. 83, texts from Clement and Minucius stating the claims of the Magi to
subdue demons, but the latter expressly cites Ostanes, and see p. 178 *infra*.

[7] *Vendidad* vii. 44, and ix. (for cleansing from defilement by a demon): incidentally the process is thought of as driving away diseases, cf. xxii. 21, p. 234,
transl. Darmsteter (*Sacred Books of the East*, iv.). In general cf. A. J. Carnoy in
*Encycl. Rel. Eth.* viii. p. 294, and above all, *Le Muséon*, ser. iii. vol. i. pp. 171 ff.

[8] Cf. Cumont, *Religions orientales*[4], p. 174; R. Campbell Thompson, ' Assyrian
Medical Texts ' in *Proc. Roy. Soc. Med.* xix. No. 3, pp. 29 ff.   One clear instance
of Persian borrowing from Babylon is the festival of Sakaia (C. Clemen, *Die
Religionen der Erde*, p. 152).

[9] *Vendidad* vii. 44 mentions healers. *Vendidad* vii. 41 specially says " a
healer shall heal a priest for the blessing of the just." *Vendidad* xx. refers to
a mythical priest-healer.

now among the Parsis in Persia a *mobed* is paid to read passages
from the *Yasna*, the *Yasts*, or the *Khordah-avesta*, in order to conjure
away the evil eye or cure a sick child.[1]  In apotropaic rites the Magi
were no doubt paramount: Plutarch mentions that side of their
activity.[2]

Such proceedings were in ancient civilizations and are in many
areas to-day the equivalent of our antiseptics and inoculations.
Man thinks himself to be surrounded by a whole world of evil powers
against whom he must arm.  Μαγεία as later understood includes
such methods of self-protection, but it includes much more ; and
in particular methods of divination by water, of influencing the
affections of others, and of inflicting physical harm on them.  In
this range it is as remote from the normal standards of Persian
priesthood as would be temple prostitution from those of the
Catholic Church, and it is quite clear that if the Magi had contact
with magic they were not professional magicians in the later sense
of μάγοι.

How then did this terminology arise ?  To answer this we must
consider what we mean and what the ancients mean by magic ; otherwise there is a danger of real confusion of thought. The modern
meaning of
magic.

In the ordinary colloquial language of educated men ' magic '
and ' magical ' have inherited most of the meanings discussed in
the previous paragraphs.  Neither has any longer any connexion
with its original Persian surroundings.  But both have retained
the rather contemptuous connotation belonging to them in Greek
and Latin literature, so that they customarily afford terms of abuse
for religious ceremonies which are regarded as superstitious.  This
usage is the natural continuation of the classical use of *magus* and
*magia*.

In the terminology used by students of the history of religion
it has been found convenient to use ' magic ' in a clearer and
narrower sense.  In this sense it means the attempt to divert the
course of nature by methods which to our science appear to be of a
non-rational kind, or which to the user appear to rest on some hidden
and peculiar wisdom : the charming of warts we call magic, birth-
control we do not.  We distinguish it from science which proceeds
by rational methods, and from religion which if it seems to influence
the course of events does so by asking some superior being or beings
to do what is needed instead of either operating directly by some

---

[1] Carnoy, *Muséon*, *l.c.* pp. 183 f.  We find an interesting dedication to
Artemis Anaitis (probably from Gjeuldi) by a woman, περίπτωμα ἔχουσα καὶ
ἐξασθεῖσα ὑπὸ τῆς ἱερείας (priestess of Anahita), Cumont, *Comptes rendus de
l'Acad. des Inscr.*, 1915, 271.  The goddess as represented on the accompanying
relief is of the type of the Ephesian Artemis.

[2] *De Iside et Osiride*, 46, p. 369 E.

kind of sympathetic action or again compelling the superior being or beings.

Now this modern use of 'magic' does not fit the ancient world.[1] Certain public practices which we should characterize as magical are not so characterized. The communal rain-making at Crannon in Thessaly is mentioned as a peculiar local claim,[2] that on mount Lykaion in Arcadia as a rite, like the *aquaelicium* at Rome [3]: it is in fact like prayers for rain or a procession to bless the crops. The *envoûtement* of citizens who disloyally failed to obey a call to go off to a colony, by burning wax images of them, is recorded in a public document at Cyrene as a perfectly natural proceeding. Like the burning of hostile armour to Lua Rua at Rome it is mentioned as a rite: no deity is mentioned.[4] Again, the use of ἐπῳδαί or spells is not confined to magicians. The doctor used them, as Sophocles, *Ajax* 584, reminds us.[5]

There is not, then, as with us, a sphere of magic in contrast to the sphere of religion. Further, the words used to designate magical acts do not for the most part possess a precise and technical meaning. φίλτρον, love-charm, is indeed fairly specialized, but it also is used in a good sense as 'winning attractiveness.' φάρμακον is *drug* as well as *poison* or *magical material*.[6] ἐπῳδή means *charm*, but Aeschylus feels no scruple in making Apollo use it metaphorically and say, "The Father (Zeus) made no spells for these troubles " (the shedding of blood), τούτων ἐπῳδὰς οὐκ ἐποίησεν πατήρ [7]; the derivative ἐπῳδός is used with no depreciatory nuance 'to charm towards' or 'to charm from.' [8] γόης, indeed, is either used literally for a wizard (as in the *Phoronis*, an epic thought to be not later than the seventh

---

[1] Cf. Fr. Pfister's admirable article 'Epode' in Pauly-Wissowa, Supp. iv. 323 ff. P. gives an excellent collection of material and conclusions which seem to me very sound.

[2] Antigonus, Ἱστοριῶν παραδόξων συναγωγή 15.

[3] Pausanias viii. 38. 4; Heraclides, *Descriptio Graeciae*, ii. 8 (Müller, *Geographi Graeci Minores*, i. 107), describes a custom on Mount Pelion which may have had this purpose, rain-making (probably) at Olbia by the priest of Zeus Olbios ; E. H. Minns, *Scythians and Greeks*, p. 476₆. Note the Pharisee rain-making ceremony of Sukkot, L. Finkelstein, *Harv. Theol. Rev.* xxii. p. 195. For rain-making in a late Jewish collection of stories, W. Bousset, *Nachr. Gött. Gel. Ges.*, 1916, p. 484.

[4] *Archiv für Religionswissenschaft*, xxiv. pp. 172 f. (As Deubner has argued, it is likely that such rites not directed to personal deities had no small part in early Roman religion.) We may compare the burning in effigy by the Holy Office of offenders whose persons could not be secured.

[5] So the son of Autolycus, *Odyss.* xix. 457 : the Cyclops can use one if he knows it (Euripides, *Cyclops*, 646).

[6] Cf. *Journ. Theol. Stud.* xxx. p. 391.          [7] *Eum.* 649.

[8] Plato, *Leges*, p. 671 A ; *Phaedo*, p. 78 A.

century B.C.[1]), or metaphorically for a quack, humbug, impostor. And yet Plato did not feel that the operation of the γόης differed *toto caelo* from ordinary cult. He makes Diotima say in her discourse on the functions of daemones : " Through their care goes the whole science of divination, the art of the priests and of all those concerned with sacrifices and initiations and spells and all divining and *goeteia*. God has no intercourse with men : it is through this race that all intercourse happens between gods and men." [2] Spells and *goeteia* are on a footing with sacrifice and divination, just as in *Rep.* 364 B religious impostors claim power obtained θυσίαις τε καὶ ἐπῳδαῖς, by sacrifice and spells, and in the passage quoted earlier from Hippocrates *mageia* is classified with other popular beliefs, and the antithesis is one of supernaturalism and non-supernaturalism. So later Pliny, before treating of curative spells, asks *polleantne aliquid uerba et incantamenta carminum,* and in answering gives among his illustrations of people's unconscious faith in this power : *quippe uictimas caedi sine precatione non uidetur referre aut deos rite consuli.* He refers to fixed public forms of prayer, and the *deuotio* used by the Decii, and Tuccia's prayer.[3]

Pfister rightly concludes, " dass kein prinzipieller Unterschied zwischen Zauberspruch und Gebet so wenig wie zwischen Zauberei und Religion besteht." [4] This is true, and incidental ancient attempts at theoretical differentiation are clearly the products of individual sophistication.[5]

What then do the ancients mean by *magia* ? Broadly speaking Magia. three things : the profession by private individuals of the possession of technical ability enabling them to supply recipes or perform rites to help their clients and damage their clients' enemies ; the use by such clients or by others of such proceedings to damage enemies ; and—corresponding to the vague modern use already mentioned— the religions belonging to aliens or on any general ground disapproved.

[1] Kinkel, *Epicorum Graecorum Fragmenta,* i. 211, No. 2 (of the Idaean Dactyls : the passage treats of their discovery of iron). For the date of the poem cf. Schmid-Stählin, *Geschichte der griechischen Literatur,* i. p. 294. Herodotus ii. 33 describes dwellers in the Sahara as γόητες, and in iv. 105 he says that the Neuri, a Scythian tribe, are probably γ. since it is reported that each of them becomes a wolf for a few days of every year and then resumes his shape. Here, as in Plato, *Rep.* p. 380 D, there is a nuance of irony.

[2] *Symp.* p. 202 E. τελεταί, translated 'initiations,' has a wider range of meaning ; cf. H. Bolkestein, *Religionsgesch. Versuche u. Vorarbeiten,* XXI. ii. p. 57.

[3] *N.H.* xxviii. 10 ff. Cf. *Gnomologium Epicteteum,* 67 (88), in H. Schenkl's *Epictetus,* ed. mai.[2] p. 492, ὥσπερ ὁ ἥλιος οὐ περιμένει λιτὰς καὶ γοητείας ἵν᾽ ἀνατείλῃ.

[4] Pauly-Wissowa, Supp. iv. 325. 7.

[5] Suidas s.vv. μαγεία, μαγική, γοητεία. Such a definition is akin to the Peripatetic idea of δεισιδαιμονία as contrasted with εὐσέβεια and with ἀθεότης (P. J. Koets, Δεισιδαιμονία).

The third use is natural. We find the supposed priest of Dionysus in Euripides, *Bacchae* 234, described as γόης ἐπῳδὸς Λυδίας ἀπὸ χθονός.[1] Again Pliny includes human sacrifice and Druidism under the head of magic.[2] In the *Acta disputationis S. Achatii* 5 the Roman magistrate is made to say *ideo magi estis quia nouum nescio quod genus religionis inducitis.* If we return for a moment to Persia we there find magic closely associated with the older worship which Zoroastrianism has sought to replace.

Roman law and magic.

Roman law had of course to deal with various practices which fall within the sphere of what we call magic. In early times the law of the Twelve Tables dealt with attempts to remove or appropriate one's neighbour's crops by spells. Later we find the law prohibiting nocturnal sacrifices, which might mean seditious meetings, or such a danger to public order as the movement repressed by the *Senatus consultum de Bacchanalibus,* and liable to punish professional activity in magic. It is clear that the presiding magistrate must have had considerable discretionary power in determining what was punishable as magic, and that under the Empire the suspicion of political intrigue intensified the official attitude against magicians.[3] It was so with *Chaldaei* or astrologers.

[1] Cf. Hubert in Daremberg-Saglio, *Dict. Antiq.* iii. 1499 f.; Pfister, *l.c.* 342 f. Philostratus, *Vit. Apoll.* iv. 16, tells how the hierophant at Eleusis sought to exclude Apollonius of Tyana as μὴ καθαρὸς τὰ δαιμόνια. This may be genuine feeling against a γόης (Farnell, *Cults,* iii. p. 168), but it is really just background for the hero's prophecy and hangs together with the idea that the θεῖος ἀνήρ has an inherent priestliness which dispenses him from ordinary requirements : cf. Porphyry, *Vita Plotini* 10 ἐκείνους (sc. τοὺς θεοὺς) δεῖ πρὸς ἐμὲ ἔρχεσθαι, οὐκ ἐμὲ πρὸς ἐκείνους. (But in Marinus, *Vita Procli* 19, we read that the philosopher should be the hierophant of the whole universe : we have to do with a man who was *pratiquant.*) Cf. Apollonius Tyan. *Ep.* 16 μάγους οἴει δεῖν ὀνομάζεσθαι τοὺς ἀπὸ Πυθαγόρου φιλοσόφους, ὧδέ που καὶ τοὺς ἀπὸ Ὀρφέως· ἐγὼ δὲ καὶ τοὺς ἀπὸ τοῦ δεινὸς οἶμαι δεῖν ὀνομάζεσθαι μάγους, εἰ μέλλουσιν εἶναι θεῖοί τε καὶ δίκαιοι. Neopythagoreanism was particularly open to accusations of magic. There is an instructive parallelism between the charges made against Apollonius and those made against the Apostles in apocryphal Acts ; cf. O. Weinreich, *Gebet und Wunder,* p. 196 ( =*Genethliakon W. Schmid,* p. 362).

[2] *N.H.* xxx. 12 f.

[3] Mommsen, *Römisches Strafrecht,* pp. 639 ff. ; P. Vallette, *L'Apologie d'Apulée,* pp. 34 ff. ; Fr. Beckmann, *Zauberei und Recht in Roms Frühzeit* (Osnabrück, 1923) ; Ed. Fraenkel, *Gnomon,* i. pp. 185 ff. The meaning of *mala carmina* has been disputed. The phrase can cover ' satire ' and ' imprecations to do harm,' for the two things are closely allied and sometimes combined ; cf. F. N. Robinson, *Studies in the History of Religions presented to C. H. Toy,* pp. 95 ff., and G. L. Hendrickson, *Am. Journ. Phil.* xlvi. pp. 101 ff. Note that Cato the elder, *De re rustica,* 160, records medical spells.

I take it that the gravamen of the charge against Apuleius lay in the fact that the disposition of Pudentilla's property was affected. For the official attitude cf. Dio Cassius lii. 36. 3 τοὺς δὲ δὴ μαγευτὰς πάνυ οὐκ εἶναι προσήκει.

They were not as a rule people of such position as to be able to get very much attention paid to their possible rights.

One text which we must consider is Constantine's rescript, dated June 22, 321, in *Codex Theodosianus* ix. 16. 3,[1] and assigned by Seeck to May 23, 318[2] : *eorum est scientia punienda et seuerissimis merito legibus uindicanda qui magicis adcincti artibus aut contra hominum moliti salutem aut pudicos ad libidinem defixisse animos detegentur : nullis uero criminationibus implicanda sunt remedia humanis quaesita corporibus aut in agrestibus locis, ne maturis uindemiis metuerentur imbres aut ruentis grandinis lapidatione quaterentur, innocenter adhibita suffragia quibus non cuiusque salus aut existimatio laederetur sed quorum proficerent artes ne diuina munera et labores hominum sternerentur.* Now it does not follow from this that magic to do harm or inspire love was grouped with weather charms and medical charms under a single category of magic in the anthropological sense.[3] There is no mention in this edict of the punishment appropriate to magi. Its purpose is one of toleration, of defining what was anyhow safe and admissible : just as a rescript of Diocletian and Maximian says, *artem geometriae discere atque exerceri publice intersit, ars autem mathematicae damnabilis interdicta est.*[4] Such definition was clearly called for. Later in the fourth century we find many condemnations for acts which on Constantine's definition of magic were regarded as licit ; these may be in part due to the official fear of treason, but are perhaps as much due to the intense popular fear of those *quos maleficos ob facinorum magnitudinem uolgus appellat,*[5] and to the feeling that it is dangerous to the community to have in its midst men who may draw down divine anger on everyone.[6] A very clear instance of the intensity of this terror of magic is a rescript of Constantius : *Multi magicis artibus ausi elementa turbare, uitas insontium labefactare non dubitant et Manibus accitis audent uentilare, ut quisque suos conficiat malis artibus inimicos ;*

Constantine's rescript.

---

[1] = *Codex Iustinianus*, ix. 18. 4.

[2] *Regesten der Kaiser und Päpste*, 62. 16, 166.

[3] Seneca, *Nat. Quaest.* iv. 6 b, 6-9, illustrates the methods used at Cleonae to avert hail by referring to the injunction in the Twelve Tables, *ne quis alienos fructus excantassit,* and Clement of Alexandria, *Strom.* vi. 3. 31, speaks of τοὺς ἐν Κλεωναῖς μάγους, but both write after the coming into being of the Ostanes literature discussed later.

[4] *Cod. Iust.* ix. 18. 2.

[5] *Cod. Theod.* xvi. 16. 4 : for the word cf. S. Augustine, *Ciu. dei*, x. 9 ; Mommsen, *op. cit.* pp. 639 f. For the state of feeling cf. J. Maurice, *Comptes rendus de l'Académie des Inscriptions*, 1926, pp. 132 ff., and later analogies in Kittredge, *Witchcraft*, pp. 358 f.

[6] Cf. Deuteron. xviii. 10-14, cited in *Mosaicarum et Romanarum legum collatio*, xv. (Seckel-Kuebler, *Iurisprudentiae anteiustinianae reliquiae*[6], II. ii. 379).

*hos, quoniam naturae peregrini sunt, feralis pestis absumat.*[1] This is hysteria. The line drawn by Constantine became normal.[2] It should be remarked that the provisions against *magici libri* did not affect the preservation of the relevant portions of the elder Pliny and the composition and preservation of the work of Marcellus of Bordeaux, and later at Byzantium of the *Geoponica.*[3] Nor is there any reason to suppose that the law took cognisance of theurgy such as is associated with the *Oracula Chaldaica* and is handled by Iamblichus, *On the Mysteries*, or of such a séance as that described by Porphyry in his *Life of Plotinus*, ch. 10, though the animus of St. Augustine's polemic against theurgy suggests that it was not negligible at the time.[4]

There is then no sphere of magic at once distinguishable from the sphere of religion and from that of science, though magic and religion together can be opposed to science, as we saw in Hippocrates (so Pliny, having incidentally handled *magicas uanitates* previously *à propos* of herbs and animals, etc., passes to a special treatment in xxx.). What gets the name of magic is a varied complex of things, mainly *qua* professional or *qua* criminal in intent or *qua* alien. We may explain the selection of μάγος as a typical name, and the formation of the noun μαγεία from it as due to the impression made on unfriendly Ionian spectators by Persian priests, with their queer garments and tiaras and mouth masks—as we see them on the relief from Dascylium—performing uncomprehended rites, uttering unintelligible prayers, and indispensable at sacrifice.[5] Egypt had what

---

[1] *Cod. Theod.* ix. 16. 5, dated December 4, 357, which Seeck, 47. 5, 203, corrects to 356. The same tone is apparent in *Cod. Theod.* ix. 16. 6 (July 5, 358 in the *Cod.*; July 5, 357 according to Seeck 204).

[2] Maurice, *l.c.* p. 187. Giving an abortive or a love philtre was punishable in any case (Paulus, *Sententiae*, v. 23. 14). In connexion with rulings on magic Paulus states that if a man dies of a drug given for his health the giver is punished (v. 23. 19).

[3] The magic cryptogram published by A. S. Hunt, *Proc. Brit. Acad.* xv., is in cryptogram no doubt because of the professional importance of secrecy.

[4] *Ciuitas dei*, x. 9, where note the distinction drawn by Neoplatonists between this *theurgia* and magic. On these rites cf. J. Bidez, *Revue belge de philologie et d'histoire*, vii. p. 1477; some knowledge of them may be behind the passage of *Confessio S. Cypriani* discussed by me in *J.T.S.* xxviii. (I hope to return to this topic: it seems to me that we may have to reckon there also with material like the *Testament of Solomon*.) A reference to these rites I suspect in Julian, *Contra Christianos*, p. 197 Ζεὺς . . . δέδωκεν ἡμῖν διὰ τῶν ἱερῶν τεχνῶν ἐπίσκεψιν. The difficulties in which Psellus found himself were raised by Christian orthodoxy; cf. J. Bidez, *Cat. MSS. alchimiques grecs*, vi. 115.

[5] For an Ionian impression compare the statement of Heraclitus *ap.* Clem. Alex. *Protr.* ii. p. 16. 24 Stählin, that he made his oracular utterances νυκτιπόλοις μάγοις βάκχοις λήναις μύσταις, " to night-roamers, magi, bacchants, maenads, initiates "; he threatens them with fiery destruction and taunts them with the

an anthropologist recognizes as magic—constraints of gods, threats to gods, and so on—and had it deeply embedded in its religion : but not in such a form that a casual Greek observer would have known of it. It was the external aspect of Persian cultus which counted, not the meaning of the rite. Increasing information in the fourth century B.C. brought with it a more favourable picture of the Magi, but even in the second century of our era the fire-worship remains a mysterious thing to Pausanias, who says that the Magus read charms, and the dry wood piled on the altar must kindle without a flame.

The terminology gained importance, as we shall see. One cause may be mentioned now. No one would *call* himself a γόης : it meant quack and had no background. But μάγος, while it meant quack, had a dignified history. Even to Greeks who thought of the Magi as barbarians they might appear to possess a certain amount of hold over the supernatural : this could arise, not from an intellectual or religious conviction but from a feeling, " they are the old priests and there may be something in them." Englishmen in the eighteenth century went to the old Royal family at Paris to be touched for the King's evil. There is even a story of George I. referring an applicant to the Pretender—with success, it is said.[1] μάγος and μαγεία were definitely adopted by the profession, as the magic papyri show.[2]

3. In the Hellenistic period we have to reckon with two factors. The Hellenistic period. One is the modification of the position of the Magi, the other the creation of supposedly Magian literature in Greek. The first of these may have affected the history of this terminology, the second certainly has.

(i.) First, the position of the caste of Magi was not what it had been. The position of the Magi. Those who were in Persia probably lacked their old official standing between Alexander's conquest and the Parthian national revival in the second century B.C., and even in that they did not have the authority which the Sassanid régime gave to them in the third

---

unworthiness of their mysteries. (At the same time it is possible that Heraclitus was influenced by Zoroastrianism ; cf. L. A. Stella, *Rendiconti Acc. Lincei*, 1927, pp. 571 ff.) It is possible that the Persians regarded Artemis of Ephesus as the same as Anahita ; they certainly used the temple ; cf. Ch. Picard, *Éphèse et Claros*, pp. 606 ff. But note the arguments of W. H. Buckler and D. M. Robinson, *Am. J. Arch.* 2nd ser. xvii. (1913) pp. 368 ff., against any substantial Persian influence on the cult of Artemis at Sardis (though their scruples as to the existence of priestesses for Anahita are weakened by *C. R. Ac. Inscr.*, 1915, 271, cited above, p. 169).

[1] E. L. Hussey, *Archaeological Journal*, x. p. 201.
[2] Cf. on them my article in *Journal of Egyptian Archaeology*, xv.

century A.D.[1]  In tradition Alexander appears as their enemy and
the destroyer of the old Avesta.[2]  Be this as it may (and it is of course
incompatible with all that we know of Alexander's policy towards
the conquered), there may well have been some relaxation of their
organization.  Magians may have sometimes married outside the
caste,[3] and it seems just possible that aliens (presumably by some
rite of adoption) were admitted occasionally to priestly positions,
just as later Tabari records that Mihr-Nars destined his first son for
the ecclesiastical career, and that Bahram-Gotz gave to him the
second position in the Church.[4]  This, like the tale of the conversion
of a Greek who is given a high religious position,[5] may be purely
legendary.  A Musulman was not perhaps sensitive to the minutiae
of Persian religion ; but the tale looks like an act of special favourit-
ism indicating the possibility of elasticity.

Whatever happened in the native haunts of the Magi, their
position *in partibus* was gravely affected.  The Persian régime
had naturally caused Magi to take up their abode in cities of
Asia Minor, at least in those cities which were garrison towns
or administrative centres.  After the overthrow of the old order
some of them stayed, and we know of them not merely in those
kingdoms which cultivated Persian traditions (Commagene, Cappadocia, Pontus), but also in Greek cities (Hypaepa and Hierocaesarea

[1] Cf. A. Christensen, *L'Empire des Sassanidae* (*D. kgl. Danske Vidensk.
Selsk. Skriften*, 7 Raekke, historisk og filosofisk Afd. i. 1, 1907), pp. 17 f., 20, 34,
64 ff. : for Sassanian assertion of faith on their coins, Herzfeld, *Paikuli*, i.
pp. 44 ff.; for a supplement to Christensen, E. Stein, *Byz.-neugriech. Jahrbücher*, i. pp. 50 ff. (political influence of this church at its height in middle of
fifth century A.D., strong from end of fourth to end of fifth).

[2] Gottheil, *Essays Drisler*, p. 35 (a prophecy).

[3] Cf. Cumont, *Textes et monuments*, i. p. 239 (in the Dinkārt); Clemen, *Religionen*, p, 161 (modern Parsis).

[4] Th. Nöldeke, *Geschichte der Perser und Araber zur Zeit der Sassaniden aus
der arabischen Chronik des Tabari*, p. 452.

[5] A. V. W. Jackson, *Zoroaster*, pp. 89 f.  Normally speaking the hereditary
principle was vital, as it still is among the Parsees (J. H. Moulton, *The Treasure
of the Magi*, pp. 132 f.) ; cf. A. Christensen, pp. 20, 34, 65, for organization, and
Clemen, *Religionen*, p. 161, for the double initiatory rites now admitting to the
Parsee priesthood a man born in the class.  In *Acta S. Anastasii*, p. 2 b 7 Usener,
we read of A. being taught Magian lore by his father.  Cf. Apuleius, *Apol.* 26 " nec
ulli temere inter Persas concessum est magum esse, haud magis quam regnare."
Philo, *De specialibus legibus*, iii. 100, says that no one was allowed to become
king among the Persians εἰ μὴ πρότερον τοῦ Μάγων γένους κεκοινωνηκὼς τυγχάνοι.
This is, however, probably only a pointed way of putting what we read in
Plato, *Alcib. I.* p. 122 A, Cicero, *De diuin.* i. 91, of the king's education by the
Magi—or a misunderstanding.  On priestly families in Zoroastrian Armenia
cf. M. H. Ananikian in Hastings, *Enc. Rel. Eth.* i. pp. 801 f. : he remarks that
there is no record of a Magian caste in Armenia.

in Lydia). Bardaisan in his *Laws of the Countries*, § 38, states that some of the Persians were scattered and lived in Media, Atropatene, Parthia, Egypt, and Phrygia, and were in every country called Magi. Now Magian colonies in the kingdoms might without difficulty keep up their traditions, though even there they could not avoid contact with the Greek culture around them[1]; but in Greek cities they were far more exposed to change. As their numbers dwindled they may very well have admitted others to their ranks by some sort of adoption. And it will be remembered that Pausanias speaks of the sanctuaries at Hierocaesarea and Hypaepa as belonging to *Lydians called Persic*, Λυδοῖς ἐπίκλην Περσικοῖς.[2] Further, a Graeco-Aramaic bilingual inscription found at Farasa (the ancient Ariaramneia-Rhodandos in Cappadocia), and assigned by H. Grégoire to the first century of or before our era, runs thus:
Σαγάριος Μαγ[αφά]ρνου στρατηγ[ὸ]ς ᾽Αριαραμινεί(ας) ἐμάγευσε Μίθρῃ.[3] That is, Sagarios became a Magos of Mithras,[4] or officiated as Magos for Mithras.[5] It would not be safe to insist in Greek of this type that the aorist must have its proper significance ' became ' rather than ' was '; but the use of the verb is really unmistakable. If Sagarios had been of the priestly Magian tribe, we should have had not Σαγάριος στρατηγὸς . . . ἐμάγευσε, but Σαγάριος μάγος . . . ἐστρατήγησε. It may further be remarked that this emphasis on Mithras belongs to the Hellenistic development of Persian religious ideas. Now in Mithraism those who had reached the fifth grade of initiation were called *Persae*, and it is quite thinkable that this implied something like St. Paul's view of Gentile Christians as belonging to the new Israel. Persia, like Israel, was a holy nation with its hope ; and, as Meyer has reminded us, Zoroastrianism was universalist.[6]

So the μάγος at Hypaepa was very likely no more necessarily of

---

[1] Cf. *Journ. Hell. Stud.* xlix. p. 114 on the mixture of Greek and Persian eschatology in the inscription on the funerary monument of Antiochus I. of Commagene. The style shows the same mixture : its superficial character is that of contemporary rhetoric, but its spirit and *innere Form* find their best analogy in Persian inscriptions and in the Sassanid inscriptions of Paikuli.

For the blending of ideas cf. also *Gnomon*, vi. pp. 30 ff., and the prophecy current under the name of Hystaspes (Ganschinietz, Pauly-Wissowa, ix. 541 f. ; an exhaustive treatment by H. Windisch, ' Die Orakel des Hystaspes,' in *Verh. d. kon. Akademie-Amsterdam*, Afd. Letterk. N.F. xxviii. p. 3, 1929).

[2] v. 27. 5. We read of an ἀρχίμαγος at Hypaepa in an inscription assigned to the third or fourth century A.D. (Kaibel, *Epigrammata Graeca*, 537, No. 903 a).

[3] *Comptes rendus de l'Académie des Inscriptions*, 1908, pp. 434 ff. Ed. Meyer, *Ursprung und Anfänge des Christentums*, ii. p. 88, assigns it to the third century B.C.

[4] So Cumont translates, *Les Religions orientales dans le paganisme romain*[4], p. 274, note 23.

[5] So Grégoire.     [6] *Ursprung*, ii. p. 73.

Persian blood than Christian *leuitae* were of Jewish blood. There is another aspect of this Dispersion to be remembered. Magi left in isolation and perhaps stripped of former revenues may well have used their prestige and their reputation as magicians and have become more or less professional magicians. We certainly meet diviners from this region ; Juvenal vi. 550 mentions *Armenius uel Commagenus haruspex.*

Magical literature.

(ii.) The second new Hellenistic factor is the coming into circulation in and after the third century B.C. of various collections of magical recipes under the names of Ostanes, Zoroaster, and the Magi. We know them from quotations in the elder Pliny, Pseudo-Dioscorides, magic papyri, the *Geoponica* and elsewhere,[1] and the elder Pliny gives us in *N.H.* xxx. 3 ff. an excellent illustration of the extent to which they had imposed on the popular imagination. The magic art, he says, undoubtedly started with Zoroaster in Persia, as all authorities agree. He quotes Eudoxus and Aristotle for the date of Zoroaster (here placed 6000 years before Plato's death) and proceeds to record the opinion of Hermippus "who wrote most carefully about that whole art and set forth 2,000,000 lines written by Zoroaster, giving the titles of his works." Pliny's actual authority may well be Apion, who appears in the *indices auctorum* but not in the text [2] ; but the tradition goes back to Hermippus, almost certainly the Hermippus who was a pupil of Callimachus.

Pliny quotes Zoroaster for a method of determining the time to sow (xviii. 200), and several times in xxxvii. on the virtues of certain stones (150, 157, 159), and records his name in his *indices auctorum.* Ostanes he does not there record, but quotes in xxviii. 69, where O. is quoted after the Magi and Hesiod, and in §§ 256 and 261 ; the Magi he quotes continually in xxviii., xxx. and xxxvii. It is quite clear that when he quotes Magi he means not ' magicians ' in a vague way, but some definite body of doctrine ; this follows from such passages as xxix. 138 *magnam auctoritatem huic animali* (sc. *gryllo) perhibet Nigidius, maiorem magi, quoniam retro ambulat terramque terebret, stridat noctibus,* and xxx. 100 *sed et alios alligant*

[1] E.g. *Catalogus codicum astrologicorum Graecorum,* ii. 192 ff, etc. Cumont, *Textes et monuments,* i. p. 33.

[2] So F. Münzer, *Beiträge zur Quellenkritik der Naturgeschichte des Plinius,* p. 130. We have a reference to Apion Περὶ μάγου in Suidas, s.v. Πάσης, II. ii. 139 Bernhardy (no doubt taken by S. from one of the sources from which he draws his explanations of proverbs; cf. A. Adler, *Suidas,* I. xix.), and in the proem of Diogenes Laertius. If this hypothesis is correct it is particularly notable that Egyptian magic is not mentioned by Pliny (a point remarked by Cumont, *Religions orientales*[4], p. 295 n. 99). This should perhaps be explained from the fact that the Persian tradition was so thoroughly established. Is it also conceivable that Apion shifted responsibility from Egypt ? I do not press this, for it is not clear to me that Apion would have regarded magic as disreputable.

*magi.* It is probable that Pliny cites from some doxographic source, giving the plural Magi like the οἱ Στωικοί, οἱ 'Επικούρειοι, οἱ Πλατωνικοί of texts recording *placita* of philosophers.[1] In xxi. 62 he gives Pseudo-Democritus as an intermediary source,[2] and it may be that this was commonly his source.

It is much to be desired that the relations of this *soi-disant* Persian material to Persian ideas should be fully investigated. Eduard Meyer has remarked on a point of contact between Ostanes and the Avesta, though noting that Persian tradition is changed.[3] We may here note the virtues ascribed to puppy's brains (xxix. 117) and to dog's gall (xxx. 82), since the dog was in Iranian theory very much an animal on the side of good : we may also note the generally apotropaeic and medicinal character of this material, which agrees with some of the scanty indications which we have found of Persian practice.

Hermippus was a writer whose attitude towards history was some- Hermippus. what credulous,[4] but it may well be that the statement about his setting forth of two million lines of Zoroaster indicates the existence of these writings in Greek by his time [5] : the number may well be either a scribal error or an exaggeration. As for the idea of genuine translation, it is not likely. Apart from the Septuagint there is very little genuine translation into Greek, but only adaptation. The Tefnut story is translated freely,[6] the ' Potter's Oracle ' may be a translation as it claims to be,[7] and I would remark that Ecphantus

---

[1] Note xxviii. 86 "innocentiores ex his." For this mode of quotation cf. my *Sallustius*, xxxviii.

[2] "Democritus . . . narrat . . . magos Parthorumque reges hac herba uti ad uota suscipienda." For this work cf. Wellmann, *Die Φυσικά des Bolos Demokritos*, i. (*Abh. Preuss. Akad.*, 1928, vii.). Ostanes was the supposed teacher of Democritus; cf. Diels, *Vorsokratiker*, ii. p. 130. In the same way Pliny seems to have received Chaldaean theories of the universe through Epigenes, whom he perhaps knew from Posidonius (W. Kroll, *Hermes*, lxv. pp. 1 ff.).

[3] *Ursprung*, ii. p. 93. An interesting indication of knowledge of Persian terminology is a gloss in Hesychius : Δεύας · τοὺς ἀκάκους (κακοὺς Bötticher) θεοὺς Μάγοι.

[4] Cf. F. E. Adcock, *Camb. Hist. Journ.* ii. p. 106, on the part which Hermippus seems to have played in falsifying tradition concerning the early Greek lawgivers. Diels, *Doxographi*, p. 151, suggests that H. acted in good faith.

[5] It does not seem to me quite safe to conclude from Pliny, as has been done, that these books were in the Alexandrian library, though the stichometric indication of their total bulk perhaps points to a library. *Explanauit* is ambiguous : probably it means ' gave a full statement of contents of.'

[6] Reitzenstein-Crönert-Spiegelberg, *Sitzungsber. Heidelb. Akad.* 1923, ii. Cf. the Greek acrostic poem with a corresponding Demotic poem of Moschion (Revillout, *Revue égyptologique*, ii. pp. 274 f.). Like our magic papyri and Coptic Gnostic books it is the product of a bilingual stratum.

[7] *Journ. Hell. Stud.* xlix. p. 114.

*ap.* Porphyry, *De abstinentia* iv. 10, gives an adaptation of the Egyptian ' negative confession of the dead man ' [1] : what was then meant by adaptation is illustrated by P Oxy 1381. 174 f., *à propos* of a work on early Egyptian history. Such a claim could be utterly false, as we see from *Corp. Herm.* xvi., which pretends to be Egyptian but is Greek commonplace, or from Philo of Byblos : and it will be remembered that Plotinus himself detected one late fabrication under the name of Zoroaster.[2] There was a popular demand for such literature, and in the third century B.C. the temptation to invent unknown works from the past was intensified by the existence of the Alexandrian Library and its desire for completeness.[3]

Provisionally, we may guess that these supposedly Persian works had a Persian atmosphere and were in part at least based on Persian ideas and perhaps actual books, but that they were in no sense like Max Müller's *Sacred Books of the East.* Their scope was not limited to magic,[4] but it was by their magical content that they

---

[1] For that cf. G. Roeder, *Urkunden zur Religion des alten Ägypten*, pp. 274 f. Similar material in Damascius on cosmogony. Joseph. *C. Ap.* i. 54 says of his *Ant. Jud. ἐκ τῶν ἱερῶν γραμμάτων μεθηρμήνευκα.*

[2] *Vita Plotini*, 16.

[3] Cf. Galen xv. 105, xvi. 5 Kühn. To this period Wellmann ascribes the Neopythagorean Ἰδιοφυῆ of Orpheus (Φυσικά *des Bolos*, i. 4). On the existence of Pythagoreanism in this century cf. H. Lewy, *Sobria ebrietas* (*Beih. z. Zeit. neut. Wiss.* ix.), p. 67. On its importance for magic cf. *Journ. Egypt. Arch.* xv. pp. 227 f. It should be remarked that the Essenes, who have often been thought to be influenced by Pythagoreanism, possessed writings of the ancients concerned with medicinal roots and properties of stones (λίθων ἰδιότητες, Josephus, *B.J.* ii. 136). These may well have been something like the Ἰδιοφυῆ, or even in some relation thereunto. (Some of the Essenes claimed the gift of prophecy : βίβλοις ἱεραῖς καὶ διαφόροις ἁγνείας καὶ προφητῶν ἀποφθέγμασιν ἐμπαιδοτριβούμενοι, *ib.* 159.) See the article on the Essenes by Cumont, *Comptes rendus de l'Académie des Inscriptions*, 1930, pp. 99 ff.

[4] Dion of Prusa quotes in *Or.* 36 a Persian tale relating to fiery destruction of the universe : his manner of quoting it *may* suggest that he came upon it casually and that it was not part of any sort of large collection of Persian material. Nigidius Figulus *ap.* Serv. *in Ecl.* iv. 10 (fr. lxvii. in Swoboda's edition, p. 83), having quoted the Orphic doctrine of the four ages of the world presided over by Saturn, Jupiter, Neptune and Pluto, adds that some, like the Magi, say that there will be an age of Apollo (cf. J. Jüthner, *Anzeiger der Akad. in Wien*, 1925, pp. 170 f.). On this doctrine M. Cumont kindly allows me to refer to his forthcoming article in *Rev. hist. rel.* 1930. Ostanes certainly dealt with angelology, and perhaps exercised considerable influence on the development of ideas on this topic ; cf. Cumont, *Religions orientales*⁴, pp. 279 f. Plut. *De defectu oraculorum* 10 refers to the theory of *daimones* as coming from the Magi or Orpheus, or some Egyptian or Phrygian. For the method of securing a happy passage to heaven in Arnobius ii. 62 cf. *Journal Eg. Archaeol.* xv. pp. 230 ff.

most impressed popular imagination, which was then more prone than now to take a book or a statement at its face value, and that they helped to crystallize the idea of magic as a Persian thing. They had a long life.[1]

4. We have now seen the main lines of the development of the term $\mu\acute{a}\gamma\sigma$. In and after the Hellenistic period it has its two meanings, Persian fire-priest and magician or quack, and these meanings occur side by side. Thus Philo is fully aware of the character of the Persian Magi and of their $\mu\alpha\gamma\iota\kappa\acute{\eta}$ and is disposed to ennoble it, writing as he does at a time when for nearly three centuries it has been a current idea that various early Greek sages had learnt wisdom from Persian and Egyptian priests. At the same time, a page earlier he uses $\mu\acute{a}\gamma\sigma$ in the derived sense.[2] Apuleius also in his *Apologia* 26 sets the two senses side by side. The derived sense is much commoner. Magi appear in Tacitus on a footing with *Chaldaei* : they are credited with rites (*sacra*) and with ways of evoking the dead.[3] They are in fact professionals to whom the private person may turn in time of need. It has been shown earlier that the term now implies no nationality in particular ; it is freely used in Egyptian magical texts, and Pliny can say *peragratis Persidis Arabiae Aethiopiae Aegypti magis*,[4] and Herodian $\tau\sigma\acute{v}\varsigma$ $\tau\epsilon$ $\pi\alpha\nu\tau\alpha\chi\acute{o}\theta\epsilon\nu$ $\mu\acute{a}\gamma\sigma\nu\varsigma$.[5] At the same time the name has a flavour of Eastern wisdom, as in Matth. ii. 1,[6] and a magus might employ Persian dress and apparatus to

Summary.

---

[1] In addition to material noted earlier cf. the Life of Severus, Patriarch of Antioch from 512 to 518, by Zacharias the Scholastic. He mentions a collection of magical books, some ascribed to Zoroaster, some to Ostanes, some to Manetho (*Patrologia Orientalis*, II. i. 62, ed. Kugener; *ibid.* 70 f. we read of mountebanks who claimed to know from Magian and Persian books where Darius had hidden treasures; *ibid.* 38 there is a reference to papers ($\chi\acute{a}\rho\tau\eta\varsigma$) with invocations of pagan gods doubtless like the $\lambda\acute{o}\gamma\sigma\iota$ of our magical papyri).

[2] *Quod omnis probus liber*, § 74 ; *De specialibus legibus*, iii. 100 ; *ib.* 93, in the ordinary sense. What he says, § 101, on the $\pi\alpha\rho\acute{a}\kappa\sigma\mu\mu\alpha$ $\tau\alpha\acute{v}\tau\eta\varsigma$, sc. $\tau\hat{\eta}\varsigma$ $\mu\alpha\gamma\iota\kappa\hat{\eta}\varsigma$, does not refer to Persia. So again Numenius *ap.* Euseb. *Praep. evang.* ix. 7 (a reference which I owe to Mr. B. S. Page) speaks of $B\rho\alpha\chi\mu\hat{a}\nu\epsilon\varsigma$ $\kappa\alpha\grave{\iota}$ $'Io\nu\delta\alpha\hat{\iota}\sigma\iota$ $\kappa\alpha\grave{\iota}$ $M\acute{a}\gamma\sigma\iota$ $\kappa\alpha\grave{\iota}$ $A\grave{\iota}\gamma\acute{v}\pi\tau\iota\sigma\iota$, but in another fragment (*ib.* ix. 8) uses $\mu\alpha\gamma\epsilon\hat{v}\sigma\alpha\iota$ of Iannes and Iambres.

[3] Cf. *Ann.* xvi. 31, where Servilia, defending herself on the charge of having had recourse to such *sacra* for divinatory purposes, says "nullos impios deos, nullas deuotiones nec aliud infelicibus precibus inuocaui quam ut hunc optimum patrem tu, Caesar, uos patres seruaretis incolumem " ; Tibullus i. 2. 61 f. "nocte serena concidit ad magicos hostia pulla deos "; Virg. *Ecl.* 8. 68 "magicis . . . sacris " ; Serv. *ad Aen.* iv. 493 "cum multa sacra Romani susciperent, semper magica damnarunt."

[4] *N.H.* xxv. 13.       [5] iv. 12. 3.

[6] Cf. Klostermann's note. They come $\dot{a}\pi\grave{o}$ $\dot{a}\nu\alpha\tau\sigma\lambda\hat{\omega}\nu$, which is vague, and they are mentioned with respect. Matthew and Luke differ in their use of $\mu\acute{a}\gamma\sigma\varsigma$.

give atmosphere.[1] In so far as he uses anything really taken from Persia, he uses it just as non-Christians used the name of Jesus in magic, or as one might imagine individual quacks in a non-Catholic country using adaptations of liturgical exorcisms, divorced from their background and combined with other elements seeking the aegis of the borrowed name. Such an analogy seems to me helpful for the understanding of the *Mithrasliturgie*.

The problem of Elymas.

5. The writer of Acts describes Elymas as μάγον ψευδο-προφήτην. This is almost intentionally vague, and it is not quite safe to infer that Elymas was a professional vending spells or performing for profit rites intended to do harm or to influence the affections of others. μάγος in such a context *may* merely be used like γόης, humbug, of a practitioner of another and hostile religion. It is probable that in such a context you mean by μάγος a man who might perfectly well be doing mumbo-jumbo even if you have not actually found him in the act.

It is not surprising to find a Jew in this context. Jewish exorcists appear in Acts xix. 13, where τῶν περιερχομένων Ἰουδαίων ἐξορκιστῶν is very contemptuous for a body including seven sons of a high priest, and classes them with the begging priests of the *dea Syra* or cheapjacks of any kind. Their spells, or spells which purported to be theirs, enjoyed widespread authority, largely due no doubt to the mysterious nature of the Jewish race and its firm claim of intimate relationship to a powerful deity whose name was surrounded with a secrecy which accentuated its value, a deity moreover who was believed to have interfered and to be prepared to interfere cataclysmically with the course of history. The temptation to Jews to embrace this career may be inferred from various prohibiters : Rab of Babylon, who died in A.D. 297, said, "He who learns a single word from a Magian is worthy of death,"[2] and the (possibly Jewish) list of prohibitions in *Didache* ii. 2 includes οὐ μαγεύσεις οὐ φονεύσεις. Burkitt has drawn attention to an interesting Syriac homily *On*

[1] Cf. Lucian, *Menippus* 6 f., which is of course localized at Babylon : so one of our supposed magical Magi *in partibus* may lie behind the picture, which may go back to Lucian's model Menippus. We may remark that M. is ordered to carry a lyre (8), and with it calms Cerberus. Cf. the new fragment of Varro, possibly from his Menippean satire Ὄνος λύρας, discussed *Cl. Rev.*, 1927, pp. 169 ff., and 1929, pp. 60 f.

[2] Cited by Strack-Billerbeck, i. 76, on Matt. ii. 1. Cf. S. Krauss, *Jewish Encyclopaedia*, ii. p. 406a, for Jewish contempt of the Magi. In general cf. L. Blau, *Altjüdisches Zauberwesen*, and *Jewish Encyclopaedia*, viii. p. 255 ; Schürer, *Gesch. jüd. Volkes*⁴, iii. pp. 407 ff. ; C. C. McCown, *The Testament of Solomon*. Jewish magic is part of the whole interesting phenomenon of heretical Judaism in antiquity, on which cf. my *Early Gentile Christianity*, pp. 54 f. ; H. Gressmann, *Die orientalischen Religionen im hellenistisch-römischen Zeitalter*, pp. 116 ff., 168.

*Magicians, Enchanters and Diviners*, in which the writer complains
that his fellow-Christians, even the clergy, resorted to magicians and
Jews. The text is ascribed in MSS. to St. Ephraim, but assigned
by Burkitt to Isaac of Antioch, who flourished in the first half of
the fifth century of our era.[1] So later the legend of Theophilus,
supposed, according to the version which Radermacher regards as
the oldest, to have lived in the time of Heraclius, mentions a Jewish
' servant of the devil ' at Adana in Cilicia : it is to him that the
Christian when tempted has recourse.[2]

Elymas is not an ordinary professional vending curses and
philtres, or if he is, he has other qualities commending him to Sergius
Paulus. He is a man of religious potentiality who has some sort of
vague position in the household of a great Roman. His status is not
unlike that of the domestic philosophers whom men of rank kept, or
of private chaplains later. Juvenal vi. gives a striking picture of a
Jewess [3] who has secured a Roman lady's confidence. That Elymas
should stand in the position ascribed to him may to us appear
strange : but in view of the religious curiosity which marked the
period we need not regard the association as impossible : the intimate
relation in which the astrologer Thrasyllus stood to Tiberius after
his successful prophecy may serve as a further analogy.[4] Moreover,

[1] *Proc. Soc. Bibl. Archaeol.* xxiii. (1901), pp. 77 f. ; T. J. Lamy's *St.
Ephraem*, ii. p. 400 ; A. Baumstark, *Geschichte der syrischen Literatur*, p. 65,
accepts the identification as fairly near certain.

[2] τοῦ διαβόλου ὑπουργός, L. Radermacher, *Griechische Quellen zur Faustsage*
(*Sitzungsber. Akad. Wien*, 206, iv., 1927), p. 164. 23.

[3] Possibly a syncretistic Jewess, as Reitzenstein infers from 544 (*Die hellenis-
tischen Mysterienreligionem*[3], pp. 145 ff.) ; but Juvenal speaks loosely. On the expulsion of Jews for proselytism from Rome in 139 B.C. cf. Reitzenstein, pp. 104 f.

[4] Cf. the *Symposiac Questions* of Plutarch with their discussions of such
topics as Jewish religion, the question of Tiberius on the death of the great Pan
(and *Cl. Rev.*, 1923, pp. 164 f.), the interest of Felix in Paul's preaching, Acts
xxiv. 24 ff., and Apion's work on the symbolism of Egyptian hieroglyphics. We
may further note Nero's sudden devotion to the statuette of an unknown deity
(Suet. *Nero*, 56) and his initiation by Tiridates (Plin. *N.H.* xxx. 17 " magos secum
adduxerat, magicis etiam cenis eum initiauerat "), or again Statius, *Silvae*,
III. ii. 101 ff. (in giving to a friend good wishes for his departure to Egypt
Statius remarks on the opportunities which he will have for learning the secrets
of the country, not merely the old question of the Nile's sources but also, 110,
" cur inuida Memphis, curue Therapnaei lasciuiat ora Canopi, cur seruet Pharias
Lethaeus ianitor aras, uilia cur magnos aequent animalia diuos ; quae sibi prae-
sternat uiuax altaria phoenix." *A propos* of *magnos*, conventional as it is, we may
observe that μέγας and μέγιστος are as divine epithets particularly common in
Graeco-Roman Egypt). Plin. *Ep.* v. 8. 4, explaining the appeal which history
makes, says " sunt enim homines natura curiosi et quamlibet nuda rerum
cognitione capiuntur, ut qui sermunculis etiam fabellispue ducantur." Cf.

Sir William Ramsay has rightly reminded us of the train of *comites* who formed the suite of a governor [1] ; we may remember the pictures which Juvenal and Lucian give us of the Greeks attendant on a great man, or again earlier the way in which Fulvius Nobilior took Ennius with him on the Aetolian war to celebrate his achievements in verse. A Roman governor might of course have other use for a magus. Josephus tells how Felix used Atomos, a Jew of Cyprian birth who pretended to be a Magus, to persuade Drusilla to leave her husband.[2] It has been suggested that Atomos and Etoimas (a strong variant here) are one and the same man : this is possible, but no more.[3]

The general character of the story.
6. The story as a whole is of the type so common later of a demonstration by results of the superior merits of Christianity. The appeal to works as a proof of Messiahship and the gift and promise of supernatural powers to the disciples are made emphatically in the Gospels.[4] In the surrounding Hellenistic world the notion of a dispassionate supernatural being was confined to certain philosophers, and any enthusiastic devotee expected wonders from the object of his devotion, particularly in any conflict, and appealed to those wonders as reasons why the indifferent public around him should side with him. The *Bacchae* of Euripides illustrates this attitude. A striking instance is afforded by a Delian inscription of about 200 B.C. recording how Apollonius, who like his father and grandfather before him was priest of Sarapis, had a vision saying that a Sarapeum must be built and the god must not live in hired places as before, and promising to find and to indicate the spot. The temple was built, and then legal proceedings were taken against the new religion. Sarapis said to Apollonius in a dream, *We shall be victorious*, and they were. A poem by Maiistas follows, celebrating the event.

---

again the knowledge which Epictetus shows of Judaic use (i. 11. 12, 22. 4 ; ii. 9. 14).

This curiosity is a factor of some importance in the spread of Christianity in the Gentile world. Christian propaganda in it must have depended largely on one individual bringing in another. It must have been so also with Mithraism, which, unlike the cults of Cybele and of the Egyptian deities, had no public ceremonies striking the imagination at once.

To this periphery of interested persons and to Christian people eager to know the earlier history of the movement Luke and Acts were perhaps addressed. It is not likely that they were gettable through the booksellers of the time.

[1] *St. Paul the Traveller*, p. 77. Cf. Friedländer, *Sittengeschichte Roms*[9], i. p. 73, iv. pp. 56 ff., on the Emperor's entourage.

[2] *Ant. Iud.* xx. 142.

[3] Literature in A. Wikenhauser's *Die Apostelgeschichte und ihr Geschichtswert* (*Neutestamentliche Abhandlungen*, viii. 3-5), p. 397. We find in Egypt domestic magicians, A. H. Gardiner, *Proc. Soc. Bibl. Arch.* xxxix. p. 32.

[4] Mt. xi. 4-6 ; Lk. vii. 21-22 ; John x. 41, xiv. 11 ; Lk. x. 17 ff.

The miracle was that the accusers were struck dumb. *"And all the people in that hour marvelled at thy power, and thou didst bring great glory to thy servant in god-stablished Delos."* [1] So again in the Alexandrine story of the dispute between the Jews and the Alexandrians before Trajan, the image of Sarapis sweated at the critical moment and there was much popular emotion in consequence. There were tumults in Rome, and many shouts were raised and many fled to the hills.[2]

The result of a miracle is πίστις, that is to say, those present or some of them take up an attitude of submissive reliance in the new δύναμις and its representatives.[3] Here the miracle takes the form of a judgement of God, like that which fell on Ananias and Sapphira, or that in the Delian story. The story is, as E. Peterson has remarked,[4] one of *heiliges Recht*; it includes the motif of the successful curse (like that of Theseus in the *Hippolytus* of Euripides). A *Gottesurteil* (with a competitive nuance) occurs in the story of Korah, Dathan and Abiram in Numbers xvi., and of Elijah and the prophets of Baal in 1 Kings xviii. There may be in it some suggestion of the out-doing of the magician at his own game : blinding is one of the things

---

[1] O. Weinreich, *Neue Urkunden zur Sarapis-Religion*, pp. 31 ff.

[2] P Oxy 1242; cf. W. Weber, *Hermes*, pp. 50, 70. On the typology of these stories cf. E. Peterson, ΕΙΣ ΘΕΟΣ. In Christian legend they are extremely common, e.g. E. A. W. Budge, *The Contendings of the Apostles*, ii. p. 367.

[3] The *Heroicus* of Philostratus illustrates well the concept of πίστις in the early third century A.D. A Phoenician visits a vine-tender who believes himself to have a special relation to the hero Protesilaus, who visits him and looks after him. The Phoenician is inclined to disbelieve things mythical, having met no eye-witnesses of their reality (φημὶ γὰρ ἀπίστως διακεῖσθαι πρὸς τὰ μυθώδη), but is sympathetic, having said earlier καὶ γὰρ ἂν χαρίζοιο τοῖς ἥρωσιν, εἰ πιστεύων ἀπέλθοιμι. The vine-tender's narratives convince him, and he says μετὰ σοῦ λοιπόν, ἀμπελουργέ, τάττω ἐμαυτὸν καὶ οὐδεὶς ἔτι τοῖς τοιούτοις ἀπιστήσει. (Cf. Eitrem, *Symbolae Osloenses*, viii.) It is like the effect of an Apostolic sermon. For the psychology of religious conviction at the time we may compare Plin. *Ep.* vii. 27 ; P. asks whether *phantasmata* have objective existence and says that he is inclined to believe in them (1) from what he hears happened to Curtius Rufus, (2) from the story of Athenodorus, (3) from his freedman's dream. So Athanasius in his *Vita S. Antonii*, 77 (xxvi. 952 Migne) represents pagan philosophers as admitting to the Saint the superiority of ἡ δι' ἐνεργείας πίστις over ἡ διὰ λόγων ἀπόδειξις.

[4] *Die Kirche*, p. 19. A similar *Gottesurteil* prophesied for the high-priest Ananias in Acts xxiii. 2 and invoked in 1 Cor. v. 5 and later formulas of ex-communication, in forms of ordeal, in Roman republican treaty-making by *fetiales*. It is described in an Epidaurian inscription, Ἀρχαιολογικὴ Ἐφημερίς, 1918, p. 168, and in the so-called Lydian confession inscriptions ; it is threatened by Apollo's prophet to a menacing unbeliever in the papyrus dialogue published by W. Schubart, *Hermes*, lv. pp. 188 ff. On the successful curse cf. G. L. Hendrickson, *A.J.P.* xlvi. pp. 101 ff.

which his type claimed to be able to do,[1] and a demonstration of
power before a personage in authority is also characteristic.[2] But the
form of the tale is not the common one of competitive thaumaturgy,
and it does not end with the conversion and cure of the opponent
as is frequent in such tales.[3] It is just possible, but this is a most

[1] F. Ll. Griffith and H. Thompson, *Demotic Magical Papyrus of London and Leiden*, col. xxiv. 31.

[2] So Pachrates before Hadrian (Preisendanz, *Pap. Graec. Mag.* iv. 2445 ff.),
Eleazar before Vespasian, his sons and officers (Josephus, *Ant. Iud.* vii. 46), and
in a Syrian story Zoroaster before the king (R. Gottheil, *Essays Drisler*, pp. 40 f.).

[3] Of this we have Jewish instances (e.g. the contest between Moses and the
Egyptian magician, the rivalry of Daniel and the Chaldaeans in dream inter-
pretation), and a striking Egyptian instance in F. Ll. Griffith, *Stories of the High
Priests of Memphis*, pp. 173 ff. (the magicians of Ethiopia and of Egypt each in
turn cause the king of the one country to be taken to the other and beaten).
Parallel motifs are common, e.g. the Eastern idea of war as fought out partly
between the gods of the two countries, the war of Ninus and Zoroaster fought
out by magic (Arnobius i. 5), the divination of different Scythian diviners in
Herodotus.
Christian instances are plentiful, as for instance the legend of St. Peter and
Simon Magus and tales discussed by me *Journ. Theol. Stud.* xxviii. pp. 414 f.;
Budge, *Monks of Kubla Khan*, pp. 16 f. In his *Contendings*, ii. pp. 495 ff., we
have rival miracles of St. Peter and St. John on the one hand and St. Paul on the
other. *Ibid.* p. 580 we have rival healings by Artemis and St. Paul; pp. 654 f. a
spontaneous *Gottesurteil*, the priests who had not believed become blind, but in
accordance with the common motif recover their sight, thanks to the Apostles.
An interesting specimen of this type of tale occurs in the *Historia Apostolica*
ascribed to Abdias, vi. 7 ff. (Fabricius, *Codex pseudepigraphus Noui Testamenti²*,
I. ii. 608 ff.). Christian missionaries, Simon and Jude, go to Persia to undo
the work of two Magi, Zaroes and Arfaxat, heresiarchs who had fled from St.
Matthew in Ethiopia. Their tenets as stated in 7 are clearly Manichee; at the
same time they are credited with power to make men immobile or blind and to
control snakes (vii. 1). In the king's army there are " sacrificatores et arioli et
magi et incantatores qui per singulas mansiones sacrificantes daemoniis dabant
responsa fallaciae suae." On the day on which the Apostles come they could
give no oracle, but the daemon of a neighbouring city's shrine tells them *cum
ingenti mugitu* that the silence is due to Simon and Jude, "qui tantam consecuti
a Deo sunt uirtutem ut nullus nostrorum audeat illis praesentibus loqui." Then
as a demonstration of power the Apostles allow the gods to speak again. The
motif is probably borrowed from the story of St. Gregory Thaumaturgus:
Greg. Nyss. *Vita G. T.* in Migne *P.G.* xlvi. 913 D, cf. *Journ. Hell. Stud.* xlv. p. 95.
The silencing of oracles is known elsewhere, e.g. *Passio S. Saturnini*, 3, in
Ruinart, *Acta Martyrum²*, 109 f., but this is more individual, and uncertain as
is the date of Abdias it is probably later than the story of Gregory. (For making a
pagan image speak cf. Budge, *Contendings*, ii. pp. 379 ff.) It is improved on, since
the prophecy which follows is wrong, and the Christians follow by foretelling
what actually happens; the Magi are saved from death only by the entreaty
of the Christians. There follows a further trial of strength. The Magi (here
apparently Zaroes and Arfaxat in particular, ch. 13) cause the eloquent men

tentative guess, to which I attach little weight, that the localization
of the story in Cyprus derives additional point from the island's
reputation for magic.  Pliny xxx. 11, having spoken of Persian magic
as the oldest, passes to Jewish as " many thousands of years subsequent to Zoroaster " and adds *tanto recentior est Cypria*.[1]  If it
really was a recent development, this may add point to the story.

7. The story as it stands is one of the vivid scenes which the Conclusion.
writer of the third Gospel and of Acts incorporates in his tale.  It
comes before us bald and unadorned, without any attempt to explain
how Paul and Barnabas came before Sergius (as for instance by
some allusion to the Cyprian connexions of Barnabas, or by the
suggestion that the governor hearing of the new preaching wished
to know of it, either in the interests of public order or from that
religious curiosity which we have considered).[2]  The proconsul's
conversion, which would have been an event of the first importance,
is just stated as though it were that of a washerwoman.  And it
has no consequences :  " No Church is said to have been founded
at Paphos (contrast the names in xvii. 34) ;  the change of Saul's
name here to Paul remains very odd, notwithstanding all the
explanations given by commentators, and the names of the Magus
are more than odd." [3]  The conclusion to which one is driven is that

---

of the kingdom first to be silent, then to speak but be unable to move, then to
be unable to see though their eyes are open.  Later when they try to repeat
this the Apostles prevent them.  Next they bring serpents, which the Apostles
cause to bite them, after which they prevent the bites from being mortal and
cause them to heal after three days of suffering.

The story is clearly late and confused, passing from Manichee missionaries
to Persian priests, vi. 10.  They have authority like that of the Magi at the
Sassanid court ; but it would be unsafe to suppose that it rests on genuine knowledge of conditions in Persia.  In the *Passio S. Symphorosae* Hadrian has his
*magi et arioli* : the source of both stories is no doubt Daniel.  Abdias shows no
such local material as we find in the *Actes des martyrs persans*, edited by Delehaye
in *Patrologia Orientalis*, ii. 4, or in the Syrian Acts of the Persian Martyrs.

[1] It may be remarked that Cyprus was well fitted to play this part.
Egyptian, Phoenician and Greek influences had long blended in it.

[2] W. M. Ramsay, *Paul the Traveller*, p. 80, justly remarks that the Western
addition in vs. 8, " For Sergius heard Barnabas and Saul very gladly," is
explanatory : it sophisticates the narrative.

[3] I quote a letter from Professor Burkitt.  I need hardly say that the
incoherence of this piece of tradition confirms the suggestion made by Schwartz,
*Nachr. Götting. Gesell.*, 1907, pp. 271 f. (cf. *Beginnings* Vol. II. pp. 125 f. and
Addit. Notes 16, 18, and 34), of a doublet in the story of Paul and Barnabas.
It is possible, as Professor Lake suggests to me, that Elymas was, like Simon
Magus, a person of far greater importance than the narrative suggests : we are
in the dark.

Luke has some definite tradition which he has incorporated *tant bien que mal*. So lame a story would not readily have been invented in Luke's time. It is a *Gottesurteil* with the proconsul as background. In a later stage of development we should have heard of the conversion and cure of Elymas, and of the subsequent fortunes and martyrdom of Sergius : that became common form.

Naïve as the tale seems to us, it served three purposes. First, it represented the Roman authorities as very sympathetic at the outset of Paul's active ministry in the Gentile world ; secondly, it gave to Paul a *Gottesurteil* comparable with that declared by Peter on Ananias and Sapphira ; thirdly, and this was perhaps important, it represented Christianity in very sharp contrast with *magia*. The claim of Christians to work miracles, coupled with the novelty of the movement, caused them to be classed with *magi*.[1] Now Acts very definitely associates *magia* with a Jewish religious adventurer here, with others of the type in ch. xix., and with a time-serving temporary Christian convert in ch. viii. : and even he is represented as awed by the authority of the Apostles (vs. 24). The story, then, was useful ; and probably neither Luke nor his audience felt the difficulties which strike us.

## Note XV. The Conversion of Paul and the Events
### immediately following it

#### By Kirsopp Lake

The Pauline allusions.    The story of Paul's conversion and the events immediately following is told in Acts ix. 1 ff., in xxii. 6 ff., in xxvi. 12 ff., is referred to in Gal. i. 13 ff., and probably in 2 Cor. xi. 32.

Neither of the references in the Pauline epistles is a complete narrative. They do not give any account of the actual vision. But it is disconcerting to note to what an extent they mention episodes immediately following it which are partly ignored in Acts and partly inconsistent with its direct statements. It is therefore desirable to divide the whole subject into two sections : (i.) The account of the

---

[1] Cf. p. 182 earlier ; Celsus *ap.* Origen, *Contra Celsum*, i. 38 ; O. Braun, *Ausgewählte Akten persischer Märtyrer*, pp. 64, 116 ; the Apostles regarded as sorcerers by unbelievers in Budge, *Contendings*, ii. pp. 106, 125, 143, 226, 362, 422, 631 ; so Christ, *ibid.* p. 381 (as by Celsus *ap.* Orig. *C.C.* i. 68, cf. Klostermann on Mk. i. 23). We may note as remarkable, Braun, p. 203, of the Eucharist, "the flesh over which the magical prayers are recited," a phrase put in the mouth of the Magi. A. Fridrichsen, *Theology*, xxii. (March 1931) pp. 122 ff., argues forcibly that the words uttered by expelled demons in the Gospels are intended to differentiate Jesus from common magicians.

'Vision' described three times in Acts. (ii.) Paul's experiences and conduct immediately after the vision, partially related both in Acts and in the Epistles.

(i.) *The Vision.*—The three accounts of the vision in Acts are almost The Vision. identical; they clearly represent a single tradition, and probably a single source. The phraseology in all three is generally similar, but manifests Luke's tendency slightly to vary his phrases when repeating the same story. Moreover this variation is much less marked in the important passages, which are generally repeated almost *verbatim*.

The vision which changed Paul's life is described in each of the Variations three passages in Acts, with only very slight verbal differences. They in the narrative. all say that he was on the road to Damascus, that a bright light shone about him, and that a voice said, "Saul, Saul, why persecutest thou me?" Saul said, "Who art thou, Lord?" and was told, "I am Jesus, whom thou persecutest." There are, however, some differences in the account of the minor circumstances. (*a*) In ix. 7 Paul's companions heard the voice, but saw nothing; but in xxii. 9 they saw the light, but heard nothing. (*b*) In ix. 4 and xxii. 7 Paul fell to the ground, but his companions remained standing; but in xxvi. 14 they all fell to the ground. (*c*) In ix. 6 and xxii. 10 Jesus tells Paul to go to Damascus, where he will be told what to do; but in xxvi. 16 f. the actual commission of apostleship—ἐγὼ ἀποστέλλω σε—is given to Paul at the time of the vision.

Of these differences the first two are unimportant, and are such as are always found in any narrative which is repeated. Any lawyer knows that complete agreement between witnesses, or the exact repetition of the same story, is a sign of fabrication or of very careful preparation. The third is in a different category, and becomes very important when taken in connexion with the continuation of the narrative in ix. 9 ff. and xxii. 12 ff., and with the narrative in Gal. i. 13 ff., which present serious difficulty.

According to Acts ix. Paul went at once to Damascus, where Ananias, Ananias of definitely described as a Christian, was commissioned by Jesus to heal Damascus. Paul's blindness and to communicate to him the gift of the Spirit, which would fit him to be a witness to Jesus. Thus the first apostolic commission of Paul was given through Ananias. The same story is told in xxii. 12-16, but with minor differences. These make it appear that in xxii. 15 Ananias was announcing Paul's call to apostleship rather than conferring anything, that baptism is regarded as cleansing from sin rather than as conferring the Spirit, and that the divine commission to preach to the Gentiles was given later to Paul himself in Jerusalem.

But of this whole episode there is no trace at all in xxvi. The commission is given to Paul at the time of the vision, there is no story of his blindness or of Ananias, and Paul goes at once to Damascus and begins to preach.

It might be thought that this difference is merely due to a natural Paul's compression of the narrative, but when Galatians is taken into account assertion in the matter becomes more serious. Paul's own words are that he is an Galations.

apostle—not from men—$\dot{a}\pi'$ $\dot{a}\nu\theta\rho\dot{\omega}\pi\omega\nu$—nor through a man—$\delta\iota'$ $\dot{a}\nu\theta\rho\dot{\omega}\pi o\nu$ (Gal. i. 1)—and "I assure you," he says, "brethren, that the gospel which is preached by me is not according to man, for I did not receive it from a man ($\pi a\rho\dot{a}$ $\dot{a}\nu\theta\rho\dot{\omega}\pi o\nu$), nor was I taught it, but through revelation of Jesus Christ" (Gal. i. 11-12), and "when it pleased God (who separated me from my mother's womb, and called me through his grace) to reveal his Son in me, that I might preach him among the Gentiles, immediately I conferred not with flesh and blood, nor did I go up to Jerusalem, but I went away to Arabia" (Gal. i. 15-17).

By no possibility can these statements be reconciled with the story that Paul did not receive his commission directly from Jesus, who merely told him to go to Damascus to receive further instructions, which were communicated to him through a man—Ananias. If Paul had wished to contradict the story in Acts, could he have selected a better phrase than that which he employs when he says that he is an apostle 'neither from men nor through a man'? Or, on the other hand, could there have been a more deadly refutation of Paul's claim that he did not 'confer with flesh and blood' than the quiet recitation of the fact that his baptism and instruction to be a 'witness' came through Ananias?

**Possible sources for story.** It must be obvious that Paul would not so warmly have protested that his commission came directly from Jesus if there had been no stories of a different nature. As has been pointed out several times in *Beginnings of Christianity*, notably by Prof. Burkitt in Vol. II. pp. 106 ff., the difficulty of 'source-criticism' in Acts is that the parallel example of the third gospel proves that Luke used sources, but also proves that he used them so skilfully that their reconstruction in any detail is hazardous, if not impossible. Undoubtedly this applies to the present problem. Certainly Luke may have been acquainted with at least two, and possibly three sources, each of which possibly contained the story of how Paul came to be a Christian. One of these sources was Paul himself; for whether the writer of Acts was or was not a companion of Paul, it cannot be doubted that he had access to the Pauline tradition. The second source was the tradition of Jerusalem, which the earlier chapters of Acts abundantly prove to have been well known to Luke. The third possible source is the tradition of Antioch. This is certain: but can we tell which, or how many of the three sources, Luke was actually following and how far he edited it?

No hypothesis is more than a guess, yet any has just as much probability as that which merely accepts the divergence of the narratives and argues that it is unimportant. It is at least not impossible that the story of Ananias was current in Jerusalem, and was used to justify the contention that Paul was, in spite of his protest, an apostle 'from men and through a man.' Unless human nature has markedly deteriorated, it is probable that the story was told in many forms, none quite correct; but that the contention was made that Paul's apostleship was secondary is clear from the warmth with which Paul denied it, and the story of Ananias, told with continual variation, has exactly the form which such a story would probably receive. The account in Acts xxvi., which approaches so much nearer to the narrative in Galatians, may be harmonized to the Pauline version. A further possibility, which from lack of evidence cannot be proved or refuted, is that Acts ix. and Acts xxii. are a combination of the Pauline and Jerusalem versions, due to the Church at Antioch rather than to Luke, nor was Luke necessarily wrong in preferring it. It is quite unnecessary to suppose that the story of Ananias is fiction : it is very probable that there was someone of that name who befriended Paul, shaken and half blind, when he staggered into Damascus, and that Jewish Christians believed that he had contributed far more to Paul's understanding than Paul himself thought that he had done.

Can we say any more about Ananias ? Not with certainty. He may have been a refugee from Jerusalem, or an original disciple of Jesus living in Damascus (see note on ix. 10) ; but special importance attaches to the points raised in the notes to ix. 10 and 17. Preuschen's view is that chapter xxii. shows that there was originally a tradition according to which Ananias merely restored Paul's sight, and that he was a pious Jew, not a Christian. This is possible, but unprovable and perhaps improbable. Certainly, however, chapters ix. and xxii. depict Ananias differently. In chapter ix. he speaks in the accents of an Hellenistic Christian of the Lucan type. He is sent by ‘ the Lord, Jesus ’ ; and Paul is offered baptism in such a way that it is equated with the gift of the Spirit. In chapter xxii. he speaks as a Jewish Christian of the most primitive type. He is sent by ‘ the God of our fathers,’ and Jesus is not described as the Lord or even as the Messiah, but as the ‘ righteous one.’ Baptism is merely the washing away of sin, and the Spirit is not mentioned. If these are two variants of the same tradition, one of them has been very much edited, and surely it is much more likely that chapter xxii. represents the source, and that chapter ix. is Luke's Hellenizing revision. Certainty is unattainable, but to my own mind the most probable guess is that Ananias was an original Christian of the most primitive Jewish type, to whom Jesus was ‘ the Righteous one.’ He befriended and perhaps healed Paul, and in spite of Paul's protests was claimed in Jerusalem as his converter. I think xxii. is nearer the source than is ix., which has been Hellenized by Luke. But, on the other hand, xxii. may be somewhat shorter than the original.

Actual rôle<br>of Ananias.

Why did Luke omit the story of Ananias in chapter xxvi. ? I think that the most probable solution is that though Luke was using fundamentally the same source as he did in the earlier chapters, he omitted this episode either because he knew that Paul himself refused to accept it or from a correct and artistic sense that it was unnecessary in a speech before Herod Agrippa. This seems more likely than any more complicated theory of a combination of sources.

Thus the general result of a consideration of this part of the story is to suggest that the narrative of Paul's conversion as given in Acts is probably a form of the story current in Jerusalem, rather than a perfect representation of the way in which Paul would have told the story.

Paul's movements after his conversion.

(ii.) *The Events immediately following the Conversion.*—There are much greater difficulties in the narrative of Paul's procedure immediately after the conversion. Galatians says that he went away to Arabia and then returned to Damascus. Only after three years did he go to Jerusalem. Acts, on the other hand, says that he spent a few days in Damascus and then went straight to Jerusalem.

Arabia.

The Arabia to which Paul refers is doubtless the kingdom of the Nabatean Arabs, at that time both powerful and prosperous. The daughter of its king Aretas had been the wife of Herod Antipas, who discarded her in favour of Herodias, and Aretas—after an interval of some years—had attacked Herod with such success that the Romans had been obliged to intervene.[1] At one time the Nabatean power had extended from Damascus to beyond the Gulf of Akaba, and the Sinai peninsula is full of inscriptions and graffiti in the peculiar Nabatean script. After the time of Pompey Damascus was lost, but the greater part of the country east of Peraea remained in Nabatean power.

The exact limits of Nabatean Arabia in the first century cannot be defined with certainty, but Aretas probably controlled all the eastern part of Transjordania. The great cities of the Decapolis, such as Philadelphia and Gerasa, were of course not included, and Machaerus, east of the Dead Sea, was, according to Josephus,[2] the frontier fortress of Herod Antipas. But south and east of these cities Aretas was the dominant power.

Paul's purpose.

Why did Paul go to Nabatean Arabia? He is not explicit in Galatians; but the general tenor of his words implies that he went in fulfilment of the commission which he had received to preach to the Gentiles. "When it pleased him to reveal his Son in me that I might preach him among the Gentiles, immediately . . . I went to Arabia." Why? The obvious answer is, to obey the command and preach. The meaning is really quite plain, and has only been made obscure by the tendency of commentators to think that Arabia means Mt. Sinai and that Paul went there for rest and contemplation, because in Paul's exegesis of the story of Hagar in Gal. iv. 25 it is said that Mt. Sinai is in Arabia, and there is a tendency to suppose that Paul never preached except where Acts says that he did. But the Epistles show how much Paul did which Acts does not record, and Mt. Sinai[3] was no more the dominant part of Arabia in the first century than it is to-day.

The account in Acts.

Acts has a very different account. It says that Paul stayed in Damascus after his conversion, and preached in the synagogues that Jesus was the Son of God until the Jews threatened to kill him, when he went secretly to Jerusalem.[4]

It is impossible to see any way of reconciling these two presentments of Paul's movements. No one could ever suppose that the period of

---

[1] See Vol. I. pp. 16 ff.

[2] *Antiq.* xviii. 5. 1, and see the footnote on p. 18 of Vol. I.

[3] It is of course by no means certain that the Biblical Sinai is the modern Sinai.

[4] Acts ix. 20 ff.

preaching in Damascus described in Acts ix. was extended over three years. No one could suppose that into this period there must be intercalated a visit to Arabia. Indeed, the natural interpretation of Gal. i. is even further from Acts. If we had only the epistle, is it not certain that we should assume that the conversion took place in Damascus, that Paul then immediately went, not to but away from Damascus, and only returned (ὑπέστρεψα, a word which surely implies that he was in Damascus when he was converted) to Damascus after a visit to Arabia ? The general tenor of the passage certainly excludes the view that the immediate result of the conversion was a short but successful mission in Damascus, whence he went to Jerusalem.

It is hard to resist the conclusion that Luke has omitted essential details, thus bringing together events which were really separate, and making it appear that Paul's preaching in Damascus followed immediately after his conversion instead of many months later.

The next episode in the story is Paul's escape from Damascus in a basket let down over the wall when he was endangered by a Jewish plot. The parallel account of this plot and Paul's escape is given in 2 Cor. xi. 32 f. The 'basket' incident, which is the spectacular part of each story, suggests that both refer to the same incident, but there is much difficulty in the details. 2 Cor. xi. 32 f. says : " In Damascus, the ethnarch of Aretas the king watched (ἐφρούρει) the city of the Damascenes in order to capture me, and I was let down in a basket through a window in the wall, and I escaped from his hands." On the basis of this passage it has often been suggested that at this time Damascus, which had belonged to the Nabateans before the time of Pompey, had again been given by Rome to Aretas. There is, however, no evidence in support of this view except the fact—which may at any moment cease to be one—that no Roman coins of the reigns of Caius and Claudius have been found in Damascus. They are extant for Tiberius and for Nero, but not for the intervening reigns. But the argument from silence is peculiarly dangerous when applied to Roman coins in an outlying corner of the Empire in the first century. There is absolutely no other evidence to support the theory that Damascus was subject to Aretas in the time of Paul. Moreover the exact wording of 2 Cor. xi. 32 f. surely suggests that Aretas did not control Damascus at this time. What Paul implies is that when he was in Damascus the ethnarch of Aretas watched the city in order to catch Paul if he came out ; φρουρεῖν is a common word for besieging a city, though it can mean 'to guard' or 'to garrison.'[1] The ethnarch may have been the representative of Aretas in the city, but I suspect that he was the Sheikh of the tribe of Nabateans who controlled the territory outside the walls. In any case he was obviously watching the gates of Damascus in order to catch Paul if he tried to get out. So long as Paul was in Damascus the ethnarch had no power to kidnap him. But Paul wanted to go elsewhere, presumably to Jerusalem, in order, as he says in

Paul's escape from Damascus.

[1] See also Ed. Schwartz, *Nachrichten d. k. Ges. d. Wiss. zu Göttingen*, 1906, pp. 367 f.

Galatians, to see Cephas. Hence he left by the unusual but simple method of a basket through the window, while the ethnarch watched the door. It is a perfectly convincing narrative.

The story in Acts.

The story told in Acts has difficulties in itself and does not agree at all with 2 Corinthians. According to it the danger to Paul came from a Jewish plot, not from Arabian hostility. But the Jews were inside Damascus. Paul was frequenting their society daily. Why should they adopt the complicated tactics of waiting for him at the gate of the city? Moreover, why, if it were a Jewish plot, should Paul go straight to Jerusalem? It would be an exaggeration to say that the story is impossible, but it looks very much like an example of the tendency to give a Jewish basis to all hostility to Paul. In any case we really have to choose between Paul's own version in 2 Corinthians and that in Acts. It is very improbable that there were two plots against him, and that he twice was let down in a basket. According to Acts, Paul escaped because the Jews inside Damascus wanted to kill him; according to Corinthians, because the Arabs outside Damascus were waiting for him; in each case they were looking for him to go by the gate, and therefore he employed an unusual route, but the difference between Jews inside and Arabs outside is considerable. It is not likely that Paul confused them, and equally unlikely that they had made common cause in a plot against him.

Assuming that the account in 2 Corinthians is the true version, why were the Arabs hostile? The answer probably is that Paul had been preaching in Nabataean Arabia for more than a year, and Acts itself is witness that constituted authority rarely tolerated the Apostle for a longer time. Galatians in this case, when correctly interpreted, supplements and explains 2 Corinthians.

After the escape from Damascus comes the first visit to Jerusalem. Here again Acts and Galatians agree that Paul went from Damascus to Jerusalem, though according to himself it was three years after his conversion, and according to Acts 'some days' after it. But there is a more serious discrepancy. According to Paul's own account he went up to talk privately (that, surely, is the implication of ἱστορῆσαι) with Peter. He saw no other apostle except James the Lord's brother. He remained quite unknown to the Christians in Judaea, and it is absurd to argue that Judaea means 'outside of Jerusalem.' But a very different story is told in Acts. He was at first suspected by the Christians, but Barnabas—whom Paul reckons among the apostles—took him and introduced him to the apostles, and he was then so far from remaining unknown that he preached with such vigour that he had to be taken out of the city and sent away to Tarsus in order to save his life from the hostility which he had aroused.

Conclusion.

All these discrepancies raise the same problem. They are of that simple and direct nature which admits of no compromise. Either we must take Paul's version, or that of Acts. Paul was a principal in the story, and he was writing nearer the events. There can be no doubt that in general his version ought to be followed.   The question remains, how far does this affect our confidence in Acts ?   It seems to me absurd to say that Acts does not suffer.   When a witness has been put in the box and proves to be slightly wrong on almost every point, and very wrong on some, his evidence on other questions is to be treated with caution.   Nevertheless those who have had most to do with witnesses are the most reluctant to define the exact limits which this caution ought to be given.   Few ever give quite accurate testimony.   Luke was collecting information ; he heard other stories besides Paul's.   If he got them confused, and sometimes did not follow Paul's own account, it is not surprising.

Would he have done so to such an extent if he had actually known Paul in the flesh ?   It seems to me doubtful, but not impossible.

## Note XVI. The Apostolic Council of Jerusalem [1]

### By Kirsopp Lake

The general problem of Acts xv. is so complicated that it can only be stated—it cannot be solved—by a process of analysis into smaller ones. *The general problem.*

The reason for this is that here, almost for the only time in Acts, we really have a parallel narrative in a contemporary source, which may fairly be taken as playing a part analogous to that of Mark as compared with the gospel of Luke.   It is analogous, however, not identical.   For whereas Mark and Luke, both being gospels, belong to the same class of literature, Acts is history and Galatians is a controversial letter, two entirely different types of composition ; moreover Mark is one of the sources of Luke, but there is no reason to suppose that Galatians was used by the writer of Acts (see Vol. II. p. 308).

In Galatians i. 11-ii. 14 Paul gives a short account of his life from his conversion down either to the time when he went to Galatia or to the time when he was writing.   The first part of this account, i. 11-24, covers the period described in Acts ix. 1-30 and has been discussed in Additional Note 15.   The second part, ii. 1-14, covers either the visit described in Acts xi. 27-30 and xii. 25 or that described in Acts xv. 1-35. *Gal. i. 11-ii. 14.*

A comparison between the epistle and these verses of Acts presents the following problems :

(i.) What is the meaning of Galatians ii. 4, 5 ?

(ii.) To which visit of Paul to Jerusalem, as described in Acts, does Galatians ii. really correspond ?

---

[1] This note was published in advance in the series of essays in honour of Israel Abrahams, under the title 'The Council of Jerusalem Described in Acts xv.,' *Jewish Studies in Memory of Israel Abrahams*, New York, 1927, pp. 244-265.

(iii.) What is the meaning of Acts xv. in general and of the apostolic decrees in particular ?

(iv.) The results of a comparison of Galatians ii. and Acts xv.

Gal. ii. 4 f.

(i.) *What is the meaning of Galatians ii. 4, 5 ?*

As so often happens in passages which present exegetical difficulties, the text is uncertain. The ordinary text found in all critical editions and in all translations of modern times is : ἀλλ᾽ οὐδὲ Τίτος ὁ σὺν ἐμοὶ Ἕλλην ὢν ἠναγκάσθη περιτμηθῆναι· διὰ δὲ τοὺς παρεισάκτους ψευδαδέλφους, οἵτινες παρεισῆλθον κατασκοπῆσαι τὴν ἐλευθερίαν ἡμῶν ἣν ἔχομεν ἐν Χριστῷ Ἰησοῦ, ἵνα ἡμᾶς καταδουλώσουσιν, οἷς οὐδὲ πρὸς ὥραν εἴξαμεν τῇ ὑποταγῇ, ἵνα ἡ ἀλήθεια τοῦ εὐαγγελίου διαμείνῃ πρὸς ὑμᾶς. "But not even Titus who was with me, being a Greek, was compelled to be circumcised, but because of the false brethren privily brought in, who came in privily to spy out our liberty which we have in Christ Jesus, that they might bring us into bondage, to whom we yielded in subjection, no ! not for an hour, that the truth of the gospel might continue with you."

This text is found in all Greek MSS. (including ℵB) except D, but not in the Old Latin version or in the Peshitto Syriac. It has in so far a claim to recognition that it has not merely much manuscript support, but provides a sentence so impossible to construe and difficult to explain that it would always invite alteration.

The Western text.

The serious rival to this text is found in D, Irenaeus, Victorinus, Tertullian, Ambrosiaster, Primasius, and the Old Latin version : ἀλλ᾽ οὐδὲ Τίτος . . . ἠναγκάσθη περιτμηθῆναι, διὰ δὲ τοὺς παρεισάκτους ψευδαδέλφους . . . πρὸς ὥραν εἴξαμεν τῇ ὑποταγῇ ἵνα ἡ ἀλήθεια κτλ., omitting the words οἷς οὐδέ before πρὸς ὥραν.

Intermediate stages between these two readings are found in Marcion, some Greek MSS. known to Victorinus, and the Peshitto Syriac, who read οὐδὲ πρὸς ὥραν εἴξαμεν κτλ., but without οἷς, and in Jerome's *Commentary on Galatians*, which implies οἷς πρὸς ὥραν εἴξαμεν without οὐδέ. The question is whether these stages represent emendations of the ordinary text or of that found in D, etc. Undoubtedly, Tertullian and Irenaeus represent an older type of text than anything found, as a whole, in our extant MSS., but in any given instance there is always the chance that they have a purely Western corruption, and that the great MSS. are right. The crucial point of the textual argument is to be found in the reading of the Peshitto and Marcion. This seems to be certainly an emendation of the one text or of the other. If we assume the text of the MSS. to have been the original, it is possible that Marcion and Rabbula (the maker of the Peshitto) struck out οἷς to improve the grammar ; if we assume the text of Tertullian and Irenaeus, they may have inserted a negative in order to exclude the exegesis that Paul really did ' yield in subjection.'

The textual problem.

It will be seen, therefore, that the real difficulty is not that the textual authorities are equally balanced, but that it is so difficult to see which of the variants is really the *lectio ardua* which explains the others.  The question is, Which is more likely to have seemed *ardua* to early scribes, and so to have first invited alteration ?  Would they have been more shocked by the suggestion that Paul had circumcised Titus, or by an anacoluthon in his statement that he did not do so ?[1]

It is, however, a curious fact that the chief importance of this textual puzzle is to show that from the beginning no one was quite sure what certain details in the passage meant.  Nor is it appreciably easier with one text rather than another.  Whether it means "Titus was not compelled, and remained uncircumcised" or "Titus was not compelled, but was circumcised as an act of grace" depends entirely on the emphasis read into the words.  So also with the ordinary text, the choice between thinking that Paul meant that he yielded but not in subjection, or thinking that he meant that he did not yield at all, is entirely doubtful apart from emphasis on certain words.

I am inclined to think that probability favours the text which omits the οἷς and the οὐδέ, and that Titus probably was circumcised.  Paul is here defending himself against attack [2] : there is, therefore, a probability that the incidents with which he deals are those which his opponents had used to prove that he was subordinate to the Apostles at Jerusalem.  Certainly this is the case with the first visit to Jerusalem, and with the interview with the Apostles on the second visit ; clearly these were facts out of which Paul's opponents had tried to make capital, and had thus forced him to give his own account of what had happened.  If we might assume that this is also the case with the episode of Titus, it would follow that he had been circumcised, that Paul's opponents had used this as an argument, and that Paul therefore found it necessary to explain that, though Titus had been circumcised, it was not under compulsion, but as an act of grace, perhaps of misplaced concession to false brethren, whose true character he did not at the time perceive.

This is the more probable view, but it may be argued on the other hand, with fair plausibility, that the incident of Titus is only mentioned in order to prove that the interview at Jerusalem was not really a permanent submission, as could be seen from the fact that Titus (who was a Gentile) was not circumcised, in spite of the pressure exercised by the false brethren, to whom he yielded only on matters of temporary importance, not on those of principle.[3]  Nor is it possible to base a decision between these two lines of argument on our knowledge of what Paul is likely to have done.  Paul argues in his Epistles against the necessity of circumcision, but on the other hand, if Acts be correct,[4]

---

[1] I have taken the foregoing paragraphs from my *Earlier Epistles of St. Paul*, pp. 275 ff.

[2] For a fresh statement of this aspect of Paul's defence in the epistle, including this verse, see J. H. Ropes, *The Singular Problem of the Epistle to the Galatians*, 1929.

[3] Or, if another text be followed, "to whom we did not yield even for a moment," or with still another exegetical possibility, "to whom we did not yield even for a moment in any real subjection."

[4] See note on xvi. 3.

he circumcised Timothy, who was, after all, a Greek, even though his mother was a Jewess, and we may safely say that no one after reading Galatians v. would ever have expected such a concession to Jewish feeling, though v. 11 (" If I preach circumcision, why am I persecuted ?") may be taken as implying that in some way he had given rise to the statement that he did recommend circumcision.

Thus the only possible summing up of the whole point seems to be that a verdict of 'not proven' ought to be returned. It is possible to make attractive statements in the spirit of an advocate for either side, but if a judicial attitude is to be observed no other verdict is conceivable. If, however, I were obliged to take sides, I should say that there is a balance of argument in favour of the view that Titus was circumcised.

Conclusion.    However this may be, the most important facts are also the clearest. The trouble began in Jerusalem, and it was concerned with the question of circumcision. Paul did not go up because of it, but it came upon him because of 'false brethren' who had been brought in unawares when owing to revelation he was already there for another purpose, which he scarcely defines but suggests to have been the care of the poor.[1]  Moreover, the leaders were ultimately convinced that he was justified in the gospel which he was preaching among the Gentiles. Peter and the other 'pillars' recognized that he was the leader of the mission to the heathen, as Peter was of the mission to the Jews. No 'terms' are mentioned. It was, according to Galatians, an unconditional surrender to the Antiochian position. But not every one was convinced, and further trouble remained. Peter came down to Antioch, and so also did emissaries from James. These latter raised, not the question of circumcision, but the terms on which Jewish Christians might properly associate with Gentiles. The position of James was one of opposition to unconditional intercourse with Gentiles, and Peter and Barnabas, who, like Paul, had been freely mingling with them, were persuaded that James was right.

It is the narrative which must be accepted as Paul's own statement of the sequence of events. It is extremely unlikely that he is wrong in his account of the matter. On the other hand it is by no means impossible that Luke has foreshortened events, and combined narratives. Galatians, therefore, not Acts, gives the final verdict, and it is a radically bad

---

[1] Paul is not very explicit on the subject. That the object of his visit was the care of the poor is implied by Gal. ii. 10, but all that Paul emphasizes is that he went up by revelation, not as a matter of obedience to the apostles in Jerusalem. It is from Acts xi., not from Galatians, that the 'relief' nature of his visit is to be gathered. The reverse is true of his final visit to Jerusalem. Acts says hardly anything about the 'relief' which Paul brought from Europe, but 1 and 2 Corinthians show that to take this to Jerusalem was one of his chief objects, and that he had been working for it for years. I think it is possible that the 'relief' element was really present on both occasions, and possibly its long-continued nature indicates that it was not due—as Acts would suggest— merely to famine, but also to the ill-judged 'communism' which must have permanently impoverished the church in Jerusalem.

method which in any way tries to squeeze the Pauline statement into harmony with the Lucan. If the two accounts differ it is Paul and not Luke who must be followed.

(ii.) *To which visit of Paul to Jerusalem, as described in Acts, does Galatians ii. really correspond?*

To this question three answers have been given. (*a*) By most of the older commentators it was held that Galatians ii. clearly corresponded to Acts xv. The best statement of this theory is certainly that given by Lightfoot in his *St. Paul's Epistle to the Galatians*, pp. 123 f. He writes as follows : " The *geography* is the same. In both narratives the communications take place between Jerusalem and Antioch : in both the headquarters of the false brethren are at the former place, their machinations are carried on in the latter : in both the Gentile apostles go up to Jerusalem apparently from Antioch, and return thence to Antioch again. The *time* is the same, or at least not inconsistent. St. Paul places the events fifteen or sixteen years after his conversion : St. Luke's narrative implies that they took place about the year 51.[1] The *persons* are the same : Paul and Barnabas appear as the representatives of the Gentile churches, Cephas and James as the leaders of the circumcision. The agitators are similarly described in the two accounts : in the Acts, as converted Pharisees, who had imported their dogmas into the Christian Church ; in the Epistle, as false brethren who attempt to impose the bondage of the Law on the Gentile converts. The two apostles of the Gentiles are represented in both accounts as attended : ' certain other Gentiles ' (ἐξ αὐτῶν) are mentioned by St. Luke ; Titus, a Gentile, is named by St. Paul. The *subject of dispute* is the same : the circumcision of the Gentile converts. The *character of the conference* is in general the same : a prolonged and hard-fought contest. The *result* is the same : the exemption of the Gentiles from the enactments of the Law, and the recognition of the apostolic commission of Paul and Barnabas by the leaders of the Jewish Church."

The strength of this position is in its affirmations. It certainly shows that there is so strong a resemblance between the circumstances of these two visits to Jerusalem that it is incredible that they were repeated so exactly on another occasion. The suggestion that they were is made worse if Galatians ii. refers to another visit actually mentioned in Acts, for that would mean that the same controversy arose twice, that Luke described it on one occasion and Paul on the other. Therefore, since Lightfoot wrote, the majority of English critics have always agreed that Acts xv. and Galatians ii. refer to the same visit.

The difficulty is not in this affirmation, but its application to the details of the story, for it entails conclusions which are very disturbing.

_____

[1] Lightfoot explains in a footnote that "this is calculated by a back reckoning of the time spent from the Apostolic Council to the appointment of Festus, the date of which is fixed independently at A.D. 60." A modern writer would probably speak less certainly ; see Turner's article on ' Chronology ' in Hastings' *Dictionary of the Bible* and Additional Note 34.

*[margin note: Paul's visit to Jerusalem : (a) Lightfoot's view ;]*

If Galatians ii. = Acts xv., it was, according to the sequence of events given in Acts, Paul's third visit to Jerusalem. He went there first soon after his conversion, a second time for the Antiochian mission to relieve the famine in Judaea, and Acts xv. is the third visit. But Paul's own statement in Galatians is that the visit described in chapter ii. was only his second; and he is emphatic on the point, because he is arguing that he was not and never had been subordinate to Jerusalem, and that the facts of his life show that he never had had an opportunity for being in such a position. He calls God to witness that he is not lying. Why should he have voluntarily weakened his position by omitting a visit to Jerusalem? The suggestion is incredible.

This point had of course been seen by the Tübingen school, but they had used it merely to discredit Luke. In England the belief was wide-spread that they had been fully answered, and no further serious attention was paid to them, except by a very few scholars who knew that the last word had not been said on the subject, but had not formulated any clear theory of their own. In Germany there were three parties—those who inherited the Tübingen tradition and thought that Acts was quite untrustworthy, those who had inherited the opposite view and believed that somehow the discrepancy between Acts and Galatians could be reconciled, and a younger generation which had for the moment given up historical criticism in favour of *Quellenkritik*, and produced an endless series of theories as to the source of Acts.

Lightfoot was, of course, fully aware of all that was going on in Germany. He was convinced that the Tübingen school was wrong in its general presentation of history, and he held that Acts was more trustworthy than most of his German contemporaries admitted.

His own solution of the difficulty was: "The answer is to be sought in the circumstances under which that visit was paid. The storm of persecution had broken over the Church of Jerusalem. One leading Apostle had been put to death; another rescued by a miracle had fled for his life. At this season of terror and confusion Paul and Barnabas arrived. It is probable that every Christian of rank had retired from the city. No mention is made of the Twelve; the salutations of the Gentile Apostles are received by 'the Elders.' They arrived charged with alms for the relief of the poor brethren of Judaea. Having deposited these in trustworthy hands, they would depart with all convenient speed. Any lengthened stay might endanger their lives. Nor, indeed, was there any motive for remaining. Even had St. Paul purposed holding con-ferences with the Apostles or the Church of the Circumcision, at this moment of dire distress it would have been impossible. Of this visit then, so brief and so hurried, he makes no mention here. His object is not to enumerate his journeys to Jerusalem, but to define his relations with the Twelve; and on these relations it had no bearing." But this explanation overlooks the fact that in Galatians Paul is clearing himself of the accusation that he is a disobedient subordinate of the apostles in Jerusalem by showing that on his visits to Jerusalem he never was subordinate to them. Surely it is inconceivable that he omitted a visit which can scarcely have been unknown, especially if he could have said that the apostles were then absent. Nor is the picture of the apostles retiring to safety and leaving the Church to presbyters a very convincing suggestion, or consistent with Acts viii. 1.

(b) A new suggestion was made in 1895 by Sir William Ramsay, who recognized that Lightfoot's argument was weak when it minimized the ' famine relief ' visit. He therefore took the obvious step of identifying the second visit in Acts with the second visit in Galatians. He thought that Acts said nothing about the details of the visit because it had been held in private.[1]  *(b) Ramsay's view;*

At the time when I first read his book Ramsay's view, though not widely accepted, seemed to me the best way out of the difficulty. I followed it up in my *Earlier Epistles of St. Paul*, and so did Mr. C. W. Emmet in his *Epistle to the Galatians* and in Vol. II. It has also been recently accepted by Prof. F. C. Burkitt in his *Christian Beginnings* and by Canon Streeter. Nevertheless the theory never won general approval ; and rightly so. The obvious difficulty is that if the whole question had really been settled beforehand by the apostles at the second visit to Jerusalem, why did they pretend to argue it all *de novo* at the meeting described in Acts xv., as though they had never discussed, much less settled, the problem ?

Nevertheless, just as there is convincing power in Lightfoot's view, that Galatians ii. must mean the same visit as Acts xv., so also is there in Ramsay's contention that Galatians ii. must refer to Paul's second visit. The problem is thus an *impasse* if we take Acts as it stands.  *(c) Schwartz's view.*

(c) The succession of critics whose work has pointed to the only possible solution is Weizsäcker, McGiffert, and Schwartz. In varying ways they all used the same key to solve the riddle. Acts xi. (the famine relief visit) and Acts xv. are both descriptions of the visit referred to in Galatians ii., derived from different sources and described from different points of view.

The clear advantages of this theory are :

(1) It is based on the known fact that Luke used 'sources,' and that in his gospel he repeats, on occasion, the same saying from Mark and from another source which is found to have been used by Matthew also. Thus the saying " There is nothing hid that shall not be revealed " comes in Luke viii. 17 and in Luke xii. 2. The first passage is from Mark, the second from Q (?) (cf. Matt. x. 26). A glance at the third appendix to Huck's *Synopse* shows at least seven other instances of this tendency to double a saying because it was found in more than one source. Nor is there anything strange in this. The characteristic is found in Matthew, and in general in almost all writers of this period who made use of 'sources.'

[1] See *Paul the Traveller and Roman Citizen*, pp. 48 ff. Prof. Burkitt, as I have learnt by correspondence with him, is impressed by this point and thinks that the fact that in Galatians Paul had a private interview with the Apostles, but in Acts a public discussion, invalidates Lightfoot's view that Galatians ii. refers to the same episode as Acts xv.

(2) It is the only theory which can do justice to the arguments set out by Lightfoot in favour of identifying Acts xv. and Galatians ii. without doing violence to the fact that Paul says that Galatians ii. was his second visit to Jerusalem. The difficulty of reconciling these points disappears when it is seen that the two stories refer to the same visit, described from different points of view.

It has not, I think, found so much favour as it might have done, because it is bound up with Schwartz's theory of chronology (see Additional Notes 18 and 34) and with his belief that John the son of Zebedee was put to death together with his brother James.

It is, however, not necessary to accept these theories because we hold that Acts xv. is a different version of the visit to Jerusalem mentioned in Acts xi. 34, so that both these accounts are parallel to Galatians ii. and both are really Paul's second visit.

The test of order.

The most exacting test which can be applied to any reconstruction of an historical narrative is whether it produces a result in accordance with the oldest tradition, especially as to the order of events. Two narratives may reasonably differ as to the importance or even the character of various episodes, but if they are of first-rate value they will not often differ as to the order in which the events happened. Now it is on this question of order that Acts xv. and Galatians differ most in the present arrangement of the narrative, but this point has sometimes been overlooked in the interest of the central difficulty of whether the visit was Paul's second or third.

According to Galatians Paul went to Jerusalem by revelation, not because of any controversy in the Church, and he hints that the visit was concerned with the care of the poor. While in Jerusalem he was attacked by 'false brethren'; there was a discussion, but he won the day; then on his return to Antioch the difficulties again arose, because emissaries from Jerusalem reopened the question, and persuaded Peter and Barnabas to desert the Hellenistic side which they had hitherto adopted.

It would, however, seem that the problem was not quite the same as it had been. In Jerusalem the question seems to have been that of circumcision. It is true that this is scarcely stated in so many words, but it certainly seems to be implied by the story of Titus. But in Antioch the question was the further one of the conditions of intercourse between Jewish and Gentile Christians. Paul, Barnabas, and Peter had mingled freely with Gentiles, and joined in their meals. But the emissaries of James held that this was improper. There is no suggestion that they were claiming that the Gentiles should be circumcised, but they did insist on a social barrier between circumcised and uncircumcised. Paul did not yield on this point, but Barnabas and Peter gave way.

Acts, as it stands, gives a different sequence of events. According to it the trouble arose in Antioch, was carried to Jerusalem by Paul and Barnabas, who went there for that express purpose, and, partly by them but still more by Peter, the Church was persuaded of the essential rightness of the Antiochian position.  But this settlement was accompanied by the imposition of three (or four) requirements, which from their nature seem to be intended to fix the conditions of intercourse between Jewish and Gentile Christians.  They would be in place as the solution of the controversy, which according to Galatians arose in Antioch between Peter and Paul, but they scarcely fit into the struggle about circumcision, which according to both Galatians and Acts was the subject of the meeting in Jerusalem.  Nevertheless, taking Acts as it stands, these conditions seem to be intended as the solution of the controversy about circumcision.  There is nothing in Acts about a new dispute in Antioch either on circumcision or on the social intercourse of Jew and Gentile, for though Paul and Barnabas quarrelled on their return, it was about a personal matter.

Thus, taking Acts as it stands, there is a serious difference between it and Galatians as to the order of events.  This difficulty used to be solved most often by the rather violent method of supposing that Paul in Galatians ii. deserted the chronological order of events and that Paul's visit to Antioch was earlier, not later, than the conference in Jerusalem.  This is Zahn's and Turner's view.[1]  It is in itself highly improbable, and would hardly have been suggested but for the apparent evidence of Acts that the trouble began in Antioch and was settled in Jerusalem.

A far more plausible solution is provided by the distinction of sources suggested above.  According to this the Antiochian tradition in Acts is represented by Acts xi. 27-30 ; xii. 25 = Gal. ii. 1 ff. ; Acts xv. 1 f.; xv. 30 ff. = Gal. ii. 11 ff.  The possibility exists that the missionary journey in xiii.-xiv. comes from this source ; Galatians, however, does not mention this journey, so prominent in Acts, partly because it was not germane to the argument, partly because the Galatians knew all about it, but it is hinted at as the natural result of the agreement reached in Jerusalem.  It is, however, also possible that the journey is misplaced. Luke on the other hand omits the temporary defection of Peter, and ascribes the estrangement of Paul from Barnabas to a personal quarrel about Mark.  The sequence of events, taking Galatians as our standard, with the sections of Acts divided according to their sources, is as follows :

| | Galatians. | Antioch source. | Jer. source. |
|---|---|---|---|
| 1. Paul's visit to Jerusalem. | Gal. ii. 1-2. | Acts xi. 27-30. | ... |
| 2. The 'Council' of the Apostles. | Gal. ii. 3-10. | ... | Acts xv. 3-29. |
| 3. Paul's return to Antioch. | implied by Gal. ii. 11. | ? Acts xii. 25. | Acts xv. 30. |
| 4. Peter's arrival in Antioch. | Gal. ii. 11. | ... | ... |
| 5. The arrival of emissaries from James. | Gal. ii. 12. | Acts xv. 1-2. | ... |
| 6. A quarrel of Paul against Peter and Barnabas. | Gal. ii. 13-14. | ? Acts xv. 36 ff. | ... |

Possibly the mission to the Gentiles in Acts xiii.-xiv. should be inserted between 3 and 4, but it seems to me more probable that we should accept

---

[1] Article on 'Chronology' in Hastings' *Dictionary of the Bible*.

Schwartz's view. It probably comes from a 'Barnabas-tradition,' is misplaced and should come after 6 (see Additional Note 34).

If we accept this reconstruction the order of events is the same in the Antiochian source of Acts as in Galatians—a visit to Jerusalem, a meeting with the apostles, a return to Antioch, and a quarrel in Antioch, instigated by emissaries from Jerusalem who influenced (Peter and) Barnabas. The order of events is thus exactly the same in both documents. The only difference is that the dispute in Antioch is represented in Acts as being about circumcision and the Law, instead of about social intercourse.

The result of the editorial manipulation of the sources was that Luke inserted the narrative of events, as he had heard them from the side of Jerusalem, into the Antiôchian tradition, in the description of the result of the trouble in Antioch, so that the defection of Barnabas is disconnected from the story of the Jewish emissaries. Thus xv. 3-35 gives the Jerusalem story of what happened when Paul and Barnabas went up to Jerusalem, as the Antiochian source also relates in xi. 27 ff. It is impossible to say whether this tradition reached Luke in a written form or not, but it clearly reflects the views of Jerusalem rather than of Antioch. It also really agrees with the other evidence in that it too, like Galatians and the Antiochian source, when read by itself, makes the controversy begin in Jerusalem.

To fit this story into the Antiochian frame Luke had to add some editorial sentences, which made the Jerusalem narrative appear the story of another incident, and forced xv. 1—the coming of emissaries from Jerusalem—into connexion with the Circumcision controversy instead of with the Intercourse controversy. He thus produced the very unconvincing story of a controversy which began in Antioch, and was then removed to Jerusalem by representatives of the Antiochian mission, who, however, said nothing about the controversy which took them to Jerusalem, until it was actually forced on their attention.

He also introduced into the narrative of the discussion in Jerusalem decrees which have *prima facie* more to do with the subject of social intercourse, but the exact importance of this point will be more conveniently discussed a little later (see pp. 210 ff.).

The Apostolic Decrees.    (iii.) *The meaning of Acts xv. in general and of the apostolic decrees in particular.*

Reading Acts xv. as a connected narrative, and merely looking for the general meaning of the decrees, it is clear that the meaning of Luke was that they represent the minimum of the Law which was to be required from Gentile Christians in lieu of circumcision. The difficulty of accepting this view is that it seems so inconsistent with Paul's position, as stated in Galatians and Romans, that it is almost incredible that he would have accepted such a compromise.[1] Moreover,

---

[1] This statement would not be accepted by Prof. Burkitt or by many other authorities. The most persuasive statement of their case seems to me to be Burkitt's *Christian Beginnings*, pp. 108-134. He argues that Paul's objection

closer investigation into the wording of the decrees confirms this doubt, and suggests that the decrees were concerned with the problem of social intercourse between Jews and Gentiles in the Christian Church, not with the problem of circumcision.

The apostolic decrees forbid three things,[1] εἰδωλόθυτα, αἷμα, and πορνεία.

(a) Εἰδωλόθυτα is the Jewish equivalent of the ordinary Greek εἰδωλόθυτα. θεόθυτα[2] or ἱερόθυτα. But from 1 Cor. viii. it seems that εἰδωλόθυτα might be used in a wider or in a narrower sense. In the narrow sense it would imply actual participation in a sacrificial meal. We are naturally inclined to look on these meals as solemn religious services. Some of them no doubt were ; but others probably resembled a dinner-party more closely than a church service. It was the custom to issue invitations to dinner in the temple, and the fiction was that the god was himself the host. For instance, Pap Oxy i. 110 says : ἐρωτᾷ σε Χαιρήμων δειπνῆσαι εἰς κλείνην (κλίνην) τοῦ κυρίου Σαράπιδος ἐν τῷ Σαραπείῳ αὔριον ἥτις ἐστὶν ιε, ἀπὸ ὥρας θ′.[3] In the wider sense the greater part of the meat sold in the shops was 'offered to idols,' as the animal from which it was taken had usually been consecrated to some god, even if it were only by the ceremonial burning of a few hairs. Thus, in this strict sense, to avoid eating things offered to idols was difficult, if not impossible. It would, however, appear that it was not quite impossible, for Paul implies that by making inquiry the Corinthians might be able to avoid such meat.

Its meaning in Acts is defined by vs. 20 as τὰ ἀλισγήματα τῶν εἰδώλων, which cannot be narrowed down to the actual participation in a sacrifice, or even to the eating of sacrificed meat,—it means idolatry, described by that part of it which was most prominent and least easy to avoid.

---

to 'Law' was only when it was regarded as the necessary basis of a right relation between God and Man—not when it was the basis of relation between human beings   Moreover the Epistles show that the decrees, thus interpreted, would have been agreeable to Paul. All this is quite true, except that the omission of any reference to αἷμα (I doubt whether the vegetarians of Romans really cover this point) seems more important to me than to Burkitt. But the point which he seems to me to pass over far too lightly is that Acts appears to regard the decrees as a substitute for the Law. In this sense I feel sure that Paul would never have accepted them. If I understand him fully Burkitt and I agree that the decrees are in fact social regulations. As such Paul might have accepted them, but Acts, at least, to me shows that Luke regarded them as the end of the controversy about circumcision, not about social intercourse.

[1] For a discussion of the text, and the reason for saying 'three' rather than 'four,' see Vol. III. pp. 265 ff.

[2] From Phrynichus, *Ecloga*, p. 159 (Lobeck's edition), it would appear that θεόθυτα was the older name. There is a good note on these words by J. Weiss in Meyer's *Kommentar* on 1 Cor. viii. 1.

[3] For further examples see Lietzmann's note on *Kultmahle* on pp. 50 f. of the 2nd edition of the commentary on 1 Cor. in his *Handbuch*.

αἷμα.

(b) Αἷμα might mean murder, and it has often been so interpreted. But murder, unlike idolatry, was not a common practice difficult to avoid, and it seems unlikely to be intended (but see p. 209). It may refer to the Jewish objection to blood as a form of food, and πνικτόν be a correct gloss on its meaning. This was based on Leviticus vii. 26, which in Leviticus xvii. 10 was specially extended to cover the 'stranger living in Israel': "Whatsoever man there be of the house of Israel, or of the strangers that sojourn among you, that eateth any manner of blood, I will even set my face against that soul that eateth blood, and will cut him off from among his people. For the life of the flesh is in the blood." The later Judaism always devised all manner of rules to safeguard the possibility of eating blood, especially by ordering that animals must be killed by effusion of blood only, and there must be no possibility of their death being hastened by any other means, such as strangulation. Thus the 'things strangled' of the Neutral text is only another way of expressing the command [1] to keep from blood. A third alternative view is that 'blood' is here used with reference to sacrifice, and is merely an instance of the contamination incurred by joining in idolatrous worship. (See Strack, ii. pp. 730-739.)

πορνεια.

(c) Πορνεία might mean fornication in a general sense; but it may equally mean 'marriage within the forbidden degrees,' which the rabbis described as 'forbidden for πορνεία.' So also in Numbers xxv. 1 f. the context makes it plain that the πορνεία of the Israelites was marriage with the women of Midian (cf. Apoc. ii. 20). (See Strack, ii. pp. 729 f.)

Once more it has been suggested that πορνεία, like εἰδωλόθυτα and αἷμα, is merely another example of the contamination of idolatry, so that the three parts of the decree are really a single command to avoid heathen worship, made emphatic by mentioning its three most prominent features. It is undoubtedly true that a sexual metaphor is often adopted in the Old Testament to describe the worship of false gods. It is also true that religious prostitution was an integral part of some if not all oriental cults. On the other hand, πορνεία is often used in the Pauline epistles, and always in the ordinary sense. Is it probable that the word is used here of religious prostitution with no hint that it is being given this special sense?

Each of the words is therefore capable of more than one shade of meaning, and three conceivable interpretations can be suggested for the decrees as a whole. (i.) They may be a food law; (ii.) they may be a command to avoid heathen worship, expressed by reference to its three salient features; (iii.) they may be a 'moral law' to avoid three notable sins. But no one of these interpretations (and I do not know of any fourth possibility) can be adopted without straining the meaning of one of the three commands, or otherwise raising difficulties. A food law is an inappropriate setting for πορνεία; a command to avoid idolatry represented by its three salient features is more consistent with the language of the commands, but the use of πορνεία in this special sense is a little

---

[1] See Strack, ii. pp. 730 ff.

unusual, and it is a serious difficulty that none of the early Christian writers interpreted the decrees in this way; a moral law seems at first less open to objection, for it was the popular view of the early Christian writers of the West, but εἰδωλόθυτα is after all not really a synonym for εἰδωλολατρεία, and 'eating sacrifices' might be thought to be almost— not quite—as out of place in a 'moral law' as πορνεία is in a food law.[1]

But the question whether these regulations were a 'food law' or a 'moral law' presents a somewhat wrong antithesis.    Assuming that εἰδωλόθυτα means principally food offered to idols, and αἷμα means food containing blood, it would still not be fair to call this a food law in the sense in which the ordinary man would now understand the phrase. An exact parallel is to be found in American law, which forbids the making of wine; that is a food law, but, in the minds of those who assent to it, its justification is that it is wrong to touch alcohol.    It is the 'wrongness,' not the 'food,' which is forbidden; and that was exactly the attitude of the Jews towards the use of blood as food.    There was therefore nothing inappropriate to their mind in putting 'blood' into the same category with idolatry and forbidden marriages, and making abstinence from it one of the conditions of intercourse between Jews and God-fearers.    For, after all, the most hopeful line of approach to the subject is to remember always that the question which necessitated such rules can only have been that of the terms on which Gentiles who were Christian God-fearers [2] could meet with Christian Jews, and these again with Jews who were not Christian.    There is at least a probability that the terms were the same as those on which God-fearers and Jews met when neither were Christian.    The problem was for Christians only a passing one, for it was soon solved by the Synagogue, which turned out the Christians, and made it a matter of no practical importance whether a Christian was a Jew or a God-fearer, as the community of Jews would not associate with him in any case.[3]    But for the moment Jewish Christians still hoped to preserve the continuity of the institution, and 'terms' were a practical necessity.

There is unfortunately very little known about the Jewish rules as to intercourse with God-fearers.    It must, however, be remembered that though God-fearers is a convenient phrase for us to use, it gives an undue clearness of definition (see Additional Note 8).    God-fearers are not a special class recognized by Jewish rules, as the 'sojourners' were in ancient Israel or in the imaginary Israel of the Talmud; the latter are the 'pious heathen' who refrain from idolatry, and in the opinion of many Jews will have a share in the World to come.    Possibly in the first century in Palestine there was a formulated statement of the amount of belief and conduct required to give a heathen the requisite degree of piety,

*Food law and moral law.*

*Jewish rules for God-fearers.*

[1] See G. Resch, *Das Aposteldekret.*

[2] See pp. 84 ff. for the caution to be observed in the use of this word.

[3] This problem was very soon replaced for the Christian community by the question of intercourse with friendly heathen; but I do not know of any evidence to show that this question was ever dealt with formally, or that anyone ever suggested that the apostolic decrees should be applied to it.

but there seems to be no proof that this was so.  More probably, perhaps, popular opinion crystallized more or less unconsciously into a general belief that such and such a man (e.g. Cornelius) was pious—that he ' feared God.'

Leviticus and the Noachian Commands.
Possibly the rules which were applied to the ' sojourners '—heathen living among Jews—may give some clues as to Jewish policy.   This can be gleaned from Leviticus, which specifically prescribes certain rules for the ' stranger within your gates.'   These resident heathen were obliged (i.) to abstain from offering sacrifice to strange gods (Lev. xvii. 7-9), (ii.) from blood (Lev. xvii. 10ff.), (iii.) from marriage within the forbidden degrees (Lev. xviii. 6-26), (iv.) from work on the Sabbath (Exod. xx. 10 f.), and (v.) from eating leavened bread during the Passover week (Exod. xii. 18 f.). These regulations were expanded and ultimately codified by the Rabbis as the Seven Commands given to the sons of Noah,[1] and therefore binding on all mankind.   They are set out in *Sanhedrin* 56 b : (i.) Obedience to law, (ii.) Abstinence from blasphemy, (iii.) Abstinence from idolatry, (iv.) Abstinence from marriage within the forbidden degrees, (v.) Abstinence from blood, (vi.) Abstinence from robbery, (vii.) Abstinence from meat cut from a living animal.

The formulation of these rules is doubtless later than Acts, and their application to ' sojourners ' is an historic fiction.   At the time when they were drawn up the Jews had no land of their own.   They were themselves the ' sojourners,' and the rules in *Sanhedrin* for the treatment of strangers living in Jewish territory were devised with a view to a restored Israel rather than based strictly on the memory of the past, just as the tractate *Middoth* gives the measurements for a future temple rather than merely the tradition of the old one.   Nevertheless the picture of the future was based on memory of the past.   In the case of the temple the memory was real, and the rules as to sojourners, so far as they represent memory, may have been based on the treatment of God-fearers.   At the time of Acts the formulation of this treatment was probably not so definite as is that of the ' sojourners ' in the *Sanhedrin*, but there is sufficient resemblance between the apostolic decrees and the Noachian rules to make it possible that both represent the regulations which controlled the intercourse of Jews and God-fearers in the middle of the first century.

The Diaspora.
It is however also possible that a somewhat different view obtained in the Diaspora.   For the reconstruction of Jewish life in Greek cities outside Palestine we have distressingly little evidence, and we do not know how far the rules found in the Talmud ever obtained in the Diaspora in the first century.   For the present purpose Philo gives no help.   He inculcates the duty of kindness to the heathen who accept the true God, but it is never quite clear whether he is speaking of proselytes or God-fearers.   More important are two striking passages in the Jewish part of the *Oracula Sibyllina*, in which the writer appeals to the heathen to mend their ways and seek salvation.

[1] According to one tradition six of these commands were given to Adam, and only the seventh was added in the time of Noah.

(1) *Or. Sib.* iv. 24-34.

ὄλβιοι ἀνθρώπων κεῖνοι κατὰ γαῖαν ἔσονται,
ὅσσοι δὴ στέρξουσι μέγαν θεὸν εὐλογέοντες
πρὶν πιέειν φαγέειν τε πεποιθότες εὐσεβίῃσιν·
οἳ νηοὺς μὲν ἅπαντας ἀπαρνήσονται ἰδόντες
καὶ βωμούς, εἰκαῖα λίθων ἀφιδρύματα κωφῶν,
αἵμασιν ἐμψύχων μεμιασμένα καὶ θυσίῃσιν
τετραπόδων· λεύσουσι δ' ἑνὸς θεοῦ εἰς μέγα κῦδος
οὔτε φόνον ῥέξαντες ἀτάσθαλον οὔτε κλοπαῖον
κέρδος ἀπεμπολέοντες, ἃ δὴ ῥίγιστα τέτυκται,
οὐδ' ἄρ' ἐπ' ἀλλοτρίῃ κοίτῃ πόθον αἰσχρὸν ἔχοντες,
οὐδ' ἐπ' ἄρσενος ὕβριν ἀπεχθέα τε στυγερήν τε.

(2) *Or. Sib.* iv. 162-170.

ἆ μέλεοι, μετάθεσθε, βροτοί, τάδε, μηδὲ πρὸς ὀργὴν
παντοίην ἀγάγητε θεὸν μέγαν, ἀλλὰ μεθέντες
φάσγανα καὶ στοναχὰς ἀνδροκτασίας τε καὶ ὕβρεις
ἐν ποταμοῖς λούσασθε ὅλον δέμας ἀενάοισιν,
χεῖράς τ' ἐκτανύσαντες ἐς αἰθέρα τῶν πάρος ἔργων
συγγνώμην αἰτεῖσθε καὶ εὐλογίαις ἀσέβειαν
πικρὰν ἱλάσκεσθε· θεὸς δώσει μετάνοιαν
οὐδ' ὀλέσει· παύσει δὲ χόλον πάλιν, ἤνπερ ἅπαντες
εὐσεβίην περίτιμον ἐνὶ φρεσὶν ἀσκήσητε.

It is noteworthy that here in both passages, besides the recognition of the true God, abstention from idolatry and idolatrous sacrifices, murder, theft, and immorality is inculcated as necessary in the first passage, and from violence, murder, and immorality (ὕβρις) in the second. This is very similar to the apostolic decrees if they be interpreted as moral requirements.[1] Of course the writer of the *Oracula* does not actually say that he was willing to associate with Gentiles who accepted his precepts, but he certainly indicates that God would receive them, and the greater may be supposed to include the less.

(iv.) *The results of a comparison between Galatians ii. and Acts xv.* Acts and
The preceding discussion has rendered probable two conclusions. (i.) Galatians compared.
The conference in Jerusalem described in Galatians ii. was concerned with the question of circumcision, and the applicability of the Law to Gentile Christians. Luke regarded the decrees as the settlement of this issue. But there is nothing in the Pauline epistles to support this view. (ii.) The actual intention of the decrees, as established by the meaning of the words, and a consideration of contemporary Jewish thought, was to facilitate the social intercourse of Jewish and Gentile Christians by

---

[1] Cognate to this, though not quite the same, is the decision of the Rabbis in Hadrian's persecution that Jews might save their lives by other infractions of the Law, but not by idolatry, incest or other sexual offences, or by homicide (*Sanhedrin* 74a, *Jer. Sanhedrin* 21b, *Jer. Shebi'it* 35a). See G. F. Moore, *Judaism*, vol. ii. p. 106, and the article on 'Martyrdom' in the *Jewish Encyclopaedia*.

establishing rules of conduct for Gentiles which would remove the possibility of offence in Jewish circles.

That is to say, the internal evidence of the decrees indicates that they, or the policy which they embody, belong to a different problem from that with which Luke has connected them. Moreover, Galatians clearly indicates that the controversy as to the conditions of social intercourse to which they really belong began in Antioch between Paul on the one side and Peter, Barnabas, and the representatives of James on the other side, after Paul, Peter, and James had come to an agreement in Paul's favour as to the original controversy with regard to circumcision and the keeping of the Law.

The explanation of Luke's confusion.

Assuming that the policy represented by the decrees is not a fiction, the critical problem is to form a reasonable hypothesis to explain why Luke represents as a 'minimum-law' requirement what was really the regulation of social intercourse.

Three points are provided by the Epistles and Acts, and by the known course of the history of Christianity.

(i.) Owing to the speedy rejection of Christians from the Jewish society the question of social intercourse between Jewish and Gentile Christians soon ceased to be a real issue. Except in Palestine Jewish Christianity had either ceased to exist or was quite unimportant before A.D. 100. It is therefore not impossible that Luke may really never have come into personal contact with the situation to which the decrees belong, just as he probably never had come into personal contact with glossolalia, and so misunderstood and misrepresented the account of it which is behind Acts ii.[1]

(ii.) Galatians ii. is clear evidence of Paul's opinion that the controversy as to circumcision had been settled and that Peter and James agreed with him, but that the controversy as to social intercourse had not been settled, that James was on the other side from himself, and that Peter and Barnabas had gone over to James.

(iii.) It is possible that attention should be paid to the fact that in Acts xxi. James mentions the decrees as a new thing, of which Paul was unaware. This might suggest that while Paul had been in Asia and Achaia the controversy had been settled. But though this is possible it would be unwise to press the point, for the speech of James is quite likely to be Lucan, and the passage can be explained as reminding Paul of what he knows, rather than as telling what he does not. Moreover, though the meaning is not quite clear, James seems to imply—as Luke would doubtless have intended—that the decrees were the minimum requirement from the Gentiles as a substitute for circumcision.

Putting these three points together—and the third can really be omitted—the most probable hypothesis seems to be that Luke either knew of the decrees as an actual document, or at least of the policy which they represent, as the settlement of a controversy between Jewish and Gentile Christians. But he did not quite know what the exact controversy was. Finding, however, in his sources an account of a rather stormy meeting

[1] See Additional Note 10.

at Jerusalem, which ended in the abolition of circumcision for Gentile Christians, he assumed that the decrees were part of the decision of this meeting, fixing a 'minimum-law' requirement, and he told the story accordingly.   In reality the decrees belong to the second controversy, and Paul had not been a party to them, though he had played a leading rôle in the previous and more important discussion as to circumcision.

So much is reasonably clear, but were the decrees the end of the dispute at Antioch described in Gal. ii. 11, and do they really belong to the Church of Antioch rather than of Jerusalem? Were they accepted by Peter and Barnabas but not by Paul?

It is relatively unimportant to decide—and it is impossible to do so— Did the whether Luke actually had seen a definite letter of the apostles embodying Apostles the decrees.   It is, of course, possible that such decrees were sent out in letter? a circular letter.   But there is no corroborative evidence, and, next to the insertion of speeches, the summarizing of a situation in a letter, supposed to have been addressed by one party to the other, was the favourite method of the writers of the period.   Like many of the speeches in Acts this letter recapitulates what has been told in the narrative.   This, and also the fact that other writers of the time appear to invent letters much as they do speeches for their heroes, suggest that this passage is Luke's own composition.   The style seems to justify such an origin.   On this point Harnack and Weiss seem to have the better of the argument rather than Zahn, who thinks the language points to the source here used by Luke. (For the use of letters in ancient writers see Additional Note 32.)   Therefore, though the point does not admit of certainty, I am doubtful if the text of Acts is that of the actual document.

More important is the question whether, apart from the epistolary form, the 'decrees' really represent a rule which in the first century claimed apostolic authority and was issued from Jerusalem.

Is there sufficient ground for believing in the existence of apostolic Apostolic authority at this period?   Loisy is the most incisive critic of this belief, authority. and his researches into Acts have led him to think, and in turn are coloured by the opinion, that 'apostolic' authority is a fiction of the editor of Acts, unsupported by the source which he was using, and without foundation in history.   I think that Loisy is wrong on this point, and that his and similar opinions are due to an erroneous interpretation of the Pauline epistles.

In Galatians and in Corinthians Paul refers by implication to the question of apostolic authority.   He rejects with great vigour all claims which involved his recognition of the superiority of the apostles in Jerusalem.   But the same epistles prove that he believed in apostolic authority as such.   His claim was not that the other apostles had no power, but that he had as much as they had, and that his was not derived from theirs.   He also was in the habit of settling questions by letters.   Moreover, Galatians certainly shows that there was a party which denied Paul's apostolic authority, except as derived from Jerusalem.   Thus the epistles themselves prove that apostolic authority was really claimed by some persons in the early Church, and that these persons were in Jerusalem is equally clear. Whether they regarded 'the Twelve' or 'James' as the chief holder of this authority is another question.

The extension in tradition of the 'James' theory is found in the Clementines, and of the 'Twelve' theory in the *Epistola Apostolorum* and in the *Apostolic Constitutions* and its sources, such as the *Didache* and the *Didascalia.*

Thus apart from the actual form of the document, which may be Lucan rather than historical, it is not improbable that a letter[1] was sent —either at the time of the conference or at some other—by the Church of Jerusalem to regulate the relations between Jewish and 'God-fearing' Christians.

## NOTE XVII. PAUL'S CONTROVERSIES

### By KIRSOPP LAKE

The work of a missionary implies controversy, and his preaching necessarily takes the form of arguments with those whom he wishes to convert. His message is always the same, but because the positions of his hearers are different he is obliged to embark on different discussions.

To reconstruct Paul's preaching and the controversies which arose from it is the central theme of any book on Paul, but it belongs only to the periphery of one on Acts, and is called for only to show how far, or how little, Acts describes the essential facts. It must be remembered that Acts and the Epistles are both imperfect from the point of view of the historian. Acts is in the main a narrative of events, told not to convey information as the historian understands it, but to create belief. It gives only a brief summary of Paul's preaching conveyed in the form of short speeches. The Epistles are in the main controversy combined with exhortation, and assume rather than describe the preaching which aroused opposition and called them forth. That is why all attempts to construct a system of Pauline doctrine—Paulinismus—from the Epistles is doomed to failure, and always produces something of which there is no trace in the Christian literature of the primitive Church, until perhaps[2] the time of Augustine, who with only

---

[1] Prof. Burkitt thinks that Rev. ii. 24 ff. is a direct reference to the decrees. This seems to me to claim too much. Οὐ βάλλω ἐφ' ὑμᾶς ἄλλο βάρος κτλ. is not a very strange way of saying 'I put no burden upon you except being faithful to the teaching you received.' It means especially that they should avoid 'Jezebel.' It is of course true that the writer has previously said that 'Jezebel' had made the faithful πορνεῦσαι καὶ εἰδωλόθυτα φαγεῖν. But this, as Westcott and Hort indicate, is a reference to Numbers xxv. 1 f. rather than to Acts xv. 20. It is probably intended metaphorically; for whatever the Jezebel-sect was it taught τὰ βάθεα Σατανᾶ, which sounds like a Gnostic cult. Still, if the point be pressed, I should not object to seeing a possible reference to the decrees in this passage.

[2] I do not think that Irenaeus is an exception. He is not an expounder of Pauline but of Johannine Christology. But it might be argued that Marcionism was an unsuccessful 'Paulinismus.'

slight exaggeration might be called the first creator of ' Paulinismus,' for
he first studied the Epistles as though they were a handbook of theology.

To some extent, therefore, any reconstruction of Pauline teaching and
controversies is fated to be subjective in method and doubtful in results,
but a comparison of Acts and the Epistles makes it plain that in his career
as a Christian missionary Paul was engaged in four great controversies.
It is impossible to fill in the details of any one of the four, but their outlines
can be sketched so as to throw light on the problem of the relative completeness or incompleteness of the picture of Paul given in Acts.

These four controversies were with the Jews, the Gentile heathen, the
Jewish Christians, and the Gentile Christians.

(i.) *Paul's Controversy with the Jews.*—Before his conversion Paul had Controversy
been engaged in controversy with Christians.  We know nothing about with Jews.
the details, but it is a reasonably safe surmise that it turned mainly on the
claims set up by the disciples in Jerusalem—that Jesus had risen from the
dead and was the man appointed by God to come from heaven and be
the judge of the living and the dead at the great day of the Lord.  He can
hardly have been much occupied in discussing the teaching of Jesus as to
the Law, for that seems to have played but little part in the teaching of the
disciples at this time.   It is not even mentioned in Acts,[1] and there is no
reference to it in the Pauline epistles.

The vision on the road to Damascus meant that Paul reversed his
judgement on this question.   Henceforth Jesus was to him assuredly the
Man who would come from heaven, and the Resurrection was the certain
fact which gave Paul this assurance.  Therefore in this controversy Paul
simply changed sides.  But it continued—Paul, now on the Christian side,
arguing in favour of the belief that Jesus had risen, the Jews denying it.

It is probably true that to the Jews this belief in the Messiahstic
of Jesus was not so important as the later developments of Hellenistic
Christianity.  To them it doubtless mattered far less that a group of otherwise reasonably orthodox Jews were under a delusion about Jesus, than that
Greek-speaking Jews such as Paul should inculcate disregard of the Law
in the mind of those who might otherwise have been converts.  But it was
not so to Paul.  To him the Resurrection was the necessary foundation
of his whole position, and he felt that those who admitted the possibility
of a resurrection ought to follow him.  Thus as between Paul and the Jews
the vital point of controversy, at least in his eyes, was the Resurrection.

The Epistles give us no examples of Paul's exposition of this position, The
though undoubtedly 1 Cor. xv. 3-9, the list of the appearances of Jesus Resurrec-
after the Resurrection, may be safely taken as a specimen of his argument. tion.
It is true that in 1 Corinthians it is used against Gentiles, not Jews, but that
is because, in doubting the resurrection of Christians as the appointed
method of immortality, the Corinthians compelled the repetition of an
argument which had once convinced them though it had not convinced
the Jews.   There are many problems involved in this passage—what, for
instance, is the proof from the Old Testament of a resurrection on the third

---

[1] In the case of Stephen the Temple not the Law is central.

day (1 Cor. xv. 4), and why does the list of the appearances of the risen Jesus differ so greatly from that in the gospels ?—but it is at least clear that in Paul's controversy about the Resurrection his main arguments were (a) the appearances of the risen Jesus, (b) the evidence of prophecy. The absence of any reference to the story of the ' empty tomb ' as told in the gospels is remarkable. It is difficult to think that Paul had never heard it ; possibly he felt that the failure of the women to find the body of the Lord was unimportant. (See K. Lake, *The Historical Evidence for the Resurrection of Jesus Christ*, pp. 190 ff., and P. Gardner-Smith, *The Narratives of the Resurrection*, pp. 10 ff.)

In Acts the argument is given at some length in the speech to Agrippa II. in xxvi. 2-23, and in the speech on the steps in xxii. 1-21, and more briefly in the speech, if it can be so called, to the Sanhedrin in xxiii. 6. In the two longer accounts the whole emphasis of the argument is on the personal experience of Paul which proved to him the fact of the Resurrection of Jesus. The shorter account is often rejected as unhistorical, but probably without sufficient reason (cf. Vol. II. pp. 295 f.).

Acts xxiii.<br>6.

According to it Paul, finding himself in a dangerous position, created a diversion in his favour by calling out " I am a Pharisee, a son of a Pharisee. I am on trial for the hope and resurrection of the dead." That Paul said this is impugned on three counts: (a) it was no answer to the charge brought against him ; (b) it was untrue that he was tried for this reason ; (c) he had no right to say that he was a Pharisee.

(a) It is indeed true that this was no legal defence to the accusation brought against him. To the accusation ' You brought foreigners into the Temple ' it is no answer to say ' I believe in a resurrection.' But neither was Stephen's speech an answer to the accusation brought against him, and, as was pointed out on p. 70, it is usual for reformers when arrested not to answer the charge, but to make a speech in favour of the reform they desire. Paul's speech is psychologically correct, and therefore not historically improbable.

(b) Similarly there is no real force in the contention that it was untrue for Paul to say that he was on trial ' for the hope and resurrection of the dead.' Technically and from the Jewish point of view this had nothing to do with it, but from Paul's—and in considering the accuracy of the narrative nothing else matters—this was the whole question. If he had not believed that his preaching about Jesus was justified by the Pharisaic doctrine of a resurrection he would never have been on trial. Everything else was to him entirely secondary. Doubtless neither side could understand the other, and the Sanhedrin would have maintained that it had no official interest in Paul's belief that Jesus was risen, provided he kept his Gentile friends out of the Temple. But Paul, in a spirit foreign to that of the lawyers, but well known to all leaders of forlorn hopes, insisted that the question of the Resurrection was central. The narrative on this point, at all events, is entirely convincing.

(c) It is, however, urged that nothing can justify Paul for claiming to be a Pharisee. Why not ? He believed, probably, that he was almost the only true Pharisee, because he alone drew the true conclusions from Pharisaic

belief.  Had he succeeded in persuading the Jews that he was right, everyone would now hold the same position and claim that Pauline doctrine was
the natural development of Pharisaism.  He merely did what all reformers
have done before and since, he threw back the picture of what he desired
on to the institution in which he had been brought up, and claimed that
that picture was the reality.  Whether Paul was right or wrong in the
abstract is an academic question.  The point at issue is whether it is
conceivable that he claimed to be a Pharisee, and on this point a comparison with the acts of other reformers and all psychological probability
support the story in Acts, and refute the critics who regard this episode
as unhistorical.

Besides this argument with the Jews, which was the reversal of that   The Law.
which he had carried on against the Christians before his conversion,
Paul had also a long-drawn-out argument as to the validity of the Law.
It is a question for the exegete of the Epistles to decide whether the
large amount of evidence contained in Romans and Galatians as to
Paul's arguments belongs really to his controversy with the Jews or to
that with Jewish Christians.[1]  It is, however, quite certain that the
question of the Law must have constantly arisen in discussions between
Paul and the Jews, and the arguments in the Epistles are undoubtedly
those which he used against Jewish opponents, whether in the Synagogue
or in the Church.

Paul did not believe that the Law was in any way whatever binding
on Gentile Christians.  This conclusion is not modified in the least,

[1] There has been a steady change of opinion on this subject during the last
hundred years.  The Tübingen school held that there was a mission of Jewish
Christians which everywhere opposed Paul, insisting on circumcision and the
observance of the Law.  It thought that a majority of Christians in the Roman
Empire were Jewish by origin and that Jewish Christianity was one of the
most important factors in the early Church.  Later Weizsäcker modified this
theory, and supported the view that even in Rome and Galatia Gentile Christians
may have been the majority.  W. Lütgert in a series of monographs went
further in minimizing the extent of Jewish Christianity.  I followed him, so
far as Corinth was concerned, in my *Earlier Epistles of St. Paul*, and recently
J. H. Ropes has contributed in *The Singular Problem of the Epistle to the
Galatians* a powerful argument against the existence of Jewish Christians or
of a Jewish Christian mission in Galatia.

Ropes holds that Jewish Christians, in the sense in which the word is usually
employed, were never more than a rare phenomenon except in Palestine.
Elsewhere the Christian Church was almost wholly made up of converted
'God-fearers' who joined the Church rather than the Synagogue.  The controversies internal to the Church were everywhere those of 'Gentile Christianity'
as illustrated by the Epistles to the Corinthians.  So far as Romans and
Galatians deal with the Law it is not because there was a Jewish-Christian
mission, in rivalry to Paul, but because Paul wished to protect his converts
from the efforts of Jewish teachers to persuade them to come over to the true
Mother Church—the Synagogue—and accept whole-heartedly all the teaching
of the Old Testament on which Paul himself relied for the proof of so much of
his teaching.

because he strongly urged in practice the same conduct as that produced by obedience to the Law. It was the fruit of the Spirit, not the work of the Law, and his central message in Galatians and Romans is that righteousness is obtained by a remodelling of man's nature, brought about by faith on the part of man, and by the Spirit given by the favour (χάρις) of God. There are many details which are doubtful, especially the relation of this change of nature to baptism. Did Paul think that the Spirit was conveyed in baptism, or, in other words, that baptism was the form chosen by God to embody his favour? I think that he did, though the matter is doubtful, and probably incapable of proof, but I am sure that many of Paul's converts thought so. But the really important point has often been overlooked in the heat of controversy about the relation between baptism and faith. Whether baptism was held to be the necessary form of the divine act of favour bestowing the Spirit may be left an open question, nor is it necessary to have a final definition of 'righteousness' or of 'faith.' The central point is that Paul clearly thought that a real supernatural change was needed and was effected. That surely is Greek, not Jewish. The Jewish position is that when the sinner repents and changes his ways he is acceptable to God. He is not changed, but his choice and his conduct are. The converted Christian in Pauline theology is a 'new creature.' Like the Fourth Gospel Paul holds that we 'become' children of God. The contrast is between this 'becoming a child of God'—whether by faith alone or by faith and baptism is immaterial—and Jewish teaching, typified in Christian literature by the parable of the Prodigal Son, in which the Prodigal is always a Son, even though a foolish one. In this respect the doctrine of Sonship in early Christianity moves, as it were, on opposite lines with regard to Christ and with regard to Christians. Its tendency is to become less 'adoptionist' with regard to Christ, but to become more so with regard to Christians. The Prodigal was not an 'adopted' son, but Paul's converts were.

In the Pauline scheme of thought there is no room for any 'Law,' presented as a requirement of conduct necessary to salvation. Salvation to him is the gift of God, not the result of right conduct. Or, to put the same thing a little differently, right conduct is the result not the cause of salvation.

In opposition to the Jews Paul maintained that the Law was not valid since the Messiah had come, and that circumcision was therefore not necessary for converts—it was an institution of the past—and, though Paul never states the point, it cannot have been necessary in his opinion for the children of Jewish Christians, for if such children were circumcised they were *ipso facto* under the Law.

There is some evidence, though not very much, which goes to show that in the first century certain Jews held that when the Messiah came the Law would cease. But that was not and never has been orthodox Jewish teaching. Paul, however, held this view (had he done so before his conversion?) and used it to support the contention that the Law, which had been promulgated because of transgressions, was now abrogated.

Such is the contention of the Epistles to the Romans and the Galatians.[1]
It must have been a prominent part of Paul's teaching, yet it is not
mentioned in Acts. Why not ? The simplest though not entirely satisfactory explanation is that in the Lucan circle the question of the Law
had been settled, and it was not necessary to discuss it. This theory is
obviously easier to accept if it be held that the writer of Acts was not a
companion of Paul and had never read the Pauline epistles.

What other views are known to have existed on this subject ? It is *The Law in
simplest to start with the position ultimately adopted in the Church. *the Didas-
*calia.*
This is set forth in the *Didascalia*, and through the *Apostolic Constitutions*, which incorporated the *Didascalia* in themselves, passed into the
general body of Christian doctrine. It held that the Law is binding on
Christians, but the Law is only that part of Exodus which precedes the
worshipping of the golden calf in Exod. xxxii. All that followed was not
Law but δευτέρωσις, *Secundatio*, ' secondary matter ' or Mishna, which was
inflicted on Jews and on Jews only in punishment for their sin in worshipping the golden calf. It was therefore not binding on any except Jews.
In this way the ceremonial law of Leviticus was excluded, though if the
generation of the *Didascalia* had been consistent it would have noted that
circumcision was included. The truth, of course, is that this treatment of
the subject is merely an artificial explanation devised in order to justify
an established situation, rather than the intellectual conviction which
produced that situation.

At a period a little earlier than that of the *Didascalia* the Church had *Marcion.*
to face the contention of Marcion that the Law was to be disregarded
because it was not the work of the God of the Christians but of an inferior
Demiurge, who was responsible for the tragedy of creation. Marcion
maintained that he was the true interpreter of Paul, and in one sense he
was certainly nearer to Paul than was the *Didascalia*. Paul knew nothing
of any distinction between Law and *Secundatio* any more than he did of
a distinction between moral and ceremonial law.

Paul's view of the Old Testament did indeed make a division in the *Paul and
Old Testament, perhaps as little tenable in the end as the distinction *the O.T.*
between moral and ceremonial law, but somewhat less subjective. He
distinguished between the Promises and the Law. The Promises had been
made to Abraham, were universal in scope, and pointed to the coming of the
Messiah, Jesus. The Law was temporary, was given because of transgression and as a means of education until the Promise was fulfilled. It then
ceased. It should be noted that this line of thought applies only to the
Torah—the Pentateuch. The Prophets were not identified by Paul—or

---

[1] The most difficult problem in these epistles scarcely concerns us here, but
in fairness to Judaism it calls for mention. Paul undoubtedly argues that
Judaism expects men to keep the whole Law without failure. Otherwise they
are accursed and doomed to death (see Rom. iii. 20, vii. 10; Gal. iii. 11).
Judaism never said or thought this. That the best of men often err was not
unknown to Israel; but repentance was always able to restore the sinner.
See Vol. I. pp. 53 ff. Why then does Paul speak as he does ? Is it mere
controversy, based on rabbinic exegesis ? It is a very difficult question.

by any other Jew—with the Law or with the Promise. The chief importance of prophecy was to foretell the future. The prophet in his lifetime was the messenger of God, exhorting and warning the people, and so far as these exhortations referred to permanent conditions they were of universal importance, but the main significance of the prophetic writings to Paul and all others of his and succeeding generations was to foretell the future, so that when the event happened it could be recognized as fulfilment. (See Is. xlviii. 3-8, and cf. the treatment in Justin Martyr, *Apolog.* i. 21 ff.)

Thus Paul's position was the rejection of the whole Law as such—the Decalogue just as much as the Law of leprosy, partly because he believed that with the coming of the Messiah the whole had been abrogated, partly no doubt because he was temperamentally opposed to that form of life which endeavours to obtain 'rightness' by establishing a code of conduct. Therefore he was quite as ready as Marcion to abandon the Law. Both Paul and Marcion held that the Law was such that it could not be fulfilled; in that sense salvation was impossible through the Law. But Paul explained this as due partly to the purpose for which the Law had been given, partly to the defect of human nature, corrupted by the transgression of Adam. Marcion explained it as due to the imperfect intelligence of the Demiurge. (See Harnack, *Marcion*, and cf. especially the chapter on Marcion in F. C. Burkitt's *The Gospel History and its Transmission.*)

Barnabas.    Another way of dealing with the difficulty of the Law, so as to accept the Old Testament as inspired scripture without observing the Law, was that of 'Barnabas,' who applied the method of allegorical interpretation to the Law, so that, for instance, the command not to eat pork meant to avoid the society of swine-like men. This system has always been used to some extent by commentators on 'sacred' books, whether Jewish, Christian, or heathen, but few ever went so far as 'Barnabas,' who maintained that the literal interpretation was the invention of the devil.

In these ways Christianity dealt with the question of the Law. Paul's view was not accepted in the sense in which he had meant it, and the distinction between Law and Promise gave place to that between 'Law' and 'Secundatio.' The reason for this is not far to seek. In spite of Paul, 'Law' in the sense of a code of conduct is a necessity for an institutionally organized society. The real objection to the Jewish Law was that it was an antiquated and impossible code which the Gentile world could not and would not accept. Circumcision especially was a Semitic custom repugnant to the Greek or Roman mind. But the Church could not exist without a law. Even Paul himself was obliged to lay down rules which formed an embryonic law. Before long a Christian law was formulated, using the 'Law,' omitting the 'Secundatio,' and adding such additional precepts as seemed necessary. It never quite gained the position of the Jewish Law, but in the Middle Ages came very near it.

Controversy with the Heathen.    (ii.) *Paul's Controversy with the Heathen.*—As soon as Paul became a missionary to the heathen rather than to the Jews, a different controversy began. Of it we have no direct examples in his epistles, and relatively few incidental references to it. The earliest is perhaps the summary given in 1 Thess. i. 9 f. where Paul claims that he succeeded in persuading the Thessalonians to "turn to God from idols, to serve a living and real God, and to wait for his son from heaven, whom he raised from the dead— Jesus who rescues us from the wrath to come." Obviously, however, this success was not reached without controversy, and his enforced departure from Thessalonica shows that he roused strong opposition. It is of course impossible to reconstruct the details of his arguments, but their general outline can probably be recovered from Rom. i. 18-32, 1 Cor. i. 18-ii. 10, Acts xiv. 15-17 (Lystra), and xvii. 22-31 (Athens). They consisted of a ' theory of history ' presented so as to support the eschatological message of impending judgement and possible salvation.

The first part of this theory is that, though there was evidence of the true God in nature, the Gentiles had refused to pay attention to it. The argument is the same as that developed in the second century by the Apologists, except that there is no trace of the doctrine, typical of the Apologists, that the Philosophers of Greece were analogous in the Greek world to the Prophets in the Hebrew, and there is a noticeable absence of the doctrine, even more typical of the Apologists, that the corruption of mankind was due to demons, though Paul undoubtedly believed in the maleficent working of devils and demons. (See O. Everling, *Die paulinische Angelologie und Dämonologie,* and Dibelius, *Die Geisterwelt im Glauben des Paulus.*)

The second part of the Pauline ' theory of history ' was that God had exhausted his patience with men, and would speedily judge and punish them. Safety, however, was offered to those who accepted Jesus as their saviour, appointed by God for this purpose of salvation, and also the pre-destined agent of God at the coming judgement (cf. Rom. ii. 16 ; Acts xvii. 31).

The main differences between the Epistles and Acts are: (*a*) the Epistles tend to emphasize the work of Jesus as saviour, Acts as judge.

(*b*) In the Epistles salvation is due to union with Jesus, which is also represented as the possession of the Spirit ' which is the Lord,' but in Acts salvation is due to repentance and baptism which conferred the Spirit. Both in the Epistles and in Acts the human deed necessary to accept the Divine offer of salvation is called ' faith,' and those who thus accept it are called οἱ πιστοί or οἱ πιστεύοντες. On the other hand both in the Epistles and in Acts salvation is also regarded as the free favour given to those who had been predestined for it, but in neither does there appear to be any real perception of the intellectual difficulty involved in the attempt to accept simultaneously theories of salvation by human faith and by divine predestination.

There are indeed other difficult questions involved, but they belong rather to the interpretation of the Epistles, which are more obscure than Acts. How far, for instance, did Paul identify the Spirit and the risen Jesus ? What part did baptism play in his scheme in relation to the gift of the Spirit ? Was it a sacrament, as it was in Johannine and Catholic Christianity, or a symbolic ceremony, as it was in Judaism which had no true sacraments ?  Possibly there is not sufficient evidence in the Epistles to justify any answer to these questions, which will nevertheless prove fundamental in any attempt to reconstruct fully Paul's preaching to the Gentiles and the controversy which it aroused.  For the commentator on Acts it is sufficient to note that they exist, for so far as Acts is concerned it cannot be doubted that the Spirit was central in the writer's doctrine of the church, and that he held it to be given normally either by baptism or by the laying on of hands.

(c) In the Epistles the salvation of men is very clearly dependent on the death of Jesus, which was an atoning sacrifice.  In Acts, however, there is at most only one reference to this doctrine—in xx. 28 ' the church of the Lord which he rescued ($\pi\epsilon\rho\iota\epsilon\pi o\iota\acute{\eta}\sigma a\tau o$) by the blood of his own one ' (see note *ad loc.*), and its absence is one of the most remarkable features of Acts.  The death of Jesus has in Acts, except in xx. 28, no soteriological significance ; it is merely a Jewish crime.  In Pauline doctrine the death of Jesus redeems men from sin ; this much is clear, even though it may be hard to say whether men make use of this redemption by faith, or by baptism, or by both, and whether they do so by an act of their own free will or by the grace of God given to the elect.  But in Acts this is not mentioned ; in strictly Jewish fashion repentance — with its corollary, faith—is all that is necessary.

Controversy with Jewish Christians.
(iii.) *Paul's Controversy with the Jewish Christians.*—Both Acts and the Epistles give more information on this subject than they do on the preaching of Paul either to Jews or to Gentiles.  From Acts xv. it is clear that there was a party in Jerusalem which insisted on the observance of the Jewish Law.  This party was the ancestor of the Nazarenes or Ebionites who continued to exist on a small scale until the end of the fourth century.  Acts taken by itself would not suggest that this party carried on a vigorous missionary propaganda throughout the Roman Empire, but the Epistles to the Romans and to the Galatians are usually interpreted to show that they did so.[1]

There are many problems with regard to the Jewish-Christian party which are likely to remain permanently obscure.  What, for instance, was its relation to James ?  And what value has the Pseudo-Clementine literature for the reconstruction of its teaching ?  But for the present purpose it is sufficient to note that (a) it maintained the validity of the Law and insisted on circumcision, but (b) regarded Jesus as the Messiah, though exactly in what sense is open to argument.

Did they think of him as the Messiah of the Psalms of Solomon, the Prince of the House of David, who would restore the Kingdom to Israel, or as the Messiah of the Book of Enoch, who would appear at the end of this world, to judge it, and to admit or to exclude from the Life of the World to Come ?  Or did they, like the later Christians, combine both

[1] In view of Prof. Ropes's book, *The Singular Problem of the Epistle to the Galatians*, this interpretation is open to grave doubt.  In any case, however, there certainly were Jewish Christians in Palestine, though there may have been extremely few elsewhere.

expectations ?   We do not know, and probably cannot know, as there is
no sufficient extant evidence.[1]

An extremely difficult and important question is the relation of James The position
to this party.

His position seems clear up to a point.   His representatives in Antioch
undoubtedly insisted on the Jewish manner of life, which must at least
mean observance by Gentile converts of whatever rules were in force at
that time for the regulation of social relationship between Jews and God-
fearers.   All the evidence seems to suggest that these rules are embodied
in the apostolic decrees.   There is, as has been said, no evidence at all
that Paul ever accepted them as part of the Christian way of life, but
there is every reason to suppose that they were current in circles where
Jewish Christians were found.   In other words, there is no reason to
suppose that Acts is wholly fiction.

Did James go further, and insist on circumcision for converts ?
Possibly he did.   But the possibility cannot be excluded that James
and others believed that the life of the ' World to Come '—though perhaps
not the 'Days of the Messiah '—would be open to pious God-fearers.   That
this view was held in some circles seems clear from the Sibylline Oracles,[2]
but before opinion can be clarified on this point we need more knowledge
on two points : (a) How far did Jews in the first century admit that
pious God-fearers had a share in the ' World to Come ' ? and (b) How far
did the first Christian eschatology contemplate the 'Days of the
Messiah' as well as the ' World to Come ' ?   On the second point it is
possible that Jesus contemplated only the speedy coming of the ' World
to Come,' and that Paul and others (notably the Johannine Apocalypse)
introduced a Christian version of the ' Days of the Messiah,' which was
not part of the teaching of Jesus.   (See Vol. I. pp. 267 ff. and 362 ff.)

If this be so, quite conceivably the position of James was that the
way of life was open to those heathen who became God-fearers, but that
they must obey the rules laid down for God-fearers.   Whether this be
so or not, it would certainly seem probable that this was the position
adopted by Peter and Barnabas under pressure from James, but refused
by Paul.   In favour of the view that James did not go further than this,
and did not insist on circumcision, is Paul's clear statement in Gal. ii. 9
that James accepted Paul's gospel to the Gentiles, which certainly did
not include circumcision.   Against it is the statement in Acts xv. 1 that
trouble was caused in Antioch by those who came down from Judaea

---

[1] It has sometimes been thought that we learn something about it from
the Pseudo-Clementine literature.   This is improbable.   The Pseudo-Clementine
literature is a work which resembles many more recent productions in being
an attempt to reconstruct Apostolic Christianity so as to edify a later generation.   Such books are neither wholly history nor wholly fiction, they are a
separate *genre*, but the historian of the early Church does well to make little
use of them.   The Pseudo-Clementines throw an immensely valuable light on
the thought of the fourth or possibly third century, but little or none on the
history of the first.

[2] See p. 209.

and insisted on circumcision. It is, however, not stated that these Judaeans were sent by James.

A possible view which seems to me to have general probability in its favour, though it cannot be demonstrated by evidence, is that James was willing, as Galatians says, to condone Paul's practice of not circumcising his converts. He did not feel that this excluded them from the World to Come, and if the World to Come was all that interested these Goyim, and Paul was content to have it so, well and good, But he, James, the brother of the Lord, and a son of David according to the flesh, did not forget the customs, and desired to remain faithful to the Law of God, given to His People. He would have been deeply shocked at the idea that Jews, however much they believed that Jesus was the Messiah, should give up circumcision, just as Protestants who have abandoned all belief in baptismal regeneration would nevertheless be shocked at any suggestion that they should give up baptizing their children.

Some such view as this would seem to do most justice to the three important pieces of evidence which we possess. (i.) Paul's statement that James accepted his preaching to the Gentiles. (ii.) The picture of James in Acts xxi. 17 ff. (iii.) The undoubted fact that James lived in Jerusalem until almost the beginning of the Jewish-Roman war, and was accepted by most of the Jews as a pious and devout worshipper in the Temple.

The position of Peter is also far from clear. It seems certain from Acts as well as from Galatians that he did not insist on the circumcision, but both he and Barnabas obviously made to James some concession which Paul refused. It is clear from Galatians that this concession concerned the social intercourse of Christians or Gentile Christians with Jews or with Jewish Christians. It is a fair guess that the decrees, or the attitude which they embody, belong to this episode, but the details must necessarily remain obscure. (See Additional Note 16.)

Controversy with Gentile Christians. (iv.) *The Controversy with Gentile Christians.*—The last controversy in which Paul was concerned was with Greek-speaking Christians who were for the most part converts from heathenism, and in any case were permeated with the religious preconceptions of the Greco-oriental world. It will probably always be doubtful how far Paul himself accepted or had inherited those preconceptions, but the Epistles to the Corinthians show that he was engaged during his stay at Ephesus in a violent controversy which turned mainly on the relation between them and the Christian message which his converts had accepted.

Stated briefly the situation was this : the Corinthians, who are doubtless to be taken as typical of Gentile Christians, believed in general that Christianity gave them the Spirit of God which so changed their nature that they became—like divine beings—immortal. It is unnecessary here to discuss the difficulties which arise if we ask the three questions which constitute the ' Pauline problem ' in relation to Gentile Christianity—(i.) How far did they or Paul think that this Spirit was the result of baptism ? (ii.) Did they or Paul think that without the Spirit life ended with the

grave ?  (iii.) How far did they or Paul identify or distinguish Jesus and
the Spirit ?  But whatever may be the answer to these problems it is
certain that controversy arose when, especially in Corinth, the converts
began to discuss the relation between the life of the Spirit and Gentile
concepts of sacrificial meals, the problems of marriage and sex, the bearing
of the life of the Spirit on personal conduct, and the connexion between the
immortality given by the Spirit and the belief in a resurrection.

On all these points Paul had definite opinions, but the most important
was his insistence that the life of the Spirit re-enforced and did not cancel
the claims of a strict Jewish code of morality, and that the gift of immortality did not exclude the Jewish belief in a resurrection.

Though the details are obscure it is clear from the Epistles to the
Corinthians that the controversy on these topics was extremely bitter, and
that Paul himself was at times doubtful whether he would succeed in
carrying his Gentile converts with him.  But in the end he won.  He failed
in his controversy with the Jews ; probably he failed, at least partially, in
his controversy with Jewish Christians, but he triumphed in this, his final
controversy, with Gentile Christians.  It was this triumph which occured
him his position in the Church—which is Gentile Christianity—and
preserved his epistles as Holy Scripture, for it is to be remembered that
though for later ages Paul lived because of his epistles, for the early
Church the epistles lived because of Paul.

Why is there not a single word about this controversy in Acts ?  That Luke's
it is a reality, not a figment of historical imagination, is proved by the silence.
epistles.  But Luke is absolutely silent on the whole matter, and if we
did not possess the epistles we should suppose that in the Apostolic age no
suggestion of quarrels ruffled the peace of Gentile Christianity.  Whether
' Luke ' was a companion of Paul or not he clearly had reliable information
as to Paul's missionary career in Ephesus and Corinth.  He cannot have
been ignorant of the controversy, and his silence is puzzling.

The only answer which we can give is that he desired to represent
the Apostolic Church as harassed by persecution from without, but never
disturbed by quarrels within.  Even in chapter xv. there is no quarrel
on such issues.  There was a momentary difference of opinion, but no
quarrel and no discussion among the leaders.  The quarrel with Barnabas,
which in Galatians is doctrinal, is merely personal in Acts.

It is the same picture which Clement of Rome drew a little later, and
is copied in all the long series of pseudo-Apostolic writings.  It is found
in the speech of Paul at Miletus, " After I am gone [if that be the right
translation, see note *ad loc.*], grievous wolves shall enter "—which implies
that they had not done so as yet.  It is only contradicted, but then in
the most convincing and absolute manner, by the epistles of Paul himself,
which show that turbulent discussion, not ' deep peace,' was as characteristic of the Gentile Church in its infancy as in its maturity.

NOTE XVIII. PAUL'S ROUTE IN ASIA MINOR

By KIRSOPP LAKE

Paul's route.    The route followed by Paul on his missionary journeys generally offers no special difficulty ; the places in Europe which he visited—Neapolis, Philippi, Amphipolis, Apollonia, Thessalonica, Beroea, Athens, Corinth— are all well known, and, except for the journey from Beroea to Athens (see note, Vol. IV. pp. 207 f.), the road which he probably took is quite obvious. This, however, is only partly true of his journeys in Asia Minor. Here the towns mentioned can indeed be generally identified, but when he refers to districts it is not always certain what Luke means, and the route which Paul followed is obscure.

The purpose of this note, therefore, is to discuss the difficulties which are found if Paul be followed on his journeys across Asia Minor.

The first journey.    Chapters xiii. and xiv. cover the first journey. The localities on Paul's way out are Perga, Pisidian Antioch, Iconium, Lystra, Derbe, and on his return he retraced his steps except that Attalia took the place of Perga.

## 1. *Perga—Antioch—Iconium*

Perga.    There is no problem connected with Perga except the doubt whether Acts necessarily means that the party landed at Perga. (See note on xiii. 13.) The text merely states that having started from Paphos, Paul and his party came to Perga. This would not exclude the possibility that they actually landed at Attalia. Ramsay (*Church in the Roman Empire*, p. 16) admits that at present Perga could not be reached by a sea-going boat, and assumes that the channel up the Cestrus was kept open by dredging. It is of course true that this was done in Ephesus, but there is no evidence that it was at Perga, and according to Strabo (p. 667) Perga was not even on the river, but five miles distant. Therefore it is quite doubtful whether the party actually landed at Perga.

Pisidian Antioch.    From Perga they went to Antioch of Pisidia. Probably one reason for going to Antioch was its large Jewish colony (Josephus, *Antiq.* xii. 3. 1). It was the chief city in the southern part of the province of Galatia, and there was doubtless a well-recognized road between it and Perga, but the course of this road is by no means certain. The most probable theory seems to be that of Ramsay (*Church in the Roman Empire*, p. 19). According to this it went up one of the eastern branches of the Cestrus to Adada, which is now called Karabavlo. Ramsay thinks that Paul was the patron saint of the city, and that the church, of which some ruins remain, was dedicated to him. Churches dedicated to St. Paul are not uncommon, and this may account for the modern name of the town ; the only objection is that as a rule in local Turkish corruptions of the name of a Greek saint the ' saint ' is usually represented by Ayo (ἅγιος).

From Adada the road to Antioch, according to Ramsay, is uncertain. There is a path along the south-eastern end of Lake Egerdir, the ancient Limnai, but Ramsay thinks that an easier road would have been one which turns to the east after leaving Adada and goes through the hills between it and Lake Karalis.

From Antioch Paul went to Iconium. Here again further knowledge Iconium. of the locality has changed opinion as to the way by which Paul is likely to have gone from Antioch to Iconium. The chief feature of the country is a great mountain ridge, known as the Sultan Dagh, the pass over which is at least four thousand feet above Antioch. The main road from Ephesus across Asia Minor to the Euphrates valley went immediately to the north of this mountain, and for any traveller coming from Ephesus the natural road would have been along this main artery of traffic as far as Laodicea, from which a branch road went to Iconium. But although Antioch seems to be quite close to this road, it is unfortunately separated from it by the whole bulk of the Sultan Dagh, and to reach it would mean going over the pass just mentioned and joining the main road at Philomelion.

It is therefore practically certain that he went along the *Via Sebaste* The *Via* which was built for Augustus by his propraetor Cornutus Aquila in *Sebaste.* 6 B.C. It went from Antioch through Selki, where the 44th and 45th milestones have been found, and Yonuslar (the ancient Pappa), where a milestone (the number is missing) is also extant. These milestones had originally the general inscription *Imperator Caesar Divi filius, Augustus, Pontifex Maximus, Consul XI, Designatus XII, Imperator XV, Tribunicia potestate XVIII, Viam Sebasten, curante Cornuto Aquila legato suo pro praetore, fecit.* After Pappa the road must have passed through the Bagharzik Deré, and probably through Bulumia to Lystra, though absolute evidence of this is not yet available.[1]

This road is doubtless referred to in a passage in the extract from the second-century *Acta Pauli*,[2] known as *The Acts of Paul and Thecla* (ii. 3). It runs as follows :

---

[1] See H. S. Cronin, 'First Report of a Journey in Pisidia,' in the *Journal of Hellenic Studies,* xxii. (1902), pp. 94 ff., esp. pp. 109 f.

[2] The *Acts of Paul* from which the commonly known *Acts of Paul and Thecla* was taken is one of the five ' Leucian ' Acts used by the Manichaeans in Africa. The *Acts of Paul* at all events was also recognized as scripture by the orthodox in Africa, and was quoted as such by Augustine in his controversy with Felix the Manichee. Tertullian, however, says that it had been recently composed by a presbyter in Asia Minor in a mistaken attempt to glorify the Apostle. The original text of the complete *Acta* is lost, but large parts of an early Coptic version have been published by Carl Schmidt, and the same scholar has recently announced the discovery of a large section of the Greek text in a papyrus of the third century. There cannot be any doubt but that the commonly current *Acts of Paul and Thecla* are an extract from this second-century document. The possibility of course remains that the author of the original book was making use of earlier sources, but there is no evidence of this. When Ramsay wrote, Carl Schmidt's discovery had not been made, and Ramsay regarded the *Acts of Paul and Thecla* as an independent work. Out of a large literature see especially Lipsius and Bonnet, *Acta Apostolorum Apocrypha,* C. Schmidt, *Die alten Petrusakten* and *Acta Pauli,* M. R. James, *Apocryphal Acts,* and ' Acta Iohannis ' in *Texts and Studies.*

Καὶ ἐπορεύετο κατὰ τὴν βασιλικὴν ὁδὸν τὴν ἐπὶ Λύστραν, καὶ εἱστήκει ἀπεκδεχόμενος αὐτόν, καὶ τοὺς ἐρχομένους ἐθεώρει κατὰ τὴν μήνυσιν Τίτου. εἶδεν δὲ τὸν Παῦλον ἐρχόμενον, ἄνδρα μικρὸν τῷ μεγέθει, ψιλὸν τῇ κεφαλῇ, ἀγκύλον ταῖς κνήμαις, εὐεκτικόν, σύνοφρυν, μικρῶς ἐπίρρινον, χάριτος πλήρη· ποτὲ μὲν γὰρ ἐφαίνετο ὡς ἄνθρωπος, ποτὲ δὲ ἀγγέλου πρόσωπον εἶχεν.

It cannot be doubted that the ὁδὸς βασιλική in this passage is the Greek rendering of *Via Sebaste*. Why however should βασιλική have been substituted for the Greek word *Sebaste*? The guess may be hazarded that the road was restored rather than built by Augustus, and that *Sebaste* was an attempt to connect with Rome an older road going back to Persian times or earlier. Augustus seems never to have neglected an opportunity, however small, of diverting old names or old customs into a closer connexion with Rome. The 'Royal road' of Herodotus is usually supposed to have gone through Ancyra, but W. M. Calder seems to have proved conclusively that it really went through Lycaonia. If so, the ὁδὸς βασιλική of the *Acta Pauli* is a characteristic survival of the ancient name of the great road which Augustus partly restored and incorporated into his system.[1]

## 2. *Lystra—Derbe*

Lystra.    Lystra is the modern Zoldera, on the northern bank of the Kopree river, opposite to and about a mile from the village of Khatyn Serai. That Zoldera is Lystra was first proved in 1885 by J. R. S. Sterrett,[2] who found a Latin inscription :

DIVUM AUG(ustum)
COL(onia) IUL(ia) FE
LIX GEMINA
LUSTRA
CONSE
CRAVIT
D(ecreto) D(ecurionum).

This inscription not improbably indicates that there was an *Augusteum* at Lystra just as there was at Ancyra and Antioch, and the question occurs inevitably whether this is not the same as the temple which Luke describes as that of Zeus. At Ancyra the *Augusteum* seems to have been outside the city, and in Lystra it may have been associated with the Lycaonian cult which Luke identified with that of Zeus (see note on xiv. 13).

The road to Lystra from Iconium is thus described by Sir W. M. Ramsay,[3] who visited Khatyn Serai in 1882, but did not cross over to

[1] Herodotus v. 52, and W. M. Calder, 'The Royal Road in Herodotus,' in the *Classical Review*, xxxix. 1 (1925) pp. 7 ff.
[2] *The Wolfe Expedition to Asia Minor* (vol. iii. of the *Papers of the American School of Classical Studies at Athens*), 1888, Inscr. No. 242, p. 142.
[3] *The Church in the Roman Empire*, pp. 47 f.

Zoldera: "Lystra is about six hours S.S.W. from Iconium. The road passes
for a mile or more through the luxuriant gardens of the suburbs, and then.
across the level plain, rising gently for twelve miles. Then it reaches a
range of hills, which stretch outwards in a south-easterly direction from
the mountainous country that bounds the vast Lycaonian plains on the
west and separates them from the great depression in which are situated
the two connected lakes Trogitis (Seidi Sheher) and Karalis (Bey Sheher,
the largest in Asia Minor). This range, which entails a further ascent
of 500 feet, diminishes in height towards the east, and sinks down to the
plain ten miles away. After crossing these hills, the road descends into
a valley, in breadth about a mile, down the centre of which flows a river
towards the south-east ; and on the southern bank of the river, about a
mile from the place where the road leaves the hills, stands the village of
Khatyn Serai, ' The Lady's Mansion.' The name dates no doubt from the
time of the Seljuk Sultans of Roum, when the village was an estate and
country residence of some sultana from Konia (as Iconium is now called).
Its elevation, about 3777 feet above the sea and 427 above Iconium, fits
it for a summer residence."

The exact site of Derbe is not known ; but at present the most probable Derbe.
suggestion is either that of J. R. S. Sterrett, who thinks that Derbe was
at Losta (or Zosta), or that of W. M. Ramsay, who thinks that it was
probably at Gudelissin. Ramsay thinks that the ruins at Losta are
merely stones which were brought from Gudelissin, which is about three
miles W.N.W. of Losta. Gudelissin has a large mound, of the kind sometimes described as Assyrian Tells, and referred to by Strabo as ' cities of
Semiramis ' ; doubtless its excavation would be interesting, and it may
be the site of Derbe. I admit, however, to the feeling, which apparently
Professor Sterrett shared, that Acts xiv. 20 implies (though admittedly it
does not state) that Paul did not stop anywhere between Lystra and Derbe.
Gudelissin is about 35 miles from Lystra, and could not be reached in one
day of ordinary travel. It would therefore not surprise me if Derbe were
ultimately found to have been rather nearer to Zoldera.

Derbe appears in Acts xiv. to have been the place where Paul turned
back and retraced his steps through Lystra, Iconium, and Pisidian Antioch
to Perga, but on this occasion it is definitely stated that Attalia was the
actual port of departure for sailing to Syrian Antioch. It should be noted
that the inaccuracy of speaking of the first great city reached instead of
the actual port of arrival, which probably made Luke say Perga instead
of Attalia in xiii. 13, is here observable in the reference to Antioch, for of
course they really landed at Seleucia.

If E. Schwartz's theory about Acts be accepted, these few verses, xiv. 21-26.
xiv. 21-26, are at least partly editorial, and put in to round out the
narrative (see pp. 201 ff. and 237 f.). It is not impossible, is even probable, but it cannot be proved. If it be accepted, xv. 40 and probably
part of the context must also be editorial. According to this theory
Barnabas probably left Paul at Iconium and returned alone to Antioch,
while Paul went on as is described in xvi. 4 ff.

If, however, the text be followed as it stands, the Apostolic Council The Council.

described in chap. xv. comes between the first and second journeys, and the second missionary journey began when Paul again left Antioch, after quarrelling with Barnabas about Mark.[1] The first part is only briefly indicated. Paul appears to have gone to Derbe by land, so that he must have gone through the Syrian Gates, crossing Cilicia to Tarsus, thence through the Cilician Gates, and so along the northern side of the Taurus through the kingdom of Antiochus to Derbe, Lystra, and Iconium.

xvi. 6.    So much is clear : the difficulty begins with xvi. 6.

The Greek of the Neutral text of this verse is διῆλθον δὲ τὴν Φρυγίαν καὶ Γαλατικὴν χώραν, κωλυθέντες ὑπὸ τοῦ ἁγίου πνεύματος λαλῆσαι τὸν λόγον ἐν τῇ Ἀσίᾳ, ἐλθόντες δὲ κατὰ τὴν Μυσίαν ἐπείραζον εἰς τὴν Βειθυνίαν πορευθῆναι καὶ οὐκ εἴασεν αὐτοὺς τὸ πνεῦμα Ἰησοῦ· παρελθόντες δὲ τὴν Μυσίαν κατέβησαν εἰς Τρῳάδα. The Western text is the same except that it reads μηδενὶ λαλῆσαι τὸν λόγον τοῦ θεοῦ ἐν τῇ Ἀσίᾳ, substitutes γενόμενοι for ἐλθόντες, and διελθόντες for παρελθόντες. Obviously these changes are unimportant for interpretation, but the later text read διελθόντες for διῆλθον and inserted τήν before Γαλατικὴν χώραν.

The value of the later text.    To adopt either of these later readings would be a violation of all recognized textual probability. A reading found in the later MSS., but in neither the Neutral nor Western text, has no claim to be considered. But it is worth asking why these changes were made by the later scribes. Διελθόντες for διῆλθον is doubtless due[2] to an attempt to understand Paul's route, and it is intimately connected with the insertion of τήν before Γαλατικὴν χώραν. The emendator clearly took Φρυγίαν as a substantive, and held that it was distinct from the ' Galatian territory.' But to express this in Greek usually requires an article before Γαλατικὴν χώραν. The emendation is therefore evidence that in the fourth or fifth century it was held that Paul travelled first through Phrygia, and then through Galatia. When in Galatia he proposed to go into Asia, but could not, and therefore went on until, κατὰ τὴν Μυσίαν, he tried to enter Bithynia. This also proved impossible, so he went through Mysia to Troas. To the scribe of the late text it seemed clear that the question of entry into Asia arose after Paul was in Galatia. Therefore he changed διῆλθον to διελθόντες, and so bears witness that κωλυθέντες ought to be interpreted as describing the state of things which led up to διῆλθον. Similarly his preference for τὴν Γαλατικὴν χώραν corroborates the opinion of modern grammarians that the original phrase meant a single district : had it meant two districts the article must have been repeated before Γαλατικὴν χώραν.

Therefore, rejecting the late text, and accepting the judgement of the late scribe as to the meaning of the original text, we must say that κωλυθέντες conditions διῆλθον and that τὴν Φρυγίαν καὶ Γαλατικὴν χώραν means two localities conceived as a single district.

---

[1] There is a different account in the *Acts of Barnabas*, but it is probably pure fiction. It confuses Antioch in Syria with Pisidian Antioch, and makes Mark a servant of a priest of Zeus in Iconium. The text is published by Lipsius and Bonnet, *Acta Apostolorum Apocrypha*, ii. 2, pp. 292 ff.

[2] See Vol. III. p. 152.

Thus the conditions which must be met by any solution of the problem The conditions of the problem.
of Paul's route between Lystra and Troas are the following :

(i.) He wished to preach in ' Asia,' but was unable to do so.

(ii.) He therefore passed through τὴν Φρυγίαν καὶ Γαλατικὴν χώραν
until he was κατὰ τὴν Μυσίαν.

(iii.) He then tried to enter Bithynia but was unable, and so went
through Mysia to Troas.

The doubtful points, which make the solution difficult, are : The doubtful points.

(a) What is the meaning of ' Asia ' ?

(b) What spot is meant by κατὰ τὴν Μυσίαν ?

(c) What is the meaning of τὴν Φρυγίαν καὶ Γαλατικὴν χώραν ?

(a) *Asia.*—This is an elusive word which is used in several senses : Asia.

(i.) The continent of Asia, as distinct from Europe. This sense is
found in geographers, but clearly cannot be the one used by Luke.

(ii.) Asia with the adjective *minor* is also used by geographers in the
same sense as it is to-day, but is equally inappropriate here.

(iii.) Far more often, especially in official documents, Asia is used in
the sense of the Roman province ; it is probably so used in 1 Peter i. 1.
But it must be remembered that Asia, like the other provinces, varied in
size from time to time. The original ' Asia ' was Mysia and Lydia, and
perhaps Caria. Phrygia was added in 116 B.C., but in 80 B.C. the *Dioceses*
of Synnada, Apameia, and Laodicea were given to Cilicia, only to be
restored to Asia in 49 B.C.

(iv.) It is also used in a narrower[1] sense of the Greek cities of the
Aegean coast (using coast in a liberal sense) with the territory adjacent to
them. This is probably the older use, as not only the provinces of the
Empire but also the kingdoms they replaced were named *a parte potiori.*
An example of this older and narrower use of ' Asia ' is given by the
' Seven Churches of Asia ' of the Apocalypse. It means the Greek cities
of the district of which the line Ephesus—Smyrna—Pergamos is the
western limit, and Laodicea the eastern. Possibly the other cities of the
Lycus valley, Colossae and Hierapolis, and even Apameia, were sometimes
included, but Strabo[2] includes them in Phrygia. Of course Strabo knew

[1] " Asia is a term about which it is very difficult to decide. The Roman
province Asia had been formed in 133 B.C., and the name seems to have soon
come into popular use, because there was no other term to denote the Aegean
coast lands. But during the first century before Christ the province was greatly
increased in size, and it is very difficult to determine after this time whether
the name Asia is used in the popular sense of the Aegean coast lands or denotes
the entire Roman province ; in short, whether it includes Phrygia or not."
(W. M. Ramsay, *The Church in the Roman Empire,* p. 150.)

[2] Very probably Apameia was just as Greek-speaking among the upper
classes in the city as was Ephesus, but the surrounding population was definitely
Phrygian. Strabo goes even further and includes the cities of the Lycus in
Phrygia, but says that Apameia was the greatest market of Asia τῆς ἰδίως λεγομένης
after Ephesus. I do not feel sure whether Asia here means the restricted district

that all this district was in the province of Asia, but as a geographer he regards west-central Asia as Phrygia, and distinguishes it from Galatia and Mysia. So far as Acts is concerned the most important evidence is given in Acts ii. 9 f., where the component parts, or some of them, of Asia Minor are described as Cappadocia, Pontus, Asia, Phrygia, and Pamphylia. Obviously Asia is here used in a sense which excluded Phrygia.

In which of these senses is 'Asia' used in Acts xvi. 6 ? The choice is clearly between the third and the fourth. It either means the province Asia, or Asia in the narrower sense of Acts ii. and the Apocalypse.

In favour of the first possibility is the place where Paul was at the time. Acts xvi. 5 brings him to Lystra or Iconium. From Iconium it was only a step to the frontier of the Roman province of Asia, but it was a long way to the 'Asian' cities in the narrower sense. The natural meaning of διῆλθον κτλ. in xvi. 6 is that they went through Phrygia, because they had been prevented from preaching in Asia, which implies that Asia was near at hand. On the other hand, none of the other words used in the passage are the names of Roman provinces, and if Asia really means 'Greek cities,' it may have been within Paul's purpose even when he was in Iconium. Of course, on Ramsay's view, that κωλυθέντες is merely an equivalent of καὶ ἐκωλύθησαν, Asia in the narrower sense is more probable ; but grammar seems to render his theory unlikely.

Mysia.

(b) κατὰ τὴν Μυσίαν. Strabo's accurate account leaves no doubt as to the general position of Mysia. It was the district from the shores of Troy to the eastern slopes of the Mysian Olympus. Thus when Paul is described as being κατὰ τὴν Μυσίαν when he considered going to Bithynia, the meaning is plain. He was not far south of the Bithynian boundary and not far east of the Mysian Olympus. If it were necessary to choose a single town, Dorylaion or Kotiaion would admirably fit all the conditions of the problem ; these towns are in Phrygia, but close to country inhabited by Galatians.[1]

It will be seen that this spot, as well as the whole of Mysia, was well inside the frontiers of the province of Asia, and also that there is no spot in the province of Galatia which could fairly be described as κατὰ τὴν

---

under discussion, or the province, or the continent, but I think that it probably means the continent. Perhaps the point really is that Asia was the name used by Greeks to describe the eastern shore of the Aegean. The inhabitants of various districts called their lands after their own names, but the Greeks, who could not use their own name, because it belonged to the country from which they had emigrated, called it all Asia. Asia is a Greek name, not used by Lydians or Phrygians or Carians or others, but only by Greeks and Romans. Hence the description which the κοινόν of Asia gives of itself is οἱ ἐπὶ τῆς Ἀσίας Ἕλληνες. Therefore also it was possible for such a city as Laodicea, with a mixed population, to belong to the κοινὸν τῆς Ἀσίας, and so to be spoken of at times as in Asia, at other times as in Phrygia.

[1] Thus the whole district from Iconium to Dorylaion was one in which Phrygians and Galatians must have been closely intermingled. It was Phrygia, but it was also Galatian country.

Μυσίαν. Nevertheless it seems to me clear that the writer did not think that this journey, ending near Dorylaion, was in Asia in his sense of the word. It is indeed possible to say—as Ramsay does—that Paul was only prevented from preaching in Asia, not from travelling across it, but the *prima facie* force of the words used is that ' Asia ' was one district, ' Phrygia and Galatian territory ' another, Mysia a third, and Bithynia a fourth. Paul originally wished to go to Asia, but could not preach there, so he went through ' Phrygia and Galatian country,' and when he could not go straight on into Bithynia he turned to the west and went to Troas.

(c) The meaning of τὴν Φρυγίαν καὶ Γαλατικὴν χώραν. This question has often been discussed in commentaries on Acts and on the Epistle to the Galatians. There is, first of all, a grammatical question. It is conceivable either that Φρυγίαν is a substantive and means ' Phrygia,' or that it is an adjective qualifying χώρα, strictly co-ordinate with Γαλατικήν, and meaning ' Phrygian.'

The majority of recent commentators take the latter view. It is quite possible, and is supported by the awkwardness of the alternate view, which gives us a substantive with an article closely tied up to another substantive with a qualifying adjective without an article. It is argued that ' Phrygia and the Galatian district ' could not be translated into Greek by τὴν Φρυγίαν καὶ Γαλατικὴν χώραν, for, as the later scribes saw, if Phrygia is a substantive, there should be an article before Γαλατικήν.

Nevertheless there is more to be said for the other view than has often been admitted in recent books. Two arguments deserve consideration.

(i.) Φρύγιος, the adjective formed from Φρύξ, was ' of three termina- Φρύγιος. tions ' in earlier Greek, but Lucian uses it as of only two,[1] and I know of no instance of the nominative with the feminine termination in Greek contemporary with the New Testament. There may be examples of which I am ignorant, and it may be merely an accident, but the spelling and use of such words is largely a matter of fashion, and it is probable that the declension of many words was in practice more irregular than grammarians have always admitted.[2] In any case Φρυγία had undoubtedly become a substantive proper name, and the first thought of any reader would be to interpret it so. Moreover it is quite possible that Γαλατικὴ χώρα was a recognized name for a certain district (probably, as is argued later, where Gaelic was predominantly spoken), and was customarily used without the article, especially in combination with another substantive. One article was enough for both. An exact parallel is given by τῆς Ἰτουραίας καὶ Τραχωνίτιδος χώρας in Luke iii. 1, where it is similarly possible to say that Ἰτουραίας is an adjective, but it can really hardly be doubted that to the ordinary reader the phrase meant ' Ituraea and the district of Trachonitis.'

(ii.) Even more powerful is the argument supplied by Acts xviii. 23, Acts xviii. where Luke writes of Paul's return from Syria to Ephesus that he ἐξῆλθεν 23.

[1] *Harmonides* 1.
[2] For an example of heteroclitism see the notes on ' Lystra,' pp. 162 f., and on ' Three Sabbaths,' pp. 202 f.

(from Antioch) διερχόμενος καθεξῆς τὴν Γαλατικὴν χώραν καὶ Φρυγίαν. Here again we have the same composite district, travelled in the reverse direction. Exactly the same words are used, but in the opposite order, and it is impossible to argue here that Φρυγία is an adjective. As before, the article comes at the beginning and is not repeated with the second phrase.

Thus I believe that there is a preponderance of sound argument for thinking that in xvi. 6 Φρυγία was intended by Luke for a substantive as it is in xviii. 23. Why Luke or anyone else used one form for Phrygia and another for ' the Galatian district ' is a further point ; but it is not impossible that he did not know, any more than most Englishmen know why they add -shire to the name of some counties and not to others, or Americans know why they say 'State of Maine' (not, be it noted, *the* State of Maine) but ' New York State.'

Accepting, then, the view that ἡ Φρυγία καὶ Γαλατικὴ χώρα means a composite entity of which one part was called ' Phrygia ' and the other ' Galatian country,' the questions arise : (i.) in what sense would these two names be applied to any one part of Asia Minor ? and (ii.) what route did Paul follow if he went through it ?

The history of Asia Minor.

The obscurity which surrounds any attempt to define what may be meant by Phrygia and Galatia is partly due to the history of central Asia Minor, which was for centuries conditioned by a series of invasions. We do not know, though archaeology will probably reveal before long, to what race the earliest inhabitants of central Asia Minor belonged. They may have been members of what is commonly called the Mediterranean race, but at present we know little about them, and though we may discover some details, it is very probable that we shall never know with certainty the nature of their language. The first event of which we have reasonably accurate information is that the Hittites, who were probably not aborigines, were the lords of Asia Minor in the third millennium before Christ. Information about the Hittites is accumulating almost daily, and though it would be improper to say that they were an Indo-European race, some of them certainly used an Indo-European language for official purposes. Their capital, or at all events one of their chief cities, was at Pteria, perhaps better known under its Turkish name Boghaz-Keui.

The Hittites carried on alternating war and commerce with Egypt and Assyria. In the second millennium before Christ their western frontier was invaded by the Greeks, and few things have been more romantic in the history of archaeology than the discovery on Hittite monuments of probable references to the Achaeans and to the names of heroes whom we had been inclined to regard as mythical rather than historical. A similar invasion of Asia Minor was carried out very successfully at the same time, or a little earlier, by the Phrygians, who came from the Balkan district, and conquered the Hittites at least so far as to occupy the western part of Asia Minor up to Iconium. The remaining power of the Hittites in eastern Asia Minor disappeared in the days of the Babylonian and Persian Empires, which, from the point of view of Asia Minor, may be regarded as invasions coming from the south and covering the middle of the first millennium.

Then the tide turned again, and the country was once more swept by invading Greeks under Alexander of Macedonia and his successors.

Just at this time, about the year 278, a new invasion began. The Gauls coming from the north were then invading all the Mediterranean lands, and they came into Asia Minor partly as invaders, partly as mercenaries. They overran Phrygia, and ultimately established a kingdom with Ancyra (the modern Angora) as its capital; their language was akin to Welsh and other Celtic dialects. Thus part of Phrygia ceased to be Phrygian, though the Galatians seem to have adopted the Phrygian cult of the Great Mother. Owing to Greek influence the territory dominated by the Gauls was called by outsiders ' Galatia,' just as owing to Latin influence the similar kingdom in the West was called ' Gallia.' It is not necessary to go into the details of the history of these Gauls. They were constantly fighting with all their neighbours, and especially with the Pontic kings to the north.

In 121 B.C. the Romans declared Galatia free, which meant subject to Rome instead of Pontus. In Pompey's reorganization of the east Galatia was put under three chiefs, of whom the survivor and ultimate king of the whole district was Deiotarus. He was succeeded in 40 B.C. by Castor, but Mark Antony reorganized the whole district, making Castor king of Galatia, Amyntas, formerly secretary to Deiotarus, king of Pisidia, and Polemon king of Lycaonia. The capitals of these three kingdoms were Ancyra, Pisidian Antioch, and Iconium. In 36 B.C. Castor died, and Amyntas was given Lycaonia and Galatia, from which he now took his title as king, Polemon being compensated by appointment to the kingdom of Pontus. Amyntas appears to have been a competent ruler, and increased his kingdom by the addition of Pamphylia and part of Cilicia. In 25 B.C. he was killed, and the Romans took over his kingdom as a province, to which they gave the name of *Provincia Galatia.* The province of Galatia thus became the Roman name of large tracts of land which had formerly belonged to other kingdoms, especially to Phrygia and to Lycaonia. It was, of course, very much larger than Galatia proper, and in large parts of it there were no Galatians at all.

Thus, to return to Acts xvi. 6, in the first century ' Galatia' or ' Galatian territory ' might conceivably have had any one of three meanings : (i.) the old kingdom of Galatia; (ii.) the larger and indistinctly defined territory where Gaelic was spoken ; (iii.) the Roman province of Galatia, which did not coincide with either (i.) or (ii.). `'Galatian territory' in Acts xvi.`

The older commentators interpreted ' the Galatian district ' in Acts xvi. 6 as the ' kingdom of Galatia.' Lightfoot's exposition of this theory is the best and most accessible.[1] He takes Asia to mean the province, and explains τὴν Φρυγίαν καὶ Γαλατικὴν χώραν as the country which had once been Phrygia and afterwards Galatia. He thinks that Paul may have gone as far as Ancyra, and that he may have intended to visit the eastern part of Bithynia. The decisive objections to this theory are that it was three hundred years since ' Galatia ' had been ' Phrygia,' and that `Lightfoot.`

---

[1] J. B. Lightfoot, *Commentary on the Epistle to the Galatians.*

Ancyra is so far from Mysia that to describe it as κατὰ τὴν Μυσίαν is impossible.

*Ramsay.*     A more attractive suggestion was made by Sir W. M. Ramsay in 1892 in a course of lectures at Oxford, and published in 1893 with the title *The Church in the Roman Empire before 170 A.D.* Few more brilliantly attractive books have ever been written, and to the present writer this book and its sequel, *St. Paul the Traveller and Roman Citizen*, were a revelation of the possibilities opened by biblical archaeology. Ramsay thought that the source of this part of Acts was characterized by a carefully accurate use of Roman official phraseology, and explained Acts xvi. 6 in the light of this theory. He took ' Asia ' to mean the province, thought that the Galatia implied by Paul's Epistle to the Galatians was the district of Lystra, Derbe, Iconium, and Antioch, which were within the province, and explained τὴν Φρυγίαν καὶ Γαλατικὴν χώραν as meaning the *regio Phrygia Galatica*, which was, he thought, the official name of the district of Lystra and the other cities mentioned.

*The Epistle to the Galatians.*     The difficulty of deciding who were the recipients of the Epistle to the Galatians is of course separate from the interpretation of Acts xvi. 6. It would be out of place to discuss it in full in this note, but it may be said that the problem resolves itself into three subordinate questions.

(i.) Were those to whom the Epistle was sent Galatians in the ethnological sense or were they Greeks, or at least Greek-speaking persons, living in a district called Galatia ? The fact that the Epistle is written in Greek, not in Gaelic, at least shows that they understood Greek, though it does not follow that they were not Gauls by birth.

(ii.) Would persons not Galatians by birth (and the inhabitants of Lystra, etc., were certainly not Galatians by blood) have cared to be addressed as Galatians merely because they lived in a province of that name ? So far as I can see we have no means of answering this question. It is futile to discuss it on the basis of modern analogies, which can generally be made to prove whichever view the writer prefers, but it seems very improbable that Greek-speaking Phrygians or Lycaonians would have described themselves as Galatians—a markedly national word—merely because for purposes of government the Romans treated their country as part of a complex to which they had given the name of Galatia.

(iii.) The fact that Acts does not describe any missionary work among Galatians loses its importance when we compare Acts' account of Paul in Corinth with the information derived from the Epistles. See note on Acts xix. 1-20. It is abundantly clear that in dealing with Paul, just as in dealing with the early church, Luke gave a selection, not a complete statement of the facts.

*Phrygia Galatica.*     But if the identification of the ' Galatians ' of the Epistle be foreign to the present purpose, the interpretation of τὴν Φρυγίαν καὶ Γαλατικὴν χώραν is, on the contrary, extremely important for the meaning of Acts. Ramsay holds that when the province of Galatia was organized its component parts were called *regiones* and described by their original names with the addition of the adjective Galatian ; so that there was *Pontus Galaticus, Phrygia Galatica*, and so on. *Pontus Galaticus* is attested by inscriptions and by Ptolemy,[1] but there is very little evidence (apparently only Galen) for *Phrygia Asiana*, and none for *Phrygia Galatica*. It is true that Ramsay quotes the *Menologium Sirletianum* for *Phrygia Galatica*, but to do so he emends the text, which is " Hi sancti martyres fuerunt sub Diocletiano imperatore in urbe Antiochiae Pisidiae ex regione Phrygiae Galaciae sub praeside Magno." Ramsay emends *Galaciae* to *Galaticae*, and so gets evidence for *Phrygia Galatica*. But surely there is no justification for this emendation. The natural construction would be to take Galaciae (the spelling of which is orthographical fashion, not a mistake) as dependent on *praeside*—' when Magnus was governor of Galatia.'

Admittedly *Phrygia Galatica* would have been a natural term for officials to use for the Phrygian districts of the province of Galatia. But that is not quite the real point. Would anyone, not a Roman official, have used the phrase ? To the inhabitants Lystra and Derbe were Lycaonian cities, Iconium probably and Antioch certainly were Phrygian cities, and it is very doubtful if anyone except an official would have troubled to qualify the statement. The Greeks living in such cities were of course Greeks, and would not have called themselves Phrygians or Lycaonians, but neither would they have called themselves Galatians.

There is another objection. *Phrygia Galatica* may have been the official title of the part of Phrygia incorporated in the province of Galatia. As has been said, there is no evidence for this, but it would not be surprising if evidence were found. It would be analogous to the undoubted use of *Pontus Galaticus*. But why should this be rendered in Greek by Φρυγία καὶ Γαλατικὴ χώρα rather than by ἡ Γαλατικὴ Φρυγία ? Ramsay indeed argues that χώρα represents an official use of *regio* to describe the subdivisions of the province. But there is no evidence for this use in Galatia except Ramsay's claim that an inscription at Antioch [2] which reads εκατονταρχην [?]εγεωναριον should be completed by reading a ρ for the missing letter, as Sterrett first thought, and not a λ as he afterwards preferred. But λεγεωνάριον is as natural a title for a centurion as ρεγεωνάριον is unusual.

Moreover, on this point we ought to be guided by Roman practice in Asia. This province was, we are told by Cassiodorus (*s. anno* 679), divided by Sulla into *regiones*, but Cicero uses *civitates* not *regiones* in describing this division, Appian says that it was κατὰ πόλεις, and *CIG.* 3902 speaks of διοικήσεις, obviously in the sense of *regiones*. It seems clear that a *regio* was not an ancient kingdom but the district surrounding a prominent city. It is rendered in Greek in several ways.

Thus the analogy of Asia gives no support to the view that in Acts xvi. 6 χώρα is likely to be the Greek rendering of *regio* used in the official sense of a division of a province, corresponding to an ancient kingdom.

Finally, perhaps decisive against Ramsay's theory is the fact that if ἡ Φρυγία καὶ Γαλατικὴ χώρα means the *regio* of the province of Galatia called *Phrygia Galatica*, it is impossible that Paul's route through this

---

[1] Ramsay, *The Church in the Roman Empire*, p. 81.

[2] Published by Sterrett in his *Epigraphical Journey in Asia Minor*.

district brought him out anywhere near Mysia. Ramsay has to argue that Paul, after passing through *Phrygia Galatica*, journeyed through the province of Asia until he came to the neighbourhood of Mysia, for though the Spirit prevented him from preaching in Asia, it did not prevent him from travelling through it. Without being impossible this seems to me very unlikely. The natural meaning of Acts is that because Paul could not preach in ' Asia ' he changed his plans and went through Phrygia, etc. —which by implication was not ' Asia.' Moreover, though Ramsay thinks that the order of words in xvi. 6, not the construction of the sentence, gives the order of events, it is hard to agree that this is probable. His theory demands that Paul first passed through *Phrygia Galatica* and then was prevented by the Spirit from preaching in Asia. But the natural interpretation of the Greek is the opposite.

Therefore, attractive though Ramsay's theory be,[1] it is probably untenable.

Paul's more probable route.

A more probable view seems to be that when Paul reached Iconium he meant to go along the main road to the Greeks of the Lycus Valley and the coast, the district which Luke calls Asia. But he had a revelation which made him change his mind, and he went north through Phrygia and territory where Galatians were numerous. If this view be accepted ' Phrygia and Galatian country ' means territory in which sometimes Phrygian and sometimes Gaelic was the language of the villagers. His route may have been through Laodicea, Amorion, and Orkistos (surely a Gaelic place) to Nakoleia and perhaps to Dorylaeum. Either Nakoleia or Dorylaeum might be said to be κατὰ τὴν Μυσίαν. He was also on the direct road to Nicaea, and certainly from Nakoleia and probably from Dorylaeum there was a straight road to Troas, ' skirting ' Mysia—if that be the meaning of παρελθών. In one or the other of these places he was once more prevented by revelation from working as he had intended— this time in Bithynia—and so turned to the left and went through Mysia to Troas.

This theory does not differ essentially from Ramsay's as to the route which Paul took, but gives a different explanation of the phrases in xvi. 6. It implies that Paul was influenced by language rather than political boundaries, and that Luke similarly describes the districts traversed in terms of language rather than in official Roman terminology. Paul was looking for places where he could preach intelligibly, that is to say, in Greek. A Greek audience could be found in Antioch of Pisidia and in Iconium. But these places were closed for any renewed preaching, and he had the choice of going beyond them to the great Greek cities of ' Asia,' or of going north to the equally Greek cities of Bithynia—Nicaea or Nicomedia. ' Asia ' was nearer, and more attractive, and he first thought of

---

[1] In my *Earlier Epistles of St. Paul* I was quite convinced by it. I thought that Paul probably kept south of the Sultan Dagh, and went up through Kinnaborion to Kotiaeon. Nor did any reviewers help my conversion, which is mainly due to the impression, made by the minute labour of writing the commentary, that Luke does not specially use Roman official language and that Ramsay's theory makes as many difficulties as it solves.

going there.  Possibly Metropolis and Apameia were sufficiently Greek
for him to have thought of them as belonging in a cultural sense to ' Asia,'
though they were usually reckoned as Phrygian.  When revelation made
him give up this plan, he turned northward and had to go through a non-
Greek country where the language mainly alternated between Phrygian
and Gaelic.  Just when he was near the great cities of Bithynia, he was
again stopped.  Not until he reached Corinth [1] could he find a city with
the three necessary but complex conditions for extensive and settled
preaching—a large Greek-speaking population (which must, however, not
be too Greek-thinking), prosperous Greek-speaking synagogues to ensure
an initial hearing for him, and a sufficiently developed anti-Judaism to
render Jewish hostility relatively unimportant when he was successful in
diverting ' God-fearers ' from the Synagogue to the Church.

There remains yet one other way of dealing with this problem.  What-    Schwartz's
ever theory be adopted to explain Acts xvi. 6, it remains almost unique   theory.
for its omission to mention the cities through which Paul passed.  He
cannot have gone from Lystra to Troas without going through a number
of well-known cities, whatever route he followed, and Luke's habit is to
mention the cities through which Paul went, even when he has nothing
more to say about them.

This is a strong point in favour of Schwartz's theory that the two
missionary journeys are really one.  According to this view the visit to
Jerusalem to relieve the famine (Acts xi. 30 and xii. 25) is the same as
the visit to Jerusalem for the Apostolic Council (Acts xv.), and in Additional Note 16 it has been argued that this is probably right.  But Acts
xi. 30, xii. 25, and xv. are all immediately followed by accounts of
a missionary journey.  If the visits to Jerusalem are the same, argues
Schwartz, so also must be the journeys which follow ; Luke has merely
made two journeys out of one and has added an end and a beginning at
the appropriate points.  According to this theory xiv. 21-28 is an editorial
patch, put in in order to bring Paul back to Antioch and Jerusalem, and

---

[1] In Lystra and in Derbe the villagers appear to have spoken Lycaonian.
It survived as a spoken language at least until the sixth century.  It is mentioned
in the life of Martha, the mother of Symeon Thaumastorites (cf. *A.S.S.* May 5,
p. 413).  Also in the Acts of the Council of Constantinople in A.D. 536 reference
is made to two Lycaonian monasteries in Constantinople—that of Modestus
and that of Eutychius.  (See Mansi, viii. 1055, and cf. K. Holl's ' Das Fortleben
der Volkssprachen in Kleinasien in nachchristlichen Zeit,' in *Hermes,* xliii. (1908)
pp. 240 ff.)  Phrygian was probably spoken in Iconium ; it was an Indo-European language and survived in outlying districts for some centuries.  In all
the cities there was naturally some knowledge of Greek, though probably not
enough to reward any prolonged stay by Paul.  But it is probable that in the
country (ἡ χώρα as opposed to τὰς πόλεις) Greek was of little use.  In any case
the lower classes were too hostile.  In Macedonia there was too much Jewish
influence ; in Athens too much really Greek scepticism ; only in Corinth was
there that peculiar Greco-Oriental stratum which was satisfactory for Paul's
preaching.

xv. 36-xvi. 9 is a corresponding patch, added in order to bring him back from Jerusalem to Troas. Both patches are marked by vagaries and absence of detail.

The main objection to this theory is that it changes the story as told by Luke more than we should like. For this reason I have struggled against accepting it, but find myself less and less able to see good reasons against it. Probably it is the most likely guess in a complex of problems which will never be settled quite satisfactorily.

If it be adopted, its corollaries should be noted. It implies the following smaller points :

(i.) Luke's account of the 'first journey' must have been an Antiochian-Barnabas source, rather than a Pauline source. This obviously explains the general tenor of the narrative far better than the theory that Luke had a single source and deliberately cut it into two. A Barnabas source (which need not mean that Barnabas had anything to do with writing it) would naturally not contain the further adventures of Paul. All that Luke did was to bring Paul into the end of it, and not notice or not know that Paul and Barnabas separated at Lystra[1] on their return journey to that city. He then also put in a short account of a journey across Asia Minor, of which he had heard something, in order to link up his narrative with the true Pauline story as given in the ' we-source,' where the characteristic fullness of detail as to the route followed really begins.

The main point therefore is that Luke had two sources : (a) a Barnabas-Antiochian source, which gave him the material for chapters xiii.-xiv. 20. This brought Barnabas back to Antioch, but did not say explicitly what Paul did. (b) A Pauline source, including the ' we-document,' whether written by Luke or used by him, which gave a detailed account of Paul's journey from Troas to Corinth and Ephesus. It did not explain how Paul reached Troas. To bring together these sources Luke put in a few connecting paragraphs characterized by a geographical vagueness quite different from either source, and presenting enormous difficulties to any commentator who tries to extract from them a precision of detail which Luke never put into them.

(ii.) There is some difficulty in seeing what were the facts about Paul's quarrel with Barnabas. As it stands in Acts at present, it is tempting to identify it with the quarrel described in Gal. ii. 11. But this can hardly be right, nor do the details agree, for in Acts the question is about Mark, and in Galatians it is about intercourse with the Gentiles. Perhaps Luke knew from his Antiochian source that Paul and Barnabas had quarrelled in Antioch, and thought erroneously that this was the same quarrel as that about Mark which had prevented Barnabas from coming to Troas with Paul.

(iii.) An extreme possibility may be mentioned. I have never felt quite so certain as both Mr. Emmet and Professor Windisch were in Vol. II. that Luke knew nothing about the Pauline Epistles. Admittedly he made little or no use of them ; but it would be an extraordinary thing that

---

[1] Or possibly Iconium, Derbe, or Antioch—the exact point is immaterial.

anyone who so clearly was either a member of the Pauline circle, or had access to its traditions, should have been ignorant of letters which were well known both in Rome and Antioch[1] so soon after Acts was written.

It seems to me not impossible that he knew the Epistles, and perhaps even thought that Christians were gaining a wrong impression of the work done by Paul, who was unfairly represented by letters written controversially and for special purposes. Is it an accident that he describes Paul's first dealings with the Romans, the Corinthians, the Ephesians, and the Thessalonians ? If it be not, it is possibly justifiable to go a step further, and emphasize the fact that Galatia is the remaining church which Paul founded and wrote to. If Luke knew this and had any interest in the foundation of the Pauline churches, he may have noted that the narrative, as it was in his sources, gave no place after xvi. 6 for the foundation of the Galatian churches. Possibly he thought that it belonged to the period, just before Paul went to Europe, for which his two main sources gave him no information. Moreover it is not impossible that he was right.

### 3. *The Route of Paul's ' Third Journey '*

Compared with the complexities of the ' second journey,' this offers few difficulties. There are indeed only two. The 'third' journey.

(i.) The meaning of τὴν Γαλατικὴν χώραν καὶ Φρυγίαν in Acts xviii. 23. Formerly[2] I interpreted this in accordance with Ramsay's theory. According to this the province of Galatia was divided into *regiones* ; the part which once had been in the kingdom of Lycaonia was called *Lycaonia Galatica*, the remainder of Lycaonia, which was in Paul's time ruled by Antiochus, being called *Lycaonia Antiochiana*. Similarly the old kingdom of Phrygia was divided between the provinces of Asia and Galatia and called *Phrygia Asiana* and *Phrygia Galatica*. Thus Paul passed first through *Lycaonia Antiochiana*, then through *Lycaonia Galatica*, *Phrygia Galatica*, and *Phrygia Asiana* successively. This theory certainly fits the facts. Paul doubtless came through the ' Cilician gate ' above Tarsus, and the direct road to Ephesus passed through these districts.

Whether this is exactly what Luke meant is another question. It calls for a remarkable mixture of terminology ; ἡ Γαλατικὴ χώρα is (according to it) a strict use of Roman phraseology, but Φρυγία is used in the ethnological sense and covers two Roman *regiones* in two separate provinces. Moreover it is hard to see why *Lycaonia Antiochiana* is not mentioned. The natural way to have expressed the facts called for by Ramsay's theory would have been διερχόμενος καθεξῆς τὴν Λυκαονίαν (both divisions) καὶ τὴν Φρυγίαν (both divisions).

A different explanation may therefore be considered favourably. Luke's habit is not to repeat phrases exactly, but to vary them. The variation is a matter of style, and does not imply a change of meaning. Here he is summarizing a long journey which covers territory that Paul

---

[1] *Testibus* Clement and Ignatius.

[2] *The Earlier Epistles of St. Paul*, pp. 260 f.

had already travelled through before. He varies the phrase for Phrygia and Galatia, but probably only means that he again went to the places in Galatia and Phrygia which he had visited before. Which these places were depends on the view taken of xvi. 6.

(ii.) The meaning of τὰ ἀνωτερικὰ μέρη in xix. 1. This passage cannot be dissociated from the previous one. Ramsay [1] thinks it merely means that Paul came by a road over the hills instead of by the main road. The alternative and more probable view is that διελθόντα τὰ ἀνωτερικὰ μέρη refers back, with variation of phrase, to the διερχόμενος καθεξῆς τὴν Γαλατικὴν χώραν καὶ Φρυγίαν in xviii. 23, so that τὰ ἀνωτερικὰ μέρη and τὴν Γαλατικὴν χώραν καὶ Φρυγίαν mean the same district. The problem cannot be separated from the interpretation of xvi. 6 and its solution can never be certain, because ἀνωτερικά is a vague phrase. It means 'higher,' and its exact significance depends on the context. It may be higher up a river, or a mountain, or from the coast. In relation to Ephesus the last seems somewhat the most probable, but the point is uncertain. Happily, unlike the obscurity of xvi. 6, it is not really very important.

## NOTE XIX. THE UNKNOWN GOD

### By KIRSOPP LAKE

The evidence concerning the altar 'to the unknown God' in Athens can best be divided into the two classes of (i.) heathen analogies and (ii.) early Christian exegesis.

### (i.) Heathen Analogies

Pausanias. (a) Pausanias i. 1. 4 says that on the road from Phalerum to Athens there were βωμοὶ θεῶν τε ὀνομαζομένων ἀγνώστων καὶ ἡρώων καὶ παίδων τῶν Θησέως καὶ Φαλήρου.

(b) Pausanias v. 14. 8 says that at Olympia by the great altar of Zeus there were other altars, including an altar 'to unknown gods'—πρὸς αὐτῷ δ' ἐστὶν ἀγνώστων θεῶν βωμός, καὶ μετὰ τοῦτον καθαρσίου Διός κτλ.

The Pergamene inscription. (c) An inscription was published in 1910 by H. Hepding from Pergamos in the precinct of Demeter, which probably belongs to the second century A.D. and may be plausibly reconstructed

ΘΕΟΙΣΑΓ(νωστοις)
ΚΑΠΙΤ(ων)
ΔΑΔΟΥΧΟ(ς)

but might equally be read θεοῖς ἁγιωτάτοις. (For a discussion of the reconstruction see especially Birt, Rhein. Mus. f. Phil., 1914; Weinreich, 'De dis ignotis quaestiones' in Archiv f. Religionswiss. xviii. (1915) pp. 29 ff., O. Kern, Hermes, xlvi. pp. 434 f., and Deissman, Paulus, App. II.)

---

[1] St. Paul the Traveller and Roman Citizen, p. 265.

(d) Diogenes Laertius, i. 110, writing early in the third century, describes how in time of pestilence the Athenians sent for Epimenides the Cretan to help them fulfil the command of the oracle to offer atonement for the city. Epimenides took black and white sheep to the Areopagus, and the story goes on: κἀκεῖθεν εἴασεν ἰέναι οἷ βούλοιντο, προστάξας τοῖς ἀκολούθοις ἔνθα ἂν κατακλίνοι αὐτῶν ἕκαστον θύειν τῷ προσήκοντι θεῷ, καὶ οὕτω λῆξαι τὸ κακόν. ὅθεν ἔτι καὶ νῦν ἔστιν εὑρεῖν κατὰ τοὺς δήμους τῶν Ἀθηναίων βωμοὺς ἀνωνύμους, ὑπόμνημα τῆς τότε γενομένης ἐξιλάσεως. Birt (Rhein. Mus. f. Phil., 1914) has shown good grounds for thinking (as is wholly probable in itself) that Diogenes was repeating an earlier tradition. To this there may be a reference in Aristotle, Ἀθηναίων Πολιτεία, of which the first lines mention the purification of the city by Epimenides the Cretan. Plutarch also (Solon xii.) says that after the Cylonian pollution and the banishment of the family of Megacles the Athenians were attacked by the Megarians, and the city became a prey to superstitious panic. The seers declared that their sacrifices proved that the city was polluted and needed expiation. For this purpose Epimenides was summoned. He helped Solon to reform the religion of the city, and Plutarch continues : τὸ δὲ μέγιστον ἱλασμοῖς τισι καὶ καθαρμοῖς καὶ ἱδρύσεσι κατοργιάσας καὶ καθοσιώσας τὴν πόλιν ὑπήκοον τοῦ δικαίου καὶ μᾶλλον εὐπειθῆ πρὸς ὁμόνοιαν κατέστησε.

(e) Philostratus in the Life of Apollonius of Tyana, vi. 3. 5, tells the story of a certain Timasion who had left his home to escape the inconvenient affection of his stepmother, which was like that of Phaedra for Hippolytus. Unlike Hippolytus, however, he had not insulted Aphrodite, but had consistently sacrificed to her. In this respect, said Apollonius, he was wiser than Hippolytus: καὶ αὐτὸ δὲ τὸ διαβεβλῆσθαι πρὸς ὅντινα δὴ τῶν θεῶν, ὥσπερ πρὸς τὴν Ἀφροδίτην ὁ Ἱππόλυτος, οὐκ ἀξιῶ σωφροσύνης· σωφρονέστερον γὰρ τὸ περὶ πάντων θεῶν εὖ λέγειν, καὶ ταῦτα Ἀθήνησι οὗ καὶ ἀγνώστων δαιμόνων βωμοὶ ἵδρυνται. It should be noted that the phrase καὶ ταῦτα Ἀθήνησι means 'especially in Athens,' and the point of the whole is that Hippolytus, who was living in Athens, was peculiarly foolish to insult the gods in a place which was so devoted to them (and they to it) that there were even altars to unknown gods. The reference is adequately annotated by the passages from Pausanias and Diogenes Laertius given above.

There is therefore no reason to suppose, as Norden has suggested, that the reference to Athens shows that the passage is taken from an episode in Athens in the supposed 'Damis' source of Philostratus, the existence of which seems disproved by E. Meyer in Hermes, 1917, pp. 399 ff. (see E. Norden, Agnostos Theos, pp. 35 ff. ; Corssen, ZNTW., 1913, pp. 309 ff. ; Harnack, 'Die Rede des Paulus in Athen usw.' in TU. xxxix. (1913) p. 39 ; Birt, Rhein. Mus., 1914, pp. 345 ff.).

(f) There is also one other piece of evidence which has sometimes but erroneously been alleged as heathen testimony to an altar to 'an unknown God' in Athens. The main topic in the Philopatris, ascribed to Lucian, is the worship of the unknown God who has an altar in Athens. If the treatise were really Lucian's this would be extremely important, but the *Philopatris* is obviously a Christian document of a much later date, and is now generally assigned to the tenth century (see Krumbacher, *Byzantinische Literaturgeschichte*, pp. 188 f.).

Conclusions. The significant point in this evidence is that it establishes the existence in Athens and at Olympia of altars to unknown gods. The reconstruction of the Pergamene inscription is too doubtful to be used with confidence. The story in Diogenes Laertius gives at least one reason why such altars were erected. The chief value of the story in Philostratus is that it shows that the anonymous altars of Athens were well known, and suggests that they were unusual elsewhere. There is no evidence for an altar to any one god who was specially called 'the unknown,' but the story in Diogenes Laertius suggests that the singular may have been used in the formula τῷ προσήκοντι θεῷ, meaning 'to the unknown god who is concerned in the matter'; ἀγνώστῳ θεῷ would be a loose but not very inaccurate paraphrase. I do not see why Wikenhauser and others are so certain that τῷ προσήκοντι was not used, though the text of Diogenes does not necessarily imply that it was.

It is perhaps noteworthy that the proper Greek idiom for an inscription on an altar usually puts the name of the god in the genitive, not in the dative as Luke does. The dative does, however, come in the Pergamene inscription in the second century, as well as in Tertullian, Jerome, and Euthalius. Apparently the fashion changed.

### (ii.) *Christian Exegesis*

Tertullian. (*a*) Tertullian in *Ad nationes* ii. 9 says : " sed et Romanorum deos Varro bifariam disposuit, in certos et electos. Tantam vanitatem ! quid enim erat illis cum incertis si certos habebant ? Nisi si Attico stupore recipere voluerunt, nam et Athenis ara est inscripta : ignotis deis."

The text of this passage is clearly defective, and there is only one extant manuscript. We may confidently accept the emendation of the first editor, Jacobus Gothofredus (1625), who printed *trifariam* for *bifariam* and inserted *incertos* between *in certos* and *et*, but *Attico stupore recipere* is more difficult. Reifferscheid prints *Atticos stupores*, following the 1634 edition of Nic. Rigaltius, and Norden emends *recipere* into *recinere*. But for the present purpose it is enough that Tertullian clearly knew a tradition of an altar in Athens to 'unknown gods.' He is making no special allusion to Acts, but rather regards these altars as a well-known characteristic of Attic practice. The same comment holds of another passage (*Adv. Marcion.* i. 9) where he says : " Invenio plane ignotis deis aras prostitutas, sed Attica idololatria est ; item incertis deis, sed superstitio Romana est." This leaves but little doubt that Tertullian quoted 'unknown gods' as a typically Attic phrase, and knew that it was generally so recognized.

Clement.
Jerome. (*b*) Clement of Alexandria (*Strom.* v. 82) and Origen (*in Joh.* x. 5) quote Acts, but do not discuss the question of the altar or its inscription.

(*c*) Jerome flatly asserts that Paul changed the plural 'gods' into the singular 'god.' In the *Comment. in Titum*, i. 12, he says: "nec mirum si pro opportunitate temporis gentilium poetarum versibus abutatur, cum etiam de inscriptione arae aliqua commutans ad Athenienses locutus sit, pertransiens enim, inquit, et contemplans culturas vestras inveni et aram in qua superscriptum est 'ignoto deo,' quod itaque ignorantes colitis hoc ego annuntio vobis. Inscriptio autem arae non ita erat, ut Paulus asseruit, 'ignoto deo,' sed ita : 'Diis Asiae et Europae et Africae diis ignotis et peregrinis.' Verum quia Paulus non pluribus diis indigebat sed uno tantum ignoto deo, singulari verbo usus est," etc.

The same inscription (to the gods of Asia, etc.) is quoted in the Euthalius. Euthalian apparatus to Acts, but there the last phrase "diis ignotis et peregrinis " is changed to the singular, doubtless in accommodation to the text of Acts. It reads : θεοῖς Ἀσίας καὶ Εὐρώπης καὶ Λιβύης, θεῷ τε ἀγνώστῳ καὶ ξένῳ· τοδὲ τὸ ἐπίγραμμα Παῦλος ἀναγνοὺς ἐδημογορεῖ. Unfortunately the date of 'Euthalius' is wholly uncertain ; in its present form the Euthalian apparatus may be a late composition, even if the original form is early, and no one knows which parts are early and which are late.

The Euthalian tradition is copied by the *Catena* of Andreas which exists in three forms, published under the names of Theophylact and Oecumenius. (See Migne, *PG.* cxxv. pp. 745 ff., 997 ff., and *PG.* cxviii. pp. 237 ff.)

(*d*) A line of interpretation, which may come from the same source Didymus. as Jerome's, but cannot be derived from him and may be entirely independent, is found in Didymus of Alexandria, according to a fragment of a catena on the epistles published in Mai's *Nova Bibliotheca Patrum*, iv. 2, p. 139. This, commenting on 2 Cor. x. 5 (αἰχμαλωτίζοντες πᾶν νόημα εἰς τὴν ὑπακοὴν τοῦ Χριστοῦ), says: δύνατον ἐκλαβεῖν καὶ οὕτως· πᾶν νόημα τὸ ὅπως ποτὲ ἔν τινι διδασκαλίᾳ φερόμενον ἀνάγκῃ καὶ βίᾳ μετοικίζοντες πρὸς τὸ πεῖσαι ὑπακοῦσαι τῷ Χριστῷ φερόμενον· οὕτω γὰρ τὸ Ἀθήνῃσιν ἀνακείμενον βωμῷ ἐπίγραμμα ἐμφαῖνον πολλῶν θεῶν νόημα ἑλκύσας ὁ ταῦτα γράφων μετήνεγκεν εἰς τὸν μόνον ἀληθινὸν θεόν, φήσας ὃν οὖν ἀγνοοῦντες εὐσεβεῖτε κτλ. Which may be bad exegesis of 2 Corinthians, but at least shows that Didymus regarded it as incontestable that there were altars at Athens to unknown gods in the plural, but not to an unknown god in the singular.

(*e*) A curiously wide-spread but late tradition affirming that the Herodotus. altar to the unknown god was connected with a special emergency in the history of Athens can be traced back partly to the tradition about Epimenides given by Diogenes Laertius, partly to another story in Herodotus.

Herodotus vi. 105 tells the story of Pheidippides, the Marathon runner, who was first sent to Sparta to suggest a treaty. On the way he met the god Pan, who complained that in spite of his constant help the Athenians never gave him any worship : βώσαντα δὲ τοὔνομα τοῦ Φειδιππίδεω τὸν Πᾶνα Ἀθηναίοισι κελεῦσαι ἀπαγγεῖλαι, διότι ἑωυτοῦ οὐδεμίαν ἐπιμελείην ποιεῦνται ἐόντος εὐνόου Ἀθηναίοισι καὶ πολλαχῇ γενομένου σφι ἤδη χρησίμου τὰ δ' ἔτι καὶ ἐσομένου. καὶ ταῦτα μὲν

'Αθηναῖοι καταστάντων σφι εὖ ἤδη τῶν πρηγμάτων πιστεύσαντες εἶναι ἀληθέα ἱδρύσαντο ὑπὸ τῇ 'Ακροπόλι Πανὸς ἱρὸν καὶ αὐτὸν ἀπὸ ταύτης τῆς ἀγγελίης θυσίῃσι ἐπετείοισι καὶ λαμπάδι ἱλάσκονται. (Cf. also Pausanias i. 28. 4 and viii. 54. 6.)

Isidore.

This story first reappears in extant Christian writings in Isidore of Pelusium's letter to Hero (Migne, *PG*. lxxviii. 1128) where the writer clearly confuses it with the story in Diogenes Laertius. After telling the story of Pan's meeting with 'Philippides' (as he and many others write the name of the runner) he continues: νικήσαντες οὖν βωμὸν ᾠκοδόμησαν καὶ ἐπέγραψαν· 'Αγνώστῳ θεῷ. ἄλλοι δέ φασι ὅτι λοιμὸς κατέσκηψεν 'Αθήναζε καὶ εἰς τοσοῦτον αὐτοὺς ἐξέκαυσεν ὡς μηδὲ τῶν λεπτοτάτων σινδόνων ἀνέχεσθαι, τοὺς νομιζομένους οὖν θεοὺς ἑαυτῶν θεραπεύοντες οὐδὲν ἀπώναντο. ἐννοήσαντες οὖν ὅτι ἔστιν ἴσως θεός τις, ὃν αὐτοὶ κατέλιπον ἀγέραστον, ὁ τὸν λοιμὸν καταπέμψας, ναὸν δειμάμενοι καὶ βωμὸν ἐπιγράψαντες· 'Αγνώστῳ θεῷ καὶ θύσαντες εὐθέως ἐθεραπεύθησαν.

Isho'dad.

(*f*) The discovery of the commentary of Isho'dad shows that the source used by Isidore may have been Theodore of Mopsuestia, who is quoted by Isho'dad without the mistake as to the altar, but in a form which renders that mistake quite natural. He says :

"About this altar, on which was written, To the hidden God, Mar Ephraim and others say, that want of rain and earthquakes sometimes happened at Athens ; and when they took counsel to make prayers collectively every day, they changed the altars of all their gods ; and when altars were at an end and there were no helps, they overturned them and threw them down ; and again they congregated and took counsel, saying, If there are no others, who is this one who does not cease to trouble us ? and they carved and set up altars to the hidden God, whoever He was ; and when the mercies of Grace revealed about the anguish of their minds, He sent them help. But the Interpreter says that the Athenians were once upon a time at war with their enemies, and the Athenians retreated from them in defeat ; then a certain Demon appeared and said unto them, I have never been honoured by you as I ought ; and because I am angry with you, therefore you have had a defeat from your enemies. Then the Athenians were afraid, and raised to him the well-known altar ; and because they dreaded lest this very thing should happen to them, having secretly neglected [one] who was unknown to them, they erected for themselves one altar more, and wrote upon it, Of the Unknown and Hidden God ; and when they wished to say this, that though there is a God in whom we do not believe, we raise this altar to His honour, that He may be reconciled to us, although He is not honoured as known ; therefore Paul did well to take a reason from this, and said before them, This hidden God to whom ye have raised an altar without knowing Him, I have come to declare unto you. There is no God whom ye know not, except the true God, who hath appointed the times by His command, and hath put bounds," etc. (See Mrs. Gibson's edition of Isho'dad, in *Horae Semiticae*, x. p. 28.)

Here the 'well-known altar' means the altar to Pan, and it is distinguished from the altar to the unknown God, but a careless reader might easily make the mistake which appears in Isidore of Pelusium, especially since the name of Pan is not mentioned.

Less complete and more confused versions of the same story are found in Bar Salibi and Bar Hebraeus, who are almost certainly dependent on Isho'dad.

(g) Finally, in a late and historically worthless Pseudo-Athanasian Pseudo-treatise, *De templo Athenarum*,[1] is a curious legend that the altar of <sup-note>Athanasius.</sup-note> the unknown God owed its inscription to a certain Apollo, who told the seven sages of Greece that by it he intended the Trinity of which the Logos was to be born of a virgin named Mary.

It will be seen that none of this evidence is of any real value, and it Conclusions. throws into relief the implication of Tertullian and the clear statements of Didymus and Jerome that there was no altar to 'an unknown God,' but only to 'unknown gods.' This makes all the more plausible the suggestion that the writer of Acts knew the altars τῷ προσήκοντι θεῷ referred to by Diogenes Laertius, that ἀγνώστῳ θεῷ is his (or possibly Paul's) paraphrase of the inscription, but that Jerome and others who knew of altars to 'unknown gods,' thought of them rather than of the altars to τῷ προσήκοντι θεῷ.

Suggestions have been made that the phrase 'unknown God' is borrowed from Gnosticism or from Hittite religion; but there is no evidence that there was ever anywhere an altar to the 'unknown God' of the Gnostics. There is indeed very little evidence that the Gnostics used this phrase. It is possible that Hittite religion had a theology which included an unknown Father-God, who was revealed by a Son-God, but the evidence is slight, and is many centuries earlier than Acts. It seems extremely improbable that either Gnosticism or Hittite religion have anything to do with the phrase. In Paul's speech the writer takes it to mean the God of the Jews and Christians, though it certainly did not have that meaning in Athens.

To sum up, it is doubtful whether there was ever an inscription which read exactly ἀγνώστῳ θεῷ. If there was, it probably was a survival from the cleansing of the city by Epimenides, and if the inscription was really in the plural it meant either 'the gods of other nations whose names are unknown,' or 'gods of importance whom it is well to propitiate, though they are not known by name.'

For the recent discussions of the subject see E. Norden, *Agnostos Theos*; R. Reitzenstein, 'Die Areopagrede des Paulus' in the *Neue Jahrbücher für klass. Altertumswiss.* xxxi. pp. 393-422; Weinreich, 'De dis ignotis quaestiones' in the *Archiv für Religionswissenschaft*, xviii. (1915); P. Corssen, 'Der Altar des unbekannten Gottes,' *ZNTW.*, 1913; Ed. Meyer, 'Apollonios von Tyana' in *Hermes*, lii. (1917); the reviews of Norden's book by Birt in the *Rhein. Museum für Philologie*, 1914, and

---

[1] Printed in Migne, *PG.* xxviii. coll. 1428 f.

by F. C. Burkitt in *JTS*. xv. (1914) pp. 455 ff. ; Th. Zahn, *Commentary on Acts*, Excursus viii. (pp. 870-882). The fullest summary of the evidence and recent literature is in Wikenhauser, *Die Apostelgeschichte und ihr Geschichtswert*, pp. 369-390.

## NOTE XX. "YOUR OWN POETS"

### By KIRSOPP LAKE

It is obvious that the use of a familiar quotation by no means implies that the user was acquainted with the book from which it was taken. Therefore, although from an early period passages in the speech of Paul at Athens have been recognized as quotations, it does not necessarily follow that either Paul or the writer of his speech was acquainted with the books from which these quotations were taken.

It is doubtful whether the phrase "as some also of your own poets have said" refers forward or backward, or possibly both. The matter seemed settled by the identification of the phrase "for we are also his offspring" as a quotation from the *Phaenomena* of Aratus, but it has been reopened by the discovery that "for in him we live and move and have our being" may be taken from Epimenides.

Aratus.

Aratus was born about 310 B.C. of a good Cilician family, either in Soli or Tarsus. He was the pupil of Menedemos and Menecrates, and the friend of Zeno the Stoic, and his writings show considerable Stoic influence. He wrote a poem to Pan, some medical works, an edition of the *Odyssey*, and other minor works which are not extant, but his most famous composition was the *Phaenomena*, a treatise in verse on Astronomy, which was very popular and used for many generations as a school book. (See H. Weinhold, 'Die Astronomie in der antiken Schule,' a dissertation at München, 1912, published in the *Zeitschrift f. Gesch. der Erziehung*, N.F. 3, pp. 143 ff.) Posidonius wrote a comparison of him and Homer, which suggests the combination of Homer and Aratus which is found (see p. 247) in Euthalius and probably in Origen. The *Phaenomena* were translated into Latin by Cicero and others, and many commentaries were written on his work. (See the edition of E. Maass, 1893 ; the same writer's 'Aratea' in *Philol. Untersuch.* xii., 1892 ; A. Westermann, Μυθογράφοι, pp. 52 ff., in which are printed the five extant lives of Aratus, all representing a common source, and Wilamowitz in the *Nachrichten d. götting. Ges. d. Wissensch.*, 1894, p. 198.)

The passage quoted from Aratus in Acts is the beginning of the poem. This was first recognized by Clement of Alexandria, *Strom.* I. xix. 91. 4 f. It runs as follows :

ἐκ Διὸς ἀρχώμεσθα. τὸν οὐδέποτ᾽, ἄνδρες, ἐῶμεν
ἄρρητον· μεσταὶ δὲ Διὸς πᾶσαι μὲν ἀγυιαί,
πᾶσαι δ᾽ ἀνθρώπων ἀγοραί, μεστὴ δὲ θάλασσα
καὶ λιμένες· πάντῃ δὲ Διὸς κεχρήμεθα πάντες.

τοῦ γὰρ καὶ γένος εἰμέν· ὃ δ' ἤπιος ἀνθρώποισι
δεξιὰ σημαίνει, λαοὺς δ' ἐπὶ ἔργον ἐγείρει
μιμνήισκων βιότοιο, λέγει δ' ὅτε βῶλος ἀρίστη
βουσί τε καὶ μακέληισι, λέγει δ' ὅτε δεξιαὶ ὧραι
καὶ φυτὰ γυρῶσαι καὶ σπέρματα πάντα βαλέσθαι.
αὐτὸς γὰρ τά γε σήματ' ἐν οὐρανῶι ἐστήριξεν
ἄστρα διακρίνας, ἐσκέψατο δ' εἰς ἐνιαυτὸν
ἀστέρας οἵ κε μάλιστα τετυγμένα σημαίνοιεν
ἀνδράσιν Ὡράων, ὄφρ' ἔμπεδα πάντα φύωνται.

(ed. Maass, 1893, pp. 3 f.)

It is interesting to note that this passage not only contains the quotation in Acts xvii. 28, but that there is a strong general resemblance between the second part of the passage and xvii. 26. A note to xvii. 28 in Codex 1739 which usually gives the comments of Origen is Ἀράτου καὶ Ὁμήρου ποιήτου. Von der Goltz, who first published this MS., read only Ἀράτ[ου] (TU. neue Folge, ii. 4, p. 44), but though the note is erased and faint the other words can be read in a bright light. The same or a similar note is found in Cod. H, Syr hl and Euthalius. It is possible that Aratus was using the earlier poem of Cleanthes to Zeus, which contains the line ἐκ σοῦ γὰρ γένος ἔσμεν. No special reference to Homer can be suggested except the familiar description of Zeus as ' father of gods and men.'

Epimenides is a half-mythical figure in Greek history whose story Epimenides was related by Theopompus and quoted from him in Diogenes Laertius and other later writers. The same story is told by him as is found in a later mythology of Rip Van Winkle. His father sent him one day into the country to drive back some sheep into the city, but he went to sleep on the road, and when he woke up discovered that nearly all his friends were dead. At last, however, he found his younger brother, who had become an old man, and learned from him what had happened. He died at the age of 157 according to Theopompus, but Diogenes says that the Cretans held that he was 299 and that Xenophanes gave a different form of the story which reduced his life to 154.

It is generally presumed that this is the same Epimenides who was reckoned among the seven sages of Greece, and there is an early tradition, found both in Plato and in Aristotle, that he purified the city after the Cylonian pollution in the method described in Addit. Note 19. That this tradition was found in Aristotle was unknown to modern scholars until the discovery of the Ἀθηναίων Πολιτεία, and Plato's statement was regarded as proof that Epimenides came to Athens at the time of the Persian war. Plato's words are as follows : τῆδε γὰρ ἴσως ἀκήκοας Plato. ὡς Ἐπιμενίδης γέγονεν ἀνὴρ θεῖος, ὃς ἦν ἡμῖν οἰκεῖος, ἐλθὼν δὲ πρὸ τῶν Περσικῶν δέκα ἔτεσι πρότερον παρ' ὑμᾶς κατὰ τὴν τοῦ θεοῦ μαντείαν, θυσίας τε ἐθύσατό τινας ἃς ὁ θεὸς ἀνεῖλε, καὶ δὴ καὶ φοβουμένων τὸν Περσικὸν Ἀθηναίων στόλον εἶπεν ὅτι δέκα μὲν ἐτῶν οὐχ ἥξουσιν, ὅταν δὲ ἔλθωσιν ἀπαλλαγήσονται πράξαντες οὐδὲν ὧν ἤλπιζον παθόντες τε ἢ δράσαντες πλείω κακά. τότ' οὖν ἐξενώθησαν ὑμῖν οἱ πρόγονοι ἡμῶν, καὶ εὔνοιαν ἐκ τόσου ἔγωγε ὑμῖν καὶ οἱ ἡμέτεροι ἔχουσιν γονῆς (Plato, *Leg.* i. 642 D, E).

Aristotle.

This seems explicit enough, and the tradition found in Plutarch and elsewhere that the purification of the city by Epimenides took place in the time of Solon was generally and naturally discounted. But the beginning of the Ἀθηναίων Πολιτεία is as follows : . . . [Μ]ύρωνος καθ᾽ ἱερῶν ὀμόσαντες ἀριστίνδην. καταγνωσθέντος δὲ τοῦ ἄγο[υ]ς [νεκρ]οὶ μὲν ἐκ τῶν τάφων ἐξεβλήθησαν, τὸ δὲ γένος αὐτῶν ἔφυγεν ἀειφυγίαν. [Ἐπι]μενίδης δ᾽ ὁ Κρὴς ἐπὶ τούτοις ἐκάθηρε τὴν πόλιν. This is at least as explicit as the statement in Plato, but is inconsistent with it and confirms the story in Plutarch. The reference is to the Cylonian pollution of which the earliest accounts are those given by Herodotus v. 71 and Thucydides i. 126. From these accounts it would appear that a certain Cylon endeavoured to make himself tyrant. The attempt failed and some of his followers were killed. In putting them to death the ruling clan in Athens, the Alcmaeonidae, violated the right of sanctuary. Later on they were punished for this crime. The trial, according to Plutarch (*Solon* xii.), was conducted by Myron, and Plutarch describes how after these events the city still appeared to be polluted according to the soothsayers and Epimenides was summoned to purify it.

Modern critics.

As between Plato and Aristotle it is hard to decide, but the general tendency of modern investigators has been to accept the Aristotelian story. Diels, especially in the *Sitzungsberichte* of the Berlin Academy, argues that the Aristotelian tradition is correct, and the story in Plato is due to a recrudescence of the question of the Alcmaeonidae in the time of the Persian war. The whole matter is very obscure and is fortunately not one of those which an editor of Acts has to decide. Obviously Epimenides is a more or less mythical figure, and Diogenes Laertius mentions significantly that there was more than one person of that name. (For modern studies see especially Diels, *Fragmente der Vorsokratiker*, vol. ii. 1², pp. 489 ff., and the same writer in the *Sitzungsberichte* of the Berlin Academy, 1891, pp. 387 ff., and Demoulin, 'Epiménide de Crète,' in the *Biblioth. de la faculté de philos. et lettres de l'Université de Liége*, fasc. xii., 1901.)

Diogenes Laertius.

There was in antiquity a considerable literature attributed to Epimenides. Aristotle mentions a collection of his oracles (Aristot. *Rhet.* iii. 17, p. 1418 a 23, cf. Plutarch *De def. orac.* 1), but the fullest account is that of Diogenes Laertius i. 111 f., who writes : ἐποίησε δὲ Κουρήτων καὶ Κορυβάντων γένευιν καὶ Θεογονίαν, ἔπη πεντακισχίλια· Ἀργοῦς ναυπηγίαν τε, καὶ Ἰάσονος εἰς Κόλχους ἀπόπλουν, ἔπη ἑξακισχίλια πεντακόσια. συνέγραψε δὲ καὶ καταλογάδην Περὶ θυσιῶν, καὶ τῆς ἐν Κρήτῃ πολιτείας· καὶ Περὶ Μίνω καὶ Ῥαδαμάνθυος, εἰς ἔπη τετρακισχίλια. ἱδρύσατο δὲ καὶ παρ᾽ Ἀθηναίοις τὸ ἱερὸν τῶν σεμνῶν θεῶν, ὥς φησι Λόβων ὁ Ἀργεῖος ἐν τῷ Περὶ ποιητῶν. λέγεται δὲ καὶ πρῶτος οἰκίας καὶ ἀγροὺς καθῆραι, καὶ ἱερὰ ἱδρύσασθαι. εἰσὶ δ᾽ οἳ μὴ κοιμηθῆναι αὐτὸν λέγουσιν, ἀλλὰ χρόνον τινὰ ἐκπατῆσαι, ἀσχολούμενον περὶ ῥιζοτομίαν. φέρεται δ᾽ αὐτοῦ καὶ ἐπιστολὴ πρὸς Σόλωνα τὸν νομοθέτην, περιέχουσα πολιτείαν ἣν διέταξε Κρησὶ Μίνως.

ἀλλὰ Δημήτριος ὁ Μάγνης ἐν τοῖς περὶ ὁμωνύμων ποιητῶν τε καὶ συγγραφέων διελέγχειν πειρᾶται τὴν ἐπιστολὴν ὡς νεαράν, καὶ μὴ τῇ Κρητικῇ φωνῇ γεγραμμένην, Ἀτθίδι δέ, καὶ ταύτῃ νέᾳ.

None of these writings is fully extant, and it is not clear how many of the titles are alternative names for the same books. The fragments which remain are collected in Diels, *Fragmenten der Vorsokratiker*, ii. 1², pp. 489 ff. (cf. also O. Kern, *De Theogoniis Orphicis*, pp. 62 ff.). Diels is inclined to postulate only two works, one in verse called Θεογονία ἢ Κρητικὰ ἢ χρησμοί, and one in prose called Καθαρμοί. H. Demoulin thinks that hardly any of the fragments are genuine. Probably he is right, but the point of importance is that a volume of literature rightly or wrongly ascribed to Epimenides was extant in the first century and that this literature included works about Minos. The quotation from Diogenes implies that one (about Minos and Rhadamanthus) was in verse and another (the Constitution of Minos) in prose.

*The fragments of Epimenides.*

The importance of these observations is due to the discovery of the following passage in the recently published commentary of Isho'dad : "This, 'In him we live and move and have our being'; and this, 'As certain of your own sages have said, We are his offspring.' Paul takes both of these from certain heathen poets. Now about this, 'In him we live,' etc.; because the Cretans said as truth about Zeus, that he was a lord; he was lacerated by a wild boar and buried; and behold! his grave is known amongst us; so therefore Minos, son of Zeus, made a laudatory speech on behalf of his father; and he said in it, 'The Cretans carve a Tomb for thee, O holy and high! liars, evil beasts, and slow bellies! for thou art not dead for ever; thou art alive and risen; for in thee we live and are moved, and have our being,' so therefore the blessed Paul took this sentence from Minos; for he took again 'We are the offspring of God' from Aratus a poet, who wrote about God, and about the seven [planets] and the twelve [signs]; saying, 'From God we begin, from the Lord of heaven, that is, Zeus; for all markets, and seas, and havens are filled with his name; and also in every place, all we men are in want of him, because we are his offspring; and he out of his goodness giveth good signs to us and to all men. He moves us to come forward to work; and he ordains all that is visible and invisible; and because of this we all worship him and say, Hail to thee, our Father, wonderful and great!'" (*Horae Semiticae*, x. 4, p. xiv.).

*Isho'dad.*

It is probable that this was taken by Isho'dad from Theodore of Mopsuestia who was one of the chief sources which he used, and this hypothesis is supported by a quotation from the *Gannat Busamé* which preserves the Nestorian tradition based largely on Theodore, and repeats the same story about Minos. (See Rendel Harris in Mrs. Gibson's edition of Isho'dad, *Horae Semiticae*, x. p. xiii, and *Expositor*, Oct. 1906.) Neither Isho'dad nor the *Gannat* mention Epimenides; Isho'dad indeed says that the author of the poem was Minos, but they prove that the phrase "for in him we live and move and have our being" came from the same poem as the description of the Cretans as liars, evil beasts, and slow bellies; and concerning this latter verse, Clement of Alexandria testifies that it was taken from a poem of Epimenides the Cretan.  For in *Stromata* I. xiv. 59. 1 he says : φασὶ δὲ Ἕλληνες μετά γε Ὀρφέα καὶ Λίνον καὶ τοὺς παλαιοτάτους παρὰ σφίσι ποιητὰς ἐπὶ σοφίᾳ πρώτους θαυμασθῆναι τοὺς ἑπτὰ τοὺς ἐπικληθέντας σοφούς, ὧν τέσσαρες . . . τὸν δὲ ἕβδομον οἱ μὲν Περίανδρον εἶναι λέγουσιν τὸν Κορίνθιον, οἱ δὲ Ἀνάχαρσιν τὸν Σκύθην, οἱ δὲ Ἐπιμενίδην τὸν Κρῆτα [ὃν Ἑλληνικὸν οἶδε προφήτην,] οὗ μέμνηται ὁ ἀπόστολος Παῦλος ἐν τῇ πρὸς Τίτον ἐπιστολῇ, λέγων οὕτως· "εἶπέν τις ἐξ αὐτῶν ἴδιος προφήτης οὕτως·

Κρῆτες ἀεὶ ψεῦσται, κακὰ θηρία, γαστέρες ἀργαί·

καὶ ἡ μαρτυρία αὕτη ἐστὶν ἀληθής." This statement is also repeated by Jerome and Chrysostom in their commentaries on Titus.

Conclusions.     Combining the testimony of Isho'dad and Clement, it seems clear that they referred the two quotations to a poem of Epimenides, and its attribution to Minos by Isho'dad is explained by the statement in Diogenes Laertius that Epimenides wrote about Minos.     Probably Minos was introduced as a speaker in the Κρητικά.

This evidence seems sufficient to justify the statement that " we live and move and have our being" is a reference to Epimenides.  It is true that as it stands in Acts this passage is not an hexameter, but it is possible that the metrical form has been lost in the course of transmission, and a very slight change suffices to restore it.  Rendel Harris, for instance, reconstructed the four lines of the poem as follows :

> τύμβον ἐτεκτήναντο σέθεν, κύδιστε, μέγιστε,
> Κρῆτες, ἀεὶ ψεῦσται, κακὰ θηρία, γαστέρες ἀργαί·
> ἀλλὰ σύ γ᾽ οὐ θνήσκεις, ἔστηκας γὰρ ζωὸς αἰεί·
> ἐν γὰρ σοὶ ζῶμεν, καὶ κινύμεθ᾽ ἠδὲ καὶ ἐσμέν.

A. B. Cook has conjectured a somewhat different Greek (see *Zeus*, i. p. 664) which is as follows :

> σοὶ μὲν ἐτεκτήναντο τάφον, πανυπέρτατε δαῖμον,
> Κρῆτες ἀεὶ ψεῦσται, κακὰ θηρία, γαστέρες ἀργαί·
> ἀλλὰ γὰρ οὐ σὺ θάνες, ζώεις δὲ καὶ ἵστασαι αἰεί·
> ἐν σοὶ γὰρ ζῶμεν καὶ κινεόμεσθα καὶ εἶμεν.

The point is of no importance, but I think they are both wrong in their first lines, for Chrysostom (*Com. on Titus*, i. 12) gives

> καὶ γὰρ τάφον, ὦ ἄνα, σεῖο
> Κρῆτες ἐτεκτήναντο· σὺ δ᾽ οὐ θάνες· ἐσσὶ γὰρ αἰεί.

There is no reason for emending this.  It is true that Chrysostom is quoting from Callimachus (*Hymn to Zeus*, lines 7 and 8) ; but in the light of Clement's evidence I think that Callimachus must himself have been quoting Epimenides, or in view of the extremely doubtful chronology of the poems of ' Epimenides ' it is possible that ' Epimenides ' was quoting Callimachus.  It is conceivable that the Epistle to Titus is quoting Callimachus, as Chrysostom says, not Epimenides, as Clement says, but scarcely possible that Clement did not know that Epimenides wrote thus.

Some scholars, however, for whose opinion I have much respect, think that Isho'dad has confused Callimachus and Epimenides, mainly on the ground that the poets would not have used exactly the same language. Personally I feel less inclined to discount the evidence of Isho'dad, but it is worth remembering that the large amount of quotation from, or reference to, Greek poets in Paul's speech at Athens is more important to the student of Acts than the exact identification of the writers. The really significant thing is that Greek quotations seem here to play the same part as the Old Testament in speeches to Jews or in a synagogue. (See further Additional Note 32.)

It is also possible, though perhaps less probable, that the passage from Epimenides had passed into a commonplace which had lost its metrical form.

One further point, however, calls for attention. Can it be an accident that the inscription " to an unknown God " which Paul takes, as it were, for his text (see Addit. Note 19) suggests more than anything else the story of the visit paid to Athens by Epimenides the Cretan, and that the striking phrase " for in him we live and move and have our being " seems to be a reminiscence from a poem by Epimenides, from which yet another quotation is found in the probably spurious epistle of Paul to Titus ?

That at least the literature of Epimenides was known in the Pauline circle, including the authors of Acts and of the Pastoral Epistles, seems almost certain. Assuming that Paul really delivered this speech before the Areopagus, an attractive picture might be drawn of how the connexion of Epimenides with the altar to the unknown God led up to a quotation from the poem of Epimenides. But obviously much the same sequence of thought can be attributed to the writer of Acts if the speech be regarded as his composition. If Titus were a genuine Pauline epistle the matter might be different, but it probably is not.

## NOTE XXI. ARTEMIS OF EPHESUS

### By LILY ROSS TAYLOR

Demetrius's claim (Acts xix. 27) that Artemis of Ephesus was wor- Acts xix. 27. shipped in all Asia and throughout the inhabited world was not exaggerated. Not only was the cult the most important of the province of Asia : it had a fame throughout the Greek and Roman world that probably no divinity except Apollo of Delphi could surpass. The city's great goddess, frequently given epithets like $\mu\epsilon\gamma\dot{a}\lambda\eta$, $\mu\epsilon\gamma\dot{\iota}\sigma\tau\eta$,[1] with her temple, which was numbered among the seven wonders of the world, was Ephesus's chief claim to pre-eminence, and the Ephesians jealously guarded her fame.

[1] Compare the Ephesian oath in Xenophon of Ephesus, *Ephesiaca* i. 11, τὴν πάτριον ἡμῖν θεὸν τὴν μεγάλην 'Εφεσίων "Αρτεμιν.

The origin of the goddess at Ephesus is shrouded in obscurity.  She
seems to have been a form of the great Asiatic mother-goddess, a divinity
of fertility who, before the Ionian colonists came, was already worshipped
without temple or image at the site of the later Artemisium beside the
ancient harbour of Ephesus.  It is likely that the Ionian settlers gave
the goddess her earliest temple and image and her name Artemis, which
she acquired as an adjunct to the local name Ephesia that she always
retained.[1]  With the name Artemis she also had attached to her many
of the legends of the maiden huntress.  Ephesus even claimed to be the
birthplace of Artemis and Apollo, though Apollo had no real share in
the cult at the shrine.[2]

There had been earlier structures before the great Artemisium was
begun in the middle of the sixth century.  By that time the shrine had
attained such fame that the whole of Asia is said to have shared in the
expense of the splendid marble temple.[3]  King Croesus of Lydia dedi
cated the columns, which were conspicuous because of the friezes in high
relief about their bases.  The temple was of enormous proportions—
about four times the size of the Parthenon.  The work on the temple
required a hundred and twenty years for its completion.  The great
shrine was burned to the ground on the night of the birth of Alexander
the Great (356 B.C.).[4]  Immediately—again, it would seem, with the aid
of all Asia—work was begun upon a new structure even more splendid
than the earlier one.  The new temple was similar in proportions to the
previous one, and it retained many of the characteristic features,
notably the frieze at the base of the columns.  Fragmentary remains
of the columns of both temples are to-day preserved in the British
Museum.  The new temple, richly adorned with works of the greatest

[1] On this name see Jessen, s.v. Ephesia, Pauly-Wissowa, 2754.

[2] For the close relation between Artemis of Ephesus and Apollo of Claros
see Picard, *Éphèse et Claros, recherches sur les sanctuaires et les cultes de l'Ionie
du Nord*, Paris, 1922.  Picard's study contains the most exhaustive collection
of the material available on Ephesian Artemis.  See also Jessen, s.v. Ephesia, 2,
Pauly-Wissowa.  For the inscriptions see Hicks in *Ancient Greek Inscriptions
in the British Museum*, iii., and Heberdey and Keil in *Forschungen in Ephesos*,
i.-iii.  New inscriptions are published from time to time in the *Jahreshefte des
öst. arch. Inst.*  Important for the temple of Artemis is the edict (*ibid.* xxiii.,
1926, 282-284) of the proconsul Paullus Fabius Persicus dating from the reign
of Claudius.  It shows the activity of Roman authorities in attempting to
prevent graft in connexion with the Artemisium.

Literary evidence for Artemis of Ephesus is abundant from Herodotus
down to the writers of the Empire.  The fullest material is found in Strabo,
xiv. 639-642, and Achilles Tat. vii. 13-viii. 14.  The temple of Artemis was
excavated under the auspices of the British Museum (see below), the city, on
the site to which Lysimachus moved it a mile away, by the Austrian Archaeological Institute.  On the topography of Ephesus see Bürchner, s.v. Ephesos,
Pauly-Wissowa, and G. Radet, *Ephesiaca*, i. and ii.

[3] Pliny, *N.H.* xvi. 213; Livy i. 45.

[4] Plut. *Alex.* 3.

painters and sculptors of the Greek world, had a place in practically every ancient list of the seven wonders of the world.[1]

Although the votive offerings of the early period show Artemis under a wide variety of types [2]—nude, draped, seated and standing figures with many attributes—the cult image was a stiff upright figure which resembled the trunk of a tree out of which the earliest image seems to have been fashioned.  In the later period the erect figure was completely covered with a symbolic adornment which suggested the goddess's character as a composite divinity of fertility.  Just when the adornment became fixed in the type under which Ephesian Artemis was widely represented in imperial times cannot be ascertained; the earliest dated representation of the type that we have is found on cistophoric coins of Ephesus and Tralles of about 133 B.C.[3]  It shows her wearing a modius and veil on her head; her figure is bound from waist to ankles in shroudlike bands; and the upper part of her body from waist to neck is covered with breasts.  About her head and among the bands of the lower part of her body are representations of animals and birds. The entire adornment seems to have been superimposed on the image.

The representa-tion of the goddess.

The head-dress, the many breasts, and the bands about the body have all been associated with other eastern representations of the mother goddess.  They are indications of the Oriental character which Ephesian Artemis always retained.  Further indications of the same character are to be found in the priesthoods and festivals of the shrine.[4]

The chief priest of Ephesian Artemis, like other priests of the Asiatic mother goddess, was a eunuch.  During the period of Persian power he acquired the Persian title *Megabyzos*, which he afterwards retained. Strabo's account (xiv. 641) has raised some questions : ἱερέας δ᾿ εὐνού-χους εἶχον, οὓς ἐκάλουν Μεγαβύζους, καὶ ἀλλαχόθεν μετιόντες ἀεί τινας ἀξίους τῆς τοιαύτης προστασίας, καὶ ἦγον ἐν τιμῇ μεγάλῃ· συνιερᾶσθαι δὲ τούτοις ἐχρῆν παρθένους, νυνὶ δὲ τὰ μὲν φυλάττεται τῶν νομίμων, τὰ δ᾿ ἧττον.  Picard [5] had drawn the conclusion from this state-ment that in Strabo's day there was a whole college of *Megabyzoi* who served the goddess in place of the single chief priest of an earlier time, but Strabo's words are not definite enough to make the suggestion certain.  Picard also holds that under the Empire there was a single high priestess who took the pre-eminent place in the cult which the *Megabyzos* had previously held, when only one priest of that title served at a time.  But though there are imperial inscriptions which mention

The priest of Artemis.

---

[1] On the temple see Bürchner, *op. cit.*; Picard, *op. cit.* chap. i. ; D. C. Hogarth, *The Archaic Artemisia* (British Museum, Excavations at Ephesus (1908)).

[2] See Picard, chap. vii., with his criticisms of Hogarth's conclusions as to the early type of the goddess.

[3] Head, *A History of the Coinage of Ephesus* (reprinted from the *Num. Chron.* 1880), iv. p. 11.

[4] The eastern character of the goddess has been ably demonstrated by Picard.

[5] Chap. iii.

individual priestesses,[1] there is no proof that they served independently of other priestesses. The organization of the hierarchy must remain in doubt. The maiden priestesses, whom Plutarch compared to the Vestals,[2] held office for a temporary period, after which they might marry.

The κοσμητεῖραι. The priestly organization included a large number of officers, both male and female. Among the most distinguished were the κοσμητεῖραι, matrons who had charge of the sacred adornment of the goddess. The office, like that of the maiden priesthood, was often hereditary in families.[3] The inscriptions record the titles of a number of officers who were associated with the great festival of Artemis—χρυσοφόροι, δειπνοφόροι, ἐνθυμίατροι, ἱεροκήρυκες, etc.

The Essenes. Associated with the cult was also a group called the Essenes who lived as a celibate brotherhood during the year of service. The city νεοποιοί. appointed officers called νεωποῖαι, later νεοποιοί, two from each city tribe to act as temple wardens. They made provisions for all repairs and all dedications in the *temenos* of the goddess.

Sacrifices to Artemis. Sacrifices to Ephesian Artemis were made chiefly with food, libations, and incense, less often, it would seem, with victims. The chief festival of the goddess was in the month which the Ephesians named Artemisium, because Artemis was said to have been born in it. The most important feature of the festival was a great procession in which all the cult objects of the shrine were carried. For this festival, and for the equestrian, gymnastic, and musical contests that accompanied it, all the Ionians of Asia were wont to come together[4]; following the ceremony there were often deliberations of a political nature.

Asylum for fugitives. One of the great prerogatives which the Artemisium shared with other shrines was the right of providing asylum for fugitives, and even in certain cases for runaway slaves.[5] Many of the latter passed into the possession of the goddess. The right, which had been extended by Mark Antony, had been abused to such an extent that it was investigated in the Roman senate in the reign of Tiberius. At that time the representatives of the Ephesians appeared in the senate with the delegates of other cities to plead their rights.[6] Their pre-eminence is indicated by the fact that they were heard before the delegates of the other cities.

Another prominent feature of the Artemisium was its importance in financial affairs. Besides caring for the great wealth of the goddess, the temple treasury functioned as a bank. It received deposits from kings, cities, and private individuals, and it lent money. Aristides refers to it as ταμεῖον κοινὸν Ἀσίας.[7]

νεωκόρος. In Acts xix. 35 the γραμματεύς of Ephesus calls the city ' sacristan ' of the great Artemis (νεωκόρον οὖσαν τῆς μεγάλης Ἀρτέμιδος). This is

---

[1] See the important inscription of Salutaris, *Forschungen in Ephesos*, ii., No. 27, line 266.

[2] *Mor.* 795 E.

[3] Cf. *CIG.* ii. 3002 γένος ἔχουσαν ἄνωθεν ἱερειῶν καὶ κοσμητειρῶν.

[4] Thuc. iii. 104.      [5] Achil. Tat. vii. 13.

[6] Tac. *Ann.* iii. 60-61.      [7] *Or.* xlii. 522 J.

the earliest known case of a νεωκόρος πόλις and the only instance where
the word is applied to the cult of Artemis. Later the phrase is common
in its application to cities possessing league temples of the imperial cult
in Asia. A city was said to be νεωκόρος or δίς, or even τρὶς νεωκόρος
τῶν Σεβαστῶν, according to the number of temples of the imperial cult
which it possessed.[1] It is not unlikely that the phrase originated in
Ephesus as a description of the city's relation to Artemis.

The fear which the success of Paul's preaching aroused among the Demetrius.
craftsmen is of great interest. There are many references to images of
the goddess in the inscriptions,[2] and many votive offerings have been
found in the excavations. But nothing so far discovered corresponds
to the ναοὺς ἀργυροῦς Ἀρτέμιδος. Hicks made the tempting suggestion
that in the description of Demetrius, Δημήτριος γάρ τις ὀνόματι,
ἀργυροκόπος, ποιῶν ναοὺς ἀργυροῦς Ἀρτέμιδος, the writer of Acts was
making a mistaken amplification of the word νεοποιός which he found in
his source and failed to understand. A Demetrius who was an eponymous
νεοποιός of his year—that is the first νεοποιός of the Ephesian tribe—
is named in an inscription which Hicks dates about the middle of the first
century after Christ.[3] He suggests that this νεοποιός may be identical
with the Demetrius of Acts. He would still retain the association of
Demetrius, who was by profession a silversmith, ̃with the image makers,
assuming that he made not ναοί but silver images of the goddess such
as are frequently mentioned in the inscriptions.

If we may trust the account in Acts, the cult of Artemis was in The
eclipse as a result of Paul's preaching, and the Ephesians were trying Ephesian
decree of
to guard the prestige of their divinity. About a century later the cult A.D. 160.
of the goddess was again on the wane, and we find the Ephesian senate
taking active measures to restore the goddess to her former prominence.[4]
Again, it was probably the growing power of Christianity which caused
the decline of Ephesian Artemis. The decree, dating from the year 160,
reads as follows :

ἔδ]οξεν τῆς πρώτης καὶ με[γίστης μητρ]οπόλεως τῆς Ἀσίας καὶ δὶς
νεωκ[όρου τῶν Σεβά]στων καὶ φιλοσεβάστου Ἐφε[σίων πόλεως τῇ
βο]υλῇ καὶ τῷ δήμῳ· περὶ ὧν εἰσήγ[ηται . . . Λ]αβέριος Ἄμοινος
φιλοσέβαστος, ὁ γραμμ[ατεὺς τοῦ δ]ήμου, ἐπεψήφισαν δὲ οἱ στ[ρ]ατηγοὶ
τῆς πόλεως φιλοσέβαστοι· [Ἐπειδὴ ἡ π]ροεστῶσα τῆς πόλεως ἡμῶν

---

[1] See W. Büchner, *De Neocoria*, Giessen, 1888. For the Jews as νεωκόροι of
their god see Josephus, *Bell. Iud.* v. 9. 4, § 283.

[2] Notably in the Salutaris inscription mentioned above.

[3] See Hicks, *Expositor*, i. (1890) pp. 401 ff. ; against his suggestion see
Ramsay, *ibid.* ii. pp. 1 ff., and Hicks's reply, *ibid.* pp. 144 ff. Cf. Picard,
pp. 127. For the inscription of Demetrius see *Ancient Greek Inscriptions in
the British Museum*, iii. 578 and p. 209.

[4] *Ibid.* No. 482B, p. 144 ( =Dittenberger, *Sylloge*³, 867). See Hicks's discussion there and his suggestion that the Salutaris inscription, which is practically contemporary with Pliny's letters about the Christians, is to be associated
with " a wave of reaction against the advance of Christianity in Asia Minor."

θεὸς Ἄρτε[μις οὐ μόνον] ἐν τῇ ἑαυτῆς πατρίδι ἀτιμᾶται, ἥν ἅ[λλων
ἁπασῶν πόλεων] ἐνδοξοτέραν διὰ τῆς ἰδίας θειότητ[ος πεποίηκεν,
ἀ]λλὰ παρὰ ["Ελλησίν τε κ]αὶ [β]αρβάρ[ο]ις, ὥστε πολλ]αχοῦ ἀνεῖσθαι
αὐτῆς ἱε[ρά τε καὶ τιμάς· ἀξία δέ ἐστιν] αὐτή τε εἰδρῦσθαι καὶ
βωμοὺς [αὐτῇ ἀνακεῖσθαι διὰ] τὰς ὑπ' αὐτῆς γενομένας ἐναργεῖς
ἐπι[φανείας]· καὶ τοῦτο δὲ μέγιστον τοῦ περὶ αὐτὴν σε[βασ]μοῦ ἐστιν
τεκμήριον, τὸ ἐπώνυμον αὐτ[ῆς] εἶναι μῆνα καλουμένου παρ' ἡ[μ]ῖν μὲν
Ἀρτ[εμισι]ῶνα παρὰ δὲ Μακεδόσιν καὶ τοῖς λοιποῖς ἔ[θνεσιν] τοῖς
Ἑλληνικοῖς καὶ ταῖς ἐν αὐτοῖς πόλεσι[ν] Ἀρτεμίσιον, ἐν ᾧ μηνὶ
πανηγύρεις τε καὶ ἱερ[ο]μηνίαι ἐπιτελοῦνται, διαφερόντως δὲ ἐν
[τῇ] ἡμετέρᾳ πόλει τῇ τροφῷ τῆς ἰδίας θεοῦ τῆς Ἐφ[εσία]ς· προσῆκον
δὲ εἶναι ἡγούμενος ὁ δῆμος [ὁ Ἐ]φεσίων ὅλον τὸν μῆνα τὸν ἐπώνυμον
τοῦ θ[είου ὀ]νόματος εἶναι ἱερὸν καὶ ἀνακεῖσθαι τῇ θεῷ [ἐ]δοκίμασεν
δ[ι]ὰ τοῦδε τοῦ ψηφίσματος [καταστῆσ]αι τὴν περὶ αὐτοῦ θρησκείαν·
διὸ [δεδόχθαι ἱερ]ὸν τὸν μῆνα τὸν Ἀρτεμισιῶνα εἶ[ναι πάσας τ]ὰς
ἡμέρας, ἄγεσθαι δὲ ἐπ' αὐταῖς μῆν[α ὅλον δι'] ἔτους τὰς ἑορτὰς καὶ τὴν
τῶν Ἀρτεμ[ισίων πανήγ]υριν καὶ τὰς ἱερομηνίας, ἅτε τοῦ μηνὸς ὅ[λου
ἀνακειμέ]νου τῇ θεῷ· οὕτω γὰρ ἐπὶ τὸ ἄμεινον τῆς [θεοῦ τιμωμέν]ης
ἡ πόλις ἡμ[ῶν ἐ]νδοξοτέρα τε καὶ εὐδ[αιμονεστέρα] εἰς τὸ[ν ἅπα]ντα
διαμενεῖ χ[ρόνον].

## Note XXII. The Asiarchs

### By Lily Ross Taylor

The Asiarchs in literature and inscriptions.
Apart from the reference in Acts, there is slight evidence in literary sources for the Asiarchs. In the time of Augustus they are mentioned by Strabo, and in the reign of Antoninus Pius or Marcus Aurelius by the writer of the letter of the Smyrneans on the martyrdom of Polycarp. They are further known from several references in late juridical sources. On the other hand there is a large amount of inscriptional evidence for them. Their names and their titles are recorded on numerous coins and stones of the cities of Asia. Moreover, similar titles like Galatarch, Bithyniarch, Lyciarch from the neighbouring provinces throw light on their character. The records of the Lyciarchs are particularly significant because they are abundant, and many of them are early in date.

The Asiarchs were the foremost men of the province of Asia, chosen from the wealthiest and the most aristocratic inhabitants of the province. Strabo (xiv. 649) describes them as οἱ πρωτεύοντες κατὰ τὴν ἐπαρχίαν, and the numerous honours claimed by the Asiarchs in cities and in the provinces bear out his words. They were holders or former holders of a yearly office in the league that was formed by the cities of Asia. Every important city claimed Asiarchs among its citizens, and Ephesus would probably have had several in the time of Paul.

The League of Asia.
The league of the cities of Asia, like other Greek leagues, was a religious organization with certain political functions. It probably existed in republican times and was active in the erection of monuments to the

goddess Roma and the Roman proconsuls. The first definite reference to it as a league (τὸ κοινὸν τῶν ἀπὸ τῆς Ἀσίας Ἑλλήνων) comes from the early days of Mark Antony's power in the East.[1] In 29 B.C., after Octavian's final victory over Antony, the league secured permission from the new ruler to erect a temple to him in common with the goddess Roma at Pergamum and to institute quinquennial games there in honour of the new cult.[2] Henceforth the chief purpose of the league was the cult of the reigning emperor and with him of the goddess Roma, who, however, speedily acquired a secondary position. The league in Asia, in many ways a prototype of the leagues formed in other provinces, became a valuable instrument of the provincial governors in securing loyalty to Roman rule. It maintained the cult of Roma and Augustus in Pergamum, and its representatives assembled each year in one of the chief cities of the province to celebrate the emperor's birthday as a festival of the league. Among the cities Ephesus ranked with Smyrna and Pergamum as the most important. In addition to the shrine in Pergamum, new league temples of the imperial cult were built in other cities. Under Tiberius a temple was constructed in Smyrna, and under either Claudius or Nero a third shrine was built in Ephesus. This shrine may have been in existence when Paul was in Ephesus. Later other temples were built, and Ephesus itself eventually had two more league shrines.

From Strabo's account of the neighbouring Lycian league [3] we can Lycian perhaps form some idea of the method by which the league elected League. its officers. In Lycia representatives of the twenty-three cities came together in the city agreed upon and cast their votes for the Lyciarch and the other chief officers of the association (ἄλλαι ἀρχαὶ αἱ τοῦ συστήματος). Each representative had one, two, or three votes, the number being determined by the size of the city which had sent him. If the Asiarchs were elected by a similar system, cities like Pergamum, Smyrna, and Ephesus would have disposed of more votes than the smaller cities and therefore would have had a better chance of securing the election of their candidates.

[1] See the beginning of Mark Antony's letter to the League, preserved in the papyrus published by Kenyon, *Classical Review*, vii. p. 476 : Μάρκος Ἀντώνιος αὐτοκράτωρ τριῶν ἀνδρῶν δημοσίων πραγμάτων ἀποκαταστάσεως, τῶι κοινῶι τῶν ἀπὸ τῆς Ἀσίας Ἑλλήνων, χαίρειν.

[2] Dio li. 20. 7-9 τοῖς δὲ δὴ ξένοις, Ἕλληνάς σφας ἐπικαλέσας, ἑαυτῷ τινα, τοῖς μὲν Ἀσιανοῖς ἐν Περγάμῳ τοῖς δὲ Βιθυνοῖς ἐν Νικομηδείᾳ, τεμενίσαι ἐπέτρεψε . . . καὶ ἔλαβον καὶ οἱ Περγαμηνοὶ τὸν ἀγῶνα τὸν ἱερὸν ὠνομασμένον ἐπὶ τῇ τοῦ ναοῦ αὐτοῦ τιμῇ ποιεῖν.

[3] Strabo xiv. 664-65 εἰσὶ δὲ τρεῖς καὶ εἴκοσι πόλεις αἱ τῆς ψήφου μετέχουσαι· συνέρχονται δὲ ἐξ ἑκάστης πόλεως εἰς κοινὸν συνέδριον, ἣν ἂν δοκιμάσωσι πόλιν ἑλόμενοι· τῶν δὲ πόλεων αἱ μέγισται μὲν τριῶν ψήφων ἐστὶν ἑκάστη κυρία, αἱ δὲ μέσαι δυεῖν, αἱ δ' ἄλλαι μιᾶς· ἀνὰ λόγον δὲ καὶ τὰς εἰσφορὰς εἰσφέρουσι καὶ τὰς ἄλλας λειτουργίας. . . . ἐν δὲ τῷ συνεδρίῳ πρῶτον μὲν Λυκιάρχης αἱρεῖται, εἶτ' ἄλλαι ἀρχαὶ αἱ τοῦ συστήματος. δικαστήριά τε ἀποδείκνυται κοινῇ . . . ὁμοίως δὲ καὶ δικασταὶ καὶ ἄρχοντες ἀνὰ λόγον ταῖς ψήφοις ἐξ ἑκάστης προχειρίζονται πόλεως.

The duration of the Asiarchate.

The Asiarch held office for a year. The title ἀσιάρχης may denote a man in his year of office or may, like any of the titles familiar in the Roman *cursus honorum*, indicate that the office had been held in the past. In one case former service is clearly indicated by the aorist participle ἀσιαρχήσας. (In the neighbouring Lycian league λυκιαρχήσας is fairly common, though λυκιάρχης also seems often to refer to a former holder of the office.) The office might be held more than once, a fact that is clearly indicated by occurrences of the title ἀσιάρχης β. In each year several Asiarchs were appointed. There was probably one who served for the entire league and there was one who functioned at the league temples in each of the cities. Thus we find titles like ἀσιάρχης ναῶν τῶν ἐν Σμύρνῃ, ἀσιάρχης ναῶν τῶν ἐν Ἐφέσῳ.[1]

The High Priest of Asia.

After the league of Asia began to devote itself to the imperial cult, the chief officer of the league was the high priest of the emperor, ἀρχιερεὺς Ἀσίας. In time several high priests were appointed in each year, one presumably as chief priest of the whole league and one to officiate at the league temples of each city.[2] Aelius Aristides, the rhetorician, writing about the middle of the second century, describes his election as Archiereus of Asia (*Oratio Sacra*, iv. 26. 101-104, ed. Keil). After his name had been presented to the assembly by the Smyrneans, he says that he got third or fourth place in the voting, but the place secured his election, presumably as high priest of the league temples in one of the cities. The titles of the Archiereis are closely analogous to those of the Asiarchs. Thus we find the simple title ἀρχιερεύς or ἀρχιερεὺς Ἀσίας, ἀρχιερεὺς β to indicate a second term of office, an isolated case of the aorist participle ἀρχιερασάμενος to denote the completion of the term of active service, and the fuller titles which indicate the association with the league temples of a particular city : ἀρχιερεὺς Ἀσίας ναοῦ τοῦ ἐν Ἐφέσῳ, ἀρχιερεὺς Ἀσίας ναῶν τῶν ἐν Σμύρνῃ.

The identity of the high priests and Asiarchs.

The similarity of titles in itself suggests that at least for the second century and later, the period to which the majority of the inscriptions belong, ἀσιάρχης and ἀρχιερεὺς Ἀσίας were alternate titles for the same office, the high priesthood of the league of Asia, but there is also more definite evidence to support the identification. In the theatre of Ephesus were discovered the following inscriptions : (*I.B.M.* 604) . . . ἀγωνοθετοῦντος Τ[ιβ.] Ἰουλίου Ῥηγείνου ἀρχ[ι]ερέως β ναῶν τῶν ἐν Ἐφέ[σῳ]. (605) . . . ἀγωνο(θ)ετοῦντος δι᾽ αἰῶνος Τιβ. Ἰουλ. Ῥηγείνου ἀσιάρχου β ναῶν τῶν ἐν Ἐφέσῳ. The similarity in the two titles held by the same man is striking, and it requires a forced interpretation of the evidence to assume, as some scholars have, that Julius Reginus held twice two separate offices of the league at the temples in Ephesus.

The titles Archiereus and Asiarch are also both given to a certain

---

[1] See the list of Asiarchs and Archiereis published by Chapot, *La Province romaine proconsulaire d'Asie*, pp. 482 ff.; cf. Ruggiero, *Dizion. Epigr.* i. pp. 728 ff.

[2] See the important article of A. Stein, 'Zur sozialen Stellung der provinzialen Oberpriester,' Ἐπιτύμβιον *Heinrich Swoboda dargebracht* (1927), pp. 300-311.

Philippos of Tralles, and here again there have been efforts to explain the evidence on the assumption that there were two different offices and two men of this name. In the letter of the Smyrneans on the martyrdom of Polycarp, dating from the middle of the second century, we learn that the people of Smyrna, eager for the death of Polycarp, appealed to the Asiarch Philippos (τὸν ἀσιάρχην Φίλιππον) to loose a lion upon him. The Asiarch refused because the games were at an end, and so Polycarp was burned alive. In the statement of the time when the martyrdom took place we find the words ἐπὶ ἀρχιερέως Φιλίππου Τραλλιανοῦ. Moreover, an inscription recording a Philippos of Tralles as Asiarch, and another mentioning a man of the same name as Archiereus of Asia, are preserved from a date that seems to correspond with Polycarp's martyrdom. (See Lightfoot, *Apostolic Fathers, S. Ignatius, S. Polycarp, Letter to the Smyrneans*, part ii. vol. ii. sect. ii. pp. 947 ff. For the inscriptions see Dittenberger, *OGIS*. 498, 499, and the discussions of date and identity there.)

A further indication of the identity of the two offices is found in the fact that the wife of the Asiarch sometimes has the title ἀρχιέρεια, high priestess, an office that was the special prerogative of the wife of the high priest of the province (*CIG*. 3677): . . . Πλω(τίου) Αὐρ. Γράτου, ἀσιάρχου καὶ Ἰουλίας Αὐρ. Ἀσκληπιοδώρας τῆς γυναικὸς αὐτοῦ ἀρχιερείας.[1] Another record is even more significant (*CIG*. 3324): Μ. Αὐρ. Ζήνων καὶ Μ. Κλ. Ἰουλιανή, ἀσιάρχαι δίς. . . . Here husband and wife are both called Asiarch, and scholars opposed to the identification of Asiarch and Archiereus of Asia have found no explanation of the title but have been forced to assume a stone-cutter's error. As a parallel for Asiarch as a title for a woman (there is no other instance of it in Asia), we may note that in Lycia the high priestess of the league is more than once referred to as Λυκιαρχίσσα. In this connexion a law of Constantine, quoted in the *Codex Justin.* v. 27. 1, is of interest. The object of the law was to make sure that the high priest should have a worthy wife. It forbade anyone enjoying the *ornamenta* of a priesthood to claim, as legitimate, children borne to him by a woman of low birth, and it explains the priesthood by offices analogous to the Asiarchate—*id est Phoenicarchiae vel Syriarchiae.*

The office of Asiarch is described as a priesthood in two other juridical sources. One of them is the following passage on immunities quoted from Modestinus in the *Digesta* (xxvii. 1. 6): ἔθνους ἱεραρχία (the word is corrupt: ἱεραρχία is Mommsen's reading, ἱερωσύνη Politianus) οἷον ἀσιαρχία βιθυναρχία καππαδοκαρχία παρέχει ἀλειτουργησίαν ἀπὸ ἐπιτροπῶν, τοῦτ᾽ ἔστιν ἕως ἂν ἄρχῃ. An even more explicit statement that the Asiarch was priest of the province comes from the scholia to the *Basilika* (ed. Heimbach, iii. 681) οἱ ἱερεῖς τῶν ἐπαρχιῶν τοῦτ᾽ ἔστιν ἀσιάρχαι καὶ οἱ λοιποί.

The evidence thus indicates that from the second century Asiarch

*The high priestess.*

*Modestinus.*

*Conclusions.*

---

[1] See also *I.G.R.* iv. 1233. Other instances are cited by Stein, *op. cit.* p. 303, n. 6, but most of them do not seem to apply.

and Archiereus of Asia were alternate titles for the same office.[1] But at an earlier time there is reason to believe thåt Asiarch was a more inclusive title than Archiereus. In the time of Paul there were two or perhaps three league temples in the province of Asia, and therefore presumably three or four high priests were chosen in each year. It is quite possible that there was at the time a considerable group of holders and former holders of the high priesthood in a city of the importance of Ephesus, and the passage in Acts seems to imply that the Asiarchs were fairly numerous there. But in the days of Augustus when Strabo wrote there was only the league temple at Pergamum, and there could not have been more than two high priests chosen in each year. How then can Strabo's statement (xiv. 649) about another city, Tralles, be explained ? συνοικεῖται δὲ καλῶς εἴ τις ἄλλη τῶν κατὰ τὴν Ἀσίαν ὑπὸ εὐπόρων ἀνθρώπων, καὶ ἀεί τινες ἐξ αὐτῆς εἰσιν οἱ πρωτεύοντες κατὰ τὴν ἐπαρχίαν οὓς ἀσιάρχας καλοῦσιν. In the intense competition between the cities of the time even the wealth of Tralles cannot account for the success of the city in securing the priesthood a number of times. If, as in Lycia, there was a proportional system in the number of votes allotted to each city, Tralles would hardly have had the maximum number of votes. When early in the reign of Tiberius (Tac. Ann. iv. 55 ff.) there was a contest among eleven cities of Asia for the site of the second league temple, the Tralliani were passed over as parum validi.

Strabo.     Moreover, Strabo presents a further difficulty. Among the Asiarchs he mentions a certain Pythodorus, a supporter of Pompey, who later had his property confiscated by Caesar, but succeeded eventually in regaining his wealth. Continuing from the passage quoted Strabo says: ὧν Πυθόδωρός τε ἦν ἀνὴρ Νυσαεὺς τὸ ἐξ ἀρχῆς, ἐκεῖσε δὲ μεταβεβηκὼς διὰ τὴν ἐπιφάνειαν, καὶ ἐν τῇ πρὸς Πομπήιον φιλίᾳ διαπρέπων μετ᾽ ὀλίγων· περιεβέβλητο δὲ καὶ οὐσίαν βασιλικὴν πλειόνων ἢ δισχιλίων ταλάντων, ἣν ὑπὸ Καίσαρος τοῦ θεοῦ πραθεῖσαν διὰ τὴν πρὸς Πομπήιον φιλίαν ἐξωνησάμενος οὐχ ἥττω τοῖς παισὶ κατέλιπε. . . . οὗτος δὴ καθ᾽ ἡμᾶς ἤκμασε. Although it is possible that Pythodoros did not hold the office of Asiarch until after the cult of the emperor was organized in 29 B.C., it is more likely from Strabo's words that he was Asiarch in the time of Pompey. It is

[1] From a late fourth-century inscription in which the producer of the quinquennial games in Asia is called Asiarch, A. Schulten (Jahreshefte des öst. arch. Inst. ix., 1906, pp. 66 ff.) concludes that the Asiarchate " bezeichnet die alle vier Jahre zu dem Amt des Provinzialpriesters hinzutretende Function des Spielgebers." This view, previously advanced by Monceaux, De communi Asiae, p. 56, is refuted for the later period by the fact that the Asiarchs are much more numerous in inscriptions than the Archiereis. See Chapot, op. cit. p. 479, n. 2. For the early empire see the discussion of Tralles above. It is impossible to base conclusions for the early empire on the late rescript of Valentinian, Valens, and Gratian which Schulten thinks settles the whole question. It belongs to a time when poverty made the onus of public office a serious problem, and it perhaps indicates that at the time Asiarchs were chosen only for the occasion of the quinquennial games. Even in the rescript there is no reason to suppose that Asiarch is not equivalent to Archiereus.

noteworthy that, though not a native of Tralles, Pythodoros was named
by Cicero as one of the most important citizens of Tralles in the year 59
B.C. (*Pro Flacco* 52, " Ubi erant illi Pythodori, Aetidemi, Lepsiones, ceteri
homines apud nos noti, inter suos nobiles ? ").

If as early as the time of Augustus the city of Tralles always had The earlier
Asiarchs in its population, and if one of them probably belongs to a time period.
before the cult of the emperor was established, it is obvious that the
Asiarchs and the Archiereis of Asia had not yet come to be identical,
as they seem to have been at least from the second century on. It
would seem that the Asiarchs were more numerous than the Archiereis,
and that they were known in the province before the imperial cult made
necessary the appointment of a high priest. My explanation (based
originally on a suggestion made to me by Professor Allen B. West) is that
from the Asiarchs designated in each year as the foremost men of Asia one
was chosen to act as high priest of the emperor, and then, as the temples
of the league were built, one was selected to serve at the league temples in
each city. Thus all Archiereis would have been Asiarchs, but all the
Asiarchs would not have acquired the distinction of the high priesthood.
As the number of league temples grew, in time there would have been a
priesthood for every Asiarch, and the two terms would thus come to be
identical in meaning. It is possible that this was already the case in the
time of Paul, or at least in that of Luke.

Even before the imperial cult was established, the Asiarchs may in fact
have had charge of league monuments, presumably shrines of Roma and of
the Roman proconsuls whose festivals and monuments persisted in Asia.
We might again use the analogy of the Lycian league, though we must use
it with caution particularly because Lycia was not yet a Roman province
when Strabo described its organization. Lycia chose only one Lyciarch a
year, an officer who, at least after the establishment of the Roman province
under Claudius, is frequently called Archiereus. But at the same time it
chose other officers (ἀρχαί). Asia apparently called all of its chief officers
Asiarchs, and, before the imperial cult became the centre of the league,
may have placed them in charge of monuments of proconsuls like Mucius
Scaevola whom she continued later to honour.

When Asiarch and Archiereus of Asia became alternate titles for the The later
same office, there were certain distinctions in the use of the two terms. period.
Asiarch, because it was briefer, was preferred for the limited space of a coin.
But in formal documents ἀρχιερεύς was the official designation of the
high priests of the emperor. It is, for instance, the term used in dating the
martyrdom of Polycarp. Asiarch, as Mommsen pointed out, is the more
popular term, used to express the pre-eminence of the office which Strabo
emphasizes. It is noteworthy that the pre-eminence of the imperial
priests is emphasized in other provinces by such expressions as πρῶτος τῶν
Ἑλλήνων, πρῶτος τῆς ἐπαρχείας (Dittenberger, *OGIS*. 544, 545, 652).
The compounds of ἀρχεῖν are very similar in the idea which they conveyed
to the popular mind. That such is the case is clear from the titles of the
high priest in the Achaean league. Under Nero he is spoken of as *primus
Achaeon* or πρῶτος τῶν ἀπ᾽ αἰῶνος (*AJA*., 1926, 393 ; *I.G.* iii. 805). Under

Hadrian he is called ἀρχιερεὺς καὶ ἑλλαδάρχης, and henceforth Helladarch is a regular adjunct of the titles of the high priest in the Achaean league. (See Stähelin, s.v. Helladarchai, Pauly-Wissowa.) The same usage is to be found in Galatarch as an additional title for the high priest of the league in Galatia. In Asia, however, Asiarch and Archiereus of Asia do not occur together as a combined title. The reason is perhaps to be found in the fact that Asiarch was an old title, already in use before the imperial cult was established, while probably Galatarch and certainly Helladarch were new inventions to express the pre-eminence of the provincial priesthood.

[On the league in Asia see Chapot, *La Province romaine proconsulaire d'Asie*, pp. 454-467 ; Kornemann, s.v. Koinon, Pauly-Wissowa, Suppl. iv.

Against the identification of Asiarch and Archiereus of Asia see the following articles in Pauly-Wissowa : Kornemann, s.v. Koinon (Suppl. iv.) ; Ruge, s.v. Lycia ; Brandis, s.v. Asiarch and Archiereus. See also in Daremberg and Saglio, Perrot, s.v. Asiarches, and A. Souter in Hastings, *Dictionary of the Apostolic Church*, i. pp. 102 f.

For the suggestion that the Asiarchs are Archiereis who have completed their term of service see Guiraud, *Les Assemblées provinciales dans l'empire romain* (1887), pp. 97-106.

In favour of the identification of the two offices see the following discussions : Lightfoot, *The Apostolic Fathers, S. Ignatius, S. Polycarp*, part ii. vol. ii. sect. ii. pp. 987 ff. (ed. of 1885) (valuable because the evidence available in 1885 is quoted in some detail) ; Marquardt, *Röm. Staatsverwaltung*, i. pp. 513 ff. ; Mommsen, *Jahreshefte des österreich. Inst.* iii. (1900), pp. 1-8 ; Dittenberger, *OGIS.* 498, n. 3 ; Fougères, *Mélanges Perrot*, pp. 103-108 (a revision of the opinion expressed in his thesis, *De Lyciorum communi*).

For a good summary of the evidence, which reaches no conclusion, see Chapot, *op. cit.* pp. 468-489.]


NOTE XXIII. THE MICHIGAN PAPYRUS FRAGMENT 1571

By SILVA NEW

The codex.    This single mutilated leaf of a codex of Acts has been dated as early as the first half of the third century and as late as the end of the fourth. In the *Harvard Theological Review* for January 1927 Professor H. A. Sanders published a facsimile of the papyrus, with a reconstruction of its contents and some discussion of its text. Since the *Harvard Theological Review* is not always accessible, and because some important suggestions have been made since Professor Sanders's publication,[1] it has seemed desirable to print the text in this volume.

[1] See especially Prof. A. C. Clark, 'The Michigan Papyrus of Acts,' *J.T.S.* xxix. (1927–1928), pp. 18 ff.

Acts xviii. 27-xix. 6; xix. 12-16

*Recto*

xviii. 27   [ . . . . . . ] ϲτΗΝ αχαϊα ΠΟΛΥ ϹΥΝϵϲ[βαλετο ταιϲ εκκλη]
28   [σι]αμ[ϲ] ϵΥΤΟΝωϹ ΓΑΡ ΤΟΙϹ Ι ΟΥ[δαι]ΟΙϹ ΔΙΑμ[ατηλεγ]
[χετο] ΔΗΜΟϹΙΑ ΔΙ α[λεγομεν]Ο ϲ ϵΠΙ[δεικνυϲ]

xix.   1   [δια τ]ωΝ ΓΡΑΦωΝ χ̄ρ̄ν̄ [ειναι] ῑ̄Η̄Ν̄ θϵΛΟΝΙ[οϲ δε]
[του π]αΥΛΟΥ ΚΑΤΑ ΤΗ[ν ιδιαν βου]ΛΗ[ν πορευ]                                    5
[εσθα]ι ϵΙϹ ΙϵΡΟϹΟΛΥΜΑ [ειπεν αυτω] ΤΟ [π̄ν̄ᾱ]
[υποστρ]ϵΦϵΙΝ ϵΙϹ Τ[ην ασιαν διελθων δε τα]
2   [ανωτ]ϵΡΙΚΑ ΜϵΡ[η ε]ρ̣χϵΤΑ[ι εις εφεσον] Κ̣Α̣Ι̣ [ει]
[πεν τοι]ϲ ΜΑθΗΤΑΙϹ ϵΙ π̄ν̄ᾱ Α Γ[ιον ελαβ]ϵΤϵ ΙΠΙ
[στευσα]ν̣Τ̣ϵ̣ϲ ΟΙ Δ' Α π ϵΚΡϵΙΝΑ[ντο προ]ϲ ΑΥΤΟ̄                              10
[αλλ ου]Δ̣ ϵΙ π̄ν̄ᾱ ΑΓΙΟΝ ΛΑΜΒΑΝ̣[ουσιν τι]ΝϵϹ Η
3   [κουσα]ΜϵΝ · Ο Δϵ ΠΑΥΛΟϹ ΠΡΟϹ ΑΥ[του]ϲ · [ει]ϲ̣ ΤΙ ΟῩ
[εβαπτ]ΙϹθΗΤϵ · ΟΙ Δϵ ϵΛϵΓΟΝ ϵΙϹ ΤΟ [ι]ωΑΝΝΟΥ
4   [βαπτι]ϲΜΑ ϵΙΠϵΝ Δϵ ΠΑΥΛΟϹ Ϊ ωΑΝΝΗϹ ϵΒ[α]
[πτισε]ν̣ ΒΑΠΤΙϹΜΑ ΜϵΤΑΝΟΙΑϹ Τω ΛΑω ΛϵΓω[ν]                          15
[εις τον] ϵΡΧΟΜϵΝΟΝ Μϵ[τ] ΑΥΤΟΝ ΙΝΑ ΠΙϹΤϵΥ[σω]
5   [σιν του]Τ̣ ϵϹΤΙΝ ϵΙϹ ΤΟΝ ῑ̄Η̄Ν̄ ΑΚΟΥ[σ]ΑΝΤϵ[ϲ δε] ₐ ι
[τουτο εβαπτι]ϲθΗϹΑΝ̣ ϵΙϹ ΤΟ ΟΝΟΜΑ ΤΟΥ κ[υ]
6   [ημων ι]η̄ῡ ΤΟΥ χ̄ῡ ιϲ α]φϵ̣ϲ̣ΙΝ ΑΜΑΡΤΙωΝ κ[αι]
[επιθεντος αυτοις το]Υ̣ ΠΑ[υλου χειρα] ϵΠϵ[πε]                            20
[σεν π̄ν̄ᾱ το αγιον επ αυ]ΤΟΥ[ϲ . . . . . . . . . ]

---

1. Sanders originally read θειν for ϲτην, but he has since seen the την clearly. Apparently the scribe wrote ΤΙΝ and changed this to a ligatured ΤΗΝ by adding an horizontal line in which the ink is a little paler. Sanders completed this line by supplying βαλετο εν ταις εκκλη, but this gives a very long line so that βαλετο ταις εκκλη is a probable conjecture.

2. No line in the fragment as reconstructed by Sanders has more than 34 letters, except this and the previous line. This has 38, which suggests that the word supplied at the end may be wrong. But the δια- seems certain, excluding διελεγετο, and no acceptable suggestion has been made.

3. The δι after δημοσια is quite clear and shows that the papyrus had the διαλεγόμενος of D. Sanders however reads δια[λεγομεν]ος επιδεικνυς rather than δια[λεγομενος] και επιδεικνυς with D, but it seems possible that the traces of letters which he reads as ος are really και.

4. θελονι[ος] is clear, but is an error for θέλοντος.

8 f. The reconstruction given is that of Sanders. Since μαθηταῖς is certain

it is much the most probable suggestion. It introduces the disciples abruptly, unlike all other texts, but it is not really difficult to understand.

10. στευσα]ντες οι δε απεκρεινα[ντο προ]s is the reading of Schubart and of Wilcken in the privately issued *Bulletin of the Bezan Club*, and is now accepted by Sanders, except that he thinks that the papyrus has Δ', as above, not Δε.

11. Prof. Sanders supplies ουσιν τι in the space towards the end of the line. It would also be possible to read ουσι τι, but the longer reading more exactly corresponds to the length of the certain supplement in the line above.

19. The reconstruction given was suggested by Prof. A. C. Clark. It avoids the necessity of supposing that contrary to his usual practice the scribe here wrote out χριστου in full. From this point to the end of the recto the lacunae are too long to justify details of reconstruction. For instance it might be επιθεντος αυτοις του Παυλου χειρας επεπεσεν το π̄ν̄ᾱ το αγιον επ αυτους . . . The one thing certain is that the codex read ἐπ' αὐτούς, not ἐπ' αὐτοῖς.

*Verso*

NΘ

xix. 12 [. . . . . . . . . . . . . . . . . . . .] επι τογc αcθενογν[τας]

    [επιφε]ρεcθα[ι α]πο τογ χρωτοc cογδα[ρια]

    η cιμικινθι[α κ]αι απαλλαccεcθαι α[π αυτω]

    [τ]αc νοcογ[s τα τ]ε πᾱντᾱ τα πονηρα ε[κπο]

13 [ρευε]cθ[αι επεχειρ]ηcαν δε τινεc κ[αι εκ]        5

    [των περιερχομενω]ν ϊογδαιων εξ[ορκι]

    [cτων ονομαξειν επ]ι τογc εχον̣τ[ας τα]

    πη̣[ατα τα πον]ηρα τ̣[ο ο]νομα τογ κ̄[ῡ ῑη̄ῡ]

    λ[εγοντες] εξ̣ορκιζομεν ϋμαc τον̣ [ῑη̄ῡ]

14 ον̣ [κηρυ]ccει ο παγλοc εν οιc και γ[ιοι σκευ]    10

    ϊα̣ [ξ̄ Ιου]δ̣αιογ τινοc αρχιερεωc ηθ[ελη]

    cαν [το α]γτο ποιηcαι εθοc εχοντεc [εξορκι]

    ζειν τογc τοιογτογc και ειcελθο[ντες]

    προc δαιμονιζομενον ηρξα[ντο επι]

    καλειcθαι το ονομα λεγοντεc π[αραγγελ]    15

    λομεν cοι εν ῑη̄ῡ ον παγλοc ο [αποστο]

15 λοc κηργccει εξελ̣θειν απο[κριθεν]

    δε το π̄ν̄ᾱ το πονηρο̣[ν ειπεν αυτοις ιη̄ν]

    [γ]ει[νωσκω κα]ι το[ν παυλον επισταμαι]

16 [υ]μ̣[εις δε τινε]c εc[τε και εφαλομενος]    20

    [ο ανθρωπος ε]π α̣[υτους . . . . . . . . . . . . . . . .]

---

4. πᾱντᾱ seems clear in the photograph, though Sanders prints πῡτᾱ, but as the suprascript line denoting an abbreviation is also clear this is probably a slip of the pen.

10 ff. The reconstruction of the lacunae in these lines is peculiarly difficult, as both in 10 and 11 the obvious suggestions do not completely fill the space, as may be seen by comparing the corresponding places in the recto. In 10 κηρυ is three letters less than the certain ντο προ in line 10 on the recto, and in 11 the gap between ιο and δαιου was filled by Sanders with the single letter υ as against ουσιν τι in the corresponding place in the recto. Sanders suggested that there was on the verso a flaw in the papyrus which rendered it unfit for use. This is possible, but a rather desperate suggestion. An alternative in line 10 is to restore [και κηρυ]σσει which fills the lacuna, but this is, if anything, too long, and gives an otherwise unknown reading.

Line 11 is still harder. The iota at the beginning is certain, but the following letter might be an alpha or an omicron. The reconstruction given above gives the spelling of Scaeva found in the codex Alexandrinus, and the fragment of a letter visible after the iota is consistent with an alpha in which the pointed angle at the left bottom corner has been chipped away so as to give a rounder appearance than usual. In the space between the initial iota and the delta in ιουδαιου there is plenty of room for five letters, but Sanders throws a little doubt on the ξ̄ which has been supplied, by pointing out that in papyri there is often a gap left after a numeral, which is also often a large letter (cf. the Michigan fragment of Matthew in the *Harvard Theological Review*, xix. (1926) pp. 215 ff.). On the other hand ιου does not fill the space, as is shown by the fact that the corresponding hole on the other side of the papyrus covers at least six letters, and probably seven.

MICHIGAN PAPYRUS 1571

*Recto*

MICHIGAN PAPYRUS 1571

*Verso*

That the general character of this text is Western is obvious at a The character glance. It has all the paraphrases common to D and the margin of the of the text. Harclean Syriac, as well as the interpolation in xix. 14. But in smaller matters of wording and order it is not exactly the text of either of these two Western authorities, as the following collation with Codex Bezae clearly shows.[1]

xviii. 28. τὸν Ἰησοῦν εἶναι Χριστόν] Χριστὸν εἶναι Ἰησοῦν (cf. εἶναι τὸν Χριστὸν Ἰησοῦν אABHLPϚ)

xix. 1 f. εὑρὼν τινὰς μαθητὰς εἶπε πρὸς αὐτοὺς] εἶπεν τοῖς μαθηταῖς unattested.

2. οἱ δὲ πρὸς αὐτόν] οἱ δὲ ἀπεκρείναντο πρὸς αὐτόν unattested.

3. εἶπεν δέ] ὁ δὲ Παῦλος πρὸς αὐτούς unattested, but cf. εἶπέν τε πρὸς αὐτούς HLPϚ, ὁ δὲ εἶπεν אA, εἶπέν τε B.

4. ὁ Παῦλος] Παῦλος c. אABHLPSϚ. Χριστόν] τὸν Ἰησοῦν c. אAB, τὸν Χριστὸν Ἰησοῦν HLPSϚ.

5. κυρίου] τοῦ κυρίου c. אABHLPSϚ.

6. αὐτοῖς] αὐτοὺς c. אABHLPSϚ.

12. χρωτὸς αὐτοῦ] χρωτός unattested. ἢ καί] ἤ c. אABHLPSϚ. πνεύματα πονηρά] πνεύματα τὰ πονηρά c. אABHLPSϚ.

13. κυρίου] τοῦ κυρίου c. אABHLPSϚ. ὁρκίζω] ἐξορκίζομεν, cf. ὁρκίζομεν c. HLPSϚ. Παῦλος κηρύσσει] κηρύσσει ὁ Παῦλος, cf. ὁ Παῦλος κηρύσσει LϚ.

14. om. Ἰουδαίου] ins. Ἰουδαίου c. אABHPSϚ. ἱερέως] ἀρχιερέως c. אABHLPSϚ. εἶχαν] ἔχοντες unattested. τοὺς τοιούτους ἐξορκίζειν] ἐξορκίζειν τοὺς τοιούτους Harclean Mg. τὸν δαιμονιζόμενον] δαιμονιζόμενον unattested. Παῦλος] Παῦλος ὁ ἀπόστολος unattested. ἐξελθεῖν κηρύσσει] κηρύσσει ἐξελθεῖν Harclean.

15. τότε ἀπεκρίθη] ἀποκριθὲν δέ אABHLPSϚ Harclean.

16. εἰς αὐτοὺς ὁ ἄνθρωπος] ὁ ἄνθρωπος ἐπ᾽ αὐτούς c. אAB.

The most striking feature of this collation is the uniformly unimportant nature of the variants. With few exceptions they are either quite unattested or are common to most manuscripts. That they are

---

[1] In a text which is so largely reconstructed it is difficult to know what variants may properly be cited, but I have tried to include only those which are certain. Thus, silence obviously does not in all cases mean agreement with D, and the text of the papyrus must be consulted whenever any question arises.

not merely another way of cataloguing individual peculiarities of D is shown by the fact that the Harclean margin when extant tends to agree with D rather than with the papyrus, though it does not always do so.

That the papyrus has not been slightly corrected to a Neutral standard is shown partly by its date, but especially by the fact that its agreements with אAB etc. are all in small variants—the more striking Western readings, both of the 'paraphrastic' and 'interpolative' types, being all retained. In a corrected MS. it is usually the striking variants which are changed, the small points which remain. In this connexion it is highly significant that the unattested variants are mostly within the Western readings, which have found no place in the Neutral text. Their lack of support is natural enough ; for we have no Greek witnesses to the Western 'interpolation' except D and the papyrus.

**The papyrus and the Western text.**     This problem of the relation of the papyrus to the Western text as a whole is of course the most important of those raised.

The Western text differs in its attestation from the Neutral in two significant directions.

(i.) It is geographically more widely spread and chronologically earlier. It is found in Carthage, Edessa, and Egypt, as well as in the unknown home of Codex Bezae, and it was apparently used by every witness to the text of Acts as well as of the Gospels in the third century, except perhaps Origen and Clement.[1]

(ii.) There is, in everything except general features, no such close agreement between the individual witnesses to the Western text as is found in the case of the Neutral text, or even more in the case of the Ecclesiastical text. On small points D, the African Latin, the Old Syriac and the third-century writers constantly disagree. In the text of the Gospels we can, indeed, distinguish with substantial accuracy between three phenomena : (a) 'Families' of manuscripts which clearly represent a single MS. Such are Family 1, Family 13 and Family II. (b) 'Texts' where there is obviously an intimate connexion between MSS. which are not, however, genetically connected. Such are the Neutral text found in Mark in אBLΔΨ 33, the Caesarean text found in Θ 565 and their associates, the African Latin found in the Gospels in Cyprian and k or in Acts in Augustine and the Fleury palimpsest. (c) 'Types'[2] of witnesses from which a definite text cannot safely be

---

[1] So far as the Gospels are concerned Origen used sometimes the Neutral and sometimes the Caesarean text (see 'The Caesarean Text of Mark' by K. Lake, R. P. Blake, and S. New in the *Harvard Theological Review*, October 1928). In Acts he seems at least to have had many Western readings, but it would be unsafe to say of him, as of Irenaeus, that he used a Western text. Clement of Alexandria in the Gospels used a Western text, but in Acts seems to show Neutral variants. However, he quotes Acts so little that it is rash to speak very positively.

[2] Types is perhaps not the happiest word. My friend Professor Blake suggests 'phase,' and the German *Gestalt* is possibly better than any English word.

reconstructed, though they are obviously connected.[1] Such is the Western text, both in the Gospels and in Acts. It is not really Western and it is not a text, but it is a ' type ' of which early examples are found in all the chief centres of the Church in the third century. We see it in varying perspective, according to the source which we are using ; we can approximate to but never completely define its readings.

To this Western ' type ' the Michigan papyrus belongs. Its importance is that it comes from Egypt, is earlier than any MS. of the Neutral text, yet has a great amount of agreement with it in details. If we suppose that the Neutral text is a third-century Egyptian revision of an older text of the Western type, the Michigan papyrus is probably the best example known of that subdivision of the ' type ' used by the reviser, who, as always happened, corrected the spectacular variants, but retained the smaller ones. To put this supposition in another form, in the Michigan papyrus and in B we have witnesses to two successive forms of the Egyptian text. Thus in a collation of the papyrus with D we would naturally have, as we do, a series of small agreements with the Neutral text, and a complementary series of unattested variants within the Western ' interpolations.'

The facts may be made plain by a more detailed consideration of one passage from the papyrus.

Acts xix. 14 f.

## Acts xix. 14-15

| The Neutral Text | The Western Text according to the Michigan Papyrus |
|---|---|
| ἦσαν δέ τινος Σκευᾶ ᾿Ιουδαίου ἀρχιερέως ἑπτὰ υἱοὶ τοῦτο ποιοῦντες · ἀποκριθὲν δὲ τὸ πνεῦμα τὸ πονηρὸν εἶπεν αὐτοῖς. | ἐν οἷς καὶ υἱοὶ [σκευ] ἰα̣ [ζ ᾿Ιου]δαίου τινὸς ἀρχιερέως ἠθέλησαν τὸ αὐτὸ ποιῆσαι, ἔθος ἔχοντες ἐξορκίζειν τοὺς τοιούτους · καὶ εἰσελθοντες πρὸς δαιμονιζόμενον ἤρξαντο ἐπικαλεῖσθαι τὸ ὄνομα, λέγοντες · παραγγέλλομέν σοι ἐν ᾿Ιησοῦ ὃν Παῦλος ὁ ἀπόστολος κηρύσσει ἐξελθεῖν, ἀποκριθὲν δὲ τὸ πνεῦμα τὸ πονηρὸν εἶπεν αὐτοῖς, κτλ. |
| τινος] τινες ℵA σκευα] σκευϊα A | |

### Critical Notes on the Western Text

om ζ D    αρχιερεως] ιερεως D hl[mg]
εχοντες] ειχαν D (hl[mg])
τους τοιουτους εξορκιζειν D
τον δαιμονιζομενον D
αποκριθεν δε] τοτε απεκριθη D

---

[1] That is to say, any reconstruction would necessarily have a large apparatus with many variants within the text. This is really the criterion. Family 1, and even more Family II, can be reconstructed so securely that in the whole of Mark there is no doubt about more than a dozen words (less than that in Fam. II). A reconstructed Neutral text would have two or three alternative readings in every chapter, the Caesarean text perhaps twice as many ; but the Western text would have variants in every verse.

The general difference between the Western type and the other readings is obvious. The Western text has the framework ἐν οἷς . . . ἠθέλησαν τὸ αὐτὸ ποιῆσαι, ἔθος ἔχοντες τοὺς τοιούτους ἐξορκίζειν followed by a detailed account of the exorcism—καὶ εἰσελθόντες πρὸς τὸν δαιμονιζόμενον ἤρξαντο ἐπικαλεῖσθαι τὸ ὄνομα λέγοντες παραγέλλομέν σοι ἐν Ἰησοῦ ὃν Παῦλος κηρύσσει ἐξελθεῖν. There are some minor variants in this account, but the important variant is within the framework. D reads ἐν οἷς καὶ υἱοὶ Σκευᾶ τινὸς ἱερέως ἠθέλησαν τὸ αὐτὸ ποιῆσαι, the Harclean margin reads " in quibus erant filii septem Scevae cujusdam sacerdotis," etc., and the Michigan papyrus has ἐν οἷς καὶ υἱοὶ . . . Ἰουδαίου τινὸς ἀρχιερέως, etc. Unfortunately it is not certain whether the lacunae cover Σκευᾶ ἑπτά or not, though the balance of probability is perhaps favourable.

Thus though the Western text type is unmistakable it varies in a manner which cannot be accidental. The rival texts with negligible variants read ἦσαν δέ τινος Σκευᾶ ἰουδαίου ἀρχιερέως ἑπτὰ υἱοὶ τοῦτο ποιοῦντες, and they continue, very awkwardly, ἀποκριθὲν δὲ τὸ πνεῦμα τὸ πονηρὸν εἶπεν αὐτοῖς.

The chief point to be noted is that the Western text tells a different story from the Neutral. According to the latter the ' sons of Scaeva ' are introduced as examples of the Jewish exorcists mentioned in the preceding verse; according to the Western it was ' at this juncture ' [1] (ἐν οἷς) that the sons of Scaeva wished to copy the Jewish exorcists. Except in the Michigan papyrus it does not say that Scaeva was a Jew. This reading appears to be the first Egyptian emendation, and due to a misunderstanding which took ἐν οἷς as meaning ' among whom.' Once this change was made it would inevitably appear that the long Western reading was unnecessary repetition, τὸ αὐτό would naturally become τοῦτο, and the ' Neutral ' revision would follow quite naturally.

One final observation may be made: The very awkward ἀποκριθὲν of the Neutral text is not found in D, which reads τότε ἀπεκρίθη, but it does appear in the Michigan papyrus, where it is not at all awkward but rather ' better ' Greek than the characteristic τότε of D. Obviously this fact supports the suggestion that the Michigan papyrus represents an Egyptian form, slightly revised, of the Western text, and that this form was the basis of the Neutral revision.

[1] For this rendering cf. Luke xii. 1, Acts xxvi. 12 (xxiv. 18 ?). These show that ἐν οἷς, meaning ' at this time ' or ' under these circumstances,' is a good Lucan idiom, though it is not very usual Greek. Its excuse would be that no one in the first century would be likely to think that Scaeva could be a Jewish priest, to say nothing of a high priest. Least of all would a writer acquainted with Jewish customs have had such an idea in his mind. He would not see how easily a more ignorant generation would inevitably connect ἐν οἷς with the Jewish exorcists just mentioned.

## NOTE XXIV. DUST AND GARMENTS

### By HENRY J. CADBURY

The book of Acts contains a series of references to gestures involving the use of dust, or of garments, or both. In spite of prolonged study by scholars, and the inferences which may be drawn from the texts and contexts of the several passages, and the citation of parallels elsewhere, the interpretation of these gestures remains without settled solution. It may therefore be advisable to look at the passages collectively and separately, and to tabulate and discuss some forms of explanation.

The passages are as follows :

(1) Acts xiii. 51 οἱ δὲ ἐκτιναξάμενοι τὸν κονιορτὸν τῶν ποδῶν ἐπ’    Acts xiii. 51. αὐτοὺς ἦλθον εἰς Εἰκόνιον. The subject is Paul and Barnabas ; the place is Antioch of Pisidia. The Jews having " contradicted the things which were spoken by Paul, and blasphemed," were filled with jealousy at the success of the gospel among the Gentiles, and " urged on the devout women of honorable estate and the chief men of the city, and stirred up a persecution against Paul and Barnabas, and cast them out of their borders. But they shook off the dust of their feet against them, and came unto Iconium."

This incident appears at first sight a literal fulfilment of the command of Jesus to his disciples as recorded in Matthew, Mark, and Luke. If Jesus' command was known to the apostles Paul and Barnabas, that would account for their acting so. In like manner if, as is certainly the case, the injunction was known to the author of Acts, that would account for his describing here the fulfilment. Luke, in fact, twice uses the expression in his Gospel, once (ix. 5) at the sending out of the Twelve (a passage parallel to Mark and clearly derived from Mark, though influenced by a like passage in Q),[1] where Jesus commands : καὶ ὅσοι ἂν μὴ δέχωνται ὑμᾶς, ἐξερχόμενοι ἀπὸ τῆς πόλεως ἐκείνης καὶ [2] τὸν κονιορτὸν ἀπὸ τῶν ποδῶν ὑμῶν ἀποτινάσσετε [3] εἰς μαρτύριον ἐπ’ αὐτούς ; the other time (x. 11) where Jesus, commanding the Seventy, tells them in such cases to go out into the city squares and say : καὶ τὸν κονιορτὸν τὸν κολληθέντα ἡμῖν ἐκ τῆς πόλεως ὑμῶν εἰς τοὺς πόδας ἀπομασσόμεθα ὑμῖν. There are items in the wording of these passages which suggest that Acts is really reminiscent of them. Note that in Acts Luke has in characteristic fashion [4] retained Mark's verb ἐκτινάσσω, while in the Gospel he changes it to ἀποτινάσσω (and ἀπομάσσομαι). The phrase in Acts ἐπ’ αὐτούς finds its explanation in the Gospel parallels ὑμῖν and εἰς μαρτύριον ἐπ’ αὐτούς (Mark εἰς μαρτύριον αὐτοῖς).

[1] The probable relation of the four passages is that Mark vi. 7-11 is used in Matt. x. 1-16 and Luke ix. 1-5, and that Q is interwoven in Matt. x. 1-16, and separately given in Luke x. 1-12. But both passages in Luke may represent some conflation with the main source of the other one.

[2] Om. καὶ ℵBCDL, etc.

[3] ἀποτινάσσετε ℵB, ἐκτινάξατε D, ἀποτινάξατε ACLW, etc.

[4] There are a series of items in Mark which are omitted by Luke in the parallel, but reappear in Acts. See note on i. 7, Vol. IV. p. 8.

Merx's
explanation.

But what is the gesture, and what does it mean ? Merx [1] has suggested that the dust of the feet means the dust which is stirred up by the feet and clings to the garments. In this case the shaking would be of the garments. But except for this passage of Acts, and possibly in Matthew x. 14,[2] we have expressions like τὸν χοῦν [3] τὸν ὑποκάτω τῶν ποδῶν of Mark vi. 11, τὸν κονιορτὸν ἀπὸ τῶν ποδῶν of Luke ix. 5, and most explicitly in Luke x. 11 καὶ τὸν κονιορτὸν τὸν κολληθέντα ἡμῖν ἐκ τῆς πόλεως εἰς τοὺς πόδας. Unless the expression is purely figurative, as it would be in modern speech, like our use of "washing one's hands of the matter," it must mean shaking dust off the shoes [4] or feet.

Rabbinic
explana-
tions.

Rabbinic commentators on the New Testament (Matt. x. 14), from Lightfoot to Strack-Billerbeck, regard the gesture as indicating that the city thus rejected is treated as the heathen. They cite the passages that indicate that dust from heathen lands, even Syria, destroyed Levitical purity, or that inculcate care to avoid imported vegetables, to burn priests' garments that have come in contact with dust derived from heathen lands, or to blow off from the feet the dust of a field in which human bones have been uncovered by ploughing. But the New Testament passages suggest that the act was not so much one of self-purification as of warning to those left behind,[5] "a testimony unto them," [6] perhaps

---

[1] A. Merx, *Die vier canonischen Evangelien*, ii. 1. pp. 178 f. on Matt. x. 14.

[2] There is some good evidence (אC 33 syr sin, etc.) for reading κονιορτὸν ἐκ τῶν ποδῶν instead of κονιορτὸν τῶν ποδῶν in Matt. x. 14.

[3] χοῦς for the classical κονιορτός is common in the LXX and thence also Rev. xviii. 19.

[4] Shoes or sandals are not mentioned in any of the passages, but I believe that they, rather than the feet, were regarded as carrying defilement. Cf. 1 Kings ii. 5. Of course Q, unlike Mark ὑποδεδεμένους σανδάλια, seems to have included a prohibition of ὑποδήματα.

[5] The gesture is explained by words of warning by the missionaries (Luke x. 11 b) or Jesus (Q, Matt. x. 14=Luke x. 12). The best protestation to others might be a solemn act of self-vindication, placing the responsibility on others. Cf. Acts xviii. 6 ; Matt. xxvii. 24 f. It might be equivalent to a curse. We may note that in the Paris magical amulet (2316. 318 v.) the witch Βασκανοσύνη declares that she goes to shut up the seven sources of water, to burn off the threshing-floor, to shake off dust (κονιορτὸν ἀποτινάξαι), and to do other malicious things. According to Dalman, *Arbeit und Sitte in Palästina*, i., 1928, p. 522, the customs continue both of shaking dust off shoes and clothes and of shaking garments (cf. below).

[6] The meaning of εἰς μαρτύριον αὐτοῖς is not absolutely clear here, and is much disputed in the other Marcan passages in the synoptic tradition, viz. Mark i. 44=Matt. viii. 4=Luke v. 14 ; Mark xiii. 9=Matt. x. 18=Matt. xxiv. 14=Luke xxi. 13 (where ὑμῖν implies αὐτοῖς). But I cannot enter into this problem. For a recent discussion of the former see S. Zeitlin, *Revue des Études Juives*, lxxxvii., 1929, pp. 79 ff., and of the latter see F. C. Burkitt, *Christian Beginnings*, 1924, pp. 145 ff. The early *Acta Barnabae*, 20, doubtless has this passage in mind in saying τὸν κονιορτὸν τῶν ποδῶν ἐξετινάξαμεν κατέναντι τοῦ ἱεροῦ ἐκείνου, cf. 21.

of a dire fate threatening them. It would be strange indeed if Paul should use against Jews who objected to his Gentile success a gesture that was to be understood principally as the strict Jew's act of purification against Gentile defilement. The shaking off of dust might mean rather that the missionaries clear themselves of all further responsibility for the impenitence of the doomed city. It might be done in anger or scorn, but those are not the main elements. It was an act towards a whole city, not towards individuals. We may note, finally, that it did not preclude a subsequent return to Antioch (xiv. 21 f.) to strengthen the souls of the disciples there. It might further mean ridding oneself of all that has to do with the city. The departing missionaries not only abandon the unreceptive city to its fate, but even avoid taking any vestige of it with them. Luke himself in the Gospel adds before ' dust ' the climactic ' even.' [1]

(2) Acts xiv. 14 ἀκούσαντες δὲ οἱ ἀπόστολοι Βαρνάβας καὶ Παῦλος, Acts xiv. 14. διαρρήξαντες τὰ ἱμάτια ἑαυτῶν ἐξεπήδησαν εἰς τὸν ὄχλον, κράζοντες κτλ. The actors are the same as before. The scene is Lystra. Upon the cure of the lame man the natives have cried in their Lycaonian language that Paul and Barnabas were gods, and are preparing to offer sacrifice to them.

Here even more certainly than in the previous passage, rabbinic testimony seems to afford the explanation. The rending of garments is the prescribed reaction against blasphemy. The rabbis have explicit regulations as to the cases when garments so torn can be sewed up again. There is also the requirement that the Sanhedrin, when hearing witnesses to a case of blasphemy, all except the witnesses,[2] must rend their garments as the blasphemous words are repeated.

This episode in Acts also has its counterpart in the gospels when at the trial of Jesus upon his admission of Messiahship we read, " And the high priest rent his clothes,[3] and saith, What further need have we of witnesses ? Ye have heard the blasphemy : what think ye ? " Luke in his gospel omits the rending of the garments and the reference to blasphemy. This is one of the cases where an item of Mark missing in Luke's parallel reappears in Acts in a different connexion.[4]

But the rending of garments even in Jewish literature is by no means

[1] The καί is certain at Luke x. 11, but is supported only by ΑΕΔ . . . min lat syr at ix. 5.

[2] By a kind of naïveté the witnesses are exempted on the assumption that they have duly rent their garments already—when they heard the original blasphemy. Mo'ed Katon f 25b.

[3] Mark xiv. 63 διαρρήξας τοὺς χιτῶνας, Matt. xxvi. 65 διέρρηξεν τὰ ἱμάτια, using the more usual noun ; but διαρρήγνυμι τοὺς χιτῶνας occurs in the Apocrypha, Judith xiv. 19 ; Ep. Jer. 30 ; 2 Macc. iv. 38. Why the undergarments rather than the cloak were rent, why the high priest who is forbidden to rend his garments in private grief (Lev. x. 6, xxi. 10) is here permitted to do so, and other questions, relevant to this scene but not to Acts, are discussed in the commentaries on Mark and Matthew. It is doubtful whether claiming to be the Messiah would be technically blasphemy at all ; words against the temple might be.

[4] See above, p. 269, note 4.

limited to cases of blasphemy. It occurs in many passages in the Old Testament of sorrow,[1] especially of painful surprise. Perhaps not one of the nearly fifty instances, not even Jeremiah xxxvi. 24, involves blasphemy. There, and in a few other Old Testament passages, it may be regarded as an act of protestation (e.g. Numb. xiv. 6).[2] And it would seem that this, rather than horror at blasphemy, was the meaning of the apostle's gesture at Lystra. It should be remembered, also, that in Hellenistic writings the torn garments are found with bared breasts in cases of entreaty,[3] and in cases of sudden irruption aiming to stop proceedings.[4] In the latter connexion note here in Acts ἐξεπήδησαν εἰς τὸν ὄχλον. A like gesture is the tearing off or throwing off of garments. That occurs with sudden acts of protestation or intervention.[5] I believe διαρρήγνυμι sometimes means to tear off clothes, just as it is used of breaking fetters and thus loosening them.[6]

Acts xvi. 22.    (3) This interpretation at once brings us to our next passage in Acts, xvi. 22 καὶ συνεπέστη ὁ ὄχλος κατ' αὐτῶν, καὶ οἱ στρατηγοὶ περριρήξαντες αὐτῶν τὰ ἱμάτια ἐκέλευον ῥαβδίζειν. The missionaries are this time in Philippi; because they have driven out from the ventriloquist slave girl the

---

[1] The rending of garments has been discussed in the articles on funeral customs of the Hebrews from the earliest times and was the subject of special monographs by C. J. G. Heidenus (Jena, 1663), Chris. J. Schröder (Jena, 1705), J. C. Wichmannshausen (Viteb. 1716). Doubtless the gesture is native in other groups also. Among the arguments used in the seventeenth century to identify the American Indians with the lost Ten Tribes of Israel was their agreement in this custom (Samuel Smith, *History of New Jersey*, 2nd edit., 1865, p. 9).

[2] The instances cited in Mo'ed Katon *f*25b in answer to the question " whence do we prove that the garments must be rent when the name of God is profaned ? " are 2 Kings xviii. 37, xix. 1. The Greek version uses βλασφημέω in the context (xix. 4, 6, 22). Similar to the inappropriateness of using the gesture of defilement in |dealing with the Jews at xiii. 51 is that of using the gesture of blasphemy in dealing with Gentiles. Cyril (Cramer's *Catena, ad loc.*), who feels it necessary to defend the use of a Jewish custom by Christians, writes : ἔθος ἐστὶν 'Ιουδαίοις ἐπὶ ταῖς κατὰ θεοῦ δυσφημίαις περιρηγνύναι τὰ ἱμάτια . . . δεδράκασι δὲ τοῦτο καὶ οἱ θεσπέσιοι μαθηταὶ Παῦλός τε καὶ Βαρνάβας . . . ἐπειδὴ δὴ τὸ δρώμενον δυσφημία τις ἦν, διέρρηξαν τὰ ἱμάτια αὐτῶν παραδοσεσι 'Ιουδαϊκαῖς καὶ ἐγγράφοις ἔθεσιν ἀκολουθοῦντες. Yet the Jews were careful not to blaspheme Gentile gods. See Josephus as cited on xix. 37, Vol. IV. p. 251.

[3] Herodian i. 13 τοιαῦτά τινα εἰποῦσα, ῥηξαμένη τε τὴν ἐσθῆτα κτλ.

[4] P Lips 37. 19.

[5] I think some instances commonly used to illustrate Acts xvi. 22 (περιρήγνυμι) and xxii. 23 (ῥιπτέω) belong here, e.g. Ovid, *Heroid.* vi. 27 *protinus exilui, tunicisque a pectore ruptis* ; Dio Chrys. *Orat.* xxxv. p. 432 M. (Dindorf ii. 42) δεῖ περιρηξάμενον ἐκπηδᾶν γυμνὸν εἰς τὰς ὁδούς ; Capitolinus, *incurrere in parietes, vestem scindere, gladium accipere, quasi omnes, posset occidere* ; Lucian, *De salt.* 83, the spectators ἐπήδων καὶ ἐβόων καὶ τὰς ἐσθῆτας ἀπερρίπτουν (see, however, p. 277, note 5).

[6] Luke viii. 29 διαρρήσσων τὰ δεσμὰ (where ῥήσσω=ῥήγνυμι), and elsewhere.

so-called Python the mob has gathered, and they have been accused before the *strategi* of disturbing the city and introducing customs unlawful for Romans. The *strategi* tearing off ' their ' clothes bid them to be scourged with rods. But whose clothes ? If those of Paul and Silas, then the matter is not a gesture at all, but the first hasty and violent steps towards scourging. This is on the whole quite probable. Wettstein gives at least five passages (Plutarch, Dion. Hal., Livy, Valer. Max.) where, in connexion with beatings by *lictores*, ῥάβδουχοι (cf. Acts xvi. 35, 38), or ὑπηρέται, the torn garments of the victims are mentioned.

But it is not impossible that the passage really means the clothes of the *strategi* themselves. Having heard the charge they express their horror and officious zeal by the violent tearing off of their own garments. The verb used is περιρήγνυμι, while in all other Biblical passages διαρρήγνυμι (rarely ῥήγνυμι) is employed of rending one's own garments. But there is abundant evidence in Hellenistic writings that περιρήγνυμι is used in just this sense,[1] as well as of stripping others for chastisement.

Such an interpretation is not new, though it has been revived by Sir William M. Ramsay.[2] It is not at all necessary for the passage, which yields fair sense and accords enough with ancient penological practice if understood of the stripping of prisoners for the lash. But in view of the ambiguity of the verb and of the pronoun,[3] and in connexion with the evidence of the interest in gestures elsewhere in the book of Acts, the possibility that the *strategi* tore their own clothes is worth remembering.[4]

---

[1] Plut. *Public.* p. 99 E ; *De virt. mulier.* p. 251 B. Cf. Wettstein *ad loc.* ; Demos. xix. 197 (p. 403 Reiske) ; Polyb. xv. 33. 4 ; 2 Macc. iv. 38. Josephus uses the middle of περιρήγνυμι in the sense of stripping oneself, e.g. *B.J.* ii. 15. 2, § 316 (cf. 322, *v.l.*) ; *Antiq.* vi. 14. 6, § 357, xi. 6. 7, § 221 (for διαρρήγνυμι Esther iv. 1, LXX), xviii. 3. 4, § 78 ; cf. Arrian, *Anab. Alex.* vii. 24. 3 περιρηξαμένους (without any object, of horror or grief) ; Alciphr. iv. 4. 4 τὸν χιτωνίσκον περιρηξαμένη τὰ μαστάρια τοῖς δικασταῖς ἐπέδειξας. But later Christian writers use the active, *Acta Thomae* 63 (cited by Moulton and Milligan s.v.) τὴν ἐσθῆτα περιέρρηξα καὶ τὰς χεῖρας ἐπὶ τὴν ὄψιν ἐπάταξα, and Cyril, as quoted above, p. 272 n. 2, uses the compound in περι- in the active as equivalent to that in δια-. In view of Luke's independence in matters of voice in other verbs it would be unwise to lay stress on his use of the active here. Cf. Diod. Sic. xvii. 35. 5 and Charito of Aphrodisias, who used the middle of περιρήγνυμι with ἐσθῆτα and even alone (like Arrian) as a gesture of grief, while with δεσμά he uses the active of διαρρήγνυμι as does Luke (note 6, p. 272).

[2] *St. Paul the Traveller and the Roman Citizen*, p. 219, cf. 217.

[3] It is possible, though not necessary, to give the rough breathing αὑτῶν if the garments are regarded as those of the *strategi*.

[4] Such confusion between actors occurs not only where our present text is obscure, but probably elsewhere also through carelessness both in the earlier and later stages of tradition. Examples of the latter, as when the short stature of Zacchaeus is transferred to Jesus, are quite common. Of earlier confusions in the material of Acts, perhaps due to such obscurity in sources as made it possible for Luke (v. 29) to suppose that the dining with publicans in Mark ii. 15 was in Levi's house, some few possibilities may be suggested. The first of these

Acts xviii. 6.

(4) Acts xviii. 6 ἀντιτασσομένων δὲ αὐτῶν καὶ βλασφημούντων ἐκτιναξάμενας τὰ ἱμάτια εἶπεν πρὸς αὐτούς· Τὸ αἷμα ὑμῶν ἐπὶ τὴν κεφαλήν· καθαρὸς ἐγώ· ἀπὸ τοῦ νῦν εἰς τὰ ἔθνη πορεύσομαι.

The scene is at Corinth, possibly in the synagogue (see verse 7), and the actors are Paul the missionary and the Corinthian Jews. The gesture is the shaking out of the garments. The verb used is the same as in xiii. 51, and the passages have in common the unusual use of the middle voice. In both passages the situation is alike, the familiar one in Acts, of Paul turning to the Gentiles when rejected by the Jews. It would be natural to connect the two gestures in meaning. To be sure, there is no dust mentioned here, and the gesture is not of the feet, but the garments. A. E. J. Rawlinson, who compares the two actions, says of this one : " St. Paul shakes his clothes because he has already deposited his sandals according to custom at the synagogue door." [1] The context, however, gives rather more than usual the interpretation of the gesture. Paul's words, " Your blood be upon your own head. I am pure, henceforth I go to the Gentiles," is doubtless the author's rendering of the gesture. More plainly than the shaking off of dust it means ' washing one's hands '— to use another figure—of other men's guilt, and the turning it back upon their own heads. The phrase ' Your blood be upon your head ' is almost certainly here due to the Old Testament, where it is quite common. The gesture also might be suspected of similar origin. But the shaking of garments is nearly as little mentioned in the Old Testament as the shaking off of dust.[2] The parallel cited is Neh. v. 13, where again symbolic actions are explained in words following : " Also I shook out my lap, and said : So God shake out every man from his house, and from his labour, that performeth not this promise, even thus be he shaken out and emptied." The Greek verb in this passage is ἐκτινάσσω (ter), the noun is ἀναβολή, which would probably be understood to mean cloak. The Hebrew נער

Neh. v. 13.

---

also has to do with garments. There is good evidence that the garments of those who were executed were removed, but not so much reason for mentioning removal of the garments of executioners as is done at the stoning of Stephen (vii. 58, and the note Vol. IV. p. 85; cf. xxii. 20 and Vol. III. p. 407, note 2). When Eutychus is raised alive after his fall it would be more natural to mention that he tasted food (xx. 11), as does Jairus's daughter and the risen Jesus, than that Paul did. The uncertainty whether it was Paul or Aquila that shaved the head in a vow at Cenchreae (xviii. 18) is notorious.

[1] On Mark vi. 11 in the *Westminster Commentary.*

[2] The gesture is not cited from the ancients in this sense. See in a different connexion the examples of waving garments, p. 275 n. 2. I. Benzinger, *Prot. Realencykl.* x. p. 525, speaks of the shaking out of one's garment as a gesture of the strongest detestation, still practised by the Arab to express his scorn. But this, too, is different from the present passage. And there is also the cabalistic Jewish custom of shaking the ends of one's garment in the ' Tashlik ' ceremony on New Year's day when sins are cast into the sea. The phrase εἰς τὴν κεφαλήν (σήν, σοί, etc.) has in classical Greek some parallels, usually with τρέπω, e.g. Aristoph. *Nub.* 39 ; *Plut.* 526 ; Phalaris, *Epist.* 102.

means either the bosom of the cloak or the arms. But the context seems to imply shaking something loose.[1] These considerations do not, however, affect the possibility that the author of Acts is imitating the Septuagint passage. But the interpretation of Paul's gesture is not the same as Nehemiah's, and still lacks from extraneous sources any illumination.

(5) Acts xxii. 22 f. ἤκουον δὲ αὐτοῦ ἄχρι τούτου τοῦ λόγου καὶ ἐπῆραν Acts xxii. τὴν φωνὴν αὐτῶν λέγοντες· Αἶρε ἀπὸ τῆς γῆς τὸν τοιοῦτον, οὐ γὰρ 22 f. καθῆκεν αὐτὸν ζῆν. κραυγαζόντων τε αὐτῶν καὶ ῥιπτούντων τὰ ἱμάτια καὶ κονιορτὸν βαλλόντων εἰς τὸν ἀέρα ἐκέλευσεν ὁ χιλίαρχος κτλ.

The scene is Jerusalem. The actors are again Paul and hostile Jews. He has just spoken of being sent by God to the Gentiles. This, as usual, precipitates the murderous rage of his fellow-countrymen. Besides their shouts the author mentions two gestures or gesticulations.

This passage is the last of our series—in many ways the most obscure, most vivid, and most abused by commentators. It may be noted that it combines the two items used in gestures heretofore—dust and garments. The context seems to suggest that these are gestures of anger and hostility, but just why the inner feelings should take on such outward form is the problem.

The casting of garments may be interpreted in several ways. It may mean throwing off, and this may be explained as intended to show that they were stripping themselves for action. One thinks of threatened stoning. ῥίπτω is used of throwing away arms in flight. It might be used of garments.[2] A similar meaning was suggested above for δια- and περιρήγνυμι. And at the stoning of Stephen this author tells us that garments were laid aside (vii. 58 ἀπέθεντο, cf. xxii. 20). The throwing of dust could be understood as a like mark of murderous intent. Though it was thrown in the air, it was intended as a threat if not as an actual missile[3] against Paul. In the absence of stones, or for fear of the soldiers guarding Paul, only dust is used.

There are, however, various alternatives. The signs may not be gestures of actual attack, but rather evidences of the excitement and rage of the crowd. Commentators call it typically oriental[4] but cite no parallels.[5] Preuschen is certainly as near the mark when he says : " Für das Aufwerfen des Staubes lassen sich keine Parallelen beibringen."

It is in fact the recent commentators on Job that feel the most assur-

---

[1] L. W. Batten in *International Critical Commentary, ad loc.*

[2] Plato, *Republic* v. 474 A, is an excellent parallel, or Dio Chrys. vii. p. 103 M. (Dindorf i. 114), cf. xxxii. p. 389 M. (i. 431).

[3] Shimei in 2 Sam. xvi. 13, where LXX has τῷ χοῒ πάσσων.

[4] Rackham : " the ordinary oriental symptoms of excitement."

[5] An interesting description of a hippodrome is given by Gregory Nazianzenus (*Or. in laudem Basilii,* xv., Migne, *P.G.* 36, 513 f.) ὅπερ οὖν πάσχοντας ἔστιν ἰδεῖν περὶ τὰς ἀντιθέτους ἱπποδρομίας τοὺς φιλίππους τε καὶ φιλοθεάμονας, πηδῶσιν, βοῶσιν, οὐρανῷ πέμπουσι κόνιν, ἡνιοχοῦσι καθήμενοι, παίουσι τὸν ἀέρα τοῖς δακτύλοις, ὡς μάστιξι κτλ. This passage is correctly quoted from Gregory Nazianzenus by John of Damascus (*Sacra par. π.* 31) but erroneously ascribed by Wettstein to Gregory Thaumaturgus.

ance about the interpretation of this passage in Acts. It is, according to
Jastrow,[1] reminiscent of Job ii. 12, where the three friends of Job when
they first saw him in his misery "lifted up their voice and wept, and they
rent every one his mantle and threw dust upon their heads towards heaven."
Buttenwieser following Weizsäcker translates ῥιπτούντων τὰ ἱμάτια ' rent
their garments,' and adds that these acts are "not an expression of wild
fanaticism, but rites customary under such circumstances. The object
is to avert from themselves the curse that is likely to fall on the blasphemous : ' He who puts himself in a state as of one accursed will not be harmed
by the curse, having made himself immune against it.' "[2]

Such an interpretation of Acts xxii. 23 would bring our series to an
interesting conclusion, for then practically all the gestures could fall under
the same heading, avoidance and deprecation of blasphemy. Whether it
be the shaking of dust from the feet at Antioch, the rending of garments
at Lystra or Philippi, the shaking of garments at Corinth, or here the
gestures with both dust and garments, it is the old prophylactic of magic
against blasphemy that is always involved. The Jews count it blasphemy
for Paul to claim a divine mission to the Gentiles, Paul counts it blasphemy
for the Jews to reject the message, the Gentile praetors or *strategi* at
Philippi count Paul's un-Roman teaching blasphemy, and of course Paul
and Barnabas shudder with horror at being worshipped at Lystra as gods.[3]

It must be admitted that if such an apotropaic purpose is the origin
of the gestures, neither the author nor the readers of Acts were probably
aware of it, certainly not in the instance at hand. For the proper gesture
for sorrow, and probably for blasphemy, was to rub dust, earth, or ashes
on the head. This is often associated with torn garments,[4] and if we are
to see this combination in Job we must suppose with Jastrow that the

*In the left margin:* Job ii. 4.    Conclu-sions.

[1] M. Jastrow, Jr., *The Book of Job*, 1920, p. 204. The same writer had
made an extensive study of ' Dust, Earth, and Ashes as Symbols of Mourning
among the Ancient Hebrews ' in *Journal of American Oriental Society*, xx.,
1899, pp. 133 ff.

[2] M. Buttenwieser, *The Book of Job*, 1922, p. 44, quoting Pedersen, *Der
Eid bei den Semiten*, 1914, p. 102. The Old Testament or Semitic civilization
in general was no poorer in gestures of disgust, aversion, etc., than it was in
vocabulary to correspond; cf. wag the head (Lam. ii. 15, Ps. xxii. 7), clap the
hand (*ibid.* and elsewhere), shake the fist (Zeph. ii. 15), pluck out the hair
(2 Esdras i. 8). But the reader of the English 'throw dust in our eyes' at
Num. xvi. 14 should be warned that this is not a literal rendering of the
Hebrew idiom there.

[3] It should be recalled that Greek writers in general and this evangelist in
particular use the verb βλασφημέω of evil speaking, not only against God but
against pagan gods (Acts xix. 37) and men (Luke xxiii. 39). Its use in the
context of Acts xiii. 51 and xviii. 6 has been already mentioned.

[4] Josh. vii. 6 ; 1 Sam. iv. 12 ; 2 Sam. i. 2, xiii. 19, xv. 32 ; 1 Macc.
iii. 47, iv. 39, xi. 71 ; Josephus, *B.J.* ii. 15. 4, § 322. See the article in
*JAOS.* mentioned in note 1. It may be added that the evidence which Jastrow
gives from Egyptian monuments of the custom of putting dust on the head
could be greatly multiplied from recent illustrated publications.

words ' towards heaven ' are a gloss. But in Acts certainly, and perhaps in Job,[1] there is no doubt that the dust was thrown into the air. This was scarcely with the object of getting it on to their own heads. Still less likely is it that ῥιπτούντων [2] refers to rending garments. I can find no authority for Weizsäcker. It might mean casting off, as has been said above, and nakedness rather than torn garments may be accounted as a sign of mourning. A quite different interpretation of the verb remains, however, to be considered. That is that it means ' waved.' This view is at least as old as Wettstein,[3] and has been argued by Field, and is adopted in many modern translations and commentaries.

Field [4] admits that " there is no good example of this use of ῥιπτεῖν," but he thinks it was so understood by Chrysostom who paraphrases as τὰ ἱμάτια ἐκτινάσσοντες, and there is a good deal of evidence that other verbs like σοβέω, ἀνασείω, perhaps ἀναριπτέω,[5] and in Latin iactare, iactatio togarum are used of the applause of spectators.[6] In the present scene one scarcely expects to find favourable applause, and whether the gesture of waving garments, if that is to be thought of here, could connote feelings other than approbation is not evident. It may be we can only consider the gestures signs of excitement.


### NOTE XXV. THE POLICY OF THE EARLY ROMAN EMPERORS TOWARDS JUDAISM

By VINCENT M. SCRAMUZZA

The first authentic relation between the Roman government and the Jewish commonwealth dates from the time of Judas Maccabee (165–161 B.C.). In his struggle to free Palestine from the political overlordship of the Seleucids and the devastating encroachments of Hellenism, that revolutionary leader made an alliance with the Roman senate and people.[7]

*The Maccabees.*

---

[1] See, however, G. B. Gray's philological note in *International Critical Commentary*, vol. ii. p. 15. The Hebrew verb seems to imply casting in handfuls as in Exodus ix. 8, 10, where we have the ' towards heaven ' as in Job, *loc. cit.*, and in Greek the verb πάσσω as in 2 Sam. xvi. 13 ; see p. 275, note 3.

[2] In spite of old attempts to distinguish (iactare vs. iacere, etc.) I shall assume that ῥιπτέω means the same as ῥίπτω, as I have assumed in the case of -ῥήγνυμι and -ῥήσσ(ττ)ω. See, however, J. H. Moulton, *Grammar of N.T. Greek*, ii. pp. 257, 386 ; W. Schmid, *Atticismus*, ii. pp. 81 f.

[3] It is not likely that it was invented by Wettstein, but I do not trace it earlier. Wettstein explains the gesture as of approval: " Qui longius aberant, his signis testabantur, se cum illis facere, qui propius adstantes clamabant."

[4] *Notes on the Translation of the N.T.*, 1899, p. 136.

[5] Following Boissonade's note on Aristaenetus, *Epist.* p. 580, editors substitute ἀνερρίπτουν for ἀπερρίπτουν in Lucian, *De salt.* 83, cited above, p. 272.

[6] See Wettstein *ad loc.*, and more fully C. Sittl, *Die Gebärden der Griechen und Römer*, 1890, p. 62, note 5.

[7] 1 Macc. viii.

The Romans gave him no immediate help, but as friends and associates of the revolutionaries they acquired one more right for interfering in the confused affairs of the Seleucid empire, and, later, in the factional strifes of the Jewish nation. When Pompey proceeded to systematize the affairs of Syria and the East in general, his intervention in Judea was invoked by both aspirants to the office of priest-king, the brothers Hyrcanus II. and Aristobulus II., as well as by the people, whose ambassadors entreated him that he would abolish the Hasmonean monarchy altogether and replace it by the old theocratic constitution of the priests.[1] Pompey decided in the interest of Rome. He abolished the kingship, reduced the area of the Jewish domains, and put an end to the independence of Judea proper by making it tributary to Rome, and placing it under the supervision of the Roman governor of Syria (63 B.C.).[2] During the Roman civil wars, the irrepressible Jewish factions, by taking sides with one or the other of the contending Roman generals, or by allying with Parthia,[3] were able to recapture for Judea a great measure of that national independence [4] which it had lost since 63 B.C. By such means the monarchy—this time dissociated from the high-priesthood—was once more revived in the person of Herod the Great by the Roman senate, on the joint recommendation of Antony and Octavian.[5]

The politics of the Jewish commonwealth were by no means the only problem Judaism thrust before the Romans. Other, and no less serious, difficulties were created by the troublesome Jewish colonies in the provinces, and in Rome itself. For instance, we know from Cicero that the Jews of Rome, by their numbers and their craft, were able to influence the political meetings of the Roman people and the decisions of the jury courts.[6] We know from him also that the synagogues of Italy and the provinces sent yearly to the temple at Jerusalem enough gold to cause some Roman statesmen to fear lest the financial balance of the empire be disturbed.[7]

To this manifold Jewish problem Augustus was to find a solution when he emerged from the battle of Actium the undisputed master of the world. The programme first worked out by him was followed by all the Julio-Claudian emperors, except Caligula. What that programme was, and how it was carried out down to the time of Nero, will be reviewed in this note, which will take up—first, the affairs of Judea; secondly, those of the Diaspora.

## I

Augustus.    When Augustus began the reconstruction of the eastern provinces (31 B.C.) he was faced with the alternative of re-establishing in Judea some arrangement like that first introduced by Pompey, that is, administering

---

[1] Jos. *Ant.* xiv. 3. 2.    [2] Jos. *B.J.* i. 7. 6-7 ; *Ant.* xiv. 4. 4.
[3] Jos. *B.J.* i. 13. 9-11 ; *Ant.* xiv. 13. 9-10.
[4] On the later vicissitudes of Judea cf. Jos. *B.J.* i. 8. 2-5 ; *Ant.* xiv. 5. 2-4.
[5] Jos. *B.J.* i. 14. 4 ; *Ant.* xiv. 14. 4-5.
[6] *Pro Flacc.* xxviii. (66-69).    [7] *Ibid.*

the country directly, or of leaving the *status quo*, that is, allowing Herod to continue as king.[1] He chose the latter course. The resourceful Herod, who had faithfully adhered to Mark Antony in the latter's struggles against Parthia and the young Caesar, found an adroit way of transferring his allegiance to the new master.[2] Augustus, for his part, received him as a friend. He not only confirmed him as king of Judea, but, on various occasions, enlarged his domains by considerable additions of Jewish and non-Jewish territories.[3]

Herod appears as the very man Rome needed at that juncture to safe- Herod. guard her interests along part of the Syrian frontier, and keep the rebellious sons of Israel well in hand. Fully aware that they hated the western invader as profoundly as they had ever hated the Seleucids, Augustus perceived that the Roman control of Judea through a vassal king of the Jewish faith would be less troublesome and more effective than direct administration. In Herod's favour it could be said also that, as he himself cleverly pointed out, he had showed by his loyal conduct towards Antony that he could be an invaluable friend to Augustus. At the same time he had proved that he fully realized he could reign only by the grace of Rome.[4] By his record, then, he could be trusted. Besides, he could hardly be surpassed as an intermediary between Judaism and Hellenism. For, notwithstanding his show of orthodox piety,[5] he steadfastly fostered Hellenistic culture not only in the mixed areas of his realm,[6] but, in a lesser degree, even in Jerusalem.[7] Such a policy, needless to say, would recommend him more strongly to the Romans. Thus between the emperor and the vassal king there grew up a mutual understanding and trust which ended only with Herod's death. The frequency of their meetings shows that Augustus had ample opportunity for guiding or, at least, seconding

---

[1] The best work on the history of Judea at this time is by E. Schürer, *Geschichte des jüdischen Volkes im Zeitalter Jesu Christi*, quoted in this article by the pages of the 2nd edition. (See also H. Grätz, *Geschichte der Juden von den ältesten Zeiten bis auf die Gegenwart*, 11 vols., Leipzig, 1853–1876; and H. Ewald, *Geschichte des Volkes Israel*, 8 vols., Göttingen, 1843–1859; W. D. Morrison, *The Jews under Roman Rule*, New York, 1890; S. Mathews, *A History of New Testament Times in Palestine*, New York, 1904; J. S. Riggs, *History of the Jewish People during the Maccabean and Roman Periods*, New York, 1900; J. Juster, *Les Juifs dans l'Empire Romain*, 2 vols., Paris, 1914; J. Felten, *Neutestamentliche Zeitgeschichte*, 2 vols., 2-3 ed., Regensburg, 1925; M. S. Ginsburg, *Rome et la Judée, contribution à l'histoire de leurs relations politiques*, Paris, 1928; Th. H. Robinson, J. W. Hunkin, F. C. Burkitt, *Palestine in General History* (Schweich Lectures, 1926), London, 1929; H. Dessau, *Geschichte der römischen Kaiserzeit*, ii. 2, Leipzig, 1930, chap. xii. § 10, pp. 706-831.)

[2] Jos. *B.J.* i. 20. 1-2 ; *Ant.* xv. 6. 5-7.

[3] Jos. *B.J.* i. 20. 1-4 ; *Ant.* xv. 6. 5-7 ; xv. 7. 3 ; xv. 10. 1-3 ; Dio liv. 9. 3.

[4] Jos. *B.J.* i. 20. 1-2 ; *Ant.* xv. 6. 5-7. Cf. Schürer, *op. cit.* vol. i. p. 307.

[5] Jos. *B.J.* i. 21. 1 ; *Ant.* xv. 11. 1-6.

[6] Jos. *B.J.* i. 21. 2-4 and 11-12 ; *Ant.* xv. 9. 5 ; xvi. 5.

[7] Jos. *B.J.* i. 21. 1-12 ; *Ant.* xv. 8 ; xv. 10. 4.

Herod's internal policies, and that the two were cordial, even affectionate, towards each other.[1] Schürer justly remarks that the unbounded confidence Augustus had in him may be seen in his recommendation to certain governors of Syria that they take counsel with Herod in all matters of importance.[2]

It would appear that Herod shaped his internal policy with a view to securing an unceasing flow of sympathy and approval from the Roman who was past master in the art of *divide et impera*. His repeated offences against the tenets of the Pharisees who at that time were in full ascendancy, his persecution of the Sadducees, and his practical suppression of the Sanhedrin where they had a preponderance,[3] may have been partly carried out with a design to show his suzerain that he was entirely detached from the aims of the Jewish race. At any rate, it was clear that he felt no need of relying on any of the Jewish parties, but rather on the support of Rome, on the assistance of the Hellenistic counsellors whom he called to his court, and on the protection of mercenary troops which he recruited from among the Gentiles.[4] But despite this political attitude towards the Jewish homeland, Herod contributed immensely to the realization of the unity of Judaism. This is shown chiefly by his appointment of Palestinian, Babylonian, and Alexandrian Jews to the exalted position of high-priest, and by his untiring championing of the rights and aspirations of the Jews of the Diaspora.[5] This last policy of his became a cardinal principle with his descendants, especially Agrippa I., as we shall see. His subjects, however, were not assuaged by such remote benefits. They felt that his rule was oppressive, and they rebelled against him in the last months of his life. The rebellion had a drawn-out and disastrous sequel, as it gathered new impetus after the king's death. To put an end to it, the governor of Syria, Quintilius Varus, had to make two armed expeditions into Palestine, but was at last able to re-establish order, thanks to his imposing forces and his stern measures of repression.[6]

The settlement of Judea after Herod.

Meantime Augustus was studying the difficult situation. His main problem was whether to continue the rule of the house of Herod, or yield to the demands of the Jewish people to free them once for all from the hated dynasty, and allow them to live according to their ancient constitution—whatever that meant—under Roman supervision. The political incapacity or insincerity of the Jewish leaders could not be more manifest. For at the very time that their representatives were beseeching the emperor for national liberty supervised by him, they rose against Sabinus, the procurator whom Augustus had sent to govern the country pending his final adjudication of the case. It was to quell this revolt that Varus made his second Palestinian expedition. Evidently, even in the face of armed opposition, Augustus thought that the Herodian policies, with all their faults, were the best under the circumstances, since he brushed aside all

---

[1] Jos. *B.J.* i. 20. 4 ; *Ant.* xv. 10. 3.    [2] *Ibid.*

[3] Jos. *Ant.* xii. 3. 2 ; xvi. 2. 3-5 ; xvi. 6. 1-8.

[4] Jos. *B.J.* i. 33. 9 ; *Ant.* xvii. 8. 3.

[5] Jos. *Ant.* xii. 3. 2 ; xvi. 2. 3-5.

[6] Jos. *B.J.* ii. 5. 1-3 ; *Ant.* xvii. 10, 9-10,

suggestions of reform and allowed Herod's dynasty to continue to rule
Palestine.   Complying with the king's will except on a few minor points,
he gave Archelaus, the eldest son, Judea, Samaria, and Idumea with the
title of ethnarch, and the promise that he would get later the title of king
if he should prove worthy of it.   Antipas received Galilee and Perea ;
and Philip got Batanea, Trachonitis, Auranitis, Gaulonitis, and Iturea.
Both ruled with the title of tetrarch.[1]

Augustus's faith in Archelaus was doomed to disappointment.   After a Archelaus.
reign of nine years that inept prince was summoned to Rome to answer
a long list of grievances lodged against him by both Jews and Samaritans,
and was deposed.   His principate was made a provincial administrative
district, in charge of a procurator of its own, over whom the governor of
Syria seems to have enjoyed a certain measure of supervision, at least in
matters of major importance.[2]   Such is the story as told by Josephus.[3]
Yet Augustus may have had in view the defence of Syria against Parthian
machinations.   We are led to this hypothesis from the coincidence that,
not many years afterwards, two other kingdoms, Cappadocia and Commagene, were reduced to the provincial status for the sake of defending
Syria.[4]   It is true that this measure was adopted some time later, in A.D.
17 ; but there is reason for believing that it had been advised by Augustus
himself.[5]   We know that the whole Syrian problem was considered unsatisfactory in Rome, and for that reason Germanicus was dispatched
thither with extraordinary powers to work out a more suitable arrangement.
The other fact, that, after the death of Philip, Tiberius joined his tetrarchy
to Syria, would seem to point out that Augustus, in default of a strong man
of the type of Herod to rule Palestine, may have revised his plans and
reached the conclusion that the entire country had better be reduced to
the provincial status.

It should not be imagined that the Romans' direct administration of The pro-
Judea (A.D. 6–41), with the exception of the last two years of Caligula's curators.
reign, was a period of tyranny.   The contrary seems to be true.   A census
was taken early for the purpose of determining the rate of taxation.[6]
Henceforth taxes were probably lighter, since, on one hand, there was no
longer a royal court to maintain, and, on the other, the Roman governor
was of the equestrian order, that is, one of the second rank.[7]   The too
frequent depositions of the high priest, whose term of office should have

---

[1] This paragraph is based on Jos. *B.J.* ii. 1-5 and 6. 1-3, and *Ant.* xvii. 8-11.
Cf. Luke iii. 1.

[2] See Mommsen, *Römische Geschichte*, vol. v., Berlin, 1885, p. 509, note 1 ;
O. Hirschfeld, *Sitzungber. der Berl. Acad.*, 1889, pp. 440-442 ; Schürer, *op. cit.*
vol. i. pp. 380-381 ; A. Domaszewski, ' Kleine Beiträge zur Kaisergeschichte,'
in *Philologus* (lxvii.), 1908, pp. 9-11.

[3] *B.J.* ii. 7. 3; ii. 8. 1 ; *Ant.* xvii. 13-xviii. 1. 1.   Cf. Dio lv. 27. 6.

[4] Tac. *Ann.* ii. 56. 4-5.   Cf. Dio lvii. 17. 7.

[5] Mommsen, *Röm. Gesch.* vol. v. p. 375.

[6] Jos. *Ant.* xviii. 1. 1.

[7] Tacitus says that " provinciae Syria atque Judaea, fessae oneribus,
deminutionem tributi orabant " (*Ann.* ii. 42. 7).

been lifelong, was probably the most patent infringement of the Jewish constitution. This policy aimed at weakening organized national opposition ; yet the Romans did not inaugurate it, but inherited it from Herod and Archelaus. The custody of the high priest's robe by the Romans was another act of suzerainty which violated ancient tradition ; but in this case also the Roman government continued a policy that had been started by Herod. A further restriction of the high priest's prerogatives was the supervision of the temple's finances by the Romans. But in all other respects the national leadership of the high priest became a greater reality, because, with the procurator living in Caesarea in deference to Jewish sentiment, he was the only great authority in the holy city. Under the new form of government, the nation " had larger room to manage their own affairs in their own way than under Herod."[1]    The Sanhedrin became once more the constitutional body governing the country,[2] as it assumed the powers once wielded by the king. Local officials, now free from Roman interference, became amenable to it. As of old, it had complete control over the administration of civil justice, while its authority in criminal cases was limited only in those instances in which it pronounced a death sentence, for the execution of which the ratification of the procurator was necessary.[3] A great privilege granted to the nation was exemption from regular military service.[4]

The provincial régime seemed degrading to the Jews, its mild character notwithstanding. It was challenged while Augustus was still living by a party of irreconcilables which may be termed the extreme left of the Pharisees.[5] They repudiated the doctrine of passive resistance elaborated in the days of Herod by conservative leaders such as Pollio and Sameas,[6] who had taught the people that it was God's will they should suffer under vexatious rulers. The new school believed in action—open, organized, ceaseless, violent action. Later on they took, or were given, the name of Zealots.[7] According to Josephus it was these men who roused the people's anti-Roman passions to white heat, and led them, in A.D. 66, to armed rebellion and to ruin.[8]

The tetrarchies.    Augustus's settlement in the tetrarchies continued unchanged for many years. As both these political districts were inhabited by a mixed population, Philip and Antipas found it advisable to make many concessions to the Hellenistic spirit of that age. Nevertheless both princes befriended the claims of Judaism, as may be seen, for instance, from their joint remonstrance against Pilate's display of heathenish emblems in Jerusalem.[9]

---

[1] G. F. Moore, *Judaism in the First Centuries of the Christian Era*, 3 vols., Cambridge, Mass., 1927–1930, vol. i. p. 82.

[2] Jos. *Ant.* xx. 10. 1.

[3] Cf. Schürer, *op. cit.* vol. ii. pp. 160 ff. ; and J. Juster, *Les Juifs dans l'Empire Romain*, 2 vols., Paris, 1914, vol. ii. pp. 133 ff.

[4] Jos. *Ant.* xiv. 10. 6. Cf. Mommsen, ' Die Conscriptionsordnung der römischen Kaiserzeit,' in *Hermes*, 1884, pp. 1-79, 210-234.

[5] Cf. Jos. *Ant.* xviii. 1. 1 and 6.    [6] *Ibid.* xv. 1. 1.

[7] See Vol. I. pp. 425 ff.    [8] Jos. *B.J.* ii. 8. 1 ; *Ant.* xviii. 1. 1 and 6.

[9] Phil. *Leg.* 38 (Mangey ii. pp. 589 f.).

Philip, who seems to have governed with moderation, died in A.D. 33 or 34. We have seen that Tiberius incorporated his territory with Syria. Caligula, however, granted it to Agrippa, a grandson of Herod (A.D. 37), together with the title of king.

The third of Herod's reigning sons, Antipas, came to a sorry end. Antipas. Tiberius allowed him to rule ; but Caligula deposed him (A.D. 39),[1] and added his tetrarchy to the kingdom of Agrippa. Probably Caligula had no other motive than simple friendship for his extraordinary favours to Agrippa. Placed in so high a position, Agrippa was to play an honourable rôle in the defence of the Jews in Judea and abroad. Two years later he received from Claudius the remaining portion of Herod's old kingdom. Thus Judea from an insignificant provincial appendage became once more the centre of a considerable Palestinian state.

A cardinal policy of Augustus, to which Tiberius adhered scrupulously, The Jews was the exemption of the Jewish race from emperor worship. The cult and worship of the living sovereign, symbolic of the relations between him and his of the subjects, was not a new thing in the Roman empire. It had been elaborated Emperor. in the Greek world, and had found universal acceptance. Since the Roman government was republican, the Greeks as well as the barbarians who fell under its sway worshipped the abstract goddess Roma. But when Augustus grafted the principate on the trunk of republican institutions, the provincials saw in his person the incarnation of the mighty power of Rome. To all of them, who had been unspeakably oppressed, he appeared as a divine agent who would save them from their long-standing ills, and partly, although not principally, for that reason they, of their own accord, worshipped him as a god. By a felicitous stroke of genius Augustus fostered this universal feeling of the subject peoples. He approved everywhere, except in Italy, the erection of statues and the building of altars and temples to him as to a god, the institution of annual feasts and other periodical celebrations, and the establishment of priestly colleges to maintain his cult either jointly with that of Roma or else alone. Participation in the imperial cult became early an outward sign of loyalty to Rome and the emperor, and, in time, a test of political conformity. All the subject peoples were bound to it, at least collectively at first, if not individually. But this politico-religious requirement imposed no hardship on their beliefs since the imperial cult did not exclude the worship of other gods, even where these gods were national and had an ethnic and political significance of their own.

In the case of the Jews, however, it was clear to Augustus that they could not comply with the emperor's cult, since their own worship of Jehovah was of the most exclusive and uncompromising character. The fact that none of our sources contains any references to difficulties in this regard between the first two emperors and the Jews would seem to indicate that they had been exempted from the general law of emperor worship.[2]

---

[1] Jos. *Ant.* xviii. 7. 2. It would seem that the foolish prince had entered into a secret alliance with Parthia, and had actually begun to accumulate provisions for a joint action against the empire.

[2] Cf. Juster, *Les Juifs*, i. p. 353.

In lieu of the common forms and implications of that cult, other forms were allowed the Jews to give expression to the ideas involved in it without doing violence to their scruples. Of course the substitute forms were obligatory for all the Jews. In common with the other subject peoples they took an oath of allegiance to the emperor on his accession to the throne and at other stated times.[1] And if they did not sacrifice to him, yet they sacrificed for him twice a day in the temple, and more solemnly on special occasions.[2] If it is true, as Philo maintains, that the victims for those sacrifices were provided by Augustus himself,[3] we may see in that a tacit acquiescence of the first emperor in what was indeed a dispensation to the Jews from the religious-political test required of all other provincials. Outside of Palestine they prayed for him in their synagogues, and, if they could not erect temples and statues to him, yet they dedicated their synagogues in his honour, and placed therein tablets, wreaths, shields, and standards, and had recourse to various other symbols, to express their devotion to him.[4]

Tiberius.

Several events during the reign of Tiberius reveal that that emperor's policy towards the religious sentiments of the Jews was modelled upon that of Augustus, that is, was one of extreme tolerance. His order to Pilate to remove from the praetorium in Jerusalem certain votive shields to which the people objected [5] ; his removal of the same official based on the latter's cruelty to a band of religious fanatics [6] ; the return to the high priest of the precious vestment which had been in the possession of the Roman procurator since the annexation of Judea in A.D. 6 [7] ; and the delicacy of the governor of Syria, Vitellius, in causing his legions to march from Antioch to Petra by a roundabout route, lest the sight of their standards should give offence to the Jews [8] ;—all these acts bear an unmistakable mark of studied consideration and respect for the religious beliefs of the Jewish subjects, and, we may state, fidelity to the conciliatory programme of Augustus.

Caligula.

Caligula broke away from this policy of toleration which had worked well. He attempted to install his statue in the temple, and force the whole nation in and outside Judea to recognize his divinity, which, strange as it may appear to us, he took quite seriously.[9] His order to that effect plunged the whole Jewish world into a state of extraordinary ferment. There would have ensued dire consequences in Judea but for the prudence and skill of the governor of Syria, the tolerant and sympathetic Petronius, who had been charged with the execution of the emperor's order. The situation was opportunely saved by the murder of

---

[1] Phil. *Leg.* 32 (M. ii. 580) ; Jos. *Ant.* xviii. 5. 3.   See also xvii. 1. 4.

[2] Phil. *Leg.* 32 and 45 (M. ii. 580, 598).

[3] *Ibid.* 23 (M. ii. 569).   But see also Jos. *C. Ap.* ii. 6.

[4] Phil. *In Flacc.* 7 (M. ii. 524).   Cf. Juster, *Les Juifs*, i. pp. 339-354.

[5] Phil. *Leg.* 38 (M. ii. 589 f.).         [6] Jos. *Ant.* xviii. 4. 1-2.

[7] *Ibid.* xviii. 4. 3.             [8] *Ibid.* xviii. 5. 3.

[9] Phil. *Leg.* 11-15 and 25 (M. ii. 556-561 and 569) ; Jos. *Ant.* xviii. 7. 2; Dio lix. 26 and 28.

the tyrant (January 24, A.D. 41), which was hailed by the Jews everywhere as a clear intervention of divine providence.[1]

The accession of Claudius marked a new era of goodwill, one might *Claudius.* perhaps say of imperial redress, to the Jews everywhere. Claudius, who took Augustus as his model in the conduct of government, adopted in regard to Palestine a policy which reproduced at once the outward marks and the informing spirit which existed under Augustus. We have seen that he ended the direct administration of Judea, and re-established the old Herodian kingdom in its whole extent. From the Roman point of view this was good politics, as it meant retreat with honour from the dangerous position taken by Caligula. Indeed, the grant of independence under a king of their own was calculated to pacify the roused nation. To say *Agrippa.* that Claudius restored to Agrippa his grandfather's kingdom simply as a reward for Agrippa's activities in placing him on the throne of the Caesars, is telling only a small part of that story. The two men had been reared together in Rome, and knew each other well. Agrippa, with his Jewish faith and blood,[2] his great ability, his mild character and attested piety, his proved patronage of the Jewish cause everywhere, and his loyalty to Rome,[3] was the ideal man (as Herod had been under Augustus) to bridge the chasm which had been created in Judea by the incapacity or the insolence of some of the Roman procurators, and still more by the sacrilegious attempts of the insane Caligula. We have no proof for asserting that Claudius outlined for his vassal king a policy of conciliation, but we may scarcely doubt that such was the case.[4] The emperor took the first propitious occasion to declare, mainly for the benefit of the Jewish world, that he would not offend his contemporaries by posing as a god.[5] Briefly, Claudius and Agrippa followed a common programme which consisted in working concertedly for the re-establishment of those peaceful relations between the suzerain and the subject race which existed under Augustus and Herod.[6] On one side, Claudius issued a number of decrees favourable to the Jews of the homeland and the Diaspora.[7] Agrippa, on the other

---

[1] Jos. *Ant.* xix. 1. 2.

[2] According to Deut. xxiii. 8 the descendants in the third generation of those who had embraced the Jewish faith were full-fledged Jews. Cf. Schürer, *Geschichte*, vol. i. p. 465, n. 27.

[3] He styles himself βασιλεὺς φιλόκαισαρ εὐσεβὴς καὶ φιλορώμαιος. See Le Bas et Waddington, *Voyage archéologique, Inscriptions*, t. iii. partie i. no. 2365.

[4] When Claudius appointed two other kings, one over the Cherusci, the other over the Parthians, he outlined for them the course of action he wished them to follow. His speeches on both occasions have been preserved in rhetorical paraphrases by Tacitus (*Ann.* xi. 16 ; xii. 11). Josephus has an account of the discussion between Claudius and Agrippa for the settlement of the Jewish question in the Diaspora (*Ant.* xix. 5).

[5] Claudius's letter to the Alexandrines, line 49, in H. I. Bell, *Jews and Christians in Egypt*, London, 1924, p. 24.

[6] Keim (in D. Schenkel, *Bibellexicon*, iii. p. 55) and Schürer (*Geschichte*, vol. i. p. 469) agree that Agrippa " was a careful imitator of old Herod."

[7] Jos. *Ant.* xix. 5. 2-3 ; xix. 6. 3.

side, inaugurated a government that must have been satisfactory to the greater number of Jews, as may be gathered from the pietistic praises of Josephus [1] and the Talmud,[2] and the hearty co-operation accorded him by the Pharisaic party.[3]

The pro-<br>curators<br>after<br>Agrippa.

Unfortunately Agrippa's untimely death ruined Claudius's hopes of establishing lasting peace in Judea. As his only son was a minor, seventeen years old, the emperor deemed it too risky to entrust the turbulent state to a regency, but, instead, placed it anew under direct imperial administration.[4] Thus Claudius, after having followed the earliest Jewish policy of Augustus, followed also his latest one, namely, that which had made Judea a province when no Jew could be found strong or wise enough to rule it. At the same time Claudius took pains to make the new measure less distasteful. He forbade Marsus, the bellicose governor of Syria, who twice had crossed Agrippa's path, to enter Judea [5]; and appointed over the sulky country excellent procurators who, by patience and kindliness, kept it at peace.[6] At the same time he restricted procuratorial interference by returning once more into the keeping of the Jews the high priest's robe. He also transferred to Agrippa's brother, Herod of Chalcis, and after his death to Agrippa II., the right to appoint the high priest and supervise the administration of the temple.[7] Again, he removed from office and punished the procurator Cumanus because he had offended the people.[8] The appointment of Felix was undoubtedly a bad one, if we judge it from the state of near anarchy into which he allowed Judea to sink. Nevertheless in passing judgement upon Claudius's responsibility for sending him to that country, one should not forget that the appointment was made at the request of the high priest Jonathan,[9] and that the procurator's wrongs were acts of omission rather than commission. One wonders what procurator could have proved successful in a country where the Zealots had been teaching a whole generation that relentless opposition to the Roman government was willed by God. The appearance of organized guerrilla warfare forced Felix to resort to acts which appeared unduly cruel to the excited populace, and, in turn, increased the fury and influence of the Zealots.[10]

Nero.

The government of Nero made the mistake of allowing Felix to continue in office. That was due to the influence of the latter's brother, Pallas, the powerful secretary of the treasury. In the main, Nero followed the Jewish policy of his predecessor. We know, for instance, that in a violent quarrel between the Greeks and the Jews of Caesarea concerning local citizenship, he gave a decision adverse to the Jews, along the lines established by Claudius in a similar case at Alexandria. But on several occasions he

---

[1] Jos. *Ant.* xix. 7. 3.    [2] *Mishnah*, Bikkurim, iii. 4.
[3] *Mishnah*, Sota, vii. 8. Cf. Schürer, *Geschichte*, vol. i. pp. 464 f.
[4] Jos. *Ant.* xix. 9. 2.    [5] *Ibid.*
[6] Jos. *B.J.* ii. 11. 6.    [7] Jos. *Ant.* xx. 1.
[8] Jos. *B.J.* ii. 12. 3-7; *Ant.* xx. 6. Cf. Tac. *Ann.* xii. 54. 7.
[9] Jos. *B.J.* ii. 12. 8; *Ant.* xx. 8. 5.
[10] Jos. *B.J.* ii. 13. 2-3; *Ant.* xx. 8. 5-6. Josephus places the rise of the Sicarii against this background.

showed them favour, if for no other reason than to please his mistress Poppaea who seems to have been a proselyte.[1]  Possibly the rapacity of his procurators may have had his connivance, as he himself, to secure the stupendous sums he needed for his extravagances, was engaged in extraordinary acts of extortion.  Josephus relates that it was an act of procuratorial extortion, coupled with the emperor's settlement of the Caesarean question, that acted as the proverbial match applied to a powder magazine.[2] In conclusion, it may be said that ancient and modern historians are too prone to accuse the Romans of oppression.[3]  Certainly no one can deny its existence ; but ultimately the responsibility for the disastrous war which ruined the Jewish nation lay in the dangerous doctrine of the intervention of God who would deliver his people from the sacrilegious foreigner.  By keeping the masses in a feverish state of expectancy, that doctrine made pacification impossible.  Worst of all, it lent itself to abuse by all sorts of cranks and rascals.[4]

## II

For one reason or another, the Jewish population scattered throughout the empire gave much concern to every emperor in the first century of the Christian era.[5]  As their colonies literally dotted the eastern portion of the empire, and were found also in every country of the west [6] ; and as every Jew, with rare exception, held himself uncompromisingly aloof from the natives, clashes often arose between the two elements.  We are told that Mithridates took from the island of Cos eight hundred talents belonging to the Jews of Asia.[7]  This story, together with Cicero's statement in regard to the huge tribute the Jewish colonies of the Diaspora sent to the temple at Jerusalem every year, affords us some idea of their numerical strength, if not of their economic well-being.  The figures of the Jewish population given by Philo and Josephus are evidently exaggerated.[8] Modern historians make more moderate estimates.  Harnack places their number in and outside Judea at four or four and a half million persons.[9] Juster brings it up to six or seven millions.[10]  In Egypt alone they were one million, or from one-seventh to one-eighth of the whole population.[11] Of that number, two hundred thousand lived in Alexandria.  It was in Alexandria, and chiefly because of their large number and their wealth,

The Diaspora.

---

[1] Jos. *Ant.* xx. 8. 11.                    [2] *B.J.* ii. 13. 7 ; ii. 14. 4.

[3] Cf. Moore, *Judaism*, i. p. 82.

[4] Cf. Jos. *B.J.* ii. 13. 4 ;  *Ant.* xx. 8. 5-6 ; Acts xxi. 38.

[5] For a good bibliography on the Jews of the Diaspora see Dora Askowith, *The Toleration of the Jews under Julius Caesar and Augustus*, Columbia Dissertation, New York, 1915.

[6] Cf. Strabo in Jos. *Ant.* xiv. 7. 2.  See also Juster, *Les Juifs*, i. pp. 180-209.

[7] Jos. *Ant.* xiv. 7. 2.

[8] *Leg.* 31 (M. ii. 577) ; *B.J.* ii. 14. 3 ; ii. 18. 1 ; vi. 9. 3 ; vii. 3. 3.

[9] *Die Mission und Ausbreitung des Christentums in der ersten drei Jahrhunderten*, 2 vols., 3rd ed., Leipzig, 1915, vol. i. p. 10.

[10] Juster, *Les Juifs*, i. p. 210.

[11] Phil. *In Flacc.* 6 (M. ii. 523) ;  Jos. *B.J.* ii. 16. 4.

that the Jews drew upon themselves the jealousy and hatred of the citizen body more violently than in any other place.

The scattered communities, large and small, were all united by strong spiritual bonds to each other and to Jerusalem. They were conscious of their formidable cohesion, and they were not afraid to flaunt their ecumenical strength in the face of governors and emperors to forestall, by intimidation, any pending measure they regarded as obnoxious. They were nowhere segregated in ghettos, as they were afterwards in the Middle Ages, but on account of their scrupulous abstention from the official cult, the social activities, the cultural aspirations, and even the diet of the peoples among whom they lived, they aroused suspicion practically everywhere.[1] As the Roman empire was an association of city-states, each with its own laws and customs, which Rome tried earnestly to respect, the problem of each Jewish community was primarily one which concerned the city-state in which it was situated. But as Rome had acquired by degrees the right of legislating for her allied and subject cities and kingdoms on matters of general policy, in fact on any and all matters, the Jews from all parts of the empire appealed to the Roman authorities to redress the hostile acts of the provincials or the adverse decisions of local magistrates. It would appear that the Roman government intervened in their favour in almost every case, and as a matter of general policy, not only because it had pledged itself to certain obligations towards the Jewish nation, but also because it had undertaken that its allied and subject cities and kingdoms should likewise fulfil those same obligations.[2] Thus, in the words of Juster, Jewish privileges were elevated to the rank of Roman laws.[3] Freedom of worship was the battle-cry of the Jews, and they obtained it readily in a world which had made freedom of worship a basic principle of international polity. But freedom of worship had an extremely wide range for the Jews who identified religion with nationality. For them it was equivalent to an independent religious, social, economic, and political existence in the midst of the Gentile communities.

Before these sweeping claims the Roman government adopted a policy of tolerance, since, as we have already hinted, it found it impolitic to resort to one of persecution. It was Julius Caesar who first laid the groundwork for the unique juridical status accorded to the Jews. There can be little doubt that he thus rewarded them for the help they gave him in his campaign in Egypt.[4] Josephus reproduces several edicts of the dictator, of consuls, praetors, and provincial governors, as well as some resolutions by the senate, forbidding the allied and subject city-states to interfere with their rights, and defining the nature of their privileges.[5] In the main, they may be listed as follows : freedom of assembly for the purpose of worship-

---

[1] On the Greek point of view see Jos. *Ant.* xvi. 2. 5.

[2] Cf. the edict to the Parians in Jos. *Ant.* xiv. 10. 8. See also *Ant.* xvi. 2. 4.

[3] *Les Juifs*, i. p. 221.

[4] Cf. Jos. *Ant.* xiv. 10. 2 ; xvi. 2. 4.

[5] *Ibid.* xiv. 10. The cities to which those edicts were issued were Delos, Ephesus, Sardis, Alexandria, Laodicea, Tralles, Pergamum, and Halicarnassus.

ping their god, the right to collect offerings for the temple, exemption from military service,[1] and a broad recognition of their corporate existence according to the laws of their fathers.   What is more significant, these privileges were not granted to the Jewish nationals (*peregrini*) only, but also to those individuals who had become Roman citizens.

These categorical instructions, however, were far from obtaining ready and universal compliance, and intermittent persecutions against the Jews sprang up in many sections of the vast empire.   The cities of Ionia, for instance, confiscated their sacred money, laid tribute upon them, brought them before their tribunals, and forced them to do services on the Sabbath.[2] Similar abuses took place in Cyrenaica and the province of Asia.   Before these acts of violence, Augustus maintained everywhere the juridical policy formulated by the great Julius, whether his answer to the complaints of the Jews was given directly by himself, or by his legates and procurators.[3] In every instance the magistrates of the cities concerned were directed to let the Jews assemble and worship freely, and organize their social life according to the customs of their fathers.

*Persecution of Jews in the Empire.*

Tiberius's attitude towards the Jews of the Diaspora was not different from that of Augustus, if we are to believe Philo.[4]   But the Jewish philosopher seems to contradict himself when he attributes to Tiberius a desire to destroy the whole Jewish race.[5]   A statement by Eusebius qualifies this passage in the sense that it was against the Jews of Rome that Tiberius's vindictive measures were aimed.[6]   Philo makes Sejanus responsible for the emperor's anti-Jewish policy.   I shall deal a little later with Tiberius's hostility to the Jewish colony in the capital.   Here I only wish to remark that it is not safe to generalize about his policy towards Judaism at large from his treatment of the Roman colony, for the reason that the two problems were in many respects unlike.   Indeed, it may be asserted that his treatment of the Jews of the capital did not influence in the least his treatment of the Jews in their homeland, where we have seen that he displayed the greatest amount of tolerance, respect, and protection of their beliefs and practices.   Of these two divergent attitudes of Tiberius, the latter has the greater claim to be considered as a basis for any *a priori* conclusion about his dealings with the Jews of the Diaspora. On this point it may be noted also that had Tiberius been hostile to the Jews of the Diaspora, Philo would have hardly described his reign as a golden age for the provinces, and Josephus would not show a tendency to praise him.[7]   But apart from these reflections, it would not seem that Tiberius, the staunch conservative, would depart from that policy of tolerance which since the days of Caesar had become a corner-stone of imperial legislation,

*Tiberius.*

[1] The Jews could not take an oath of allegiance to the imperator since they would have to swear by pagan deities and on standards surmounted by eagles.

[2] Jos. *Ant.* xvi. 2. 3-4.          [3] *Ibid.* xvi. 2. 5 ; xvi. 6. 1-7.
[4] *Leg.* 24 (M. ii. 569).          [5] *Ibid.*
[6] *Eccl. Hist.* ii. 5. 7.

[7] Cf. P. Manfrin, *Gli Ebrei sotto la dominazione romana*, 3 vols., Roma, 1888–1892, vol. iii. p. 218.

and from which no other ruler departed, save Caligula.  As a matter of fact, Tiberius " ordered the provincial governors to change none of the existing customs " regarding the Jews.[1]

Caligula.     Before Caligula had completed the first year of his reign, the world witnessed the beginning of a revolution in the form of government established by Augustus.  With a tenacity born of madness the new ruler endeavoured to establish a monarchy of the Hellenistic type.  His order to the Jews to worship him was but one aspect of that general policy. We have seen how that order affected Palestine.  In the Diaspora the most conspicuous chapter of that tragic story was written in Alexandria.  There the Greek, or citizen, population had developed an intense hatred of the Jews, since the latter, dissatisfied with the Ptolemaic régime, had welcomed the Roman invader.  The Jews enjoyed in the Egyptian capital more fully than anywhere else all those privileges and immunities for which, as we have seen, they also strove in Ionia, Asia, and Cyrenaica.  Since the time of the early Ptolemies they had formed in every sense a city within a city.  They lived under a communal constitution of their own, had their own record offices and law-courts, an ecclesia, an ethnarch, and, from Augustus on, a council in lieu of the ethnarchate.[2]  This unique juridical position placed them on such a near equality of privilege with the citizens that they had felt they could derive no additional advantage from the status of full, or *de jure*, citizenship which Ptolemy Philopator (221–203) tried to impose on them.  Therefore they resisted the king's attempt.[3]

The problem in Alexandria.     Under the Roman rule, however, they claimed that they were Alexandrian citizens *de jure* from the mere fact that they were native members of the Alexandrian Jewish community.  That is, they contended that there were two classes of Alexandrian citizens, themselves and the native Greeks, the citizenship of both races being juridically the same.  In all likelihood the reason for this new claim was their discovery that the Roman government would not admit to Roman citizenship any native of Egypt and Alexandria who did not first possess Alexandrian citizenship.  The Jewish contention reached an acute stage when Caligula's order that they worship him furnished an occasion to the Alexandrians to drive them from their houses, desecrate their synagogues, briefly, to make them feel that they were aliens in Alexandria, as Flaccus himself, the Roman prefect, had decided.  A state of war developed.  From both camps embassies were sent to Rome to lay the facts before the emperor.  The illustrious Philo was chairman of the Jewish embassy.  Apion, the first magistrate of Alexandria and a formidable polemist,[4] headed the Greek party. Caligula having been assassinated meantime, the solution of the troublesome question was left to his successor.

The edict of Claudius in Josephus.     Until recently our sole knowledge of Claudius's decision was gathered from an edict which Josephus ascribes to him, and quotes in full.[5]  But

---

[1] Phil. *Leg.* 24 (M. ii. 569).          [2] Phil. *In Flacc.* 10 (M. ii. 527-528).

[3] Cf. 3 Macc. iii. 2, 30.

[4] He is the man against whom Josephus wrote two books Περὶ ἀρχαιότητος Ἰουδαίων (*Contra Apionem*).

[5] *Ant.* xix. 5. 2.

this document offers serious difficulties. In the opening sentence, wherein the writer, that is, Claudius, poses the *status quaestionis*, it is stated explicitly that the Ptolemies had granted the Jews a citizenship equal to that of the Greeks (ἰσοπολιτεία), and it is implied that Augustus had confirmed it. . In the conclusion, however, where we should expect Claudius to settle above all other things that very question, he refers to it no longer, but, instead, issues a general order to the Alexandrians to respect the ancient privileges of the Jews. Some scholars have accused Claudius of inconsistency, while others have charged Josephus with forgery. The latter view rests on more solid ground, because, for one thing, Josephus has been found unreliable on other occasions. Besides, it does not seem likely that the imperial chancery at Rome, whence the decree emanated, was less acquainted with Alexandrian constitutional questions than the prefect Flaccus. Philo clearly states that the latter declared the Jews to be aliens in Alexandria.[1] This creates a serious problem, for it is hard to believe in general that an imperial legate could wilfully distort an imperial edict of so fundamental a character, and specifically that Flaccus could say that the Jews were aliens if Augustus had in truth enacted that they were citizens. The term ἰσοπολιτεία of the Josephean document is thus open to suspicion, and the suspicion is increased when Josephus, writing a few years later against Apion whom he knew to be well posted in Alexandrian affairs, does not say a word about ἰσοπολιτεία but states simply that Claudius confirmed to the Jews their ancient privileges.

Claudius's authentic decree was discovered eight or nine years ago in a Philadelphia (Egypt) papyrus, and published with great scholarship by H. I. Bell under the title *Jews and Christians in Egypt*, London, 1924. It is in the form of a letter addressed by the emperor himself to the city of Alexandria.[2] After disposing of other matters which are foreign to our subject, the emperor exhorts the Alexandrians to " offer no outrage to the Jews in the exercise of their traditional worship but permit them to observe their customs as in the days of Divus Augustus." [3] Then he continues : " I bid the Jews not to busy themselves about anything beyond what they have held hitherto . . . nor to strive in gymnasiarchic or *cosmetic* games, but to profit by what they possess, and enjoy in a city not their own an abundance of all good things." [4] From these and other passages it is clear that Claudius denied to the Jews the right of Alexandrian citizenship, and forbade them to seek after it [5] ; while, at the same time, he preserved

*The text of the edict in the Philadelphian papyrus.*

---

[1] *In Flacc.* 8 (M. ii. 527).

[2] One may debate whether this letter is a different document from the edict quoted by Josephus, or is the basis upon which the Jewish historian constructed his own version.

[3] Claudius's letter, lines 85-88 (Bell, *Jews and Christians*, p. 25).

[4] Claudius's letter, lines 88-95.

[5] Legitimate sons of citizens only might be ephebi and take part in the activities of the gymnasium. Exclusion from the gymnasium was equivalent to exclusion from eligibility to citizenship.

for them their ancient customs and immunities, above all, freedom of worship.[1]

**The wider edict of Claudius.**

Claudius holds a more important place in regard to the Jewish question on account of another edict of his, also reproduced by Josephus, in which he lays down for the whole empire the same principle he had adopted for Alexandria.[2] Henceforth the Greeks everywhere were to permit the Jews to keep their ancient customs without opposition, and the Jews were forbidden to take a hostile attitude towards the pagan beliefs. This decree has been universally regarded as a new charter of liberties for the Jewish communities of the Diaspora.[3] And such it is. But it is also a clear demarcation of how far their privilege may extend. The Jews are given full liberty to be faithful observers of their laws individually and collectively in the midst of the heathen peoples, but not the liberty to make Jews of others. Thus the way was opened anew, and this time definitely, for that imposing imperial legislation which through stress and storm assured the Jews in every city of the empire a privileged position, at the same time stopping them from embarking on wholesale propaganda. Claudius's edict, so much needed after the ill-advised policy of Caligula, became a legal standard by which were regulated the relations between each Jewish community and the city that harboured it.[4] This is evident, among other instances, from Nero's settlement of the Greco-Jewish controversy at Caesarea.

**Jews and Latins.**

If the contact between Jews and Greeks created new problems throughout the East which were primarily political, the contact of Jews and Latins gave rise to preoccupations which were chiefly moral. In this respect, however, Judaism did not stand alone, but was one of many foreign cults which undermined Latin conservatism in religion and morality. For the sake of public safety and morality, the senate had endeavoured to stamp out the spread of those cults in Italy as early as the year 186 B.C. The Jewish religion was in many respects like other eastern cults. But in others it was different. While a morbid emotionalism may have been the chief attraction of the oriental cults in general, the appeal of Judaism is to

**In Rome.**

be sought in its uncompromising exclusiveness. The Jewish community in Rome exhibited from its infancy such an aggressive spirit of proselytism as to determine the government to banish the chief propagandists from the city (139 B.C.).[5] Despite this setback, the community grew in numbers

---

[1] On the extent of Jewish self-government in Alexandria see E. R. Goodenough, *The Jurisprudence of the Jewish Courts in Egypt : Legal Administration by the Jews under the Early Roman Empire as described by Philo Judaeus,* New Haven, 1929.

[2] *Ant.* xix. 5. 3.

[3] Cf. G. La Piana, ' Foreign Groups in Rome during the First Centuries of the Empire,' in *Harvard Theological Review,* 1927, p. 378.

[4] Cf. Petronius's order to the people of Doris (Jos. *Ant.* xix. 6. 3).

[5] Val. Max. *Epit.* i. 3. 3. According to Friedländer (*Darstellung aus der Sittengeschichte Roms,* 9th ed., 4 vols., Leipzig, 1919–1921, vol. iii. p. 206) the passages in question do not refer to the leaders of a Jewish colony in Rome,

and influence until it could affect, as we have seen, Roman politics and juries. It displayed its weight in the course of the civil wars, and had a hand in the Clodian riots. The degree of power and respectability it had Julius attained was recognized by Caesar, who, at the time he dissolved those clubs Caesar. and associations which could produce no proof of long standing,[1] exempted the Jewish synagogues.[2] The appreciation of the Roman Jews was amply attested by their remarkable demonstration of grief at his funeral.

Augustus maintained for them the privileges they had won under Augustus. Caesar, when he once more suppressed all colleges which could not give evidence of ancient and honourable standing or of senatorial approval.[3] But he went further in that he exempted the Jews by name.[4] His understanding of their beliefs was such that if the distribution of free corn happened on the Sabbath, when the Jews entitled to it could not participate, he would order a special distribution to be made for them on the following day.[5] It is possible that in recognition of such a marked benevolence one of the Roman synagogues honoured him by taking the name Augustensis,[6] probably at a time when the poorest folks in the capital adopted the cult of the Genius Augusti.

Some modern historians have given much prominence to Tiberius's Tiberius. harsh treatment of the Jews of Rome, but it would seem that the punishment meted out to them was part of a larger legislative programme aimed against oriental aliens in general, and undertaken for the purpose of purifying Italy from imported superstitious practices. The restoration of the old Roman morality and religion had been one of the major policies of Augustus. As this end could be attained best by discouraging foreign beliefs, Augustus took that course and, among other things, forbade the practice of astrology.[7] In this light the praise he gave his grandson Caius for refusing to worship at the temple in Jerusalem acquires new significance.[8] Clearly the first emperor's sympathy for the Jews did not mean approval of their proselytizing activities.

---

which could not exist as early as 139 B.C., but to those persons who had come to Rome as ambassadors of the Maccabees. Yet it is difficult to account for the power and prestige of the Jewish colony at Rome at the time of Cicero, if its beginning be identified with the importation of war prisoners by Pompey after 63 B.C. Cf. Radin, *The Jews among the Greeks and Romans*, p. 228. On the Jewish colony of Rome see, besides the work of La Piana cited above, p. 292, note 3; A. Berliner, *Geschichte der Juden in Rom*, 2 vols., Frankfurt a. M., 1893; H. Vogelstein und P. Rieger, *Geschichte der Juden in Rom*, 2 vols., Berlin, 1896–1895; G. Blustein, *Storia degli Ebrei in Roma dal 140 avanti Cristo ad oggi*, Roma, 1920.

[1] Suet. *Jul.* 42.

[2] Jos. *Ant.* xiv. 10. 8; xiv. 10. 12.

[3] Suet. *Aug.* 32.

[4] Cf. Jos. *Ant.* xvi. 2. 5; xvi. 6. 1-7; Phil. *Leg.* 40 (M. ii. 591-592).

[5] Phil. *Leg.* 23 (M. ii. 568-569). This section of Philo's treatise gives a full account of Augustus's attitude on the Jewish problem.

[6] Cf. *C.I.G.* 9902, 9903; *C.I.L.* vi. 29757; *Notizie degli Scavi*, 1900, p. 88.

[7] Dio lvi. 25. 5.                    [8] Suet. *Aug.* 93.

Just a few years after his death certain extraordinary events revealed the hopeless task of keeping oriental practices under control in the capital, and determined Tiberius to adopt repressive measures.  About the same time that the Roman aristocracy was soliciting from astrologers and magicians more eagerly than ever the revelation of signs announcing the death of the emperor,[1] a noble profligate, aided by the priests of Isis, by posing as Anubis seduced a Roman matron in the goddess's temple [2] ; and four Jewish rogues embezzled from another noblewoman, who had accepted the Jewish faith, some costly presents which at their instigation she had sent to the temple in Jerusalem.[3]  The almost contemporary occurrence of these scandals roused public opinion to a pitch of indignation, and gave Tiberius the psychological opportunity for taking a strong hand in the matter.  By a resolution of the senate astrologers and magicians from Mesopotamia and Egypt as well as Jews were deported to Sardinia and other provinces.[4]  If this stern measure was extended to all the Jews in Rome, it would be clearly a departure from the policy of Caesar and Augustus.  But it would rather seem that Tiberius's legislation in this regard was essentially punitive, that is, it was aimed against that crowd of fakes, charlatans, and rogues who had been convicted of guilt, or were highly suspected [5] ; and, if we follow Dio, against those fanatic Jews who, despite imperial disapproval, engaged more or less openly in making converts among the native Romans.[6]  A different interpretation seems hardly admissible, unless we disregard Dio's testimony and construe as calculated euphemism Philo's statement which I quote in a note,[7] and which I refer to this case, since I know of no other punishment inflicted by Tiberius upon the Jews.[8]  Indeed, as it has been said before, Philo not only holds Tiberius in high esteem, but he even absolves him of the charge of malevolence against his co-religionists, and blames Sejanus for the excessive zeal with which they were hunted and deported.

Caligula.

Caligula's order to the Jews to worship him does not seem to have distressed the Jewish community in Rome.  One reason may be found in

---

[1] Tac. *Ann.* ii. 27-32 ; Dio lvii. 15. 8.

[2] Jos. *Ant.* xviii. 3. 4.                                    [3] *Ibid.* xviii. 3. 5.

[4] Tacitus (*Ann.* ii. 85, 5) and Josephus (*Ant.* xviii. 3. 5) say that 4000 men were sent to Sardinia as militia.  The Latin historian states also that all who did not renounce their religion within a stated time were to be banished from Italy.  Cf. Suet. *Tib.* 36.

[5] Philo's statement is as follows : καὶ τοῖς πανταχόσε χειροτονουμένοις ὑπάρχοις ἐπέσκηψε (i.e. Tiberius) παρηγορῆσαι μὲν τοὺς κατὰ πόλεις τῶν ἀπὸ τοῦ ἔθνους, ὡς οὐκ εἰς πάντας προβάσης τῆς ἐπεξελεύσεως, ἀλλ' ἐπὶ μόνους τοὺς αἰτίους—ὀλίγοι δὲ ἦσαν (*Leg.* 24, M. ii. 569).

[6] τῶν τε Ἰουδαίων πολλῶν ἐς τὴν Ῥώμην συνελθόντων καὶ συχνοὺς τῶν ἐπιχωρίων ἐς τὰ σφέτερα ἔθη μεθιστάντων, τοὺς πλείονας ἐξήλασεν (Dio lvii. 18. 5a = Joann. Antioch. fr. 79, § 4 b, M. v. 20-22).

[7] See note 5 above.

[8] Probably Tiberius ordered the provincial governors to watch closely over the collection and destination of the temple tribute, and punish those found guilty of offences similar to that of the four notorious rogues of the capital.

the character of the capital city, which, despite its moral looseness, was still a citadel of old-fashioned Latin ideals, and stony ground for the growth of emperor-worship and other radical Hellenistic customs.  It is conceivable that the senatorial party may have aided Jewish resistance in the capital, while, at the same time, the presence of King Agrippa may have been of real help to the community at least in delaying compliance with the emperor's order.  At any rate it would seem that while the Jews of Palestine were passing through a harrowing ordeal during their negotiations with Petronius, and those in Alexandria were losing their properties, their lives, and their ancient privileges, the Jews of the capital went through no embarrassment worth recording.  The complete silence of Philo and Josephus on this point, not to speak of the pagan writers, would point to that conclusion.

Claudius, like Tiberius, took measures of repression against the Jewish Claudius. community of Rome while being friendly to those of the Diaspora.  Our information on this subject is gathered from Acts xviii. 1-2, which states that " Claudius had decreed that all the Jews should leave Rome " [1] ; from Suetonius, who says that "he expelled from Rome the Jews for having made (or who made) constant disturbances at the instigation of Chrestus " [2] ; and from Dio Cassius, who stresses the point that the Jews were not driven out owing to their great numbers, but were forbidden to hold meetings, though still allowed to continue their traditional mode of life.[3]  To these witnesses should be added a reference by Orosius to a passage in Josephus to the effect that in the ninth year of Claudius's reign the Jews were expelled from Rome.  But Orosius adds that he prefers the version of Suetonius we have already given, and then states that he does not know whether only the Jews were expelled or the Christians also.[4] It is hopeless to endeavour to harmonize these varied statements.  Scholars have arrayed themselves into three main camps.  One regards the statement by Suetonius as a culmination of other measures against the Jews ; another construes Dio's passage as a correction of that of Suetonius ; the third holds the view that one statement is equivalent to the other.  If Chrestus be identified with Christ, as it seems he should be, the date assigned by Orosius (A.D. 49) appears quite plausible, and, as a consequence, the statement of Suetonius may very well be regarded as a culmination

---

[1] διὰ τὸ διατεταχέναι Κλαύδιον χωρίζεσθαι πάντας τοὺς Ἰουδαίους ἀπὸ τῆς Ῥώμης.

[2] "Iudaeos impulsore Chresto assidue tumultuantes Roma expulit" (Claud. 25).

[3] τούς τε Ἰουδαίους πλεονάσαντας αὖθις, ὥστε χαλεπῶς ἂν ἄνευ ταραχῆς ὑπὸ τοῦ ὄχλου σφῶν τῆς πόλεως εἰρχθῆναι, οὐκ ἐξήλασε μέν, τῷ δὲ δὴ πατρίῳ βίῳ χρωμένους ἐκέλευσε μὴ συναθροίζεσθαι (lx. 6. 6).

[4] "Anno eius nono expulsos per Claudium urbe Iudaeos Josephus refert. Sed me magis Suetonius movet qui ait hoc modo : Claudius Iudaeos impulsore Christo adsidue tumultuantes Roma expulit, quod, utrum contra Christum tumultuantes Iudaeos coherceri et comprimi iusserit, an etiam Christianos simul velut cognatae religionis homines voluerit expelli, nequaquam discernitur" (vii. 6. 15-16).  W. M. Ramsay argues that Orosius's date is one year too early (St. Paul the Traveller, 16th ed., London, 1927, p. 254), but see also Additional Note 34, p. 459.

of the anti-Jewish measures of Claudius.   The fact that the notoriously unreliable Orosius asserts that he got his information from Josephus opens his testimony to serious suspicion for the reason that Josephus has nowhere a statement on that subject.   On the other hand, the date A.D. 49 bears all the marks of circumstantial credibility, for it was just in the period A.D. 47–52 that Claudius was engaged in a very earnest campaign for the suppression of foreign cults and the restoration of the old Roman religion.[1] At any rate there are a few conclusions we may safely draw from our sources, viz. :

(a) The practical difficulty of expelling all the Jews, which Dio points out, suggests that Suetonius's statement should be interpreted in the sense that only those individuals were expelled who took actual part in the disorders.

(b) In this connexion it may be added that, despite the naïve doubting of Orosius, the Christians too would have been expelled, since they were engaged in the quarrel as actively as the Jews.

(c) The main body of the Jews was left unmolested.

(d) Their worship was not prohibited, but only hedged with certain rigid regulations.

(e) These restrictions were not directed at the Jews only, but were part of a general campaign against the oriental cults.   For Claudius had at heart the preservation of the old Roman religion and morals,[2] and for that reason he too banished astrologers from Italy.[3]   There can be no doubt that in this respect he was carrying out the policy inaugurated by Augustus and continued by Tiberius.   That policy accorded hospitality to foreign religions, but considered them a menace the moment they took advantage of that hospitality to make converts among the Italians.   On the other hand, it should be noted that as Dio groups Claudius's regulation of the Jewish community with the suppression of the clubs which had been re-introduced by Caligula,[4] and with the abolition of taverns and restaurants,[5] the seeming anti-Judaism of Claudius may have amounted to nothing more than a few measures taken for better police protection, and not for theological reasons.

Nero.

We have stated that on one occasion Nero showed himself friendly to the Jews of Jerusalem as a favour to Poppaea.   It is likely that she also exerted herself in behalf of the Jews of Rome when, after the disastrous fire of A.D. 64, the emperor or the mob was seeking scapegoats.   Aliturus, a court jester of Jewish nationality, through whom Josephus obtained that same year the release of two friends who were prisoners in Rome,[6] and Epaphroditus, Nero's secretary a libellis and apparently a proselyte,[7] may

---

[1] See the evidence from Tacitus, Ann. xi., xii., collected on p. 460 below.

[2] See Tac. Ann. xi. 15 ; xii. 23. 3 ; Dio lx. 23. 1.

[3] Tac. Ann. xi. 52. 3.                    [4] Dio lx. 6. 6.

[5] Dio lx. 6. 7.                          [6] Jos. Vita 3.

[7] Jos. Ant. i. 8 ; C. Ap. ii. 41.   Josephus dedicated to him the Jewish Antiquities and Against Apion (Vita 76 ; C. Ap. i. 1 ; ii. 1 ; ii. 41).   R. Laqueur denies that Epaphroditus, the patron of Josephus, was Nero's secretary a libellis (Der jüdische Historiker Flavius Josephus, Giessen, 1920, pp. 26 ff.).

have worked with Poppaea in the defence of the Jews of the capital. Their intercession must have proved effective if it be true that the Jews, who, as Christian tradition would have it, were suspected of arson, were able to divert the suspicion from themselves to the innocent Christians.  The important fact is that they escaped punishment.  As Nero has not been painted by Jewish tradition in dark colours,[1] despite the fact that it was he who ordered the disastrous war of A.D. 66, the conclusion may be drawn that he did not appear to the Jews as an enemy.

### Note XXVI. Roman Law and the Trial of Paul

#### By Henry J. Cadbury

The law and institutions of Rome appear in the book of Acts frequently and in many forms.  There are references to Roman army officers and detachments of the military service.[2]  The provinces of Rome are mentioned and cities with Roman municipal organization.  The scenes at Lystra and Ephesus bring us temptingly near to the imperial cult without making any explicit mention.  The names of Sergius Paulus, Claudius Lysias, Publius of Malta, and of Paul himself, raise questions of Roman personal nomenclature, while the problem of individual status as citizens or otherwise is raised in the dialogue between Paul and Lysias and elsewhere, and also by the mention of the synagogue of Libertini.  Roman penal procedure lies behind the stories of Paul's experiences in several cities in the Empire.  Various forms of punishment, including the stocks, beating, and imprisonment (with its various forms of greater or less severity), figure in the narrative of Acts, as well as the securing by bond, or the complete dismissal of the charges and the acquittal of the prisoner. *(margin: Roman institutions in Acts.)*

On all these the commentary has attempted to throw such light as our knowledge of Roman institutions under the Early Empire permits, but there is one more extensive and continuous narrative of Roman procedure which calls for further treatment—the concluding legal experiences of Paul as related at the end of Acts.  From Acts xxi. 33 to the end of the book the Apostle is a prisoner of Rome.  The whole last quarter of the book of Acts has to do with his changing experiences in different places and under different officials, but always he is in the hands of the law. *(margin: Paul's trial.)*

Though many of the legal details in these chapters have been dealt with in notes as they appeared, it is desirable to set down more fully in this essay a few of the more salient points of this series of events, and particularly to note the questions of Roman law which they raise.  These questions, unfortunately, cannot always be satisfactorily answered from other sources. From the legal viewpoint the story of Paul has been frequently studied.

---

[1] Vogelstein and Rieger (*op. cit.* vol. i. p. 91) record a Talmudic legend according to which Nero was not slain in the civil war, but disappeared and became a Jew.  The famous R. Meir was said to be his descendant.

[2] See Additional Note 33.

Mommsen.

Special mention should be made of the work of Theodor Mommsen, who, after collecting all the information available on Roman criminal procedure in his monumental work, *Römisches Strafrecht*,[1] attempted to relate it to the account in Acts by an essay, ' Die Rechtsverhältnisse des Apostels Paulus.'[2]   In many other forms the problems involved have been discussed by modern scholars,[3] though recent lives of Paul are disappointingly meagre in their attempts to get at the legal background of the story.

The general difficulties: (1) the treatment in Acts.

The difficulties to which reference has been made are partly inherent in the account of Acts. Although the author, among many other claims for him, has been attributed a considerable legal interest and even legal knowledge,[4] the narrative in Acts is an untechnical account with apologetic motive.   It is doubtful whether the writer had access to any official records such as are known to us from the Egyptian papyri and are paraded and perhaps actually known in some of the later Christian *acta*.   No claim of his actual presence can be made for the events, since except during the voyage to Rome the ' we ' of the supposed eyewitness diary is not employed in this section.   We may take it for granted that the writer regarded the charge against Paul as ill-founded and lacking in legal basis.   The treatment by officers of the law when favourable was a mark of God's favour for Paul, and when unfavourable was due to the malicious influence of the Jews, or to the venal character of the magistrate.   But even seeming defeat for the messenger of the Gospel nevertheless means for the author divine intervention trampling over obstacles.   Amid such motives mere legal record is hardly to be anticipated in Acts.

[1] 1899.   His *Römisches Staatsrecht*[3], 1887–1889, also contains much relevant material.   The older standard work was Gustav Geib, *Geschichte des römischen Kriminalprocesses*, 1842.   I am not aware that any of the many more recent general works on Roman law or on criminal law supersede Mommsen.

[2] *ZNTW*. ii., 1901, pp. 81 ff., republished in *Gesammelte Schriften*, iii. pp. 431 ff. The subject was briefly dealt with by O. Eger in his rectorial address at Basle, *Rechtsgeschichtliches zum N.T.*, 1919, and it was made the subject of a thesis by N. G. Veldhoen, *Het Proces van den Apostel Paulus*, Leiden, 1924.   This work was not available to the present writer, being out of print and apparently not accessible in any American library.   A popular account with slight reference to Roman law is ' Der Prozess des Apostel Paulus ' by E. Springer in *Preussische Jahrbücher*, 218 (1929), pp. 182-196.

[3] See, for example, Septimus Buss, *Roman Law and History in the N.T.*, 1901 ; U. Holzmeister, ' Der heilige Paulus vor dem Richterstuhle des Festus,' *Zeitschrift für katholische Theologie*, xxxvi., 1912, pp. 489 ff., 742 ff.   The latter is an extensive defence of the accuracy of Acts xxv. 1-12.   It depends for Roman law almost exclusively on Mommsen.   In spite of its assurance that at every point Acts can be vindicated it discloses to the discriminating reader many of the unsolved problems in regard to the whole process of Paul.

[4] M. von Aberle, *Tüb. Theol. Quartalschrift*, xxxvii., 1855, pp. 173 ff.   Cf. D. Plooij, *Expositor*, December 1914, pp. 511 ff. ; February 1917, pp. 108 ff. ; J. I. Still, *St. Paul on Trial*, 1924.   All three writers argue independently that Acts was written as a kind of brief for Paul's trial.   Cf. the *iuris studiosum* of Luke in the Canon of Muratori, and see Vol. II. pp. 179 ff.

On the other side, however, our difficulty is partly due to the lack of precise information available from the sources for ancient Roman law. In spite of the long and skilful labours of the students of jurisprudence a layman like the present writer receives the impression from modern books that a curiously large number of the questions raised in the book of Acts are without answer from contemporary records. Much of our knowledge of Roman law for this era comes by inference from suggestions of historians and orators. Cicero particularly gives us considerable insight into conditions in his time.[1] The systematic codification belongs to a later period, and often covers only in the most summary way such questions as we ask.[2] Along certain lines the Egyptian papyri have provided an extraordinarily full amount of information.[3] This must be gratefully acknowledged, while we express the hope that from this or some other source more light will fall on the trial and appeal of Paul.

*(2) our limited knowledge of Roman law.*

The subject may be divided into four stages :

*Division of the subject.*

1. Paul under Arrest by Claudius Lysias.
2. Paul in Custody under the Procurators.
3. The Appeal to Caesar.
4. The Outcome of the Action against Paul.

### I. *Under Arrest by Claudius Lysias*

The first stage of Paul's experience must be described as police proceedings rather than process of law. While he was engaged innocently enough in the Temple, certain Jews of Asia suspected him of having brought Greeks into the area forbidden to non-Jews. They raised a cry against him which nearly led to his being lynched outside the Temple. But the Roman garrison under Claudius Lysias, receiving word of the disturbance, intervened, and withdrew Paul safely into the barracks.

*Arrest by Claudius Lysias.*

This is the account in Acts, and it can be understood in accordance with our knowledge derived elsewhere. The maintenance of law and order in the Roman provinces lay ultimately in the hands of the Roman executive. This in Judea was the procurator. Only rarely and under special com-

*The Procurator.*

---

[1] See A. H. J. Greenidge, *The Legal Procedure of Cicero's Time*, 1901 ; Emilio Costa, *Cicerone giureconsulto*, i., 1911. An interesting sketch of 'Procedure in the Courts of the Roman Provincial Governors' (*Classical Journal*, xxv., 1929, pp. 93-101) by E. J. Urch, though based on Cicero's writings, especially the Verrine orations, is suggestive for procedure of Roman procurators in the next century.

[2] Even the later codes give much more attention to civil than to criminal law. See the quotations in S. Buss, *op. cit.* pp. 375 f.

[3] See R. Taubenschlag, *Das Strafrecht im Lichte der Papyri*, 1916. The same writer deals briefly but explicitly with ' Le procès de l'apôtre Paul en lumière des papyri ' in *Bulletin international de l'Académie polonaise des sciences et des lettres*, Classe de philologie, Classe d'histoire et de philosophie, 1919–1920 (Krakow, 1922–1924), pp. 55-59. His parallels deal mainly with denunciation to the police, arrest, imprisonment, examination by torture, consultation of a judicial college, the assessors.

mission did he have any superior except the emperor who personally appointed him. Twice Josephus [1] mentions intervention in the affairs of the Judean procurator by governors (*legati Augusti*) of the province of Syria, but in both cases the difficulties were not with small matters, for the procurator's personal fitness was in question, and wide special powers were granted the *legati* in each case, as Tacitus informs us.[2] As magistrate the procurator of Judea was supreme.

But it was impossible for the procurator to deal directly with all matters of order. He was provided with certain military forces [3] which were intended in the main for police purposes. Though their headquarters were with the procurator himself at Caesarea, a considerable detachment was necessary at Jerusalem. And in the time of Felix we find just such a garrison there under command of Claudius Lysias. His action is readily understood as the quelling of riot, the protection of an individual from the mob, and the arrest of an apparent disturber of the peace.

Native police.

Somewhat more obscure is the question of native police in Palestine. Part of the so-called auxiliary troops of the procurator were recruited from non-Italians, and in Palestine doubtless included Samaritans and Syrians, if not Jews, but they were responsible to Roman officers. It is probable that some purely Jewish police authorities existed, but their character and scope remain unknown. A central court, the Sanhedrin, and local courts already existed when the Romans took control. Of their judicial functions we shall speak later. That they had some police authority seems probable, under entirely Jewish rules, but tolerated by the Romans. There were, for example, the Sagan and Seganim, the στρατηγός and στρατηγοὶ τοῦ ἱεροῦ.[4] They are usually supposed to have held police powers. Quite

---

[1] *Antiq.* xviii. 4. 2, § 89, the dismissal of Pilate by Vitellius ; *ibid.* xx. 6, §§ 118 ff. (= *B.J.* ii. 12. 3 ff., §§ 232 ff.), the dismissal of Cumanus by Quadratus. On the relation of procuratorial Judea to provincial Syria see Additional Note 25.

[2] *Ann.* vi. 32, xii. 54. The status is not easily determined. For one definitely expressed view the following may be cited from A. Souter in Hastings, *D.A.C.* ii. p. 286 : " It is inexact to speak of Judaea as a province at this period. It remained from the beginning down to the time of Vespasian a client-State, whether ruled by one king or by a number of princes, or by a Roman procurator in company with an ἀρχιερεὺς καὶ ἐθνάρχης. The king was subordinate to the governor of the province Syria. The procurator's position, however, was like that of the *praefectus Aegypti*. He took the place of the highest ruler (the Emperor), but neither Judaea nor Egypt was part of the Roman Empire in the strict sense of the term (T. Mommsen, *Gesammelte Schriften*, vol. iii., *Juristische Schriften*, 1907, p. 431, n. 1, contradicting his earlier work, *The Provinces of the Roman Empire*, Eng. trans. vol. ii. p. 185)."

[3] See Additional Note 33.

[4] See Acts iv. 1 and note. To the bibliography there on the Sagan may be added E. E. Briess, *Wiener Studien*, xxxiv. (1911) pp. 356 f., and A. Schwarz, *Monatsschrift für Geschichte und Wissenschaft des Judentums*, lxiv. (1920), pp. 30-55. At the time of Paul's arrest Herod Agrippa II. had some kind of authority over the temple, e.g. he named the στρατηγὸς τοῦ ἱεροῦ. But Acts does not hint that he was consulted by Festus just for that reason.

relevant to the case of Paul is also the statement that the Romans permitted the Jews or their Sanhedrin to execute any foreigners who, contrary to the notices posted in Greek and Latin at the parapet, entered the inner courts of the Temple, even if they were Roman citizens.[1] Certainly the inscriptions themselves, of which one in Greek is preserved,[2] imply a strict authority to enforce the prohibition. Even if we had to concede that the authority to execute sentence belonged only to the Romans, some power at least to arrest—and we are speaking here of police authority—must have been in Jewish hands.

The duties of the local authorities, whether Roman or native, did not end with the arrest of the accused or suspected persons. Not every case that came to their attention could be referred to the supreme authority. The governor of the provinces, or in Judea the procurator, could not attend to petty matters. It was necessary for native courts or subordinate officers to exercise two functions : (i.) the final disposal of many cases, and (ii.) the preparation of information for cases to be submitted to the higher jurisdiction. These questions therefore emerge in relation to the story in Acts : What authority had the Sanhedrin to try and to sentence ? How would Lysias decide whether he was competent to deal with Paul's case ? If he was not, what steps would he take to prepare the case for the procurator's decision ?

There is much to be said in favour of supposing that the Jewish authorities had wide judicial functions.[3] It was the general policy of Rome to leave local matters of many sorts to be settled in native courts by native law. This was part of the autonomy of favoured cities and was jealously safeguarded. It was perhaps guaranteed to subject districts by the law of the province. The local authorities could doubtless be held responsible by the Romans for not exercising such authority in matters of public welfare,[4] while private cases—especially where no Romans were involved—must have often been in their hands. The degree of autonomy permitted in such matters doubtless differed in different areas. Egypt,

*Their func-tions.*

---

[1] Josephus, *B.J.* vi. 2. 4, §§ 125 f. According to Josephus, *Antiq.* xii. 3. 4, § 145, similar foreign endorsement of the sanctity of the temple from Gentile contamination had been included in a decree of Antiochus the Great μηδενὶ ἐξεῖναι ἀλλοφύλῳ εἰς τὸν περίβολον εἰσιέναι τοῦ ἱεροῦ.

[2] See on Acts xxi. 28.

[3] Beside the general works referred to throughout this Note see, on the extent of Jewish legal authority in Palestine and elsewhere, L. Mitteis, *Reichsrecht und Volksrecht in den östlichen Provinzen des römisches Kaiserreichs*, 1891, pp. 90 ff. ; D. Askowith, *The Toleration and Persecution of the Jews in the Roman Empire*, Part I., 1915, pp. 182 ff. ; H.-P. Chajes, ' Les Juges juifs en Palestine ' in *Revue des Études juives*, xxxix., 1899, pp. 39 ff. ; J. Langen, ' Das jüdische Synhedrium und die römische Procuratur in Judäa,' in *Tübingen Theologische Quartalschrift*, xliv., 1862, pp. 411 ff. ; E. Stapfer, ' Le Sanhédrin de Jérusalem au premier siècle,' *Revue de théologie et de philosophie*, xvii., 1884, pp. 105 ff.

[4] Cf. Acts xix. 40; John xi. 48; Josephus, *B.J.* ii. 12. 2, § 229. But in none of these cases is it absolutely certain that the accountability of the native officials to Rome is intended in any official sense.

for example—no matter how deep in the Ptolemaic and earlier times the roots of the complicated legal system may lie—under the Roman Empire formed a single well-organized unity with no conspicuous division or transition between native and Roman procedure.

The Sanhedrin.

In Palestine in particular we know that the Sanhedrin and possibly local courts are mentioned. The extended scope of their authority is assumed in many records and not merely in the Talmud, which may be suspected of idealizing. Religious issues would certainly be the first to be referred to the Sanhedrin if the matter were one of Jew against Jew. But for the Jews religion involved the Jewish law as a whole, and the Romans, too, doubtless allowed the native court considerable latitude, including civil and criminal competence as well as merely religious. The limitation on Jewish authority in cases affecting non-Jews, especially Roman citizens, would doubtless be found in matters involving capital punishment, and in what we may class as offences against the Roman State or Emperor.

The competence of the Sanhedrin to try Paul.

The book of Acts, in spite of its obscurity, suggests that Paul might conceivably have been tried by the Sanhedrin. Most explicitly is this expressed when the Jewish spokesman complains to Felix (xxiv. 6c, 7, 8a) : " We wished to judge him (i.e. Paul) according to our law. But Lysias the tribune intervening took him out of our hands with much violence, bidding his accusers to come before thee." But the words quoted are in none of the Old Uncial MSS. and may not be the work of the original author. For once he cannot be accused of a seeming slight contradiction between parallel accounts.[1]

[1] The genuineness of the passage, however, has found some supporters. See Holzmeister, *loc. cit.* p. 768. The insertion is good evidence that the early readers like ourselves did not find it unavoidably evident in Acts or in their understanding of the legal situation that the Jews were incompetent to try the case. Of course, both the author of Acts and the interpolator could draw their conclusions from the trial story of Jesus and the part which the Sanhedrin plays there. The author knew the forms of that story which we read in Mark and in his own gospel. The interpolator may well have known and been influenced by John, especially xviii. 31 and xix. 7.

Uncertainty whether it was Lysias or the Sanhedrin that was ' about to ' find out about Paul—i.e. whether the case was under Roman or Jewish jurisdiction—has likewise led to the variants μέλλων, μέλλον, μέλλοντες, μελλόντων, μέλλοντα at xxiii. 20. Which is the original form or even the original meaning is hard to decide. In the parallel at vs. 15 the plural is almost without variant, and at first sight seems to imply the Sanhedrin as the investigator, not Lysias. If a reading in vs. 20 is to be preferred that makes the original story consistent (intrinsic probability) we shall understand that verse in the same way, but if the reading is to be preferred which the later scribes are most likely to have changed (transcriptional probability) we shall understand the verse in another way. Cf. Vol. III. p. 219. On further examination it will be found that even vs. 15 is not quite definite in itself : " Do you," is the command to the chief priests and elders, " make representations to the tribune together with the Sanhedrin, that he (i.e. the tribune) bring down him (i.e. Paul) to you (just who

But even with these words omitted the book of Acts suggests that in the Possible in- early stages the Jews had a certain competence to try the case. It would terpretation. be possible to interpret the facts behind the story thus :

It was largely an accident that Paul fell into the hands of Lysias. The Jews, unless they had lost their self-control, might have arrested him, tried him, and sentenced him. The tribune intervened because (a) the matter seemed to be a case of excessive disorder ; (b) the Jews seemed likely to lynch Paul without a real trial ; (c) he mistakenly supposed Paul to be a well-known Egyptian and a raiser of insurrection. Both because he was not a Jew, and because the presumed offence was treason against Rome, the Egyptian's case belonged to the jurisdiction of the Romans rather than to that of the Sanhedrin. Even later both Lysias and the procurators pay considerable deference to the opinion of the Sanhedrin about Paul, and it would not more seriously impugn the accuracy of Acts than would many an alternative view to suppose that as a matter of fact what Lysias first undertook and what Festus finally proposed was an actual trial of Paul by the Sanhedrin, the Roman officer's own presence being intended only to guarantee the prisoner a fair hearing and military protection from open lynching or secret violence. Final decision by the Sanhedrin was prevented in the first instance by that council's own failure to agree at its first hearing, and by the discovery by Lysias of a plot that made it essential for Paul's safety to remove him immediately to custody at Caesarea until a second hearing to secure a verdict from the Sanhedrin was possible. In the second instance, under Festus, Paul avoided being again exposed to the jurisdiction of the Sanhedrin by his appeal to Caesar.

Such may well have been the author's own understanding of the story. Whether such a view agrees on the one hand with the normal legal procedure under the circumstances, and on the other hand with the actual development in Paul's case, are two quite other questions.

An alternative view would be that the jurisdiction of the Roman An alter- authorities entered much earlier and more completely into the progress of native. events. The scene before the Sanhedrin was no real trial, but merely Lysias's attempt to get information as to why the Jews cried out against Paul. This, indeed, more than once is said to be the reason (xxii. 30, xxiii. 28). Whether such an investigation was a customary way of formulating a case, as has been suggested in the case of the trial of Jesus [1] before

---

are meant ?) as though going to investigate (? decide) more carefully the facts about him." But it is almost impossible to reproduce or explain the uncertainty of reference in the Greek. At xxv. 3 there is no statement at all of the item of legal procedure which was to be the ostensible object of summoning Paul to Jerusalem as requested by his enemies on a later occasion.

[1] See for example R. W. Husband, *The Prosecution of Jesus*, Princeton, 1916. How the accuser was decided upon is a subject on which Roman law must have had definite rules. But we cannot deal with this or even with the far more relevant question as to the charge against Paul. An attempt to adjust the various informal statements in Acts to our imperfect knowledge of the criminal law of Rome we gladly forgo. What Paul was accused of puzzled the Romans.

the Sanhedrin, or whether Lysias regarded the Sanhedrin as experts in the Jewish law, who, like Agrippa, could perhaps explain the matter to a Roman who was puzzled at the furore of the whole controversy, Paul's appearance before the Sanhedrin was not the hearing of the accused before the competent tribunal.   And later, too, except for a suggestion that may simply mean that being tried at Jerusalem was as good as surrendering Paul to the fury of the Jews (as no doubt it was), the competent judge is the procurator (ἐπὶ σοῦ xxiii. 30, xxiv. 19, ἐπ᾽ ἐμοῦ xxv. 9).

On this view the Sanhedrin is probably not to be considered here at all as a competent final court.   Paul was from the start a prisoner in the hands of Roman authorities and would scarcely be turned over to the Jewish ones.   Not even at xxv. 9 does Acts suggest that the Romans considered leaving the verdict to the Jews.   The latter appear throughout as the accusers.   In the trial scenes of Jesus, submission of his case by Pilate to the Sanhedrin is definitely proposed.   Doubtless there were matters in which such reference was usual.   Jesus was not a Roman citizen, why should not the Jews deal with him ?   The explanation usually given is that the trial (or execution ?) of capital cases was not entrusted to the Sanhedrin.   We have the dialogue in John xviii. 31 :

Pilate : Take ye him and judge him according to your law.

The Jews : We have not authority to put any man to death.

The Gospel story, however, is far from certain evidence that the Sanhedrin had full jurisdiction in cases involving Jews or Jewish offences apart from the infliction of the death penalty,[1] and its action about Jesus is a debatable question that need not be settled here.   The two cases were not alike.   It is true that Paul, too, if accused of bringing Gentiles into the Temple, was probably held on a capital charge.[2]   But not only was the occasion two

---

It still puzzles us.   Did it puzzle Luke ?   Perhaps he thought he knew.   Perhaps he really did not care what accusation the Jews brought against his hero, and he certainly had no thought that Paul was guilty of anything that one ought not to be guilty of.

[1] Even with regard to the death penalty and the Sanhedrin no uniformity of opinion exists.   Some hold that it could pronounce sentence but not execute, some that it could do neither, and some that it could do both.   The literature on the subject, centring in the gospel story, is enormous.   The case of another Christian, James the brother of Jesus, much nearer to the time of Paul's arrest, suggests far more drastic limitations of the Sanhedrin's power.   According to Josephus, *Antiq.* xx. 9. 1, § 202, the new procurator was informed that without his consent the high priest had no right even to assemble the Sanhedrin.

[2] Yet we do not know that the guilt of a Jew who brought Gentiles into the Temple was regarded as the same as the guilt of the alien trespassers themselves.   Further, the accusation varies between a *fait accompli* (xxi. 28 κεκοίνωκεν) and an intention (xxiv. 6 ἐπείρασεν βεβηλῶσαι).   On the other hand, the particular offence of which Paul was accused was apparently so exceptionally treated by Rome that the Jewish court was competent to sentence to death and execute even a Roman citizen who was guilty of it.   This is the plain implication of Josephus, *B.J.* vi. 2. 4, §§ 124-126.

or three decades later : the prisoner now was a Roman citizen as well as
a Jew, and his initial arrest had been made by Roman, not by Jewish,
officers of law. It was this last consideration which really left the matter
in the hands of Claudius Lysias. He did not at first know that the prisoner
was a Roman.

Lysias's next step was to examine the prisoner. Whether he intended The first ex-
to dispose of the case himself, or whether he expected from the first to amination.
refer it to the procurator, the tribune would be compelled to make an
inquiry as to the grounds on which Paul might be thought guilty. Acts
makes plain that the scourging was inquisitorial, not punitive. This method
of examination was usual in the Roman Empire as under other govern-
ments, was legal, and presumably often effected its purpose. It was
forbidden, however, in the case of Roman citizens. On this we have other
testimony besides the book of Acts. Paul's assertion of his rights promptly
stopped this form of inquiry.[1]

The tribune's next step would naturally be to hear Paul's accusers. The hearing
Who were they ? Paul is represented as saying that they ought to be of the
certain Jews of Asia, presumably those who had seen him in the temple and accusers.
who thought that he had brought in Trophimus, an Asian Greek. These
at least were the appropriate witnesses to summon. But Lysias prefers
to consult the Jewish officials.

In what capacity do these persons now meet with Paul and Lysias ?
The language used suggests that the author means the Sanhedrin. But
surely it was not meeting as a court competent to try Paul. Nor did
Lysias associate with himself this Jewish body in the way in which the
Roman governors called the citizens into *conventus* as assessors for the
provincial assizes. It has been suggested that in the case of Jesus the
Sanhedrin served to formulate the charge and prepare the evidence to
submit it to the Roman procurator.[2] This is quite likely in that case, but
scarcely so in the one before us. The author has been doubtless influenced
both here and in the trial of Stephen by details reported concerning the
trial of Jesus, and on that account his narrative here may lack in historical
exactness. Yet it is plain that the responsibility for preparing the case
for an ultimate decision rested on Lysias himself. To clear his own mind,
to find out why the Jews so bitterly assailed Paul, he listened to the
Sanhedrin as representing the plaintiff.

In fact, throughout the scenes that follow, ' the chief priests and
Sanhedrin,' ' the chief priest, Ananias, and some elders,' ' the chief priests
and the first men of the Jews,' ' the chief priests and elders of the Jews '
appear as Paul's accusers. Whether they acted on their individual initiative we do not know. Perhaps they acted rather as representatives of the
nation, whose privileges they believed Paul had violated.

A cognate question, and one similarly difficult to answer, would be the The charge.
charge against Paul. From what has already been said we shall hardly

---

[1] See on this incident notes on xxii. 24-29. On torture ($\pi\epsilon\iota\theta\alpha\nu\acute{\alpha}\gamma\kappa\eta$) in
the papyri see U. Wilcken, *Archiv für Papyrusforschung*, ii. p. 119, and the
article of R. Taubenschlag cited in note 3, p. 299.

[2] See R. W. Husband, *op. cit.*

expect Luke to formulate it in precise terms of Roman criminal law. In fact his view is that it could not be so stated since there was no provable offence, and the underlying hostility of the complainants rested on their own prejudice and some misunderstanding. Luke, it is true, here and even in the Gospel makes some rather definite charges,[1] but they must be taken as his understanding of the ' constructive ' crimes for which accusations were preferred. The Roman officials find the accusations mystifying. They see that they are in reality strife about Jewish religious matters and are not cognizable.

The decision of Lysias.

The ultimate decision of Lysias was to refer the case to the procurator. When was that decision reached ? Not, I think, when the plot against Paul's life was discovered. That led Lysias to arrange a change of place of custody, not a change of jurisdiction. Except for his own safety's sake Paul might have been heard by the procurator at Jerusalem when the latter made his next visit. Even later, long after his removal to Caesarea, a hearing at Jerusalem before the procurator is a possibility. The letter that Lysias wrote is not evidence that he had just decided to refer the case to the procurator. Rather it means that instead of being able to explain the case verbally when Felix came to Jerusalem, Lysias must now refer it in writing. It would be more convenient and natural for the procurator to deal with Paul's case in Jerusalem. Paul, Lysias, the accusers were all there, and from them could be secured all the information available for a decision. When, however, the prisoner was removed to Caesarea, it was necessary for the accusers also to appear there, and such immediate reference of the matter as Lysias must or could make was in writing.[2]

But at what earlier point it became clear to Lysias that Paul's case would have to come before the procurator we cannot tell from Acts, nor do other sources of information indicate how the decision was made. It would be interesting to know whether Roman citizenship in itself ensured him a higher hearing.[3] Yet surely in case of slight punishment, or the acquittal or dismissal of his case, a Roman citizen in the provinces did not always have to wait for the governor's arrival.

## II. *In Custody under the Procurators*

The Procurators.

The next stage in Paul's case is at Caesarea, where it came first before Felix and afterwards before Festus.

[1] See particularly Luke xxiii. 2, Acts xxiv. 5 f.

[2] At xxiv. 22 Felix gives as reason (or excuse) for delaying a decision that he would wait until Lysias also should reach Caesarea.

[3] On the privileges which distinguished Jews who were Roman citizens from Jews who were not see J. Juster, *Les Juifs dans l'Empire Romain*, 1914, ii. pp. 162 ff., ' Influence du *Status Civitatis* des Juifs sur leur situation en droit pénal.' Apart from the two advantages mentioned in connexion with Acts, immunity from scourging and right to appeal to the emperor, many of the items are quite debatable. Attention may be called to the difficulties which Acts itself presents concerning the exact extent of citizens' prerogative as mentioned below.

The authority of the procurators of Judea [1] is apparently like that of the proconsuls in senatorial provinces, of *legati* in imperial provinces, and of the prefects in Egypt. Of the administration of the last of these a considerable amount is now known from the papyri. Beside the larger areas with their senatorial and imperial governors, not a few small sections of the Empire were kept as independent units, and received directly appointed commissioners from Rome. These bore the less honourable name ' procurator ' (not to be confused with certain strictly financial officers of the same name), but they exercised final authority (under the emperor) over the area assigned to them. Judea was such an area during most of the period covered by Acts, and Pilate, Felix, and Festus are usually reckoned among the incumbents of this office. *Their authority.*

Their procedure in cases referred to them was simple. Their hearings were held only at limited places, in the Judean procuratorship probably only at Caesarea and at Jerusalem. The cases were often only briefly heard, and it was in the procurators' power to make immediate decision. It was also apparently in their power indefinitely to postpone decision.[2] In these circumstances, defendants held in custody remained, like Paul, as prisoners. No doubt with such arbitrary power the procurator was in position to yield to ' undue influence ' and to be bribed—either to acquit, to condemn, or to postpone. Accusations of such motives like those in Acts are to be found in Josephus as well as in the histories of the larger provincial governors. There were Roman laws to punish such maladministration when it was proved. *Their procedure.*

The questions of Roman law which this stage in Paul's experience suggests include these : *Legal problems.*

On whose initiative was a case that had been referred to the procurator called to trial ? Was it of the accusers ? Of the inferior officer that remanded it ? Of the defendant ? Or was it automatically put on the calendar ? The accounts in Acts imply nothing as to this in the first instance, though after Paul had been kept prisoner to the end of Felix's term of office, a plea for the hearing of the case is made by the Jews. Had the prisoner himself no means of moving for an early trial and decision ? Or was the procurator as independent in the determination when to hear and decide a case as he was free to render a favourable or unfavourable verdict ?

We have no doubt that delays in court procedure were often excessive, then as now. The Egyptian papyri imply that defendants frequently complained of this. Apparently they were at the mercy of the supreme magistrate and, unless the language of the petitions is merely formal, often

---

[1] Beside general works on Roman law or on Jewish history see H. Regnault, *Une province procuratorienne au début de l'Empire Romain,* Paris, 1909 ; O. Hirschfeld, *Die kaiserlichen Verwaltungsbeamten bis auf Diocletian*[2], 1905, pp. 371-409. For a brief English discussion of procurators see H. Mattingly, *The Imperial Civil Service of Rome,* 1910.

[2] " Rechtsmittel, um das Statthaltergericht zur Erledigung der Klage zu nötigen, kennt die römische Ordnung nicht," Mommsen, *ZNTW.* ii., 1901, p. 93. Cf. the story of Lampon quoted from Philo, *infra,* p. 330.

entreated prompt hearing as a favour. On the other hand, the plaintiff anxious to secure vengeance might also pray for a speedy hearing.[1] A delayed decision might be a favour to neither side, though if the accused were held in custody during the delay, as was Paul, he suffered a kind of punishment through the delay itself. It is possible that Felix held Paul a prisoner for two years just as " a favour to the Jews." The author of Acts, however, does not use that phrase of the long delay by Felix—though he is free in suggesting unworthy motives for a doubtless unworthy procurator [2]—but merely of the brief period during which the office was being transferred to his successor Festus. It looks from Acts as though a general discharge of prisoners whose cases were still *sub judice* was to be anticipated upon the retirement of the governor from office. The failure of Felix so to release Paul was the favour to the Jews.[3]

Adjourned cases.

The situation that confronted Festus with a prisoner held over from a previous term must have been a not unusual one,[4] and definite provisions for dealing with it must have existed quite as much as in the case of prisoners remanded to the procurator's bench in the first place. Acts implies that the accusers moved for a new hearing. The previous hearings could serve no purpose now. Even if a record of them was available no verdict had been rendered. A new hearing was demanded by the Jews and Festus intended to grant it. They asked that it be held in Jerusalem. Festus passed the suggestion on to Paul.[5] The alternative would seem to us to be a hearing in Caesarea. But again these questions emerge : (a) Were the alternatives hearings before the same procurator at two different seats of sessions—Caesarea and Jerusalem ? If so, the Jews might prefer the latter and Paul might prefer the former, and the procurator might well inquire as to the preference of each side ; but could Paul determine the decision between them ? Moreover, in what sense would he call being tried in Jerusalem being ' surrendered ' ($\chi\alpha\rho\acute{\iota}\sigma\alpha\sigma\theta\alpha\iota$) [6] to the Jews ? Did he

---

[1] Cf. Luke xviii. 2-7.　　　　　　[2] See note on xxiv. 24.

[3] The Western text implies that it was specially ' on account of Drusilla.'

[4] Josephus, *B.J.* ii. 14. 1, § 273, says that Albinus the successor of Festus released persons imprisoned for robbery by former procurators, bribed to do so by the prisoners' relatives. The verb is δεδεμένους simply, as in Acts xxiv. 27. Was not Paul as good as sentenced to prison under Felix ? In like manner Archelaus is said at his father's death to have released those whom Herod had imprisoned (*ibid.* ii. 1. 2, § 4 ; 2. 5, § 28).

[5] Acts describes Festus's motive quite unfavourably. See note on xxv. 9. It was natural for the governor to think it possible to get more information on the case at Jerusalem. Thus when the Jews were accused by the Samaritans before Quadratus, he deferred giving a reply at Tyre, where he was at the time, saying he would render a verdict when on arriving in Judaea he should have learned the truth more accurately (Josephus, *Antiq.* xx. 6. 2, § 128 ; cf. *B.J.* ii. 12. 6, § 241). This he did, holding hearings at Lydda and possibly at Samaria as well.

[6] Acts xxv. 11. The verb is not used in the Gospels of Pilate's surrender of Jesus to the wish of the Jews, but rather in quite the opposite sense of the release of Barabbas (Acts iii. 14).

mean that in Jewish territory his life was in danger of plots ?   Or did he
mean that the psychological climate of Jerusalem was less propitious to an
unprejudiced decision there by the procurator ? [1]   Or (b) did it mean, as
already suggested and rejected, that the alternatives were a trial before the
Jewish or the Roman authorities ?

As usual, Acts has a parallel but slightly variant account of the Jews' The two
request in Festus's report (xxv. 14-21).   There Festus says that they asked accounts in Acts.
a verdict of condemnation ($\kappa a \tau a \delta i \kappa \eta$, not a hearing in Jerusalem as in
xxv. 3), and that he had declined their request on the ground that it is not
customary for Romans to surrender ($\chi a \rho i \zeta \epsilon \sigma \theta a \iota$) any man before the
accused has the accusers face to face and has an opportunity of defence
concerning the charge.   In continuing the story, Festus repeats what the
author had told us, that he asked Paul whether he wished to go to Jerusalem
and there be tried.   But this time there is no phrase like $\epsilon \pi' \epsilon \mu o \hat{v}$ to show
that the Roman procurator would conduct or even witness the trial.
The variant account therefore leaves us no more clear about the alternatives
or general procedure.

Two further considerations bearing on the disposition of Paul's case Paul's posi-
suggest themselves :  (i.) he was a native [2] not of Judea but of Cilicia, and (1) Cilician,
(ii.) he had besides the rights of a Roman citizen.   Could either of these (2) Roman.
facts relieve the procurators of Judea of final responsibility ?   According
to Luke (xxiii. 7), Pilate, on learning that Jesus was a Galilean, referred
his case to Herod Antipas.   Felix also made inquiry as to Paul's province
(Acts xxiii. 34, cf. note there).   Unfortunately, our other sources do not
tell us whether the jurisdiction for a criminal case could be shifted from the
place of alleged crime or arrest to the place of the accused's domicile.[3]   It
is possible that the reference of Jesus to Herod, if historical,[4] was merely
to secure the advice of Herod about the case.   The verb $\dot{a} \nu a \pi \dot{\epsilon} \mu \pi \omega$ cannot
be pressed as the technical term for remanding to higher authority,[5]
for it is used both when Pilate refers Jesus to Herod, and later when Herod
refers Jesus to Pilate (Luke xxiii. 11).   In Acts also no real use is made of
the information that Paul was a Cilician.   Yet the question (which has
some parallels in the Acta of martyrs) [6] is hardly mentioned without some

[1] Compare Pilate's intimidation by those who were insistent on Jesus'
execution as represented in the Gospels.

[2] Native in the literal sense is perhaps not quite the right word.   Presumably
not birthplace but ' domicile ' would supply the alternative jurisdiction.   By
domicile Paul was a Cilician and Jesus a Galilean, but there is a tradition that
Paul was a native, not of Tarsus, but of Gischala in Galilee, just as there is a
tradition that Jesus was a native, not of Nazareth, but of Bethlehem in Judaea.

[3] On 'Domicil' and 'Thatort' see Mommsen, Römisches Strafrecht, pp. 357 f.

[4] Its historicity has been questioned.   See articles mentioned Vol. IV. p. 47.

[5] It is so used in the papyri, but also for referring to a lower authority.   See
Preisigke, Fachwörter and Wörterbuch, s.v.

[6] See Preuschen on Acts xxiii. 34.   Compare the similar initial question
put to litigants by Absalom (2 Sam. xv. 2), " Of what city art thou ? "
and the Homeric $\tau i s \ \pi \acute{o} \theta \epsilon \nu \ \epsilon i s \ \dot{a} \nu \delta \rho \hat{\omega} \nu$ ; ($\pi \acute{o} \theta \iota \ \tau o \iota \ \pi \acute{o} \lambda \iota s \ \dot{\eta} \delta \grave{\epsilon} \ \tau o \kappa \hat{\eta} \epsilon s$ ;) of Od. a 170
(Il. Φ 150).   Josephus may be suspected of echoing Homer rather than

*arrière pensée*, merely because it was one of the items to be filled in in the *questionnaire* about each prisoner. Did it matter whether the province to which the prisoner belonged was ' Senatorial ' or ' Imperial ' ? Cilicia at this time would mean the imperial province *Cilicia et Syria et Phoenice.*[1]

The power of the procurator to refer cases.

Of the Roman citizen's right to appeal his case to Rome we shall speak in the next section. Had the procurator any opportunity to take similar action on his own initiative ? It seems almost certain that he must have been able to submit a criminal proceeding to the emperor if the issue involved appeared to him of too much importance or difficulty. Just how much all the evidence on this point amounts to I do not know. But since in Acts neither the procurators nor the author himself seem to contemplate such a disposition of the case, at least on the procurator's initiative, there is no need to canvass the problem further.

We may conjecture that if the procurators had such a right in special cases it was not limited to Roman citizens. Josephus several times speaks of persons sent by the *legati* of Syria or the procurators of Judea to Rome for trial or execution. It is plain that in many cases the prisoners were not Roman citizens. They were the leaders of rival groups in controversy or the ringleaders of brigandage or revolt.[2] As accused by the Jews in Acts xxiv. 5 (κινοῦντα στάσεις πᾶσι τοῖς Ἰουδαίοις τοῖς κατὰ τὴν οἰκουμένην πρωτοστάτην τε τῆς τῶν Ναζωραίων αἱρέσεως) Paul might well seem to a procurator such a person and a fit candidate for reference to the emperor. He had already been confused by Claudius Lysias with a notable raiser of insurrection (xxi. 38). His own words are in defence against charges of tumult or *seditio* (xxiv. 12, 18).

The necessity of reference to Rome.

On the other hand, mention must be made of the view held by Mommsen that the procurator not only might but must refer to Rome a case like Paul's. He said explicitly : " Dies bestätigt die vortreffliche Schilderung des Prozesses des Apostels Paulus. Der Statthalter meint über den Sachverhalt berichten zu müssen (Acts xxv. 27 ἄλογον γάρ μοι δοκεῖ πέμποντα δέσμιον μὴ καὶ τὰς κατ' αὐτοῦ αἰτίας σημᾶναι). Nach

---

formally reporting Roman procedure when he tells us how a certain Jew, Jesus son of Ananias, who cried incessantly "Woe to Jerusalem," was brought before the procurator Albinus, scourged, and asked τίς τ' εἴη καὶ πόθεν ; (*B.J.* vi. 5. 3, § 305).

[1] There is, however, some doubt whether Cilicia may not have had its separate government under the early empire. See Marquardt, *Römische Staatsverwaltung*², i. p. 384 ; Ruggiero, *Dizionario epigrafico*, ii. pp. 228 f.

[2] *Ant.* xvii. 10. 10 Varus ; xx. 6. 3 (=*B.J.* ii. 12. 6) Quadratus ; xx. 8. 5 (=*B.J.* ii. 13. 2) Felix. But there is another instance (*Vita* 3) when Felix sent some priests to Rome to plead their cause before Caesar against whom Josephus says the charge was slight and trifling. But since these priests were relatives of Josephus his evidence is not to be understood as indicating that the ostensible accusation was for a minor offence. The cases where provincials not citizens were sent to Rome for trial are said to be exceptional. See Mommsen, *Strafrecht*, p. 241 and note 2 ; Juster, *op. cit.* ii. p. 162, note 4 ; Schürer, *GJV.*, 4th ed., p. 468, note 80.

eingelegter Provocation indess ist er nicht mehr berechtigt ein Urtheil, auch nicht ein freisprechendes zu fällen (Acts xxvi. 32) ; das Gericht ist damit abgelehnt." [1]

Such a view would quite alter our understanding of Paul's case. For though the procurators had supreme authority (*ius gladii*) over Jews in Palestine who were not Roman citizens (*peregrini*), a final decision of Paul's case according to Mommsen was never really in the hands of either Felix or Festus, since Paul's citizenship was a recognized fact, and the penalty to which he would be liable if convicted was severe. But, though Mommsen uses Acts xxv. 27 [2] to support his view, the whole story of Acts implies quite the opposite. And yet Mommsen may be right about the general procedure under the circumstances. Half a century later Pliny, as governor of Bithynia, in writing about the Christians to the emperor Trajan distinguishes his treatment of those who were Roman citizens from that of the others. Simply because of their citizenship he seems to have made no effort to dispose of their cases under his own jurisdiction. He says : " Quia cives Romani erant, adnotavi in urbem remittendos." [3]

Besides deciding cases themselves or sending the accused to Rome for trial or on appeal, a third method of dealing with Roman citizens by the governors of the provinces may be mentioned, though there is no hint that it was thought of in Paul's case. This was the practice of trying the accused in the province and of retaining him in custody while a written account of the trial and probably a suggested verdict was sent up to the emperor. Mommsen recognized the existence of such a procedure, and regarded it as a limitation of the *ius gladii* providing a middle position between the competence of governors to issue and inflict sentence even upon Roman citizens, and the incompetence of governors to condemn or even try Roman citizens at all on capital charges. He says that even the *ius gladii* seems often to have been provided or at least administered with limitation, that while the governor was entrusted with the conduct of the trial and the pronouncement of the verdict, before the infliction of the

A third possibility.

---

[1] *Römisches Strafrecht*, p. 243, note 1.

[2] He gives apparently no other evidence (see the criticism of Juster, *op. cit.* ii. pp. 162 f. note 6). The fact that the *potestas gladii* is occasionally mentioned in the titles of procurators (Dessau, *Inscr. Lat. Selectae*, 1368, 1372, 9200) might seem to imply that it was exceptional and that procurators, like governors of the senatorial provinces under the early principate, did not have the right. Cf. B. Kübler, *Geschichte des römischen Rechts*, 1925, pp. 224 f. But the cases of procurators with the right of the sword (see the Index of Dessau, vol. iii. 1, pp. 403 ff.) do not appear to offer us any simple classification. Josephus comes as near as his style permits to saying explicitly that Coponius the procurator had the *ius gladii* (*B.J.* ii. 8. 1, § 117 μέχρι τοῦ κτείνειν λαβὼν παρὰ Καίσαρος ἐξουσίαν, cf. *Antiq.* xviii. 1. 1, § 2 ἡγησόμενος 'Ιουδαίων τῇ ἐπὶ πᾶσιν ἐξουσίᾳ), but whether by this description of the first procurator of Judea Josephus means us to assume the same of the later incumbents or whether he mentions it precisely because it was not usual does not appear.

[3] *Epist.* x. 96. 4.

punishment he must send for the imperial authorization.[1] Mommsen's example is the interesting case of the Christian Attalus, a Roman citizen brought before the governor of Gaul in the time of Marcus Aurelius. The passage reads as follows : μαθὼν ὁ ἡγεμὼν ὅτι ʿΡωμαῖός ἐστιν, ἐκέλευσεν αὐτὸν ἀναληφθῆναι μετὰ καὶ τῶν λοιπῶν τῶν ἐν τῇ εἱρκτῇ ὄντων, περὶ ὧν ἐπέστειλεν τῷ Καίσαρι καὶ περιέμενεν τὴν ἀπόφασιν τὴν ἀπʼ ἐκείνου.[2]

The trial of Antipater.

This is certainly an intelligible and economical procedure. One wonders that it was not done or at least recorded oftener. A recent writer [3] finds a like example in the trial of Antipater, son of Herod the Great, before Varus, *legatus* of Syria in 5 B.C., though he admits that the accounts in Josephus [4] obscure the supreme jurisdiction of the *legatus* by the prominence given the king.[5] Furthermore, before there was time for Varus to hear from Augustus, Antipater was implicated in new charges which led to his execution. It is probably true that Antipater was a Roman citizen inheriting the privilege bestowed on his grandfather Antipater,[6] but it may be doubted whether as king and father Herod was compelled to turn the case over to Varus. And in both this example and the preceding it is not clear that if the governor suggested a verdict, and if that verdict was approved by the emperor, it would be treated as the governor's verdict in the first instance.[7] This type of proceeding, if not wholly relevant to the reports of Paul's trial in Acts, suggests at least the multiplicity of possible courses and our lack of complete data about them.

## III. *The Appeal to Caesar*

The appeal to Caesar.

The appeal to Caesar is an item so distinct that it might seem to raise few doubts. It may be well to state briefly a simple understanding of this stage in the proceedings, and then to indicate the objections to it suggested both from the side of Acts and from the side of the Roman law.[8]

If I mistake not the situation is usually understood as follows. When Festus found Paul a prisoner awaiting trial he expected as governor to

---

[1] *Römisches Strafrecht*, p. 244.

[2] Eusebius, *H.E.* v. 1. 44, quoting the letter from Vienne and Lyon.

[3] E. Täubler, ʻ Relatio ad Principem,ʼ *Klio*, xvii., 1921, pp. 98 ff.

[4] *B.J.* i. 32 ; *Antiq.* xvii. 5. The letter to Caesar is mentioned at § 640 and § 133 respectively. I think even Täubler mistakenly refers to Varus the imprisoning of Antipater and the sending of a report to Augustus in *Antiq.* In *B.J.* both Herod and Varus send reports.

[5] Similar exaggeration may be suspected in the part played by Agrippa in Acts xxvi. (but see note 1, p. 313) and by Antipas in Luke xxiii. 7-12.

[6] Josephus, *B.J.* i. 9. 5, § 194=*Antiq.* xiv. 8. 3, § 137.

[7] The opinion mentioned is that of Täubler, *loc. cit.*

[8] The special bibliography on this topic includes among older works J. C. Santorocci, *De provocatione Pauli*, Marburg, 1721 ; J. T. Krebs, *De provocatione Pauli*, Leipzig, 1753, and more recently U. Holzmeister, ʻ Der heilige Paulus vor dem Richterstuhle des Festus,ʼ in *Z. für kath. Theol.* xxxvi., 1912, pp. 489 ff., 742 ff. An investigation in this field was promised by O. Eger, *op. cit.* notes 31, 53, but he writes me that he has not been able to complete it.

decide his case. The case was now at least in Roman hands, and the governor had by law absolute authority with one exception. That exception was that Roman citizens might appeal directly to the Roman emperor against a capital or other severe verdict. Paul as a citizen exercised this right and made formal appeal. The procurator was then bound to send the case forward. The further hearings at Caesarea [1] were intended only to secure the necessary information for describing the case in the document forwarded to the emperor relating to the prisoner. And so Paul came to Rome.[2]

There is no doubt that Roman law was acquainted with such processes of appeal as the one here suggested.[3] Apparently two technical terms have to be considered, *provocatio* and *appellatio*.

(*a*) The *provocatio* [4] goes well back into Roman history.[5] It was the *Provocatio.* right of a citizen to appeal against the verdict of a magistrate. The recognition of this right was made obligatory by the *Lex Valeria* of 509 B.C., and was subsequently strengthened by various laws which provided sanctions for its enforcement and prevented the evasion of the right by plea of martial law or even by new legislation.

The magistrate involved under the republic was mainly the consul, though he came to delegate his powers to subordinates. The appeal from his verdict under the republic was to the people as a whole meeting in their ' largest assembly,' i.e. to the *comitia centuriata*. The verdicts from which an appeal could be made were at first those involving capital and corporal punishment, and subsequently those involving heavy fines. When this

---

[1] Acts makes no suggestion that Agrippa's opinion was intended to be more than advisory. But if Paul's alleged offence was against the temple, Agrippa may have been more nearly concerned with the matter, since Josephus tells us that Herod of Chalcis had authority over the temple, the sacred money, and the choice of high priests as had also his descendants (*Antiq.* xx. 1. 3, §§ 15 f.) until the end of the war. Among the latter he evidently means Herod Agrippa II., for he says (*ibid.* xx. 9. 7, § 222) that he had been entrusted with the care (ἐπιμέλεια) of the temple.

[2] The following summary from A. R. Gordon in Hastings, *D.A.C.* ii. p. 617, may be quoted as typical: "The rehearing of the case before Felix's successor, the brave and honourable Porcius Festus, would no doubt have resulted in the Apostle's acquittal, had he not chosen, in the exercise of his rights as a citizen, to entrust his life and liberty to Roman justice rather than expose them to the malice of his enemies in Jerusalem (xxv. 10 f.). The appeal was allowed by Festus, after a brief deliberation with his *consilium* (vs. 12), and Paul was sent to Rome with a dimissory letter strongly in his favour (vss. 26 f.)."

[3] Beside the general works on Roman law there is a full monograph dealing with methods of appeal in the early empire by J. Merkel, *Abhandlungen aus dem Gebiete des römischen Rechts*, Heft ii., 1883. See also Pauly-Wissowa, articles on *appellatio, intercessio*, and (when it appears) on *provocatio*.

[4] For English readers the *provocatio* is discussed but not quite acceptably in P. M. Schisas, *Offences against the State in Roman Law*, 1926.

[5] By the story of Horatius the origin of *provocatio* was carried back to the time of the kings.

latter extension was made, and what was the maximum amount of fine that could be inflicted without being subject to the right of appeal, are two details in the history of the *provocatio* on which the authorities give us no certain information.

**Limitations of *provocatio*.**     The right of *provocatio* had several limitations. In some crimes it was not allowed. It was not granted to certain persons, viz. women (?), slaves, and foreigners. It was, in fact, the prerogative of Roman citizens. Further, the right of *provocatio* could be suspended by a decree of the legislative bodies. Either a *quaestio extra ordinem* of the *comitia* or a *senatus consultum* could authorize the consul to try cases with unrestricted *ius gladii*. The *senatus consultum ultimum* suspended *provocatio* by declaration of martial law. The purpose of later legislation, as already noted, was to prevent all such forms of suspension.

Above all, the right of *provocatio* was limited geographically. It was effective only within the walls of Rome and a mile beyond them. This area was called *domi*. In territory beyond that (called *militiae*) the consul was vested with unrestricted power, as though on the field of battle. The distinction was outwardly expressed by the removal of the axes from the lictors' *fasces* when the consul came within the area of the city which was subject to *provocatio*.

It is often assumed that the right of *provocatio* had been extended to citizens in the *area militiae* in the time of Paul under the empire, and even as early as Cicero's time under the republic, so that Roman citizens condemned by the provincial governors enjoyed the privileges they would enjoy at Rome. This is very likely correct. Unfortunately, we have no record of any law making such an extension, and the incidents or evidence cited as indicating that the extension had been made is not conclusive.

**Greenidge.**     Greenidge,[1] contrary to accepted opinion, argued that the right of appeal on grounds of citizenship was guaranteed by law only in Rome, and was never extended during the republic to the provinces. He believed it was rather by custom than by legal checks that provincial governors were restrained from inflicting the extreme penalty on Roman citizens, and that Verres was accused not of violating the law but of injuring the name of Rome in the eyes of provincials by violent or degrading treatment of its citizens. In Rome a citizen could appeal ; outside of Rome even among barbarian peoples his citizenship was a passport to respectful treatment and immunity.[2]

[1] *The Legal Procedure of Cicero's Time*, pp. 410 ff., and more fully ' The "Provocatio Militiae" and Provincial Jurisdiction ' in *Class. Rev.* x., 1896, pp. 225 ff.

[2] Josephus, *B.J.* ii. 14. 9, § 308, describes as unprecedented the actions of the procurator Gessius Florus in A.D. 66 at Jerusalem : ἄνδρας ἱππικοῦ τάγματος μαστιγῶσαί τε πρὸ τοῦ βήματος καὶ σταυρῷ προσηλῶσαι, ὧν εἰ καὶ τὸ γένος Ἰουδαῖον ἀλλὰ γοῦν τὸ ἀξίωμα Ῥωμαικὸν ἦν. But this statement does not deny that (legally or illegally) earlier procurators executed Roman knights by more honourable forms of punishment or used flogging and crucifixion for Roman citizens who were not of equestrian rank.

At the other extreme Mommsen and others have believed that the Mommsen. governors, so far from possessing power of the sword over citizens with no right of appeal, did not exercise that power at all, at least before the third Christian century.   At the beginning of the empire citizens, if accused on a capital charge, could not be tried at all in the provinces, for the governors had no competence to condemn to death even subject to *provocatio*.   The accused was to be sent to the emperor.   In other words, the old right of *provocatio* at Rome had had three effects :

(i.) It actually made capital sentence on citizens outside of Rome useless, because whether the sentenced party actually appealed or remained silent he had to be sent to Rome.

(ii.) It required that citizens, who because of absence from Rome were, in accordance with the earliest local limitations of *provocatio*, not able to employ it, should be sent to Rome for trial.

(iii.) It made the magistrate in effect prosecutor rather than judge, and his hearing was to secure evidence by which he might ask for a verdict at the bar of the superior court where alone such verdicts could be pronounced with validity.

(*b*) *Appellatio.*—Besides the *provocatio* Roman law had another institu- *Appellatio.* tion called the *appellatio*, which though quite as obscure in its history and development as the *provocatio* may be more briefly described.[1]   It also was claimed to be, and doubtless was, of great antiquity.   It, too, aimed to protect the citizen from the unjust acts of the magistrate.   It will be remembered that to avoid despotism the republican constitution provided for a plurality of holders in each magisterial office.   Each consul had his colleague who could veto his action, and further, the tribunes of the plebs were empowered to interfere in like manner.

The *appellatio* was the request made by a citizen to the magistrate's colleague or to the tribune to intervene (*intercessio*) to protect him.   The *appellatio* was not applied quite alike in civil and in criminal law, and was perhaps more frequent in the former.   Apparently it could be exercised at more than one stage in the proceedings.   It was resorted to as a precautionary defence rather than for the purpose of reversing a verdict already rendered, for the reversal of a verdict once given was scarcely provided for in Roman law.

Under the principate the procedure of both *provocatio* and *appellatio* Modification in the Empire. was considerably modified.[2]   In the first place, the two classes were apparently reduced in practice to one.   Both names were then used indiscriminately, though it is uncertain which of the older processes ought to be considered the true ancestor of the appeal to the emperor.[3]   We may argue

[1] Reference may be made to Merkel, *op. cit.*

[2] The difficulty of determining procedure under the emperors is increased by the fact that different emperors followed different courses, and by the possibility that civil cases were handled differently from criminal and cases of remission from cases of appeal (cf. note 1, p. 334).

[3] Besides Merkel, *op. cit.* pp. 41 ff., and general works, cf. A. H. J. Greenidge, ' The Greek Evidence for the Origin of the Imperial Appeal ' in *Class. Rev.* viii., 1894, pp. 142 ff.

that since the sovereign people was replaced by the sovereign prince the *provocatio* formerly addressed to the people was now addressed to the emperor.[1]  The earliest imperial law on the subject (*Lex Iulia de vi publica et privata*) is later so described by Paulus [2] and Ulpian,[3] i.e. the appeal to the emperor which it provided for was formerly an appeal to the people. On the other hand, since all magisterial rights, including the tribunician, were lodged in the emperor, himself " a magistrate and *maior collega* of all other magistrates, a request for intervention addressed to him would properly be called *appellatio*."[4]

Unsolved problems.

Other changes of minor importance which were made under the principate are known to us, but on the matters which affect the trial of Paul our information is unfortunately not certain.  Let us set down some of the unanswered questions :

(i.) Was the right of appeal under the empire permitted to all citizens of Rome from acts of provincial governors involving capital punishment, or was it extended to others than citizens—in fact to all residents of the Empire ?

(ii.) If distinction was made in the case of citizens, how was citizenship established ?  By papers carried by the citizen wherever he travelled ? [5]

(iii.) On what charges was appeal to Rome authorized ?  Or was it

---

[1] *Provocatio ad populum* as such appears to have been already practically abolished by the legislation of Sulla.  Regular courts at Rome (*quaestiones perpetuae*) heard appeals formerly submitted to the *comitia*.  These *quaestiones perpetuae* were under the early empire theoretically exempt from the control of the princeps.

[2] *Sententiae*, v. 26. 1 : " lege Iulia de vi publica damnatur, qui aliqua potestate praeditus civem Romanum antea ad populum, nunc imperatorem appellantem necaverit necarive iusserit, torserit, verberaverit, condemnaverit inve publica vincula duci iusserit.  Cuius rei poena in humiliores capitis in honestiores insulae deportatione coercetur."

[3] *Digest*, xlviii. 6. 7.

[4] J. L. Strachan-Davidson, *Problems of the Roman Criminal Law*, 1912, vol. ii. p. 176.

[5] The same question arises about other privileges of citizens, e.g. the immunity from examination by scourging.  Epictetus, iii. 24. 41, and Suetonius, *Claudius*, xxv., suggest how serious it was for one to claim Roman citizenship falsely.  But how could Paul or others (Silas) be proved to be claiming it falsely or truly ?  The Roman name was superficial evidence, but the magistrate would require some means of identifying the accused.  It would be easy to invent a Roman name as an alias.  On the other hand the census-lists would contain the names of Roman citizens at the time of the last assessment and at the place of *origo*, but even at Tarsus Paul would have to identify himself as the Paulus listed as a Roman citizen.  Were birth-certificates of Roman citizens such as those discovered in recent times (cf. H. A. Sanders, *Class. Philol.* xxii., 1927, pp. 409 ff.; *Memoirs of the American Academy in Rome*, ix., 1931, pp. 61 ff., where earlier literature is named) carried around by them when they travelled like a modern passport ?

extended to all charges ?  And if, as seems likely, it was valid only when allowed by the provincial governor,[1] what items was he expected to take into consideration ?

(iv.) Could the authorized appellant make claim only after sentence was passed ?  Could he appeal against trial by the governor as a court of first instance, or against some detail of procedure after the proceedings had once begun ?

(v.) In cases where the provincial governor had not the right to condemn, or at least not the right to condemn without allowing appeal, had the governor no right to acquit ?  And if he had this right could it be exercised at any stage in the proceedings or only before appeal was made ?

(vi.) Was the provincial governor regarded as having had the emperor's *potestas* including the *ius gladii* delegated to him by the emperor, so that the restrictions on his authority were due only to the place of his jurisdiction (*militiae*) ?  or was the office of proconsul or procurator in itself incompetent to deal with certain cases, whether as the court of first instance or as a final court ?

(vii.) Was there any difference in the procedure when the governor was a *procurator* rather than a *legatus* or when he was either of these imperial appointees rather than the proconsul over a senatorial province ?

If now we confront these questions and the preceding summary of legal procedure with the story in Acts, several points emerge.  As for the questions it may be said : Answers suggested by Acts.

(i.) Acts does not indicate that the right of appeal was limited to Roman citizens.  Though Paul's citizenship is claimed in connexion with flogging, it is not mentioned as validating his appeal to Caesar.

(ii.) There is no evidence as to how Paul proved his citizenship.  He states it, and his word is apparently accepted at once.  This can scarcely be a complete representation of the actual procedure.

(iii.) The charge on which Paul was accused, and the penalty to which he was subject, though not explicit, were doubtless understood to be serious, e.g. *maiestas* and death (Acts xxv. 11) respectively, so that we cannot infer that in minor cases also appeals were possible ; but the appeal was not allowed by the procurator automatically.  He first consulted his *consilium* (xxv. 12).  Then he decided (xxv. 25 ἔκρινα) to send Paul to the emperor.

(iv.) Paul's appeal takes place after certain hearings by the procurators and before formal sentence is pronounced.  It appears to be not so much an appeal from the jurisdiction of the procurator as a device to escape either the jurisdiction of a lower court (the Sanhedrin) to which Festus seemed inclined to commit him, or trial by Festus himself in an atmosphere prejudicial to a fair hearing or under circumstances that would expose Paul to a violent death by lynching or assassination.

---

[1] On the allowing of an appeal see Mommsen, *Gesammelte Schriften*, iii. pp. 386 ff.  In like manner a delegation to the emperor was ' allowed ' by Festus (Josephus, *Antiq*. xx. 8. 11, § 194).  Similar requests by the Jews to send an embassy to the emperor are made to Varus (Josephus, *Antiq*. xvii. 11. 1), Fadus and Longinus (*ibid*. xx. 1. 1), Petronius (Philo, *Legat. ad Gaium*, 33, § 247), Flaccus (Philo, *In Flaccum*, 12, § 97).

(v.) It is explicitly said that Paul could have been freed if he had not appealed to Caesar.[1] But whether a release without further trial before the procurator is meant is not told us, nor why, if no further hearing was needed, the appeal seemed to Agrippa absolutely to prevent Festus from releasing Paul: " This man could have been set free if he had not appealed to Caesar." Nevertheless the dialogue definitely implies that at least at some stage in the proceedings a sentence of acquittal was possible in the provinces for those accused as Paul had been if the prisoner himself did not appeal.[2]

(vi.) There is an interesting but obscure phrase of Paul's in xxv. 10, " I stand at Caesar's judgement-seat where I ought to be judged." This might imply that the provincial $\beta\hat{\eta}\mu\alpha$ was regarded as representing the emperor. Eger[3] has attempted to confirm this by phrases from the papyri, and there can be no doubt that the procurator held his authority by delegation from the emperor. It would be difficult, however, to regard the appeal as from the emperor to the emperor, and this phrase may be taken as an appeal not against the jurisdiction of the procurator, but against the Jewish court to whom Festus threatened to expose Paul. He insists on a Roman trial.

The limited value of Acts.

If Acts could be regarded as an impeccable account of Roman procedure couched in technical phraseology, its answers to our questions, in the absence of other information, would have to satisfy us, not only about its own intention, but also about contemporary procedure. But its trustworthiness in legal detail can, under the circumstances, be neither affirmed nor denied categorically.[4] Neither legal nor Biblical experts agree in their verdict about it. Possibly we should read further between the lines.

We might well suppose, for example, that though Roman citizenship is not mentioned, it was the basis of Paul's plea. It was disclosed to the authorities at an early stage of the trial (xxii. 25); it was reported by Lysias when the case was referred to Felix (xxiii. 27). It was a fact of which any

---

[1] We may suspect that both then and earlier the only real obstacle to the release of Paul by the procurators was not legal difficulty, but a lack of courage on their part to do justice against Jewish protest. So at least we are intended to understand the actions of Pilate and of Felix, and this may be the meaning of Acts xxviii. 19, " When the Jews opposed [my release] I was compelled to appeal to Caesar."

[2] We may add that the legal evidence from other sources indicates that the remanding to Rome of a prisoner implied that the governor was not satisfied as to his innocence—in other words that he believed that there were reasonable grounds for the prisoner's being held under arrest until the case could be tried in the competent tribunal. In some cases he could write to Rome for advice. In the case of the Christians Pliny followed both courses.

[3] *Op. cit.* note 28 : τὸ ἱερώτατον τοῦ ἡγεμόνος βῆμα.

[4] Mommsen's criticism of xxviii. 18 f. (*ZNTW.* ii., 1901, p. 93 note) and Schwartz's criticism of xxv. 9 (*GGN.*, 1907, p. 295 note) are typical of the verdict of hopelessness which details in Acts elicit. I may add that Luke's accuracy about the census in Luke ii. 1 does not seem to me to have been vindicated yet in spite of many attempts.

review of the case would make Festus cognizant.  Shall we assume that
the author knew the rights of appeal involved in Roman citizenship?
On the other hand, his references to citizenship do not inspire confidence.  It is true that the same legal situation which authorized appeal
to Rome also forbade corporal punishment.  The *leges* that provided for
*provocatio* had the effect of preventing sentence to flogging as well as execution of the sentence.  Yet both times that Paul objects as a citizen to
flogging, his objection emphasizes that he is uncondemned (ἀκατάκριτος
xvi. 37, xxii. 25).  No doubt to flog a non-Roman for examination was as
usual as the modern "third degree" in America, but it would appear as
though the author believed that a citizen when duly condemned could be
flogged.[1]  A similar point of view perhaps emerges in the passage (xxv. 16)
where the " custom of the Romans " is definitely cited.  Festus says such
custom does not allow a man to be condemned before he has a chance to
meet his accusers and make his defence.  Again the implication is that it is
because he is unheard, or rather unsentenced, that Paul is to be protected
from severe punishment, and not merely because he is a Roman.

Another suggestion may be made about the so-called appeal to Caesar.
The author of Acts doubtless understood it as does his reader as a provi-
dential step to get Paul to Rome.  Paul intended in this way both to escape
from danger and to achieve his desired goal.  But, assuming the accuracy
of the narrative, may we not read behind it a different development ?
Paul was appealing, not to Rome, but against Jerusalem.  As already said,
he desired a Roman trial.  He argued that as the representative tribunal
of the emperor the procurator's court ought not to surrender him to his
enemies; therefore he said, "I stand at Caesar's judgement-seat where I
ought to be judged."  But the procurator, twisting Paul's grandiloquent
words, took them as an appeal to Caesar at Rome, and consequently
disposed of an awkward case by reference to the emperor.  From the
historian's viewpoint it was an inspired manœuvre, for it brought Paul to
his goal at Rome.

### IV.  *The Outcome of the Action against Paul*

Our uncertainty as to the exact nature of procedure in general, and of    The result of
Paul's case in particular, follows us in endeavouring to understand the    the appeal.
sequel to the appeal.  Presumably prisoners sent to Rome for trial,
whether at their own initiative or another's, whether citizens or not, were

---

[1] On the other hand the wording of Acts xxii. 29 καὶ ὁ χιλίαρχος δὲ ἐφοβήθη
ἐπιγνοὺς ὅτι Ῥωμαῖός ἐστιν καὶ ὅτι αὐτὸν ἦν δεδεκώς suggests that our author
thought that even the imprisonment of a Roman citizen by Lysias was culpable.
In support of the record of Acts that (whether legally or not) Paul was beaten,
imprisoned, stoned, etc., are his own words in 2 Cor. xi. 23 ff., including ἐν
φυλακαῖς περισσοτέρως . . . τρὶς ἐραβδίσθην, ἅπαξ ἐλιθάσθην, but on the other
hand the letters of Paul say nothing of his Roman citizenship.  M. Jones,
*St. Paul the Orator,* 1910, p. 168, believes that some of these punishments only
Romans could have administered, and that the author of Acts, " in pursuance
of the definite purpose of the book, has kept them out of sight."

treated much alike. They would be escorted under guard. It has been conjectured that special military appointments were made for this purpose.[1] Paul and other prisoners were sent forward in care of Julius, a centurion of the *cohors Augusta*. *Litterae dimissoriae* were prepared to accompany the prisoner or to explain the case.[2] We are led to suppose that the memorandum by Festus after consultation with Agrippa was quite favourable to Paul.

The expenses of the trial.   The expenses of the trial are a question on which we have no real information. Ramsay repeatedly emphasizes that for both parties the expenses would be quite heavy, and he uses this consideration to infer that Paul had some considerable means at his disposal,[3] and that the accusers, on the other hand, unless they felt some real necessity to press the case, would be likely to let it drop.[4]

It is not clear, however, that Paul, who was in the habit of constant travel and preaching at his own expense, would find either the journey to Rome, or residence there as a prisoner, more expensive than his usual manner of life. It is possible that his transportation was at government expense. I think food on voyages was always provided by individual passengers rather than by the ship's owner (so at Acts xxviii. 10). Paul would hardly be expected to pay the expense of his Roman escort, and if he paid the expenses of his friends (Aristarchus or (?) Luke) even that would not be new (cf. xx. 34 τοῖς οὖσιν μετ' ἐμοῦ). We are informed that prisoners were able to engage in their own business.[5] It is possible that Acts xxviii. 30 (see note) means by ἐν ἰδίῳ μισθώματι much the same thing, self-support on his own wages.

Another expense of modern appeals may also have been spared in Paul's case—the expense of witnesses and attorneys. Though the Jews employed Tertullus in an earlier trial, Paul is always represented as speaking for himself. Mommsen seems to regard the employment of an *advocatus*, ῥήτωρ or συνήγορος, as unknown in trials before the emperor in criminal cases.[6] The superior courts probably did not require witnesses from either party. But how the evidence was presented we cannot be sure. Certainly

---

[1] See Additional Note 33, p. 444. Some appellants to the emperor travelled not as prisoners at all, but at most were on bond to appear at his court.

[2] Cf. Acts xxiii. 25 ff., xxv. 26. The term and its synonym *apostoli* are attested in later law, when a time limit for demanding and presenting them was fixed with penalties attached. See the discussion of J. C. Naber, *Mnemosyne*, N.S. 1, 1922, pp. 1 ff.

[3] *St. Paul the Traveller*, pp. 311 ff.

[4] *The Teaching of Paul*, pp. 355, 362.

[5] Ulpian, *Dig.* iv. 6. 10 *rei suae superesse*.

[6] *Römisches Strafrecht*, pp. 264 f. According to Merkel, *op. cit.* p. 91, both parties in a provincial appeal had to appear before the *iudex ad quem*. The free city was represented by σύνδικοι. The substitution of agents for the parties to the appeal was allowed in *causae pecuniariae*, not in *causae capitales*. At a later time the whole reference of the case was made in writing. No parties appeared before the Court of Appeal. The records of the first hearings became the basis of final decision.

some appeals to the emperor included considerable personnel on both sides—whether as witnesses, or as pleaders and sympathizers.

The Palestinian Jews would more probably have to incur their own expense if they decided to go in person, or to send their representatives to press the case in Rome.   Unlike Paul, they might have no desire on their own account to be at Rome.   Possibly under such circumstances they would entrust the prosecution of their interests to the local Jews at Rome. Josephus[1] tells us that the Roman Jews supported in large numbers the complaint made to the emperor by the Palestinian Jews against Archelaus, though fifty representatives were sent from Palestine, and when Josephus himself and others went to Rome to use their influence in attempting to secure acquittal from the emperor of certain Jewish priests sent to Rome by Felix, they relied on two local Jews—Aliturus, Nero's favourite actor, and Poppaea, Nero's wife.[2]   It is not inconceivable that in Paul's case the Palestinian Jews, if they wished to press their cause, would be likely to enlist the Jews of Rome, and that the object of Acts xxviii. 21 is to indicate that no such move against Paul had been made.

In the first century in Rome prisoners, sent up on appeal from provinces, were apparently entrusted to the *praefectus praetorio*.   Some Latin MSS. reading *praefectus* are understood to mean that this was done to the prisoners brought by Julius.   The corresponding Greek, using στρατοπεδ-άρχης, may mean the same (see note *ad loc.*).[3]   *The custody of prisoners.*

Acts describes the custody as light.   It was the *custodia militaris*.[4] Paul had privacy and company very much as he desired them, and there was opportunity to preach and perhaps to work.   Whether the descriptions of his status given in Philippians belong to this time or not, they offer no contradiction.

Of a trial of Paul Acts tells us nothing.   Cases appealed from the provinces in the time of Claudius and Nero were apparently heard by the emperor in person.   Of this we have evidence in papyri and in history.[5] But they, as well as earlier and later emperors, also delegated authority.   *Paul's trial in Rome.*

---

[1] *Antiq.* xvii. 11. 1, § 300 ;  *B.J.* ii. 6. 1, § 80.

[2] *Vita*, 3, § 16.

[3] Cf. Vol. III. p. 253, Vol. IV. p. 345 and Addit. Note 33.

[4] See the article by Hitzig on ' Custodia ' in Pauly-Wissowa, iv. col. 1897 ff., and, largely dependent on it, Wikenhauser, *Die Apostelgeschichte*, pp. 360 f.   An interesting account of both more and less severe custody at Rome is given by Josephus, *Antiq.* xviii. 6. 7, §§ 203 f., and 10, § 235, in connexion with the changing fortunes of Agrippa I.

[5] The papyri afford analogies rather than evidence.   The cases in the papyri to be mentioned below are not strictly appeals like Paul's, they are more like the hearings of embassies.   Taubenschlag in his article cited above, p. 299, note 3, says explicitly, " Seulement nous ne trouvons pas de cas dans les papyri, où un citoyen romain en appellerait au tribunal impérial ; mais il faut dire, que nous ne possédons pas de matériel concernant un procès intenté devant la cour impériale.   Dans les papyri l'unique procès qui soit déroulé devant l'empereur provient d'un cas ordinaire et non d'une provocation (cf. P Oxy 33 et Mommsen, *Strafrecht*, 265 ; Taubenschlag, *Strafrecht*, 95₁)."

The *praefecti praetorio* here again became prominent.[1]   We are told that under Nero appeals were directed to the Senate for decision.   There is also the statement that appeals from the provinces were delegated by Augustus to *consularibus viris, quos singulos cuiusque provinciae negotiis praeposuisset.*[2]   Even when the emperor himself heard a case he was assisted by his friends who formed his *consilium*, which, in turn, became, a body of legal experts.[3]   All this seems fairly certain.   But who served as accusers ?   How was the case called, and when ?   On what basis was it decided ?   As to the latter point, we may at least conjecture that it was settled not strictly on the basis of evidence, law, or precedent, but in accordance with the feelings of the court of appeal.   Such, at least, had been the basis of treatment of appellants in earlier Roman history.   It was, as its name implies, an appeal for favour, at least in part. Although the procedure in pardon is as obscure as in appeal, the pardon was an extensive item in the procedure of the principate,[4] difficult to distinguish from the emperor's functions as a court of first or second instance.

Procedure in appeals.

Certain elements of procedure are known to us from another type of appeal for which we have some slight evidence [5]—the appeal to the provincial governor or to the emperor from a non-Roman local court, as, for example, of a free Greek city like Athens or Cos.   The fragmentary documents [6] speak of the appeal as addressed either to the proconsul or to the emperor, and they seem to specify the conditions to be observed by the city government.   It must satisfy the governor of the merits of its case if the appeal is to the governor ; if it is to the emperor it must supply some

---

[1] There is no evidence before the third century that these *praefecti* constituted the authority before which cases submitted to the emperor at Rome were tried.   Rather were they responsible for the custody of the prisoners awaiting trial.   This affects our understanding of πραιτώριον in Philip. i. 13 (see Lohmeyer in Meyer[3] *ad loc.*).   If Paul is writing from Rome *praetorium* must refer not to the emperor's palace nor to his judicial court but to the praetorian guard or its barracks.   Conversely if the passage in Philip. i. 13 is understood to refer to the high judicial authority before which Paul was tried, then the place of writing must be in the provinces, as at Caesarea (Acts xxiii. 35, see note), Ephesus (see note on Acts xix. 23-41), etc.

[2] Suetonius, *Aug.* 33.

[3] Cuq, 'Mémoire sur le Consilium Principis' in *Mémoires présentés par divers Savants à l'Académie des Inscriptions et Belles Lettres*, 1884.   The trial of Appianus (late A.D. 2) in P Oxy 33 implies a hearing, in the presence of the emperor, of a proconsul and of the Senate, or at least part of it.   Cf. Vol. IV. p. 322.

[4] See J. Merkel, 'Über die Begnadigungscompetenz im römischen Strafprocesse' (*Abhandlungen aus dem Gebiete des römischen Rechts*, Heft i.), 1881, especially pp. 33 ff. ; A. H. J. Greenidge, 'The Power of Pardon possessed by the " Princeps," ' *Class. Rev.* viii., 1894, pp. 429 ff.

[5] See Mommsen, *Zeitschrift der Savigny-Stiftung für Rechtsgeschichte*, Röm. Abt. xi., 1890, pp. 34 ff. ( =*Gesammelte Schriften*, iii. pp. 386 ff.).

[6] *C.I.A.* iii. 38; Paton and Hicks, *The Inscriptions of Cos*, No. 26.

sort of bond.  In either case it must elect its representatives.[1]  Possibly
in the extant inscriptions the city itself, or its representative, is the
appellant.  The safeguards are aimed to prevent merely malicious appeals [2]
or the wilful avoidance of trial.[3]  Whether cases like the appeal of Paul
had like elements of procedure is, of course, uncertain.

An interesting light on procedure before the emperor is given by various  Philo's
extant accounts of deputations of Alexandrian Jews and Gentiles who  evidence.
appeared before the emperor.  It is to be admitted that the hearing of an
appealing prisoner remitted on a criminal charge may well have differed
in many respects from occasions in which the emperor gave an audience
to two rival petitioning delegations representing divergent interests in
some city or province of the empire.  Yet Philo describes the proper procedure in the latter circumstances much as we should picture the trial of
Paul.  The passage is worth quoting in full.  Philo, himself one of the Jewish
delegation to Caligula in A.D. 40, complains of the shabby treatment they
had received, and contrasts it with what would have befitted a fair judge :

δικαστοῦ μὲν γὰρ ἔργα ταῦτα ἦν· καθῆται μετὰ συνέδρων ἀριστίνδην
ἐπιλελεγμένων, ἐξεταζομένης ὑποθέσεως μεγίστης ἐν τετρακοσίοις ἔτεσιν
ἡσυχασθείσης καὶ νῦν πρῶτον εἰσαγομένης ἐπὶ μυριάσι πολλαῖς τῶν
Ἀλεξανδρέων Ἰουδαίων, ἑκατέρωθεν στῆναι τοὺς ἀντιδίκους μετὰ τῶν
συναγορευσόντων, ἐν μέρει μὲν ἀκοῦσαι τῆς κατηγορίας, ἐν μέρει δὲ τῆς
ἀπολογίας πρὸς μεμετρημένον ὕδωρ, ἀναστάντα βουλεύσασθαι μετὰ τῶν
συνέδρων, τί χρὴ φανερῶς ἀποφήνασθαι γνώμῃ τῇ δικαιοτάτῃ.[4]

Of equal interest are the accounts of similar hearings in the papyri.[5]  The papyri.
They are all apparently written from the anti-Jewish standpoint.  They
purport to give accounts of the proceedings before the emperor in person.

---

[1] ἐὰν δὲ ἐκκαλέσηταί τις ἢ ἐμὲ (i.e. the emperor) ἢ τὸν ἀνθύπατον, χειροτονείτω
συνδίκους ὁ δῆμος.

[2] ἐπηρείας [χάριν].                         [3] διὰ τοὺς φυγοδικοῦντας.

[4] Legatio ad Gaium, 44, § 350, p. 597 M.

[5] The principal papyri involved are P Lond i. p. 227 + P Par 68 = BGU.
341 ; BGU. 511 + P Cairo 10448, BGU. 588, P Oxy 33, P Oxy 1242, P Oxy
1089.  Cf. also P Lond 1912.  The discussion of these papyri has produced a
considerable literature most of which is listed in H. I. Bell, Jews and Christians
in Egypt, 1924, p. 10, note 1.  Add E. von Dobschütz in Amer. Jour. of Theol.
viii., 1904, pp. 728 ff. ; A. von Premerstein in Philologus, Supplementband xvi.,
Heft ii., 1923; E. Meyer, Ursprung und Anfänge des Christentums, iii., 1923,
pp. 539 ff. ; H. I. Bell in Beihefte zum ' Alten Orient,' ix., 1926 ; and Clark
Hopkins in Yale Classical Studies, i., 1928, pp. 171 ff.  See particularly W. Weber
in Hermes, l., 1915, pp. 47 ff., who draws many parallels between the papyri
and the trial of Paul and at the end emphasizes that both are literature of the
same type.  On the Jewish problem at Alexandria new discussions (for example,
S. Loesch, Epistula Claudiana, Rottenburg a. N., 1930) and even new materials
continue to appear.  Of the second item in the above list, the so-called Isidorus
Acts, two new papyrus fragments have been found, one at Berlin (published
in the Sitzungsberichte of the Berlin Academy, 1930, pp. 664 ff., by Uxkull-
Gyllenband) and one in London published in Archiv für Papyrusforschung,
x., 1931, pp. 5 ff., by H. I. Bell.

He is attended by his *consilium*, and the proconsul may also be in attendance. Both parties are present in numbers. They have their spokesmen and ῥήτορες, but they are sometimes treated as units and dealt with collectively. At other times individuals are subject to individual sentence direct from the emperor. We can only conjecture that these were cases of *seditio* and that the members of the delegation were at the same time representatives or ringleaders of the opposing factions, and that they were held guilty personally if their faction was decided to be in the wrong. We may note further the references to the interest or intervention in the Jewish cause of the wives of the emperors or women closely connected with the emperor—Agrippina under Claudius and Plotina under Trajan.[1] Evidently the Gentile authors regarded the Jewish prejudice of the court as partly domestic intrigue. A Christian under Nero might well fear the influence of Poppaea.[2]

Of particular interest is the fact that these Alexandrian *acta martyrum*, as they have been called, evidently are not mere contemporary documents. They are a literary genre.[3] They represent a topic of composition— historical tracts with a purpose, circulated in later times as a form of literature. While the book of Acts does not give the hearing before the emperor, the earlier stages as presented are at least a literary analogy to the anti-Semitic propaganda of the Gentile documents.

Inscription in Cyrene.    A still closer parallel to the case of Paul is furnished by a more recent discovery, the inscriptions of Augustus in Cyrene.[4] In the second of the

---

[1] *BGU*. 511, lines 7 f.; P Oxy 1242, lines 26, 31 f. Josephus, *Antiq.* xx. 6. 3, § 135, mentions Agrippina as intervening for the Jews against Cumanus, Celer, and the Samaritans at the instigation of Herod Agrippa II. One inevitably compares the Jewish 'queens' mentioned in Acts—Drusilla and Bernice. Cf. Vol. IV. p. 296. We may compare in other stories the intervention of the official's wife in the fate of Jews: a concubine (?) of Artaxerxes present when relief is asked for the Jews (Neh. ii. 6, see commentaries), a concubine of Ptolemy Physcon entreating his mercy for the Jews (Josephus, *C. Apion.* ii. 5, § 55), Herodias suggesting to Herod Antipas the execution of John the Baptist (Mark vi. 24=Matt. xiv. 8), Pilate's wife urging him because of a dream to clemency toward Jesus (Matt. xxvii. 19).

[2] She intervened for the Jewish delegations mentioned by Josephus in *Vita*, 3, § 16 (under Felix), and in *Antiq.* xx. 8. 11, § 195 (under Festus). We have beside in Josephus reference to the intervention of Antonia (*Antiq.* xviii. 6. 4-7) and Agrippina (*Antiq.* xx. 6. 3) on behalf of the Agrippas.

[3] See especially Weber and von Premerstein in the articles cited in note 5, p. 323.

[4] First published by G. Oliverio, *Notiziario Archeologico* of the Ministero delle Colonie, Fasc. iv. (1927), pp. 13 ff. The juristic aspects, including a reference to the parallelism with Paul's trial, are most fully dealt with by A. von Premerstein, *Zeitschrift der Savigny-Stiftung*, xlviii. (1928), Röm. Abt. pp. 419 ff., especially pp. 458-466, and by L. Wenger in *Abhandlungen der Bayerischen Akademie der Wissenschaften*, xxxiv., 1928, 2. Abhandlung, especially pp. 71 ff. English readers have access to the text and English translation in an article by J. G. C. Anderson in the *Journal of Roman Studies*, xvii., 1927, pp. 33 ff.

five edicts (lines 40-55) dated in the year 7-6 B.C. the emperor exonerates·
from blame Publius Sextius Scaeva, apparently the proconsul of the province, for sending up to him as prisoners three men who had declared that
they knew and wished to tell the emperor a matter that concerned his
welfare and the public interests. They proved to have no such information.
The emperor therefore released them from their custody and dismissed
them. Two of the men from their names are plainly Roman citizens, the
third is explicitly called a freedman.

Here is apparently the earliest recorded case of the sending of citizens
from the provinces to Rome for imperial jurisdiction. It should be
observed that thus early the emperor served as court of final appeal
even for a senatorial province like *Creta et Cyrene*. There is no evidence
that the Senate was consulted.[1] Like Paul the prisoners were sent
as δέσμιοι.[2] Their custody in Rome is described as παραφυλακή,
which has been supposed to mean light custody. One of the prisoners
is retained on another charge and is given still greater freedom than
formerly, being merely forbidden to depart without the emperor's
instructions.

Though much in the inscription remains obscure, this much is
clear, and it provides a tantalizing parallel to the narrative of Paul.
The prisoners from Cyrene apparently confess that they have lied
about the information they have for the emperor.[3] Were they afraid
of an unfavourable sentence if the proconsul had his way, much as
Paul was ? Or, on the other hand, was the proconsul without
the *potestas gladii* ? In a more general way the decrees show that
long before Trajan wrote his detailed advice to Pliny in Bithynia,
the emperor kept his hand on the various affairs of provincial
administration.

With regard to one matter of procedure, an interesting and novel Lake and
suggestion made some years ago by Professor Lake and subsequently by Ramsay.

---

[1] Contrast line 12, where the emperor makes a provisional arrangement
until the Senate can deliberate. Cf. von Premerstein *loc. cit.* and in *Klio*,
xxii., 1929, pp. 162 ff. On the other hand D. McFayden, *Classical Philology*,
xvi., 1921, pp. 34 ff., and xxiii., 1928, pp. 388 ff., disputes the inference that
the emperor had *imperium maius* over the governor. Rather he thinks for
senatorial provinces the emperor's action was merely a *cognitio* or investigation
of the facts. See his fuller study, ' The Rise of the Princeps' Jurisdiction
within the City of Rome,' *Washington University Studies*, x., 1923, pp.
181-265.

[2] Line 46; cf. δεσμώτας in Acts xxvii. 1, 42.

[3] Or have been lied about. Unfortunately the charge against them, if there
was one, is not clear, nor is it clear what blame would be attributed to the
proconsul—whether for imprisoning Roman citizens and sending them to Rome,
or whether for not punishing them in a more summary fashion. It is to be hoped
that further discussion of scholars will clarify some of these points. That
prisoners could hope to escape immediate punishment by claiming to have
information of importance to the emperor is suggested by Josephus, *Antiq.*
xviii. 6. 5, § 169 ; *B.J.* iii. 8. 9, § 404 ; cf. vi. 7. 1, § 360.

Professor Ramsay [1] deserves consideration.  It may be most conveniently presented in Professor Lake's own words, taken from the *Theologisch Tijdschrift*, xlvii. (1913) pp. 356 ff.:

The problem of the end of Acts.

" The real difficulty of the last chapter of Acts is best put in the form of a question.  Why does Luke seem to stop his narrative in the middle of an incident ?  We are told with sufficient detail, and considerable vividness of style, why Paul was arrested in Jerusalem, why the hearing of his case was removed to Rome, and how he was treated on his arrival in the city. But just when the story seems to be leading up to a trial in Rome it suddenly comes to an end, not in the least as though the writer were breaking off hurriedly and unexpectedly, but with a sentence which obviously was as carefully composed for a conclusion as the opening words of Acts were for a beginning.

" Moreover, all the hints [2] afforded by the narrative and by the Epistles

[1] The history of the articles involved has been unearthed only with some effort.  The argument of Professor Lake was first published in the January 1909 issue of the *Interpreter*, v. pp. 146-156, under the title, ' What was the end of St. Paul's trial ? '  In the July issue of the same volume (pp. 438 f.), in making a reply to the criticism of Vernon Bartlet, Professor Lake added the example of the case of Lampon in Philo which J. H. A. Hart had suggested to him.  Professor W. M. Ramsay in the *Expositor* for March 1913, pp. 264-284, published under the title ' The Imprisonment and Supposed Trial of St. Paul ' a similar argument, relying on the legal knowledge of Professor J. S. Reid and including the example of Lampon.  This was reprinted as chapter li. in his *Teaching of Paul in Terms of the Present Day* (1913), pp. 346-382.  Almost simultaneously Professor Lake reprinted his earlier article (embodying the note about Lampon) in *Theologisch Tijdschrift*, xlvii. (June 1913) pp.356-365.  It is this last that is republished here. Bartlet's objections were published in the *Interpreter*, v., 1909, pp. 329 f., and in the *Expositor*, May 1913, pp. 464-467.

[2] The points which seem to be cogent are the emphasis on the more or less favourable opinion of the Roman authorities as compared with the hostility of the Jews, and the hint in Acts xxvi. 32 of future acquittal by the emperor, rather than a suggestion that Paul made a mistake in appealing.  Yet certainly these indications are not decisive ; no one would build on them.  More important is the evidence outside the Acts which points to a release of Paul.  This is—

(*a*) In the Pauline Epistles (omitting the Pastorals) :

(1) Philemon 22, " But withal prepare me also a lodging ; for I hope that through your prayers I shall be granted unto you."

(2) Philip. i. 23 ff. " But I am in a strait between the two . . . yet to abide in the flesh is more needful for your sakes."

(3) Philip. ii. 24, " I trust in the Lord that I myself shall also come shortly." These passages seem to point to an expectation of release ; why should we assume that it was falsified ?

(*b*) The general consensus of opinion that it is difficult to find room for the Pastorals before the end of Acts, and the fact that if they have to be placed after Acts they certainly imply an acquittal.  Professor Bartlet will not admit this, but it is the weak point in his position, and deserves fuller treatment.  At

seem to point to an issue favourable to Paul, for there is a continuous and surely intentional emphasis throughout the book on the fact that Paul was never found guilty by any Roman court.  I find it hard to think that Luke would have written in this way, if he had known that the last and most important trial of all was unfavourable to his argument.

" Thus it is really a most difficult thing to answer the question, why Luke stopped when he did.

" Two explanations seem to be popular.  The first is that Luke intended to write a third book in which the trial before Caesar would be described.  In spite of the vogue given to this theory by various popular writers, such as Sir William Ramsay, it is in itself exceedingly improbable. That is to say, it is not impossible that Luke wrote a third book in which he described the further spread of Christianity; but it is exceedingly unlikely that he chose to split an important narrative between the two books. *The possibility of a third volume of Luke-Acts.*

" It might, it is true, be urged that the division between the Gospel and Acts afforded an actual example of just such a splitting of one narrative—that of the Ascension—between two books.  But this is not really the case.  As the opening verses of Acts show, Luke regarded his Gospel as covering the whole of the earthly ministry of the Lord, from his Birth to his Ascension.[1]  The reason why the Acts returns to the story of the parting of Jesus from his disciples is that Luke wished to amplify and correct the statement at the end of the Gospel.  If the end of Acts really presents a parallel in form to the end of the Gospel, it ought to contain a short statement of the end of the trial of Paul, and it is not impossible, though improbable, that this statement was taken up and expanded in a third book which has not survived.

" To split the narrative of a single incident between two books is common enough in the less reputable forms of serial fiction, but it is not the method of an historian, and whatever view be taken of the accuracy of his narratives, there is no doubt that Luke was consciously a writer of history.

" The other explanation is that Luke stopped when he did because at the time events had gone no further.  In other words, he was writing before the trial of Paul was finished.  This view has recently been advocated by Harnack in his *Neue Untersuchungen zur Apostelgeschichte*.  Still, as he himself points out, there are serious objections to so early a date for Acts. For instance, there is certainly some evidence, though I admit that it is not very strong, for the view that the Lucan books were written after the *The early date theory.*

---

present I must admit that if I thought that St. Paul was condemned at his first trial I should regard the Pastorals as undoubtedly spurious ; and I fancy that many would take the same view.

(c) The evidence of Clement of Rome, that St. Paul reached τὸ τέρμα τῆς δύσεως before his death.  It is hard to think that a Roman could ever have meant Rome itself by this expression.

[1] This is true whatever text be read.  The words ἀνεφέρετο εἰς τὸν οὐρανόν only explain διέστη and do not affect the broad sense of the narrative.

fall of Jerusalem. It is equally certain that a strong case can be made out for the growth of legend and a change of doctrine with regard to the Ascension, and some critics think that this development is impossible so early as A.D. 60, though it is hard to see that this legendary growth is more than what might have taken place within twenty years of the Resurrection, or even sooner. Finally, and to my own mind most important of all, there is exceedingly good ground for thinking that Luke was acquainted with the writings of Josephus. If this be true, there is good reason for thinking that Acts was written between A.D. 90 and 100. But this makes it more difficult than ever to understand why Luke does not mention the end of the trial. For if it be true that Domitian persecuted the Christians (and there is little reason to doubt it), the definite acquittal of Paul by the Emperor would have been so strong an argument that it could hardly have been passed by.

The two remaining possibilities.

" Thus one is driven to a choice between two alternatives. (1) In spite of the apparent indications given in Acts, Paul really was condemned and executed. (2) That the end of the trial, though favourable to Paul, was of such a nature that it added nothing to Luke's implied argument, and was from this point of view even a little disappointing.

Reasons against a condemnation of St. Paul.

" Either of these alternatives would explain the facts. I would, however, argue that the former is really excluded, not only by the general impression created by the Acts, but by the facts that in writing to Philemon Paul looks confidently forward to release, and that the Pastoral epistles seem certainly to imply that this release actually took place. This last point is only weakened and not invalidated if the authenticity of the Pastoral epistles be denied, for in any case they represent an early and valuable tradition as to the life of the apostle.

The possibility of an indecisive end to the trial.

" Thus one is driven to consider the remaining possibility, and ask whether it is conceivable that the end of the trial was favourable to Paul but disappointing to Luke.

" What was the situation ? Paul had been arrested in Jerusalem by the Jews ; but being a Roman citizen, had been protected by the Roman procurator, who also took cognizance of the case, and insisted that the Jews should accuse Paul before him. He was, however, definitely the judge and not the accuser ; Paul was not accused of anything by the Romans, and in modern language the case might be described as ' The Jews v. Paul.'

" The Procurator could not quite understand the case, and asked Paul if he would go to Jerusalem to be tried ; but the apostle stood on his rights as a Roman citizen, and insisted on being tried in Caesar's court. On this the Procurator sent the case to Rome. It must not be forgotten that the word ' appeal ' in the English version gives a somewhat wrong connotation. Paul did not appeal against a verdict, but against the proposed change of the venue of the court. The nature of the case was not altered in the least by being removed to Rome. Strictly speaking, it is doubtful whether one can even say that the case was changed from one court to another. Probably all that may be said is that the case was moved from Caesar's court sitting in Caesarea under the representative of Caesar, to

the same court sitting in Rome under Caesar himself.   Thus it remained
the case of ' The Jews *v.* Paul.'

" What happened when Paul reached Rome ?

" To understand the passage in its proper proportions one must re-  Luke's<br>interests.
member that Luke has—at least in the latter chapters of the Acts—two
main interests.   He wishes in the first place to show that the Roman
authorities were not hostile to Christianity, and in the second that the
Jews deliberately rejected it, in spite of their own scriptures.

" Both of these interests are displayed in the account of Paul at Rome,  Their mani-<br>festation in<br>the story of<br>Paul in<br>Rome.
and this is only slightly obscured by the fact that both are illustrated by
the same incident—the meeting of Paul with the Jews.

" Luke says that Paul immediately summoned the Jewish community
together and explained to them the situation.

" ' He called together those that were the chief of the Jews ; and when
they were come together he said unto them: "I, brethren, though I had
done nothing against the people, or the customs of our fathers, yet was
delivered prisoner from Jerusalem into the hands of the Romans ; who,
when they had examined me, desired to set me at liberty, because there
was no cause of death in me.   But when the Jews spake against it, I was
constrained to appeal unto Caesar ; not that I had aught to accuse my
nation of.   For this, therefore, did I call you to see and to speak with me ;
for because of the hope of Israel am I bound with this chain." '

" That is to say, he maintains that he has done nothing which a Jew
ought not to have done, and is anxious to persuade the community in
Rome that they ought not to be hostile to him.   It is noticeable that the
word used for ' call ' ($\pi\alpha\rho\epsilon\kappa\acute{\alpha}\lambda\epsilon\sigma\alpha$) is probably the word which would
be used for summoning of a friendly witness.   It is perhaps not too
much to suggest that one of Paul's objects was to provide himself with
testimony on the question of the Jewish law, though too much stress must
not be put on this point, as the words need not necessarily imply any more
than the invitation to come to speak with him.

" To Paul's speech the Jews reply by announcing their ignorance of the
whole matter.   'We neither received letters from Judea concerning thee,
nor did any of the brethren come hither and report or speak any harm of
thee.'

" This was their quite sufficient answer to the question of Paul.   He
naturally wanted to know what were the intentions of the prosecutors
in the case against him ; and he is told that they had neither come to
Rome, nor instructed their representatives in the city.   Therefore, with
this satisfactory incident Luke turns off to his other main interest and
describes how the Jews rejected Paul.   This is the underlying motive of the
whole of the next few paragraphs, which are therefore unimportant for
our present purpose.   But in Acts xxviii. 30 Luke returns to the former
motive, and tells us that Paul 'abode two whole years in his own hired
dwelling, and received all that came in unto him, preaching the kingdom
of God, and teaching the things concerning the Lord Jesus Christ with all
boldness, without hindrance.'

" The real difficulty is not in the meaning of these words, but in their

implication ; and my suggestion is that this difficulty may be entirely due
to our ignorance of the practice of Roman law, and that the passage was
probably perfectly intelligible when it was written.

Roman prac-
tice when a
prosecutor
defaulted.

"The situation was that the defendant in the case of 'The Jews v.
Paul' was waiting trial, and that the prosecutors failed to appear.  Now,
what was the practice in such cases ?  So far as I can find out no one knows;
therefore one has a certain right to proceed to conjecture.  It is surely
extremely probable that the practice in such a case must have been to
quash the whole proceedings and release the prisoner.  It is scarcely less
probable that practice had fixed a stated time after which proceedings
should be quashed in this manner.  Thus I would suggest that if we knew
enough about early Roman law we should probably find that a ' complete
biennium ' was this stated time, and that the meaning of Luke's statement is that the prosecutors never put in an appearance in Rome, and
that Paul waited the statutory time necessary for his release without ever
hearing anything more of the matter.

The meaning
of ' two
years.'

"There is, moreover, one small piece of evidence (for which I am
indebted to Mr. J. H. A. Hart) which suggests that two years really was a
recognized period for this purpose.  In the *In Flaccum* Philo tells the story
of a certain Lampon who got into trouble on a charge of *maiestas* against
Tiberius.  He was innocent, but was kept in custody for two years, and
this period is described as the *longest time*.  Taken in connexion with
Acts, this seems to imply that a case had to be heard within two years.
It is, however, necessary to admit that this, though the most obvious
interpretation, is not absolutely certain, for the Greek is . . . Λάμπων μὲν
ἀσεβείας τῆς εἰς Τιβέριον Καίσαρα δίκην σχὼν καὶ ἐπὶ διετίαν τριβομένου
/τοῦ πράγματος ἀπείρηκώς. ὑπερθέσεις γὰρ καὶ ἀναβολὰς ὁ δικαστὴς
ἐθελοκακῶν ἐσκήπτετο βουλόμενος, κἂν ἀποφύγῃ τὸ ἔγκλημα, τὸν γοῦν
περὶ μέλλοντος ἀδήλου φόβον πρὸς μήκιστον χρόνον ἐπικρεμάσας αὐτῷ
ζωὴν ὀδυνηροτέραν θανάτου παρασχεῖν.  The parallel to Paul's case is
obvious, and I would read into Philo the explanation that μήκιστον χρόνον
is an explanation of διετίαν, and means 'the longest time legally possible';
but I am in fairness bound to admit that it may only mean that the
ingenuity of the δικαστής was exhausted by the end of two years, that
μήκιστον χρόνον is only ' a very long time,' and that the likeness to
Paul's case is merely accidental coincidence, though I think this very
improbable.

Luke's
reticence.

"To render this suggestion more acceptable it is necessary to do two
things.  The first is to discuss the question : why did not Luke say this
explicitly ?  The answer to this is twofold.  In the first place, it is not
impossible that the phrase ' waited two full years without hindrance '
was as explicit in the ears of the first century as 'served his time' would
be in connexion with a convict of the present day.  We should not need
to be told that a convict who had ' served his time ' was released.  The
one fact implies the other.  In the second place, it must be remembered
that the liberation thus obtained by Paul through mere lapse of time was
not a point on which Luke would have wished to lay stress.  His object
was to show that Christianity was not forbidden by the Romans, and the

automatic release of Paul—not because he had been proved innocent, but because the prosecutors had not thought the case worth the trouble of a journey to Rome—was of no use to him as an argument. What was of value was the fact that all through these two years Paul had exercised his claim to teach, and no objection had been raised by the authorities. On that point he does lay emphasis, but the automatic release of the prisoner was unsatisfactory; it was no use as a precedent, and no advocate lays emphasis on the weak points of his argument. Thus it may fairly be claimed that the interpretation suggested really satisfies the conditions of the problem, as laid down previously, for it supplies an end to the trial which was favourable to Paul but disappointing to Luke from the point of view of Christian Apologetic.

" The other thing which remains to be done is to show cause for think- Our ignor-
ing that our knowledge of the Roman law on such a point is so small as to ance of
justify a conjecture. Roman law

" Here I am unfortunately without any first-hand knowledge; but I can find neither book nor scholar claiming any certain information on the point at issue. Above all, I would direct attention to an article by the late Dr. Greenidge in the *Classical Review*, vol. x. (1896) pp. 225 ff. on ' The *Provocatio Militiae* and Provincial Jurisdiction.' From this it will be seen that the whole question of the ' Appeal to Caesar ' on the legal side is most obscure and difficult. It is clear that the right of *provocatio* from a provincial court to Rome was not established in the time of Cicero, and the law which extended the right of *provocatio ad populum* (or *ad Caesarem*) from Rome to the provinces is uncertain. It seems, however, that the *Lex Iulia*, if it did not establish, at least controlled the right of appeal.

" When one turns from the question of legal theory to that of practice, the matter is no easier. There are in the Early Empire only four cases which bear on the question.

" Two of these are mentioned by Pliny, who tells us in his famous letter to Trajan (xcvi. 4) that, in dealing with the Christians in his province, he sent to Rome those who were Roman citizens. This seems to imply that it was the custom for citizens to be sent to Rome if accused of capital offence. But in another place he tells us that Marius Priscus scourged and strangled a Roman knight in the province of Africa. The third case is given by Suetonius who tells us in his Life of Galba (c. 9) that he crucified a guardian for poisoning his ward: ' *Implorantique leges et civem Romanum se testificanti, quasi solatio et honore aliquo poenam leva- turus, mutari multoque praeter ceteros altiorem et dealbatam statui crucem iussit.*'

" The fourth case is that of Paul. Clearly the practice of Pliny and the case of Paul point to a fixed practice of a change of venue to Rome in the case of citizens accused of a capital offence, while the cases of Marius Priscus and of Galba point in the opposite direction.

" Probably the distinction between senatorial and imperatorial pro- vinces affects the question. But it is at least plain that the whole matter is quite obscure, and that it is not surprising that we do not know precisely what happened in the necessarily rare event of a prosecution collapsing for lack of a prosecutor after the case had actually been brought to Rome.

Conclusions.    " There is then fair reason for venturing to conjecture that Luke means that the case against Paul came to nothing owing to the continued absence of the prosecuting Jews, and that after two years he was released.

" I would repeat that the strong points of this suggestion are :

" 1. It relieves us from the necessity of thinking that Luke left off in the middle of an incident.

" 2. It supplies us with a conclusion favourable to Paul, such as seems to be hinted at in other parts of the book.

" 3. It is at the same time a conclusion which, inasmuch as it afforded no legal precedent, was not really satisfactory to Luke's apologetic view, and was therefore more likely to be hinted at by him than to be explicitly stated.

" On the other hand, the weak point is plainly the absence of any direct evidence, which prevents the suggestion from rising at present above the level of an attractive conjecture. Perhaps some student of Roman law may be able to throw some more light on the question."

The case of Lampon.    There is little to be added to Professor Lake's statement of the case, or the parallel presentation by Professor Ramsay. The case of Lampon is, as Ramsay himself admits (*op. cit.* pp. 365, 378 f.), really not analogous to that of Paul at Rome, as in Alexandria it is the prefect, not the accusers, who allow the case to drag on and there is no appeal to Rome possible. Lampon's situation is more like Paul's two years in Caesarea under Felix.

The evidence of Pliny.    I may mention, however, a case mentioned by Pliny to the Emperor Trajan (*Epist.* x. 56) of a person exiled for life by Julius Bassus, the proconsul of Bithynia in A.D. 98. The decrees of Bassus had been subsequently rescinded and the Senate had granted a new trial to all those whom he had sentenced provided they appealed within the space of two years (*datum a senatu ius . . . ex integro agendi dumtaxat per biennium*). Since this person continued to remain in the province and had not acquainted the proconsul with his case (*adiisset docuissetque proconsulem*), Pliny inquired what should be done with him. Trajan's reply (*ibid.* x. 57) points out that the man had two years given him for appeal if he thought himself aggrieved (*per biennium agendi facultatem habuerit, si existimabat se iniuria relegatum*), and ordered him now, more than a decade later, to be sent as prisoner to the praetorian prefects at Rome (*vinctus mitti ad praefectos praetorii mei debet*).

The Latin text does not speak in terms of appeal, still less of appeal from the proconsul to the emperor. Rather it suggests that the case is to be heard afresh (*ex integro*) by a subsequent proconsul. The term, however, is a *biennium* fixed apparently by special decree of the Senate. This may show that such a period of grace was customary. Yet again we must confess that the Bithynian's case is far from a complete parallel to the proposed solution of the διετία of Acts xxviii. 30.

One piece of evidence not known to Lake and Ramsay should be here mentioned. It has already been cited by Eger [1] in connexion with the An edict appeal of Paul, but not on the hypothesis that the case against Paul went of Nero. by default. It is an imperial edict, published many years ago, among the papyri (*BGU*. 628 *recto*) and now attributed to the reign of Nero.[2] It deals precisely with criminal cases submitted to the emperor whether by appeal or by reference as a court of first instance, and with the avoidance of delay in the arrival of the two parties.[3] The emperor recalls how his 'divine parent'[4] had fixed a time limit before which accused and accuser from the provinces had to appear and to wait for each other. If they both failed to appear the case was dropped from the calendar. The emperor apparently went on to refer to a new (?) definition of the suitable term for such delay, a term which varied according as the cases originated in Italy or came from across the Alps or from across the sea. By exception a longer term, however, is allowed in capital cases. For them the time limits are fixed as nine months in Italy, and for transalpine cases and those from across the sea a year and six months.

The text, which unfortunately is badly mutilated, as finally restored by Mitteis [5] is as follows :

### Col. I

#### Exemplum edicti

In multis benefactis consultisque divi parentis mei id quoque
iure nobis praedicandum pu[t]o [q]uod causas qu⟨a⟩e a[d] principalem
notionem [vel] provocatae vel [rem]issae fuissen[t i]mposita qua-
dam nec[ess]itate | de[c]idenda[s es]se pers[p]exit ne [aut] prob[i] h[o]mines
5 [c]onflictar[e]ntur · diu[t]ina mor[a a]ut call[id]iores fructum [ca]pere
[ali]quem p[rot]rahend[a] lite au[c]uparen[tu]r, quod [c]um animadver-
[ti]sset iam p[er] multo[s] annos ev[en]ire ed[i]xit salub[ri]ter praefini-
t[is] temp⟨o⟩r[ibus] intra qu⟨a⟩e cum [ex p]rovinciis [a]d a[gend]um veni-
[sse]nt utrae[qu]e [p]arte[s] *l* nec disce[de]rent priusqu[am] ad disceptan-
10 [du]m i[ntrodu]cti f[uis]se[nt aut] scirent fore u[t al]tera parte audi-

---

[1] *Rechtsgeschichtliches zum N.T.* pp. 20 ff.

[2] So L. Mitteis in *Grundzüge und Chrestomathie der Papyruskunde*, II. i. 281, and others. Mommsen had placed it in the third century. It is apparently this document which, though unmentioned, was at the basis of J. S. Reid's statement to Ramsay (*op. cit.* p. 365) about procedure in the third century.

[3] The danger of injustice in such circumstances was not remote. With the words in Col. I. lines 5 ff. compare the phrases quoted above, p. 323, notes 2 and 3, from the inscription of Cos.

[4] Probably Claudius. See Cassius Dio lx. 28, and Seneca, *Apocolocynt*. xii. 19 f. Cf. Suetonius, *Claudius* 15. That this was a new procedure under Claudius is obviously implied. Dio seems to date the promulgation of the rule in A.D. 46.

[5] *Op. cit.* II. ii. 417 f. For an earlier attempt by the same writer see *Hermes*, xxxii., 1897, pp. 630 ff. Slightly different both as regards assured readings and conjectures is the same text as published by Bruns, *Fontes iuris Romani*[7], 1909, pp. 251 ff. It is still worth while to consult the discussion by É. Cuq in *Nouvelle Revue historique de droit français et étranger*, xxiii., 1899, pp. 111 ff.

ta ser[v]aret[u]r sententia aut [sec]undum praese[nte]m pronuntia-
[retur ; sin vero] neut[er] litiga[nti]um adfuisset, ex[cid]ere tum eas [ ].
[lites ex or]dine cognitionu[m] offici nostri.  E[t . . .]rcules iam
[dudum] id obtinendum fuit [cu]m a prescripto eius edi[c]ti satis super-
15 q[ue tempo]ris quasi conive[n]tibus nobis tra[ns]cocurrerint
e[t . . . . . . .iu]dex in pr[ . . . . . .] . . di . . . .[ . . .inte]rposito tem-
[pore . . . . . . . .]io [ . . . . . . .]ation[ . . . . . . . . . . . .] conti[ . .].

(Some lines missing)

[ . . . . . . . . . . . . . .]s in Italia q[ . . . . . . . .]edi[ . . .] . . .
[ . . . . . . . . . . . .]t sex menses t[ran]salpinis
20 [autem . . . . . . .]m annum qui nis[i] adfuerint vel
defensi fuerint cum [cont]roversiae eorum noscantur

## Col. II

sciant fore et stetur sentent[i]ae et acc[us]atores
ad petendam poenam in re [c]ogantur.  Sed quoniam
capitale[s] causae aliquid a[u]xilium conctationis ad-
mittun[t e]t accusatoribus et rei[s] in It[a]lia qu[i]dem
5 novem [me]nses dabuntur t[ra]nsalpinis audem et trans-
marinis annus et sex menses intra quos nisi «a»
adfuer[in]t fore iam nu[n]c sciant ut cu[m] prosecu-
toribus [v]eneant quod n[e]que grave n[e]que durum
videri pote⟨st⟩ si ⟨i⟩is tam prol[i]xum tempus i[nd]ulserim
10 et opinor qui aliqua di[gn]itate censer[i] possunt
tanto [ . . .] . .i debe[nt] so[lli]citi [esse u]t iis quae praecepta
sunt ma[t]urato obsequantur cu[m] praesentem repu-
tent interesse hones[t]atis suae ut quam primum
molestia carent.  Appella[ti]ones vero quae ad magis-
15 tratus et sacerdotia et alios honores pertinebunt
habe[ant] formam tem[po]ris sui.  Set ea [qu]aequae sunt
er [ . . . . . . .]rump[ . . . . .]umqu . .ad notion[em]

(Some lines missing)

The bearing
of this text.
The bearing of this text on the general, if not the particular, subject
of our inquiry is obvious.  It is a contemporary document giving imperial
prescription.  It deals with cases *quae ad principalem notionem vel provocatae vel remissae*[1] *fuissent*.  It shows that time limits were definitely
fixed, that both accused and accusers had to be present before the allowed
term expired, and that if neither appeared the appeal was dropped.  The
maximum limit given is, however, eighteen months in capital cases, not

---

[1] Are two different classes of cases meant ?  Cf. Dio Cassius, lii. 21. 1 ; 22.
5 τὰς δίκας τάς τε ἐκκλήτους (or ἐφεσίμους) καὶ τὰς ἀναπομπίμους.  Cf. lii. 33. 1.
On the untechnical character of Dio's language see *Class. Rev.* viii., 1894, pp. 143 f.

two years as Lake conjectured,[1] and the present text omits to say what happens if the accuser fails to appear within the allotted time. Possibly the accusers were then summoned by process of law or by force, or were condemned for negligence or contempt of court. But there is perhaps a hint that in these circumstances the accused was set free.[2] It seems to contemplate that the accused is under bail or at liberty, not controlled in his movements by the officers of the government. As Eger says, while this edict does not solve the riddle of Paul's case, it prevents all too limited conclusions, and that is in itself an advantage for the knowledge of historical truth. It suggests, for example, as did Lake, that the case of Paul really never came to trial at all, or at least never ended in either acquittal or condemnation. It may be objected to such a solution that it does not fulfil the tone of foreboding in Paul's farewell at Miletus (Acts xx. 22-25), and still less the divine promise that Paul should appear before Caesar (Acts xxvii. 24 Καίσαρί σε δεῖ παραστῆναι). But exactness in fulfilment of prophecies is curiously neglected by the author of Acts. These would not be the only examples.[3] They are perhaps only variants of other divine promises, found in Acts xxi. 11 and xxiii. 11 respectively, that Paul should be arrested in Jerusalem and should testify at Rome. While his journey to Jerusalem is filled with foreboding, his journey to Rome is rather filled with an optimism that makes at least a relatively favourable outcome not unexpected. And even if his case was dismissed and Paul released without trial, it is quite likely that the dismissal required an appearance of the appellant before the supreme court for the very declaration of dismissal. In that event Paul would appear before Caesar.

Such an outcome in Paul's case would be tantamount to a victory—a victory by default.[4] It is just the kind of victory that Acts seems else-

---

[1] Of course διετία might mean a year and a fraction, as τριετία in xx. 31 means two years and three months (xix. 8. 10), but not necessarily much more. But the διετίαν ὅλην of Acts xxviii. 30 can hardly mean only a year and a half. Per contra see Ramsay, op. cit. pp. 352 note, 377. Even so the two years of Lake may be right for the earlier rule of Claudius. The eighteen months of the decree are according to the new regulation; the term for capital cases under the old regulation, if named originally in the document, is not now to be read there. Even if Paul's case fell in Nero's reign it may have been earlier than the decree.

[2] See the discussion of Mitteis, Hermes, xxxii., 1897, pp. 634 ff.

[3] See note on xxi. 11.

[4] The Greeks used δίκη ἐρήμη of a case won by default. The forms ἐρημοδίκιον, eremodicium, occur later of failure to appear to take part in a suit at the appointed time. But I am not quite sure that they are exactly suited to a situation where a defendant in an appeal is released because the accusers do not arrive at the capital before the statutory period of time has expired. Another term, earlier, though not classical, is φυγοδικέω, -ης, -ία (e.g. P Thead 15. 19; P Ryl 65. 14; Bull. de corr. Hell. x., 1886, p. 400, and Inscrip. of Cos, No. 26 cited above, p. 322, note 6). It is used not only of the defendant and in ordinary trials, but in appeals. In connexion with it is mentioned the fixing of a time limit, and some sort of money penalty. Our fullest information,

where to describe—actions quite inconclusive in outcome so far as law is concerned, but in effect favourable to Paul and to his work. While we may still admit that some reference to the dismissal of the case,[1] as Gallio dismissed the case at Corinth, would be more according to our expectation, we may at least add this one more, as perhaps as likely as any, to the other explanations of the peculiar ending of Acts.

Later tradi-
tions.

Of other outcome of the trial of Paul Acts gives no certain clue, and we may not in this place lengthen our note by discussing the various extra-canonical traditions, involving either condemnation and martyrdom, or release and subsequent journeys, or—in inverted order—both. The tradition that he met death by the sword at Rome under Nero is familiar and not unlikely, though the evidence for it is not as early as we should like, and the traditions of martyrdom are in general among the most unreliable of early Christian literary remains. If condemned to death, the last privilege that Paul, a Roman citizen, could claim was death by decapitation in preference to other modes of execution. The journey of Paul to the West and the journeys to the East with subsequent re-imprisonment are so easily inferred from his own expressed hope of a journey to Spain (Rom. xv. 24, 28) and from the pastoral epistles respectively that the traditions which affirm them cannot command our confidence.[2]

Pfister's
suggestion.

Room must be given here, however, to mention one possible explanation of these traditions of the subsequent fate of Paul, since it supplies one more to the many solutions offered for the end of Acts (Vol. IV., pp. 349 f.). It is the suggestion of Fr. Pfister.[3] Like the proposal of Lake and Ramsay, it has not received the attention that it may deserve. He calls attention to the fact that the *Acta Pauli*, giving journeys of Paul and ending with his martyrdom at Rome, may have originated as a parallel rather than as a supplement to the closing chapters of the canonical Acts. The places mentioned are in part the same, and the

---

however, on Roman procedure in cases of default comes from later times and from civil suits. See Bethmann-Holweg, *Der römische Civilprozess*, iii. pp. 300 ff., and the articles by Th. Kipp in Pauly-Wissowa, s.v. 'Contumacia' and 'Eremodicium.'

[1] E. Schwartz, *GGN.*, 1907, p. 298, believed that Acts xxviii. 17 ff. is a remnant of an original account in which a trial and acquittal of Paul was reported and in which the Roman Jews took some part in the proceedings before the emperor.

[2] I cannot agree with Professor Lake (or rather with his statement of long ago to which he himself might not now entirely subscribe) in giving any weight to the arguments for Paul's release mentioned above, p. 326, note 2, since (a) the letters of imprisonment are perhaps not written in Rome at all, (b) the pastoral epistles as they stand are probably not genuine, and even as spurious or mixed concoctions are no real evidence for even a tradition of release, and (c) neither Clement's τὸ τέρμα τῆς δύσεως nor any other passage persuades me that Paul went to Spain [consentio invitus K. L.].

[3] *Der Reliquienkult im Altertum*, i., 1909, pp. 266-278, and *Zeitschrift für die neutestamentliche Wissenschaft*, xiv., 1913, pp. 216-221.

journey leads to Rome and to death.  But the two accounts were in some respects exclusive rivals, and at a time when both were highly regarded it seemed necessary to treat the *Acta Pauli* version as a subsequent experience to the records of our Acts.  But obviously the death of Paul could not have occurred twice.  Pfister believes that the canonical Acts originally ended with such a record—the conclusion of Paul's case, his condemnation, and his martyrdom.  To make room for the originally parallel version of the apocryphal literature he thinks that this ending of our Acts was removed, and the book was left in its mutilated state in order to permit the continuation of the story as current in other favourite early Christian writings.  The mistaking of doublets for successive episodes is a common error.  To lengthen the career and to extend the journeys of a hero is also characteristic of growing legends in honour of the dead and great.

Against this theory are of course to be weighed the various alternative *Objections.* suggestions about the ending of Acts mentioned at the end of the Commentary.  The last sentence of the book is too formal to have been left there merely as the result of mutilation, and too Lucan to be a subsequent redactor's patching.  It has also been pointed out that as they stand Luke and Acts are volumes of almost identical length,[1] which suggests that the original author divided his material to fit a uniform (and standard) length of book roll, and planned them as they are.

But there is much that is attractive in Pfister's theory.  Those who *Favourable* believe that Luke planned and wrote a third volume (Vol. IV. pp. 244, *points.* 349) would assign the further story of Paul to it instead of to a suppressed ending of Acts.  We do not now know exactly in what form the writings represented by the apocryphal Acts first circulated.  Pfister believes that the further career of Peter as well as of Paul were combined in the extra-canonical records, so that one who read them after the canonical Acts would get a sequence something like this :

A.  Paul's last journey to Rome (Acts xxvii.-xxviii.).
B.  Paul's trial, condemnation, and execution (Acts [ultimately suppressed]).
C.  Paul's departure for Spain.
D.  Peter's arrival in Rome.
E.  Peter's encounter with Simon Magus (cf. *Acta Petri cum Simone*, etc.).
F.  Peter's martyrdom (cf. *Acta Petri*).
G.  Paul's last journey to Rome (cf. *Acta Pauli*).
H.  Paul's trial, condemnation, and martyrdom (cf. *Acta Pauli*).

By omitting B the repetition of B and H is resolved, and a possible order of events is left.  For the connexion of C and D attention may be called to the so-called Vercelli *Acts of Peter*,[2] which describe first

---

[1] A. Ruegg, *Theologische Studien und Kritiken*, lxix., 1896, pp. 94 ff.  The Gospel of Matthew is also of almost exactly the same length.

[2] For English translation see M. R. James, *The Apocryphal N.T.*, 1924, pp. 304 ff., and note the editor's comment about the *Acts of Paul* on p. 306.

Paul's departure from Rome for Spain (1-3) and thereafter the arrival of Peter at Rome (4 ff.), etc. It will be recalled that the Canon of Muratori also suggests that another volume than Acts, but by the same *Lucas*, dealt with these two events—*semote passionem petri evidenter declarat sed profectionem pauli ad urbes ad spaniam proficiscentis*.[1] As far as our present judgement goes, both of these writings belong not far from A.D. 200.

Pfister's suggestion may seem to be cutting the Gordian knot of the close of Acts. There is no textual evidence for any earlier form of the book than that which we possess. The same may be said, however, in the case of Mark and the Epistle to Diognetus, both of which are presumably now mutilated at their close. Readers of Acts would feel no surprise if after the gloomy predictions and close escapes it continued to carry Paul's case to a fatal outcome. Their surprise is that it leads to no outcome at all. And certainly no other evidence that we possess is authoritative enough to disprove that as a matter of fact the two years in Rome was followed by the Apostle's crown of martyrdom.

## Note XXVII. The Winds

### By Kirsopp Lake and Henry J. Cadbury

The ancient names of the winds.

The difficulty in identifying the names of the winds in ancient literature is chiefly because they were originally not related to the points of the compass, which of course did not exist, nor always to the position of the sun, but were often based on the names of countries from which the winds blew. Obviously this led to confusion. The direction of a wind blowing from Africa is not quite the same in Greece as it is in Italy, and a wind described as Libyan in Egypt would be from the west, while in Sicily it would be from the south.

Naturally, however, as time went on there was an attempt to standardize the names of the winds and to state more accurately what their relation was to the position of the sun. But this in turn led to a further difficulty. The apparent position of the sun is not the same in the winter as it is in the summer, and a wind which comes from the setting of the sun would be approximately W.S.W. in the winter and W.N.W. in the summer. It was therefore necessary to distinguish between the wind which blew from the rising or the setting of the sun at the equinox or at the two solstices. Thus there were three ' sunrise ' and three ' sunset ' winds, varying in the

---

[1] See below, Addit. Note 37, p. 495, and contrast Vol. II. pp. 210 f., where the usual emendations are made and an opposite meaning given. Pfister believes that this passage can be translated as it stands: "But the Acts of all the apostles were written in one volume. Luke compiled for 'most excellent Theophilus' what things were done in detail in his presence, just as also he separately declares plainly the passion of Peter and the departure of Paul from the city [Rome], when he departed for Spain."

Mediterranean district about thirty degrees each side of east and west. There were also the hot and cold winds which blew from or against the noonday sun. Between the north wind on the one hand and the south on the other there was a considerable gap before the solstitial winds were reached, and obviously as soon as the matter was approached scientifically an attempt would be made to fill up the gaps and provide a system of names for the winds spaced equally round the horizon.

The classical example of this system is Aristotle, *Meteorolog.* ii. 6, Aristotle. p. 363 a, which runs as follows :

Γέγραπται μὲν οὖν, τοῦ μᾶλλον εὐσήμως ἔχειν, ὁ τοῦ ὁρίζοντος κύκλος· διὸ καὶ στρογγύλος. δεῖ δὲ νοεῖν αὐτοῦ τὸ ἕτερον ἔκτμημα τὸ ὑφ᾽ ἡμῶν οἰκούμενον· ἔσται γὰρ κἀκεῖνο διελεῖν τὸν αὐτὸν τρόπον. ὑποκείσθω δὲ πρῶτον ἐναντία κατὰ τόπον εἶναι τὰ πλεῖστον ἀπέχοντα κατὰ τόπον, ὥσπερ κατ᾽ εἶδος ἐναντία τὰ πλεῖστον ἀπέχοντα κατὰ τὸ εἶδος· πλεῖστον δ᾽ ἀπέχει κατὰ τόπον τὰ κείμενα πρὸς ἄλληλα κατὰ διάμετρον. ἔστω οὖν τὸ μὲν ἐφ᾽ ᾧ Α δυσμὴ ἰσημερινή, ἐναντίος δὲ τούτῳ τόπος, ἐφ᾽ οὗ τὸ Β, ἀνατολὴ ἰσημερινή· ἄλλη δὲ διάμετρος ταύτην πρὸς ὀρθὴν τέμνουσα, ἧς τὸ ἐφ᾽ οὗ Η, ἔστω ἄρκτος· τούτῳ δ᾽ ἐναντίον ἐξ ἐναντίας τὸ ἐφ᾽ οὗ Θ, μεσημβρία· τὸ δ᾽ ἐφ᾽ οὗ Ζ ἀνατολὴ θερινή, τὸ δ᾽ ἐφ᾽ οὗ Ε δυσμὴ θερινή, τὸ δ᾽ ἐφ᾽ οὗ Δ ἀνατολὴ χειμερινή, τὸ δ᾽ ἐφ᾽ οὗ Γ δυσμὴ χειμερινή. ἀπὸ δὲ τοῦ Ζ ἤχθω διάμετρος ἐπὶ τὸ Γ, καὶ ἀπὸ τοῦ Δ ἐπὶ τὸ Ε. ἐπεὶ οὖν τὰ μὲν πλεῖστον ἀπέχοντα κατὰ τόπον ἐναντία κατὰ τόπον, πλεῖστον δ᾽ ἀπέχει τὰ κατὰ διάμετρον, ἀναγκαῖον καὶ τῶν πνευμάτων ταῦτα ἀλλήλοις ἐναντία εἶναι, ὅσα κατὰ διάμετρόν ἐστιν. καλεῖται δὲ κατὰ τὴν θέσιν τῶν τόπων τὰ πνεύματα ὧδε, ζέφυρος μὲν τὸ ἀπὸ τοῦ Α· τοῦτο γὰρ δυσμὴ ἰσημερινή. ἐναντίος δὲ τούτῳ ἀπηλιώτης ἀπὸ τοῦ Β · τοῦτο γὰρ ἀνατολὴ ἰσημερινή. βορέας δὲ καὶ ἀπαρκτίας ἀπὸ τοῦ Η· ἐνταῦθα γὰρ ἡ ἄρκτος. ἐναντίος δὲ τούτῳ νότος ἀπὸ τοῦ Θ· μεσημβρία τε γὰρ αὕτη ἀφ᾽ ἧς πνεῖ, καὶ τὸ Θ τῷ Η ἐναντίον· κατὰ διάμετρον γάρ. ἀπὸ δὲ τοῦ Ζ καικίας· αὕτη γὰρ ἀνατολὴ θερινή. ἐναντίος δ᾽ οὐχ ὁ ἀπὸ τοῦ Ε πνέων, ἀλλ᾽ ὁ ἀπὸ τοῦ Γ λίψ. οὗτος γὰρ ἀπὸ δυσμῆς χειμερινῆς πνεῖ, ἐναντίος δὲ τούτῳ· κατὰ διάμετρον γὰρ κεῖται. ὁ δ᾽ ἀπὸ τοῦ Δ εὖρος· οὗτος γὰρ ἀπ᾽ ἀνατολῆς χειμερινῆς πνεῖ, γειτνιῶν τῷ νότῳ· διὸ καὶ πολλάκις εὐρόνοτοι λέγονται πνεῖν. ἐναντίος δὲ τούτῳ οὐχ ὁ ἀπὸ τοῦ Γ λίψ, ἀλλ᾽ ὁ ἀπὸ τοῦ Ε, ὃν καλοῦσιν οἱ μὲν ἀργέστην, οἱ δ᾽ ὀλυμπίαν, οἱ δὲ σκίρωνα · οὗτος γὰρ ἀπὸ δυσμῆς θερινῆς πνεῖ, καὶ κατὰ διάμετρον αὐτῷ κεῖται μόνος. οὗτοι μὲν οὖν οἱ κατὰ διάμετρόν τε κείμενοι ἄνεμοι, καὶ οἷς εἰσιν ἐναντίοι· ἕτεροι δ᾽ εἰσὶ καθ᾽ οὓς οὐκ ἔστιν ἐναντία πνεύματα· ἀπὸ μὲν γὰρ τοῦ Ι ὃν καλοῦσι θρασκίαν· οὗτος γὰρ μέσος ἀργέστου καὶ ἀπαρκτίου· ἀπὸ δὲ τοῦ Κ ὃν καλοῦσι μέσην· οὗτος γὰρ μέσος καικίου καὶ ἀπαρκτίου. ἡ δὲ τοῦ ΙΚ διάμετρος βούλεται μὲν κατὰ τὸν διὰ παντὸς εἶναι φαινόμενον, οὐκ ἀκριβοῖ δέ. ἐναντία δὲ τούτοις οὐκ ἔστι τοῖς πνεύμασιν, οὔτε τῷ θρασκίᾳ, οὔτε τῷ μέσῃ (ἔπει γὰρ ἄν τις ἐφ᾽ οὗ τὸ Μ · τοῦτο γὰρ κατὰ διάμετρον), οὔτε τῷ Ι, τῷ θρασκίᾳ· ἔπει γὰρ ἂν ἀπὸ τοῦ Ν · τοῦτο γὰρ κατὰ διάμετρον τὸ σημεῖον, εἰ μὴ ἀπ᾽ αὐτοῦ καὶ ἐπ᾽ ὀλίγον πνεῖ τις ἄνεμος, ὃν καλοῦσιν οἱ περὶ τὸν τόπον ἐκεῖνον φοινικίαν.

The figure
implied.
Thus the geometrical figure which Aristotle is describing, with the letters arranged as he indicates, would be thus :

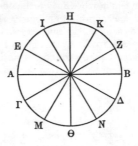

Aristotle's
meaning.
The meaning is that if you draw a circle to represent the horizon, one diameter of it will represent the rising and setting of the sun at the equinox, that is, due east and west, from which points blow the winds Apeliotes and Zephyros. Another diameter drawn at right angles to the first gives north and south—Boreas (also called 'Απαρκτίας) and Notos. The rising of the sun at the winter solstice gives a point one-third of the way between east and south. This is Euros. Opposite to it is Argestes, which is north of Zephyros by a similar third of the way to north. In the same way Kaikias is north of east and Lips south of west by the same margin. Between Argestes and Boreas comes Thraskias, and between Boreas and Thraskias comes Meses. Aristotle then states that there is no name for the points opposite to Thraskias and Meses, but as he also says that the wind opposite to Meses is called Libonotos, and that Phoenicias is the local [1] name of the wind opposite to Thraskias, that is, between Euros and Notos, he must merely mean that Libonotos and Phoenicias are not universally recognized names. The result may be represented by the following diagram :

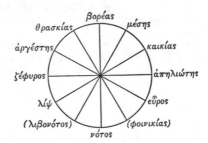

It will be seen that this system gives a list of twelve winds based upon the identification of the points at which the sun rises and sets at the equinox and at the winter and summer solstices, together with a line drawn at

[1] The only district in which a S.S.W. wind could naturally be called 'Phoenician' is the east end of the southern coast of Asia Minor.

right angles to the diameter connecting the equinoctial rising and setting.
This would give eight points, unequally arranged, and it was not difficult
to add two extra lines which fill in the big gaps between the solstitial
risings and settings and north and south, thus giving twelve points.

That this system was still in force in the first century is shown by the Pliny.
following extract from Pliny who gives almost the same description, with
the added advantage that he also gives the Latin names of the winds. It
is especially noticeable that he recognizes the existence of other local names,
and that though he is writing Latin his own preference appears to be for
the Greek words. The only serious difference between him and Aristotle
is that Aristotle says that βορέας and ἀπαρκτίας are synonyms, and Pliny
makes βορέας the same as Aristotle's μέσης, moving μέσης to a point
between its original position and due east—or almost exactly N.E.
Pliny's words (*N.H.* ii. 47) are:

Veteres quattuor omnino servavere per totidem mundi partes—ideo
nec Homerus plures nominat—hebeti, ut mox iudicatum est, ratione;
secuta aetas octo addidit nimis subtili atque concisa. proximis inter
utramque media placuit, ad brevem ex numerosa additis quattuor. sunt
ergo bini in quattuor caeli partibus, ab oriente aequinoctiali subsolanus, ab
oriente brumali volturnus. illum apelioten, hunc Graeci eurum appellant.
a meridie auster et ab occasu brumali Africus; notum et Liba nominant.
ab occasu aequinoctiali favonius, ab occasu solstitiali corus; zephyrum
et argesten vocant. a septentrionibus septentrio, interque eum et exortum
solstitialem aquilo, aparctias et boreas dicti. numerosior ratio quattuor
his interiecerat, thrascian media regione inter septentrionem et occasum
solstitialem, itemque caecian media inter aquilonem et exortum aequi-
noctialem ab ortu solstitiali, Phoenica media regione inter ortum brumalem
et meridiem, item inter Liba et notum conpositum ex utroque medium
inter meridiem et hibernum occidentem Libonotum. nec finis. alii quippe
mesen nomine etiamnum addidere inter borean et caecian, et inter eurum
notumque euronotum. sunt enim quidam peculiares quibusque gentibus
venti, non ultra certum procedentes tractum, ut Atheniensibus sciron,
paulo ab argeste deflexus, reliquae Graeciae ignotus. aliubi flatus idem
Olympias vocatur. consuetudo omnibus his nominibus argesten intellegi.
et caecian aliqui vocant Hellespontian, et eosdem alii aliter. item in Nar-
bonensi provincia clarissimus ventorum est circius nec ullo violentia inferior,
Ostiam plerumque recto Ligustico mari perferens. idem non modo in
reliquis partibus caeli ignotus est, sed ne Viennam quidem eiusdem
provinciae urbem attingens: paucis ante milibus iugi modici occursu
tantus ille ventorum coercetur. et austros in Aegyptum penetrare negat
Fabianus. quo fit manifesta lex naturae, ventis etiam et tempore et fine
dicto.

Thus the list of names in Latin and Greek is:

|        |            |                      |
| ------ | ---------- | -------------------- |
| E.     | Subsolanus | = ἀπηλιώτης          |
| E.S.E. | Vulturnus  | = εὖρος              |
| S.     | Auster     | = νότος              |

| | | |
|---|---|---|
| W.S.W. | Africus | $= \lambda \acute{\iota} \psi$ |
| W. | Favonius | $= \zeta \acute{\epsilon} \phi \upsilon \rho o \varsigma$ |
| W.N.W. | Corus, Sciron, Olympias | $= \acute{a} \rho \gamma \acute{\epsilon} \sigma \tau \eta \varsigma$ |
| N.N.E. | Aquilo | $= \beta o \rho \acute{\epsilon} a \varsigma$ |
| N. | Septentrio | $= \acute{a} \pi a \rho \kappa \tau \acute{\iota} a \varsigma$ |
| N.N.W. | Thrascia | |
| E.N.E. | Caecias, Hellespontia | |
| S.S.E. | Phoenica, Euronotus | |
| S.S.W. | Libonotus | |
| N.E. | Meses | |

Though Pliny does not say so, it is clear that the last names in the Latin column are really Greek.

*A rival system.*  This dodecagonal system was natural enough for a generation which relied chiefly on the observation of the sun, and when it had to be scientific endeavoured to unite the observation of the sun with the geometry of a circle. There are, however, traces of another system which is octagonal and gives only eight winds. These are found especially in the ancient ' wind roses ' such as that at Athens. It may be surmised that this was due largely to the difficulty of trisecting an angle and the ease with which it can be bisected. Thus instead of making the difficult twelve-pointed roses, architects confined themselves to an eight-pointed rose to which they gave the names of the eight principal winds, slightly changing the meaning of Argestes, Lips, Kaikias, and Euros so that they were identified with north-west, south-west, north-east and south-east.

*The modern system.*  Two other points should be noted. The modern nautical division of the compass gives a circle divided into thirty-two points—a development of the octagonal system. Therefore the ancient winds of the dodecagonal system do not quite coincide with any point of our compass. On the other hand the modern mathematical division of a right angle into 90 points or degrees, and the circle into 360, agrees with the dodecagonal system and is doubtless connected with it. Moreover, the ancient names, to judge from the monuments we possess, do not mean a point so much as a segment of a circle. Thus, for instance, Notos does not mean a wind which blows from due south, but a wind which blows from that segment of a circle which is one-twelfth part of the circumference and includes our ' due south ' as its middle point.

For the reader of Acts the importance of this discussion is its bearing on the interpretation of the four references to winds in xxvii. 12-14. These winds are $N \acute{o} \tau o \varsigma$, $\Lambda \acute{\iota} \psi$, $X \hat{\omega} \rho o \varsigma$, and $E \mathring{\upsilon} \rho a \kappa \acute{\upsilon} \lambda \omega \nu$.

*$\Lambda \acute{\iota} \psi$.*  (i.) $\Lambda \acute{\iota} \psi$ (vs. 12). According to the Aristotelian system described above, $\Lambda \acute{\iota} \psi$ is the wind which is the twelfth part of the circle or 30° south of west and comes from the winter setting of the sun. We must not, however, expect in Acts the meteorological precision of Aristotle or of Pliny, and contemporary evidence shows that the meaning of $\Lambda \acute{\iota} \psi$ was by no means so fixed a point as these scientific writers would imply. In the LXX $\Lambda \acute{\iota} \psi$ generally means south, but in the papyri—far more important

for our purpose—it invariably means west. This appears from documents giving the boundaries of estates in which the four points of the compass are regularly ἀπηλιώτης, νότος, λίψ, and βορρᾶς. Compare, for instance, *Flinders Petrie Papyrus* 1 (*Cunningham Memoirs*, xi.), the will of a Libyan written in 237 B.C. in which the boundaries of his property are described as

$$απο \; μεν \; απηλιω[του$$
$$Θεωνος \; Α_κ̣ωναπιμωντος \; και \; Συλωτος \; του \; Φαλοιτος \; απ[ο$$
$$δε \; τ̣ο̣υ \; αυλη \; κοινη \; απο \; δε \; λιβος \; οικος \; ιερος \; του \ldots . .$$
$$απο \; δε \; βορρα \; οδος \; δημοσια.$$

Similarly in the *Oxyrhynchus Pap.* (47, 245, 248, 273) ἡ πρὸς λίβα τοπαρχία is universally recognized to mean 'the western toparchy.' Thus for the commentator of Acts it is a serious question whether Lips should be interpreted in accordance with the LXX, with the scientific terminology of Pliny, or, seeing that the ship in question came from Alexandria, in accordance with Egyptian custom. To us it seems that the papyri are the best guide.

(ii.) Χῶρος (vs. 12). This word appears not to be found elsewhere in Greek. It represents the Latin word *Corus* (or *Caurus*) and is as much a Latinism as κεντυρίων.[1] Pliny in the passage quoted on p. 341 identifies the Latin winds Favonius and Corus with Ζέφυρος and Ἀργέστης, that is to say, Corus is the wind which blows from the setting of the sun at the summer solstice—about W.N.W. Thus in Acts xxvii. 12 κατὰ λίβα either means west or west with a tendency to south, and κατὰ χῶρον ought to mean west with a tendency to north. It is obvious that this gives a perfectly intelligible meaning to the phrase κατὰ λίβα καὶ κατὰ χῶρον, and means a harbour looking a few points either side of west. It suits the harbour of Phineka in Crete fairly well. (See note *ad loc.*)

The combination of Greek and Latin words in Luke's description of the storm and of the harbour of Phoenix suggests the possibility that he was influenced by the mixed speech of sailors, partly Alexandrian and partly Italian. If so, κατὰ λίβα and κατὰ χῶρον may be merely a conflation of two descriptions of the harbour in Crete for which they were making. It is true that κατὰ λίβα does not mean quite the same as κατὰ χῶρον, but the divergence is no more than will always be found by anyone who asks questions from a Levantine as to the place towards which he is going, or the names of the winds, or indeed about any subject on earth. He will

[1] The alternative Latin spellings (see *Thesaurus linguae Latinae*, iii. 658) *Chaurus* and *Chorus* suggest a Greek origin, unless they are due to the analogy of Greek loan-words in Latin. On the other hand, in the only other early Greek writing except Acts known to contain the word (Galen, Περὶ χυμῶν, Kühn, xvi. pp. 403, 406) it is spelt κῶρος. The uncertainty about ancient wind names may be further illustrated in this case by the fact that numerous ancient writings identify *Caurus* or *Corus* with one of the S.W. rather than with the N.W. winds, which indeed suits better with λίψ, while Vitruvius now treats *caurus* and *corus* as the same wind (i. 6), now as different (in his 24 point table).

always answer all questions, but the answers are rarely either consistent or correct. Probably the Levantine sailor of to-day is not very different from the sailors of Luke's voyage. (See also E. J. Goodspeed in *Expos.*, August 1903, pp. 130 ff., 'Did Alexandria influence the Nautical Language of St. Luke ? ' Deissmann, *Bible Studies*, pp. 141 f., and A. Rehm, article on 'Libs' in Pauly-Wissowa, xiii.)

Νότος.  (iii.) Νότος (vs. 13). The meaning of Νότος is of course clear—it is the south wind. Unlike the other names of winds in Acts it gives rise to no difficulty, and calls for no comment.

Εὐρακύλων.  (iv.) Εὐρακύλων (vs. 14). This wind like Χῶρος is not found anywhere else. It appears to be a hybrid word of which the first half is Greek and the second half Latin. But it is not only hybrid : it is apparently contradictory, for Euros means the wind which comes from the rising of the sun at the winter solstice, that is to say, it is E.S.E., and Aquilo is the Latin name for the wind which comes from the east of north and, according to Pliny, corresponds to the Greek Βορέας. It is hard to see what a wind can be which was a mixture of N.N.E. and E.S.E. Perhaps one is justified in guessing that Euros was popularly used for ' east ' and Aquilo for ' north ' so that Εὐρακύλων means north-east, but we do not know of any evidence by which to support this guess. ' Combination names ' for winds are natural and well attested, cf. Λιβονότος and Εὐρονότος, but there is no evidence of a name combined out of two languages or of one combined of Εὖρος with a north wind. The other reading for the name of the wind is Εὐροκλύδων,[1] and presumably the second part of that word means wave, so that it might reasonably be taken to mean a rough south-easterly wind. There is, however, no evidence on the point, for Εὐροκλύδων is as unknown a word as Εὐρακύλων is. One can only say that the syllable εὐρο- implies an easterly wind of some sort. Moreover, the one really certain point about this wind is that it threatened the ship with the danger of running on to the Syrtis. No wind with any trace of south in it could possibly have done this. Whatever the name of the wind was, it must have been blowing from about N.E. Therefore the most probable guess is that Euraquilo is the true reading, that it means approximately N.E., and is a remnant of the hybrid language of Alexandrian, Italo-Greek sailors.

[For a discussion of the names of the winds in antiquity the older literature, such as Kaibel, ' Antike Windrosen,' *Hermes*, xx., 1885, pp. 579-624, must be corrected by the article of Albert Rehm, 'Griechische Windrosen,' in the *Sitzungsberichte d. k. Bayerischen Akademie d. Wissen. zu München, philosophisch-philolog. Klasse*, May 1916, whose results were also independently reached two years later by Mr. D'Arcy Wentworth Thompson in the *Classical Review* for May–June 1918 (xxii. pp. 49 ff.).]

---

[1] Or Εὐρυκλύδων. The definition of τυφών in *Etym. Magn.* p. 772. 30, τυφὼν γάρ ἐστιν ἡ τοῦ ἀνέμου σφοδρὰ πνοή, ὃς καὶ εὐρυκλύδων καλεῖται, is plainly dependent on the Antiochian text of Acts *l.c.* with its ἄνεμος τυφωνικός, ὁ καλούμενος Εὐρυκλύδων.

NOTE XXVIII.  Ὑποζώματα

By HENRY J. CADBURY

[For literature on Paul's voyage to Rome see above, pp. 324 f., adding R. Ricard, 'Navigations de S. Paul,' in *Études Religieuses*, lxiv., 1927, pp. 448-465, and W. Stammler, 'Apostelgeschichte 27 in nautischer Beleuchtung' (*Greifswalder Studien zur Lutherforschung* 4), 1931. The names of many of the older monographs will be found collected in Cabrol-Leclercq, *Dictionnaire d'Archéologie Chrétienne*, x. (1931) coll. 1327 ff. The fullest and latest bibliography on ancient navigation in general is to be found at the end of F. Miltner's article 'Seewesen' in Pauly-Wissowa-Kroll, *R.E.*, Supplementband v. (1931), coll. 906-962. Miltner's discussion of 'Hypozom und Sprengwerk,' coll. 944 f., was not yet available when this note was set in type, nor was the article 'Hypozoma' by R. Hartmann in the preceding Supplementband, coll. 776-782, consulted. Both writers incline to the fourth solution (*d*) below, though they make no use of Egyptian analogies.]

In the account of the storm that fell upon the ship in which Paul was sailing near Crete the author of Acts (xxvii. 16 f.) has written: νησίον δέ τι ὑποδραμόντες καλούμενον Καῦδα ἰσχύσαμεν μόλις περικρατεῖς γενέσθαι τῆς σκάφης, ἣν ἄραντες βοηθείαις ἐχρῶντο ὑποζωννύντες τὸ πλοῖον. Among the many difficult questions raised by the interesting story none is more obscure than the participle in this sentence, ὑποζωννύντες. The verb ὑποζώννυμι is used of girding on garments. Of ships it occurs also at Polybius xxvii. 3. 3, where the Rhodian prytanis who wished his people to be ready to aid the Romans in the war against Perseus "advised the Rhodians to undergird (ὑποζωννύειν) forty ships, so that if circumstances required their help they might not have to make preparations to meet the demands of the Romans, but being in a state of readiness might be able to act instantly in any way they decided" (ἵνα ἐάν τις ἐκ τῶν καιρῶν γένηται χρεία, μὴ τότε παρασκευάζωνται πρὸς τὸ παρακαλούμενον, ἀλλ' ἑτοίμως διακείμενοι πράττωσι τὸ κριθὲν ἐξ αὐτῆς). In both these passages it is possible to regard the force of the verb as quite general, referring to preparation of the ships for action. A similar use of διαζώννυμι occurs in Appian, *Bell. Civ.* v. 10. 91, where it is said that Pompey, instead of attacking the ships of Octavian that survived defeat and storm, paid no attention to the enemy, as they overhauled (?) their ships to the best of their ability (ἐκ τῶν δυνατῶν διαζωννυμένους τὰ σκάφη) and sailed away with a favourable wind to Vibo. In Acts this meaning would be the more likely if βοήθειαι is a general term for various nautical expedients as I am inclined to think (see Vol. IV. pp. 332 f.) rather than for concrete objects used. Grammatically the clause 'girding the ship' is subordinate to 'used helps,' but it is possible in this writer for the participle to express the main idea.

It has usually been assumed, however, that the verb ὑποζώννυμι in these passages is technical, and refers to the use of ὑποζώματα. That the latter is a technical term there can be no doubt. In the fourth century before Christ the ὑποζώματα were part of the equipment of an

*ὑποζώννυμι.*

Athenian man-of-war. They were ropes or hawsers, removable from the ships by untying. But the exact arrangement of them when in use, and the object of their use, generations of discussion have not fully determined. Since the question is an extensive one, and may perhaps have no bearing on the passage in Acts, the full discussion of it has been left for this Additional Note.

ὑποζώματα.    The ὑποζώματα of ships are mentioned first in Greek literature in Plato (*Republic* x. 616 c, *Laws* xii. 945 c). But contemporary inscriptions, in which the names and equipment of vessels in the Athenian navy were listed in official inventories, were published by August Böckh in his *Urkunden über das Seewesen des Attischen Staates*, Berlin, 1840. These records, dating from about 372 to 332 b.c., frequently mention the ὑποζώματα. Their publication brought the discussion to a new point.

It had, for example, been sometimes held that the ὑποζώματα were planks of wood. This view was taken by Proclus in his commentary, ii. p. 200. 25, on Plato, *Rep. loc. cit.*, and in certain scholia on that passage and on Aristoph. *Equites*, 279.[1] But the Attic inscriptions distinctly include the ὑποζώματα among the hanging gear (σκεύη κρεμαστά) with sail, tackle, curtains (both white and hair curtains), hawsers and iron anchors, not with the other class of equipment made of wood (σκεύη ξύλινα) which included oars, rudders, ladders, mast, yards, props and poles.

The quota on each ship was apparently four. A circumstance of interest to the reader of Acts is that when by decree of the Athenian people in 324 b.c. a group of ships were provided by the state for the founding of a colony under Miltiades, it was specially noted that they were each to have two extra ὑποζώματα. The destination of the colonists is described merely as ὁ Ἀδρίας (cf. Acts xxvii. 27), Böckh, *op. cit.* pp. 452, 457 ff. If the enormous tesserakonter made by Ptolemy Philopator is described by Callixenus (*apud* Athenaeus v. 37, p. 204 a) as 'getting' twelve ὑποζώματα, it means that the normal quota would have been six, since the vessel has double prow, double stem, four tillers (πηδάλια, instead of the usual two ; see note on Acts xxvii. 40).

The Attic records also indicate that the ὑποζώματα could be detached [2] and attached to the ships or transferred from ship to ship. They could be kept in the naval arsenal [3] or on the acropolis. Whether they were put in

---

[1] ζωμεύματα] . . . ξύλα τῶν νεῶν. Plutarch, *Romulus* 7, refers to the σκάφη in which the infants were exposed as being preserved with letters inscribed on χαλκοῖς ὑποζώσμασι.

[2] In Aristophanes, *Equites* 278 f., a man is accused of having stolen ζωμεύματα for the Peloponnesian's triremes. They are thought to be a pun on ὑποζώματα. So at least the glossators (and Hesychius) thought.

[3] See now especially the full specifications for the σκευοθήκη of Philo built at the Peiraeus between 347 and 329 b.c. (*I.G.* ii. 2, 1054, line 74, republished in Dittenberger, *Sylloge* [3], No. 969, and E. S. Roberts and E. A. Gardner, *Inscriptions of Attica*, No. 126). Long shelves, running around three of the walls of this stone building, were provided for ὑποζώματα and other σκεύη κρεμαστά. The σκεύη ξύλινα were stored in a νεώσοικος or wooden shed. See V. Marstrand , *Arsenalet i Piraeus og oldtidens byggereregler*, Copenhagen, 1922.

place when the vessel sailed is not so clear.  But there are references to vessels at the dock of which one says ὑπέζωται, and there are enumerations of the ὑποζώματα on ships at the docks including the ships which the Boule in the time of Euainetus has provided with ὑποζώματα (ὑπέζωσεν). That the verb in these cases at least is technical seems likely, whatever its use in Acts xxvii. 17.  It may mean, however, that the ὑποζώματα were supplied, not necessarily that they were put in place.[1]

Unfortunately, however, these records do not indicate the position and use of the ὑποζώματα, nor do the other passages where either noun or verb occurs.  To solve this question appeal has been made variously (1) to the context of these passages, (2) to other passages where in connexion with ships other expressions are used, (3) to ancient representations of ships in art,[2] and (4) to modern nautical usage.  It should be recalled, however, that the identification of ὑποζώματα with any of these nautical phenomena is in each case unprovable.  It may, perhaps, be further suggested that possibly more than one use of ὑποζώματα existed.  Four main theories have been proposed depending on each of two alternatives—the alternative of whether the ὑποζώματα went round the ship or along one axis of the ship, and the alternative whether they ran from end to end or from side to side.

*The theories suggested.*

(i.) EXTERIOR.—They were conceived usually both before and after Böckh as enveloping the hull of the ship.  In favour of this view is the ὑπο- which ought to mean that they were girded underneath.  It was thought that their object was to keep the planks of the ship tight against the ribs, and possibly to protect the exterior of the ship from some of the force of the waves.[3]  But whether they ran horizontally or vertically was not generally agreed.  Some writers while favouring one form have admitted that the other probably was in use also.[4]

*Exterior bands.*

---

[1] There is no reference to the applying of ὑποζώματα especially at the time of storm, unless this passage in Acts be one.  But none of the evidence is incompatible with the view that ὑποζώματα were serviceable to prevent damage from storm.  Ropes with such effect are mentioned in Horace, *Carm.* i. 14. 6 f. : "Ac sine funibus vix durare carinae possint imperiosius aequor."

[2] The most fully illustrated treatment of the subject appears to be A. Köster, *Das antike Seewesen,* Berlin, 1923, to whose cuts and plates references will be made hereafter.  Cf. also E. Assmann, art. 'Seewesen' in A. Baumeister, *Denkmäler des klassischen Altertums,* iii., 1888, and Fr. Moll, *Das Schiff in der bildenden Kunst,* Berlin, 1929.

[3] This latter object is perhaps implied in the use of σπεῖραι in Lucian, *Toxaris* 19 (p. 528), where the travellers in a storm are said to have drawn some cables around (over, or after) the ship ἔτι καὶ σπείρας τινὰς ἐπισυρομένους, ὡς τὸ ῥόθιον ἐπιδέχεσθαι τῆς ὁρμῆς.  But these σπεῖραι may have been like the cables and anchors in Plut. *De garr.* 10, p. 507 A νεὼς μὲν γὰρ ἁρπαγείσης ὑπὸ πνεύματος ἐπιλαμβάνονται σπείραις καὶ ἀγκύραις τὸ τάχος ἀμβλύνοντες. A like manœuvre is found by some authorities in a later phrase of Acts, χαλάσαντες τὸ σκεῦος (see note Vol. IV. p. 333).

[4] Pollux, *Onomasticon* i. 89, has a definition which equates the ὑπόζωμα with the middle part of the rudder, and which cannot be brought into connexion with any of the matters we are discussing.

Vertical exterior bands.

(a) *Vertical.*—That they were vertical seems to suit best both the use of ὑπό- and the purpose of holding the planks. The planks ran lengthwise of the ship's hull, and a rope passed under the keel and fastened either at the gunwale on opposite sides, or joined on deck and pulled tight by twisting, or by a windlass, would hold the planks as the hoops hold the staves of a barrel. Such a practice has existed in various quarters until modern times. It is technically known as frapping.[1] Evidently several such bindings would be useful at intervals from fore to aft. This view has been held among others by James Smith, *The Voyage and Shipwreck of St. Paul*, 1848, 4th ed., 1880, pp. 108 f., 210-215 ; W. M. Ramsay, *St. Paul the Traveller*, 1896, p. 329 ; H. Balmer, *Die Romfahrt des Apostels Paulus und die Seefahrtskunde im römischen Kaiserzeitalter*, 1905, pp. 344 ff. ; E. Preuschen, *Berliner philologische Wochenschrift*, xxviii., 1908, col. 1430.

Longitudinal exterior bands.

(b) *Longitudinal.*—For the longitudinal use many equally good authorities gave their vote. It was pointed out, for example, that the length of the ὑποζώματα of the great tesserakonter of Philopator is specified as 600 cubits, and that since the vessel was 280 cubits long and at most 38 cubits in beam, a rope passing completely round the hull near the gunwale and fastened could be little less than 600 cubits long. It has further been argued that several longitudinal lines occur one below the other in the ancient representations of ships, and that in one bronze of the prow of a boat these appear plainly as ropes fastened.[2] It has been supposed that these are not decorative features but ὑποζώματα. This view of ὑποζώματα has been held among others by Böckh, *op. cit.* pp. 133-138 ; A. Breusing, *Die Nautik der Alten*, 1886, pp. 170-176 ; Cecil Torr, *Ancient Ships*, 1894, p. 41 ; and the later article by the same author, s.v. ' Navis ' in Daremberg-Saglio *Dictionnaire des Antiquités*, iv. pp. 32 f. ; von Goerne, *Neue kirchliche Zeitschrift*, 1898, p. 364.

Interior bands.

(ii.) INTERIOR (or STRAIGHT).—The discussion in English of the ὑποζώματα has been given quite a different turn by two articles in the *Harvard Studies in Classical Philology* in which not an exterior but an interior use of ὑποζώματα was proposed. Of these two studies the first is by E. G. Schauroth, vol. xxii., 1911, pp. 173-179, the second by Frank Brewster, vol. xxxiv., 1923, pp. 63-77. Since they seem not yet to have been included in the criticism of Acts their arguments may be briefly summarized.

---

[1] A similar manœuvre, by which a sheet with some sort of caulking material is held with ropes over the exterior of a hole in the hull, is not unknown in modern times according to W. K. L. Clarke, *Expos. Times*, xxvi., 1915, p. 377.

[2] Plate 40 in Köster, *Das antike Seewesen*, opposite p. 117. It has been debated whether the simple lines on some illustrations really stand for cables. The twisted rope strands in this bronze are therefore important. Another derivative of ζώννυμι applied to ships, ζωστῆρες, is often thought to have been marks or stripes indicating the height or draught of a ship. Heliodorus, *Aethiop.* i. 1 ; cf. Euripides, *Cyclop.* 505 f., and references in Daremberg-Saglio, *Dictionnaire des Antiquités*, iv. p. 32, note 13.

(c) *Transverse.*—Mr. Schauroth's theory is that the ὑποζώματα " were undergirders of rope, or perhaps chains, transversally stretched across the ship's hold under the deck, and attached at either end to one of the stout rib pieces. If two or more ropes were thus attached in one place, it would be possible by means of a bar or lever inserted between them, to twist them as taut as desired and so brace up the ship for an emergency. The same device, I am told, is to-day employed on many canal boats."

Mr. Schauroth points out that ropes passed under the keel of a trireme would not really support much of the hull, since the overhanging sides necessary for the three banks of oars would hold the ropes out from the lower part of the hull. He notes that Thucydides i. 29 uses the verb ζεύξαντες in connexion with the overhauling of old ships to make them seaworthy, and that Appian, *Bell. Civ.* v. 10, 91, uses διαζωννυμένους. Both these words " would be appropriate for a brace passed through and across a ship's hold." The literal force of ὑπο- ' under ' in ὑποζώματα may have been entirely lost, as it has been in other compounds.[1] Mr. Schauroth's main evidence is a passage in the *Argonautica* of Apollonius of Rhodes (i. 368) and the famous astronomical passage in Plato's *Republic.* The former reads :

νῆα δ᾽ ἐπικρατέως Ἄργου ὑποθημοσύνῃσιν
ἔζωσαν πάμπρωτον ἐϋστρεφεῖ ἔνδοθεν ὅπλῳ
τεινάμενοι ἑκάτερθεν, ἵν᾽ εὖ ἀραροίατο γόμφοις
δούρατα καὶ ῥοθίοιο βίην ἔχοι ἀντιόωσαν.

On this passage he says, " I call attention to the words ἔνδοθεν and ἑκάτερθεν—' from within ' and ' from both sides.' Böckh, Shaw, and other commentators [including now also G. W. Mooney, 1912] found the passage inexplicable on account of the mention of girding a ship on the inside; and because they did not understand it, decided that the text must be corrupt, and the lines rejected as they stand. . . . According to the view I have adopted, there is nothing extraordinary about the statement of Apollonius: in fact it is quite simple, for where else would such a girder be more likely to be drawn taut than on the inside of a ship? "

The passage in Plato's *Republic* x. 616 c reads : καὶ ἰδεῖν [ἔφη] αὐτόθι κατὰ μέσον τὸ φῶς ἐκ τοῦ οὐρανοῦ τὰ ἄκρα αὐτοῦ τῶν δεσμῶν τεταμένα— εἶναι γὰρ τοῦτο τὸ φῶς σύνδεσμον τοῦ οὐρανοῦ, οἷον τὰ ὑποζώματα τῶν τριήρων, οὕτω πᾶσαν συνέχον τὴν περιφοράν. Mr. Schauroth thinks in brief that the light instead of encircling the sphere ran diametrically across it, its ends (ἄκρα) being stretched to fastenings (δεσμοί) and so holding together the whole periphery.

Mr. Schauroth's case could be still further strengthened by other evidence. For instance in the *Republic* it was previously said of the light

---

[1] Pp. 175 f. He believes that certain compounds of ὑπο- come to mean actually inside. We may note that in English ' over ' in the nautical ' over-haul ' does not mean above deck exclusively.

that it was ' straight (εὐθύ) like a pillar.' If the verb ζεύγνυμι is to be brought into this connexion several other passages besides the one in Thucydides which he cites when the same verb ζεύγνυμι is used of ships could have been quoted, as was, indeed, done long ago by J. G. Schneider.[1] The medical use of ὑπόζωμα (διάζωμα) as the diaphragm of mammals or as ' the division between the thorax and abdomen of insects,' and the anatomical associations in Plato, *Laws* xii. 945 ο καθάπερ νεὼς ἢ ζῴου τινὸς οὓς τόνους [2] τε καὶ ὑποζώματα καὶ νεύρων ἐπιτόνους . . . προσαγορεύομεν, suggest taut inner braces rather than enveloping cables.[3]

Interior longitudinal bands.

(d) *Longitudinal.*—Mr. Brewster accepts from Mr. Schauroth the view that the ὑποζώματα were not passed outside the hull, but differs in supposing that they extended from end to end instead of from side to side. He quite rightly shows that neither the Plato nor the Apollonius passages determine this. In the latter ἑκάτερθεν may mean ' at each end ' as well as ' at each side.' Further, it is plain that the Latin word *tormentum* means a rope stretched from prow to stem. Isidore, *Etym.* (ed. Lindsay, Oxford, 1911), 19. 4. 4 defines it : " Tormentum funis in navibus longus, qui a prora ad puppim extenditur quo magis constringantur. Tormenta autem a tortu dicta." Vitruvius x. 15. 6 speaks of ropes on a battering-ram three in number and eight digits thick fastened just as in a ship from stem to stern continuously : " ita religati, quemadmodum navi a puppi ad proram continenter." The corresponding passage in Athenaeus, *De machinis* (ed. C. Wescher, p. 24), though it does not compare these cables to those on ships, mentions three eight-digit ropes used to undergird the ram and employs the verb ὑποζώννυται : ὑποζώννυται δὲ ὅλος ὁ κριὸς ὅπλοις ὀκταδακτύλοις τρισί.

Mr. Brewster questions the utility of rope cross-braces such as Mr. Schauroth suggested,[4] but his main argument is based on a feature of ancient boats revealed in pictures of Egyptian ships.[5] This is in brief a rope

---

[1] ζυγόν is used in more than one sense of ships. Possibly Theognis 513 νηός τοι πλευρῆσιν ὑπὸ ζυγὰ θήσομεν ἡμεῖς refers to props or braces against the sides of the ship, but it is quite obscure. See E. Harrison, *Studies in Theognis*, 1902, p. 326. E. Assmann brings also ζεῦγμα and ζύγωμα into connexion with the ὑποζώματα.

[2] The MSS. read ζῴου and ἐντόνους, for which editors have conjectured πλοίου and τόνους respectively. The latter word is now found, and in juxtaposition to the term ὑποζώματα, in an inventory of captured tackle on the Peiraeus inscription mentioned on p. 354, note 1.

[3] The use of δια- in διαζώννυμι (Appian *loc. cit.*) and διάζωμα, and perhaps the κατὰ μέσον in the gloss of Hesychius, *sub voce* ζωμεύματα] ὑποζώματα : σχοινία κατὰ μέσον τὴν ναῦν δεσμευόμενα, suit better a diameter than a circumference. Plato's light was also κατὰ μέσον.

[4] P. 76. He believes that wooden beams would serve the purpose better. In the older days, when ὑποζώματα were thought to be of wood, Taylor translated the word in Plato (vol. i. p. 471) ' transverse beams of ships.'

[5] E.g. A. Köster, *Das antike Seewesen*, pp. 21, 22, 25, and the picture from Deir-el-Bahari reproduced independently (and not reversed as in Köster, p. 25)

stretched above decks from stem to stern intended to prevent the boat from breaking its back amidships by binding the stem and stern together. Such damage to ships is technically called ' hogging,' and a hogging truss is said to be used occasionally in modern times.[1] The Egyptian pictures are dated by Egyptologists in the thirteenth century and even in the twenty-eighth century B.C. The ends in some cases are fastened to ropes passed under the keel at the end rather than to a single end piece.[2] The rope is held taut by being raised from the deck with props or twisted by a stick in the middle.[3] Mr. Brewster understands the βοηθεῖαι of Acts as props [4] and supposes that a hogging truss is the meaning of ὑποζώματα.

Mr. Brewster sums up his argument as follows (p. 77) : " We know from

---

herewith. It dates from about 1600 B.C., and represents an Egyptian ship of the Punt Expedition.

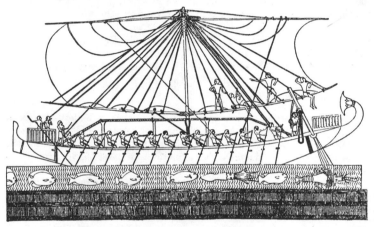

[1] This identification was suggested briefly by E. Warre, *Journal of Hellenic Studies*, v., 1884, 217 ; by J. Cook Wilson at the Oxford Philological Society in 1902 (reported in *Classical Review*, xvi., 1902, p. 234), and by E. K. Chatterton, *Sailing Ships, the Story of their Development from the Earliest Times to the Present Day*, London, 1909, p. 63.

[2] This is at least Mr. Brewster's opinion, and he identifies with these loops the *mitra* of the Romans defined by Isidore of Seville, *Etym.* 19. 4. 6, as "funis qua navis media vincitur."

[3] The detail of the stick, passing between the long twisted ropes and itself lashed at the ends (one end to one of the props) to prevent untwisting, appears plainly in a representation of an Egyptian sea-going ship, *c.* 2600 B.C.

[4] The evidence for this meaning is the Peshitto rendering here (Eb. Nestle, *zeitschrift für die neutestamentliche Wissenschaft*, viii., 1907, 75). The Syriac used here translates ἱστος at Ezek. xxvii. 5 (LXX) and at *Acta Thomae*, 3. Wettstein *ad loc.* says, without citing evidence, that in writers on building βοήθειαι is the word applied to props used to support a falling structure.

the Egyptian monuments that the pre-classical navigators used a rope-truss to keep their ships from hogging. We know that the Greek and Roman sailors used rope-cables, called in Greek ὑποζώματα and in Latin *tormenta*, to strengthen their vessels, and especially to enable them to stand stormy weather. From the references to them in Athenaeus and Vitruvius, these cables probably ran from stem to stern and were used as trusses. From the account in the *Argonautica* it appears that they ran inside the boat and not on the outside. From the account in Acts it appears that ' supports ' were used with them, a term which neatly applies to the device depicted by the Egyptians, but seems to have no real meaning on either of the other theories. Finally, we have Isidore's definitions, one of which, that of *tormentum*, well fits the Egyptian rope-truss; and the other, that of *mitra*, might fit the ropes encircling the overhangs fore and aft which we see in the Egyptian pictures. The Egyptian monuments prove that the rope-truss was in use for more than fifteen hundred years. We know now something of the intimate connexion of Crete with Egypt, of the extensive commerce of the former and of its influence on Greece. It is certainly probable that this ancient device passed on to the Greeks and from them to the Romans. The form of the device fits the evidence found in the Greek and Roman writers. On the whole, therefore, it seems probable that the ὑποζώματα were nothing but the ancient rope-truss which we see pictured by the Egyptian artists."

Conclusion.     The exact meaning of ὑποζώματα must apparently be left at present *sub judice*. The identification with the hogging truss is, perhaps, the most probable and attractive. There are several steps still necessary for the identification of such a device with the manœuvre described in Acts, which it is well to recapitulate.

(1) There is no clear pictorial evidence from the Greek and Roman sources that such a truss was used. E. Assmann, who in Baumeister's *Denkmäler* [1] really anticipated the modern arguments, thinks some of the

---

[1] Vol. iii., 1888, pp. 1594, 1604 f., 1614. He is followed by H. Droysen, *Heerwesen und Kriegführung der Griechen* (K. F. Hermann, *Lehrbuch der griechischen Antiquitäten*, ii. 2), Freiburg, 1889, p. 289; E. Lübeck, *Das Seewesen der Griechen und Römer*, Progr. Hamburg, 1. Teil, 1890, pp. 51-53; Köster, *loc. cit.* pp. 20 ff., 140 ff. The last adopts the view that the ὑποζώματα were sometimes of quite a different type (the one we have discussed under *b*). Brewster does not intimate that the view had been repeatedly sponsored in Germany for thirty-five years since Assmann first proposed it.

I may quote also a letter of Mr. P. M. B. Lake, who apparently without knowing either the German or American publications writes as follows to Professor Lake:

" A noticeable feature in all the representations of Egyptian vessels (which varied very little in many centuries) is the ' hogging truss ' extending from end to end of the ship's structure, consisting of a cable secured at bow and stern and kept in tension by vertical struts or crutches placed at intervals along its length. It is probable that from time to time, for the purpose of increasing trade, it was desirable to increase the length of ships, and apparently

Greek and Roman coins, pottery and reliefs, especially the smaller (Telephos) frieze of the great altar at Pergamum,[1] show a construction at the stem intended for the attachment of such a truss. It would not be fastened to the stem- or stern-post. Ancient ship-builders had difficulty enough in fastening these to the keel.[2] Other strain on them would be avoided.

In some of the representations of the Egyptian ships there is apparently a rope passed from gunwale to gunwale under the keel near the end. Each end of the rope is provided with a little loop,[3] and a beam was presumably passed across the deck and projected sufficiently to be held through these loops. To this beam the long truss would be fastened. " In the river ships of Egypt this binding rope appears often to be replaced by a corresponding wooden construction, which would become thus a so-called strut piece such as the river steamers from New York and Chicago use." It is the like construction which Baumeister attributes to classical times in the Mediterranean on the basis of pictorial elements which others who did not understand the Egyptian technique failed to notice. *Egyptian ships.*

(2) It would be necessary next to identify either part or all of this device with the ὑποζώματα. The word *tormentum* is so defined by Isidore as to imply such a truss, but not anywhere are ὑποζώματα so described. Assmann like others saw the origin of the ὑπο- in the encircling pieces *The tormentum as ὑπόζωμα.*

---

the naval architect of that day was faced with the same difficulty as his brother of to-day, when he attempted to do this, i.e. longitudinal weakness, and he got over this with the ' hogging truss.' A rope strop was placed round the bow and stern of the vessel. Its pointed ends and great sheer made them peculiarly adaptable for this. Then a heavy rope stretched fore and aft along the deck was secured to them, and this fore and aft rope set up tight with vertical props and crutches, the whole forming a truss or a girder that resisted the ' hogging' or drooping of the extremities of the vessel in a sea-way. The strops placed round the bow and stern were not for the purpose of binding the ship together there, but simply for the purpose of having something substantial to secure the ends of the fore and aft truss to. It is quite possible that it was the setting up of this ' truss' that St. Luke described as ' they used helps, undergirding the ship.' He saw them placing the strops round the bow and stern and, with his lack of nautical knowledge, very naturally thought that they were doing this to strengthen the sides, not noticing the rope that was running fore and aft and its subsequent setting up."

[1] For the clearest reproduction of this item in the frieze see Assmann in *Jahrbuch des deutschen archäologischen Instituts*, iv., 1889, p. 100; cf. iii., 1888, p. 92. I do not identify this detail among the plates of the frieze, *Altertümer von Pergamon*, published by the Berlin Museum, 1910, Band iii. 2 Tafeln.

[2] Korth, *Die Schiffsbaukunst*, Berlin, 1826, pp. 7 ff.

[3] These loops appear in the cuts on p. 21 of A. Köster's *Das antike Seewesen*. It should be added that Miltner, *loc. cit.* col. 945, distinguishes the ὑποζώματα as cables temporarily attached to these ropes from a more permanent similar bow-string arrangement fastened to wooden frames at each end of the deck (*Sprengwerk*). The latter are represented in the ship pictures of early Roman coins, but not in Greek sources.

at stem and stern. He says : " Das vielumstrittene ὑπόζωμα ¹ dürfte der Untergürtung durch die Zurrings wegen sogar wörtlich genommen werden, obgleich sein Synonym διάζωμα auf den geringen Wert der Präposition hindeutet."

**The use of ὑποζων-νύντες.**

(3) It would be necessary to suppose that the verb ὑποζωννύντες in Acts xxvii. 17 was not (see this note *ad init.*) a general word for overhauling, but a reference to resort on this occasion to the use of regular ὑποζώματα. But it is strange that nowhere else is the noun used of merchant ships but always for ships of war. It might be supposed that the technical ὑποζώματα represent some sort of temporary rope trusswork intended to reinforce fighting ships which were exposed to special strain in action because of the use of their beaks in ramming. In this case, instead of regarding the participle in Acts and various other words in other writings as references to the ὑποζώματα, we should rather apply them to quite different and at present undetermined aspects of the ship's equipment.

## Note XXIX.—The Titles of Jesus in Acts

### By Henry J. Cadbury

**The names applied to Jesus.**

The names applied to Jesus in New Testament times were quite varied. Often they were interchangeable and carried no special difference of thought. Certain writers had doubtless their favourite expressions for him,² just as for the Supreme Being different parts of the Old Testament used more or less consistently Yahweh (J in the Hexateuch, Psalms i.-xli.), Elohim (E and P in the Hexateuch, Psalms xlii.-lxxxiii.), or Yahweh Elohim (Deuteronomy and D passages elsewhere). In writings like Luke-Acts the variation of phrase may likewise be due to underlying sources. But the evidence, so far as it goes, suggests that the New Testament author copied

¹ I do not know why Assmann uses the singular. No instance of the word except in the plural is known to me. Possibly for the purpose of twisting with a stick it was always double. The crutches or props of the Egyptian truss seem to Assmann to solve the riddle of the wooden παραστάται mentioned in Greek sources, as others (see above) find in them the equally puzzling βοήθειαι of Acts. In a more recently discovered inscription of Peiraeus (*Berliner philologische Wochenschrift*, ix., 1889, col. 490, and since published in *Inscr. Graecae*, ii. 5, No. 792 *b*, p. 194) two other words are associated with the ὑποζωμάτων, the κορυφαῖα ὑποζωμάτων and the ὑποζωμάτων κ . μματα. E. Assmann, in the same volume of the *Wochenschrift*, coll. 971 f., suggests that the former were the ropes encircling the bow and stern to which the ὑποζώματα were fastened, the latter, which he reads as κέμματα, were the props.

² Few modern Christians who affect the sonorous combination ' our (the) Lord and Saviour Jesus Christ ' realize that in the New Testament it is the distinctive phrase only of one brief and late letter, Second Peter, which uses it four times (once without Jesus Christ). ' Saviour ' of Jesus occurs regularly in the narratives of Gnostic Gospels and in the fragmentary P Oxy 840.

his sources less precisely than the editors of the Old Testament, and that the variety of nomenclature for Jesus which he exhibits is due rather to his general liking for variation of phrase and to his particular sense of the fitness of certain expressions for certain speakers or situations. Owing to this ' dramatic ' taste of the author it is essential under the several terms discussed to differentiate references to Jesus by the narrator himself, references to him by the actors in the story in different situations, and instances of direct address to Jesus.

A complete study of the terms for Jesus used in Acts is not here necessary. The Editors of this series dealt fully with the most important of them—Christ (Messiah), Son of man, Son of God, Servant, Prophet, and Lord—in the last chapter of Volume I. on ' Christology.'[1] The origin and meaning of the terms does not now concern us. It will be sufficient here to indicate such facts about the usage in Acts as deserve special consideration.

1. *Jesus.*—This ('Ιησοῦς) is the regular Greek translation of the Hebrew Jesus. Joshua. The latter assumed a shorter form Jeshua (ישוע) in later times, which explains also the $\bar{e}$ in the Greek spelling. Among the Biblical instances Joshua the son of Nun, and Jeshua the son of Jehozadak, high priest in the time of Zerubbabel, are well known. The Greek spelling occurs in the LXX (with some exception) for the Hebrew name. It is included in the title of Ecclesiasticus. It is used in the New Testament at Luke iii. 29, Acts vii. 45, and Hebrews iv. 8 of ancient Hebrews, and of Jews of the early Roman Empire at Col. iv. 11, by Josephus frequently (see Niese, Index, *s.v.*), and in many other Jewish sources.

The name perhaps means ' JHVH is salvation,' and of this etymology the author of Matt. ii. 21 is doubtless reminding us.[2] But the etymology was rarely conscious to those who named their children so. With us, too, all names have an etymology, but it is rarely thought of in connexion with those who carry them. The child was often named for some kinsman (Luke i. 61) or the name was selected from current names. Jewish households often chose the names of famous Biblical characters. Paul the Benjamite was named Saul after the most famous person of his tribe's history. Jesus' brothers and parents bore such names as Jacob, Judah, Simeon, Joseph and Miriam (Mark vi. 3). The name Jesus therefore carried no special force with it. The disuse of the name for modern christenings in certain parts of Christendom has given it a uniqueness which it did not possess in Jesus' own lifetime.

---

[1] Many of the terms are discussed here and there in the commentary in Vol. IV. For a study in part parallel to the present note see E. D. Burton, ' Titles and Predicates of Jesus occurring in the Pauline Epistles,' *International Critical Commentary: Galatians*, 1920, pp. 392-417. *The Words of Jesus*, by G. Dalman, contains (pp. 234 ff.) a discussion of those terms which are found in the Gospels.

[2] The shorter (and original ?) form has nothing to do with JHVH. Jeshua occurs in other Semitic languages, and Joshua the Hebrew conqueror may be identical with Iashuia of the Amarna letter (Knudtzon 256). See A. T. Olmstead, *History of Palestine and Syria*, 1931, pp. 197, 201.

The name Jesus without any addition is constantly used by the evangelists of the historical figure as the subject of their narrative ; in the epistles, on the contrary, the name alone is correspondingly rare.[1] In some of the instances it is conceivable that it is used of the historical character as distinct from the more present and permanent aspects of his career. But the distinction is not carried through obviously. In Revelation it is used freely and not of the historical figure primarily. In Hebrews when the humanity of Christ is conspicuous the simple 'Ιησοῦς is often used. But it is characteristic of that epistle to introduce it at the close of a sentence and in apposition to some preceding description.[2] In Acts the simple word is comparatively rare. In several instances its use is quite in accordance with that in the gospels. There are also some instances where, as in Hebrews, it is used effectively as a loose appositive at the end of a clause.[3] Otherwise the undefined ' Jesus ' is mainly used where he is spoken of either by or to non-Christians,[4] and with reference to his past career.[5] We have also in Acts (τὰ) περὶ τοῦ 'Ιησοῦ[6] and τὸ ὄνομα τοῦ 'Ιησοῦ.[7] In visions he is spoken of or calls himself 'Ιησοῦς.[8] Preaching, especially about the past, is called τὰ περὶ τοῦ 'Ιησοῦ,[9] and as the subject of preaching, especially as an example of the resurrection, the simple 'Jesus' is used.[10] Since, however, in most of these circumstances longer expressions are used at other times, there does not seem to be in Acts any peculiar use of the simple 'Ιησοῦς.

Ναζωραῖος. 2. ὁ Ναζωραῖος.—The title ὁ Ναζωραῖος for Jesus is found in Acts ii. 22, iii. 6, iv. 10, vi. 14, xxii. 8, xxvi. 9. It is never used independently as ' the Nazarene ' has been in modern times, but always after 'Ιησοῦς or 'Ιησοῦς Χριστός. The same is true of its use in Luke xviii. 37 and elsewhere. It is true also of ὁ Ναζαρηνός which is used in Luke iv. 34 (from Mark i. 24), xxiv. 19, and in Mark. The plural οἱ Ναζωραῖοι meaning Christians is found in Acts xxiv. 5, its first known instance.[11]

The title with Jesus means probably ' from Nazareth,' like 'Ιησοῦν τὸν ἀπὸ Ναζαρέθ in Acts x. 38.[12] The name 'Ιησοῦς was common. One way the

---

[1] In Rom. x. 9, 1 Cor. xii. 3 (cf. Phil. ii. 10 f.), it seems to be used in a kind of formula of confession or malediction. In 2 Cor. iv. 5, 10, 11, 14, six instances occur in close succession, and we may compare Gal. vi. 17, 1 Thess. iv. 14.

[2] See ii. 9, iii. 1, iv. 14, vi. 20, vii. 22, xii. 2, 24.

[3] Cf. Cadbury, The Making of Luke-Acts, p. 218; add perhaps Acts v. 42, xvii. 3B, xx. 21B.

[4] ii. 22, 32, xiii. 32, xvii. 7, xix. 13, 15, xxv. 19.

[5] E.g. iv. 13.

[6] xviii. 25, xxviii. 23 (contrast 31).

[7] iv. 18, v. 40, ix. 27, but not later in the book, while longer phrases with ὄνομα occur throughout.

[8] vii. 55, ix. 5 (=xxvi. 15). Cf. xvi. 7 τὸ πνεῦμα 'Ιησοῦ.

[9] See above, note 6. I assume that τὰ περὶ τῆς βασιλείας τοῦ θεοῦ, on the other hand, is futuristic.

[10] Acts iv. 2, viii. 35, xvii. 18.

[11] See further Additional Note 30, p. 386.

[12] Cf. Matt. xxi. 11; John i. 45.

Jews had of distinguishing men of the same name was to indicate their provenience.[1]

The form of the adjective Ναζωραῖος has elicited some discussion among Hebraists. And the problem has been further complicated by the attempt to find the prophetic passage alluded to in Matt. ii. 23 Ναζωραῖος κληθήσεται.[2] While it is plain that the evangelist here associates Ναζωραῖος with Nazareth it is claimed that philologically and chronologically the connexion is impossible. It has even been inferred that Ναζωραῖος is a pre-Christian title and that a place named Nazareth never existed but is deduced from the title. All these points have been sufficiently dealt with by George F. Moore in Vol. I. pp. 426 ff., ' Appendix B. Nazarene and Nazareth.'

Matt. ii. 23.

It remains only to refer to some further discussions which have been in part called forth by the recent interest in the Mandaean material. The adherents of the religion from which these documents emanate are regularly called Nazarenes. Those who assume that the Mandaean religion is pre-Christian add an argument against the historicity of Jesus to those which W. B. Smith, for example, in *Die vorchristliche Jesus*, 1911, tried to derive from Epiphanius and from the implication of pre-Christian usage in Matt. ii. 23.[3]

The<br>Mandaeans.

3. χριστός.—Next to ' Nazarene ' the most purely identifying addition to ' Jesus ' is the word ' Christ.' But this is not a primitive usage, and the Book of Acts is noteworthy in the fact that so often ' Christ ' is still a title rather than a name. This of course is true of the cases where it occurs alone. Harnack[4] counts these as fourteen in number in Acts, and calls attention to the peculiarly loose connexion of Jesus in five cases—an

χριστός.

---

[1] Cf. Saul of Tarsus, John of Gischala, etc. Other ways of distinguishing were the use of surnames, the use of a patronymic genitive, or a reference to the profession.

[2] The usual source assigned is נצר ' branch ' in Isaiah xi. 1, etc. Eus. *Dem. Ev.* vii. 2, p. 349, thought of Lev. xxi. 12. H. Smith, *J.Th.S.* xxviii., 1926, p. 60, connects it with נזיר in Gen. xlix. 26 (perhaps a Josephite Messiah). Others have associated it with ' Nazirite,' Judges xiii. 7, " a Nazirite (נזיר = ἅγιον) shall the child be " ; cf. Luke i. 35 ἅγιον κληθήσεται, which is almost certainly due to the passage in Judges. Cf. C. Burrage, *Nazareth and the Beginnings of Christianity*, 1914. The Greek O.T. manuscripts or versions attest the forms Ναζαραιος, Ναζηραιος and Ναζιραιος, but not Ναζωραιος.

[3] Among articles discussing the term may be mentioned G. H. Box, Hastings' *D.C.G.* ii., 1908, pp. 235 f.; E. Nestle, *Expos. Times*, xix., 1908, pp. 523 f.; E. A. Abbott, *The Fourfold Gospel*, II. *The Beginning*, 1914, Appendix I. ' Nazarene and Nazorean,' pp. 309 - 350 ; M. Lidzbarski, *Mandäische Liturgien*, 1920, pp. xvi. ff. (*Abhandl. d. Gesell. d. Wissensch. zu Göttingen*, N.F. xvii. 1); H. Zimmern, ' Nazoräer (Nazarener),' *ZDMG.* lxxiv., 1920, pp. 429 ff. ; G. F. Moore, *Beginnings of Christianity*, vol. i., 1920, pp. 426 ff. ; E. Meyer, *Ursprung und Anfänge*, ii., 1921, pp. 408 f., 423 ff. ; W. Caspari, *ZNTW.* xxi., 1922, pp. 122-127 ; Strack-Billerbeck, *Kommentar zum N.T.* vol. i., 1922, on Matt. ii. 23; G. Dalman, *Orte und Wege Jesu*, 1919, chap. iii. *ad init.*

[4] *The Date of the Acts*, Eng. trans. p. 104.

appositive or predicate usage of one or the other which indicates that the words are still thought of separately. We have already noted this phenomenon in another connexion. How far from being a mere name with forgotten etymology χριστός is for our author is shown, I believe, further by his use of it for the Old Testament Messiah without special reference to Jesus [1] and its occurrence in the predicate as in ii. 36 καὶ κύριον αὐτὸν καὶ Χριστὸν ἐποίησεν ὁ θεός. Unlike κύριος the Greek word χριστός applied to a person must have seemed to Greek ears unintelligible.[2] Its usage in an etymological sense is therefore all the more striking in a writer like Luke. His use of the verb χρίω at Acts iv. 27 after the Psalmist's phrase τοῦ χριστοῦ αὐτοῦ (i.e. the anointed of the Lord) shows that he understands the etymology, and the same may well be the reason for his choice of the verb elsewhere (Luke iv. 18, Acts x. 38). Whether perfect participles like ἐκλελεγμένος (Luke ix. 35, contrast Mark ix. 7 ὁ ἀγαπητός, and compare Luke xxiii. 35 ὁ χριστὸς τοῦ θεοῦ ὁ ἐκλεκτός), ἀποδεδειγμένος (Acts ii. 22), and προκεχειρισμένον (Acts iii. 20) further reveal the author's consciousness of the force of the verbal χριστός is uncertain.

Ἰησοῦς
,χριστός. ·

The limited use of the combination Ἰησοῦς χριστός is also important evidence in Luke's writings of the continuance of χριστός as a title rather than as a name. In Paul, it is well known, that combination is very frequent and is purely appellative. In Acts at most eleven occurrences are well attested by the MSS. Seven of these are used with τὸ ὄνομα and so may be regarded as " of the nature of a formula." [3]    In the same way I would regard two others, viz. ix. 34 and x. 36, in which Jesus Christ is spoken of as the agent of cure or of the message of good news. This leaves two other cases, but in them occurs the fuller formula ' Lord Jesus Christ.' [4]

The result of the evidence in Acts concerning χριστός is certainly to compel us to acknowledge that for this writer it is not a proper name. Harnack regards its titular character as a mark of the relative primitiveness of the Christology of Acts as compared with Paul. But it should be recalled that relative primitiveness in nomenclature is not the same as relative priority in date. Besides the possibility that some of Luke's occurrences are due to sources—some would say to Aramaic sources—it is possible that χριστός = Messiah is a successful attempt at archaism. No other New Testament writer so fully puts us en rapport with the Jewish Messianic background of the gospel. The canticles of Luke i., ii. illustrate his dramatic ability in this as well as in other respects. The Lord's Christ of Luke ii. 26 alone of N.T. passages (except the quotation in Acts iv. 26) reproduces the accurate idiom which requires the possessive κυρίου with χριστός.[5]

---

[1] Luke ii. 26, iii. 15, xxiv. 26, 46 ; Acts ii. 31.

[2] Cf. Vol. I. p. 347. Is it for this reason that Aquila uses ἠλειμμένος (from ἀλείφω) in place of χριστός of the LXX at 1 Sam. ii. 35, Psalm xxvii. 8, lxxxiii. 10, lxxxviii. 39 and 52 ? or had the Christian use of the LXX seemed to necessitate a changed rendering of the term for Jewish Greek readers ?

[3] Harnack, The Date of the Acts, p. 104.

[4] See below, note 2, p. 360.

[5] At Luke ix. 20 and xxiii. 35 ὁ χριστὸς τοῦ θεοῦ takes the place of ὁ χριστός without genitive in Mark viii. 29, xv. 32.

In ii. 11 χριστὸς κύριος [1] if not a mistranslation for χριστὸς κυρίου is another definite use of χριστός as appellative. But in the later part of Acts in Gentile surroundings all uses of χριστός become less frequent. The additions by scribes in later MSS. show how little they appreciated that Luke used it in accordance with Jewish thought.[2]

4. κύριος.—In dealing with the word κύριος for Jesus it is necessary κύριος. to distinguish its use in narrative from its use in discourse, and in the latter its use in direct address to Jesus must be separately treated.

In the gospels as a whole the narrative rarely substitutes titles for the name of Jesus. This is true of such terms as Son of man, Son of God, Christ, etc., and it is nearly true of κύριος. Occurrences of κύριος in the narrative are conspicuous because of their fewness, and they appear to be more numerous in the later books. No instances occur in Mark except in the appendix, nor in Matthew, but John has five occurrences and Luke thirteen occurrences.[3] To judge from the extant fragment, the Gospel of Peter used ὁ κύριος constantly. While it may be unfair to compare Acts with gospels, since a restraint practised by evangelists in writing of Jesus' lifetime might not be felt in recording later history in which thought of the risen Lord coloured all references to him, yet both the frequent use of κύριος in the Third Gospel and its use in certain passages in Acts dealing with the Lord's earthly career suggest that it is not one of the words that Luke regards as appropriate only for the spoken parts of his actors.

Both in narrative and in discourse Acts like the LXX uses κύριος of God. Many cases of κύριος in Acts, perhaps the majority, are quite ambiguous, since they could mean either God or Jesus. Both these and the cases when it plainly means God may well be omitted from consideration.[4]

[1] It has been suggested that the combination was a recognized pre-Christian Jewish Messianic expression. It occurs at Lam. iv. 20 ; Ps. Sol. xvii. 36, xviii. title, xviii. 8 ; Luke ii. 11. In the first instance alone is it certainly a mistranslation. In Ps. Sol. xviii. the instances being in the genitive permit of interpretation as χριστὸς κυρίου. For a discussion of the term, which, as it does not occur in Acts, does not concern us now, see *Psalms of Solomon* by Ryle and James, pp. 141 f.

[2] Among the conclusions of C. Ryder Smith, ' The Names Christ and Jesus in the Acts,' *Expository Times*, xix., 1907–1908, pp. 45 f., are these : 1. " This writer never uses Jesus Christ except in reporting the words of others." 3. " The term Christ, when used alone, is always used distinctly as a Jewish title." 4. " The term Christ, whether used alone or in combination with Jesus, never occurs except in relation to a Jewish environment."

[3] Cf. Hawkins, *Horae Synopticae*, 2nd ed., 1919, p. 43, who, however, reckons that it is used of the risen and ascended Christ twenty times in Acts, forty-six in the Epistles, and twice in Revelation.

[4] It may be observed that when employed of Jesus κύριος is regularly used with the article. The apparent exceptions (ii. 36, x. 36) are easily explained. With κύριος of God, Luke often (not always) omits the article. This includes the forms πνεῦμα κυρίου, ἄγγελος κυρίου, χεὶρ κυρίου, where by a usual idiom neither the genitive nor its (construct) noun has an article. Cf. Bousset, *ZNTW*. xv., 1914, p. 162.

There remain, however, several instances where Jesus is spoken of by the actors or is spoken to by them. In the former cases the use is frequently that of the narrative, i.e. ὁ κύριος has become a fixed surrogate for Jesus and is not a conscious title. Acts ii. 36 supplies one of the clearest cases of κύριος as a title of Jesus,[1] just as it supplies clear evidence of χριστός as a title.

Lord Jesus.    The combination 'Lord Jesus' occurs several times in Acts. Instances in which Christ is added have been considered above and are not numerous, even if doubtful cases are included.[2] Like 'Jesus Christ' both 'Lord Jesus' and 'Lord Jesus Christ' occur frequently in connexion with the name,[3] or as the subject of belief or testimony or preaching.[4] Perhaps we may regard this also as due to the use of a formula. On the other hand its occurrence in the mouth of Christians speaking to Christians in passages like i. 21, xi. 17, xv. 11, 26, xx. 21, 24, 35, xxi. 13, suggests that it was regarded by Luke as the appropriate way to speak of him within the Christian circle. Certainly for use within that circle Luke has no other term for Jesus except the simple ὁ κύριος.[5]

κύριε in the vocative is the least significant use of the word. It is much the same as 'sir.' It would be used of polite address to men, both acquaintances and strangers, and certainly carries no special suggestion of an exalted station of the person addressed.[6]

The situation with regard to κύριος in Acts seems therefore to be almost the reverse of that in regard to χριστός. For ὁ κύριος when used of Jesus in Luke-Acts is a stereotyped title rather than a conscious ascription of Lordship. ὁ κύριος has been generally regarded as a late title, not native in the Palestinian Christianity. Whether it comes from Northern Syria and Semitic sources [7] or from the Hellenistic world is a subject still open to

---

[1] At first sight this passage seems parallel to Paul's confession that Jesus is Lord (1 Cor. xii. 3; Rom. x. 9; Phil. ii. 11). It should, however, be recalled that it is not so much the author's natural use but the kind of parallelism of Psalm ii. quoted at iv. 26 that led to the explicit καὶ κύριον καὶ χριστόν.

[2] There is no consensus of MSS. for including χριστός at iv. 33, xx. 21, xxviii. 31. This leaves only xi. 17 and xv. 26.

[3] viii. 16, xv. 26, xix. 5, 13, 17, xxi. 13.

[4] iv. 33, xi. 17, xvi. 31, xxviii. 31.

[5] See also Luke xxiv. 34. It is instructive to compare the three similar passages, Luke xxii. 61 (contrast Mark xiv. 72), Acts xi. 16, and xx. 35, where remembering the Lord's word is spoken of.

[6] In the gospels more definite appellations for Jesus in address are διδάσκαλε, ῥαββεί (ῥαββουνεί), and in Luke ἐπιστάτα. Occasionally κύριε is used in place of these. Under these circumstances it perhaps implies more respect than the usual κύριε ( = 'Sir') or than Matthew's ἑταῖρε (xx. 13, xxii. 12, xxvi. 50) or Luke's ἄνθρωπε (v. 20, xii. 14, xxii. 58, 60). The LXX shows that κύριε stands for a Semitic vocative with a possessive like adonai.

[7] Cf. W. Bousset, Kyrios Christos, 1913, 2nd ed., 1921, and dissenting J. G. Machen, The Origin of Paul's Religion, 1921, pp. 293 ff.; F. C. Burkitt, Christian Beginnings, 1924, pp. 42 ff.

debate. The possibility of LXX influence on the nomenclature of Jesus cannot be left out of account.[1] Attempt has been made to account for the distribution of κύριος in Luke's writings by source division. In the Gospel it has been assigned to the Special Lucan Source which critics have called L.[2] In Acts Bousset believed it was limited to sections which either were from non-Palestinian sources or were worked over by the evangelist himself.[3] In both books I believe adequate explanation of the occurrences of κύριος would be found in the author's own free and unconscious use of the term, rather than in any systematic derivation from sources. It is, for example, often found, like the purely titular use of χριστός, in connexion with πιστεύω (πίστις, πιστός)[4] or ὄνομα.[5]

Before leaving the term κύριος notice should be made of the expression Lord of all. in Acts x. 36 οὗτός ἐστιν πάντων κύριος. Although the expression is parenthetical and ejaculatory, the antecedent of οὗτος is probably Jesus (see commentary ad loc.). The absence of the article, though grammatically intelligible on account both of the predicate position and of the inarticular dependent genitive, leaves us uncertain as to whether the Greek reader felt in πάντων κύριος the definiteness of a real title. Similar expressions are not infrequent of God. From the Apocrypha and Pseudepigrapha of the Old Testament may be cited, with the help of the index to Charles's edition, the following :

---

[1] See the monumental posthumous work of Count W. Baudissin, *Kyrios als Gottesname in Judentum und seine Stelle in der Religionsgeschichte*, 1926–1929. For the recent voluminous literature on the title see Preuschen-Bauer, *Wörterbuch*, coll. 722 f.     Cf. Baudissin, *op. cit.* iv. p. 68.     Add E. von Dobschütz, ' Κύριος Ἰησοῦς ' in *ZNTW*. xxx., 1931, pp. 97 ff. The LXX use of κύριος for JHVH doubtless tended to enhance the meaning of κύριος when once applied to Jesus. If Paul implied gradation by his "gods many and lords many" (1 Cor. viii. 5), that was due to the relation he found between God and Jesus rather than to an accepted connotation of the word κύριος in Gentile circles as inferior to θεός.

[2] B. Weiss, *Die Quellen der synoptischen Überlieferung*, 1908, pp. 134, 137, 144, 156, 164 ; B. S. Easton, *JBL*. xxix., 1910, p. 149 ; *JBL*. xxx., 1911, p. 84 ; *Gospel according to St. Luke*, 1926, p. xxvi. It might be also claimed as characteristic of ' Proto-Luke.' So Streeter, *The Four Gospels*, p. 212 ; V. Taylor, *Behind the Third Gospel*, 1926, p. 265, regards its use in Proto-Luke as in point of development earlier than that in Paul or Acts. It has long been accounted a characteristic of Luke the Evangelist. See Hawkins, *Horae Synopticae*, 2nd ed., 1919, p. 43.

[3] ' Der Gebrauch des Kyriostitels als Kriterium für die Quellenscheidung in der ersten Hälfte der Apostelgeschichte' in *ZNTW*. xv., 1914, pp. 141-162.

[4] Acts v. 14, ix. 42, xi. 17, 21, 23, xv. 11, xvi. 15, 31, xviii. 8, xx. 21. The list includes cases where Ἰησοῦς or Ἰησοῦς χριστός are added as well as some where κύριος may mean God. Bousset, *loc. cit.* p. 150, claims that the term ' belief ' is also late.

[5] Acts viii. 16, ix. 28, xix. 5, 13, 17, xxi. 13.

Ruler of all (τοῦ πάντα δεσποτεύοντος θεοῦ),[1] 3 Macc. v. 28; (ὁ τῶν πάντων δυνάστης), vi. 39.

King of all (τῷ βασιλεῖ τῶν πάντων),[2] Tobit x. 13 א.

Sovereign of all (ὁ πάντων δεσπότης), Wisd. Sol. vi. 7, viii. 3.

Father of all, Apoc. Mos. xxxv. 2, xxxvii. 4.

God of all (δέσποτα ὁ θεὸς πάντων), Sirach xxxvi. (xxxiii.) 1, xlv. 23 (Heb.), l. 22; Jubilees xxii. 10, 27, xxx. 19, xxxi. 13, 32; Apoc. Mos. xxxii. 2, xlii. 8.

For 'Lord of all' we may cite the *Assumption of Moses* iv. 2.[3] In Hecataeus's account of Moses God is called τῶν ὅλων κύριον.[4]

The expression τῶν ὅλων in the last instance is probably neuter like τοῦ ὅλου. It would be a natural term for philosophers and laymen to use of the 'universe.' τῶν πάντων may also be neuter, but in Acts x. 36 is almost certainly personal, referring to men or gods.[5]

For the application of the phrase to Jesus one naturally turns to Romans x. 12 οὐ γάρ ἐστι διαστολὴ 'Ιουδαίου τε καὶ ῞Ελληνος. ὁ γὰρ αὐτὸς κύριος πάντων. But I know of no evidence that the title had any general currency in Christian speech.

βασιλεύς. 5. ὁ βασιλεύς.—The term king is rarely used of Jesus in the earliest Christian literature. In Luke-Acts it occurs in the mouths of non-Christians. In the 'Hosanna cry' Luke has changed Mark's " Blessed is he that cometh in the name of the Lord. Blessed is the coming kingdom of our father David " to " Blessed is the king that cometh in the name of the Lord." As in the other gospels the cross of Jesus bears the *titulus* " King of the Jews." But Luke twice besides makes specific the charge that Jesus thought himself χριστὸς βασιλεύς (Luke xxiii. 2) or was thought to be βασιλεὺς ἕτερος (Acts xvii. 7). I refrain from translating these expressions. To many readers they would associate Jesus with an emperor rather than with a local prince (see Vol. IV. p. 206), but they are evidently chosen

---

[1] Cf. the phrase κύριον τὸν πάντων δεσπότην in the free Greek paraphrase of Job v. 8.

[2] Cf. Josephus, *Antiq.* xiv. § 24 βασιλεῦ τῶν ὅλων.

[3] The Latin is *domine omnis*. Only the Greek Esther (xiii. 11) has κύριος εἶ πάντων. There is said to be a corresponding Aramaic title (Dalman, *Adonaj*, 1889, p. 83). Still closer is the expression used by Plutarch, a pagan writer, about a pagan god. When Osiris was born a voice came: ὡς ὁ πάντων κύριος εἰς φῶς πρόεισιν (Plutarch, *De Iside et Osiride*, 12, p. 355 E). The lines attributed to Menander (Ps.-Justin, *De monarchia*, 5) or Diphilus, another comic poet (Clem. Alex. *Stromata*, v. 14; Euseb. *Praep. evangel.* xiii. 13), with τὸν ὄντα κύριον πάντων ἀεὶ καὶ πατέρα need not be Christian forgery (Kock, *Comicorum Atticorum Fragmenta*, ii. p. 580) any more than Plato, *Epist.* vi. p. 323 D.

[4] Diodor. Sic. xl. 3, 4 (Müller, *Fragm. histor. Graec.* ii. 392). Cf. ὁ δημιουργὸς τῶν ἀπάντων of God in 1 Clem. xxvi. 1, lix. 2, and δημιουργὸς τῶν ὅλων in *Ad Diognetum*, vii. 2.

[5] We may compare for the personal use the way in which in the papyri petitioners apply to their patrons such flattering titles as τὸν πάντων βοηθόν, τὸν πάντων σωτῆρα καὶ ἀντιλήμπτορα.

for their political implications.   For this author, then, βασιλεύς is not an established religious title for Jesus.

6. *Son of Man.*—The terms Son of man and Son of God occur of Jesus **Son of Man.** each once in Acts.   It is strange that Son of man occurs at all, since it is the self-designation of Jesus as speaker and is limited in the Gospels (including John) to places where Jesus is speaking of himself.   It is not used at all even in the Epistles of the New Testament or in the Apostolic Fathers. Its rare occurrences (as in Acts vii. 56, Revelation i. 13, xiv. 14 [1]) show by their setting or context that it is due in each case to the influence of the apocalyptic passage in Daniel vii. 13.   It therefore throws little light on the much disputed gospel usage, and in its turn is but little illuminated by that.   That Acts accepts an apocalyptic rôle for the risen Jesus is confirmed from other passages and would not need the dying words of Stephen as support.   The story of the Ascension facilitates a literal belief in the Son of man standing [2] on the clouds at God's right hand.

7. *Son of God.*—The single occurrence of Son of God in Acts is in ix. 20.   **Son of God.** The newly converted Paul " preached Jesus in the synagogues of Damascus that he was the Son of God." [3]   One may suggest that the phrase is not specially chosen, since the next verse but one ends with a clause similarly constructed, " that this was the Christ."   No argument is needed to prove that Luke accepted the belief that Jesus was God's son or that he regarded the title as equivalent to Christ.   The former is implied in Acts xiii. 33 where Psalm ii. 7 is quoted, " Thou art my son, this day have I begotten thee," [4] not to mention passages in Luke's gospel.   That earlier volume also illustrates the parallelism of Christ and Son of God as in Acts ix. 20 and 22 in the adjacent sentences [5] :

> xxii. 67  εἰ σὺ εἶ ὁ χριστός, εἰπὸν ἡμῖν.
> xxii. 70  σὺ οὖν εἶ ὁ υἱὸς τοῦ θεοῦ ;

Indeed, the last sentence following directly upon a reference to the Son of man suggests that it too should be included in Luke's equation.   So within the compass of four verses of the Gospel ὁ υἱὸς τοῦ ἀνθρώπου, ὁ υἱὸς τοῦ θεοῦ and χριστός seem to be used interchangeably and to be interpreted three verses later by χριστὸς βασιλεύς (xxiii. 2).

8. ὁ δίκαιος.—The adjective δίκαιος is used of Jesus in Acts iii. 14, **The Righteous** vii. 52, and xxii. 14.   Unlike other New Testament passages where it is used **One.** of Jesus [6] it has in each case the article and no noun.   This suggests that it

---

[1] Also in Hegesippus *apud* Eusebius *H.E.* ii. 23, and probably in the Gospel according to the Hebrews (Jerome, *De vir. ill.* 2).   Both passages have to do with James the Just.

[2] Elsewhere he is more often spoken of as ' seated ' on the right hand.

[3] Neither at viii. 37 or elsewhere does the MS. evidence justify us in reading ' Son of God.'

[4] This form is also given to the Voice from heaven at the Baptism in the Western text of Luke.

[5] These questions seem to divide into two Mark's (xiv. 61) σὺ εἶ ὁ χριστὸς ὁ υἱὸς τοῦ εὐλογητοῦ ;

[6] 1 Peter iii. 18; 1 John ii. 1.

is a title rather than simply a descriptive adjective. Of course ὁ δίκαιος can mean generically the righteous person, and this is doubtless its force in James v. 6, 1 Peter iv. 18, and in the quotation of Paul and Hebrews from Habakkuk ὁ δίκαιός μου ἐκ πίστεως ζήσεται. In favour of regarding ὁ δίκαιος in Acts as a title is its definite reference to Jesus and its complete substitution for a name or pronoun referring to him. The Similitudes of Enoch xxxviii. 2 apparently attest ‘the righteous one’ of the Messiah in pre-Christian Judaism, but one doubtful [1] instance hardly suffices to prove that it was a fixed term.[2] Against supposing that Acts is so using it is the free way in which it is expanded by a similar adjective in iii. 14 to τὸν ἅγιον καὶ δίκαιον. In other respects also it seems to retain in Luke-Acts an untechnical meaning.[3] If ὁ δίκαιος subsequently was established in Christianity as a title for Jesus it would doubtless be read into these passages just as it was read predictively into the Wisdom of Solomon, especially under the influence of ii. 18 εἰ γάρ ἐστιν ὁ δίκαιος υἱὸς θεοῦ, and into Isaiah iii. 10 δήσωμεν τὸν δίκαιον ὅτι δύσχρηστος ἡμῖν ἐστιν. C. C. Torrey says “The ‘Just one’ ὁ δίκαιος of Acts iii., vii. and x. (sic) comes especially from Isaiah liii. 11,” [4] but that judgement is due to the same over-emphasis on the influence of that part of Scripture as will meet us in considering the next title.[5]

ὁ παῖς.

9. ὁ παῖς.—Of particular interest among the terms used of Jesus in Acts is παῖς. The passages are four in number, two in the speech of Peter in Solomon’s Porch iii. 13, 26, and two in the prayer of the disciples iv.

---

[1] The reading is uncertain, and of course we do not know whether δίκαιος lies behind the Ethiopic. In Enoch liii. 6 occurs ‘the righteous and elect one.’

[2] See H. Dechent, ‘ Der “ Gerechte ” eine Bezeichnung für den Messias,’ Theol. Studien und Kritiken, c., 1927–28, pp. 439 ff. The title appears to be more characteristic of James the brother of Jesus. It had become a surname of the Athenian statesman Aristides. Compare the Latin surname Justus borne by three New Testament characters (Acts i. 23, see note, xviii. 7, Col. iv. 11). On the history of δίκαιος as a royal, or at least an honorary, title see M. Rostovtzeff in Yale Classical Studies, ii., 1931, p. 9 note.

[3] So of Jesus in Luke xxiii. 47 δίκαιος (not ὁ δίκαιος) replaces Mark xv. 39 υἱὸς Θεοῦ (not ὁ υἱὸς τοῦ Θεοῦ). Here, unless we see a far-fetched echo of Wisdom of Solomon ii. 18 (see above), Luke is simply putting in the centurion’s mouth the more colourless ‘ innocent ’ for the more technical or ‘ superstitious ’ Son of God. It is a curiosity and a mark of Luke’s association of ideas that two of the occurrences of φονεύς in Acts are in two of the passages named using ὁ Δίκαιος or δίκαιος, viz. iii. 14 and vii. 52, while the only other occurrence of φονεύς in Acts (xxviii. 4) has Δίκη or δίκη in the context. Cf. Matt. xxiii. 35; James v. 6.

[4] ‘ The Influence of Second Isaiah in the Gospels and Acts,’ Journal of Biblical Literature, xlviii., 1929, p. 29.

[5] It is possible that ὁ ἅγιος in iii. 14, cf. ὁ ἅγιος τοῦ θεοῦ Luke iv. 34 (= Mark i. 24), John vi. 69, and ὁ ὅσιος (τοῦ θεοῦ) of Psalm xvi. 10, Acts ii. 27, xiii. 35, quite as much deserve to be regarded as Jewish or Christian Messianic titles as ὁ δίκαιος, but I have not included them in this study. Another term, Son of David, is also omitted here, since it is implied rather than actually used in Acts.

27, 30. The word is followed in each case by a genitive pronoun ($a\mathring{v}\tau o\mathring{v}$ or $\sigma o v$) meaning 'God's,' and in all the instances but one by an appositive 'Jesus.' The two instances in the prayer use the festal adjective 'holy.'

The questions arise : (i.) why is this term for Jesus limited in Acts and indeed practically in the New Testament [1] to these occurrences ? and (ii.) what meaning or connotation does the term convey ? It may be noted in the first place that like several other appellations of Jesus it is limited to the spoken parts. Two instances are in prayer, and their formal character [2] is further attested by the limitation of the phrase in other early Christian literature to liturgical usage. All the instances have been carefully collected and studied of late by A. von Harnack.[3] They include among the next earliest writings the *Didache* and the Epistle of Barnabas. The liturgical character of the expression has been generally acknowledged. *Resulting problems.*

The explanation of this liturgical character is, however, not unanimous. The common and simplest view is that what is liturgical is also ancient. It is claimed that the term $\pi a\hat{\iota}s$ represents a primitive Christology. It was so primitive that it is not found even in Paul. Acts quite accurately limits it to the earliest chapters and to the earliest Christians, Peter and the rest. Such, at least, is one explanation. *A primitive Christology.*

Burkitt [4] has lately suggested a somewhat later origin. He thinks that $\pi a\hat{\iota}s$ came into Christology from the LXX. It belongs, therefore, not to Palestinian but to Hellenistic Christianity. We have here the same controversy as prevails more extensively about the title $\kappa\acute{v}\rho\iota o s$. The ordinary meaning of $\pi a\hat{\iota}s$ is child. It suggests relationship to parents less than $v\iota\acute{o}s$, and its emphasis is rather upon youth. On the other hand, like certain similar words in other languages it may also be used for 'servant,' and as a matter of fact in the LXX it is used no less often than $\delta o\hat{v}\lambda o s$ to translate עֶבֶד.[5] The Hebrew words for 'son' or 'child,' on the other hand, are otherwise rendered.[6] It seems altogether likely, therefore, that though $\pi a\hat{\iota}s$ elsewhere in Luke-Acts may mean 'child,' or even 'son,'[7] in these passages it means 'servant.' In the Old Testament, however, 'servant of God' has become a common metaphor of religious speech. It is applied by *Derived from the LXX.*

---

[1] At Matt. xii. 18 is quoted of Jesus Isaiah xlii. 1 $\iota\delta o\mathring{v}$ $\acute{o}$ $\pi a\hat{\iota}s$ $\mu o v$ $\check{o}\nu$ $\mathring{\eta}\rho\acute{\epsilon}\tau\iota\sigma a$.

[2] Dibelius in *ZNTW.* xvi., 1915, pp. 123 ff., argues from its own wording that Acts iv. 24-28 has behind it older formulations of a kerygmatic or liturgic character.

[3] See below, p. 367. Harnack had earlier given a considerable list in his note on Barnabas vi. 1.

[4] *Christian Beginnings*, pp. 35-41.

[5] Most translators used both words. But $\pi a\hat{\iota}s$ is found exclusively in Genesis and indeed (with only three exceptions) in the whole Pentateuch. In the Book of the Twelve, on the other hand, the few instances of עבד are all rendered by $\delta o\hat{v}\lambda o s$. What Greek or Semitic original lies behind Matt. viii. 5 ff. ($\pi a\hat{\iota}s$ *ter*), Luke vii. 2 ff. $\delta o\hat{v}\lambda o s$ . . . $\pi a\hat{\iota}s$ . . . $\delta o\hat{v}\lambda o s$, is uncertain.

[6] Thus בֵּן becomes $v\iota\acute{o}s$ over 4000 times, and $\pi a\hat{\iota}s$ twice. Other words are יֶלֶד, $\pi a\iota\delta\acute{a}\rho\iota o\nu$, $\pi a\iota\delta\acute{\iota}o\nu$.

[7] Luke ii. 43, vii. 7, viii. 51, 54, ix. 42; Acts xx. 12.

pious men to themselves and by other speakers to notable persons in history. We are familiar with such phrases as ' thy servants the prophets.' In the mouth of an Old Testament writer ' thy servant ' means ' I.' And like ' thy ' we have the possessives ' his ' or ' Lord's.' With such genitives παῖς is used and is often further defined by the proper name, like Moses (especially in Joshua), Jacob (especially in 2 Isaiah), Abraham, Job, Israel, David, Zerubbabel. In precisely the same manner we have in Psalms of Solomon xii. 7 Ἰσραὴλ παῖδα αὐτοῦ, xvii. 23 Ἰσραὴλ παῖδά σου, and in Luke's own gospel Ἰσραὴλ παιδὸς αὐτοῦ (i. 54), Δαυεὶδ παιδὸς αὐτοῦ (i. 69). These are all as liturgical as any of the passages with παῖς . . . Ἰησοῦς. . . . Indeed, twice ' thy servant David ' occurs in the same context of a prayer as ' thy servant Jesus,' viz. Acts iv. 25, *Didache* ix. 2. The liturgical idiom is therefore an Old Testament form of expression. That is only natural, but is it an echo of a specific Old Testament passage or person ?

**Relation to Is. liii.**    This question is answered usually in the affirmative and with complete assurance. The use of παῖς with Jesus is generally regarded as a definite reference to the so-called Suffering Servant of parts of Isaiah, notably Isaiah liii. It may be an act of temerity to question this origin. Whether as mediated through the LXX as Burkitt proposed, or based on a tradition about Jesus or even a pre-Christian tradition of the Messiah reaching back through Semitic channels, the παῖς in Acts iii. and iv. is invariably interpreted as a reference to the 'Ebed Yahweh of Second Isaiah. Conversely the influence of the Isaiah passages on early Christology is fortified by references to these passages in Acts, with the further assumption that because they are liturgical their concepts are early. Such a connexion was questioned in Vol. I. p. 391, but in view of its all but general acceptance it is worth while to indicate how little basis it has to rest on.

The use of Isaiah's figure in early Christian interpretation is exceedingly scanty. Modern expositors, hard put to it to find predictions of Christ's death in the Old Testament, seize upon Isaiah liii. as the proof text. But there is little evidence that it played so central a rôle. Paul and Luke refer frequently in a general way to the Scriptural expectation of Christ's passion, but Paul never uses Isaiah's words and Luke but once (Acts viii. 32 f.).

The abundance of the vicarious clauses in Isaiah liii. also attracts modern commentators with their preconceived notion of what primitive Christology must have been like. Luke, however, as I have pointed out elsewhere,[1] not only omits ' vicarious ' phrases found in Mark, but the one time that he does quote Isaiah liii. almost unbelievably escapes all the vicarious phrases with which that passage abounds.

A third reason for associating the παῖς of Acts iii. and iv. with Isaiah's figure is that 1 Peter explicitly applies the same to Jesus and that these passages in Acts are assigned precisely to Peter or to Peter and his companions. The precariousness of all arguments from likeness to prove the Petrine origin either of Peter's speeches or Peter's epistles is fully discussed in the note on the speeches.[2]

---

[1] *The Making of Luke-Acts*, p. 280, and note.    [2] See p. 410.

It may be admitted that παῖς σοῦ or αὐτοῦ was used of Jesus in early Christianity in a liturgical way, and that that usage was derived from the Old Testament. How characteristic it is and how easily adopted from the Old Testament is shown by the way in which the Epistle of Barnabas twice adds it to LXX quotations.[1]  But that the usage applies to a specific Old Testament passage or group of passages seems most unlikely in view of its wide distribution in the LXX.[2]  More probably it is used of Jesus as of other Old Testament personages both famous and anonymous.  That Acts does not use it elsewhere may be due to the sources, or to the decreasing Biblical language of the volume as it proceeds, or to psychological reasons less tangible or rational.[3]

The position I have taken does not seem to me to be invalidated by anything in the two fullest and most recent discussions of the subject : A. von Harnack, ' Die Bezeichnung Jesu als " Knecht Gottes " und ihre Geschichte in der alten Kirchen ' in *Sitzungsberichte* of the Berlin Academy for 1926, pp. 212-238, and L. L. Carpenter, *Primitive Christian Application of the Doctrine of the Servant.*[4]

Beginning with the assumption that the names of Jesus have Christo- Harnack. logical meaning,[5] Harnack's argument appears to be that since παῖς θεοῦ is no ordinary designation for Jesus, and since the passages on the servant of Isaiah are quoted of Jesus in the early Christian literature, the two must be connected.  He lays stress on the sacral, festal, elevated style of the passages in which the word occurs.  He thinks the frequent use of ἅγιος with it is a sign of Messianic significance, and he notes its tendency to recur in the formula διὰ ᾽Ιησοῦ τοῦ παιδὸς σοῦ.  But he admits that the title is used of other noteworthy historical figures, and except for passages where Isaiah is actually quoted,[6] as in Matt. xii. 17 f., the passages which he lists show, I think, scarcely any evidence of echoing Isaiah.  Harnack indeed

---

[1] vi. 1 and ix. 2.  These are not, I think, specifically Christological or Christian interpolations, but rather the usual patching of Old Testament with like material where Scripture is quoted freely in order to make its reference more explicit.

[2] Neither Luke nor other early Christian writers use δοῦλος κυρίου of Jesus or of the Old Testament characters, except Rev. xv. 3 τὴν ᾠδὴν Μωύσεως τοῦ δούλου τοῦ θεοῦ.  Cf. θεράπων of Moses in Hebr. iii. 5.

[3] In the *Didache* it occurs four times but only in the prayers of the eucharist; in 1 Clement three times but only in the liturgical prayer (chap. 59); in the Martyrdom of Polycarp twice, in the prayer of Polycarp (14), and once in the doxology (20).  Students of the *Didache* have long recognized that the use of 'servant' goes back to Jewish forms of prayer.  The same may be said of the frequent 'holy.'  For examples see the Kiddush and Shemoneh 'Esreh.

[4] Durham, North Carolina, 1929; see especially pp. 59-71.

[5] His first sentence is " Man kann die Geschichte der Christologie an den Bezeichnungen (Namen) Jesu zur Darstellung bringen."

[6] This probably includes the passages in Barnabas in which Isaiah l. 8 and 10 are used ; the former without παῖς being quoted so as to include it, the latter being used to bring παῖς into a quotation of Psalm xxxiv. 12.

urges that in all four passages in Acts the author has Isaiah in mind.[1] His evidence is :

| Acts | Isaiah |
|---|---|
| iii. 13 ἐδόξασεν τὸν παῖδα αὐτοῦ Ἰησοῦν· ὃν ὑμεῖς παρεδώκατε. | lii. 13 ἰδοὺ συνήσει ὁ παῖς μου καὶ δοξασθήσεται σφόδρα. |
| | liii. 6 καὶ κύριος παρέδωκεν αὐτὸν ταῖς ἁμαρτίαις ἡμῶν. |
| iv. 27 τὸν ἅγιον παῖδά σου Ἰησοῦν ὃν ἔχρισας. | xlii. 1 Behold my servant whom I uphold (LXX less similar). |
| v. 30 ἴασιν. | liii. (presumably vs. 5 τῷ μώλωπι αὐτοῦ ἡμεῖς ἰάθημεν). |

The weakness of the evidence is manifest. The nearest parallel to ὃν ἔχρισας is Matthew's version (xii. 18, not LXX) of Isaiah xlii. 1 ὃν ᾑρέτισα. In Acts this relative clause certainly applies to a different title of Jesus (χριστός) in a different Old Testament passage (Psalm ii. 1 f. quoted Acts iv. 25 f.). The ἴασις of Acts iv. 30 together with the words καὶ σημεῖα καὶ τέρατα is a characteristic Lucan generalization of the sign of healing (τὸ σημεῖον τοῦτο τῆς ἰάσεως iv. 22) which has been central in the preceding chapters.

Counter arguments.

Against von Harnack's assumption of Isaian influence and Messianic meaning we may note (i.) that ἅγιος is a mark of the same ' erhabener, poetischer, sakraler Rede ' as is the term παῖς σου : it is used in the quoted contexts of Luke-Acts of the prophets, in the quoted context of the Didache of the ' holy vine of David,' ' holy father, in behalf of thy holy name ' ; (ii.) that παῖς (unlike κύριος or χριστός) is not used without the addition of the proper name Jesus. Just as we have ' thy servant Noah,' ' thy servant David,' so we have with only the slightest exception [2] ' thy servant Jesus.' Harnack calls this an ancient formula. Of course Second Isaiah [3] and Fourth Ezra [4] and the Apocalypse of Baruch [5] do not give their figure the Messiah's proper name. But if the term designated a

[1] Op. cit. p. 217 and note 3. Cf. C. C. Torrey, Journal of Biblical Literature, xlviii., 1929, p. 32 : " Jesus is actually called ' the Servant,' with obvious reference to Second Isaiah, in several passages in the first chapters of Acts (iii. 13, 26, iv. 27, 30). In nearly every case the context shows that the suffering Servant is especially in mind, and in one passage the purpose of the suffering is set forth." The passage (iii. 26) intended does not, however, connect " turning away everyone of you from your iniquities " with suffering. See note on the passage.

[2] For example in Acts and Didache only one out of the four instances in each has omitted Jesus, and even in these there is some evidence for it. Harnack accepts it in Did. x. (second instance) on the evidence of the Coptic version. At Acts iii. 26, besides the Antiochian text, Ἰησοῦν is added after τὸν παῖδα αὐτοῦ by A (Ropes has overlooked this) and by the important minuscules 13 and 31.

[3] The intention of the Servant passages where Cyrus, Israel, or Jacob are not named and the correctness of the readings where they are named I cannot discuss here.

[4] vii. 29 ' my servant the Messiah,' but thereafter (four times) ' my servant.'

[5] lxx. 9 ' my servant the Messiah.'

function fulfilled in Jesus it seems probable that his name would not have to be added so regularly.

It is not easy to be certain about the meaning of a term so ambiguous and yet so simple as παῖς. In later Christianity it easily fused with υἱός when applied to Jesus.[1] There is general agreement that in the earlier days it meant ' child ' or ' servant,' and more probably the latter than the former. In Acts and in other primitive occurrences it is not a term for sonship. Whether it is reminiscent of the figure in Second Isaiah, or whether it is rather a somewhat archaic term not so much redolent of a given section of Scripture as suggestive of the language in which the notable figures of sacred history are described, cannot be settled with certainty. It is sufficient here to warn against the too easy assumption of dependence on Second Isaiah's 'Ebed Yahweh.[2]

Even where parts of Isaiah liii. are plainly quoted by early Christians it is important not to assume that the whole chapter is in the quoter's mind. The Christian use of Old Testament passages usually called attention to the actual part quoted, or even less than the whole quotation, in a quite verbal and literal sense. Thus Matt. viii. 17 quotes Isaiah liii. 4a, b, of Jesus' cures, Matt. xii. 17 f. quotes Isaiah xlii. 1 f. of his avoidance of publicity, Luke [3] at xxii. 37 quotes Isaiah liii. 12d, the phrase καὶ μετὰ ἀνόμων ἐλογίσθη, and Acts viii. 32 f. applies Isaiah liii. 7 f. to Jesus in some sense not clear to us. Only in 1 Peter ii. 22-24 do we have a continuous application to Jesus of several successive items from Isaiah liii.

In their atomistic use of Scripture the early Christians were very different from the modern theologian [4] who, gathering together the four

[1] The Latin, apparently out of dislike for *puer*, came early to render παῖς as *filius*. This rendering was welcome to Christians not only in the New Testament but also in the Latin of the Old Testament and of 4 Ezra, etc. The occurrence of παῖς κυρίου and υἱὸς Θεοῦ in Wisdom ii. 13 and 18 respectively may have helped Christian readers to regard the terms as synonyms. A preference like that of the Latin is strikingly illustrated by the Peshitto which in translating παῖς at Acts iv. 25 of David uses 'ebed, but at iv. 27, 30 of Jesus uses bar.

[2] It is probably misleading to refer to the figure or figures in Isaiah as ' the servant.' There is always in Hebrew and Greek a possessive, usually ' my.' It also is not quite true to the underlying text to speak of ' the Servant of the Lord ' or 'Ebed Yahweh. Even if the early Christian passages were regarded as dependent they attest παῖς κυρίου only at Barnabas vi. 1. Only late and probably in the sense of υἱός do we get παῖς θεοῦ. παῖς θεοῦ is also pagan and is so used by Celsus (Harnack, op. cit. p. 224) often: θεὸς ἢ θεοῦ παῖς. (At Corp. Herm. xiii. 14, which Harnack following Bousset quotes, the mss. read θεὸς πέφυκας καὶ τοῦ ἑνὸς παῖς, not θεοῦ παῖς.)

[3] It is customary to regard the quotation of Isaiah lxi. 1, 2a, in Luke iv. 18 f. as ' servant Christology.' But the original passage is not associated with 'ebed or παῖς, and it was the verb ἔχρισεν (as at Acts iv. 26, 27) that suggested the Christological value of the text to the early Christian.

[4] An illustration, limiting itself, however, to only two passages, is in Harnack's assumptions loc. cit., e.g. p. 216 : " Diese Stelle [Isaiah xlii. 1 f.] zusammen mit c. 53 hat es unzweifelhaft veranlasst Jesus als den hier prophezeiter

'servant passages' of Isaiah, derives from them a complete concept, treating them as a whole, and then assumes that this Christological concept underlies the passages mentioned, and even such passages as have no more echo of Isaiah than the simple παῖς.

ἀρχηγός.    10. ἀρχηγός.—A very attractive term for Jesus, though hardly a title, is ἀρχηγός. It occurs in Acts iii. 15 τὸν δὲ ἀρχηγὸν τῆς ζωῆς ἀπεκτείνατε and Acts v. 31 τοῦτον ὁ θεὸς ἀρχηγὸν καὶ σωτῆρα ὕψωσεν, and also in Hebrews ii. 10, xii. 2. The noun besides its literal meaning of leader (perhaps military) has come to suggest the progenitor of a race or group, or the originator of certain human institutions, especially of benefactions.[1] It is often paired with αἴτιος, just as in Hebrews ii. 10 we have ἀρχηγὸς τῆς σωτηρίας but in Hebrews v. 9 αἴτιος σωτηρίας αἰωνίου. The rare τελειωτής of Hebrews xii. 2 is doubtless due to the etymological contrast of ἀρχή and τέλος, but is scarcely the proper correlative of ἀρχηγός. If we are looking for contrast we may see it rather in what Bengel calls the *magnificum antitheton* of Acts iii. 14 f., which calls Barabbas a murderer and Jesus ἀρχηγός τῆς ζωῆς. The translation 'pioneer' fails to indicate the beneficent results of pioneering implied in the word. The phrase occurs occasionally in later Christian literature.[2] In pagan mythology the word is used characteristically of the hero, but it is not therefore a divine title and ought not to be understood in Acts and Hebrews as showing the apotheosis of Jesus.[3]

σωτήρ.    11. σωτήρ.—The same beneficent suggestion inheres in the word σωτήρ. It occurs twice in Acts, at v. 31 and xiii. 23, and in the former passage is associated with ἀρχηγός. The word in Christian usage has changed from emphasis upon earthly and present to spiritual and post-mortem blessings. Its use in the New Testament is less common than one would suppose, and less explicitly of salvation from sin than in modern speech. In Luke, for

---

'παῖς' zu erkennen und demgemäss ihn in die Gebete als den 'παῖς θεοῦ' einzuführen ; denn wunderbar hatte sich in ihm erfüllt, was diese beiden Weissagungen vorhergesagt. Die übrigen παῖς-Stellen in Jesajas kommen neben ihnen nicht in Betracht." Among American scholars B. W. Bacon has most emphasized the 'Isaian type of Christological doctrine,' e.g. *Jesus the Son of God*, 1911, p. 100 ; *Jesus and Paul*, 1921, pp. 107 ff. ; *The Apostolic Message*, 1925, pp. 281 ff. ; *The Story of Jesus*, 1927, pp. 312 ff. ; *Journal of Biblical Literature*, xlviii., 1929, pp. 59 ff. (cf. Torrey, *ibid.* pp. 24 ff.).

[1] Besides modern dictionaries one may consult among commentators Knowling on Acts iii. 15, Moffatt on Hebrews ii. 10. Philo uses ἀρχηγέτης.

[2] The expression at the close of 2 Clement (xx. 5) which refers to Jesus as τὸν σωτῆρα καὶ ἀρχηγὸν τῆς ἀφθαρσίας illustrates both passages in Acts, while the letter about the martyrs at Lugdunum in Eus. *H.E.* v. 2, 3 contains for Jesus among phrases from Revelation the term ἀρχηγῷ τῆς ζωῆς τοῦ θεοῦ, probably in dependence upon Acts.

[3] E. Rohde, *Psyche*[3] (1903), i. 169, ii. 348 (Eng. Trans. 1925, pp. 146, 527 f.). Cf. C. Clemen, *Primitive Christianity and its Non-Jewish Sources*, Eng. Trans. 1912, p. 203, against Grill, *Untersuchungen über die Entstehung des vierten Evangeliums*, i., 1902, p. 331, n. 5.

example, it occurs only in the rather nationalistic lyric canticles at i. 47 (of God) and ii. 11 of Jesus as born σωτήρ, ὅς ἐστιν χριστὸς κύριος, ἐν πόλει Δαυείδ. At Acts xiii. 23 also Jesus is spoken of as a Saviour for Israel from the seed of David. This Old Testament use of the term suited also its current Hellenistic employment as an honorific title (often with εὐεργέτης, cf. Luke xxii. 25) of victorious generals or peace-giving kings or emperors. It has been thought, indeed, that some New Testament passages definitely contrast the Christian saviour with the imperial saviour.[1] Even John's ' Saviour of the world ' has parallels in the imperial usage of the first century.[2] And for both Jesus and the emperor the custom of worship adds to the word a sense of divinity until ' god and saviour ' are used of both.

Another quite different thought inheres in the word, though less often than in its cognates σώζω and σωτηρία. That is ' healing.'[3] The German rendering ' Heiland ' perpetuates but over-emphasizes this, though perhaps not more than long association has come to over-emphasize ' salvation from sin.' It is not unlikely that just as in Acts iii. 15 ἀρχηγὸς τῆς ζωῆς lays stress on the life-giving and healing power of Jesus, so ἀρχηγὸς καὶ σωτήρ in v. 31 means much the same.[4]

12. προφήτης.—The term ' prophet ' can hardly be regarded as a title Prophet. of Jesus in Acts.[5] In other writers we meet the term used of him both indefinitely as of any prophet and also with the article as of a special expected prophet. In Luke's gospel Jesus is frequently spoken of as a prophet.[6] Even the references to him as one of the ancient prophets[7] are quite indefinite.[8] The more definite term with the article, ὁ προφήτης, in Luke vii. 39 is limited to Codex Vaticanus with very slight support. The ὁ προφήτης used of Jesus in John i. 21-25, vi. 14, vii. 40, is perhaps the

---

[1] E.g. Phil. iii. 20 ἡμῶν γὰρ τὸ πολίτευμα ἐν οὐρανοῖς ὑπάρχει ἐξ οὗ καὶ σωτῆρα ἀπεκδεχόμεθα.

[2] Cf. Deissmann's *Light from the Ancient East* (4th German, translated into 2nd English edition), pp. 363 f., and the works of Harnack, Wendland, Lietzmann, and Otto which he names. These writers and E. Lohmeyer, *Christuskult und Kaiserkult*, 1919, think that Paul and others in using the terms κύριος, σωτήρ, etc. of Jesus were at least conscious of, if not influenced by, the like nomenclature for the emperor. Such comparison is denied by W. Foerster, *Herr ist Jesus*, 1924, and K. Prümm, ' Herrscherkult und neues Testament ' in *Biblica*, ix., 1928, pp. 3 ff., 129 ff., 289 ff. It is manifest that political if not religious comparison is in the mind of the author of Luke-Acts in his use of βασιλεύς (see above, p. 362). On κύριος as emperor title and its influence see further the articles mentioned by Baudissin, *op. cit.* ii. 286 ff., iv. 13 f., 191.

[3] Cf. Harnack, *Mission and Expansion of Christianity* (any edition), book ii. chap. ii.

[4] Cf. ἀρχηγὸς τῆς σωτηρίας in Hebrews ii. 10 in a spiritual sense.

[5] See Vol. I. pp. 403-408.

[6] iv. 24, vii. 16, xiii. 33, xxiv. 19.

[7] See my article, ' Jesus and the Prophets,' in the *Journal of Religion*, v., 1925, pp. 607 ff.

[8] Luke ix. 8 and 19 προφήτης τις τῶν ἀρχαίων.

expected Elijah.[1]  Perhaps another Old Testament prophecy, Deut. xviii.
15, 19, of a prophet like untó Moses was understood of a special expected
prophet rather than of the prophet available at any given time, as modern
students of the Hebrew understand it.  At any rate, it is quoted in Acts
iii. 22, vii. 37, apparently as though it was fulfilled solely in Jesus.[2]
These quotations in the speeches of Peter and Stephen are the only suggestions of the title for Jesus in Acts.

ὁ ἴδιος.       13. ὁ ἴδιος.—A very doubtful reference to Christ is to be found in Acts
xx. 28 when the passage is read τὴν ἐκκλησίαν τοῦ θεοῦ [3] ἣν περιεποιήσατο
διὰ τοῦ αἵματος τοῦ ἰδίου and translated 'through His Own's blood,' that
is, through the blood of one that was God's Own.  This use of ὁ ἴδιος as
equivalent to ὁ ἴδιος υἱός was suggested by B. Weiss, but Hort said it
could not be justified by Greek usage.  Moulton,[4] however, thought that
the use of ὁ ἴδιος in the papyri, added to the names of relatives addressed
in letters, gave some colour to regarding τοῦ ἰδίου as an independent
phrase, neither agreeing with τοῦ αἵματος nor requiring υἱοῦ to be supplied.
The plural οἱ ἴδιοι occurs several times in the New Testament, including
Acts.  The singular ὁ ἴδιος still lacks adequate evidence [5] to justify us in
regarding it as an independent substantive, or consequently as a title of
Jesus.  Unfortunately the passage is complicated by textual and theological controversy.

The       14. ὁ ἐρχόμενος.—We should include here, perhaps, also the term
'Coming  ὁ ἐρχόμενος.  In Acts xix. 4 and in the gospels it is used of Jesus as the
One.'  'Coming One.'  Its use in the New Testament suggests that it was a way of
referring to the expected Messiah, with special reference to the futurity of
his coming.  Indeed ὁ ἐρχόμενος is really equivalent to a future participle
of the verb 'to be' or to our adjective 'future.'  In Acts loc. cit. and

---

[1] The first passage seems to differentiate them.  Whether *the* prophet or
*a* prophet is to be understood has been debated not only at John i. 21 (see
Origen, *ad loc.*) but even at John vii. 52 (A. Carr, *Expositor*, Sept. 1903, pp.
219 ff.).  Matt. xxi. 11 is another possible instance.

[2] The *Assumption of Moses*, x. 15, finds this prediction fulfilled in Joshua
the son of Nun.  This is natural enough, but is it possible that in our Chris-
tianized MS. we have already comparisons between the first Ἰησοῦς and the
second ?  The passage in Deuteronomy lies behind the pseudo-Clementine
writings, which employ 'the true prophet' as a standing designation of Jesus.
Of course in Deuteronomy the Greek, as the Hebrew, does not mean so much
that the prophet is like Moses, as that he will be raised up by God as Moses
was.

[3] The reading τοῦ θεοῦ has as a variant τοῦ κυρίου.  These variants and
their consequent bearing on τοῦ ἰδίου are discussed by Ropes, Vol. III. *ad loc.*,
and in the literature there cited.

[4] *Expositor*, April 1901, p. 277 ; *Grammar of New Testament Greek*, i. p. 90 ;
cf. *Vocabulary of Greek New Testament*, p. 298.

[5] At first sight the Michigan Papyrus of Acts xix. 2 seemed to supply something of a parallel when read (*Harv. Theol. Rev.* xx., 1927, p. 4) πιστεύσαντες τὸ
ἴδιο(ν) τοῦ κ(υρίο)υ.  More careful examination of the very obscure original
writing eliminates this reading.  See Addit. Note 23.

elsewhere the modifying phrases [1] make the term inconspicuous, and perhaps the whole expression should be treated as untechnical. The unmodified ὁ ἐρχόμενος appears only in Luke vii. 19 f. = Matt. xi. 3. There is no evidence that it was a Jewish or Christian technical term.[2]

15. "*Head of the Corner.*" — Neither 'stone' nor 'corner-stone' belongs obviously among the titles of Jesus in the Book of Acts. The words of Peter in iv. 11 are an echo of Psalm cxviii. 22, introduced for the purpose of the address. But neither the term nor the use of the passage is isolated in early Christian usage. This frequency of occurrence suggests that there was a degree of stereotyping in what seems mere metaphor or quotation made *ad hoc*. We may therefore use this opportunity to supplement with a few observations the note in Vol. IV. p. 43.

Head of the Corner.

The passage runs in the Greek: οὗτός ἐστιν ὁ λίθος ὁ ἐξουθενηθεὶς ὑφ' ὑμῶν τῶν οἰκοδόμων, ὁ γενόμενος εἰς κεφαλὴν γωνίας. In the LXX the text is λίθον ὃν ἀπεδοκίμασαν οἱ οἰκοδομοῦντες οὗτος ἐγενήθη εἰς κεφαλὴν γωνίας. In Acts therefore we have a free paraphrase, though the same author had quoted verbatim the LXX version at Luke xx. 17 following Mark (xii. 10 = Matt. xxi. 42).

The Psalm quotation is associated in early Christian literature with other quotations on 'stones.' At Luke xx. 17 it is followed not by the next verse of the Psalm as in Mark and Matthew, but by words which, though not an exact quotation, are parallel to Daniel ii. 34 f., 45, Isaiah viii. 14 f. With the last-named passage is combined at Romans ix. 33 the later Isaian verse, xxviii. 16. The same combination—a striking example of the relation between Paul and 1 Peter, and of the recurrence of the same combinations of *testimonia* or proof texts—occurs in 1 Peter ii. 2-6, and between them Psalm cxviii. 22 again. And finally two of these passages and one more 'rock' text (Isaiah l. 7) are used in the Epistle of Barnabas vi. 2-4. For later catenae of texts with this linking idea see Cyprian, *Testimonia*, ii. 16 f.; Aphraates, *Hom.* i. 6 f.[3]

These passages show that λίθος became practically a term for Jesus and that the name was associated with prophecy. The chapter heading of Cyprian, *loc. cit.*, is *Quod idem et lapis dictus sit*, and Justin Martyr speaks twice in the dialogue with Trypho (xxxiv. 2, xxxvi. 1) of Christ as λίθος as one of the headings under which prophecy could be collected. The rabbinic usage was evidently not very different. Of course God himself is known in the O.T. as a rock, and the rabbis thought of God as building

The Stone.

---

[1] Acts xix. 4 μετ' αὐτόν. The expression is to be compared with John's words about the Messiah ὀπίσω μου of Mark i. 7 and parallels. At the triumphal entry ὁ ἐρχόμενος ἐν ὀνόματι τοῦ κυρίου in all the gospels is due to Psalm cxviii. 26. So also Luke xiii. 35 = Matt. xxiii. 39.

[2] R. Eisler's view that the 'aphiqomen of the Talmud = ἀφικόμενος = ὁ ἐρχόμενος (*ZNTW*. xxiv., 1925, pp. 172 ff.) is without foundation. See H. Lietzmann, *ibid.* xxv., 1926, pp. 1 ff., and R. Harris, *What was the Afikoman?* (*Woodbrooke Essays*, No. 2), 1927, especially p. 7.

[3] Cf. Rendel Harris, *Testimonies*, i. pp. 30 f.; E. C. Selwyn, *St. Luke the Prophet*, 1901, pp. 188 ff.

on rock foundation.[1] The stone of Psalm cxviii. 22 is also definitely applied in rabbinic literature to Abraham, David, and perhaps even the Messiah.[2]

The phrase κεφαλὴ γωνίας translates פנה ראש at Psalm cxviii. 22, and this LXX rendering is retained in the N.T. occurrences generally. Symmachus translated the same passage by ἀκρογωνιαῖος. The same rare Greek word appears at Isaiah xxviii. 16 (and at Ephesians ii. 20 and 1 Peter ii. 6, both dependent upon it). At Job xxxviii. 6 is the phrase λίθος γωνιαῖος. In these passages also the Hebrew includes the word פנה. But what is the architectural feature intended by the phrases? Is it a stone at the bottom, side, or top of a building? The reference to foundations at Isaiah xxviii. 16 (θεμέλια bis) and Ephes. ii. 20 (τῷ θεμελίῳ) and our own custom of dedicating corner-stones makes a bottom corner seem natural. It is said that Oriental unlike Greek builders also laid stress on a somewhat different but very large type of corner foundation.[3] But the use of head (in Hebrew, Greek, and English) in Psalm cxviii., and the fact that the stone sometimes seems to crown and complete the structure, allows us to make other conjectures. The last stone laid at the top of a corner would have architectural significance in binding the walls together where they meet. Recently J. Jeremias [4] has proposed another position, viz. the top or peak of a wall supporting a gable. This would indeed be in a conspicuous place, often over a door-way, and would be the final and crowning feature of the masonry.

Conclusions.

It does not fall within the scope of this note to discuss the position of eminence ascribed to Jesus by the author, as implied by his choice of titles.[5] We do not expect of him an exact theological description. He accords exactly neither with later theological definitions nor even with the free but more nearly contemporary viewpoint of Paul. That Luke thought highly, superhumanly, of Christ we have no doubt. The modern reader should recall, however, that Jesus is not called God, and that neither Lord nor Son of God are quite the equivalent.

On the other hand, he has no idea of making a clear distinction of fields between the present operations of God and of Jesus. Otherwise we should have had less ambiguity in the use of κύριος in the book. There is ambiguity or variety, too, in the descriptions of the source of guidance. Jesus

[1] See Strack-Billerbeck, Kommentar, i. pp. 732 f., on Matt. xvi. 18.
[2] Ibid. pp. 875 f. Cf. Sanday-Headlam, I.C.C. Romans, p. 281.
[3] J. A. Robinson, St. Paul's Epistle to the Ephesians, 1903, pp. 67 ff.; cf. 163 f.
[4] 'Der Eckstein,' in Ἄγγελος i. (1925), pp. 65-70; cf. idem ' κεφαλὴ γωνίας ' in ZNTW xxix., 1930, pp. 264 ff.; H. Gressmann in Palästina-Jahrbuch, vi. (1910), pp. 38-45.
[5] On the Christology of Acts see, besides Vol. I. pp. 345 ff., K. Lake, 'The Theology of the Acts of the Apostles,' Amer. Journ. of Theol. xix., 1915, 489 ff. ; W. Lock, ' Christology of the Earlier Chapters of the Acts,' Expositor, August 1891, pp. 178 ff., as well as many more general works; A. H. McNeile, New Testament Teaching in the Light of St. Paul's, 1923, pp. 116 ff.; C. A. Scott in Hastings, D.A.C. i., 1916, pp. 177-184.

or God appears to Paul in visions.  The Holy Spirit also is an alternative source of guidance, and once we have the spirit of Jesus (xvi. 7).  It is well known that in the same context (xvi. 6-10) guidance is described as coming besides from the Holy Spirit, a vision, or God.

Between Jesus and the Spirit there is as little of a formulated relation as between Jesus and God.[1]  The Spirit is spoken of as sent through Jesus (ii. 33).  A strange feature of Luke's theology is the apparent equivalence of angel and spirit as in Acts viii. 26, 29, 39.[2]  This equivalence would facilitate our understanding of " no resurrection, neither angel nor spirit," as consisting of two rather than three members.[3]  With such a substitution the familiar triad becomes God, Christ, angels, and precisely this combination occurs in Luke ix. 26, where in place of Mark's " when he cometh in the glory of his Father with the holy angels " (viii. 38) Luke has " when he cometh in his own glory, and the glory of the Father, and of the holy angels." [4]

NOTE XXX.  NAMES FOR CHRISTIANS AND CHRISTIANITY IN ACTS [5]

By HENRY J. CADBURY

*Order of Discussion*

| Disciples | Christians | Sect |
| Brethren | Nazarenes | Flock |
| Friends | Galileans | Gospel |
| Saints | Church | Word |
| Righteous | Congregation | Faith |
| Believers | Fellowship | Way |
| Saved | | |

The names by which a new movement or its adherents come to be known are seldom a matter of conscious selection.  The movement    *The growth of nomenclature.*

---

[1] Acts vii. 55 mentions successively the Holy Spirit, God and Jesus, but with no idea of a trinitarian relation.

[2] A like confusion occurs in Hermas and Tertullian.

[3] Acts xxiii. 8 ; hence the following word ' both,' but see the note *ad loc.*

[4] The eschatological context facilitated the triad, as at 1 Tim. v. 21, since the angels take part at the judgement.

[5] Cf. the various articles in Bible dictionaries, and especially Harnack, *Mission und Ausbreitung des Christentums*, 4th edit. 1923, i. pp. 410 ff., or the corresponding section, viz. book iii. chap. iii. and Excursus I. in earlier editions and English translations of the same work.  Unless otherwise specified, references to Harnack's *Mission* in this note are to vol. i. of the English translation of the second edition which was published in 1908 under the title *The Mission and Expansion of Christianity in the First Three Centuries*.  His *Entstehung und Entwickelung der Kirchenverfassung*, 1910 (translated the same year and cited as *Constitution and Law of the Church*), is partly parallel and partly independent.  For bibliographies of discussions of the terms see under each in Preuschen-Bauer, *Wörterbuch des N.T.*, 1924–1928.

spontaneously comes into being. New religions or sects often arise without any intention of separateness. The members find themselves isolated or set apart by unpremeditated circumstances. Their opponents often become aware of their difference before they do themselves, or find reason to name them. Thus nicknames sometimes precede names.

A need for designation comes upon the members themselves slowly and unexpectedly. The terms used arise naturally and accidentally. In course of time they become fixed. At first they are quite fluid; several are used at once or in different regions.[1] But their original expressiveness by shortening or stereotyping is finally lost to view.

The history of early Christianity was probably no exception in these respects. Its early literature reveals a nomenclature that agrees with the typical processes described. Even in the Book of Acts we find no final or hardened terminology, but an informality and variety of expression which is natural to the formative stages.

μαθητής in the Gospels.

Perhaps the most characteristic name for the Christians in Acts is μαθηταί, disciples. In the gospels it is used for the personal associates of Jesus, sometimes the group otherwise known as the Twelve or the Apostles, sometimes apparently a wider group.[2] But the immediate adherence to the living Jesus gives μαθητής in the gospels a tangible character that cannot be expected in later times.

Luke.

Luke's gospel differs little from the others in its use of μαθηταί. Frequently they appear in contrast with the crowd.[3] Sometimes a small group like the Twelve is meant, though only the context gives indication.[4] In the gospel the singular μαθητής is used of a generic disciple, but never of a specific person. But the wider usage often appears in Luke's editorial passages, and though he can hardly be expected to match Mark's pragmatic scheme of a two-fold audience for Jesus with an esoteric group of disciples, it is apparent, especially towards the end of the Gospel, that Luke regards the adherents of Jesus as no small or closed group.[5] The most expressive instance is at the entry into Jerusalem when he speaks of ἅπαν τὸ πλῆθος τῶν μαθητῶν.

Acts.

The book of Acts evidently uses the term in no limited sense. It can now use ἀπόστολοι freely. It has also the 'eleven'[6] and once the 'twelve.' The latter is at vi. 2, where we read προσκαλεσάμενοι δὲ οἱ δώδεκα τὸ πλῆθος τῶν μαθητῶν. Here we have the disciples in contrast

---

[1] Hence they do not make room for each other in a sequence that can be traced and used for assessing the relative antiquity of passages in which they occur. On the indefiniteness of Christian nomenclature cf. pp. 69 f.

[2] On the use of μαθηταί, ἀπόστολοι, and οἱ δώδεκα in the Synoptic gospels see C. H. Turner, J.Th.S. xxvi., 1925, pp. 231-237.

[3] ὄχλος, λαός, or other named persons. See Luke viii. 9 (cf. 4), ix. 14, 16, x. 23 κατ᾽ ἰδίαν, xii. 1, 22 (cf. 13), xvii. 22 (cf. 20), xx. 45.

[4] In Luke xvii. 5 'the apostles' seems to resume 'the disciples' of vs. 1.

[5] Cf. Luke xxiii. 49 πάντες οἱ γνωστοὶ αὐτῷ, xxiv. 9 τοῖς ἕνδεκα καὶ πᾶσι τοῖς λοιποῖς, 33 τοὺς ἕνδεκα καὶ τοὺς σὺν αὐτοῖς, Acts i. 14 σὺν ἀδελφοῖς αὐτοῦ, 15 the brethren were an ὄχλος of 120 persons.

[6] Acts ii. 14; cf. Luke xxiv. 9, 33.

with the twelve and the same τὸ πλῆθος as in Luke xix. 37. With this noun (see note on iv. 32 and below, p. 389) should be compared the verb in vi. 1 πληθυνόντων τῶν μαθητῶν, 7 ἐπληθύνετο ὁ ἀριθμὸς τῶν μαθητῶν.

The main difference in the use of μαθητής in Acts is the detachment of the word from Jesus. Only once has the noun a possessive referring to him, Acts ix. 1 τοὺς μαθητὰς τοῦ κυρίου.[1] While in the gospel a genitive referring to Jesus is either expressed or easily implied, in Acts οἱ μαθηταί seem to require no such implicit addition.[2] Individuals like Ananias, Timothy, Mnason are called μαθητής, and the woman Dorcas (Tabitha) is called μαθήτρια.[3] ' To make disciples ' (μαθητεύω) is also used once in Acts.[4]

It is not difficult to suppose that Luke's use of the word μαθητής corresponds with the actual use in the times which he describes. That Jesus seemed to his contemporaries a kind of teacher or rabbi or prophet, and that like men of those types he gathered a group of followers about him called disciples, is as probable as anything about him can be. All four gospels use μαθητής of his followers, and they refer to ' disciples ' of John and ' disciples ' of the Pharisees with the same word. The rabbinic references to Jesus also mention his ' disciples ' (תלמידים).[5]

In his second volume Luke implies the continuance of the same term in an absolute sense for adherents of the religion preached about Jesus, including many who had never known him after the flesh and who lived in foreign lands. It is possible that once by the adjective ἀρχαῖος he distinguishes for us an original μαθητής,[6] but he does not confine the word to the original group. Indeed he strangely does not use the word at all in the first five chapters of Acts.[7] Its uneven distribution has given rise to the suggestion that its occurrence is due to a source.[8]

Such a development as Luke implies is entirely natural. The chief reason for suspecting Luke's usage of disciple for Christians in the apostolic age is the absence of the term from Paul. Indeed, outside the historical books no writers of the New Testament use the term. Later it revives in Christian literature, being used retrospectively of the disciples mentioned in the gospels and also of contemporaries.

---

[1] In ix. 25 Paul's disciples are definitely so described. Perhaps the same possessive is implied at xiv. 20.

[2] This observation is important for correcting the impression that the μαθηταί of Acts xix. 2 and Apollos were disciples not of Jesus but of John the Baptist and that they are evidence of the continuance of a movement founded by him. See notes on xviii. 24-28, xix. 1, and W. Michaelis, ' Die sog. Johannes-Jünger in Ephesus,' *Neue kirchliche Zeitschrift*, xxxviii., 1927, pp. 717-736.

[3] ix. 10, xvi. 1, xxi. 16 ; ix. 36.      [4] xiv. 21.

[5] See the baraita in *Sanhedrin* 43a.      [6] xxi. 16.

[7] μαθητῶν was read by the Textus Receptus at i. 15 for ἀδελφῶν and by the English Authorized Version. The Uncials D and 81 support this, and some modern editors prefer it against BℵAC.

[8] See note on ix. 36, Vol. IV. p. 109 ; R. Schütz, *Apostel und Jünger*, 1921. E. Meyer, *Ursprung und Anfänge des Christentums*, i., 1921, pp. 133 ff., distinguishes a *Jüngerquelle* and a *Zwölferquelle* in Mark.

It is of course possible that Luke has read the usage of a later age into his narrative. He can scarcely be conscious of doing so, for in the case of another term, Christians, he signalizes the first occasion of its occurrence. On the other hand, Luke's use of disciple in the Acts may be due rather to its earlier use in the gospel. The two volumes were for him a unity, and in a sequel to the gospel he may have felt that the term would easily be understood. Finally, in spite of the lack of other evidence, the usage of μαθητής for Christian may have continued at least in some quarters from Jesus to Ignatius without real interruption. Which of the alternatives really explains the use of the term in Acts we appear to have no means of knowing.

ἀδελφοί.   Another frequent term for the Christians in Acts is οἱ ἀδελφοί, the brothers. Not counting its use in address in speeches it occurs about as often in the book as οἱ μαθηταί,[1] beginning with i. 15 ἀναστὰς Πέτρος ἐν μέσῳ τῶν ἀδελφῶν. This usage is of course different from that of ἀδελφός of actual kinship, and from the somewhat wider use of the word as neighbour, or fellow, the one with whom one has to do. If the word occurred only in the vocative of address, or without the article, we might hesitate to call it a generic term. But many instances in Acts, as well as frequent occurrences in the letters of Paul,[2] who also uses it in the singular with the name of an individual Christian, leave no doubt of its early and definite use for the members of the Christian group. It is used in Acts both in speech and in narrative, both in the Palestinian and in the Aegean sections of the book.

The term therefore requires little comment. In a few instances it would be possible to see in the term some contrast with the apostles, unless we understand by it ' the *other* brethren ' in such passages as i. 15 ἀναστὰς Πέτρος ἐν μεσῳ τῶν ἀδελφῶν, xi. 1 οἱ ἀπόστολοι καὶ οἱ ἀδελφοὶ οἱ ὄντες κτλ., xii. 17 ἀπαγγείλατε Ἰακώβῳ καὶ τοῖς ἀδελφοῖς ταῦτα, xxi. 17 ἀσμένως ἀπεδέξαντο ἡμᾶς οἱ ἀδελφοί, 18 τῇ δὲ ἐπιούσῃ εἰσῄει ὁ Παῦλος σὺν ἡμῖν πρὸς Ἰάκωβον, πάντες τε παρεγένοντο οἱ πρεσβύτεροι. But at xv. 23 οἱ ἀπόστολοι καὶ οἱ πρεσβύτεροι ἀδελφοί the word seems to be applied to the apostles and elders.[3]

[1] The two terms cannot be contrasted either in meaning or in application in Acts. At xviii. 27 f., probably in order to vary his language, the author brings the synonyms together : προτρεψάμενοι οἱ ἀδελφοὶ [at Ephesus] ἔγραψαν τοῖς μαθηταῖς [at Corinth] ἀποδέξασθαι αὐτόν [Apollos], ὃς παραγενόμενος συνεβάλετο πολὺ τοῖς πεπιστευκόσιν. See note Vol. IV. p. 12, and Vol. III. pp. 6 f., where the importance of the variant μαθητῶν is emphasized.

[2] Cf. also John xxi. 23 and 3 John.

[3] See note *ad loc.* Some authorities, however, read καί before ἀδελφοί. Probably the passage means ' the Christian apostles and elders,' not ' the apostles and elder brethren.' Luke does not hesitate to use two nouns that are titles in apposition, e.g. ἀνήρ with another noun. The ἄνδρες ἀδελφοὶ καὶ πατέρες vii. 2, xxii. 1 means ' fellow-Jews, both of my own age and older.' ἄνδρες of course is frequent in other writers too, used in address as ἄνδρες Ἀθηναῖοι xvii. 22. So ἄνδρες ἀδελφοί means gentlemen who are Jews, or fellow-Jews.

The use of the term is natural and easy, and its origin need not be imitative. Probably the Jews referred to each other as ' brethren.' Acts itself gives evidence of such a usage not only when a Christian Jew is addressing fellow-Jews but with reference to the mutual relations of non-Christian Jews.[1]

It is interesting that a like usage within Gentile religious communities seems to be evidenced by an increasing number of documentary sources.[2] It means that a usage indigenous in Jewish Christianity would seem entirely congenial in the Greek lands as the gospel spread. It is unnecessary to regard it as a Gentile coinage and as, therefore, used anachronistically in the earliest parts of Acts.

On the other hand it is by no means certain that the usage goes back to Jesus himself.[3] If μαθηταὶ Ἰησοῦ (μου) became οἱ μαθηταί, so ἀδελφοί μου could become οἱ ἀδελφοί, but it seems to me more likely that anachronism lies rather in the gospels, e.g. Matt. xxiii. 8, than that οἱ ἀδελφοί depends primarily on the parlance of Jesus. The metaphorical extension of the term from blood brothers to spiritual kindred would commend itself independently and repeatedly to successive groups.[4] The term continues to appear in Christian literature until the close of the third century.[5]

It is possible that the Christians were known as the ' Friends,' [6] and οἱ φίλοι. if so the best evidence is in Acts xxvii. 3 where we are told that at Sidon Paul was permitted πρὸς τοὺς φίλους πορευθέντι ἐπιμελείας τυχεῖν. Of course it is possible that here τοὺς φίλους means, even without the possessive, ' his friends,' [7] but the other rendering is natural. It is probable that philosophic groups called their fellow-members friends, and it has been supposed that " Luke with his classical culture has permitted himself

---

[1] xxii. 5, xxviii. 21.  Cf. Rom. ix. 3.  In the case of the Jewish ' church ' the use was perhaps more racial than religious—as Paul adds, loc. cit., οἱ συγγενεῖς μου κατὰ σάρκα.

[2] The instances collected by Deissmann, Bible Studies, pp. 87 f., Moulton and Milligan, Vocabulary, s.v. (cf. p. xvii), Preuschen-Bauer, Wörterbuch, s.v., include members of the monastery-like group of the Serapeum in Egypt, of a ξυστικὴ σύνοδος in Rome, and of the σεβόμενοι θεὸν ὕψιστον (cf. p. 92) on the Black Sea.

[3] The few instances of the term on Jesus' lips are all towards the close of the gospels : ' my brethren ' in Matt. xxviii. 10, John xx. 17, ' thy (Peter's) brethren ' in Luke xxii. 32.  Hebrews ii. 12 finds the expression for Jesus in Ps. xxii. 23.

[4] Mark iii. 34 f. and parallels, x. 29 f. and parallels.

[5] Cf. Harnack, Mission, p. 406.

[6] Harnack, Mission, book iii. chap. iii. Excursus I.

[7] Cf. 3 John 15 ἀσπάζονταί σε οἱ φίλοι· ἀσπάζου τοὺς φίλους κατ᾽ ὄνομα.  In the examples of Moulton-Milligan, Vocabulary, p. 671, the article is often used in Greek where we should use a possessive.

No account is taken in this Additional Note of certain other terms which could have lost their possessive implication and become names for the Christians, e.g. ἀγαπητοί (Acts xv. 25, see note) and οἱ ἴδιοι (Acts iv. 23, xxiv. 23).

this once to use the classical designation." [1] Harnack and others suppose the name to have a Gentile origin. Possibly, too, it is connected with the term Friends of God (or of the Lord). Luke himself once represents Jesus as saying λέγω ὑμῖν τοῖς φίλοις μου (Luke xii. 4), and the expression 'friends' in contrast with slaves is emphasized in speaking of his disciples in John xv. 14 f. Friends of Jesus (or of the Lord) probably goes back to Friends of God (or of the Lord)—the famous designation of Abraham in the Old Testament and in Islam.[2] In early Christian literature these longer phrases are much more common than the simpler 'friends.' [3] But neither of them survived long. When the phrase Friends of God was revived by a mystical group in Germany in the fourteenth century, or the title Friends by the Quakers in England in the seventeenth century, it was a matter of coincidence in terminology rather than of dependence.[4] The latter, however, welcomed the term when they found it in Acts as justifying their name as 'scriptural.' [5]

ἅγιοι.　'Saints' (ἅγιοι) as a title for Christians is found in Acts ix. 13, 32, 41, xxvi. 10, of which the last passage refers to the first. Thus it is rare in Acts and limited to accounts of Paul's conversion and the adjacent scenes.[6] It is, on the other hand, the usual name for Christians in the Pauline epistles. Like other terms it probably has implicit originally a possessive, 'the holy ones of God.' So we have 'thy saints' in ix. 13. A like phrase was used of the angels [7] in the Old Testament, and of worthies

---

[1] Harnack, *Mission*, p. 421. With this opinion agrees Fr. Hauck in his essay 'Die Freundschaft bei den Griechen und im Neuen Testament' in *Festgabe für Theodor Zahn*, 1928, p. 220, thinking it more likely that Luke took over the name from Gentile usage rather than that he meant to use it as an actual self-designation of the Christians. F. J. Dölger, Ἰχθύς, 1910, i. pp. 134 f., also regards φίλοι as equivalent to ἀδελφοί in the language of the cults. See J. Moffatt, *Love in the N.T.*, 1929, p. 47.

[2] Peterson, 'Der Gottesfreund' in *ZKG*. xvii., 1923, pp. 161-202. A noteworthy occurrence is Wisd. Sol. vii. 27.

[3] Harnack in his later edition adds examples, especially from Irenaeus.

[4] In both cases the origin of the name is quite obscure. On the former see Rufus M. Jones, *Studies in Mystical Religion*, chap. xiii.; on the latter, T. Edmund Harvey, *Quaker Language*, 1928, pp. 23, 29.

[5] Wm. Sewel, *The History of the Quakers*, Burlington, 1774, p. 783 (first edition in Dutch in 1717, pp. 756 f.).

[6] Such limitation is one of the curious phenomena of Luke's style, of which I hope to publish fuller collections. There are a few other expressions pretty much limited to the same sections of Acts. It is remarkable that source theorists have not made more of them. The passages are of course all Palestinian, which reminds us that in Paul οἱ ἅγιοι sometimes seems to mean precisely and *par excellence* the Judaean Christians. See K. Holl, 'Der Kirchenbegriff des Paulus in seinem Verhältnis zu dem der Urgemeinde' in *Sitzungsberichte der Preussischen Akademie*, 1921, p. 938. But Harnack denies Paul this special usage.

[7] E.g. Deut. xxxiii. 2 (not LXX), Job v. 1, xv. 15, Zech. xiv. 5, Ps. lxxxix. 5, 7, Ecclus. xlii. 17, Dan. iv. 14 (17), etc., Enoch i. 9, etc. See R. H. Charles on the last passage.

of the past. Possibly the last is the meaning of 'the saints' in Matt.
xxvii. 52 whose bodies rose from the dead at the time of Jesus' crucifixion.
Originally, at least, the word [1] had probably an eschatological rather
than an ethical significance, though of course the ethical element is not
wanting. The Jews used it of members of the Messianic kingdom.[2] It
has been suggested that the Christians identified themselves with the
*hasidim* of the Psalms (though that is never ἅγιοι but always ὅσιοι in the
LXX).[3] The name may be connected with the Hasidaeans of 1 Macc.
ii. 42, vii. 13, but in any case it was taken up by Enoch and made the
name of the Elect. Compare, for instance, Enoch xxxviii. 4, "From
henceforth (i.e. after the coming of the Messiah) those who possess the
earth shall not be able to endure the glory of the Saints, for the Lord of
Spirits will make his light to shine forth from the faces of the Saints and
the elect righteous ones." [4]
The use of the participle in the phrase κλῆρον (κληρονομίαν) ἐν τοῖς
ἡγιασμένοις at xx. 32, xxvi. 18 [5] perhaps confirms the eschatological force
of ἅγιοι in Acts and suggests that its etymology was not entirely forgotten.
See, however, p. 72 note 2. Perhaps along with 'brothers' ἅγιοι was
the name which the author supposed was used by the Christians of themselves. If so, xxvi. 10 is anachronistic.
The righteous (οἱ δίκαιοι) in the plural has a sound of Old Testament    δίκαιοι.
piety as it has in the singular [6] ; and as its occurrences in the Greek Jewish
literature seem scarcely to indicate a definite party, so its early Christian
usage seems hardly synonymous with the believers as a whole. The
nearest approach to such a meaning is perhaps a variant in Acts xiv. 2,
where Codex Bezae reads οἱ δὲ ἀρχισυνάγωγοι τῶν Ἰουδαίων καὶ οἱ

---

[1] On the meaning and history of the adjective, including its use in Greek
literature, see A. Fridrichsen, *Hagios-Quados* ( = *Videnskapsoelskapets Skrifter*,
ii. Hist.-Filos. Kl. Nr. 3), Kristiania, 1916 ; Ed. Williger, *Hagios* : *Untersuchungen zur Terminologie des Heiligen in den hellenisch-hellenistischen Religionen*
( = *Religionsgesch. Versuche und Vorarbeiten*, xix. 1), Giessen, 1922 ; R. Asking,
*Der Begriff der Heiligkeit im Urchristentum* ( = *Forschungen zur Religion und
Literatur des A. und N.T.*, N.F. 29), Göttingen, 1930.

[2] Cf. Is. iv. 3, Ps. xxxiv. 9, Tobit viii. 15, Dan. vii. 18, 22. In Christian
and perhaps in Jewish usage the risen saints are hardly to be distinguished
from angels. So ἅγιοι at 1 Thess. iii. 13 is ambiguous, and the author of
*Didache* xvi. 7 changes one meaning to the other in quoting Zech. xiv. 5.

[3] The name, translated as ὅσιοι, is frequent in the Psalms of Solomon
(viii. 40, ix. 6, x. 7, etc.). The Christian use is probably due to the Jewish.
The attempt of Geffcken, *Der Ausgang des griechisch-römischen Heidentums*,
1920, pp. 226, 319 f., note 24, to find a use of οἱ ἅγιοι of adherents of a pagan
religion in the Isaurian inscription Μᾶ Παππᾶ θυγάτηρ παρθένος κ[ὲ] κατὰ γένος
ἱέρεια τῆς θεοῦ κ[ὲ] τῶν ἁγίων is unsuccessful. See Williger, *loc. cit.* The
inscription may be late (Ramsay) and τῶν ἁγίων may be neuter (Williger).

[4] See Vol. I. pp. 87 ff., and for further references to Enoch cf Strack-
Billerbeck, ii. p. 691.

[5] Paul in Col. i. 12 says τοῦ κλήρου τῶν ἁγίων.

[6] Cf. on ὁ δίκαιος, p. 364.

ἄρχοντες τῆς συναγωγῆς ἐπήγαγον αὐτοῖς διωγμὸν κατὰ τῶν δικαίων, καὶ ἐκάκωσαν τὰς ψυχὰς τῶν ἀδελφῶν. But the passage is evidently conflate, and the phrase οἱ δίκαιοι cannot be attributed with certainty even to the Western text, still less to the primitive text of Acts.

The believers.
The English term 'believers' may be represented in Greek by the adjective οἱ πιστοί or by a present, aorist, or future participle of πιστεύω. All these uses occur sporadically in early Christian literature. None is unrepresented in Acts, but it is doubtful how far any of them are for the writer stereotyped into fixed terms. The rarity of their occurrence and the fact that they occur also with modifiers like τοὺς πιστεύοντας ἐπί σε (xxii. 19), πιστὴν τῷ κυρίῳ (xvi. 15), τοῖς πεπιστευκόσι διὰ τῆς χάριτος (xviii. 27),[1] increases our doubt. Even when they are used absolutely they sometimes appear as adjectival adjuncts to nouns as in γυναικὸς Ἰουδαίας πιστῆς (xvi. 1), περὶ δὲ τῶν πεπιστευκότων ἐθνῶν (xxi. 25).

πιστοί.
The absolute οἱ πιστοί occurs at x. 45 οἱ ἐκ περιτομῆς πιστοί, and in the Western text of xii. 3 ἡ ἐπιχείρησις αὐτοῦ ἐπὶ τοὺς πιστούς. We have assumed (Vol. IV. p. 192) that even the singular πιστή of Acts xvi. 15 means a woman 'believer.'[2] This active sense of the adjective instead of its usual passive sense as faithful, trustworthy, is notable and hardly to be found outside of Christianity.

Forms of πιστεύω.
Of the participles the perfect from the very nature of that tense's meaning lends itself to use as an established term and occurs at xxi. 20, perhaps also xv. 5, xviii. 27, xix. 18. The aorist, in its two occurrences, ii. 44, iv. 32, is, however, more nearly an absolute usage.[3] None of the terms established themselves in other early Christian literature, though οἱ πιστοί occurs in 1 Tim. iv. 3, 12, and in Ignatius.[4]

οἱ σωζό-μενοι.
Another participial phrase for the Christians is οἱ σωζόμενοι in Acts ii. 47. We may connect it with οἱ πιστεύοντες since Luke himself so often associates the verbs.[5] But the question arises here as for other

---

[1] In this instance we should note (what was not included in the commentary) that an alternative rendering would attach the amphibolous διὰ τῆς χάριτος to the verb συνεβάλετο : " And when he arrived he was very helpful because of his grace." This rendering does better justice to the article τῆς and to the use of χάρις in Acts vi. 8 and leaves the perfect participle alone as we should expect, without a useless modifier.

[2] This interpretation is preferred by some also at 1 Cor. vii. 25 γνώμην δὲ δίδωμι ὡς ἠλεημένος ὑπὸ κυρίου πιστὸς εἶναι.

[3] At ii. 44 there is some good evidence for reading the present participle, which, except for this variant, scarcely can be found absolutely in Acts. The limitation of the aorist participle (in the plural with the article) to the two passages on community of goods is a phenomenon characteristic of this author.

[4] Other miscellaneous instances, including non-Christians who speak of the Christians as οἱ πιστοί and the Latin pistores and fideles, are cited by Harnack, Mission, i. pp. 403 f., note. The use of πιστοί as the name for civil officers (G. M. Harper, Jr., ' Village Administration in Syria ' in Yale Classical Studies, i., 1928, pp. 123-127) has no connexion except to show that the adjective, like the English ' trusty,' could become a noun.

[5] See Vol. IV. p. 174 (at end).

terms in this list, whether it is used *ad hoc* or whether it has a more established character. In favour of the former attention is usually called to the use of the verb σώζω in the preceding verses 21 and 40 ; in favour of the latter we have not merely as parallel the question in Luke xiii. 23 εἰ ὀλίγοι οἱ σωζόμενοι (not σώζονται), but twice [1] in Paul the contrasting groups οἱ σωζόμενοι and οἱ ἀπολλύμενοι are mentioned, much as in Acts xxiv. 15 we have δίκαιοι and ἄδικοι. Something has been said elsewhere [2] on the term. In addition to the question already raised three others may be suggested :

(i.) Is the verb wholly passive in meaning ? Or may it have a more active and voluntaristic sense ? At ii. 40 the passive form σώθητε is usually rendered ' save yourselves,' and it would seem quite as legitimate to construe a form σωζόμενοι that is grammatically either middle or passive as implying the initiative of believing.

(ii.) Why is the present tense used ? Certainly not because salvation is regarded as a continuing process. The normal time to which salvation is assigned is future, both in Paul and in the other New Testament writers. It is an eschatological consummation.[3] The present is sometimes explained by the grammarians as indicating that salvation is thought of as being anticipatorily present now, or as meaning those who from time to time are saved.[4] It is better to regard the participle as timeless and to recall with J. Weiss [5] that such presents occur particularly with eschatological sentences. The considerations under both (i.) and (ii.) warn us against assuming too easily that the term was fatalistic. Contrast xiii. 48.

(iii.) How should οἱ σωζόμενοι be translated ? ' Those that were being saved ' implies too definitely that salvation is a process and includes this life. ' Those that were saved ' or ' the saved ' implies too definitely that salvation is completed or assured. " Such as should be saved " of A.V.[6] was a paraphrase and no doubt nearly correct but without Greek warrant. Without a real present passive participle English can supply no translation really as satisfactory even as ' the perishing ' is for οἱ ἀπολλύμενοι.[7]

' Christian ' occurs in Acts in two well-known passages. At xi. 26, after Christian. speaking of a year's ministry by Paul and Barnabas at Antioch, the author

---

[1] 1 Cor. i. 18 ; 2 Cor. ii. 15.

[2] Pp. 39 f., Vol. IV. p. 30. Cf. also W. Wagner, ' Über Σώ̓ϛειν und seine Derivata im N.T. ' in ZNTW. vi., 1905, pp. 205-235.

[3] For οἱ σωζόμενοι see Is. xxxvii. 32, xlv. 20 ; but we can hardly call it, with R. C. Trench, " a technical expression of the LXX for the Jewish remnant." Cf. also Clement, 1 Cor. lviii. 2 ἐλλόγιμος ἔσται εἰς τὸν ἀριθμὸν τῶν σωζομένων διὰ Ἰησοῦ Χριστοῦ. But at Rev. xxi. 24 the term is not well attested in the text.

[4] A. T. Robertson, *Grammar of the Greek New Testament*, p. 1116, who notes the iterative or distributive imperfect προσετίθει in the passage.

[5] On 1 Cor. i. 18 in Meyer's *Kommentar*.

[6] At Acts ii. 47 (due to the Vulgate *qui salvi fierent*), but not at 1 Cor. i. 18 or 2 Cor. ii. 15. The translation of this passage was a matter of considerable concern to the makers of the Revised Version and their critics.

[7] Though unfamiliar to theological parlance ' the escaping ' is an excellent opposite to ' the perishing.'

says : ἐγένετο δὲ . . . χρηματίσαι τε πρώτως ἐν 'Αντιοχείᾳ τοὺς μαθητὰς Χριστιανούς. Agrippa interrupting Paul at his hearing in Caesarea (xxvi. 28) says : ἐν ὀλίγῳ με πείθεις Χριστιανὸν ποιῆσαι.

The word has received considerable attention for many years. It will be sufficient to refer the reader to the items listed in the bibliographies [1] and on xi. 26 (Vol. IV. p. 130). Among the questions discussed are :

The spelling of the word.

1. The spelling of the word as Χρηστιανός. This is well attested in the earliest authorities we have for the name, as is less frequently Χρηστός for Χριστός.[2] The unintelligibility of Χριστός as a name (see p. 358 and Vol. I. p. 347) and the intelligibility of Χρηστός which is not only a good Greek adjective but also a personal name [3] may have contributed to popularize this spelling. Possibly phonetic laws entered into the preference, but it may be doubtful whether at least with the itacism current when Acts was written η and ι were very differently pronounced. The early fathers certainly connected the word with χρηστός, χρηστότης, and in their apologies made the most of this connexion,[4] while at other times they ridiculed the ignorance of their opponents for making the mistake of spelling the name *Chrestiani*.[5]

The meaning of the ending *-ianus*.

2. The formation of the name is in accord with the usual Latin method of adding *-ianus, -ιανός* to a personal name, as in 'Ηρῳδιανοί Mark iii. 6, xii. 13. Two inferences may be drawn : (i.) the word χριστός had come

---

[1] See especially Preuschen-Bauer, s.v. For English readers attention may be called to J. B. Lightfoot, *Apostolic Fathers*, part ii. vol. i., 1885, pp. 401-404 ; P. W. Schmiedel, 'Christian, Name of,' in *Ency. Biblica*, coll. 752-763 ; A. Carr, *Horae Biblicae*, 1903, pp. 328 ff. ( = *Expositor*, June 1898, pp. 456 ff.) ; Th. Zahn, *Introduction to the N.T.*, Eng. trans., 1909, ii. pp. 191 ff. ( = § 40, note 10). Among monographs on the name in other languages mention may be made of the older and thorough programme by R. A. Lipsius (Jena, 1873) and the recent article by P. de Labriolle (in *Bulletin Du Cange*, v., 1930, pp. 69-88).

[2] The most important instance is in Suetonius (*Claud.* 25), *Iudaeos impulsore Chresto adsidue tumultuantes Roma expulit;* where we wish especially to know whether the historian's information was that trouble centred around a Messiah (Christian or Jewish). The spelling Chrestian was that of the first hand in Codex Sinaiticus of the New Testament (*ter*) and Codex Mediceus of Tacitus, *Ann.* xv. 44. On the spelling in *e* see, beside the words of Blass (Vol. IV. p. 130), Gercke (see below) ; Harnack, *SAB.*, 1915, p. 762 ; A. Jacoby, *Byzantisch-neugriechische Jahrbücher*, i., 1920, pp. 148 ff. ; E. Meyer, *Ursprung und Anfänge des Christentums*, iii., 1923, pp. 307 note, 505 note. The reverse change is illustrated by spelling Crescens Κρίσκης, -κεντος as at Justin, 2 *Apol.* vi. 2 ; Tatian, *Orat. ad Graec.* xix. 1. The spelling in η or *e* for Christ or Christians prevails in inscriptions, especially in Greek. See Labriolle, *op. cit.* pp. 85 f. An instance on papyrus is cited, Vol. IV. pp. 240 f.

[3] The abundance of the name Chrestus can be easily illustrated. See indices to *CIL.* and *CIG.*, or Preisigke, *Namenbuch*, s.v.

[4] Justin, 1 *Apol.* iv. 5 ; Clem. Alex. *Strom.* ii. 4 ; also Gregory of Elvira as cited in Harnack, *Mission*, 4th edition, i. p. 412. Quite different is Justin's statement about the word Christ in the second *Apology*, vi. 3.

[5] Tertullian, *Apol.* 3 ; *Ad nat.* i. 3 ; Lactantius, *Div. Inst.* iv. 7. 5.

to be regarded as a proper name (see p. 357) when this derivative was formed, (ii.) the termination is Latin rather than Greek. This does not prove that the word is a Latin formation. But the fact that among original Greek surnames so few have the ending in -ιανός [1] at least suggests that Christians may be primarily a Latin formation. Whether a Latin formation would be made first, as Acts says ' Christians ' was, at Antioch of Syria, is to say the least uncertain. But the alternatives are either that Acts is mistaken [2] or that the name is one of the exceptional Greek formations in -ιανός. It is sometimes inferred from the form that it was made by Gentiles rather than by Jews or Christians. Acts does not say so ; it does not even say that Christians was first used of Gentile converts, though in a single context it refers to two innovations at Antioch—preaching to Gentiles, and this name.

3. The use of the name. The fact that in its first occurrences, including 1 Pet. iv. 16 εἰ δὲ (sc. τις πάσχει) ὡς Χριστιανός, μὴ αἰσχυνέσθω, beside the two in Acts, one may understand that the term is applied by non-Christians has suggested that the word is a nickname.[3] In none of the three passages is a derogatory sense certain. At 1 Pet. iv. 16 it is possible that the author is applying the title himself and glorying in it as a worthy cause for suffering (cf. vs. 14), " delighting," as Acts says, " that they had been found worthy for the sake of the name to suffer disgrace." At Acts xxvi. 28 (see note) the exact nuance escapes us, baffled as we are by the combination of a word-play in a foreign tongue, of uncertainty in the textual reading, and probably of an unusual Greek idiom. At Acts xi. 26, while the author definitely calls our attention to the use of the name— first at Antioch—he does not say by whom it was coined, and the verb he uses [4] gives no indication of the spirit in which it was applied.

*The use of the word.*

---

[1] See E. Nachmanson, in *Mélanges de Philologie offerts à M. Johan Vising*, Göteborg, 1925, pp. 273 f., with the collections on which he depends, viz. P. Meyer, ' Die Cognomina auf -anus griechischen Stammes auf den römischen Inschriften, I.' in *Beilage zur Jahresbericht des städtischen Gymnasiums in Bern. Ostern,* 1886, and M. Lambertz in *Glotta,* iv. (1913) pp. 78 ff., v. (1914) pp. 99 ff. The last-named writer (*loc. cit.* v. pp. 149 f. note) illustrates the interesting use of a name in -ιανός to form a patronymic cognomen or supernomen.

[2] So A. Gercke (see next note) asserts that the name really began at Rome. It may be worth while to warn the reader that the evidence for the name formerly found by reading on a graffito from Pompeii (hence before A.D. 79) the letters HRISTIAN (*CIL.* iv. 679) has to be abandoned.

[3] See A. Gercke, ' Der Christenname ein Scheltname ' in *Festschrift zur Jahrhundertfeier der Universität Breslau,* 1911, pp. 360 ff.

[4] Why the author chose the word χρηματίσαι for the passage rather than a more usual locution is not manifest, but he has a rich vocabulary and is sometimes influenced by an occurrence of a word to use it soon again, often in a different sense. See x. 22 ἐχρηματίσθη. The sequence χρηματίσαι Χρηστιανούς is scarcely a conspicuous assonance. Besides, this author is not much given to sound figures. Except for the established Greek word-play of Luke xxi. 11 λιμοὶ καὶ λοιμοί, the only instance in his writings worth notice is Acts xvii. 25 ζωὴν καὶ πνοήν (see note). Cf. E. Russell, *Paronomasia and Kindred Phenomena*

It may be worth while to add that Luke's statement implies not merely that the first occurrence of the name was at Antioch, but that there were subsequent occurrences known to him.[1] One wonders whether he does not therefore deliberately avoid using it on other occasions (except xxvi. 28). Such avoidance, together with his note about the word's first incidence, would constitute an interesting mark of studied care in nomenclature,[2] corresponding to other evidence about his use of words, and giving some assurance of care in the avoidance of anachronism in the matter of other terms that we are considering. Apart from this the absence of the word from the earliest Christian literature, including 1 Clement, and indeed from all the Apostolic Fathers except Ignatius, suggests that as a matter of fact it was not a name early accepted by the Christians themselves.

Nazarenes.    Nazarenes (Ναζωραῖοι) is used at Acts xxiv. 5 of the Christians. Tertullus the rhetor speaking on behalf of the Jews calls Paul a ringleader of the αἵρεσις τῶν Ναζωραίων. The epithet agrees with one form of the word Nazarene applied to Jesus.[3] If in the case of Jesus it was derived from his home in Nazareth, its application to his followers would be secondary to that. If on the other hand it has a different origin, it may have been applied to Jesus and his followers independently, but for the same reason. The context of Acts allows us to suppose that it was a term of reproach, though whether originally so or only in its acquired connotation cannot be determined. In such reproach may be found the significance of the scripture prediction given in Matt. ii. 23. But there is no evidence that the usage continued. The instance in Acts is unique in early Christian literature as the name of a group.[4] When the name appears again it is the name of a special sect or of some sects, of which one is said by Epiphanius to be pre-Christian. The name was also used by the Mandaeans of themselves, though this is not evidence of its early origin and continuous use,

---

*in the New Testament*, 1920, p. 14. The intransitive active in the sense of ' be named ' is abundantly illustrated by the papyri (Preisigke, *Wörterbuch*, ii. coll. 753 f.). It has been thought to indicate an official or legal name (Schubart, *Archiv für Papyrusforschung*, v., 1913, p. 114), though it is used of abbreviation of names and of cognomina (Lambertz, *Glotta*, iv., 1913, pp. 79, 135; v., 1914, pp. 116 note, 150 note). Modern discoveries make unnecessary and improbable the view that it suggests a divine nomenclature (F. Gardiner, *JBL*. l., 1931, pp. xxxvi f.).

[1] πρώτως is often corrected to πρῶτον in this passage and other Hellenistic writings against manuscript evidence. But it is not the equivalent but a late Greek formation indicating ' for the first time ' and implying that the same thing occurred again, whereas πρῶτον permits a change of subject or a change of verb.

[2] See pp. 417 ff.        [3] See pp. 356 f.

[4] This statement must perhaps be limited to Greek use of the name. Two Latin writers, Tertull. *Adv. Marc.* iv. 8 (*C.S.E.L.* xlvii. p. 437), and Jerome, *Comm. in Esaiam*, v. 18, xlix. 7, lii. 5 (Migne, *P.L.* xxiv. 87, 484, 517), say the Jews revile (Christ) Christians under the name *Nazareni*, the latter says thrice a day in prayer. In the latter connexion we may note that Acts assigns the term to Jewish opponents and that a prayer against *Minim* (heretics, Christians) is known from Jewish sources.

and it was used by the Persians and Mohammedans of the Christians.
For recent discussions of the term, given an undue significance by the
recent interest in Mandaism, we may refer to the Additional Note on the
Titles for Jesus.[1] In spite of its solitary character there is no reason to
suspect the occurrence of the term in Acts. It doubtless represents a
genuine usage among the varieties of names applied to the believers.

Galileans, on the other hand, is certainly geographical in its origin and   Galileans.
may very likely be used in this sense in Acts (i. 11, ii. 7). No doubt on
the lips of Jews in Jerusalem (ii. 7) it might involve scorn,[2] and it was
revived by Julian the emperor in his criticism and abuse of the Christians.
Like Nazarenes its early currency for the Christians in a general sense has
hardly more than a single certain instance in the first centuries—a passage
in Epictetus.[3] And it need not be included among the terms for Christians
in Acts.

In the word ἐκκλησία the Christians found an enduring term for their   ἐκκλησία.
movement and one which served satisfactorily many needs of nomenclature.[4] Much about its origin remains obscure.[5] In our first Christian
literature—the letters of Paul—it already appears as an accepted term.
Whether, as Matt. xvi. 18, xviii. 17 implies, it can be carried back to the
lips of Jesus is difficult and perhaps unimportant to decide—difficult
because the first passage is involved in long-standing controversy between
Catholics and Protestants, unimportant because in any case a Semitic
word would have to be sought as the original, and the original word would
be of quite different history. We do not indeed know what word would
be so used. The Old Testament equivalent would be קהל, Aramaic קהלא,
but there is reason for supposing an Aramaic word corresponding to כנסה
would be employed.[6]

The term was perhaps first selected in Greek and by Greek Christianity.   The origin
Yet its origins are in Judaism, and it is this Jewish Greek term, with its   of the word.
LXX associations of dignity and of intimate relation with God rather than
the usages of secular Greek, or any memory of etymology,[7] that gave the

---

[1] See p. 357, note 3.

[2] Cf. John vii. 41. But the angels hardly used it in scorn (Acts i. 11).

[3] Arrian, *Diss.* iv. 7. 6. The *Philopatris* also uses the word, and would
belong to the second century if it were correctly included among the works of
Lucian, but it is of much later date.

[4] Harnack, *Mission*, pp. 407 ff., emphasizes the many advantages of this
'masterly stroke'; cf. his *Constitution and Law of the Church*, 1910, pp. 15-18.

[5] See especially F. Kattenbusch, 'Der Quellort der Kirchenidee' in *Festgabe
für A. von Harnack*, 1912, pp. 143 ff., and K. L. Schmidt, 'Die Kirche des
Urchristentums' in *Festgabe für Adolf Deissmann*, 1927, pp. 258-319. See also
Vol. IV. pp. 53 f.

[6] See K. L. Schmidt, *loc. cit.* pp. 274-280.

[7] The term may have been chosen to render קהל partly on the basis of
likeness of sound. It may have seemed to the early Christians to be akin to
ἐκκλητοί, κλητοί, or ἐκλεκτοί, but "there is no foundation for the widely spread
notion that ἐκκλησία means a people or a number of individual men *called out*
of the world or mankind " (F. J. A. Hort, *The Christian Ecclesia*, 1897, p. 5).

term its appropriateness. It had, of course, frequent use in secular speech of an official or unofficial assembly. It is even maintained that it was used by the semi-religious associations.[1] But the Christians used it not in contrast with the Gentile ἐκκλησία [2] but like other terms, e.g. ἅγιοι, to express in the first instance their claim to be the true ἐκκλησία of revealed religion. So it happened that Christianity usurped the term, leaving, however, to Judaism the other LXX word for religious assembly, συναγωγή, as an almost undisputed possession.[3]

The definitive character of ἐκκλησία to express the Christian community is shown incidentally by many circumstances. For example, Latin Christianity made no effort to translate it, but transliterated it as *ecclesia*.[4] The opponents of Christianity recognized ἐκκλησία as the distinctive name of the movement. While it is often given with the genitive θεοῦ it needs no such description. The single word expresses the exclusive character of the Christian religion.

Early variations of meaning. At least three Christian uses of the term emerge as early as Paul: (i.) the universal collection of Christians everywhere; (ii.) the local group of believers; (iii.) the actual assembly of believers at worship. Something of the cult-character of the LXX term remains in all three of these uses. It is not certain which of them is the oldest, and particularly whether the first derives from the second or *vice versa*. In the sense of a local group the word naturally can take localizing expressions, like ἐν Κορίνθῳ, or even κατ᾽ οἶκόν τινος,[5] or can become plural, ἐκκλησίαι. In the universal sense the term has a kind of superterrestrial character.[6]

In Acts. In the book of Acts—to turn now to our present study—the distinction between the local and the general use is of special difficulty, for the reason that in some of the occurrences the church in Jerusalem is still the only church,[7] and that in others it seems even without the localizing definition [8]

---

[1] So J. Weiss on 1 Corinthians in Meyer's *Kommentar*, 9th edition, 1910, p. xvii, following W. Liebenam, *Zur Geschichte und Organisation des römischen Vereinswesens*, 1890, pp. 272 f.

[2] The contrast before long is thought of. So Origen, *Contra Celsum*, iii. 30.

[3] For συναγωγή of Christianity, except for possibly James ii. 2, the occurrences are late and heretical (partly Jewish-Christian), and in any case few. See Schmidt, *loc. cit.* pp. 271 f.; Harnack, *Mission*, p. 408 note, and his earlier note on Hermas, *Mand.* xi. 9.

[4] This fact is frequently stressed and rightly, though Deissmann, *Light from the Ancient East*, English translation, 2nd edition, 1927, pp. 112 f., notes that also in its secular uses ἐκκλησία was retained by Latin writers rather than translated. An example from a bilingual inscription is quoted Vol. IV. p. 248.

[5] 1 Cor. xvi. 19; Rom. xvi. 5; Col. iv. 15; Philemon 2.

[6] Cf. Harnack, *Mission*, pp. 408 f.

[7] The first occurrence is at v. 11, since only the Antiochian text uses the word at ii. 47.

[8] We have, however, viii. 1 τὴν ἐκκλησίαν τὴν ἐν Ἱεροσολύμοις, xi. 22 τῆς ἐκκλησίας τῆς οὔσης ἐν Ἱερουσαλήμ, and in a more universal sense ix. 31 ἡ ἐκκλησία καθ᾽ ὅλης τῆς Ἰουδαίας καὶ Γαλιλαίας καὶ Σαμαρείας.

to be spoken of as the church *par excellence*.[1] But elsewhere it is clear that the author assumes that other cities have their church also, and even at Jerusalem the unmodified ἐκκλησία may signify no pre-eminence. The instances of the plural ἐκκλησίαι are, however, few and near together.[2] For the church in its wider use of a divine institution the best instance is characteristically enough in the pastoral address of Paul at Miletus. It has probably the defining genitive θεοῦ.[3] It has been noted[4] that Christians are first called οἱ ἀπὸ τῆς ἐκκλησίας at Acts xii. 1. Finally we may observe that the author shows that Christian appropriation of the word has not for him in the least prevented its quite correct use also of secular gatherings in the theatre at Ephesus,[5] nor in application to the congregation of Israel τῇ ἐκκλησίᾳ ἐν τῇ ἐρήμῳ.[6] But set as it is in a speech full of the undertone of parallelism between Judaism and Christianity it is possible that this last instance is not used without a side glance at the Christian terminology.

Of the ἐκκλησία as the actually gathered assembly [7]—the third of its πλῆθος. three Christian usages—the book of Acts happens to provide no example. The idea is perhaps represented at iv. 32, vi. 2, 5, xv. 12, 30 and xxi. 22 *v.l.* by the word πλῆθος, which occasionally is used elsewhere of the religious assemblies of Jews or Gentiles. To the full discussion of this term on iv. 32 (Vol. IV. pp. 47 f.) nothing here needs to be added. No other New Testament writing uses πλῆθος so, but it occurs in the Apostolic Fathers, e.g. Ignatius, *Smyrn.* viii. 2 ὅπου ἂν φανῇ ὁ ἐπίσκοπος, ἐκεῖ τὸ πλῆθος ἔστω· ὥσπερ ὅπου ἂν ᾖ χριστὸς Ἰησοῦς, ἐκεῖ ἡ καθολικὴ ἐκκλησία. This passage, like some of the other occurrences, suggests that πλῆθος means the ordinary group of Christians as distinct from their leaders. Harnack speaks of the oldest occurrence of πλῆθος meaning the whole church as 1 Clement liv. 2, the next oldest as Hermas, *Mand.* xt. 9.[8]

The Christian group or movement was concretely expressed by other Other de- terms. Some of these were merely occasional, others were deliberate scriptions. metaphors usually based on Jewish ideas or expressions. In the book of κοινωνία. Acts κοινωνία is sometimes so understood at ii. 42 ἦσαν δὲ προσκαρτε- ροῦντες τῇ διδαχῇ τῶν ἀποστόλων καὶ τῇ κοινωνίᾳ, τῇ κλάσει τοῦ ἄρτου

---

[1] Cf. xi. 26, xiii. 1 (see the note, pp. 56 f., on οὖσα); xiv. 27, xv. 3 (all of Antioch); xviii. 22 (notoriously uncertain, see note); xx. 17 (Ephesus).

[2] xv. 41, xvi. 5, another instance of uneven distribution of words in Luke-Acts. But the distributive phrase in the singular xiv. 23 κατ' ἐκκλησίαν implies ἐκκλησίαι in the plural.

[3] xx. 28, *v.l.* κυρίου. Whether ἐκκλησία is used in Acts in the Catholic sense is discussed in Vol. IV. p. 107. It is not so used in 1 Clem.

[4] Harnack, *Mission*, p. 407 note.

[5] Acts xix. 32, 39, 41. It would be easy to multiply illustrations of this typical combination (an ἐκκλησία held in a theatre) in the ancient world.

[6] Acts vii. 38.

[7] E.g. 1 Cor. xi. 18, xiv. 19, 28, 35. The opposites are ἐν οἴκῳ xi. 34, xiv. 35, or (παρ') ἑαυτῷ, xiv. 28, xvi. 2.

[8] *Sitzungsberichte der Preuss. Akademie*, 1909, p. 61. Cf. Irenaeus *apud* Eus. *H.E.* v. 20. 6.

καὶ ταῖς προσευχαῖς.[1]  But there are too many other possibilities for this passage (see note *ad loc.*) and too few parallels for such a usage [2] to confirm this suggestion that early Christianity was known as the ' Fellowship.'

αἵρεσις.  αἵρεσις is applied by non-Christians to Christianity in Acts xxiv. 5, 14, xxviii. 22.  xxiv. 14 suggests that a Christian speaker would disclaim the title.[3]  The word is difficult to translate (see v. 17, xv. 5 note, xxiv. 5). Its connotations were (before Christianity) philosophical quite as much as religious, and not unfavourable.[4]  I suppose it refers to the teaching rather than to the group of adherents, though the two are easily interchanged. It occurs also in later Christian literature both of a heretical doctrine and of a schismatical group.  But in Latin "till far down into the third century (cf. the usage of Cyprian) *secta* was employed by Christians quite ingenuously to denote their fellowship.  It was not technical, of course, but a wholly neutral term." [5]

The flock.  In Acts xx. 28 Paul is represented as admonishing the Ephesian elders to pay heed to themselves and to the whole flock (παντὶ τῷ ποιμνίῳ).  That the church is meant is plain from the context, but it might well be supposed that the word flock, herd, is a figure adopted for this passage,[6] rather than as an established term.  But the ' pastoral' terminology had long before entered the Jewish (not to mention earlier Semitic) religion, and its occurrence in other Christian writings about as early as Acts [7] suggests that it was a term readily resorted to, if not fully established, in Christian parlance.

εὐαγγέλιον.  For the Christian religion as the object of preaching Luke uses in his two works, apart from more roundabout phrases, two words, εὐαγγέλιον and λόγος, but the latter much more frequently than the former.  A study of the former word [8] shows that it occurs in Christian writing prior to Luke, e.g. in Paul and Mark, and was known to him, but is used by him most sparingly, namely twice in Acts, both times in speeches of the Christians.  But he uses the corresponding verb very frequently (εὐαγγελί- ζομαι), though it is not used only of the Christian gospel but of good tidings on other themes.  It is an interesting fact that " the kingdom of

---

[1] Cf. A. Carr, 'The Fellowship (κοινωνία) of Acts ii. 42 and Cognate Words ' in *Expositor*, May 1913, pp. 458 ff.

[2] E. Lohmeyer, on Phil. i. 5, says that the religious term κοινωνία never signifies in Paul the fixed bond of believing brethren to each other.

[3] Cf. Vol. IV. p. 298.

[4] See, however, Dittenberger, *Sylloge*, 3rd edition, 675. 28 (2 B.C.) γίνωνται δὲ καὶ ἄλλοι ζηλωταὶ τῆς αὐτῆς αἱρέσεως cited by Preuschen-Bauer *sub voce*.

[5] Harnack, *Mission*, p. 409 note.

[6] Cf. ἐπισκόπους (which may mean simply ποιμένας, cf. 1 Pet. ii. 25) and ποιμαίνειν τὴν ἐκκλησίαν in the same verse, and in the next λύκοι βαρεῖς . . . μὴ φειδόμενοι τοῦ ποιμνίου.  Uncanonical examples include Ps. Sol. xvii. 45 and the Parable of the Seventy Shepherds in Enoch xc.

[7] 1 Pet. v. 2, 3; 1 Clem. xvi. 1, xliv. 3, liv. 2, lvii. 2.  Luke xii. 32 attributes the term to Jesus.

[8] Cf. A. Harnack, *Constitution and Law of the Church*, Eng. trans., 1910, pp. 275 ff.

God appears as the sole object of the good tidings only in the Gospel and not in the Acts, and that, on the other hand, Jesus Christ is the object only in the Acts and not in the Gospel." [1] These phenomena suggest that Luke's procedure is conscious and deliberate, but why he avoids the noun while using the verb so freely is a question not easily answered.

λόγος in the sense of Christianity is, on the other hand, more charac- λόγος. teristic of Luke than of other New Testament writers.[2] In the gospel, to be sure, he uses it sparingly and writes it fully—τὸν λόγον τοῦ θεοῦ,[3] but in Acts there are twenty-two instances of ὁ λόγος τοῦ θεοῦ (τοῦ κυρίου), and ὁ λόγος by itself is used in the same sense fourteen times. Harnack [4] has called attention to the materialization of the term in Acts. It is not hypostatized as a person as in John, not even I think at xx. where it is mentioned alongside of God (παρατίθεμαι ὑμᾶς τῷ θεῷ καὶ τῷ λόγῳ τῆς χάριτος αὐτοῦ), but it is a concrete thing, as the expression ὁ λόγος τοῦ θεοῦ ηὔξανεν [5] and others show, which seem to mean not merely the preaching but the whole Christian enterprise.[6] Compare viii. 21 οὐκ ἔστιν σοι μερὶς οὐδὲ κλῆρος ἐν τῷ λόγῳ τούτῳ.

Harnack speaks of the materialization of λόγος. It is possible that in πίστις. Acts the same process has begun also with the word πίστις. The mere occurrence of many of these terms without dependent genitive and with an article gives them at least the appearance of names made definite, οἱ ἀδελφοί, or ὁ ὁδός, or ὁ λόγος. ἡ πίστις certainly reaches the stage of an objective belief in other early Christian literature, most plainly in Jude 3, 20, the Pastoral Epistles, and even in Galatians (i. 23 and perhaps iii. 23-25). The instances in Acts that may fall under like classification are vi. 7 πολύς τε ὄχλος τῶν ἱερέων ὑπήκουον τῇ πίστει, xiii. 8 ζητῶν διαστρέψαι τὸν ἀνθύπατον ἀπὸ τῆς πίστεως, xiv. 22 παρακαλοῦντες ἐμμένειν τῇ πίστει, xvi. 5 αἱ μὲν οὖν ἐκκλησίαι ἐστερεοῦντο τῇ πίστει.[7]

The most unusual of the names for Christianity found in Acts is the ὁδός. unmodified ὁδός. The expression with dependent genitives κυρίου or θεοῦ occurs at xviii. 25, 26, and is quite in accordance with Jewish idiom. There

---

[1] Ibid. p. 290.

[2] See ibid. pp. 332 ff., for Luke-Acts especially pp. 334-339. Cf. Schniewind, Die Begriffe Wort und Evangelium bei Paulus, Diss. Bonn, 1910, pp. 10-53.

[3] v. 1, viii. 11 (for Mark's τὸν λόγον), viii. 21 (for Mark's τὸ θέλημα τοῦ θεοῦ), xi. 28.

[4] Loc. cit. pp. 337 f.        [5] vi. 7, xii. 24, xix. 20.

[6] Possibly this is the case also in vi. 4 διακονία τοῦ λόγου. The αὐτόπται καὶ ὑπηρέται τοῦ λόγου of Luke's preface is not only the closest parallel to this passage, but by its omission of τοῦ θεοῦ and by its materialization of the term λόγος provides a further illustration of the affinity of the language of this preface to the language of Acts. Cf. Expositor, June 1921, pp. 439 f.

[7] Compare the notes on the first three of these passages, Vol. IV. pp. 66, 144 f., and 167 f. respectively. It is possible to give the article a context reference in xiii. 8 ' his faith,' xv. 9 ' their faith.' Two of the passages belong to the summaries of Acts (cf. p. 396) in which also ὁ λόγος is a common expression. At another of these summaries (xix. 20) the Western text had ἡ πίστις τοῦ θεοῦ for τοῦ κυρίου ὁ λόγος.

is also little exceptional in ὁδός with a limiting pronoun or relative clause as at xxii. 4 ταύτην τὴν ὁδόν, xxiv. 14 τὴν ὁδὸν ἣν λέγουσι αἵρεσιν, but the cases of an unmodified ἡ ὁδός are sufficient to imply that the author used it with a distinctiveness which our English manner would indicate by either quotes or capital—the 'way' or the Way.[1] The instances are ix. 2 ἐάν τινας εὕρῃ τῆς ὁδοῦ ὄντας, xix. 9 κακολογοῦντες τὴν ὁδὸν ἐνώπιον τοῦ πλήθους, xix. 23 ἐγένετο δὲ τάραχος οὐκ ὀλίγος περὶ τῆς ὁδοῦ, xxiv. 22 ἀκριβέστερον εἰδὼς τὰ περὶ τῆς ὁδοῦ. In every case some later scribes revealed their consciousness of the peculiarity of the phrase by adding 'this' or 'of God' or 'of the Lord.'[2] To what is said about the term at ix. 2 (Vol. IV. p. 100) nothing need here be added.[3]

## Note XXXI. The Summaries in Acts

### By Henry J. Cadbury

The summaries in Acts and the plan of the book.

Attention has already been called in Vol. II. pp. 175 ff. to certain generalizing statements in the Book of Acts because of their alleged bearing on the general plan of the volume. The suggestion has sometimes been made that these sentences of a general character dealing with the growth of the church have been so placed among the more specific narratives as to divide the book into a distinct series of six 'panels,' and that these panels show the author's own plan of division, and perhaps even a systematic chronological arrangement. The suggestion as made is not convincing. The 'panels' cannot be limited to six and no more, and their placing seems to depend on the writer's sources and the scope of the information available rather than on any logical or chronological schematization of his own. The summaries are, however, a noteworthy feature of the Book of Acts, and it is desirable to inquire further what is their literary history and historical value.[4]

The analogies in the Gospels.

The gospels present us with some interesting analogies. In these as in Acts we have a number of separate scenes, sometimes connected with general summaries. But it seems quite likely that the history of these is not quite the same as of those in Acts. For example, the individual

---

[1] Such absolute terms are illustrated in Luke's ὁ λόγος (sc. τοῦ θεοῦ) and τὸ ὄνομα (v. 41).

[2] Cf. Ropes on ix. 2 (Vol. III. p. 83).

[3] It is stated there, however, too simply that Tao in Chinese means 'way,' for the word, though conventionally so rendered, has really the greatest variety of meanings.

[4] On the summaries in Acts see Vol. II. pp. 175 ff. (the statement of Turner is to be found in Hastings' Bible Dictionary, i. p. 421); the criticism of J. de Zwaan, Harvard Theological Review, xvii. (1924) pp. 101-110; also from another angle J. I. Still, St. Paul on Trial, pp. 26-31. From the formgeschichtliche viewpoint see M. Dibelius, 'Stilkritisches zur Apostelgeschichte' in Εὐχαριστήριον Hermann Gunkel dargebracht, part ii. pp. 34-35, and H. J. Cadbury, The Making of Luke-Acts, Index, s.v. 'Summaries.'

incidents lying behind the gospel of Mark have doubtless had a long In Mark. history as scattered apophthegms or anecdotes and miracle-tales. They were *disjecta membra* without biographical purpose, and were only brought together when a more biographical intention led Mark and others to ' draw up a narrative ' of Jesus' career. The summaries in the gospels, whether of teaching or healing or both, are not so primitive as the individual stories, and have been largely distilled out of them. They are an indication of an individual author.[1] Their purpose is that of generalizing and of thus filling the lacuna which is felt when a continuous narrative is to be made out of detached scenes. They represent the latest part of Mark, and specially reveal his editorial motives.

The later evangelists use these sections of Mark with great freedom. Matthew Desiring a still more connected story they show a tendency to repeat and and Luke. multiply them. Matthew, for example, uses Mark i. 39 twice (iv. 23 ; ix. 35), Mark iii. 7-12 twice (iv. 24, 25 ; xii. 15, 16) :

| Mark i. 39. | Matt. iv. 23. | Matt. ix. 35. |
|---|---|---|
| καὶ ἦλθεν κηρύσσων εἰς τὰς συναγωγὰς αὐτῶν εἰς ὅλην τὴν Γαλιλαίαν καὶ τὰ δαιμόνια ἐκβάλλων. | καὶ περιῆγεν ἐν ὅλῃ τῇ Γαλιλαίᾳ, διδάσκων ἐν ταῖς συναγωγαῖς αὐτῶν καὶ κηρύσσων τὸ εὐαγγέλιον τῆς βασιλείας καὶ θεραπεύων πᾶσαν νόσον καὶ πᾶσαν μαλακίαν ἐν τῷ λαῷ. | καὶ περιῆγεν ὁ Ἰησοῦς τὰς πόλεις πάσας καὶ τὰς κώμας, διδάσκων ἐν ταῖς συναγωγαῖς αὐτῶν καὶ κηρύσσων τὸ εὐαγγέλιον τῆς βασιλείας καὶ θεραπεύων πᾶσαν νόσον καὶ πᾶσαν μαλακίαν. |

| Mark iii. 7-12. | Matt. iv. 24-25. | Matt. xii. 15-16. |
|---|---|---|
| καὶ ὁ Ἰησοῦς μετὰ τῶν μαθητῶν αὐτοῦ ἀνεχώρησεν πρὸς τὴν θάλασσαν· καὶ πολὺ πλῆθος ἀπὸ τῆς Γαλιλαίας ἠκολούθησεν, καὶ ἀπὸ τῆς Ἰουδαίας καὶ ἀπὸ Ἱεροσολύμων καὶ ἀπὸ τῆς Ἰδουμαίας καὶ πέραν τοῦ Ἰορδάνου καὶ περὶ Τύρον καὶ Σιδῶνα, πλῆθος πολύ, ἀκούοντες ὅσα ποιεῖ ἦλθαν πρὸς αὐτόν. καὶ εἶπεν τοῖς μαθηταῖς ἵνα πλοιάριον προσκαρτερῇ αὐτῷ διὰ τὸν ὄχλον ἵνα μὴ θλίβωσιν αὐτόν· πολλοὺς γὰρ ἐθεράπευσεν, ὥστε ἐπιπίπτειν αὐτῷ ἵνα αὐτοῦ ἅψωνται ὅσοι εἶχον μάστιγας. καὶ τὰ πνεύματα τὰ ἀκάθαρτα, ὅταν αὐτὸν ἐθεώρουν, προσέπιπτεν αὐτῷ καὶ ἔκραζον λέγοντα ὅτι Σὺ εἶ ὁ υἱὸς τοῦ θεοῦ. καὶ πολλὰ ἐπετίμα αὐτοῖς ἵνα μὴ αὐτὸν φανερὸν ποιήσωσιν. | καὶ ἀπῆλθεν ἡ ἀκοὴ αὐτοῦ εἰς ὅλην τὴν Συρίαν· καὶ προσήνεγκαν αὐτῷ πάντας τοὺς κακῶς ἔχοντας ποικίλαις νόσοις καὶ βασάνοις συνεχομένους, δαιμονιζομένους καὶ σεληνιαζομένους καὶ παραλυτικούς, καὶ ἐθεράπευσεν αὐτούς. ἠκολούθησαν αὐτῷ ὄχλοι πολλοὶ ἀπὸ τῆς Γαλιλαίας καὶ Δεκαπόλεως καὶ Ἱεροσολύμων καὶ Ἰουδαίας καὶ πέραν Ἰορδάνου. | ὁ δὲ Ἰησοῦς γνοὺς ἀνεχώρησεν ἐκεῖθεν. καὶ ἠκολούθησαν αὐτῷ πολλοί, καὶ ἐθεράπευσεν αὐτοὺς πάντας, καὶ ἐπετίμησεν αὐτοῖς ἵνα μὴ φανερὸν αὐτὸν ποιήσωσιν. |

[1] Cf. K. L. Schmidt, *Der Rahmen der Geschichte Jesu*, e.g. p. 105.

Luke—the volume to which Acts is a sequel—does the same. Thus Mark i. 28 is used by Luke three times : iv. 14, iv. 37, and vii. 17 :

| Mark i. 28. | Luke iv. 14. | Luke iv. 37. | Luke vii. 17. |
|---|---|---|---|
| καὶ ἐξῆλθεν ἡ ἀκοὴ αὐτοῦ εὐθὺς πανταχοῦ εἰς ὅλην τὴν περίχωρον τῆς Γαλιλαίας. | καὶ φήμη ἐξῆλθεν καθ᾽ ὅλης τῆς περιχώρου περὶ αὐτοῦ. | καὶ ἐξεπορεύετο ἦχος περὶ αὐτοῦ εἰς πάντα τόπον τῆς περιχώρου. | καὶ ἐξῆλθεν ὁ λόγος οὗτος ἐν ὅλῃ τῇ Ἰουδαίᾳ περὶ αὐτοῦ καὶ πάσῃ τῇ περιχώρῳ. |

Elsewhere Luke takes the liberty of interchanging and rearranging Mark's summaries.[1] Even the repeated references to Jesus' journeying to Jerusalem in Luke ix. ff. may be due to Mark x. 1 and x. 32, together with other references to ἡ ὁδός in viii. 27, ix. 33, and x. 17. Luke's summary of his daily routine at Jerusalem (xxi. 37 and 38) is due to scattered references in Mark.

The analogy of Kings and Chronicles.

The method by which Matthew and Luke repeat Mark's summaries is known to us because we possess Mark. It is a natural method, and is doubtless used by other writers dependent on sources, though we are not always able to 'control' the evidence. An excellent illustration of the repetition of a summary in another Biblical deuterograph is found in the account of Solomon's wealth in Chronicles. The statement of 1 Kings x. 27, "And the king made silver to be in Jerusalem as stones, and cedars made he to be as the sycamore trees that are in the lowland, for abundance," is repeated verbatim in 2 Chron. i. 15, and also in 2 Chron. ix. 27. Indeed the whole summary of 1 Kings x. 23-29 is largely repeated in both passages in Chronicles in the following manner : 1 Kings x. 23-28a (except x. 26a) = 2 Chron. ix. 22-28 (except ix. 25a, 26 = 1 Kings iv. 26, 27a); 1 Kings x. 26-29 = 2 Chron. i. 14-17. The author of Chronicles has not only retained the summary where he found it in Kings near the end of the account of Solomon's reign, but he has also introduced it in the very beginning of his account of Solomon.[2] Probably in this case the repetition is unintentional. The secondary author first used his material out of its place in the source, and then repeats it in copying his source in regular order. So Matthew uses Mark ix. 43-48 on ' offences ' not only in the Sermon on the Mount (v. 29-30) but also in its proper place (xviii. 8-9), or the cure of the blind (Mark x. 46-52) not merely in his collection of cures (ix. 27-31) but later in his parallel narrative (xx. 29-34).

Luke.

In other parts of Luke-Acts it is natural to suspect that the same

---

[1] For further details see my *Style and Literary Method of Luke*, pp. 108 ff.

[2] For other repetitions in the chronicler's work see 1 Chron. viii. 29-38 = ix. 35-44 ; xxi. 5 = xxi. 20a, and Ezra ii. 1-iii. 1 = Neh. vii. 6-73. The editor of Kings himself apparently repeats his own summary in 2 Kings xiii. 12, 13 = xiv. 15, 16. Of course in some cases repetition is not due to the use of a source, or to inadvertence, but an author deliberately repeats himself for the sake of resuming a narrative after interrupting it. This I think explains 1 Macc. ix. 34 = 43, xv. 13, 14 = 25, and perhaps Acts viii. 1, 4 = xi. 19, 20 (see below). It is not clear what is the reason for 2 Samuel viii. 6c = 14c.

method is at work as in the parts dependent on Mark. Thus the nativity stories of Luke i. and ii. are broken up [1] into 'panels' by summaries something like those of Acts :

Luke i. 80 τὸ δὲ παιδίον ηὔξανεν καὶ ἐκραταιοῦτο πνεύματι.
Luke ii. 40 τὸ δὲ παιδίον ηὔξανεν καὶ ἐκραταιοῦτο πληρούμενον σοφίας καὶ χάρις θεοῦ ἦν ἐπ' αὐτό.
Luke ii. 56 καὶ Ἰησοῦς προέκοπτεν ἐν τῇ σοφίᾳ καὶ ἡλικίᾳ καὶ χάριτι παρὰ θεῷ καὶ ἀνθρώποις.

Perhaps we can trace the ultimate source of these to Judges xiii. and 1 Samuel ii. (chapters that otherwise greatly influenced these birth stories) where we read :

Judges xiii. 24 καὶ ἡδρύνθη τὸ παιδάριον καὶ εὐλόγησεν αὐτὸ Κύριος.
1 Sam. ii. 21 καὶ ἐμεγαλύνθη τὸ παιδάριον Σαμουὴλ ἐνώπιον Κυρίου.
1 Sam. ii. 26 καὶ τὸ παιδάριον Σαμουὴλ ἐπορεύετο καὶἦνἄγαθον καὶ μετὰ Κυρίου καὶ μετὰ ἀνθρώπων.

A particularly interesting example of the creation of summaries is Luke vii. 21. As the parallel in Matt. xi. 2 ff. shows, Luke gets from his source the question of John and the reply of Jesus (Luke vii. 22 ff.), but one is tempted to suppose that the summary which so well fits the reply is the work of Luke.[2]

The summaries in Acts have doubtless a similar history behind them. Acts. In the first part of Acts particularly, a number of separate scenes have been gathered together from quite different sources. The summaries serve as caesuras between scenes, or rather as connective tissue by which memorabilia are turned into the beginnings of a continuous narrative.[3] It may be assumed, then, as probable that the summaries in Acts

[1] These summaries serve both to divide and to point the parallel between the accounts of Jesus and John. Cf. A. Fridrichsen in *Symbolae Osloenses*, vi. (1928), pp. 36 f.

[2] Matthew, just as he prepares for Mark's summary about Jesus' teaching (vii. 28 f.) by inserting right before it a long collection of Jesus' sayings (v. 1-vii. 27), here prepares for the summarized reply from Q about works of mercy, not by a summary of cures, as does Luke, but by prefixing a series of incidents collected or altered from his sources which precisely justify the words " the blind see (ix. 27 ff.) and the lame walk (ix. 1 ff., cf. viii. 5 ff.), the lepers are cleansed (viii. 1 ff.), and the poor have good news preached to them " (x. 1 ff.). (Are the plurals in Matthew, e.g. viii. 28, ix. 27, and the diagnosis of the centurion's servant as a second case of paralysis (viii. 6, contrast Luke vii. 2), intended to justify the plurals in the answer of Jesus ?)

[3] This characteristic of the summaries provides the modern editor of Acts as of the gospels with an embarrassing problem in paragraphing. He is in doubt whether to connect the summary with what precedes or with what follows. If he separates it from both he has not indicated its true purpose as a transition in the structure of the book. Modern literary form has no device for handling this material properly.

(1) are later than the intervening panels ;
(2) are derived by generalization from some of the specific adjacent material ;
(3) are peculiarly liable to free treatment by the final editor and especially to combination ;
(4) when similar to one another in subject matter they may be due to Luke's well-known tendency to express himself independently but similarly on the same theme, but also may be derived by repetition from an underlying written source ;
(5) in the latter case (if derived from a written source and repeated) the variation is due to the author's tendency to paraphrase. Of two similar summaries there is some probability (in accordance with p. 394) that the second occurrence represents the original position of the summary in the source.

The relation between the parallel and repeated summaries in Acts presents characteristics confirming these conclusions. The clearest parallelism is the following :

Acts viii. and xi.

Acts viii. 1, 4 ἐγένετο δὲ ἐν ἐκείνῃ τῇ ἡμέρᾳ διωγμὸς μέγας . . . οἱ μὲν οὖν διασπαρέντες διῆλθον εὐαγγελιζόμενοι τὸν λόγον.

Acts xi. 19, 20 οἱ μὲν οὖν διασπαρέντες ἀπὸ τῆς θλίψεως τῆς γενομένης ἐπὶ Στεφάνῳ διῆλθον . . . λαλοῦντες τὸν λόγον . . . εὐαγγελιζόμενοι τὸν κύριον Ἰησοῦν.

Turner's 'panels.'

Another series is that used by Turner and others as the basis of their panels [1] :

Acts vi. 7 καὶ ὁ λόγος τοῦ θεοῦ ηὔξανεν, καὶ ἐπληθύνετο ὁ ἀριθμὸς τῶν μαθητῶν ἐν Ἰερουσαλὴμ σφόδρα, πολύς τε ὄχλος τῶν ἱερέων ὑπήκουον τῇ πίστει.

Acts ix. 31 ἡ μὲν οὖν ἐκκλησία . . . ἐπληθύνετο.

Acts xii. 24 ὁ δὲ λόγος τοῦ θεοῦ ηὔξανε καὶ ἐπληθύνετο.

Acts xvi. 5 αἱ μὲν οὖν ἐκκλησίαι ἐστερεοῦντο τῇ πίστει καὶ ἐπερίσσευον τῷ ἀριθμῷ καθ' ἡμέραν.

Acts xix. 20 οὕτως κατὰ κράτος τοῦ κυρίου ὁ λόγος ηὔξανεν καὶ ἴσχυεν.

Acts xxviii. 30 f.    Paul's two years at Rome.

To these should be added perhaps ii. 47b, v. 14 (see below), and

Acts xi. 21 πολύς τε ἀριθμὸς ὁ πιστεύσας ἐπέστρεψεν ἐπὶ τὸν κύριον.

Acts xi. 24 καὶ προσετέθη ὄχλος ἱκανὸς τῷ κυρίῳ.

In these we find with variations numerous repeated terms, especially the combination ηὔξανεν καὶ ἐπληθύνετο which occurs also in Stephen's speech of the growth of the people of Israel (vii. 17) and which may be due to the Old Testament idiom, much as the summaries in Luke i. and ii. are founded on the Old Testament. Note that in xi. 19-21 a summary of this series is combined with one of the preceding.

---

[1] See Vol. II. p. 177, note.

Much the most complicated parallelism is between ii. 41-47 and the Acts ii., iv. and v. two passages iv. 32-35, v. 11-14. The parallelism in these passages is graphically presented below, iv. 33a and v. 13a being omitted and i. 14 added.

(1)     ii. 41.

οἱ μὲν οὖν ἀποδεξάμενοι τὸν λόγον αὐτοῦ ἐβαπτί-σθησαν, καὶ προσετέθησαν ἐν τῇ ἡμέρᾳ ἐκείνῃ ψυχαὶ ὡσεὶ τρισχείλιαι.

| (2)   ii. 42. | i. 14. | ii. 46. |
|---|---|---|
| ἦσαν δὲ προσκαρτεροῦντες τῇ διδαχῇ τῶν ἀποστόλων καὶ τῇ κοινωνίᾳ, τῇ κλάσει τοῦ ἄρτου καὶ ταῖς προσ-ευχαῖς. | οὗτοι πάντες ἦσαν προσ-καρτεροῦντες ὁμοθυμαδὸν τῇ προσευχῇ σὺν γυναιξὶν καὶ Μαριὰμ τῇ μητρὶ Ἰησοῦ καὶ σὺν τοῖς ἀδελφοῖς αὐτοῦ. | καθ᾽ ἡμέραν τε προσ-καρτεροῦντες ὁμοθυμαδὸν ἐν τῷ ἱερῷ, κλῶντές τε κατ᾽ οἶκον ἄρτον, μετελάμ βανον τροφῆς ἐν ἀγαλ-λιάσει καὶ ἀφελότητι καρ-δίας. |
| (3)   ii. 43a. | v. 11. | v. 5b. |
| ἐγίνετο δὲ πάσῃ ψυχῇ φόβος · | καὶ ἐγένετο φόβος μέγας ἐφ᾽ ὅλην τὴν ἐκκλησίαν καὶ ἐπὶ πάντας τοὺς ἀκού-οντας ταῦτα. | καὶ ἐγένετο φόβος μέγας ἐπὶ πάντας τοὺς ἀκούοντας. |
| (4)   ii. 43b. | v. 12a. | |
| πολλὰ δὰ τέρατα καὶ σημεῖα διὰ τῶν ἀποστόλων ἐγεί-νετο. | διά τε τῶν χειρῶν τῶν ἀποστόλων ἐγείνετο σημεῖα καὶ τέρατα πολλὰ ἐν τῷ λαῷ. | |
| (5)   ii. 44-45. | iv. 32, 34-35. | |
| πάντες δὲ οἱ πιστεύσαντες ἐπὶ τὸ αὐτὸ εἶχον ἅπαντα κοινά, καὶ τὰ κτήματα καὶ τὰς ὑπάρξεις ἐπίπρασκον καὶ διεμέριζον αὐτὰ πᾶσιν καθότι ἄν τις χρείαν εἶχεν· | τοῦ δὲ πλήθους τῶν πισ-τευσάντων ἦν καρδία καὶ ψυχὴ μία, καὶ οὐδὲ εἷς τι τῶν ὑπαρχόντων αὐτῷ ἔλε-γον ἴδιον εἶναι, ἀλλ᾽ ἦν αὐτοῖς πάντα κοινά. . . . οὐδὲ γὰρ ἐνδεής ἦν τις ἐν αὐτοῖς· ὅσοι γὰρ κτήτορες χωρίων ἢ οἰκιῶν ὑπῆρχον, πωλοῦντες ἔφερον τὰς τει-μὰς τῶν πιπρασκομένων καὶ ἐτίθουν παρὰ τοὺς πόδας τῶν ἀποστόλων· δι-εδίδετο δὲ ἑκάστῳ καθότι ἄν τις χρείαν εἶχεν. | |
| (6)   ii. 46a. | v. 12b. | i. 14a. |
| καθ᾽, ἡμέραν τε προσκαρ-τεροῦντες ὁμοθυμαδὸν ἐν τῷ ἱερῷ, | καὶ ἦσαν ὁμοθυμαδὸν πάντες ἐν τῇ Στοᾷ Σολομῶνος. | οὗτοι πάντες ἦσαν προσ-καρτεροῦντες ὁμοθυμαδὸν τῇ προσευχῇ. |

(7)    ii. 46b.

κλῶντές τε κατ' οἶκον
ἄρτον, μετελάμβανον τρο-
φῆς᾽ ἐν ἀγαλλιάσει καὶ
ἀφελότητι καρδίας,

ii. 42.

ἦσαν δὲ προσκαρτεροῦντες
τῇ διδαχῇ τῶν ἀποστόλων
καὶ τῇ κοινωνίᾳ, τῇ κλάσει
τοῦ ἄρτου καὶ ταῖς προσ-
ευχαῖς.

(8)    ii. 47a.

αἰνοῦντες τὸν θεὸν καὶ
ἔχοντες χάριν πρὸς ὅλον
τὸν λαόν.

iv. 33b.

χάρις τε μεγάλη ἦν ἐπὶ
πάντας αὐτούς.

v. 13b.

ἀλλ' ἐμεγάλυνεν αὐτοὺς ὁ
λαός.

(9)    ii. 47b.

ὁ δὲ κύριος προσετίθει
τοὺς σωζομένους καθ'
ἡμέραν ἐπὶ τὸ αὐτό.

v. 14.

μᾶλλον δὲ προσετίθεντο
πιστεύοντες τῷ κυρίῳ
πλήθη ἀνδρῶν τε καὶ γυ-
ναικῶν.

It is evident that the same summary material is reproduced here twice. Some of the verbal likenesses are striking. The last two passages together practically equal the first.[1] They envelop between them the two concrete cases of communistic giving—Barnabas and Ananias—and may perhaps be the original setting of a summary partly derived from those definite cases and repeated in chapter ii. As has been noticed by others, ἐγίνετο δὲ φόβος fits better in chapter v. than in chapter ii.[2] Indeed chapter ii. has an earlier summary in verses 41 f., and we have here an illustration of agglutinative processes in such material. With this last-named passage should be compared, for their references to numbers, i. 15 and iv. 4 ; cf. i. 14 πάντες ἦσαν προσκαρτεροῦντες ὁμοθυμαδὸν τῇ προσευχῇ.

Similarly, after the summary in chapter v. 11-14 there is added a further summary about the healings in verses 15 and 16 : ὥστε καὶ εἰς τὰς πλατείας ἐκφέρειν τοὺς ἀσθενεῖς καὶ τιθέναι ἐπὶ κλιναρίων καὶ κραβάττων, ἵνα ἐρχομένου Πέτρου κἂν ἡ σκιὰ ἐπισκιάσει τινὶ αὐτῶν. συνήρχετο δὲ καὶ τὸ πλῆθος τῶν πέριξ πόλεων Ἰερουσαλήμ, φέροντες ἀσθενεῖς καὶ ὀχλου-μένους ὑπὸ πνευμάτων ἀκαθάρτων, οἵτινες ἐθεραπεύοντο ἅπαντες. With this should be compared viii. 6 and 7, προσεῖχον δὲ οἱ ὄχλοι τοῖς λεγομένοις ὑπὸ τοῦ Φιλίππου ὁμοθυμαδὸν ἐν τῷ ἀκούειν αὐτοὺς καὶ βλέπειν τὰ σημεῖα ἃ ἐποίει· πολλοὶ γὰρ τῶν ἐχόντων πνεύματα ἀκάθαρτα

[1] Compare L. Dieu in Revue Biblique, xxx. (1921) pp. 93 ff.

[2] Very plausible is the suggestion endorsed by Moffatt, Introduction to the Literature of the New Testament, p. 311, that some displacements have occurred in these passages. Better sequence would be secured if iv. 33 were placed after iv. 31, and v. 12a between v. 14 and v. 16. Perhaps these were scribal disloca-tions akin to the frequent early textual variants found in the transitional parts of the gospels (Schmidt, op. cit., passim). Still, it must be confessed that Luke like Paul may not always have presented his ideas in the most logical order. Typical of the extensive and varied speculation about sources and dislocation is the condensed footnote of Wendt on v. 14 in Meyer's Kommentar, 9th edition, 1913, p. 122. We may further note by way of parallelism between that verse and ii. 47 that each is followed by a reference to the carrying of persons, viz. iii. 2, the lame man at the Beautiful Gate, and v. 15, 16, the sick brought to be cured.

βοῶντα φωνῇ μεγάλῃ ἐξήρχοντο, πολλοὶ δὲ παραλελυμένοι καὶ χωλοὶ ἐθεραπεύθησαν, and xix. 11 and 12, δυνάμεις τε οὐ τὰς τυχούσας ὁ θεὸς ἐποίει διὰ τῶν χειρῶν Παύλου, ὥστε καὶ ἐπὶ τοὺς ἀσθενοῦντας ἀποφέρεσθαι ἀπὸ τοῦ χρωτὸς αὐτοῦ σουδάρια ἢ σιμικίνθια καὶ ἀπαλλάσσεσθαι ἀπ᾿ αὐτῶν τὰς νόσους, τά τε πνεύματα τὰ πονηρὰ ἐκπορεύεσθαι. These summaries of healings in some respects go beyond anything in the gospels ; the shadow of Peter is effective and Paul's body gives power to handkerchiefs. But they are influenced by the gospels—by Mark more than by Luke's version of it (cf. Mark i. 26 ; vi. 56 et al.).[1] It is probable that they are also influenced by the individual healings recorded in Acts. Thus the sick in v. 15 and 16 are called ἀσθενεῖς (cf. iv. 9), in viii. 7 παραλελυμένοι (cf. ix. 33) and χωλοί (cf. iii. 2).

It is possible that other generalizations are made on the basis of specific instances as in the case of these healings. A generalizing tendency is to be found also in the gospel of Luke (Style and Literary Method of Luke, pp. 115 ff.). Thus the summaries of generous if not communistic charity in Jerusalem discussed above (see Additional Note 12) may have been distilled by this author or his predecessor[2] out of cases like

Generalizing summaries.

---

[1] The vulgar κράβαττος of Mark, though eschewed in Luke (and Matthew), appears in Acts v. 15 and ix. 33 (perhaps it is avoided in ix. 34). For other examples of items in Mark omitted by Luke in his parallel but apparently used in Acts see notes on i. 7 and xii. 4. Indeed, the whole summary of Acts v. 15, 16 is closely parallel to Mark vi. 56, part of a section omitted by Luke. See note on Acts v. 15 f. The Marcan passage in turn probably illustrates the generalization from specific details. Mark vi. 56, according to Rawlinson ad loc., "appears to be a generalized description modelled on the episode " of the woman with the issue of blood. Probably the reference to the tassel in Mark vi. 56 (ἵνα κἂν τοῦ κρασπέδου τοῦ ἱματίου αὐτοῦ) occurred in Mark v. 27 or 28 as well as in Matt. ix. 20 and Luke viii. 44, ἥψατο τοῦ κρασπέδου τοῦ ἱματίου αὐτοῦ, and by haplography was omitted in Mark and by D and some Latin authorities in Luke. (A different explanation is offered in Streeter, The Four Gospels, p. 313.) Note the κἄν at Mark v. 28, vi. 56, Acts v. 15, but this usage is not employed again by either author.

[2] The probable source of these summaries is discussed at length by Kirsopp Lake on pp. 141 ff. The evidence of Aramaic origin for them is more than balanced by their Hellenistic traits, which include the formula in iv. 32 καρδία καὶ ψυχὴ μία, the proverbial πάντα κοινά, etc. iv. 34 οὐδὲ γὰρ ἐνδεής τις ἦν ἐν αὐτοῖς is at least as likely to be due to the LXX Deut. xv. 4 ὅτι οὐκ ἔσται ἐν σοὶ ἐνδεής as to a Semitic form of it. The ideas as well as the language depend perhaps upon Hellenic ideals going back ultimately to Plato and (the biographers of) Pythagoras. See beside M. Dibelius's article cited in the note on iv. 32, the note on ii. 44 in Wettstein, and especially H. von Schubert, ' Der Kommunismus der Wiedertäufer in Munster und seine Quellen' in Sitzungsberichte der Heidelberger Akademie der Wissenschaften, Philos.-histor. Klasse, x., 1919, pp. 33 ff. This Hellenistic influence, which deserves more attention for its historical as well as its verbal significance, is compatible with the view that to Luke himself rather than to his sources must be assigned the origin of these summaries.

those of Barnabas and of Ananias, though in their present form they ill
agree with them.[1]

Again, if we may adopt a reconstruction something like that of E.
Schwartz discussed in Vol. II. pp. 153 f., it is not impossible that the
references in Acts xi. 19, 20 to the preaching of Jerusalem Christians in
Cyprus and of Cypriote Christians in Antioch contain generalizations from
the career of that same Cypriote of Jerusalem, Barnabas of Acts iv. 36,
who preached in both places, though Acts (xi. 22-26, xiii. 4-12) now
(erroneously ?) attributes to him in both cases a later rôle and an association
in both places with Paul.[2]

Conclu-
sions.

The summaries in Acts cannot therefore be regarded as a limited series
of definite ' rubrics of progress.' De Zwaan has well shown how they
represent different classifications, and how they imperceptibly shade off
into other phrases indicating missionary successes. They vary from formal
pauses to mere casual participial constructions (e.g. vi. 1, xv. 41, xviii.
23). Between those which give definite new information and those which
give mere generalities no line can be drawn. Sometimes we doubtless have
both combined as at Acts vi. 7 with its unique reference to the conversion
of priests. " Accordingly, as in the Gospel, it seems inadvisable to regard
these phrases as keystones in Luke's edifice. The author undeniably cares
for a sort of rhythm in his narrative, and undoubtedly Acts is divided into
a series of ' panels,' but these latter are numerous, are not of equal length,
and do not include the whole contents of the book." [3]   In the first part of
the book they are limited to the Judean scene and to the church as a whole ;
later as the career of Paul is followed they acquire a more local and personal
character. Thus we hear of conversions in Thessalonica or Corinth, of the
spread of the word at the Syrian or the Pisidian Antioch, and of Paul's own
preaching of the Kingdom of God at Ephesus or in Rome.

Their position also is probably not uniform. Sometimes they are merely
the expanded conclusion of a definite incident. At other times they are
doubtless prefatory in their nature. A decision between these alternatives

[1] " Baur has observed that the single case of the field sold by Barnabas
(iv. 36) does not fit the general representations, ii. 45, iv. 32, 34, 35. They
appear to have been merely created out of that story and the legend of Ananias
and Sapphira and to be employed as filling between these stories and those of
the persecution of the apostles ; they contain, however, such extensive repetition
that without assuming radical editing no explanation is possible " (E. Schwartz,
' Zur Chronologie des Paulus,' *Nachrichten zu Göttingen*, 1907, p. 282, n. 1).
The summary, iv. 32-35, which describes the giving of all real estate by all the
Christians as the regular custom quite takes the original point out of the generous
act of Barnabas (iv. 36). By the generalization of the particular, the particular
loses its significance. So Dibelius and De Zwaan.

[2] Cf. Schwartz, *loc. cit.* p. 273, n. 1, " I cannot suppress the suspicion that
in the ἄνδρες Κύπριοι xi. 20 Barnabas himself lurks." We may add the conjecture that in the ἄνδρες Κυρηναῖοι of the same verse ' lurks ' a generalization
of Λούκιος ὁ Κυρηναῖος xiii. 1. See, however, the commentary on xi. 20
' Cypriotes and Cyrenians.'            [3] De Zwaan, *loc. cit.* p. 106.

is often difficult because the sentences under discussion are located in the interstices of the narrative. Except for purposes of punctuation and paragraphing a decision between final and initial classification is not necessary, though more often than most editors, I think, I would treat them as preparatory to the sequel.[1] Not only Luke vii. 21 suggests such treatment, but the μὲν οὖν found in viii. 4 and ix. 31 and xi. 19. xvi. 5 is an expression that ought to begin a new paragraph. The question becomes of particular interest in the case of the last sentence in the book.[2] It is usually treated as one of the panel-markers, but if it should be regarded as looking forward, the hypothesis of a third volume to Theophilus would receive additional support.[3]

Still other positions are possible for the summaries. It may be claimed that xvi. 5 is neither at the beginning nor at the end of a section but in the middle. In other cases general statements occur at some interval before or after the specific instance they deal with. Thus viii. 3 anticipates ix. 1 ff., while on the other hand xii. 25 concludes xi. 27-30.[4] In some cases what seem to be unexplained dislocations or repetitions, often attributed to combination of sources, might, if we knew the geography and chronology better, prove to be merely general editorial statements of the author somewhat carelessly placed out of context. Harnack speaks of it as "altogether characteristic of Luke's style of narrative that details of a story are here and there inserted later or again earlier than their proper place (compare also St. Luke's gospel)."[5] Of the numerous examples that he gives some are due to the rather illogical position of general statements in the Book of Acts. Other instances could no doubt be added.

How far the summaries came to our author along with his materials cannot now be determined. Whether thus derived or whether added by the final author, they give us tantalizing suggestions for determination of sources. They have been extensively used by the analysts, and naturally so. But at whatever stage they arose they are undoubtedly pieces of editorial workmanship, devised by the author or his predecessor for the creation of a continuous narrative out of the raw materials. "They serve a double purpose—to divide and to connect. They give continuity and historical perspective, but they are also of later vintage than the single

[1] Dibelius, loc. cit., shows how i. 13-14, ii. 43-47, iv. 32-35, v. 13, 14, vi. 7, ix. 31, xii. 24, prepare for the following sections.

[2] See de Zwaan, loc. cit. pp. 106 ff.; Harnack, Acts of the Apostles, chap. i. Appendix iii.

[3] See Vol. IV. p. 349 for this hypothesis.

[4] So at least it is usually understood in spite of the well-attested ὑπέστρεψαν εἰς Ἰερουσαλήμ. If we may suppose Luke was somewhat freer in his order of sentences, xii. 25 can be understood as a detached conclusion to xi. 21-26. The similar mission of inspection to Samaria in viii. 14-24 is immediately followed by the similar verse viii. 25 ὑπέστρεφον εἰς Ἰεροσόλυμα. If, on the other hand, πληρώσαντες in xii. 25 is to be taken as a participle of purpose (see note on xxv. 13), then this is the main statement of the mission to Jerusalem and xi. 30 is anticipatory. See note on xii. 25.

[5] Acts of the Apostles, pp. 226 f.

episodes. They are associated with the adjacent incidents which they generalize. They indicate that the material is typical, that the action was continued, that the effect was general. They fill in the lacunae. Like the first and last of the three colophons of John's gospel they suggest that there was plenty more material of the same kind. Simple deductions from collections of detail, they come into existence the moment those collections pass in the least degree out of the most amorphous stage, and they serve a useful literary purpose. Any modern life of Christ illustrates in later stages the incurable tendency to generalize from episodes." [1]

The historical value of the summaries is therefore open to question. The inherent difficulty of generalizing judgements and memories, the obviously late and derivative character of the descriptions distilled out of the specific scenes, the natural tendency to exaggerate the growth and influence of Christianity, and the editorial demands which made these summaries necessary—all these factors justify a reasonable doubt about their contents. On the other hand we are really not sure how much additional data Luke and his predecessors may have had beyond the specific items they have passed down to us. Certain items are mentioned with a definiteness and brevity that imply that his knowledge or his sources were more complete. In that case the summaries may rest on more information than we ourselves now have access to. They can be judged if at all only each for itself.

## Note XXXII. The Speeches in Acts

### By Henry J. Cadbury

Speeches in ancient literature.

1. Mention has been made elsewhere [2] of the custom prevalent in the ancient world of adorning historical works with imaginative speeches of the actors, and of the conformity of the book of Acts to this custom. The speeches of Acts are an extensive element in its composition—amounting to roughly one-fifth of the whole volume—and are one of its most striking features. The ordinary reader scarcely realizes what a difference they make to the book as a whole, relieving its somewhat monotonously narrative character. Jerome speaks of persons who neglected the Acts of the Apostles because it gave an impression of cold narrative—*nudam historiam*.[3] It is the speeches which relieve this impression, lending a variety to the contents and interpreting the narrative. Like the choral passages in the Greek drama they explain to the reader the meaning of the events. It is the speeches which specially interest the theologically inclined, as the majority of attentive readers of Acts have usually been. Even as a purely literary artifice they still accomplish what was no doubt an original purpose of this cherished custom—an effective dramatic result. Several of them are among

---

[1] *The Making of Luke-Acts*, pp. 58 f.
[2] Vol. II. pp. 13 f.          [3] Vol. II. p. 236.

the best known parts of the New Testament, and the skill, tact, or vigour of their language has created a strong impression. In brevity, variety, appropriateness and force they compare favourably with the similar productions of contemporary writers, such as the interminable harangues of Dionysius of Halicarnassus, or the ill-placed moralizings or vapid Biblical paraphrases of Josephus, or the monotonous monologues in the gospel of John.

2. The principal speeches may be listed as follows :      The principal speeches in Acts.

### Peter

(i.) Peter to the other disciples on the choice of a successor to Judas, i. 16-22 (18, 19 may be an editorial parenthesis).
(ii.) Peter to the multitude at Pentecost, ii. 14-36 (cf. 38, 39, 40b).
(iii.) Peter to the multitude at Solomon's Porch, iii. 12-26.
(iv.) Peter to the Sanhedrin, iv. 8-12 (cf. 19b, 20).
(v.) Peter and the Apostles to the Sanhedrin, v. 29b-32.
(vi.) Peter to Cornelius and others, x. 34-43 (cf. 47).
(vii.) Peter's report at Jerusalem, xi. 5-17.
(viii.) Peter's advice at the Council, xv. 7-11.

### James

(i.) James's advice at the Council, xv. 14-21.
(ii.) James and the elders' advice to Paul, xxi. 20-25.

### Stephen

(i.) The martyr's last defence, vii. 2-53 (cf. 56, 59b, 60b).

### Paul

(i.) Paul's address in the synagogue at Antioch of Pisidia, xiii. 16-41 (cf. 46 f.).
(ii.) Paul's address at Lystra, xiv. 15-17.
(iii.) Paul's address at Athens, xvii. 22-31.
(iv.) Paul's address to the Ephesian elders at Miletus, xx. 18-35.
(v.) Paul's defence on the barracks' stairs in Jerusalem, xxii. 1, 3-21.
(vi.) Paul's defence before the Sanhedrin, xxiii. 1, 6b.
(vii.) Paul's defence before Felix, xxiv. 10-21.
(viii.) Paul's defence before Agrippa, xxvi. 2-23 (cf. 25-27, 29).
(ix.) Paul's addresses to the Jews at Rome, xxviii. 17-20 and 25-28.

The longest addresses by non-Christians are :

(i.) The advice of Gamaliel to the Sanhedrin, v. 35-39.
(ii.) The address of the γραμματεύς at Ephesus, xix. 35-40.
(iii.) The accusation of Tertullus, xxiv. 2-8.
(iv.) Recapitulations of Paul's case by Festus to Agrippa, xxv. 14-21 and 24-27.

Mention may be made also of the prayers, e.g. at i. 24 f. and iv. 24-30, and of two letters—(a) that issued by the Council at Jerusalem, xv. 23-29, (b) the record of Paul's case sent by Claudius Lysias to accompany the prisoner to Felix, xxiii. 26-30.

Besides these the spoken parts in Acts include many dialogues such as those of Peter with Ananias and Sapphira, v. 1-11 ; Peter with Simon Magus, viii. 19-24 (cf. Paul to Bar-Jesus, xiii. 10 f.) ; Philip with the eunuch of Queen Candace, viii. 30-37 ; Peter with Cornelius or his messengers, x. 21-33 ; Paul and Silas with various groups in Philippi (xvi. 15, 17 f., 20 f., 28, 30 f., 36, 37) or Corinth (xviii. 6, 14 f.). There are also reported as in dialogue form not a few divine utterances in dreams or visions or by angels, as to Peter (x. 13-15, xii. 8), to Cornelius (x. 4-6), to Ananias (ix. 10, 11 f., 15 f.), and to Paul (ix. 5 f., xvi. 9, xviii. 9 f., xxii. 18-21, xxiii. 11, xxvii. 24).

It is unnecessary to make for the reader a complete listing of every spoken sentence in the book. But the easy shading from formal address to dialogue shows how naturally the author adopted in his own narrative the medium of direct discourse. A modern author would be more likely to avoid the appearance of direct quotation unless he was really able to quote.[1] The letters also, quite as much as the speeches, were in the ancient world more readily invented than actually supplied. They are therefore appropriately included in a discussion of the speeches, particularly in a discussion of the possibility of the fictitious origin of the speeches.

The value of the speeches.

3. Though each speech deserves and rewards independent study it is worth while to inquire collectively about them—and especially to ascertain as far as possible the probability of their origin. How far do they represent what was actually said on the occasion indicated ? Is there behind some or all of them some written or oral tradition which the author used ? May we leave unchallenged the natural assumption of a simple-minded modern reader that when Acts gives the words of Peter or Paul they are words really uttered by the apostles ? Or shall we concede to the ultimate author the occasion, the thoughts, and the words of every speech ?[2]

[1] There is evidence that ancient writers, who freely invent speeches, when by some chance an actual speech is preserved, do not quote it at all. Cf. Vol. II. p. 14. What seems to our modern tastes a like perversity is the fact that probably short speeches given in indirect form, as the familiar ones in Caesar's *Commentarii*, have far more claim to accuracy than those fuller and more life-like speeches in direct discourse with which finished ancient historians abounded. The latter are mere rhetorical exercises, while the former are rough notes of the actors or their contemporaries. Cf. H. St. J. Thackeray, *Josephus the Man and the Historian*, p. 42.

[2] On the speeches in Acts, aside from discussions of the separate speeches noted in commentaries, see the literature mentioned by J. Moffatt, *Introduction to the Literature of the N.T.* p. 284. A conservative view is urged by F. H. Chase, *The Credibility of the Acts of the Apostles*, 1902, *passim* ; A. T. Robertson, *Luke the Historian in the Light of Research*, 1920, chapter xvii., ' The Speeches in the Acts ' ; A. Wikenhauser, *Die Apostelgeschichte und ihr Geschichtswert*, 1921, pp. 146-156. The present writer has dealt with the subject in Vol. II. pp. 13 f. and in *The Making of Luke-Acts*, pp. 184 ff. See also W. Soltau, ' Die

(a) These questions do not permit a single sweeping and categorical answer.[1] Certainly it is only fair to inform the modern reader of the literary artifice prevalent in antiquity, and to warn him how widely the standard observed in speech-writing differed from our modern striving for original records to quote, for verbal accuracy, and for all the pomp of quotation marks and references. But, without more knowledge of the sources than is available to us in the case of Acts, it is impossible to know just how far this or any other ancient writer is writing his speeches ' out of his own head.' Perhaps a single writer is not always consistent. Josephus, for example, where we can confront his *Antiquities* with their Old Testament source, sometimes merely transforms into his own prosy platitudes the substance of the original passage, sometimes inserts in inappropriate scenes long diatribes of his own composing. In the more nearly contemporary parts of his histories he has also evidently invented speeches.[2] In composing their speeches the pagan historians probably rarely relied on any real knowledge of what was said, and this applies both to those who frankly accept this custom like Thucydides and to those who criticize its excesses like Polybius. Nevertheless even they prevent our assuming a general

*The custom of antiquity.*

---

Herkunft der Reden in der Apostelgeschichte' in *ZNTW.* iv., 1903, pp. 128-154. The speeches sometimes are dealt with collectively in the commentaries, e.g. Alford, *New Testament*, Prolegomena to Acts; Jacquier, *Les Actes des Apôtres*, 1926, pp. cclix-cclxxxvi, following his earlier treatment in his *Histoire des livres du N.T.* iii. 159 ff., and in *Revue Biblique*, xii., 1915, pp. 161 ff. Groups of speeches are discussed in articles, etc., e.g. (i.) the speeches of Peter, M. Kähler in *Theol. Studien und Kritiken*, xlvi., 1873, pp. 492-536; P. de Ambroggi, *Scuol. Catt.* series 6, vol. xi., 1928, pp. 81 ff., 161 ff., 243 ff.; (ii.) the speeches of Paul, Fr. Bethge, *Die Paulinischen Reden der Apostelgeschichte*, Göttingen, 1887; R. Knowling, *The Testimony of St. Paul to Christ*, 1905, Index, s.v. 'Acts, Addresses.' Quite especially to be recommended for English readers is the essay by P. Gardner, ' Speeches of St. Paul in Acts,' in *Cambridge Biblical Essays*, 1909, pp. 379-419 ; (iii.) the speeches addressed to Gentiles in Acts xiv. and xvii., H. Gebhardt in *ZNTW.* vi., 1905, pp. 236 ff. Most voluminous is the bibliography on individual speeches. See the German items on Stephen's speech prior to 1913 listed by Wendt's *Kommentar*, p. 137 (cf. *Theol. Studien und Kritiken*, lxxiii., 1900, p. 541, note), to which may be added W. Mundle, *ZNTW.* xx., 1921, pp. 133 ff., and the discussion by E. Meyer in his *Ursprung und Anfänge des Christentums*, iii., 1923, pp. 158 ff. The most important discussion in English is by B. W. Bacon in *Biblical and Semitic Studies* (by members of the Semitic and Biblical Faculty of Yale University), 1902, pp. 213-276. Paul's speech at Athens (besides earlier discussions) was subjected to the study of a great variety of scholars by the appearance in 1913 of Norden's stimulating book entitled *Agnostos Theos*.

[1] Chase, *op. cit.* p. 108, admits : '' How far this editing penetrated into the fabric of the discourses is a question to which no certain and uniform answer can be given,'' but on p. 295 he declares : '' It is a moral impossibility for them to have been conceived and composed by him [Luke].''

[2] See now H. St. J. Thackeray, *Josephus the Man and the Historian*, pp. 41-45.

rule of pure invention by the occasional instances where the substance of a reported speech is confirmed by some independent evidence. While the Christian writer need not be expected to differ from contemporary habits in these matters merely because he was a Christian, he may at least be allowed such benefit of doubt as we would grant to Dio Cassius or Tacitus. The presumption, however, is strong that his speeches are generally without basis of definite information—even when the accompanying narrative seems thoroughly reliable.

The general nature of the speeches in Acts.

(b) When we turn from general presumptions to the actual speeches in Acts it is difficult to reach any more certain conclusion. There are, however, some considerations bearing on the probable historicity of the speeches that at least deserve to be mentioned. The occasions of the speeches do not seem to suggest any immediate written record. There is no reason to suppose that notes were taken either in short-hand or in long-hand when the speeches were being delivered. Even those given before Jewish or Roman tribunals were scarcely taken down in writing. While the Egyptian papyri indicate a widespread ability to read and write and the extensive use of written records in matters of civil law, they make no suggestion that the proceedings of original courts were taken down in full. Even the early Christian forgers of apologetic *Acta* did not invent and insert long speeches of the defendants or martyrs.

There remains, however, the possibility that the words uttered by the apostles were orally transmitted by the hearers or repeated by the speakers themselves in subsequent narration of the event. In either case the probability is against any extensive verbal agreement of the ultimate record with the original.[1] Memory must have considerably condensed the actual

---

[1] The speeches having once become famous, men naturally prefer to accept them as authentic utterances of the actors. The funeral oration of Pericles (Thucydides ii. 35-46) is so regarded in spite of Thucydides' explicit warning about his practice (i. 22), and its omission of thoughts attributed to such an ἐπιτάφιος by Aristotle, *Rhet.* i. 7, and others. (On the speeches of Thucydides see R. C. Jebb, *Essays and Addresses*, pp. 359 ff. Like the speeches in Acts they each raise the question: was the historian himself present ? See G. B. Grundy, *Thucydides and the History of his Age*, 1911, especially pp. 19 ff.) The classicists are among the most inclined to plead for the historicity of the scene of Paul at Athens. See E. Curtius, *Expositor*, Nov. 1907, p. 455 ( = *Sitzungsberichte* of the Berlin Academy, 1893, p. 938): "Whoever disputes the historical value of the account of St. Paul in Athens tears one of the most important pages from the history of the human race." Cf. Blass, *Acta apostolorum*, 1895, pp. x, 191. Ed. Meyer, *op. cit.* iii. p. 105, says: "Wie man diese Scene für erfunden hat erklären können, gehört zu den Dingen, die mir immer unverständlich geblieben sind."

So in more modern times the farewell words of John Robinson to the Pilgrims sailing for America are quoted as authentic though derived from Winslow's *Brief Narration* published in 1646, and reprinted in A. Young's *Chronicles of the Pilgrim Fathers*, 1841. Winslow's *Narration* only claims to represent the substance of what was said, and modern historians doubt its value except as giving the most general impression of any actual speech.

utterance, and, indeed, the speeches that we have are all relatively brief
and succinct and capable of explanation as summaries of longer addresses.
But the same summary character of the speeches in Acts (perhaps one
should describe them as illustrative excerpts rather than summaries) is
equally attributable to the manner of composition by a historian with a
dramatic imagination.

(c) One thing at least cannot be denied the ultimate author of Acts, 'Lucan'
whom out of convenience if not out of conviction we may call Luke, and style.
that is the language and style in which the speeches are written. The
evidence for this agreement in style need hardly be presented here, as it is
obvious to any attentive reader of the Greek text of the Lucan writings,
and can be presented to others only by those tedious and rather misleading
methods of indicating identity of style which usually rouse suspicion by
their necessarily mechanical manner. Even those persons who incline to
consider the speeches in Acts close approximations to addresses actually
given by Peter, Stephen, and Paul, will probably admit that the voice is the
voice of Luke.

(d) Besides the characteristics which the speeches share with the Peculi-
vocabulary of Luke and Acts, they share with each other some elements of arities com-
likeness that go beyond mere style and vocabulary into the subject matter speeches.
itself. This again argues their common origin in the mind of the editor.

(i.) Like other quoters of Scripture he has his favourite quotations. The
same proof texts appear in the mouths of the several speakers, e.g. Acts ii.
27 (Peter) = xiii. 35 (Paul); iii. 22 (Peter) = vii. 37 (Stephen) [1]; iv. 24
(the disciples) = xiv. 15 (Paul). Cf. Acts xiii. 33 = Luke iii. 22 (Western
text); Acts ii. 34 = Luke xx. 42 f. (from Mark); Acts xxviii. 26 f. = Luke
viii. 10 (from Mark); Luke iv. 18 = Luke vii. 22 (from Q).[2] Common
expressions occur in different addresses (e.g. Acts xxvii. 34 οὐδενὸς γὰρ
ὑμῶν θρὶξ ἀπὸ τῆς κεφαλῆς ἀπολεῖται = Luke xxi. 18 καὶ θρὶξ ἐκ τῆς
κεφαλῆς ὑμῶν οὐ μὴ ἀπόληται; Acts vii. 48 οὐχ ὁ ὕψιστος ἐν χειροποιήτοις κατοικεῖ = xvii. 24 οὐκ ἐν χειροποιήτοις ναοῖς κατοικεῖ.

Even more impressive is the way in which one passage in Acts explains Inter-
the line of argument which the very terseness of a speech elsewhere makes exegesis of
obscure through omission. Thus in both the passages where "Thou shalt O.T. texts.
not suffer thy holy one to see corruption " is quoted, the death and burial
of David is emphasized (Acts ii. 29, xiii. 36). But the reason for the
emphasis is not explained on the surface. The underlying style of

---

[1] Even when the same proof text is not repeated it is apparently in the
writer's mind. Acts xiii. 47 quotes Isaiah xlix. 6; Acts xxvi. 17 f. uses its
parallel Isaiah xlii. 6 f.; Acts xvii. 24 f. is reminiscent of the preceding verse,
Isaiah xlii. 5. See Vol. II. pp. 92, 96, 100; but the whole LXX passages should
be examined. So the phrase ' both Lord and Christ ' in Acts ii. 36 is probably
reminiscent of Ps. ii. 2 quoted in iv. 26. See Vol. IV. pp. 25 f. At v. 30 and x. 39,
where the same phrase of Deut. xxi. 22 f. is used, the speaker is in both cases
Peter.

[2] E. Norden, *Agnostos Theos*, pp. 6 ff., points out the likeness between the
speeches, which he thinks shows how small was the conventional stock of
materials used in missionary preaching.

argument is, however, precisely that of the Ethiopian's question in viii. 34,
" Concerning whom does the prophet say this ?  concerning himself ?  or
someone else ? "  David being the author of the psalms, the escape from
corruption must be the fate of either David or of another.  Since David
" died and was buried and his tomb is with us to this day," " fell asleep,
and was added to his fathers and saw corruption," David's words in the
psalm refer not to himself, but to another, viz. Christ.

The logical steps may be listed thus :

A. Scripture says thus and so.
B. This must apply either to the speaker or to another.[1]
C. It can be proved not to apply to the speaker.
D. Therefore since it was fulfilled in Jesus, it may be applied to him.

Nowhere in Acts are all four steps given in a single passage, but the scheme
is clear.  That the author of Acts gives in one passage steps which he omits
in another confirms our impression that the scheme belongs to him.  Doubtless Jewish exegesis followed similar lines.  Passages which did not fit the
author were without further ado appropriated by the rabbis to the Messiah.
(Cf. Mark xii. 35 ff. and parallels for a more complicated problem.)

The following passages illustrate the different methods in Acts :

ii. 25-32 include A, C, D.  B is not explicitly stated.  C, on the contrary,
is emphasized in 29, " the patriarch David . . . is both dead and buried
and his tomb is among us until this day," and so in xiii. 36 (see note).[2]

viii. 30-35 includes A and B, while C and D are at most implied in the
briefly described episode.  B is most explicitly stated in 34, " About whom
is the prophet saying this ?  about himself ?  or about another ? "

At ii. 33 f. one may suspect that the proof texts (A) have been in part
deferred, e.g. Ps. cx. 1, and in part omitted.  ii. 34, " For David did not
ascend into the heavens," seems like a typical expression of C.  But Ps.
cx. 1 is perhaps not sufficient to account for the whole of the expression
τῇ δεξιᾷ οὖν τοῦ θεοῦ ὑψωθεὶς τήν τε ἐπαγγελίαν τοῦ πνεύματος τοῦ
ἁγίου λαβὼν παρὰ τοῦ πατρὸς ἐξέχεεν τοῦτο ὃ ὑμεῖς βλέπετε καὶ ἀκούετε.
οὐ γὰρ Δαυεὶδ ἀνέβη εἰς τοὺς οὐρανούς. The important part of the
quotation Ps. cx. 1 is κάθου ἐκ δεξιῶν μου parallel to τῇ δεξιᾷ τοῦ θεοῦ.
But it has been suggested, e.g. by Chase, The Credibility of Acts, p. 151,
that the author had in mind some words of a psalm that spoke more

[1] Another way of stating B is to say : " This scripture applies either to the
speaker's own time or to another era."  It is this contrast which is implied, I
think, in xiii. 36 ἰδίᾳ γενεᾷ (see note, possibly also γενεάν in viii. 33), in xiii. 33
σήμερον, in Luke iv. 21 σήμερον, and elsewhere.

[2] The extant tomb as disproof of immortality (and divinity) for personages of
the past was a type of argument that may have been already familiar to some
Gentile readers of Acts.  It was a scandal to pious worshippers of Zeus that the
Cretans claimed to be able to show sightseers his tomb.  It was this which led
to the words of Epimenides quoted in part in Titus i. 12 and in part in Acts
xvii. 28a (see pp. 249 ff.).  Cicero declared he would not worship Julius Caesar
because his tomb exists (Philippic i. 13).  The absence of any tomb for Moses
(Deut. xxxiv. 6) favoured the growth of traditions more than mortal about him.

definitely of ascension or exaltation, presumably Ps. lxviii. 19 with its
words ἀναβὰς εἰς ὕψος . . . ἔλαβες δόματα. (The ἐξέχεε is due to Joel iii.
1 f. quoted in verses 17 f. For the later καὶ κύριον καὶ Χριστόν see note 1,
p. 407.) Only by supplying the missing step B do the adverbs γάρ (here
and in xiii. 37) and οὖν (in ii. 30) have meaning.

That not all the Scriptures implied are quoted in Acts is clear from
xiii. 15 where the reading of law and prophets is mentioned, but the lections
are not specified. On the basis of the words ἐτροποφόρησεν (18) and
ὕψωσεν (17) they have been conjectured to have included Deuteronomy i.
and Isaiah i., while the pronoun in τοῦ λαοῦ τούτου Ἰσραήλ is perhaps a
further allusion to the unquoted lections.

(ii.) In a similar way Acts xiv. 15 ff. and xvii. 22 ff., the two addresses The
to Gentiles, supplement each other. The latter as it stands is syncopated. to the
Beginning with the inscription 'To the Unknown God' the author turns Gentiles.
to God's provision for man's welfare. What is the connexion? Norden,
like earlier commentators, recognized this difficulty, but said that the lost
step in the argument is to be supplied by the common Stoic thesis : " God
himself is invisible, but we recognize him from his works." [1] But, as in the
case of the link missing in the arguments from Scripture, so here the clue
may be found in other speeches in Acts itself. The speech at Lystra is a
close parallel to that at Athens. The god whom Paul and Barnabas came
to proclaim " in past generations allowed all nations to go their own ways,"
that is, he was to them an unknown god as he was to the Athenians.
" And yet," the speech continues, " he did not leave himself without
witness, in that he did good, sending you rains from heaven and fruitful
seasons, filling your hearts with food and gladness." The unknown God,
then, is evidenced by his good works.[2] He is " unknown, and yet well
known." Thus the short address at Lystra supplies—in the Lucan litotes
οὐκ ἀμάρτυρον—the connecting link that was missed in the Athenian
speech, while its own purpose and thought is in turn illuminated by the
fuller contents of the latter. The general parallelism of the two speeches
becomes more evident than ever.

(iii.) The speech of Stephen comes to an abrupt end, possibly for quite The speech
intentional reasons on the author's part, but passages in other speeches of of Stephen.
Acts fill the lacuna in such a way as to indicate common authorship. W.
Soltau actually argued that these other speeches were derived from one
originally fuller speech. To be sure, no Christian reader can fail to think
of the parallels between Moses' rejection and that of Jesus. Perhaps we
may be expected to see for ourselves that the promise, the law, and the
temple of the Old Testament are only types of Christianity. The speech
of Stephen, however, barely reaches the Christian application in vii. 52.

---

[1] *Agnostos Theos*, p. 24; cf. p. 29.

[2] Norden calls this Stoic. No doubt the Stoics held that God is knowable
from his works, cf. Rom. i. 19 f. But the authors of Acts and of Wisdom of
Solomon give the motif a characteristically (Jewish ?) moral tone by their argument from the *goodness* of his deeds. With ἀγαθουργῶν of Acts xiv. 17 cf. Wisd.
xiii. 1 ἐκ τῶν ὁρωμένων ἀγαθῶν οὐκ ἴσχυσαν εἰδέναι τὸν ὄντα and parts of Job.

The transition from Abraham, Moses, or David is not actually made. But the promise to Abraham occurs in iii. 25, to Moses in iii. 22, quoting the same scripture as at vii. 37, to David at ii. 25-35, xiii. 32-37, and to the prophets at iii. 18, xiii. 27, cf. vii. 52, and in each case the application to Jesus is made plain. The rejection of Jesus (like that of Moses vii. 24-28, 40) is explicitly mentioned at iii. 13-15, and God's overruling establishment of him, τοῦτον ὁ θεὸς ἀρχηγὸν καὶ σωτῆρα ὕψωσεν, at Acts v. 31 (as of Moses vii. 35 τοῦτον ὁ θεὸς καὶ ἄρχοντα καὶ λυτρωτὴν ἀπέσταλκεν).

The speeches in Acts, and the Epistles.

4. (a) In opposition to the evidence for a single mind behind the speeches, it has been usual for apologetic critics to find evidence in the speeches which connects them with the thought and even with the manner of speech of Peter and Paul. There is enough likeness between Paul's speeches, especially that at Miletus, and his authentic epistles to lend colour to this argument, if it be supposed that Pauline language could not be shared or even definitely imitated by Luke, but could come to the historian only through the tradition of Paul's reported speeches. But the Pauline idiom is not unlike the natural idiom of Luke,[1] and elsewhere than in Paul's own speeches (e.g. in the account of the Last Supper) coincidences in language between the two writers are to be found. Some have claimed that the Pauline phrases are used in a sense which shows that the author misunderstands them, or that they are only superficial imitations. Probably the language of Paul's speeches in Acts cannot be pressed against either their actual derivation from him or their free composition by one who knew him, but neither can it be used to prove that the records in Acts still echo his spoken words.

Between Peter's speeches and the epistle or epistles attributed to him there is a similar likeness, but scarcely striking, and the argument is weaker on account of the inferior claim for authenticity which can be made for the epistles of Peter. We may also compare the epistle of James with passages in Acts assigned to him. This method of argument clearly overreaches itself when the second epistle of Peter is used, or when in the reverse direction the similarity of the language of Peter's speeches in Acts is used as an argument for the genuineness of 2 Peter.

The kind of coincidence between the speeches in Acts and the epistles attributed to the same person may be illustrated by the following examples:

## The Speeches of Peter

Peter.

i. 17 ἔλαχεν τὸν κλῆρον τῆς διακονίας ταύτης. 2 Peter i. 1 τοῖς ἰσότιμον ἡμῖν λαχοῦσιν πίστιν. The verb occurs only twice again in the New Testament.

i. 18 ἐκ μισθοῦ τῆς ἀδικίας. 2 Peter ii. 15 μισθὸν ἀδικίας ἠγάπησεν.

ii. 23 προγνώσει τοῦ θεοῦ. 1 Peter i. 2 κατὰ πρόγνωσιν θεοῦ πατρός (cf. i. 20). The noun does not occur again in the New Testament.

iii. 6 ἀργύριον καὶ χρυσίον οὐχ ὑπάρχει μοι. 1 Peter i. 18 οὐ φθαρτοῖς ἀργυρίῳ ἢ χρυσίῳ ἐλυτρώθητε.

---

[1] Hawkins, *Horae Synopticae*, 2nd edit., pp. 189 ff.

iii. 16 ἡ πίστις ἡ δι᾽ αὐτοῦ. 1 Peter i. 21 δι᾽ ὑμᾶς τοὺς δι᾽ αὐτοῦ πιστοὺς εἰς θεόν.[1]

iii. 19 μετανοήσατε οὖν καὶ ἐπιστρέψατε . . . ὅπως ἂν ἔλθωσιν καιροὶ ἀναψύξεως κτλ. 2 Peter iii. 11 ff. ἐν ἁγίαις ἀναστροφαῖς καὶ εὐσεβείαις, προσδοκῶντας καὶ σπεύδοντας τὴν παρουσίαν τῆς τοῦ θεοῦ ἡμέρας. In both passages seems to be the idea that the day of the Lord can be hastened.

v. 30, x. 39 ξύλον of the cross. So 1 Peter ii. 24. But so also Paul in Acts xiii. 29 and Gal. iii. 13 (quoting Deut. xxi. 23).

x. 28, 1 Peter iv. 3 ἀθέμιτος. Not again in the New Testament.

x. 34 οὐκ ἔστιν προσωπολήμπτης ὁ θεός. 1 Peter i. 17 τὸν ἀπροσωπολήπτως κρίνοντα.

x. 42 κριτὴς ζώντων καὶ νεκρῶν. 1 Peter iv. 5 κρίνοντι ζῶντας καὶ νεκρούς. Similarly 2 Tim. iv. 1, and other early Christian writings. See references on p. 122 of Vol. IV.

xv. 11 διὰ τῆς χάριτος τοῦ κυρίου Ἰησοῦ πιστεύομεν σωθῆναι. Parallels to this usage are said to be in 1 Peter's instances of χάρις.[2]

### The Speeches of James (and the Apostolic Decree)

xv. 13. ἄνδρες ἀδελφοί ἀκούσατέ μου. James ii. 5 ἀκούσατε ἀδελφοί James. μου ἀγαπητοί.

xv. 14 ὁ θεὸς ἐπεσκέψατο λαβεῖν ἐξ ἐθνῶν λαόν. James i. 27 ἐπισκέπτεσθαι ὀρφανοὺς καὶ χήρας.

xv. 17 ἐφ᾽ οὓς ἐπικέκληται τὸ ὄνομά μου ἐπ᾽ αὐτούς, James ii. 7 τὸ καλὸν ὄνομα τὸ ἐπικληθὲν ἐφ᾽ ὑμᾶς.

xv. 23, James i. 1 χαίρειν at the beginning of a letter. Not again in the New Testament except the letter of Claudius Lysias at Acts xxiii. 26. Hence Bleek could say that the phrase, which really is a common epistolary formula, occurred among apostolic letters only in these two.

### Speeches of Paul

xiii. 21 Σαοὺλ υἱὸν Κείς, ἄνδρα ἐκ φυλῆς Βενιαμίν. This allusion is Paul. particularly appropriate in the mouth of one who was himself a Benjamite (Rom. xi. 1, Phil. iii. 5) named Saul.

xiii. 34 f. associates two Old Testament quotations because they have the same catchword (ὅσιον, -α). This is characteristic also of Paul's letters.[3]

xiii. 39 ἀπὸ πάντων ὧν οὐκ ἠδυνήθητε ἐν τῷ νόμῳ Μωυσέως δικαιωθῆναι, ἐν τούτῳ πᾶς ὁ πιστεύων δικαιοῦται. It is unnecessary to quote passages in Paul's letters where justification by faith in contrast with the law is spoken of. There is, at least superficially, a striking Paulinism here. See note ad loc.

xiii. 41 quotes Hab. i. 5. Hab. ii. 4 is one of Paul's favourite texts (Rom. i. 17, Gal. iii. 11).[4]

---

[1] F. H. Chase, op. cit. p. 121, regards this coincidence, πίστις (-ος) διά, as 'remarkable.'

[2] Jacquier, Les Actes des Apôtres, ad loc.

[3] Cf. Chase, op. cit. pp. 180 f.      [4] Ibid. p. 194.

xiv. 15-17 and xvii. 22-31 show affinity with the Wisdom of Solomon, both in general argument and in wording (see note on xvii. 29). Romans i. 18 ff. also shows affinity with the Wisdom of Solomon and to some extent with these speeches. (See notes on xiv. 16 and xvii. 30.)

Another line of similarity between these speeches and Paul is shown by 1 Thess. i. 9 f. (see Vol. IV. p. 166).

xiv. 15 θεὸν ζῶντα. Rom. ix. 26 (from LXX), 2 Cor. vi. 16, 1 Thess. i. 9, 1 Tim. iii. 15, iv. 10; also Heb. iii. 12, ix. 14, x. 31, 1 Peter i. 23 (?), etc.

xvii. 28 ἐν [1] αὐτῷ γὰρ ζῶμεν καὶ κινούμεθα καὶ ἐσμέν. This is now believed to be a quotation from the poet Epimenides. See Additional Note 20. But the quotation from a certain prophet in Titus i. 12 Κρῆτες ἀεὶ ψεῦσται, κακὰ θηρία, γαστέρες ἀργαί is from the same author, probably from the same poem, and perhaps from the same quatrain.

xvii. 31, Rom. i. 4 ὁρίζω of Jesus as ordained by God. So also Acts x. 42 (Peter).

xx. 18-35. This speech shows the nearest approximation to Pauline language. Those who maintain the genuineness of the speech and the accuracy of its wording explain this as due to the fact that like Paul's letters this is a pastoral rather than a missionary speech like the earlier ones in Acts.[2] The resemblance in language to the Pastoral Epistles is particularly close.[3] Those who deny the authenticity of the speech will scarcely explain the verbal likeness as due to imitation.[4] It is doubtful whether the author of Acts had any real acquaintance with Paul's letters, least of all with the Pastorals. A general knowledge of Paul's style and the similarity of subject matter would account for some of the likeness. It is not like Paul's letters to quote a saying of Jesus as in xx. 35.[5] The references to Paul's departure and the prediction of false teachers sound exactly like pseudonymous farewells, such as those in the Pastorals, Jude, and 2 Peter.[6]

The Pauline expressions include [7] :

---

[1] The ἐν cannot any longer be regarded as remarkably close to the mystical ἐν of Paul's formula ἐν χριστῷ.

[2] It may also be noted that this speech has the best claim to be included in the memoirs of the eyewitness, since ' we ' passages very nearly envelop it.

[3] See W. Lock, *The Pastoral Epistles*, p. xxv.

[4] But see Schulze's article mentioned below, note 7.

[5] Mention of repentance (xx. 21) is noticeably infrequent in Paul's letters. Acts xxvi. 20 again puts the word (both noun and verb) on Paul's lips.

[6] Not to mention apocalyptic passages in *Test. XII. Patr.*, *Ascension of Isaiah*, iii. 23-31, etc. To predict the coming of false teachers is a favourite kind of *vaticinium ex eventu*. Instances in early Christian pseudonymous writings include *Didache* xvi. 3, *Epistola Apostolorum* 50.

[7] Cf. Blass, *Acta apostolorum*, Editio philologica, 1895, p. x (following Lekebusch). Also H. Schulze, *Theol. Studien und Kritiken*, lxxiii., 1900, pp. 119-125, where the basis for the farewell speech at Miletus is represented as being 1 Thess., and a large number of parallels are given.

19 δουλεύων τῷ κυρίῳ.

19 μετὰ πάσης ταπεινοφροσύνης. So Eph. iv. 2.

21 Ἰουδαίοις τε καὶ Ἕλλησι.

21 πίστιν εἰς τὸν κύριον ἡμῶν Ἰησοῦν [Χριστόν].

22 f. For the suspense of Paul's approaching journey to Jerusalem see Rom. xv. 30 ff. See Vol. IV. p. 229.

24 ὡς τελειῶσαι τὸν δρόμον μου. Cf. 2 Tim. iv. 7 τὸν δρόμον τετέλεκα.

24 ὡς τελειῶσαι . . . τὴν διακονίαν. Cf. 2 Tim. iv. 5 τὴν διακονίαν σου πληροφόρησον; Col. iv. 17 τὴν διακονίαν . . . πληροῖς.

24 τὴν διακονίαν ἣν ἔλαβον παρὰ τοῦ κυρίου Ἰησοῦ. Cf. Col. iv. 17 τὴν διακονίαν ἣν παρέλαβες ἐν κυρίῳ.

24, 32 χάρις of God.

28 τὴν ἐκκλησίαν τοῦ θεοῦ.[1]

31 γρηγορεῖτε.

31 νουθετῶν.

32 οἰκοδομῆσαι.

32 κληρονομίαν ἐν τοῖς ἡγιασμένοις.[2] Cf. Acts xxvi. 18 κλῆρον ἐν τοῖς ἡγιασμένοις, Col. i. 12 τοῦ κλήρου τῶν ἁγίων.

34 f. αἱ χεῖρες . . . οὕτω κοπιῶντας. Cf. 1 Cor. iv. 12 κοπιῶμεν ἐργαζόμενοι ταῖς ἰδίαις χερσιν,[3] Eph. iv. 28 κοπιάτω ἐργαζόμενος ταῖς χερσίν.

The remaining words of Paul in Acts, mostly his speeches of defence, offer little parallel to the letters. The following examples, though the best, are scarcely very significant:

xxi. 13 ἑτοίμως ἔχω.　2 Cor. xii. 14 (1 Peter iv. 5 v.l.).

xxi. 13 ὑπὲρ τοῦ ὀνόματος.　Rom. i. 5; also in Acts v. 41, ix. 16, xv. 26.

xxiii. 6 ἐγὼ Φαρισαῖός εἰμι, υἱὸς Φαρισαίων. Cf. Phil. iii. 5 κατὰ νόμον Φαρισαῖος.

xxiv. 16, 1 Cor. x. 32, Phil. i. 10 ἀπρόσκοπος. Not again in the New Testament.

The value of these coincidences is due to the fact that in each case the speaker in Acts is identical with the author to whom the epistles quoted are traditionally assigned. Apologists for the speeches in Acts call attention to these resemblances and use them to confirm both the verbal accuracy of the speeches and the traditions of authorship for the letters, even such doubtful ones as the Pastorals and the Catholic Epistles.

There is, however, a form of confutation which so far as I am aware is overlooked even by less conservative scholars. What shall we say if an equally good array of coincidences can be made between the same speeches and the epistles attributed to other writers ? If the speeches of Peter and Stephen are as full of echoes of the letters of Paul and James, are not the agreements between the speeches of Peter and the letters of Peter, etc., to be explained otherwise than as ultimately derived from the same mind ? *Similarities in other epistles cancel these arguments.*

[1] The variant τοῦ κυρίου would be less like Paul.

[2] Probably due to Deut. xxxiii. 3 f.

[3] It is an interesting coincidence that 1 Cor. was probably written at Ephesus. Cf. Paley, *Horae Paulinae*, ch. iii. No. vi.

It is not necessary to accept or to reject the doubtful traditions of author-ship for the Pastorals, 2 Peter or James, to feel that such unobserved coinci-dences across lines of common alleged origin cancel the arguments where the writer and speaker quoted respectively are by attribution the same. The following partial collection of examples will illustrate the point. Other cases have already been included in the preceding list.[1]

### Speeches of Peter

**Peter.**

ii. 22 δυνάμεσι καὶ τέρασι καὶ σημείοις. Cf. Hebr. ii. 4 σημείοις τε καὶ τέρασι καὶ ποικίλαις δυνάμεσι.

ii. 39 τοῖς εἰς μακράν. Apparently of the Gentiles, as at Ephesians ii. 13, 17.

ii. 40 γενεὰ σκολιά. So Phil. ii. 15.

iii. 15 τὸν ἀρχηγὸν τῆς ζωῆς, v. 31 ἀρχηγὸν καὶ σωτῆρα. Cf. Hebr. ii. 10 τὸν ἀρχηγὸν τῆς σωτηρίας.

iii. 25 quotes Genesis xxii. 18. The almost identical passage, Genesis xii. 3, is quoted in Gal. iii. 8.

iv. 11 quotes Psalm cxviii. 22. The same passage in slightly different wording is quoted by Jesus in Mark xii. 10 = Luke xx. 17 = Matt. xxi. 42.

iv. 28 (the prayer of the early disciples) προορίζω. The same verb in Paul's letters five times.

viii. 21 μερὶς οὐδὲ κλῆρος. Cf. Col. i. 12 τὴν μερίδα τοῦ κλήρου.

x. 35 ἐργαζόμενος δικαιοσύνην. Cf. Hebr. xi. 33.

x. 36 εὐαγγελιζόμενος εἰρήνην. Cf. Eph. ii. 17.

x. 38 καταδυναστεύω. James ii. 6. Not elsewhere in the New Testament.[2]

xv. 11 διὰ τῆς χάριτος τοῦ κυρίου Ἰησοῦ πιστεύομεν σωθῆναι καθ' ὃν τρόπον κἀκεῖνοι. Salvation by faith through grace for both Jew and Gentile sounds Pauline enough superficially, like Acts xiii. 39 (Paul).

### Stephen's Speech

**Stephen.**

vii. 24 καταπονέω. 2 Peter ii. 7, but not again in the Greek Bible.

vii. 38 λόγια ζῶντα. Cf. Hebr. iv. 12.

vii. 53 τὸν νόμον εἰς διαταγὰς ἀγγέλων. Gal. iii. 19 νόμος . . . διαταγεὶς δι' ἀγγέλων.

### Speeches of James

**James.**

xv. 10 ζύγος of the law. Cf. Gal. v. 1.

xxi. 21 περιπατεῖν in figurative (ethical) sense. So in the epistles of Paul and John.

xxi. 24 φυλάσσω of the law. Cf. Rom. ii. 26, Gal. vi. 13.

[1] With a good reference apparatus, like that, for example, in Alford's *New Testament*, the reader may compile his own lists.

[2] Other affinities of this speech with the Epistle of James are noted by Alford, *ad loc.* μηδὲν διακρινόμενος occurs in this speech and in James i. 6. In Acts xi. 12 and xv. 9 the active of the verb is used. The cognates to προσωπολήπτης x. 34 occur in James ii. 1 and 9 and in Paul.

*Speeches of Paul*

xiii. 17 παροικία. 1 Peter i. 17 only.                                        Paul.

xiii. 10 παντὸς δόλου καὶ πάσης ῥᾳδιουργίας. Cf. 1 Peter ii. 1 πᾶσαν κακίαν καὶ πάντα δόλον.

xiii. 33 quotes Psalm ii. 7, as does Hebr. i. 5, v. 5, and (in Western MSS.) Luke iii. 22.

xviii. 21 τοῦ θεοῦ θέλοντος. Cf. James iv. 15 and Vol. IV. p. 231.

xx. 28 τῷ ποιμνίῳ . . . ἐπισκόπους, ποιμαίνειν τὴν ἐκκλησίαν. Cf. 1 Peter ii. 25 πρόβατα . . . ἐπὶ τὸν ποιμένα καὶ ἐπίσκοπον τῶν ψυχῶν ὑμῶν, v. 2 ποιμάνατε τὸ ἐν ὑμῖν ποίμνιον τοῦ θεοῦ [ἐπισκοποῦντες], κτλ.

This use of the pastoral figure in the speech at Miletus is the most notorious likeness to 1 Peter. It has been noted by commentators from Ephrem Syrus [1] to the most modern times.[2] The same epistle shows other connexions besides those already noted. It is true that οἴκεται (1 Peter ii. 18) occurs in a Petrine narrative at Acts x. 7.[3] But in the Pauline narrative xvi. 5 ἐστερεοῦντο τῇ πίστει reminds us of 1 Peter v. 9 στερεοὶ τῇ πίστει. The phrase 'good conscience' is employed in Acts xxiii. 1 (Paul) and 1 Peter iii. 16, 21, as well as in 1 Tim. i. 5, 19. The passage which was under discussion between Philip and the eunuch, Isaiah liii., in spite of exaggerated claims for its influence elsewhere,[4] really shows the most extensive influence in 1 Peter.

The likeness between 1 Peter and the speeches of Paul contributed to the dictum about Acts of the Tübingen school that Paul Petrinizes, while the converse statement that in Acts Peter Paulinizes doubtless received support from such passages as Acts xv. 11. A more satisfactory modern view, without regard to the genuineness of 2 Peter and the Pastorals for example, will incline rather to see in all the coincidences listed not so much personal influence or identity of origin, but a common Christianity mediated by the historian and shared by others, or even commonplaces of vocabulary or expression more general than any religious boundary. It would be possible to increase from outside the New Testament [5] the range in parallels, and thereby to reduce the specious significance of both of the lists presented above.

(*b*) Another favourite line of argument for the historicity of the speeches The in Acts is the primitive character of their theology.[6] The author, it is said, 'primitive theology' of the speeches.

[1] See Vol. III. p. 445.

[2] E.g. Streeter, *The Primitive Church*, 1929, p. 126: "The exhortation, 'tend the flock of Christ,' is much nearer to the speech attributed to *Paul* in Acts xx. 28 than are any passages in the Epistle to speeches of *Peter* in that book."

[3] Jacquier, *Les Actes des Apôtres*, p. 315, finds in such correspondences the influence of Peter. εὐσεβής of the same verse (and verse 2) in Acts occurs elsewhere in the N.T. only at 2 Peter ii. 9.

[4] Cf. p. 369.

[5] On the fallacy in the notation "not elsewhere in the New Testament," see my *Style and Literary Method of Luke*, p. 6.

[6] On the theology of Acts see literature listed in Additional Note 29, p. 374, note 5.

lived long after Paul had transformed the primitive gospel, and yet, especially in the earlier parts of Acts, the speeches of Peter and Stephen represent quite correctly the pre-Pauline conceptions of Jesus' death and resurrection. No archaeological *tour de force*, it is thought, could enable the historian to orient himself so completely in the past, nor would he try to do so. Only a true tradition of what was said by the early missionaries could explain the archaic content of their reported addresses.

An answer to this argument would carry us far afield into the problems of the development of thought in the early Church. There is danger of arguing in a circle, since our ideas of early Christianity, with which the speeches in Acts are said to conform so exactly, are derived in large part from those very speeches. Nor is it entirely clear that such simple theology as theirs, emphasizing Jesus' resurrection and the fulfilment of scripture, became extinct everywhere in the Church in the second half of the first century. And if by ' primitive ' theology we mean un-Pauline, it is evident that the speeches in the two parts of Acts are so similar that we cannot at the same time argue the genuineness of those in 2 Acts because they coincide with Paul's letters, and the genuineness of those in 1 Acts because they differ from them.

The parallel afforded by Luke's use of Mark.

(c) Perhaps the strongest argument in favour of a genuine element in the speeches of Acts is the parallel case of the words of Jesus in Luke. In Acts we are dealing with a writer who, as the verbal likenesses to the gospels of Mark and Matthew make plain, in his former volume carried over short sayings of his actors and dialogue, if not long formal addresses, with very slight change from his written sources. May we not infer that he did the same thing with the words of Peter and Paul ? Why should we attribute to him in his second volume a habit of freely composing speeches when in his first volume, where we have opportunity to examine his method, he transfers speech material from his source to his own manuscript with a minimum of verbal alteration ?

To this objection it may be answered that a variety of method is not impossible, especially if the author was dealing with different kinds of material. Non-Christian writers apparently do not always follow the same course consistently throughout their works. Their treatment of written sources is not always so free as when they are composing speeches of their own. The sayings of Jesus had a gnomic character, a written tradition, and perhaps a general currency which secured for them a more faithful reproduction than seemed necessary to Luke in trying to picture the life and words of the apostolic missionaries.[1] Perhaps even Luke's gospel contains

[1] It is important to remember how dependent the ultimate historian is upon the earlier history of his material and upon its divergent methods of transmission. According to its literary type alone a difference of transmission was determined for each item, and the speeches in Acts stand at the opposite pole from the apophthegms of Jesus. Cf. M. Dibelius, *Stilkritisches zur Apostelgeschichte*, 1923. Apparently at a later date the apostolic speeches of Acts came to be treated with a like conservatism. It is at least noticeable that the variation of wording between the Neutral Text and the Western, which is so noteworthy

one address of Jesus that is the author's own elaboration of a single primitive motif. This is the address in Luke iv. 18-27. The nucleus is the brief proverb on the prophet found in the similar passage in Mark vi. 4. But Luke has shifted the scene to an artistic position at the forefront of Jesus' ministry and has developed the theme in characteristic fashion. A definite Old Testament lection is provided as the text for the sermon as in the addresses to Jewish audiences in Acts, and along with the subject of the rejection of the prophet by his own people the converse experience is emphasized of his welcome and success with the alien or Gentile. For the latter theme a comparison with the speeches in Acts as well as its narrative —especially the emphasis in Stephen's speech on God's acts of revelation upon foreign soil—seems to prove that both speeches are attributable to the mind of the author.[1]

It may be added that the speeches in Acts and in Luke iv. are generally more formal in setting than the sayings of Jesus which we know to be taken over from written sources. The Greek and Roman writers who invent speeches place them, as does Acts, either before some regularly constituted assembly or at some dramatic moment in an exciting narrative. In Luke's gospel the occasional nature of the comments of Jesus is emphasized. In Greek literature the nearest parallels are the collections of apophthegms or the table-talk of the philosophers ($\dot{a}\pi o\phi\theta\dot{\epsilon}\gamma\mu a\tau a$, $\sigma\upsilon\mu\pi\dot{o}\sigma\iota a$, $\dot{a}\pi o\mu\nu\eta\mu o\nu\epsilon\dot{\upsilon}\mu a\tau a$). In Acts the occasions of the speeches correspond very closely to those at which the non-Christian historians introduce their own dramatic compositions.

(d) If the variety of manner in the speeches in Acts be cited as evidence of their diverse or primitive origin, this feature quite as much as the similarities which they exhibit may be explained as part of Luke's skill. In all his writing there is a combination of unmistakable individuality with constant variation. The speeches to Gentiles in Acts xiv. and xvii. are of very different tenor from those addressed to Jews, although they are like each other in some of their underlying arguments. The Old Testament quotations are replaced by citations from Greek poets[2] or are represented by mere echoes of the psalter. The speeches of chapters vii. and xx. further

*Variation a Lucan characteristic.*

---

a feature of Acts and a mark of early freedom with which its text was treated, is conspicuously less in the speeches than in the narrative. See Wendt, *Die Apostelgeschichte* (Meyer's *Kommentar*, 9th edit.), p. 56.

[1] I am inclined to think an excellent parallel to Luke's speeches in Acts is to be found in the Canticles of Luke i., ii. Of course Luke's versatility shows itself in the more poetic quality of these passages, but I concur in Harnack's opinion (*Luke the Physician*, p. 215) that they are Luke's own composition. Of course there are many rival opinions, and certainty is not possible. Spoken parts of Acts show many of the phenomena of the Canticles.

[2] Similarly the pastoral address in xx. takes its only formal quotation appropriately from the words of Jesus. References to John the Baptist and even quotation of his words may suit Peter speaking in Jerusalem or Caesarea (i. 22, x. 37, xi. 16), but, in spite of xviii. 25, do they suit Paul at Pisidian Antioch or at Ephesus (xiii. 24 f., xix. 1 ff., see note)?

represent the varieties within the editor's repertoire. It is barely possible that the Pauline phrases in the latter are deliberate efforts at imitation. Elsewhere the editor certainly is consciously adopting a style suited to the circumstance. This is most obvious in the way in which he confines the Semitic spelling of Σαούλ for Σαῦλος to the dialogue in ix. 4 = xxii. 7 = xxvi. 14 and ix. 17 = xxii. 13, and of Συμεών for Σίμων (Πέτρος) to the words of James in xv. 14 (see note).

Proper names.

The author seems to show a similar adaptation of language to environment in his use of proper names elsewhere. This is sometimes so consistent as to be attributable neither to sources nor to unconscious adjustment, but to conscious dramatic purpose. Nothing else will explain the definite transition at Acts xiii. 9 (see note) from Saul to Paul. It is like the use of Simon in Luke (and Mark, contrast Matt. iv. 18, viii. 14) prior to the incident where his renaming as Peter is mentioned. After that he is called Simon only in words quoted, not in the narrative. In the incident of Cornelius the phrase is always " Simon that is surnamed Peter " in discourse, and simple " Peter " in the narrative.[1] (Also the angel says to him, " Rise, Peter, kill and eat.") The author's consciousness of his method is clear in Acts xxvi. where on account of the specially Greek character of the scene [2] he explains the Hebraic form Σαούλ by prefacing it by the words " speaking to me in the Hebrew language." For other marks of the author's sensitiveness to linguistic differences see Acts ii., xiv. 11, xxi. 37, xxi. 40, xxii. 1, xxviii. 2 (βάρβαροι), and especially his treatment of foreign words.[3]

For the distribution of the two forms of Jerusalem—Ἰερουσαλήμ and Ἱεροσόλυμα—while no absolute and conscious rule seems to have guided the author, the best explanation still seems to be a similar adjustment to environment, the Hebrew form prevailing in Luke and 1 Acts, the declinable Greek form in 2 Acts.[4]

Semitic and Greek atmosphere.

The Semitic atmosphere of Luke i. and ii. is partly produced by the use of such words as Ἰούδα (elsewhere the Hellenized Ἰουδαία), Ἰσραήλ in narrative (i. 80, ii. 25 ; so also Acts v. 21 ; elsewhere only in discourse), Γαβριήλ (i. 19, 26 ; elsewhere angels are not named). Just as in Luke's gospel the canticles of chapters i. and ii. show the most Semitic style, so in Acts the speeches to Jewish audiences or on Jewish soil contain the most obvious Semitic idioms as well as the bulk of the Old Testament quotations, For the former see the idioms with στόμα or πρόσωπον in i. 16, iii. 13,

---

[1] This distinction can be used for making an interesting grammatical observation. See JBL. xlviii., 1929, pp. 422 f.

[2] See pp. 61 and 419, note 3.

[3] See Style and Literary Method of Luke, pp. 154-158. Similar habits of the authors of 1 and of 4 Maccabees are described in my Making of Luke-Acts, p. 230, note 28. For all this interest the author has not scrupled to use a Greek proverb in an Aramaic speech (xxvi. 14), nor has he apparently considered that the letter of Lysias to Felix should have been in Latin (so Jacquier), nor apparently has he thought out the scene at Pentecost.

[4] Harnack, Acts of the Apostles, pp. 76 ff. ; R. Schütz, Apostel und Jünger, 1921, pp. 20 f., and in ZNTW. xi. (1910), pp. 181 ff. On influences affecting the spelling see J. A. Montgomery, JBL. xlix., 1930, pp. 277 ff.

19, 21, iv. 25, vii. 45, xiii. 24, xv. 7 (also xvii. 26, xxii. 14), and the *parallelismus membrorum* in ii. 14, 24, etc.[1] Conversely it is possible, as has been argued by Blass, that the classical element in Luke's style comes to the front in the Gentile setting of the later chapters of Acts, and particularly in the speeches of Paul to the Athenian audience [2] and in the presence of the cultivated Agrippa. The latter speech, according to our author, gave the king an impression of Paul's great learning.[3]

Such variations of style adapted to the atmosphere of the narrative and the setting of the speech might well go further than matters of grammar and diction. If the writer was sensitive to such influences it would not be too much to attribute to him some control over the selection of religious terms and even religious ideas. It may be just such adaptation which leads to the use of the word εὐαγγέλιον in the speeches at Acts xv. 7 and xx. 24, a word that Luke has omitted in his gospel when Mark puts it in Jesus' mouth. Harnack [4] considers it an instance of deliberate imitative

Variation in religious terms.

---

[1] The parallel structure and other Biblical elements of style recur in strongly emotional spoken passages in Acts like viii. 21, 23, xiii. 10, 11, xxvi. 16 ff. Acts xx. 18-35 has a marked use of pairs of words.

[2] This is not so easily demonstrated by vocabulary, for the words, if rare, are as much Hellenistic as classical. The quotations of course give the speech a literary character. See items listed in Vol. IV. p. 209. Grammatically we may note the good participial construction καίγε (or -τοι, or -τοιγε) and the ' comparative of politeness ' in δεισιδαιμονεστέρους. (See W. Knodel, *Die Urbanitätsausdrücke bei Polybios*, 1908, pp. 32 ff. Another case in a speech is at xxv. 10 κάλλιον. πλείων is the only real comparative in Acts.) But we must not overlook the Biblical echoes even in xiv. 15-17 and in xvii. 22-31. Formal quotations would have been out of place, and God could not be spoken of to these audiences as "the God of Abraham, Isaac and Jacob " as in iii. 13, but passages in the Psalter (and Deutero-Isaiah) have affected the descriptions of the Creator in xiv. 15 and xvii. 24, of divine providence in xvii. 26, and of divine judgement in xvii. 31.

[3] Perhaps ' reading ' would be a better rendering of γράμματα. In John vii. 15 similar surprise appears to refer to Jesus' knowledge of the Scriptures. The same meaning is possible in Acts, and we may assume that Acts intends us to understand that the passages of Scripture alluded to in xxvi. 22 f. were quoted by Paul so fully as to impress Agrippa with Paul's Biblical learning.

The possibly classical or poetical idioms in xxvi. 2-23 include ἥγημαι (2; see Blass-Debrunner, *Grammatik*, § 341), ἴσασι (4 ; *ibid.* § 99. 2), ἀκριβεστάτην (5 ; *ibid.* § 60. 1), vocative at the end (7 ; *ibid.* § 474. 6), ἕνεκα (21 ; *ibid.* § 35. 3). Poetical or secular Hellenistic are the proverb in 14 (see note), the proverbial ἐν γωνίᾳ in 26, the phrases οὐρανόθεν and ὑπὲρ τὴν λαμπρότητα τοῦ ἡλίου in 13 (neither of them in the parallel accounts of ix. and xxii.), the apology τῇ Ἑβραΐδι διαλέκτῳ (14, not in ix. or xxii.) for the Semitic Σαούλ, Σαούλ. In spite of its parallelism to the best style of Luke, e.g. to his preface (see notes on 5 and 16), the chapter is also made poetic by certain Jewish or Christian semi-liturgic elements. And for ' noon ' it uses (13), instead of μεσημβρία as at xxii. 6, the very phrase, ἡμέρας μέσης, condemned by the purist Phrynichus (ed. Lobeck, pp. 53, 54, 465).

[4] *Constitution and Law of the Church*, p. 288. See Vol. IV. pp. 172 f., 261.

style. The use of ' Son of Man ' by Stephen and of παῖς θεοῦ by the apostles in Acts iii. and iv. may be further instances of archaism.[1]

**The Lucan canticles.**

Here as elsewhere the problem of the canticles in Luke i. and ii. aligns itself with the problem of the speeches. Of them also it has been claimed that only authentic tradition can explain their archaic and appropriate character. But is it inconceivable that the pious Christian imagination could recover the religious atmosphere of those who were waiting for the consolation of Israel ? Was it after all so different from the wistful longing of the end of the Gospel (xxiv. 21) or even of a later day (Acts xxvi. 6, 7) ? The strongly Semitic style of these chapters was at least tolerated by an author who could write good Greek if he wanted to, and who was not averse to recasting his sources. To compose these chapters would require a little more skill but very little more dramatic appreciation than to leave them in the Semitic dress of a source. For one who could so consistently use the phraseology of the LXX it would not be difficult to reproduce the simplest ideas of Jewish piety. And that is all that the canticles do.[2]

**The source of the speeches.**

5. Whether the speeches in Acts are the work of the ultimate historian or not is a question that could be answered only by a knowledge of the sources of that volume similar in extent to the knowledge which synoptic study gives of the methods and sources used in composing Luke. But it

[1] See Additional Note 30, pp. 363 and 364 ff. respectively.

[2] On Luke's variation of vocabulary, especially to suit the language of the speakers, see my *Making of Luke-Acts*, pp. 221-230. On the variation of terms for Jesus see Additional Note 29. Besides the terms already mentioned may be noted :

βεβηλόω (xxiv. 6 ; see note on κοινόω in xxi. 28).

ἔθνος of the Jews (xxiv. 2, xxvi. 4 ; see note) *vs.* λαός.

Ἰσραηλίτης (only in addresses to Jews), *vs.* Ἰουδαῖοι. Cf. on the infrequency of the term, Juster, *Les Juifs dans l'Empire Romain*, i. 173. In 1 Maccabees ' Israel ' is used in the narrative with few exceptions, while ' Jews ' occurs in the documents and in regard to diplomatic relations (H. W. Ettelson, *The Integrity of 1 Maccabees*, p. 301).

Χαναάν in vii. 11, xiii. 19, only in reference to the past history. The same is true of the rare occurrences in late Jewish literature (e.g. Neh. ix. 24).

Ἑβραῖοι and Ἑλληνισταί in vi. 1, *vs.* Ἰουδαῖοι and Ἕλληνες. See Additional Note 7, p. 71.

υἱοὶ Ἰσραήλ in Luke i. 16, Acts v. 21 (here only in narrative), vii. 23 (from LXX), vii. 37, ix. 15, x. 36.

One may well doubt if the Christians would be so called in Acts by a Christian speaker, as they are by others in xi. 26 and xxvi. 28, or an αἵρεσις as in xxiv. 5, xxviii. 22 (see the qualification ἣν λέγουσι αἵρεσιν in xxiv. 14). This word and Nazarenes are assigned to Jewish speakers. On the other hand, non-Christians would not refer to them as ἅγιοι. For all these terms see Additional Note 30. We may doubt, too, if the author would use in narrative such expressions as ἀστεῖος τῷ θεῷ (vii. 20), τὴν ἐκκλησίαν τοῦ θεοῦ (xx. 28), πάσῃ συνειδήσει ἀγαθῇ πεπολίτευμαι τῷ θεῷ (xxiii. 1), τὸν ἀρχιερέα τοῦ θεοῦ (xxiii. 4), or expressions like ἅγιος παῖς (iv. 27, 30), ὁ τόπος ὁ ἅγιος (vi. 13, xxi. 28), ἄγγελος ἅγιος (x. 22, contrast x. 3).

remains possible, if not probable, that these speeches are in many cases not of older vintage than the composition of the ultimate editor. The ' we ' passages, if they were a written source, do not necessarily include any extensive discourses. The first person pronoun disappears at some distance from the speeches in xx. 18 ff. and xxviii. 17 ff. There is no close connexion between the contents of these speeches and the adjacent diary.

It is equally impossible to associate securely the earlier speeches in Acts with any written source. The various theories of Greek sources for the earlier chapters do not depend upon any clue in the speech matter, nor do they lead to any identification of the speeches with the adjacent material. Torrey's theory [1] of a continuous Aramaic source behind Acts i. 1-xv. 35 involves, to be sure, a literal translation of everything—whether narrative or discourse. But Torrey's theory is far from proved, and the phenomena in the speeches permit of another explanation. It is noteworthy that most of Torrey's evidence for an Aramaic source is derived from the speech material in these fifteen chapters rather than from the narrative. His most tangible evidence of unlikeness between these chapters and the rest of Acts is the abundance of Old Testament quotation in the former. But these Old Testament quotations are almost exclusively in the speeches.[2] So are a large number of the cases of Semitic idiom which he enumerates.[3] If the speeches are the free composition of the final editor they cannot serve to prove the existence of an underlying source. It is perhaps significant that those Greek and Latin historians for whose narrative we can discover the underlying source evidently did not follow that source in their speeches.[4] Whatever scepticism one may feel about source theories in Acts elsewhere —whether in Greek or Aramaic—scepticism is doubly justified in the case of the speeches. In fact the strongest argument *against* Torrey's theory is in the use of the LXX rather than of some Semitic form of the Old Testament in the quotations in the speeches. At xv. 17 the LXX form of Amos ix. 12 οἱ κατάλοιποι τῶν ἀνθρώπων is certainly a mistranslation due to the confusion of אדם and אדום. But in its original Semitic

*The earlier speeches.* (margin note)

---

[1] C. C. Torrey, *The Composition and Date of Acts*, 1916.

[2] One is tempted to use in reply to Torrey his own words (*Ency. Bibl.* col. 2863) about 1 Maccabees, which also has speeches more abundantly in the first chapters. He says : " The greater frequency of poetical passages in the first half of the book, noticed by Westcott (Smith's *D.B.*), is simply due to the difference in character of the subject matter and the narrative, and cannot be used as an argument for diversity of authorship."

[3] Torrey gives six ' especially striking ' examples of mistranslation. Five of these are in discourse material, as are more than half of all his other examples, including the most impressive cases. I have dealt more fully with Torrey's argument in *A.J.Th.* xxiv., 1920, pp. 436-455. That Semitic idioms are not always due directly to a source is shown by the recent study of Joseph Waldis, from which it appears that often the more Semitic-looking phrases in the LXX have no corresponding idiom in the Massoretic Text. Conversely phrases in Acts which seem Semitic are rendered by the Peshitto as though they had been written in simple Greek idiom.

[4] Cf. p. 405.

form the quotation would not have served the point of the speech at all.

Of course the historicity of the speeches would not be established if it were proved that they were derived from earlier written sources. For they could still be attributed, though at an earlier stage, to the convention of ancient historians rather than to reliable tradition of actual addresses. If we accept, for example, Torrey's theory for Acts i.-xv., we may still regard the addresses included in those chapters as the work of historical imagination on the part, not of Luke, but of his Aramaic predecessor.

The<br>difficulties<br>in the<br>speeches. 6. If, on the other hand, the speeches are the work of the final editor, it would not be surprising to find them less reliable than the matter derived from narrative sources. Many of the difficulties in the book of Acts are found in these speeches,[1] and it may well be that they are due to the fact that this style of dramatic composition is more liable to error and anachronism than is the reproduction of narrative sources. The variations in the account of Paul's conversion do not seriously impugn the authenticity of the story as a whole, but they illustrate the author's freedom and variety of expression, and two of the versions, be it remembered, are in Paul's speeches. Similarly the apparent anachronism and chronological error in the passage about Judas and Theudas are in a speech of Gamaliel, not in strict narrative. Even the address in Luke iv. which we have associated with the speeches in Acts provides in its present position an anachronism in its reference to Capernaum which well illustrates how easily such errors are made by an author composing speeches.[2]

On the other hand, if neither speeches nor narrative rest *verbatim* on written sources, we may expect when we have parallel accounts that they will vary in details, and that sometimes the speech will seem more authentic or complete than the narrative, as well as sometimes the reverse. Such differences are notorious in the accounts of Paul's conversion. References to them are common and are to be found in the Commentary on xxiii. 30 and elsewhere. A noteworthy addition in xxii. 17-21 is an account of a vision to Paul in the temple.

Differences<br>between<br>speeches<br>and<br>narrative. Other instances of parallel accounts, with some items mentioned first in the second account, are :

(a) The conversion of Cornelius in x. and Peter's account of it in xi. 1-18. See Vol. IV. pp. 123 f. The mention of the men as numbering six (xi. 12) is a striking addition.

(b) The decision of James and the Council in Jerusalem in xv. 19-22, and the letter embodying their decision in xv. 23-29, and more briefly James's reference in xxi. 25. In the matter of the ' decrees ' the text, both Neutral and Western, shows a consistency between these three passages.

---

[1] E.g. Acts xxiv. 17 εἰς τὸ ἔθνος μου. Cf. Vol. II. pp. 323 f., 332 ff., 337, 343.

[2] Other suspected items in the speeches would include the account of Judas in i. 18 f., the inscription to the Unknown God (singular) in xvii. 23 (see Additional Note 19), the mention of ἐπίσκοποι of Ephesus, and of heretical teachers in xx. 28-30, etc. If the narrative rests on sources and the speeches do not, it is only fair that the narrative should not be encumbered with the burden of suspicions which only the speeches arouse.

(c) The account of Paul's stay in Ephesus in xix. and his review of it in xx. 18-35. The latter has a definite reference to plots of the Jews (19), to Paul's working with his hands (34), and to the time of his sojourn as three years (31), none of which occur in the narrative.

(d) Paul's arrest and first trial in xxi. 27-xxiii. 22 and the tribune's letter about it in xxiii. 26-30. Besides some puzzling variations in presentation (see Vol. IV. p. 294) the letter contains a statement not in the preceding narrative that the accusers also had been instructed to go to Caesarea (cf. xxiv. 8 v.l.).

(e) Paul's arrival and arrest and trial in Jerusalem in xxi. 16 ff. and his own account of it before Felix in xxiv. 10-21. The second account gives an enumeration of days (11 " not more than twelve ") that could scarcely be calculated by the reader from the narrative, and a reference to the purpose of Paul's visit to Jerusalem (17 " offerings and alms to my own nation ") which alone in Acts suggests the collection so fully mentioned in the letters of Paul.

(f) Festus's first contacts with Paul's case in xxv. 1-12 and his summary of it to Agrippa in private in xxv. 13-21, and his public summary in xxv. 24-27. The motive for the hearing is first mentioned at xxv. 26 f.

(g) Paul's summary to the Jews in Rome of his arrest and appeal to Caesar in xxviii. 17-20.

There are also many shorter spoken summaries of preceding narratives.

Besides the instances given of cases where the speech supplies what the narratives do not, we may mention further facts emerging in the spoken parts of Luke's writings (cf. note on xxiii. 30):

Luke i. 36.  Gabriel calls Elizabeth a kinswoman[1] of Mary.

Luke iv. 23.  Jesus refers to things he has done in Capernaum.

Luke x. 13 (from Q).  Jesus mentions mighty works done in Bethsaida and Chorazin.

Luke xxiv. 24.  Two disciples speak of some of their number as going to the tomb and finding it empty ;  34 the eleven and others report that Jesus had appeared to Simon.  The only anticipation of either of these is the doubtful verse xxiv. 12 (a ' Western non-interpolation ' probably due to John xx. 6 f.) which tells at most of Peter's visit to the grave and of his seeing only the grave clothes.

Acts i. 3.  Jesus' appearances lasted forty days (this is not in a spoken part ;  it is, however, a repeated narrative).  The account in Luke xxiv. makes no reference to the number of days.  Acts xiii. 31, a speech, says " many days."

Acts i. 18 f.  The account of Judas' death, if regarded as part of the speech, has no parallel in the preceding narrative.

Acts x. 41.  " Chosen witnesses, who ate and drank with him after he rose from the dead."  This is barely anticipated in the narrative of Luke xxiv. 30, 42 f.  συναλιζόμενος in Acts i. 4 probably does not mean ' eating ' (see note).

---

[1] But συγγενίς may mean merely a member of the same race, rather than any closer kin.  In that case there is scarcely any new or unexpected information in the word.

xx. 35. A saying of Jesus quoted in Paul's speech that was not given in the Gospel.

Details of Paul's origin and early life emerge in the spoken parts thus : a Tarsian (ix. 11, xxi. 39) or Cilician (xxiii. 34) by birth (xxii. 3), educated at Jerusalem at the feet of Gamaliel (xxii. 3), a Pharisee (xxvi. 5) and the son of Pharisees (xxiii. 6), a Roman citizen (xvi. 37, xxii. 25 ff.) by birth (xxii. 28).

It cannot be denied that some of these additions are quite surprising, and that in many other cases without any tangible addition of this kind the speeches give a quite different impression than was given in the narrative. Sometimes this may be due to a different emphasis which the situation seems to require (see xxii. 12 and note, and a similar addition at x. 22), or to generalization (see xxvi. 10 and note). But it extends beyond what a modern historian would be willing to leave to the scrutiny of critical readers.

The argument for a written source behind the speeches is sometimes put precisely on this ground—their inappropriateness to the occasion. It is pointed out that Stephen's address [1] and some of Paul's defences as reported in the closing chapters are quite irrelevant to the charges, and could never be due either to the original actor or to the ultimate editor, but are adapted from some written source. Evidently the source theorists cannot have it both ways at once. They cannot argue for the written transmission of speeches because they both do and do not exactly fit the circumstances. Whether such incorporation of alien material is the best explanation of any of the addresses to which it has been applied may best be discussed in connexion with the several speeches. The same may be said of Norden's slightly different explanation of the Athenian address of Paul.

The difficulty of judging the speeches.

7. By what standard shall we judge the speeches in Acts ? It is difficult for the modern reader to fix a fair and sympathetic criterion. Evidently it would be unjust to expect the ancient writer to conform to modern requirements in this or in other phases of literary composition. Of certain demands of our so-called scientific history he was entirely ignorant. He was evidently free from some of the more extreme tastes about rhetorical speeches in ancient historical writing. Contemporary *literati* would have regarded his efforts with scorn. Educated Christians of a later time found much to apologize for in the crudeness of all their scriptures, and they did well in the end to glory in the contrast between secular fine writing and the inspired ' Word of God.' [2] Even Luke, cultivated though he was, could not pass muster by the Atticist standards. Critics of the secular school would

---

[1] But Stephen's address, in so far as it is a review of history, is said to be quite in the Jewish manner. Abrahams, *Pharisaism and the Gospels*, Second Series, 1924, p. 18, note 1, says it is ' in the true form' of Jewish protestation of faith in God in history (cf. *ibid.* First Series, 1917, p. 8, on the ' Jewish lines ' of the similar historical speech in Acts xiii.). Its remarkable relation to Jewish tradition when the latter differs from the LXX shows (see notes on vii.) that either Luke or the sources on which he depended were not limited to the familiar written text for their ideas of history.

[2] See Norden, *Antike Kunstprosa*, 1898, pp. 512 ff.

scrutinize his speeches particularly. They were the most prized parts of the classical historians and the most carefully composed parts in contemporary historiography. But Luke did not follow their models.

Impartiality of judgement about the speeches is hard for the modern Christian reader. They include the most familiar parts of the book. Some of them have long associations and the prestige of apostolic names. The commentator who studies them in detail and *con amore* must detach himself to secure the more general view. But it is difficult to suppose that the Areopagus speech or the address before Agrippa could have secured such continuous admiration unless there were real skill in them, even if the skill was Luke's rather than Paul's.

It would be interesting if in judging them we could do so by Luke's own standards. Behind them it is perhaps possible to see something of his own conscious judgement and intention. One can hardly doubt, for example, that we owe to his own desire for variety and representativeness the present selection of materials in the speeches. Thus for Paul he gives us an address in a Jewish synagogue, an address before Gentiles, and a pastoral farewell to Christians. It is scarcely an accident that the first of these occurs near the beginning of his ' first missionary journey.' A similarly programmatic character is apparently intended by Luke's expansion and transference to an early position of Jesus' speech at Nazareth. The principal Gentile speech is given a setting that is of great historical interest. Luke betrays at least some of the sense of associations which Athens and the Areopagus would have for any Greek (see Vol. IV. pp. 211 ff.). The occasion and audience of the speech at Miletus is equally dramatic for the purpose. It serves besides to review the whole character of Paul's pastoral work. If the later apologetic speeches of Paul seem less varied—two of them rehearse his conversion—and more uninteresting, we may suspect that other motives determined Luke's recurring emphasis in the closing chapters.[1] Here the author is emphasizing whatever may be said of the guiltlessness of Paul's position, by repeated insistence on the irrelevance to Roman law of the charges against him, the Pharisaic orthodoxy of his belief in the risen Jesus, and the supernatural revelations which both caused and justified his career as a Christian missionary to the Gentiles.

We are, of course, in no position to know fully the problem which the speeches constituted for the editor of Acts. Even if they were available to him in part from his sources, which is improbable, their effective presentation was not easy. Even for quoting Scripture he was without many of the conveniences which we enjoy to-day, as I have indicated elsewhere.[2] There were many aspects of the speeches which tested his dramatic skill.

We note, for example, how often he has the speakers interrupted, only to continue with a final word. This certainly gives a lifelike impression which a more formal ending would not do. In several instances the interruption follows close upon some special word in the speech, e.g. ii. 36 " you crucified," vii. 51-53 ending " you did not keep it [the law]," xvii. 31

[1] See *Making of Luke-Acts*, chap. xx.
[2] *Making of Luke-Acts*, p. 326.

" raising him from the dead," xxii. 21 " Gentiles," xxiii. 6 " hope and resurrection of the dead," xxvi. 23 " resurrection " (?) or " Gentiles " (?). He
takes pains to give the impression made by the speech, or often the con-
flicting impressions that followed it.

The indica-
tion of
quotation.

One slight problem of composition that scarcely occurs to the modern
reader, or even to the commentator, is that of indicating the close of formal
quotations. The beginning of the quotation is easily indicated by words
like ' saying ' or ' as follows.' But the ancient writer could not indicate
even by punctuation the end of the quoted passage, and of course he
neither knew nor would have used our modern ' end of quotation ' or the
telegraphic ' unquote.' [1] But a skilful writer could often so arrange his
wording as to help the reader to discover promptly the change of speakers.
The end of a letter quoted could be shown by ἔρρωσθε. This is done at
xv. 29, and according to ℵ 81 ἔρρωσο is read at xxiii. 30. In narrative the
author could add at the end, " As he spoke thus," " When they heard," etc.
But quotations within speeches provided a more difficult problem.[2] The
end of a quotation in Acts is sometimes marked by a new vocative. Thus
in ii. the long quotation from Joel in 17-21 is followed immediately by
ἄνδρες Ἰσραηλῖται, and the long one from Psalm xvi. in 25-28 by ἄνδρες
ἀδελφοί.[3] In like manner in vii. 51 a vocative addressed to the audience
follows immediately upon a citation from Isaiah lxvi. In xiii. 25 a vocative
ἄνδρες ἀδελφοί follows the quotation from John the Baptist. In the speech
to Agrippa in xxvi. 19 Paul, after quoting at length the words of commission
received at his conversion, continues, " And therefore, King Agrippa, I was
not disobedient to the heavenly vision." [4] For shorter or informal quotations the author perhaps felt that the reader would rightly guess the point
of transition, but the instances that I have given show a skill, perhaps
unconscious to the author himself, that is likely to escape the modern
reader's notice.

Conclusion.

Even though devoid of historical basis in genuine tradition the speeches
in Acts have nevertheless considerable historical value. There is reason
to suppose that the talented author of Acts expended upon them not only
his artistic skill, but also a considerable amount of historic imagination.
Like Thucydides and the other best composers of speeches he attempted

[1] Homer and the epic poets often had a concluding as well as an introductory
" Thus he spoke."

[2] Such skill was even more severely taxed in the Greek dialogue, where
neither the introduction of new speakers nor the mere change of speakers could
be shown by stage direction, but had to be indicated by the spoken text. Cf.
A. R. Bellinger, ' Lucian's Dramatic Technique,' in Yale Classical Studies, i.,
1928, pp. 3 ff.

[3] Cf. Loisy, ad loc.

[4] The reader is helped after quotations by an emphatic adverb, e.g. τότε
i. 12, vii. 4, or pronoun, iii. 26 ὑμῖν, vii. 35 τοῦτον, xiii. 23 τούτου, xv. 19 διὸ ἐγὼ
κρίνω, or by the repetition of a quoted word, xvii. 29 γένος. To prevent the
reader from assuming too soon that a quotation is closed, repeated phrases like
ὁ θεὸς εἶπεν (vii. 7, not in LXX ; for a different explanation see JBL. xlviii.,
1929, p. 416) or λέγει κύριος (xv. 18) were useful.

to present what the speakers were likely to have said. Probably these addresses give us a better idea of the early church than if Luke had striven for realism,[1] better than if, baffled by the want of genuine tradition, he had forgone all effort at portrayal of the apostles' preaching. They indicate at least what seemed to a well-informed Christian of the next generation the main outline of the Christian message as first presented by Jesus' followers in Palestine and in the cities of the Mediterranean world.[2] They attest the simple theological outlook conceived to have been original by at least one Christian of the obscure period at which Acts was written.

## NOTE XXXIII. THE ROMAN ARMY

### By T. R. S. BROUGHTON

Acts has several references to the Roman army, and in the background of the story there is always a dimly perceived and changing mass of tribunes, centurions, and soldiers who sometimes limit the freedom and sometimes preserve the lives of the Christians who are in the foreground.

To describe the details which happen to be mentioned without explaining the system to which they belong seemed undesirable, if not impossible, nor is there any one book, at least in English, to which reference could conveniently be made. The following paragraphs therefore give (i.) a general description of Roman military organization in the first century, (ii.) a discussion of the units of the Roman army in Syria and Palestine, (iii.) a note on the three most difficult references to military units in Acts.

### (i.) The Organization of the Roman Army in the First Century

(a) The Legion.—The regular army was divided into legions varying Legions. in number with the military needs of the Empire.

The strength of a legion was about 6000 men divided into ten cohorts (σπεῖραι); these in turn were each divided into three maniples and six centuries. The tactical unit was the maniple, the administrative unit the cohort. There was also a body of legionary cavalry numbering in the first century 120 horse.[3] The commander of all forces in Syria was the imperial Officers.

---

[1] Cf. Gardner, loc. cit. p. 416. It is of interest to compare a later attempt in the Didache to give " the teaching of the Lord to the nations through the twelve apostles." That author knew and used some early Christian literature still known to us (Matthew, Barnabas, and perhaps Hermas).

[2] The primitive theology of 1 Acts " is, if nothing more, a triumph of archaeology," J. M. Thompson, Miracles in the New Testament, 1911, p. 140.

[3] There has been doubt of the continuance of the legionary cavalry after the Augustan reorganization. The statement of Josephus, B.J. iii. 6. 2 εἵπετο δ' αὐτῷ τὸ ἴδιον τοῦ τάγματος ἱππικόν · ἴδιοι γὰρ ἑκάστου τάγματος εἴκοσι πρὸς τοῖς ἑκατὸν ἱππεῖς, seems clear and definite.

legate, but each legion also had as commander a legate of the senatorial order. With him were a group of subordinate officers, *beneficiarii, stratores, corniculari*, as an office staff. The legionary tribunes, six in number, whether senatorial, *laticlavi*, or equestrian, *angusticlavi*, combined military and administrative duties such as going the rounds, the care of the list of soldiers in the corps, etc. They were usually young men doing military service at the beginning of their official career. In Greek they are regularly called χιλίαρχοι. The camp prefect, who also had a staff, was usually a veteran from among the *centuriones primipili*, thoroughly acquainted with the details of the service, and could in certain cases perform the duties of the legate of the legion in the latter's absence.

**Non-com. officers.** Of the subordinate officers the most important was the centurion, who was in command of a *centuria*, nominally of 100 men. There were 59 to a legion, and the first century had double the usual number of men. The centurions were ranked in a regular hierarchy from the *primus pilus*, who took part in the councils of war, to the *hastatus posterior* of the tenth cohort. This hierarchy represented the usual order of promotion. The centurions had closest contact with the soldiers of the line, and regulated duties, immunities, and punishments, so that the discipline of the legions depended chiefly on them. Officers subordinate to the centurions were the *optiones, imaginiferi, vexillarii*, etc. From these the centurions were promoted. Centurions were transferred from cohort to cohort and legion to legion as they were advanced in the service.[1] In general the centurion's opportunity for promotion ended with his appointment to the post of *primus pilus* or of camp prefect.

**The legionary soldiers.** The legionary soldier was *ipso facto* a Roman citizen, levied from a Roman town, or given Roman citizenship upon his entry into the service. The legal term of service was twenty years, but legionary soldiers were often kept in service for longer periods, particularly in the first century A.D. The centurions, whose position was more advantageous, often stayed **Pay and rewards.** still longer. The soldier's pay was probably a denarius a day, out of which he had to equip himself, secure any simple luxuries, or bribe the centurions for remissions of duties.[2] At the end of his service he received with his discharge a sum of money and a piece of land either in Italy or, as was more usual in the Empire, in soldier settlements in the provinces. Colonies were often set out in frontier lands with the double purpose of defence and development. In the east, however, the legions were resident in lands long since settled and developed; so soldier colonies were less numerous, and in general the veterans, of whom many were orientals by birth, soon merged into the people about them.[3]

**Recruiting.** After the Augustan reorganization the method of recruitment of the legions was in some measure local. At least the eastern and the western portions of the Empire became largely separate areas of recruitment,

[1] See Cagnat, Dar. et Sag., art. 'Legio,' vi. p. 1056; Domaszewski, *Rangordnung d. röm. Heeres*, pp. 90 ff.

[2] Tacitus, *Ann.* i. 17; cf. Pliny, *Hist. Nat.* xxxiii. 45.

[3] For further information see Pauly-Wissowa, art. 'Legio,' and literature there cited; Parker, *The Roman Legions.*

Africa, which in the time of Trajan had many soldiers from Asia Minor and Syria, being in the eastern area. In this policy two considerations were involved. The developed cities of the east, in the absence of Roman towns, had to be treated from the point of view of recruitment as analogous to the Roman cities of the west; and it was an advantage in each area to have soldiers already inured to the climate of their place of service. As a result, legions originally recruited in the west were early filled with Syrian soldiers. Antony had already recruited many Syrian soldiers into his legions. In the time of Vespasian the Legio III. Gallica, on the march to Italy in his interest, was composed of Syrians who, says Tacitus, saluted the rising sun, " as the custom of the Syrians was." [1] Vespasian made Italy no longer liable to recruitment for the legions, and later on the levy became more purely local.[2]

(b) *The Auxiliary Troops.*—Accompanying the legions in each province were auxiliary troops. These consisted of cavalry divisions or *alae* (ἴλαι), and of divisions either wholly or in large part consisting of infantry or *cohortes* (σπεῖραι). Special corps also were formed to meet special needs, such as slingers, archers, dromedary corps, etc. In the Augustan reorganization these troops were successors to the allied corps of the Republican army, and supplied all the light-armed troops and almost all the cavalry used in the provincial armies. They were an integral part of the garrison forces, the cohorts being attached to the various legions, between five and seven to a legion, while the *alae* of cavalry were directly under the commander of the provincial army. In procuratorial provinces such as Judaea the garrison probably consisted almost wholly of auxiliary forces. They were recruited from the various dependent and allied peoples, of peregrine right, tribal names such as *Lucenses, Astures, Ituraei* being common in both eastern and western units. In the east, however, cohorts from cities also appear in the first century A.D., e.g. *Ascalonitani, Canatheni, Sebasteni.* Additional geographical titles such as *Dacica, Syriaca,* etc., probably refer to the service of cohorts in those regions before being moved, and are distinguishing epithets. Honorary cognomina, such as *Augusta, Claudia, Traiana,* are common, and in many cases refer to the organization of the unit under the emperor designated.[3]

A soldier in a cohort or an ala was normally not a Roman citizen, but regularly received citizenship at the end of his term of service. The *cohortes* and *alae civium Romanorum voluntariorum* were special formations. Free birth was a general condition of entrance into the legions, and this rule was broken only in cases of great national danger. Augustus only twice [4] used slaves and freedmen in the legions—during the Pannonian revolt and after the defeat of Varus. From Macrobius [5] we learn that in Germany and Illyricum he levied several cohorts of freedmen which he termed

*(margin note: Auxiliaries.)*

*(margin note: Voluntarii.)*

---

[1] *Hist.* iii. 24.

[2] See Pauly-Wissowa, art. ' Dilectus '; Mommsen, *Gesammelte Schriften*, vi. pp. 20 f.

[3] See Cichorius, Pauly-Wissowa, art. ' Cohors '; Cheesman, *The Auxilia of the Roman Army.*

[4] Suetonius, *Aug.* 25 ;   Dio Cass. lv. 31-32.        [5] *Sat.* i. 11. 33.

*voluntariae.* This is the probable origin of the *cohortes civium Romanorum voluntariorum,*[1] but the presence of *cohortes ingenuorum* among the volunteers suggests that the levy was not extended to freedmen until the freeborn had been exhausted. The *cohortes classicae* were probably cohorts originally formed from the fleet where freedmen could serve, and turned to service on land.

The composition of auxiliary cohorts. An auxiliary *cohors peditata* was composed of infantry only, a *cohors equitata* of both infantry and cavalry. Most of the cohorts were of the latter type. A *cohors quingenaria* had a nominal strength of 500 men if *peditata*, if *equitata* of 380 infantry and 120 cavalry ; a *cohors miliaria* had double the number in either case.[2] In practice there might be some modification. The *Cohors I. Aug. Lusitanorum* in A.D. 156 numbered, without its centurions and decurions, 363 foot, 114 horse, and 19 dromedarii.[3] Of 23 cohorts in Vespasian's army in A.D. 67, 10 had 1000 infantry each, and 13 had 600 infantry and 120 cavalry each.[4] In a *cohors miliaria peditata* there were 10 centuries, in a *quingenaria* 6. In a *cohors miliaria equitata* the infantry were divided into 10 centuries, in a *quingenaria* into 6 ; the cavalry were divided into *turmae*, but the number is uncertain. In the *Cohors I. Aug. Lusitanorum* above mentioned there were 6 centuries and 3 turmae. Each century was commanded by a centurion, each turma by a decurion, while other officers subordinate to them, the *optio, signifer*, etc., are found. Cohorts, if *quingenariae*, were commanded by *praefecti, ἔπαρχοι,* or if *miliariae*, by *tribuni, χιλίαρχοι* (cf. Acts xxi. 33). The post of tribune was equal in rank to the military tribuneship of a legion.

The majority of the alae were *quingenariae*, really of 480 men and 544 horses,[5] while the *miliariae* were composed of 1008 men and 1104 horses.[6] An *ala quingenaria* was divided into 16 turmae of 30 men and 34 horses each,[7] a *miliaria* into 24 turmae of 42 men and 46 horses each.[8] The commander of an ala was the *praefectus alae, ἔπαρχος ἴλης,* the highest military position in the equestrian career. A *decurio* was in charge of each turma, and there were the usual subordinate officers, *optio, armorum custos, librarius,* etc.

The number of cohorts and alae. The numbers of cohorts and alae levied probably varied somewhat from time to time as need arose for light-armed troops and cavalry. Apart from special instances, such as the Thracians, whose qualifications as bowmen made them useful on every frontier, large numbers of auxiliary troops continued to live during their term of service in the province in which they were levied. It is questionable how far even Vespasian after the revolts and unrest of the years A.D. 68–70 carried out any deliberate policy of crushing the national feeling of the auxiliary units by transferring them to distant regions or mingling the soldiers with levies from other lands.[9] It is certain that cohorts were transferred, e.g. an *ala Sebastenorum* which had previously

---

[1] Mommsen, *Res Gestae*[2], p. 72.     [2] Hyginus, *De castr. mun.* 27.
[3] *B.G.U.* 696.     [4] Jos. *B.J.* iii. 4. 2.
[5] Domaszewski, Hyginus, *De cas. mun.* p. 52.
[6] Hyg. *op. cit.* 16.
[7] *C.I.L.* iii. 14 ; Domaszewski, *l.c.*     [8] Hyg. *l.c.*
[9] See Cheesman, *The Roman Auxilia*, pp. 67 ff.

been in Palestine was changed to Mauretania,[1] while an *ala I. Thracum Mauretana* appears in Palestine in a diploma of A.D. 86. We find, however, that many transferred cohorts soon begin to be recruited from the region to which they have been transferred.[2] Other cohorts such as the *II. Italica Civium Romanorum* and the *II. Classica* which were in Syria in the first century remained there long into the second.

From the military *diplomata* [3] little can safely be inferred as to the total number of alae and cohorts in any province. They are strict evidence only for the presence of particular alae and cohorts at a particular time. Some inference may be made from the number of legions, as the number of cohorts of which we have evidence in any province ranges from five to eight to a legion. The instance of the *Cohors I. Vindelicorum miliaria*, Diploma lxvi., A.D. 157, Dacia Superior, for which Cichorius, Pauly-Wissowa, art. 'Cohors,' assumes a previous stay in Palestine from the presence in the cohort of a Jew from Caesarea named Bar Simso, shows how incomplete our evidence must be.

### (ii.) *The Roman Army in Syria and Palestine*

At the end of the Mithridatic war it was evident that the Roman occupation of Syria was a necessity for the preservation of peace and order in the east. Rome was now for the first time in direct contact with the Parthians, who controlled Mesopotamia and continually interfered in the affairs of the various client-kingdoms of Armenia and of Syria. Pompey's aggressions beyond the Euphrates left a heritage of intermittent warfare, which was relieved by dissensions in the Parthian royal household and by the difficulty of securing united action from a large body of semi-independent Parthian chieftains. Within the province the client-princes of northern Syria, Sampsiceramus of Emesa, Alchaudonius of Rhambae, and others required the backing of Roman forces to offset Parthian influence upon them, and the presence of Roman troops was everywhere demanded to prevent dynastic quarrels and ensure internal peace.[4] But peace was difficult to ensure. The raids of the Bedouins of the Arabian desert were a continual source of trouble, and the Jews resented the Roman yoke. To meet the needs of external and internal defence the Roman governor of Syria was given merely the resources usual to provincial governors, the legions voted him by the senate, and the right of levying in case of need both Roman citizens and provincials within his province.[5]

*[marginal note: The army in Syria.]*

---

[1] *C.I.L.* viii. 9358, 9359, 21044 ; Mommsen, *Gesamm. Schr.* vi. p. 553.

[2] See Cheesman, *l.c.*

[3] *Diplomata* were certificates of honourable discharge given to soldiers in the Roman auxiliary forces at the end of their service. These usually contain not only the name and unit of the recipient but the names of other units serving in the province. These are published in *C.I.L.* iii.

[4] See Mommsen, *Rom. Hist.*, Dickson's trans., iv. pp. 428 ff.; Bouchier, *Syria as a Roman Province*, is a simple and abbreviated account.

[5] Marquardt, *Staatsverwaltung* [2], i. p. 536 ; cf. Cicero, *Ad Att.* v. 18. 2 ; *Ad Fam.* xv. 1. 5.

An estimate of the normal garrison of Syria between 62 B.C. and the outbreak of the civil wars is hardly possible. Gabinius as governor, 57 B.C., gathered forces for an invasion of Parthia but was prevented by insurrections of the Jews,[1] and by his mission to restore Ptolemy of Egypt to his throne.[2] The province was taken over in 55 B.C. by Crassus, who invaded Parthia with a force of 7 legions, 4000 horse, and about 4000 light-armed men, probably allied troops.[3] Not 10,000 of this army escaped from Carrhae, and Cassius, after quelling a Jewish insurrection with the help of Antipater of Idumea, could muster but two weak legions to face the Parthian invasion of 51 B.C.[4]

Similarly, during the period of the civil wars, Syria, from the military point of view, was in a quite abnormal condition. Pompey, Cassius, and Antony in succession levied troops on Syrian soil, while the Parthians took advantage of the confusion to overrun the province. Syrian detachments assisted Pompey in the earlier portion of the civil war,[5] but after the battle of Pharsalia the province supported Caesar, and an army of Jews, Arabs, and Syrians under Mithridates of Pergamum and Antipater of Idumea came to relieve Caesar in Alexandria.[6] Judaea became an ethnarchy with Hyrcanus as high priest and Antipater as actual governor.[7] In northern Syria the single legion which Caesar left under the command of his kinsman Sextus Caesar was corrupted by the Pompeian, Caecilius Bassus, who managed to resist the troops sent against him until Cassius returned to the east in 44 B.C. Cassius won all the forces there to his command [8] and levied troops in Syria for the campaign of Philippi.[9] During the confusion following Philippi, the Parthians overran Cilicia, much of Asia, and the whole of Syria except Tyre, and placed their own nominee in the high-priesthood at Jerusalem, but they were driven out by Antony's lieutenant, Ventidius Bassus. Sosius, appointed by Antony to protect Syria, aided Herod to regain Jerusalem, which was finally captured in 37 B.C. The total strength of the two armies was 11 battalions of infantry, 6000 cavalry, about 30,000 in all, exclusive of the Syrian auxiliaries who were no inconsiderable number.[10] For his Parthian campaign in 36 B.C. Antony mobilized about 100,000 men, of which 60,000 were Roman legionaries among whom Orientals had been recruited.[11] 10,000 were Spanish and Gallic auxiliaries,

[1] Jos. *Ant.* xiv. 7. 2.

[2] Dio Cassius xxxix. 56. 3 ; Jos. *B.J.* i. 8. 7 ; Plutarch, *Antony*, 3.

[3] Plut. *Crassus* 20.

[4] Cicero, *Ad Att.* v. 20. 3 ; *Ad Fam.* xv. 14. 2 ; Jos. *Ant.* xiv. 7. 3 ; *B.J.* i. 8. 9.

[5] Appian, *B.C.* ii. 49 ; ii. 71.

[6] Jos. *Ant.* xiv. 8. 1-2 ; *B.J.* i. 9. 3-4.

[7] Jos. *Ant.* xiv. 8. 3 ; *B.J.* i. 10. 4.

[8] Jos. *B.J.* i. 10. 10 ; Dio Cass. xlvii. 26 f. ; Cic. *Ad Att.* xiv. 9. 3.

[9] Jos. *B.J.* i. 11. 4 ; *Ant.* xiv. 11. 2.

[10] Jos. *B.J.* i. 17. 9 ; *Ant.* xiv. 16. 1. τέλος, here translated battalion, means legion in Appian, *B.C.* v. 87, but it is unlikely that it means legion in this passage.

[11] Jos. *B.J.* i. 17. 1 ; *Ant.* xiv. 15. 10.

and 30,000 more came from Syria and Asia Minor as contingents of the allied kings.[1] Of this army more than 30,000 were lost.[2] Before Actium, Antony increased his army to 30 legions, two-thirds of whom were orientals,[3] and perhaps seven of these remained in Syria and Egypt.[4] During these years Syria was the prey of invaders and of rival claimants for power in Rome, and the people of the province, pressed into service in large numbers and heavily taxed, passively obeyed whatever power was in command. An extensive orientalization of the Roman army in the east resulted from the levies of Cassius and of Antony, and a large supply of auxiliary forces, light-armed troops, and bowmen was raised locally by the princes of the client kingdoms. These probably maintained armies for the most part raised from their own kingdoms, but sometimes had detachments of Roman soldiers stationed in their realms ; for instance, at the time of Caesar's death the garrison of Damascus, which was then at least within the kingdom of the Nabatean Arabs, was composed of Roman soldiers.[5] In 29 B.C. Herod had a Roman legion to guard Jerusalem,[6] but in general used troops raised within his kingdom. The best portion of the garrison at Jerusalem at the time of the deposition of Archelaus was a body of some 3000 Sebastenians of the royal forces.[7] Herod also had mercenaries,[8] and was followed to his mausoleum by his guards, Thracians, Germans, and Gauls.[9]

Augustus rightly considered Syria the point of greatest strategic import- Augustus. ance in the east. It controlled the natural routes to and across the Euphrates, and since the province of Asia was without a garrison, was the only eastern province with an army. The defence, therefore, of the whole Roman east, and the support for the client-princes of Galatia, Armenia, Cappadocia, and of Syria itself, depended upon the Syrian army, and Augustus made it an imperial province under a legate of proconsular rank with legions under his command. It appears that at first there were only three legions under the command of the Syrian legate, since in 4 B.C. Varus left one of the three Syrian legions in Jerusalem to preserve order while Archelaus presented to Augustus [10] his claim to succeed his father Herod, but the number was later increased to four, perhaps at the time of Gaius Caesar's expedition to the east, by the transference of the Legio XII. Fulminata from Egypt to Syria.[11]

---

[1] Plut. *Antony*, 37. 3.  [2] Plut. *Ant.* 50. 1 ; 51. 1.
[3] Kromayer, *Hermes*, 1898, p. 68, and cf. Jos. *Ant.* xiv. 15. 10.
[4] *Hermes*, 1898, p. 65.  [5] Jos. *Ant.* xiv. 11. 7.
[6] Jos. *Ant.* xv. 3. 7.
[7] Jos. *B.J.* ii. 3. 4 τὸ μέντοι πολεμικώτατον μέρος, Σεβαστηνοὶ τρισχίλιοι, Ῥοῦφός τε καὶ Γρᾶτος ἐπὶ τούτοις, ὁ μὲν τοὺς πέζους τῶν βασιλικῶν ὑπ' αὐτὸν ἔχων, Ῥοῦφος δὲ τοὺς ἱππεῖς . . . προσέθεντο Ῥωμαίοις.
[8] Jos. *B.J.* i. 15. 6 ἔχουσαι καὶ μισθοφόρους μιγάδας.
[9] Jos. *B.J.* i. 33. 9 καὶ περὶ τὴν κλίνην οἵ τε υἱεῖς καὶ τὸ πλῆθος τῶν συγγενῶν, ἐφ' οἷς οἱ δορυφόροι καὶ τὸ Θρᾴκιον στῖφος Γερμανοί τε καὶ Γαλάται, διεσκευασμένοι πάντες ὡς εἰς πόλεμον.
[10] Jos. *B.J.* ii. 3. 1 ἐν τῶν τριῶν ἀπὸ Συρίας ταγμάτων ; cf. ii. 5. 1 ; *Ant.* xvii. 10. 9.
[11] Strabo, xvii. 1. 12 ; 1. 30 (still three legions in Egypt) ; Pauly-Wissowa, art. ' Legio,' xii.[2], 1235, 1243, 1706 ; Parker, *The Roman Legions*, p. 92.

There certainly were four legions in Syria in A.D. 23.[1]  The comparatively peaceful conditions within and without the province after 27 B.C. until the time of Nero necessitated no larger force.

The four regular legions in Syria during the first century A.D. were the X. Fretensis, III. Gallica, VI. Ferrata, and XII. Fulminata.

Legio X. Fretensis.

The Legio X. Fretensis was Caesar's tenth legion, re-levied after his death. It gained the title Fretensis from the campaign under Octavian against Sextus Pompey at the Sicilian straits.[2]  Veterans from the legion were settled in colonies in Italy during the triumvirate.[3]  The legion was sent to Syria, probably before A.D. 6,[4] certainly by A.D. 17,[5] when it was encamped at Cyrrhae. Veterans of the legion shared in the Claudian colony of Ptolemais. It was in Corbulo's army in A.D. 58.[6]  A detachment from this legion went under Cestius Gallus against Jerusalem in A.D. 66.[7]  After the campaign in Galilee in A.D. 67 it was with V. Macedonica at Caesarea.[8] In A.D. 69 it came to Titus before Jerusalem by way of Jericho,[9] and at the end of the war became the permanent garrison of Judaea, encamped on the then desolate site of Jerusalem.[10]

Legio III. Gallica.

The Legio III. Gallica had probably been XV. of Caesar's Gallic army, and when handed over to Pompey in 53 B.C. became Pompey's III. It retained this number under Caesar at Munda.[11]  It was part of Antony's Parthian army,[12] and when taken over by Augustus after Actium was stationed in Syria where it remained, and shared in the Claudian colony of Ptolemais about A.D. 45. With VI. Ferrata it was important in Corbulo's army in Armenia, and in A.D. 64 built the castellum of Zialta there.[13]  It sent a detachment under Cestius Gallus against Jerusalem in A.D. 66, and must have fought under Vespasian in Galilee. It was, however, moved to Moesia, where it repelled the inroads of the Roxolani, and was important in the movement that brought Vespasian to the throne, marching to Italy in his interest.[14]  After a winter at Capua[15] it was sent back to Syria, where it remained a long time with its headquarters perhaps at Raphaneae, which XII. Fulminata vacated on being moved to Melitene.[16]

---

[1] Tacitus, *Ann.* iv. 5 " dehinc initiô ab Suriae usque ad flumen Euphraten, quantum ingenti terrarum sinu ambitur, quattuor legionibus coercita."

[2] Mommsen, *Res Gestae*[2], p. 69.     [3] *C.I.L.* v. 4191, 4987 ; x. 3887.

[4] See Pauly-Wissowa, art. ' Legio,' xii.[1] 1235.

[5] Tacitus, *Ann.* ii. 57.     [6] Tacitus, *Ann.* xiii. 40.

[7] Jos. *B.J.* ii. 18. 9.     [8] Jos. *B.J.* iii. 6. 1 ; 7. 21 ; 9. 1.

[9] Jos. *B.J.* v. 1. 6.

[10] Jos. *B.J.* vii. 1. 2-3 ; *Vita*, § 422. Mention of a veteran of this legion, enrolled in A.D. 68 and discharged in A.D. 94, and therefore a soldier of the army of Titus before Jerusalem, is found in the diptych of M. Valerius Quadratus, discovered in 1909 at Philadelphia in the Fayûm. See Deissmann, *Light from the Ancient East*, 4th ed., Eng. translation, 1927, p. 442, n. 2, for further literature.

[11] *Bell. Gall.* viii. 54 ; *Bell. Civ.* iii. 88. 2 ; *Bell. Hisp.* 30. 7.

[12] Plut. *Antony*, 42.     [13] *C.I.L.* iii. 6741, 6742, 6742a.

[14] Tacitus, *Hist.* ii. 74 ; ii. 85 ; Suetonius, *Vesp.* 6.

[15] Tacitus, *Hist.* iv. 3.     [16] Jos. *B.J.* vii. 1. 3.

The Legio VI. Ferrata was originally part of Caesar's army,[1] and in the campaigns of Caesar in Egypt and Pontus was reduced to an effective of 1000 men,[2] who were finally settled at Arelate. The name remained and VI. Ferrata after Philippi was one of Antony's veteran legions in Syria.[3] After Actium the legion was stationed in Syria by Augustus, perhaps also at Raphaneae.[4] After the defeat of Paetus it fought in Armenia under Corbulo.[5] Returning to Syria it sent a detachment against the Jews with Cestius Gallus.[6] In A.D. 69 it went to Europe under Licinius Mucianus in Vespasian's interest.[7] It returned to Syria after the return of III. Gallica,[8] and two years later reduced the kingdom of Commagene.[9] It remained in Syria and took part in Trajan's eastern expedition,[10] and after the Jewish war under Hadrian was moved to Palestine where it made its camp at Caparcotna in Galilee.[11]

*Legio VI. Ferrata.*

There was a Legio XII. under Octavian's command at Perugia, 41–40 B.C.,[12] which probably had been Caesar's twelfth legion.[13] This legion was probably stationed in Egypt during the earlier years of Augustus, since there were three legions each in Egypt and in Syria at that time,[14] but by A.D. 23 at the latest Syria had four legions.[15] The title Fulminata appears on the epitaphs of veterans of the twelfth legion settled in 16 B.C. at Patrae.[16] The legion shared in the Claudian colony of Ptolemais. Corbulo left it in Syria during his advance into Armenia in A.D. 58, but it took part in the unfortunate Armenian campaign of Paetus in A.D. 62,[17] and was returned to Syria by Corbulo.[18] It then had its camp at Raphaneae.[19] It was led by Cestius Gallus against Jerusalem in A.D. 66.[20] Suetonius, *Vesp.* 4, says it lost an eagle on this expedition, but Jos. *B.J.* ii. 19. 7-9 is silent on this point. In A.D. 69 Titus increased the army before Jerusalem from three to four legions using XII. Fulminata,[21] but it did not retrieve the disgrace of its former defeat, and was transferred to Cappadocia, where it served as garrison for a hundred years.[22]

*Legio XII.*

In addition to these four regular legions in Syria, during the reign of Nero V. Macedonica was brought from Moesia, XV. Apollinaris from

*Additions under Nero.*

---

[1] *Bell. Gall.* viii. 4. 3.      [2] *Bell. Alex.* 69. 1.      [3] Appian, *B.C.* v. 3.

[4] *C.I.L.* iii. 14165[13]; Cohen, *Description des monnaies*, i.[2] p. 307, nos. 431-432.

[5] Tacitus, *Ann.* xv. 26; Dessau, *I.L.S.* 9108.

[6] Jos. *B.J.* ii. 18. 9.      [7] Tacitus, *Hist.* ii. 83.

[8] Tacitus, *Hist.* iv. 39.      [9] Jos. *B.J.* vii. 7. 1.

[10] Dessau, *I.L.S.* 9471.

[11] *C.I.L.* iii. 6814-6816; *Ann. epig.*, 1920, 78.

[12] *C.I.L.* xi. 6721, nos. 28-30.

[13] *C.I.L.* xi. 6721, no. 29; the Paterna of 27 B.C., *C.I.L.* xi. 1058.

[14] Strabo, xvii. 1. 12; 1. 30; Jos. *Ant.* xvii. 10. 9; *B.J.* ii. 3. 1; 5. 1.

[15] Tacitus, *Ann.* iv. 5.      [16] *C.I.L.* iii. 504, 507, 509.

[17] Tacitus, *Ann.* xv. 6.      [18] Tacitus, *Ann.* xv. 26.

[19] Jos. *B.J.* vii. 1. 3.      [20] Jos. *B.J.* ii. 18. 9.

[21] Jos. *B.J.* v. 1. 6; Tacitus, *Hist.* v. 1.

[22] Jos. *B.J.* vii. 1. 3; *C.I.L.* viii. 7079; Dio Cassius, lv. 23. 5. On these particular legions see Pauly-Wissowa, art. 'Legio,' xii.[2] 1376 ff.

Pannonia, and IIII. Scythica probably also came from Moesia to assist Corbulo's campaign in Armenia ; all these were stationed in Syria. After the Jewish war V. Macedonica, which had encamped at Emmaus and had been prominent in the operations about Jerusalem,[1] was brought back to Moesia. XV. Apollinaris, which had been active in the Jewish war at Jotapata and Gamala,[2] and in the siege of Jerusalem,[3] was returned to Pannonia in A.D. 71.[4] IIII. Scythica was sent to Syria in the early years of Nero[5] and served in Paetus's unfortunate campaign in Armenia,[6] returning to Syria after its defeat.[7] It sent a *vexillatio* of 2000 men with Cestius against Jerusalem in A.D. 66.[8] In A.D. 69, while one portion of the army lay before Jerusalem and the other was moving on Rome to secure the principate for Vespasian, this legion was for a few months the only garrison toward the Euphrates border. After the Jewish war it remained a long time in Syria with its headquarters probably in the north near Antioch.[9]

Auxiliaries in Syria in the first century.

The evidence for the auxiliary troops in Syria in the first century is scanty : a diploma, *Ann. epig.*, 1927, 44, A.D. 88, mentions three alae and seventeen cohorts ; a second, Dessau, *I.L.S.* 2724, which probably dates from the Parthian expedition of Trajan, or perhaps from the expedition of Verus (see Dessau, *l.c.*), names five alae and fifteen cohorts ; while another, *I.L.S.* 9057, A.D. 157, names four alae and sixteen cohorts. Some scattered inscriptional and literary evidences also occur. Regarding the following list of alae and cohorts which were in Syria in the first and second centuries A.D., the reader is referred to Pauly-Wissowa, articles 'Ala' and 'Cohors' by Cichorius, to the indices of the *Année epigraphique*, and the appendices of Cheesman, *The Roman Auxilia* :

ALAE.　II. Flavia Agrippiana, *I.L.S.* 2724 ; *C.I.G.* ii. 3497.
　　　　Augusta Syriaca, *I.L.S.* 2724.
　　　*I. Flavia Civium Romanorum, *Ann. epig.*, 1927, 44.
　　　*Bosporana, *Ann. epig.*, 1922, 109, A.D. 54 ; *C.I.L.* iii. 6707.
　　　　Colonorum, *Ann. epig.*, 1895, 78.
　　　　I. Ulpia Dromadariorum Miliaria, *I.L.S.* 9057.
　　　　I. Flavia Gaetulorum, *I.L.S.* 2724 ; in Moesia A.D. 99, *C.I.L.* iii. Diploma xxx.
　　　*Gallica, *Ann. epig.*, 1927, 44.
　　　*Thracum Herculiana Miliaria, *I.L.S.* 2724, 9057 ; *C.I.L.* xii. 1357, on Euphrates in the first century.
　　　*Miliaria, in Syria in first century, Pliny, *Epistles*, vii. 31.
　　　*II. Pannoniorum, *Ann. epig.*, 1927, 44 ; used in Trajan's Dacian war, *Bull. de Corr. hell.* iv. 507.

[1] Jos. *B.J.* v. 2. 3 ; 11. 4 ; vi. 1. 7 ; 4. 3.　　[2] Jos. *B.J.* iii. 7. 34.
[3] Jos. *B.J.* v. 11. 4.　　　　　　　　　　　　　[4] Jos. *B.J.* vii. 5. 3.
[5] Tacitus, *Ann.* xiii. 35, and see discussion in Pauly-Wissowa, xii.[2] 1558.
[6] Tacitus, *Ann.* xv. 6-17.
[7] Tacitus, *Ann.* xv. 26 ; Dio Cassius lxii. 22. 4.
[8] Jos. *B.J.* ii. 18. 9.
[9] See Pauly-Wissowa, art. 'Legio,' xii.[2] on the particular legions and their history.

VII. Phrygum, *Ann. epig.*, 1899, 177 ; cf. *C.I.L.* ii. 4201, 1st cent. ; xiv. 171 ; in Palestine A.D. 139.

Praetoria, *I.L.S.* 2724 ; in Pannonia A.D. 80, *C.I.L.* iii. Diploma xii.

I. Ulpia Singularium, *I.L.S.* 9057, 2724 ; *C.I.L.* x. 6426 ; *Ann. epig.*, 1911, 161.

*Sebastenorum, 1st century, Jos. *Ant.* xx. 6. 1 ; *B.J.* ii. 12. 5 ; *Ant.* xix. 9. 2.

*III. Augusta Thracum Veterana Gallica, *Ann. epig.*, 1927, 44 ; *C.I.L.* ii. 4251.

COHORTS.*I. Ascalonitanorum, *I.L.S.* 2724 ; *Ann. epig.*, 1927, 44 ; cf. Jos. *B.J.* iii. 12.

*Augusta I., *I.L.S.* 2683, after A.D. 6 ; *Ins. Gr. Res Rom.* iii. 1136, Agrippa II. ; and perhaps Acts xxvii. 1.

*IV. Bracaugustanorum, *Ann. epig.*, 1927, 44 ; in Palestine A.D. 139.

I. Flavia Chalcidenorum Sagittariorum equitata, *I.L.S.* 2724 ; see Dessau's reading, 9057, note 9 ; and text of 9057.

II. Ulpia Equitata Civium Romanorum, *I.L.S.* 2724, 9057.

I. Flavia Civium Romanorum Equitata, *I.L.S.* 2724 ; in Palestine A.D. 139.

*II. Classica Sagittariorum, *I.L.S.* 2683, after A.D. 6 ; *Ann. epig.*, 1927, 44 ; *I.L.S.* 9057.

*IV. Callaecorum, *Ann. epig.*, 1927, 44.

*I. Flavia Canathenorum, *C.I.L.* viii. 2394-2395, 17904 ; in Rhaetia, A.D. 166, *C.I.L.* iii. 6001, Diploma lxxiii. ; probably in Palestine during the first century although Canatha was under Agrippa II., Mommsen, *Ges. Schr.* vi. p. 101.

I. Ulpia Dacorum, *I.L.S.* 9057 ; in Syria until late Empire, *Not. Dig.* Or. 33. 33.

III. Dacorum Equitata, *I.L.S.* 2724.

IV. Gallorum, *I.L.S.* 9057.

VII. Gallorum, *I.L.S.* 9057 ; in Moesia earlier, *I.L.S.* 1999.

*II. Miliaria Italica Civium Romanorum Voluntariorum, *I.L.S.* 9168, A.D. 69 ; 9057 ; *Ann. epig.*, 1927, 44, and probably in Palestine early in the first century ; see below.

*I. Ituraeorum, *Ann. epig.*, 1927, 44.

*Lucensium, *Ann. epig.*, 1927, 44.

*I. Lucensium Equitata, *Ann. epig.*, 1927, 44 ; *I.L.S.* 2724 ; in Pannonia A.D. 80, *C.I.L.* iii. Diploma xi.

IV. Lucensium Equitata, *I.L.S.* 2724.

*I. Miliaria, *Ann. epig.*, 1927, 44 ; *Bull. Corr. hell.* xxi. 45. Musulamiorum, *Ann. epig.*, 1897, 44.

I. Numidarum, *Ann. epig.*, 1897, 44 ; in Lycia Pamphylia A.D. 178, *C.I.L.* iii. Diploma lxxvi.

*I. Augusta Pannoniorum, *Ann. epig.*, 1927, 44 ; *I.L.S.* 9057 ; in Egypt A.D. 83, *C.I.L.* iii. Diploma xv.

*II. Pannoniorum, *Ann. epig.*, 1927, 44.

II. Ulpia Paflagonum Equitata, *I.L.S.* 2724, 9057.

III. Ulpia Paflagonum Equitata, *I.L.S.* 2724, 9057.

I. Ulpia Petraeorum Miliaria Equitata, *I.L.S.* 2724, 9057 ; *Ann. epig.*, 1911, 161.

V. Ulpia Petraeorum Miliaria Equitata, *I.L.S.* 2724, 9057.

I. Ulpia Sagittariorum Equitata, *I.L.S.* 2724.

*I. Sebastena, *Ann. epig.*, 1927, 44, perhaps in Palestine A.D. 139.

I. Sugambrorum Equitata, *I.L.S.* 2724, but from Moesia.

I. Claudia Sugambrorum, *I.L.S.* 9057 ; in Moesia A.D. 134, *C.I.L.* iii. Diploma xlviii.

*IV. Thracum Syriaca Equitata, *Ann. epig.*, 1927, 44 ; *C.I.L.* ii. 1970.

I. Thracum or II. Thracum, see Dessau, *I.L.S.* 9057, n. 9 ; *I.L.S.* 2724 ; cf. *C.I.L.* iii. 8261-8262 ; *I.L.S.* 2733, in Moesia.

*II. Thracum Syriaca Equitata, *I.L.S.* 9057 ; *Ann. epig.*, 1927, 44.

III. Augusta Thracum Equitata, *I.L.S.* 9057 ; *C.I.L.* x. 6100 ; vi. 31856 ; *Ann. epig.*, 1888, 66 ; 1911, 161.

III. Thracum Syriaca Equitata, *Ann. epig.*, 1911, 161.

\* distinguishes alae and cohorts which were present in Syria and Palestine during the first century A.D.

Judaea in
A.D. 86
and 139.
The following alae and cohorts were in Judaea in A.D. 86, according to *C.I.L.* iii. Diploma xiv. :

| | |
|---|---|
| ALAE : Veterana Gaetulorum | I. Thracum |
| I. Thracum Mauretana | II. Thracum |
| COHORTS : I. Augusta Lusitanorum | II. Cantabrorum |

None of these is original with Syria, but the possibility of Syrian recruits is not excluded. In A.D. 139 the following appear in Syria Palestina, according to Diploma cix. :

| | |
|---|---|
| ALAE : Gallorum et Thracum | I. Galatarum |
| Antoniniana Gallorum | II. Galatarum |
| VII. Phrygum | III. Bracarum |
| COHORTS : I. Thracum miliaria | IV. Bracarum |
| I. Sebastenorum miliaria | IV. Petraeorum |
| I. Damascenorum | VI. Petraeorum |
| I. Montanorum miliaria | V. Gemina Civium |
| I. Flavia Civium Romanorum | Romanorum |

Note that while many of these are from the eastern portion of the empire, only one is from Judaea itself, and three are from Syria. The two cohorts of Roman citizens were probably originally freedmen, one of Flavian foundation and the other the result of the union of two previously existing cohorts.[1]

---

[1] See *Journal of Roman Studies*, 1928, pp. 57 ff., on the meaning of *Gemina*.

It will be observed that there is evidence for the presence of many of these cohorts in Syria in the first century A.D. Cohorts such as the Petraeorum were not formed before the time of Trajan, and several of the cohorts above noted are known to have been in Moesia and Pannonia during the first century. The Jewish wars, the formation of the province of Cappadocia, and the expeditions of Trajan and of Verus, demanded fresh alignments of troops, but a few cohorts, e.g. II. Italica C.R. and II. Classica, are known to have been in Syria before Vespasian's day and to have continued there afterwards. Many other auxiliary cohorts were used in Palestine and Syria during the first century, as auxiliary forces were gathered by various governors, Varus,[1] Petronius,[2] Cestius,[3] Vespasian,[4] and Titus,[5] to meet disturbances and revolts among the Jews, but their names have not come down. A general survey, however, of the auxilia shows that in the first century the basis of recruitment in the auxilia was largely local, that the majority of the auxiliary units served in the province in which they were raised, and that despite later changes the system of local recruitment and service was never abandoned completely. Whatever the people from which the various units drew their names and origin, a goodly proportion of the soldiers recruited belonged both in the first century and later to the province in which the unit served.[6]

The legions which formed the garrison of Syria were divided between the northern and the central regions of the province, near the cities of Antioch and Emesa. Legionary soldiers were not regularly used in Judaea unless on special occasions. It is true that a legion was stationed at Jerusalem to keep order while the succession to Herod was being decided,[7] and that the legions could always be called upon in case of need. The garrison of Judaea under the procurators was regularly composed of Syrian auxiliary cohorts. Among the royal troops under Herod and Archelaus were 3000 Sebasteni, characterized by Josephus[8] as the most warlike portion. The inclusion of these Sebasteni among the Roman auxiliary cohorts upon the reduction of the ethnarchy may be the origin of the *cohortes* and *ala Sebastenorum* which later appear. *The distribution of troops in Syria.*

Caesarea, not Jerusalem, was the military headquarters for Judaea.

[1] Jos. *B.J.* ii. 5. 1 τὰ λοιπὰ δύο τάγματα καὶ τὰς σὺν αὐτοῖς τέσσαρας ἴλας ἱππέων.

[2] Jos. *B.J.* ii. 10. 1 σὺν τρισὶ τάγμασι καὶ πόλλοις ἐκ τῆς Συρίας συμμάχοις.

[3] Jos. *B.J.* ii. 18. 9 πεζῶν τε ἓξ σπείρας καὶ τέσσαρας ἴλας ἱππέων, πρὸς αἷς τὰς παρὰ τῶν βασιλέων συμμαχίας.

[4] Jos. *B.J.* iii. 4. 2 τούτοις εἴποντο ὀκτωκαίδεκα σπεῖραι · προσεγένοντο δὲ καὶ ἀπὸ Καισαρείας πέντε καὶ ἱππέων ἴλη μία, πέντε δ' ἕτεραι τῶν ἀπὸ Συρίας ἱππέων; also large forces from the client kings.

[5] Jos. *B.J.* v. 1. 6 πρὸς οἷς αἵ τε τῶν βασιλέων συμμαχίαι πολὺ πλείους καὶ συχνοὶ τῶν ἀπὸ τῆς Συρίας ἐπίκουροι συνῆλθον; Tacitus, *Hist.* v. 1.

[6] See Cheesman, *The Roman Auxilia*, pp. 57 ff. ; Mommsen, *Ges. Schr.* vi. pp. 20 ff.

[7] Jos. *B.J.* ii. 3. 1 ἐν τῶν τριῶν ἀπὸ Συρίας ταγμάτων, ὅπερ ἄγων ἧκεν, ἐν τῇ πόλει καταλείπει.

[8] Jos. *B.J.* ii. 3. 4.

The soldiers there were mainly Syrians,[1] many from Caesarea itself and Sebaste (Samaria),[2] and readily took the part of their countrymen against the Jewish community.   Of the troops at Caesarea there are mentioned an *ala Sebastena* and five cohorts of infantry,[3] which were there under Agrippa I.   Later appear four cohorts and one ala,[4] among which Mommsen conjectures were a Cohors I. Sebastenorum, I. Ascalonitanorum, and I. Canathenorum.[5]   In Acts x. 1 mention is made of a *cohors Italica* which must have been present about A.D. 40.   No *cohors Caesariensium* is known.

The garrison of Jerusalem.     The garrison of Jerusalem itself was probably not as large as the turbulent population required.   The Roman government (perhaps mistakenly) tried to conciliate the Jews.   In response to Jewish demonstrations [6] Pilate sent back to Caesarea the standards of the garrison, which were offensive to the Jews on account of the images of Caesar on them.   It is possible that there were some legionary soldiers in the garrison of Jerusalem, since Jos. ii. 13. 4-5 speaks of the hoplites, heavy-armed soldiers, whom Felix used to disperse the following of the false prophets and of the Egyptian impostor, but hoplite does not necessarily mean a legionary soldier.[7]   Since any additions to the garrison of Jerusalem were brought from Caesarea it is probable that like the garrison there it was in the main composed of Syrians whose contempt for Jewish religious practices was the cause of serious tumults in both places.[8]   We cannot estimate the number of soldiers in the garrison,

---

[1] Jos. *B.J.* ii. 13. 7 τὸ γὰρ πλέον 'Ρωμαίοις τῆς ἐκεῖ δυνάμεως ἐκ Συρίας ἦν κατειλεγμένον.

[2] Jos. *Ant.* xx. 8. 7 μέγα δὲ φρονοῦντες ἐπὶ τῷ τοὺς πλείστους τῶν ὑπὸ 'Ρωμαίοις ἐκεῖσε στρατευομένων Καισαρεῖς εἶναι καὶ Σεβαστηνούς; Jos. *Ant.* xix. 9. 1 Καισαρεῖς καὶ Σεβαστηνοὶ τῶν εὐποιῶν αὐτοῦ λαθόμενοι τὰ τῶν δυσμενεστάτων ἐποίησαν . . . καὶ ὅσοι στρατευόμενοι τότε ἔτυχον, συχνοὶ δ' ἦσαν, οἴκαδε ἀπῆλθον . . . ; xix. 9. 2 πρὸ πάντων δὲ ἐπέστειλε τῷ Φάδῳ Καισαρεῦσι καὶ Σεβαστηνοῖς ἐπιπλῆξαι τῆς εἰς τὸν κατοιχόμενον ὕβρεως καὶ παροινίας εἰς τὰς ἔτι ζώσας, τὴν ἴλην δὲ τῶν Καισαρέων καὶ τῶν Σεβαστηνῶν καὶ τὰς πέντε σπείρας εἰς Πόντον μεταγαγεῖν, ἵν' ἐκεῖ στρατεύοιντο, τῶν δ' ἐν Συρίᾳ 'Ρωμαϊκῶν ταγμάτων ἐπιλέξαι στρατιώτας καταρίθμους καὶ τὸν ἐκείνων ἀναπληρῶσαι τόπον.   οὐ μὴν οἱ κελευσθέντες μετέστησαν.

[3] Jos. *Ant.* xix. 9. 2.

[4] Jos. *Ant.* xx. 6. 1 ἀναλαβὼν τὴν τῶν Σεβαστηνῶν ἴλην καὶ πεζῶν τέσσαρα τάγματα (=cohorts ?); *B.J.* ii. 12. 5 Κουμανὸς δὲ ἀναλαβὼν ἀπὸ τῆς Καισαρείας μίαν ἴλην ἱππέων καλουμένην Σεβαστηνῶν ἐξεβοήθει τοῖς πορθουμένοις.   Cf. *B.J.* iii. 4. 2 προσεγένοντο δὲ καὶ ἀπὸ Καισαρείας πέντε (σπεῖραι) καὶ ἱππέων ἴλη μία, when Vespasian was collecting forces to advance into Galilee.

[5] *Ges. Schr.* vi. p. 553.

[6] Jos. *B.J.* ii. 9. 3 ὑπερθαυμάσας δὲ ὁ Πιλᾶτος τὸ τῆς δεισιδαιμονίας ἄκρατον ἐκκομίσαι μὲν αὐτίκα τὰς σημαίας 'Ιεροσολύμων κελεύει; *Ant.* xviii. 3. 1 καὶ Πιλᾶτος θαυμάσας τὸ ἐχυρὸν αὐτῶν ἐπὶ φυλακῇ τῶν νόμων παραχρῆμα τὰς εἰκόνας ἐκ τῶν 'Ιεροσολύμων ἐπανεκόμισεν εἰς Καισάρειαν.

[7] The 1500 soldiers which Varus hastily levied from Berytus when on his march to relieve Sabinus in Jerusalem, Jos. *B.J.* ii. 5. 1, are termed ὁπλῖται. Although Berytus was a Roman colony these were not their regular legionary soldiers.

[8] Jos. *B.J.* ii. 12. 1 ; ii. 13. 7.

which must have varied from time to time, but Claudius Lysias could detach 200 soldiers, 70 horse, and 200 δεξιολάβοι to accompany Paul to Caesarea.[1] The unrest and brigandage of the years preceding the outbreak of war in A.D. 66 doubtless necessitated increased garrisons both in Jerusalem and in places of the region such as Jericho,[2] but the additional forces sent to Jerusalem in the time of Florus were merely a matter of cohorts,[3] and, in fact, Florus agreed[4] to leave the city, adding to the garrison but a single cohort of the forces he had brought from Caesarea. Ascalon apparently, like Sebaste, left undefended in A.D. 65,[5] was garrisoned in A.D. 67 by one cohort of infantry and one cohort of cavalry.[6] Joppa remained ungarrisoned in A.D. 66.[7]

### (iii.) Three Passages in Acts of Special Difficulty

(a) Acts x. 1.—This refers to Cornelius at Caesarea as a centurion ἐκ σπείρας τῆς καλουμένης 'Ιταλικῆς—that is ' of the cohort called Italian.' Probably this was the Cohors II. Italica Civium Romanorum,[8] which must have been in Syria before A.D. 69, for a certain Proculus of this cohort was an optio in the vexillatio of the Syrian army which accompanied Mucianus to Italy to win the principate for Vespasian.[9] This is shown by an inscription published by Dessau (I.L.S. 9168) which says Proculus Rabili f. Col. Philadel. mil. optio coh. II. Italic. c. R. Fa[us]tini, ex vexil. sagit. exer. Syriaci, stip. VII., vixit an. XXVI., Apuleius frater f.c.

---

[1] Acts xxiii. 23. See note ad loc. for the variations in the text and the difficulty of interpreting in this case.

[2] Jos. B.J. ii. 18. 6 οἱ δὲ στασιασταὶ καταλαβόμενοί τι φρούριον, ὃ καλεῖται μὲν Κύπρος, καθύπερθεν δ᾽ ἦν 'Ιεριχοῦντος, τοὺς μὲν φρουροὺς ἀπέσφαξαν.

[3] Jos. B.J. ii. 14. 6 ὁ δὲ μετὰ στρατιᾶς ἱππικῆς τε καὶ πεζικῆς ἐπὶ 'Ιεροσολύμων ὥρμησεν, but from ii. 15. 6 it appears that he came with but one cohort, which was followed by two more from Caesarea, ii. 15. 3 παρεγίνοντο δὲ δύο σπεῖραι, of which he left one, since the people asked him not to leave the one which fought, i.e. which had accompanied him.

[4] Jos. B.J. ii. 15. 6 τῶν δὲ πάντα περὶ ἀσφαλείας καὶ τοῦ μηδὲν νεωτερίσειν ὑποσχομένων, εἰ μίαν αὐτοῖς καταλείποι σπεῖραν, μὴ μέντοι τὴν μαχεσαμένην.

[5] Jos. B.J. ii. 18. 1 ἀντέσχεν δ᾽ οὔτε Σεβαστὴ ταῖς ὁρμαῖς αὐτῶν οὔτε 'Ασκάλων.

[6] Jos. B.J. iii. 2. 1 ἡ δὲ 'Ασκάλων . . . ἐφρουρεῖτο γὰρ ὑπό τε σπείρας πεζῶν καὶ ὑπὸ μιᾶς ἴλης ἱππέων, ἧς ἐπῆρχεν 'Αντώνιος.

[7] Jos. B.J. ii. 18. 10 ὁ δὲ Κέστιος . . . αὐτὸς μὲν εἰς Καισάρειαν ἀφικνεῖται, μοῖραν δὲ τῆς στρατιᾶς προέπεμψεν εἰς 'Ιόππην, προστάξας, εἰ μὲν καταλαβέσθαι δυνηθεῖεν τὴν πόλιν, φρουρεῖν.

[8] On the Italian cohort see Ramsay, Expositor, Sept. 1896, pp. 194-200 (= Was Christ born at Bethlehem? 1898, pp. 260-269); Schürer, 'Die Σπεῖρα 'Ιταλική und die Σπεῖρα Σεβαστή,' Zeitschr. f. wissenschaftliche Theologie, xviii., 1875, pp. 413-425. Italica as a cognomen for other auxiliary cohorts is attested by a passage of Arrian, Ect. 13 (Cappadocia), and C.I.L. vi. 3654 (Rome); a cohors I. Italica civium Romanorum Voluntariorum is mentioned in a cursus honorum at Ostia, C.I.L. xiv. 171.

[9] Tacitus, Hist. ii. 83.

This cohort is also mentioned in *C.I.L.* vi. 3528, referring to a tribune of the cohort in Rome, but no date can be ascertained for this inscription. The full name of the cohort is found by comparing *C.I.L.* xi. 6117 and the inscription cited above, *Cohors II. Miliaria Italica Civium Romanorum Voluntariorum quae est in Syria,* while the persons to whom dedication in the former was made, L. Maesius Rufus, Maria, and Maesia, were probably of Syrian origin.

Mommsen [1] thought that *cohortes civium Romanorum voluntariorum* began in the enrolment of freedmen in the auxiliary cohorts.[2] Only in periods of great stress were freedmen enrolled in the legions, and such soldiers were termed *voluntarii,* or *volones.*[3] Augustus made use of such troops in the legions on only two occasions, during the Pannonian revolt and after the defeat of Varus.[4] In addition, Macrobius [5] says that Augustus enrolled in Germany and Illyricum several cohorts of freedmen which he termed *voluntariae.* The Cohors II. Italica was probably a corps of freedmen and similar in origin, but the title Italica shows some connexion with Italy, and it is not itself one of these cohorts, since it is found only in the east. It is possible, as Cheesman suggests,[6] that the remainder of the four thousand Oriental freedmen, votaries of Egyptian and Jewish cults, who were enrolled in the army A.D. 19 by way of removing votaries of these cults from Italy, and sent to Sardinia to reduce the brigands there, where the pestilential climate might soon complete their ruin,[7] were finally transported to Syria. Like the *cohortes voluntariorum* in Dalmatia,[8] and other auxiliary cohorts in general,[9] this cohort came to be composed of local recruits of peregrine status. At any rate it appears in A.D. 69 in the inscription above cited as a regiment of archers, and its *optio,* though a Roman citizen, was a native of Philadelphia (Rabbat Ammon), and, as the name shows, certainly not of Roman stock. So also the Cohors II. Classica, which was in Syria in A.D. 6,[10] appears in A.D. 88 as II. Classica Sagittariorum.[11] The Cohors II. Italica remained in Syria for a considerable period after the Jewish war.[12] Of its presence in Caesarea at the time of the reference in Acts x. 1 there is no proof, but it seems probable that it is the cohort meant.

[1] *Res Gestae*[2], p. 72.

[2] Cf. Cheesman, *The Roman Auxilia,* p. 65.

[3] Livy, xxii. 57. 11; xxiii. 35. 6; Festus, ed. Lindsay, p. 511; Script. Hist. Aug. *Vita Marci,* 21.

[4] Suetonius, *Aug.* 25; cf. Dio Cass. lv. 31-32.

[5] *Sat.* i. 11. 33.                                      [6] *Op. cit.* p. 66.

[7] Tacitus, *Ann.* ii. 85 "actum et de sacris Aegyptiis Iudaicisque pellendis factumque patrum consultum, ut quattuor milia libertini generis ea superstitione infecta, quis idonea aetas, in insulam Sardiniam veherentur, coercendis illic latrociniis et si ob gravitatem caeli interissent, vile damnum; ceteri cederent Italia, nisi certam ante diem profanos ritus exuissent."

[8] Cheesman, *op. cit.* p. 67.

[9] Mommsen, *Ges. Schr.* vi. pp. 77 ff.

[10] Dessau, *I.L.S.* 2683.                              [11] *Ann. epig.,* 1927, 44.

[12] *Ann. epig.,* 1927, 44, in A.D. 88, and *I.L.S.* 9057, in A.D. 157.

On the person of Cornelius the centurion little can be added. As a centurion he was certainly a Roman citizen, but as he served in an auxiliary cohort we cannot decide whether he was born free or not. He cannot have obtained his citizenship by purchase in the manner of Claudius Lysias,[1] who, despite his non-Roman origin, rose to the still higher military position of χιλιάρχος or tribune,[2] since his gentile name, Cornelius, is not that of any of the emperors. He may have belonged to one of the families liberated by Sulla (see note on x. 2). He was not of Jewish stock, although interested in the Jewish religion, but a Gentile, and had won the respect of the Jewish community by his acts of charity. The presence of his family and household in Caesarea suggests that he had settled there at the end of his term of service, but such suppositions are conjectural, since he might well have connexions in Caesarea if the unit with which he served was garrisoned there for a considerable period.

(b) Acts xxvii. 2.—This describes Paul at Caesarea as given into the custody of Julius, a centurion of the σπεῖρα Σεβαστή.

Acts xxvii. 2.

This σπεῖρα Σεβαστή has been interpreted [3] as referring to the *cohortes Sebastenorum*, i.e. auxiliary cohorts of Samaritans such as had formed part of Herod's garrison in Jerusalem.[4] These, with an *ala Sebastenorum*, were probably the main portion of the garrison of Agrippa I. in Caesarea,[5] and were incorporated into the Roman army and used in the Jewish war.[6]

The objection to this ingenious explanation is that σπεῖρα Σεβαστή means *cohors Augusta*, not *cohors Sebastenorum*. Conceivably there has been a confusion in the Greek either of Luke or of the text of Acts, but there is no evidence of this. Moreover there is sure evidence that there was a Cohors Augusta in Syria in the first century, for Dessau [7] mentions a Quintus Aemilius Secundus who in the time of Augustus served under Quirinius in Syria as prefect of the Cohors Augusta I., also of the Cohors II. Classica. The displacement of the numeral may be merely a stone-cutter's error. The same cohort perhaps reappears in the time probably of Agrippa II. at Eitha in Batanea, σπείρης Αὐ[γούστης].[8] As a Cohors III. Augusta [9] is known in the early Empire, one must admit Cohors I. Augusta as a possible identification for the σπεῖρα Σεβαστή in Acts.

It is perhaps surprising that a centurion of a Syrian auxiliary Cohors

---

[1] On purchase of citizenship under Claudius see Dio Cassius, lx. 17.

[2] Acts xxiii. 22.

[3] On the Augustan cohort see Schürer, *Zeitschr. f. wissenschaftliche Theologie*, xviii., 1875, pp. 413-425 ; Mommsen and Harnack, ' Zu Apostelgeschichte 28, 16,' *Sitzungsberichte Berl. Akad.*, 1895, pp. 492 ff., Mommsen's part of which appears in his *Gesammelte Schriften*, vi. pp. 546 ff. ; E. Meyer, *Ursprung und Anfänge d. Christentums*, iii. p. 480.

[4] Jos. *B.J.* ii. 3. 4 ; ii. 4. 2.        [5] Jos. *Ant.* xix. 9. 2.

[6] Jos. *Ant.* xx. 6. 1 ; *B.J.* iii. 4. 2.

[7] *Q. Aemilius Q. f. Pal. Secundus [in] castris divi Aug. s[ub] P. Sulpi[c]io Quirinio le[gato] C[a]esaris Syriae honoribus decoratus, pr[a]efect. cohort. Aug. I. pr[a]efect. cohort. II. Classicae*, etc., *I.L.S.* 2683.

[8] Cagnat, *I.G.R.R.* iii. 1136 ; Dittenberger, *OGIS.* 421.

[9] *C.I.L.* vi. 3508.

Augusta should have been given charge of an important prisoner on the road to Rome, for we should expect at least a legionary centurion or else one of the *frumentarii* to perform this duty.  In the absence, however, of evidence that these were organized as cohorts, or given the cognomen Augusta, the question must be left open.

Acts
xxviii. 16.

(c) Acts xxviii. 16.—According to the Western text (see Vol. III. note *ad loc.*) the centurion Julius, upon reaching Rome, gave Paul and his companions over to the στρατοπέδαρχος, or camp commander.[1]  This is the reading which appears in the Latin *Codex Gigas* as *princeps peregrinorum.* Mommsen has conjectured[2] that this official, who when Mommsen wrote was only known to have existed in the third century A.D. as head of the *castra peregrina*, was also existent in A.D. 62, and is referred to here.  A recently discovered African inscription of the time of Trajan[3] which proves the existence of the *princeps peregrinorum* at that time lends great support to this conjecture.  The *castra peregrina* was a centre for legionary officers on furlough in Rome, and was a base for the *milites peregrini* or *frumentarii.* These officials, probably originally charged with business relating to the supply of food for the armies, fulfilled other functions also—the bearing of important messages, imperial secret police, etc., and were general liaison officers between the legions in the provinces and legionary centurions on furlough at Rome.[4]  Mommsen, *l.c.*, and in his *Römisches Strafrecht*, p. 316, basing his argument, however, chiefly on this passage of Acts, suggests that the *frumentarii* had the care during transport of prisoners who were to be tried at Caesar's court.  The *frumentarii* and all the officials of the *castra peregrina*, including even the *princeps peregrinorum*, were of centurial rank.[5] Nevertheless it must be remembered that *princeps peregrinorum* is an interpretation, not an accurate rendering, of στρατοπέδαρχος, which may refer to the head of the Praetorium (see note on xxviii. 16).

[See ' Exercitus,' ' Legio,' ' Dilectus,' ' Auxilia,' ' Cohors,' and ' Ala,' in Pauly-Wissowa, and the corresponding articles in Daremberg and Saglio ; and also Cagnat, *L'armée romaine dans l'Afrique du Nord*; Domaszewski, *Die Rangordnung des römischen Heeres* ; Cheesman, *The*

[1] Acts xxviii. 16.

[2] Mommsen, *l.c.*  The view, however, that the person to whom prisoners thus brought to Rome were entrusted was not the *princeps peregrinorum* but the prefect of the praetorian guard finds support in Pliny, *Ad Traianum*, Ep. 57. In this passage Trajan directs Pliny to send a certain Julius Bassus, who had been condemned to banishment and who had not within the two years allowed him either appealed his case or left the province, in chains to the prefects of the praetorian guard.  Paul at Rome may have been in the hands of the prae-torians, Ep. ad Philip. i. 13 ὥστε τοὺς δεσμούς μου φανερούς ἐν Χριστῷ γενέσθαι ἐν ὅλῳ τῷ πραιτωρίῳ, but the interpretation of this verse and its connexion with Rome are very doubtful.

[3] *Contes rendus de l'Académie des Ins. et Belles-lettres*, 1923, p. 197.

[4] See Pauly-Wissowa, art. ' Frumentarii ' ; Mommsen, *l.c.* ; and see especially T. Ashby and B. Reynolds, *Journal of Roman Studies*, 1923, pp. 151 ff.

[5] Domaszewski, *Rangordnung d. röm. Heeres*, pp. 28, 104, 267.

*Roman Auxilia*; Parker, *The Roman Legions*; and Marquardt, *Römische Staatsverwaltung* [2], ii. pp. 307 ff. On the Roman army in Palestine and Syria reference may be made to Bible dictionaries and commentaries, and also to S. Buss, *Roman Law and History in the New Testament*, 1901, pp. 339 ff.; E. Egli, 'Das römische Militär in der Apostelgeschichte,' *Zeitschr. f. wissensch. Theologie*, xxvii., 1883, pp. 10 ff.; Schürer, *Geschichte d. jüdischen Volkes im Zeitalter Jesu Christi* [4], i. pp. 458-466; A. Bludau, 'Die Militarverhältnisse in Caesarea im apostolischen Zeitalter,' *Theologischpraktische Monatschrift*, xvii., 1907, pp. 136-143.]

## NOTE XXXIV. THE CHRONOLOGY OF ACTS

### By KIRSOPP LAKE

There are two points from which the study of the chronology of the Apostolic age can be attacked. It is possible to begin with the established Christian tradition of the third century, or with the more nearly contemporary records of the end of the first century. In practice the Christian tradition means Eusebius, and the records of the first century mean Josephus and Tacitus, though in each case subsidiary evidence may occasionally be added from other writers, such as Orosius, Suetonius, and Dio Cassius. The results reached by these two methods do not differ greatly, but the road travelled is not the same. {*The method of chronological investigation.*}

The drawback to following the early writers is that their statements are often sadly lacking in chronological clearness. The drawback to following Eusebius is that, though he had access to writings of great value which are now lost, he was treating Acts as a document of inspired accuracy, providing unquestionable data, while we are investigating it critically. Moreover, in dealing with the early period he was himself chiefly relying on Josephus, with more faith in him and with less knowledge of Latin authorities than we should have. Nevertheless Eusebius was an historian of the first rank, and no writer on the chronology of Acts can pass him by, even though he may feel strongly that the only results which can be confidently accepted must depend on Josephus and Tacitus. For the period covered by Acts he probably had few authorities better [1] than we have, and his methods were such that it is safer to start with the references in Acts to contemporary events and with those early authorities which supplement and clarify this evidence.

---

[1] Doubtless he possessed the works of Julius Africanus, but it is by no means certain that, for the first century, Africanus had more accurate information than Josephus. He may have used Justus of Tiberias, but no one can say whether Justus was superior to Josephus. On the question of the sources of Eusebius see especially E. Schürer, 'Zur Chronologie des Lebens Pauli,' *ZWTh.*, 1898, pp. 21 ff., and Erbes, 'Die Todestage der Ap. Paulus und Petrus,' *TU.* N.F. iv. i. (1899).

Contem-
porary
events.

References to contemporary events are unfortunately very few, and the difficulty is enhanced in two directions—the dates of these events are themselves an obscure problem, and their relation to the main narrative of Acts is far from clear.

Use has, as a rule, been made of the following references to contemporary events :

(1) xii. 23.  The death of Herod.
(2) xi. 28 and xii. 25.  The famine in the time of Claudius.
(3) xiii. 7.  The proconsulship of Sergius Paulus in Cyprus.
(4) xviii. 2.  The edict of Claudius banishing the Jews from Rome.
(5) xviii. 12.  Gallio's proconsulship in Achaea.
(6) xxiv. 27.  The succession of Porcius Festus to Felix.

Of these only the first, fifth, and sixth can be fixed at all definitely, and there is much difficulty about the sixth.  The third proves to give no help, and the fourth is very problematic.

The whole chronology of i.-xv. hangs on the first two points, and the discussion of them and their relation to the structure of Acts is a complicated and baffling problem.  The fifth point is central for the chronology of xvi.-xxi., and the sixth—if it could only be settled—would fix the date of Paul's hearing before Festus and Agrippa, and give a reasonably clear chronology for the last chapters of Acts.

## I. *The Death of Herod Agrippa I.*

Our knowledge of the date of Agrippa's death depends entirely on the information given in Josephus, and this in turn on the method of dating employed.

Methods
of dating.

There are three ways in which the years of a king's reign may be reckoned : (i.) The actual lapse of years, counting from the date of accession. (ii.) The official Roman method of counting each year as beginning with the opening of the calendar year, so that—with the Eastern reckoning —the first year was the same as the last year of the preceding king, and the second year of each reign began with the autumn following the accession. (iii.) The chronographic method, by which the first year, not the second, began with the opening of the calendar year next after the accession.

Thus the chronographic method was apt to give every ruler one year less than the official, while the actual count of elapsed time agreed for part of each year with the official and for part of it with the chronographical method.

Jewish dates are further complicated by the fact that the official Hellenistic world—including the Jews—reckoned that the year began in the autumn, but there was a Jewish sacred calendar which began with Nisan— the month containing the Spring equinox.  The Babylonian Talmud [1] gives the rabbinical tradition that the dates of kings were reckoned in the official manner, taking 1 Nisan as the first day of the new year.

[1] *Rosh ha-Shanah,* f. 2a.

It does not seem that Josephus had any fixed method of chronology.
He probably copied his sources. Thus in dealing with the chronology of the
siege he takes the official years of the reigning emperor, but in treating the
story of Herod the Great he seems to follow the actual years of elapsed
time. There is no trace of the Talmudic method or of the chronographic.
It is therefore necessary in each case to see which system of chronology seems
to be consistent with the various statements.

In the case of Agrippa the statements in the *Antiquities* are
entirely consistent if Josephus be supposed to follow Agrippa's actual
years.

In *Antiq.* xviii. 6. 10 Josephus describes how at the time of Tiberius's
death (March 16, A.D. 37) Agrippa was in prison (see Vol. I. pp. 14 ff.), and
gives an amusing account of how the keeper of the prison varied the
severity of his imprisonment in accordance with the reports of the Emperor's
health. Finally, when Tiberius's death was certain, Agrippa was treated
with great consideration, though not released. When Caligula reached
Rome he was inclined to release Agrippa immediately, but Antonia persuaded him to wait for a decent interval. Soon after this—a few days—he
sent for Agrippa and gave him the tetrarchy of Philip with the title of
King. Josephus's words are as follows : τῇ δὲ ὑστεραίᾳ λόγος τε πλείων
ἦν κατὰ τὴν πόλιν ἰσχυριζόμενος ἐπὶ τῇ τελευτῇ τοῦ Τιβερίου, ἐθάρρουν
τε οἱ ἄνθρωποι φανερῶς ἤδη θροεῖν, καί τινες καὶ θυσίας ἐπετέλουν,
ἐπιστολαί τε ἀφίκοντο παρὰ τοῦ Γαίου, ἡ μὲν πρὸς τὴν σύγκλητον τοῦ
Τιβερίου διασαφοῦσα τὴν τελευτήν, καὶ τὴν αὐτοῦ παράληψιν τῆς
ἡγεμονίας γενομένην, ἡ δὲ πρὸς Πείσωνα τὸν φύλακα τῆς πόλεως τοῦτό
τε ἀγορεύουσα, καὶ τὸν Ἀγρίππαν ἐκέλευεν ἐκ τοῦ στρατοπέδου μετα-
στῆσαι εἰς τὴν οἰκίαν, ἐν ᾗ πρότερον ἢ δεθῆναι δίαιταν εἶχεν. τότε ἐν
θάρσει λοιπὸν ἦγεν τὰ περὶ αὐτῆς· φυλακὴ μὲν γὰρ καὶ τήρησις ἦν,
μετὰ μέντοι ἀνέσεως τῆς εἰς τὴν δίαιταν.

Γάιος δὲ ὡς ἐπὶ Ῥώμης παρῆν ἄγων τοῦ Τιβερίου τὸ σῶμα ταφάς τε
αὐτοῦ ποιεῖται πολυτελεῖς νόμοις τοῖς πατρίοις, Ἀγρίππαν τε αὐθημερὸν
λύειν ὄντα πρόθυμον κώλυμα Ἀντωνία ἦν, οὔ τι μίσει τῷ πρὸς τὸν
δεδεμένον προμηθείᾳ δὲ τοῦ Γαίου εὐπρεποῦς, μὴ δόξαν ἀπάγοιτο ἡδονῇ
δεχομένου τὴν Τιβερίου τελευτὴν ἄνδρα ὑπ' ἐκείνου δεδεμένον λύων ἐκ
τοῦ ὀξέος. διελθουσῶν μέντοι οὐ πολλῶν ἡμερῶν μεταπεμψάμενος αὐτὸν
εἰς τὸν οἶκον ἀποκείρει τε αὐτὸν καὶ μεταμφιέννυσιν, εἶτα δὲ τὸ διάδημα
περιτίθησιν τῇ κεφαλῇ καὶ βασιλέα καθίστησιν αὐτὸν τῆς Φιλίππου
τετραρχίας· δωρησάμενος αὐτῷ καὶ τὴν Λυσανίου τετραρχίαν, ἀλλάττει
τε σιδηρᾷ ἁλύσει χρυσῆν ἰσόσταθμον. ὑπάρχην δὲ ἐπὶ τῆς Ἰουδαίας
ἐκπέμπει Μάρυλλον.

It is clear from this narrative that the accession of Agrippa to the
tetrarchy of Philip, from which begins his reign as king, must have been
neither much before nor much after May 37. It is important to note that
in any case it must have been after 1 Nisan, which in that year was either
March 5 or April 3.

After Agrippa had reigned three years over the tetrarchy of Lysanias
—that is to say in his fourth year (spring of A.D. 40 to spring of
A.D. 41)—a quarrel between Antipas and Caligula was settled by the

banishment of Antipas to Lyons[1] and the appointment of Agrippa as tetrarch of Galilee.

The statement of Josephus is as follows : (*Antiq.* xviii. 7. 2) Γάιος δὲ ἅμα τε προσαγορεύων τὸν Ἡρώδην, πρῶτον δὲ αὐτῷ ἐνετύγχανεν, ἅμα τε τοῦ Ἀγρίππου τὰς ἐπιστολὰς ἐπιὼν ἐπὶ κατηγορίᾳ τῇ ἐκείνου συγκειμένας, κατηγόρει δὲ αὐτοῦ ὁμολογίαν πρὸς Σηιανὸν κατὰ τῆς Τιβερίου ἀρχῆς καὶ πρὸς Ἀρτάβανον τὸν Πάρθον ἐπὶ τοῦ παρόντος κατὰ τῆς Γαΐου ἀρχῆς, παράδειγμά τε ἦν αὐτῷ τοῦ λόγου μυριάσιν ἑπτὰ ὁπλιτῶν ἀρκέσουσα κατασκευὴ ἐν ταῖς Ἡρώδου ὁπλοθήκαις ἀποκειμένη, ἐκινεῖτό τε ὑπὸ τῶν εἰρημένων καὶ ἤρετο τὸν Ἡρώδην, εἰ ἀληθὴς ὁ περὶ τῶν ὅπλων λόγος. τοῦ δέ, οὐ γὰρ ἦν ἕτερα εἰπεῖν διὰ τὸ ἀντιφθέγξασθαι τὴν ἀλήθειαν, εἰπόντος εἶναι τὰ ὅπλα, πιστὰ ἡγούμενος εἶναι τὰ ἐπὶ τῇ ἀποστάσει κατηγορούμενα, τὴν τετραρχίαν ἀφελόμενος αὐτὸν προσθήκην τῇ Ἀγρίππου βασιλείᾳ ποιεῖται καὶ τὰ χρήματα ὁμοίως τῷ Ἀγρίππᾳ δίδωσιν, αὐτὸν δὲ φυγῇ ἀιδίῳ ἐζημίωσεν ἀποδείξας οἰκητήριον αὐτοῦ Λούγδουνον πόλιν τῆς Γαλλίας.

Agrippa and Claudius.

Shortly afterwards Caligula died and Claudius succeeded him. Josephus (*Antiq.* xix. 5. 1), after describing the end of the manœuvres of the politicians and soldiers, continues : Κλαύδιος δὲ τοῦ στρατιωτικοῦ πᾶν ὅ τι ἦν ὕποπτον ἐκ τοῦ ὀξέος ἀποσκευασάμενος διάγραμμα προὐτίθει τήν τε ἀρχὴν Ἀγρίππᾳ βεβαιῶν, ἣν ὁ Γάιος παρέσχε, καὶ δι᾽ ἐγκωμίων ἄγων τὸν βασιλέα· προσθήκην τε αὐτῷ ποιεῖται πᾶσαν τὴν ὑπὸ Ἡρώδου βασιλευθεῖσαν, ὃς ἦν πάππος αὐτοῦ, Ἰουδαίαν καὶ Σαμάρειαν. καὶ ταῦτα μὲν ὡς ὀφειλόμενα τῇ οἰκειότητι τοῦ γένους ἀπεδίδου· Ἄβιλαν δὲ τὴν Λυσανίου καὶ ὁπόσα ἐν τῷ Λιβάνῳ ὄρει ἐκ τῶν αὐτοῦ προσετίθει, ὅρκιά τε αὐτῷ τέμνεται πρὸς τὸν Ἀγρίππαν ἐπὶ τῆς ἀγορᾶς μέσης ἐν τῇ Ῥωμαίων πόλει. In *B.J.* ii. 11. 5 he adds : καὶ τῷ μὲν δήμῳ διατάγματι τὴν δωρεὰν ἐδήλου, τοῖς ἄρχουσιν δὲ προσέταξεν ἐγχαράξαντας δέλτοις χαλκαῖς τὴν δόσιν εἰς τὸ Καπετώλιον ἀναθεῖναι.

This reconstitution of the kingdom of Herod the Great took place in the first year of Claudius, who began to reign in January A.D. 41. Thus Agrippa when he became king over Judaea had already been 'king'—over the tetrarchies—for more than three years, but probably had not yet finished his fourth, as his fourth year of kingship began in the spring or early summer of A.D. 40.

He reigned over Judaea, according to Josephus, three years (*Antiq.* xix. 8. 2) : τέτταρας μὲν οὖν ἐπὶ Γαΐου Καίσαρος ἐβασίλευσεν ἐνιαυτοὺς τῆς Φιλίππου μὲν τετραρχίας εἰς τριετίαν ἄρξας, τῷ τετάρτῳ δὲ καὶ τὴν Ἡρώδου προσειληφώς, τρεῖς δ᾽ ἐπιλαβὼν τῆς Κλαυδίου Καίσαρος αὐτοκρατορίας, ἐν οἷς τῶν τε προειρημένων ἐβασίλευσεν καὶ τὴν Ἰουδαίαν προσέλαβεν Σαμάρειάν τε καὶ Καισάρειαν.

Taking into account the ancient method of counting this must mean that he had not yet finished his seventh year as king, or his third year as king of Judaea. He began to reign as 'king' about the beginning of May A.D. 37; became king of Judaea before the corresponding date in 41; his seventh

[1] Though in *B.J.* ii. 9. 6 (in the MSS., not in the editions) Josephus says 'to Spain.'

year therefore ended in May 44, and he died before this date. Moreover the expression chosen by Josephus indicates that his death came at about the end of his seventh year—τρίτον ἔτος αὐτῷ βασιλεύοντι τῆς ὅλης Ἰουδαίας πεπλήρωτο.

The dates in Agrippa's life can therefore be fixed thus :

> First year :  May 37—Spring 38
> Second year :  May 38—Spring 39
> Third year :  May 39—Spring 40
> Fourth year :  May 40—Spring 41
> Fifth year :  May 41—Spring 42
> Sixth year :  May 42—Spring 43
> Seventh year :  May 43—Spring 44 [1]

The beginning of his first, second, third and fourth years were under Caius, and the three following were under Claudius.[2]

These direct statements of Josephus are confirmed by the letter (quoted at length on p. 453) sent by Claudius to the Jews in answer to their complaints because after the death of Herod the custody of the sacred garments of the high priest had been taken from them. This letter (*Antiq.* xx. 1. 2) is dated in the fifth tribunicial year of Claudius, that is, A.D. 45, which fits exactly with the previously obtained date, A.D. 44, for the death of Herod Agrippa I.

Thus, if the evidence of Josephus stood alone, there would be no reason for any doubt but that the death of Agrippa was in the year A.D. 44. The reason for doubting this is numismatic. **Numismatic evidence.**

The coins of Agrippa I. are given in F. W. Madden's *Coins of the Jews*, pp. 131 ff. The general type when the Emperor is not mentioned is clear. On one side is an umbrella, encircled by the inscription ΒΑΣΙΛΕΩΣ ΑΓΡΙΠΑ,[3] and on the other side three ears of corn springing from one stalk, and, sometimes at least, giving the date in years of his reign. Dated coins are known for his fifth, sixth, and seventh years and appear to be unquestioned by numismatists. There is also one which may belong to his fourth year, but the form of the Δ which gives the date is very curious, and the coin cannot be regarded as free from suspicion (see note 4 on p. 132 of Madden, *op. cit.*).

All these coins fall within the period of Agrippa's reign as defined by the statements in Josephus, and the fact that there are none known before his fourth (or possibly fifth) year may indicate that he issued

---

[1] The only statement in Josephus inconsistent with this dating is a passing remark in *B.J.* ii. 11. 6 where the length of his reign over Judaea is rightly described as three years, but his rule over the tetrarchies is described as also three years—which is an error on any system of reckoning, and in view of the detailed statement in the *Antiquities* may be disregarded.

[2] It is true that the end of his fourth year was under Claudius as well as the beginning of his uncompleted seventh year. This might have justified Josephus in saying that he reigned four years under Claudius, but it did not force him to do so.

[3] Not ΑΓΡΙΠΠΑ as elsewhere.

no coins until Claudius gave him Judaea, in the fourth year of his 'kingship.'

There are, however, two more dated coins quoted by Madden belonging to the eighth and ninth years of Herod. So far as the description given in Madden's *Coins of the Jews*, pp. 129 ff., goes, there is no reason to dispute the genuineness of the coins except that their chronology disagrees with Josephus; and if their authenticity be accepted, it is certainly more probable that Josephus made a mistake than that coins of Agrippa were issued with a date later than his death. But, incredible as it may seem, no competent observer seems to have studied the coins, which were in the collection of the Rev. B. C. Reichardt of Damascus. No one seems to know where they are now.[1]

If it be accepted that the coin of the 'ninth year' is genuine, it must mean that he lived on into the ninth year of his reign inasmuch as the year of his accession cannot be doubted, and the ninth year reckoned from his accession would be Spring 45 to Spring 46.

Is it possible to reconcile this with the statements of Josephus? Only if on his coins he was using the Jewish sacred year, became king before 1 Nisan A.D. 37, and died after 1 Nisan A.D. 44. None of these points can be proved, and one seems almost impossible.

(a) It is quite uncertain whether Agrippa used this sacred year. That it was used by the kings rests entirely on the Babylonian Talmud, unconfirmed by any other evidence.

(b) Can Agrippa have been made king by Caius earlier than 1 Nisan 37? Tiberius died on March 16, and 1 Nisan was either March 5 or April 3. It is surely impossible to put earlier than April 3 the end of the interval of retirement or mitigated imprisonment in which Caius kept Agrippa until it seemed decent to promote one whom his predecessor had imprisoned.

(c) Finally, as will be shown, some scholars think that there is reasonable evidence that the death of Agrippa was on March 5. In the year A.D. 44 1 Nisan was March 7 or April 5. Thus it is unlikely that his eighth year had begun, even on this reckoning, before his death.

So far, then, the evidence of Josephus and of the coins contradict each other : it is conceivable that an 'eighth year' coinage had been prepared before his death and was issued after it, but the 'ninth year' is inexplicable. Either Josephus is wrong, or the coin is a forgery.[2] In support of the longer reign suggested by the coins quotation may be made of Tacitus, who states that after the deaths of Agrippa and Sohaemus, Judaea and Ituraea were added to the province of Syria. This change he dates as effected in A.D. 49. This statement, though not impossibly inconsistent with the death of Herod in 44, would be easier to understand if he lived on until 46 or 47. Possibly there is some connexion between this and the way in which Tacitus makes Cumanus and Felix contemporary governors of two small districts—Galilee

---

[1] I have made many inquiries, and I hope that this statement may bring them to light.

[2] It is of course possible that the coins were misread, but no one who saw them seems to have doubted the readings.

and Samaria—while Josephus makes them successive procurators of Judaea (see pp. 464 ff.).

In support of the chronology of Josephus is one other line of argument E.Schwartz. by which E. Schwartz[1] has tried to clinch the case for A.D. 44 and to identify the exact date as that of the *dies natalis* of Caesarea on March 5.[2]

According to Josephus,[3] Agrippa died at Caesarea, συνετέλει δ᾽ ἐνταῦθα Herod's θεωρίας εἰς τὴν Καίσαρος τιμήν, ὑπὲρ τῆς ἐκείνου σωτηρίας ἑορτήν τινα games at ταύτην ἐπιστάμενος, which is presumably a translation of *ludos pro salute Caesaris* or *pro valetudine Caesaris*. E. Schwartz thinks that it was the repetition of a similar feast instituted in 9 B.C. by Herod the Great at the founding of Caesarea, to be held every fifth year. Josephus's account is given in *Antiq.* xvi. 5. 1: περὶ δὲ τὸν χρόνον τοῦτον συντέλειαν ἔλαβεν ἡ Καισάρεια Σεβαστή, ἣν ᾠκοδόμει δεκάτῳ μὲν ἔτει πρὸς τέλος ἐλθούσης αὐτῷ τῆς ὅλης κατασκευῆς, ἐκπεσούσης δὲ τῆς προθεσμίας εἰς ὄγδοον καὶ εἰκοστὸν ἔτος τῆς ἀρχῆς ἐπ᾽ ὀλυμπιάδος δευτέρας καὶ ἐνενηκοστῆς πρὸς ταῖς ἑκατόν. ἦν οὖν εὐθὺς ἐν καθιερώσει μείζονες ἑορταὶ καὶ παρασκευαὶ πολυτελέσταται· κατηγγέλκει μὲν γὰρ ἀγῶνα μουσικῆς καὶ γυμνικῶν ἀθλημάτων, παρεσκευάκει δὲ πολὺ πλῆθος μονομάχων καὶ θηρίων ἵππων τε δρόμον καὶ τὰ πολυτελέστερα τῶν ἔν τε τῇ Ῥώμῃ καὶ παρ᾽ ἄλλοις τισὶν ἐπιτηδευμάτων. ἀνετίθει δὲ καὶ τοῦτον τὸν ἀγῶνα Καίσαρι κατὰ πενταετηρίδα παρεσκευασμένος ἄγειν αὐτόν· ὁ δ᾽ αὐτῷ πᾶσαν τὴν εἰς τὰ τοιαῦτα παρασκευὴν ἀπὸ τῶν οἰκείων διεπέμπετο τὴν φιλοτιμίαν ἐπικοσμῶν.

In this account κατὰ πενταετηρίδα presumably means at intervals of four years—recurring in the fifth year—like the Olympiads. In building Caesarea and in instituting these games Herod was following the example of many other cities of which Suetonius (*Augustus* 59 f.) says: "Provinciarum pleraeque super templa et aras ludos quoque quinquennales paene oppidatim constituerunt. Reges amici atque socii et singuli in suo quisque regno condiderunt, et cuncti simul aedem Iovis Olympii Athenis antiquitus inchoatam perficere communi sumptu destinaverunt Genioque eius dedicare."

There is also an obvious probability that in Caesarea, where the τυχή of The *dies* the city was at least cognate to the *genius* of Caesar, the feast in honour of the *natalis* of emperor would be the same as the *dies natalis* of the city. The date of the Caesarea. *dies natalis* is fixed by Eusebius, in speaking of the Martyrdom of Hadrian (*Mart. Pal.* xi. 30), as Δύστρου πέμπτῃ μηνὸς πρὸ τριῶν νώνων Μαρτίων, γενεθλίων τῆς κατὰ Καισάρειαν νομιζομένης Τύχης ἡμέρᾳ, that is, March 5.

The date on which the games in honour of Caesar were founded by Herod the Great is fixed by Josephus (*Antiq.* xvi. 5. 1) as the twenty-eighth year of Herod in Olympiad 192 (12–8 B.C.). This must be 10–9 B.C., since he puts the journey of Augustus to Syria in the seventeenth year of Herod, and this journey is fixed as the summer of 20 B.C. (Josephus, *Antiq.* xv. 10. 3 and Dio Cassius liv. 7). Taking four-year intervals from 9 B.C. the games would come round in A.D. 44.

---

[1] 'Zur Chronologie des Paulus' in *Gött. Nachrichten* for 1907.

[2] The identification, so far as the year is concerned, was made earlier by Wieseler (*Chronologie*, pp. 133 ff.).

[3] *Antiq.* xix. 8. 2.

Schwartz is obviously justified in thinking that the feast in honour of Caesar which Agrippa was celebrating at the time of his death may have been the feast instituted by Herod the Great, and in fixing the date as March 5, A.D. 44. The combination is most attractive; but the date in March is contradicted by Acts. According to Acts xii. Agrippa put Peter in prison in the days of unleavened bread of his last year: after this he went to Caesarea and died there. Seeing that in A.D. 44 the 1 Nisan cannot have been earlier than March 17, the feast at which Herod was present cannot have been that of Caesarea on March 5; though it is possible that Peter's imprisonment was in 43, and that Herod died before the next Passover. Luke's tendency to compress his narrative lends some plausibility to this suggestion.

*Difficulties in this theory.*   Thus, just as the year is rendered doubtful by the existence of a coin belonging to the ninth year of Agrippa, the connexion with the quinquennial feast in Caesarea (assuming that this was that which became the *dies natalis* of the city) is rendered doubtful by Acts. Schwartz indeed does not mention the coin, and brushes Acts aside as legendary and influenced by the analogy of the Passion; but this is scarcely convincing.

However, it should be remembered that—apart from the question of the coins—Schwartz's theory may be right on every point except the day of the month. There is no proof that the quinquennial feast in honour of Augustus in the first century was on the same day of the year as the *dies natalis* in the fourth. There is at most a presumption. Moreover, this presumption is largely counterbalanced, if not outweighed, by the fact that the *Quinquennalia* were instituted in connexion with the celebration of the conquest of Egypt and the defeat of Antony (cf. Dio Cassius li. 19). Antony died in August, and the month *Sextilis* obtained its present name of August for that reason—it was especially the Emperor's month. In Lyons, at all events, the *Quinquennalia* were celebrated on August 1. (Cf. Suetonius, *Claudius* 2.)

Therefore it seems quite as likely that Agrippa I. may have died in August 43 as in May 44, and this would leave ample room for the story as told in Acts.

The further fact that Josephus says nothing about the quarrel of Agrippa with the Sidonians, and that Acts says nothing about the feast in honour of Caesar, is relatively unimportant—the two descriptions do not exclude each other.

## II. *The Famine in the Time of Claudius*

The date of the famine described in Acts xi. 28 depends on the information supplied by Josephus, and to a less extent by Suetonius and Tacitus.

*The letter of Claudius.*   Josephus says in *Antiq.* xix. 9. 2 that when Agrippa died Claudius passed over his son (Agrippa II.) because of his age and sent Cuspius Fadus as Procurator. He quotes the following letter (*Antiq.* xx. 1. 2) from Claudius to the Jews acceding to their request, made through the younger Agrippa, to retain the keeping in Jerusalem of the high-priestly garments, which Fadus had originally demanded from them: Κλαύδιος Καῖσαρ Γερμανικὸς

δημαρχικῆς ἐξουσίας τὸ πέμπτον ὕπατος ἀποδεδειγμένος τὸ τέταρτον
αὐτοκράτωρ τὸ δέκατον πατὴρ πατρίδος Ἱεροσολυμιτῶν ἄρχουσι βουλῇ.
δήμῳ Ἰουδαίων παντὶ ἔθνει χαίρειν. Ἀγρίππα τοῦ ἐμοῦ, ὃν ἐγὼ ἔθρεψα
καὶ ἔχω σὺν ἐμαυτῷ εὐσεβέστατον ὄντα, προσαγαγόντος μοι τοὺς ὑμετέ-
ρους πρέσβεις εὐχαριστοῦντας ἐφ' ᾗ πεποίημαι τοῦ ἔθνους ὑμῶν κηδεμονίᾳ,
καὶ αἰτησαμένων σπουδαίως καὶ φιλοτίμως τὴν ἱερὰν ἐσθῆτα καὶ τὸν
στέφανον ὑπὸ τὴν ἐξουσίαν ὑμῶν εἶναι, συγχωρῶ καθὼς ὁ κράτιστος καί
μοι τιμιώτατος Οὐιτέλλιος ἐποίησεν. συγκατεθέμην δὲ τῇ γνώμῃ ταύτῃ
πρῶτον διὰ τὸ ἐμαυτοῦ εὐσεβὲς καὶ τὸ βούλεσθαι ἑκάστους κατὰ τὰ
πάτρια θρησκεύειν, ἔπειτα δὲ εἰδώς, ὅτι καὶ αὐτῷ βασιλεῖ Ἡρώδῃ καὶ
Ἀριστοβούλῳ τῷ νεωτέρῳ, ὧν τὴν πρὸς ἐμαυτὸν εὐσέβειαν καὶ τὴν περὶ
ὑμᾶς γινώσκω σπουδήν . . . ταῦτα ποιήσας, πρὸς οὓς ἔστι μοι πλεῖστα
δίκαια φιλίας κρατίστους ὄντας κἀμοὶ τιμίους. ἔγραψα δὲ περὶ τούτων
καὶ Κουσπίῳ Φάδῳ τῷ ἐμῷ ἐπιτρόπῳ. οἱ τὰ γράμματα κομίζοντες
Κορνήλιος Κέρωνος, Τρύφων Θευδίωνος, Δωρόθεος Ναθαναήλου, Ἰωάννης
Ἰωάννου. ἐγράφη πρὸ τεσσάρων καλανδῶν . . . ἐπὶ ὑπάτων Ῥούφου καὶ
Πομπηίου Σιλουανοῦ. The lacuna after καλανδῶν is supplied in the
Latin version of Josephus by the addition of ' July.' This date is often
accepted, but it rests on very slender evidence. If it be taken the letter
is dated June 28, in the fifth tribunate of Claudius (i.e. A.D. 45), in the
consulship of Rufus and Pompey. According to Schwartz these were
consuls in 46, and he regards their names as a wrong insertion in the
letter.[1]

Thus Fadus, if Josephus be trusted, must have been procurator in 45.
He was succeeded by Tiberius Alexander, and he in turn by Cumanus.
Josephus gives no precise chronology of Fadus, Tiberius, and Cumanus,
but he places the death of Herod of Chalcis (*Antiq.* xx. 5. 2) in the eighth
year of Claudius (A.D. 47–48) in the time of Cumanus, and puts the death of
Claudius (Oct. A.D. 54) in the time of Felix, the successor of Cumanus
(*Antiq.* xx. 8. 1), so that if the letter of Claudius to Fadus be genuine we
can fix the following dates :

The succession of procurators.

| | | |
|---|---|---|
| June 28 (?), A.D. 45 | . . | . Fadus |
| A date in A.D. 47–48 | . . | . Cumanus |
| October A.D. 54 | . . | . Felix |

Thus Tiberius Alexander must have been procurator not earlier than
45 and not later than 47–48. Thus in all probability the year 45 belongs to
Fadus, 46 to Tiberius Alexander, and 47 to Cumanus, though part of 45 and
part of 47 may also belong to Tiberius Alexander.

---

[1] I cannot find the evidence for these men as consuls in 46. Plooij says that
they were *consules suffecti* in 45, but the basis of his statement appears to be
Liebenam's *Fasti Consulares*, and he in turn merely takes his statement from
Josephus. There appears to be no conclusive evidence either way, but there
were so many *consules suffecti* in the imperial period that it is quite possible that
Josephus is right. The Rufus whom he mentions may be the Curtius Rufus who
is mentioned by Tacitus, *Ann.* xi. 21. (See *Prosopographia Imperii Romani*,
vol. v. p. 142, s.v. Rufus and Curtius Rufus.)

The relation of Judaea to Syria.    There is, however, a difficult problem in connexion with this period, because, according to Tacitus,[1] Judaea and Ituraea were added to the province of Syria after the death of Agrippa and of Sohaemus. Tacitus puts this change in the year 49. He does not, of course, necessarily mean that Agrippa died in that year, though in view of the doubts expressed above the point is significant.

This statement raises an important question in the history of Roman government. If Judaea became part of the Imperial Province of Syria, governed by a legate *pro praetore*, what was the real relation of the Procurator of Judaea to the Legate of Syria ? Apparently the Legate had some jurisdiction, for Vitellius when Legate of Syria dismissed Pontius Pilate, and in A.D. 52 Quadratus, Legate of Syria, intervened when Cumanus, or Cumanus and Felix, had brought Judaea and Samaria to the verge of insurrection. But it is not quite clear whether Vitellius intervened *jure suo*, or by virtue of a special commission from the Emperor.[2]

The Famine.    During this period of confused administration and obscure chronology Josephus describes a severe famine in Jerusalem, which was partly alleviated by the charity of Helena of Adiabene, who supplied the population with corn from Alexandria and dried figs from Cyprus (*Antiq.* xx. 2. 5). But the question is open to discussion whether Josephus intended to put this famine in the time of Fadus, of Tiberius Alexander, or of both.

In *Antiq.* xx. 5. 2 Josephus says that Fadus was succeeded by Tiberius Alexander, who was the son of Alexander the Alabarch of Alexandria, the brother of Philo, but had abandoned Judaism. ἦλθε δὲ Φάδῳ διάδοχος Τιβέριος Ἀλέξανδρος . . . τοῖς γὰρ πατρίοις οὐκ ἐνέμεινεν οὗτος ἔθεσιν. ἐπὶ τούτοις, he continues, καὶ τὸν μέγαν λιμὸν κατὰ τὴν Ἰουδαίαν συνέβη γενέσθαι, and he then refers back to the account of Helena's generosity, which had been previously related. The Greek MSS. and Eusebius all read ἐπὶ τούτοις, but the Epitome has ἐπὶ τούτου, which Niese accepts and prints in his text, presumably on the ground that ἐπὶ τούτοις means nothing in this context. But this was probably the reasoning of the maker of the Epitome, and as a matter of textual criticism ἐπὶ τούτοις is overwhelmingly supported by the evidence of the MSS. and by transcriptional probability. What then can ἐπὶ τούτοις mean ? Two renderings are possible. (i.) ἐπὶ τούτοις might mean, as it does in Eusebius, ' under these circumstances,' or almost ' at this time.' (ii.) As the equivalent of ἐπὶ τούτων, ' in their (i.e. Fadus and Tiberius Alexander's) time.' This use of the dative is found in 2 Macc. ii. 8, and Schürer (*GJV*. 3rd ed. i. p. 567) quotes inscriptions with the same idiom (*CIG*. No. 4713 sq., and Kaibel, *Inscr. Gr. Siciliae et Italiae*, No. 2421. 2).

It must be admitted that the general tenor of the account of Josephus implies that the events described after he has mentioned the accession of Tiberius Alexander took place in his time. But some confusion is created

---

[1] " Ituraei et Iudaei defunctis regibus Sohaemo atque Agrippa provinciae Syriae additi," Tacitus, *Ann.* xii. 23.
[2] For doubt as to the exact rank of Cumanus and Felix see pp. 464 ff.

by the fact that he gives the whole story of the conversion of Helena and
Izates to Judaism and Helena's consequent visit to Jerusalem at the place
in his general narrative to which its beginning belongs, so that he gives the
story of the famine—as part of the incident of Helena and Izates—before
it would have naturally come in his narrative. He then goes back and
picks up the thread of his story, and mentions the famine, when he comes
to it, with a reference to the fuller account which he has already given.
For this reason it is perhaps preferable to take ἐπὶ τούτοις as meaning
'under these conditions' rather than 'in their time.' It does not, however,
make much difference. If the famine came in the time of Tiberius
Alexander it was in A.D. 46. If it had begun in the time of Fadus it was
a year earlier.

There is an obscure earlier mention of the famine in Josephus in *Antiq.* iii. 15. 3, where he refers to it as in the reign of Claudius in the high-priesthood of Ishmael. This Ishmael is unfortunately not mentioned elsewhere, but it is noticeable that in *Antiq.* xix. 8. 1 Josephus says that Agrippa removed Matthias from the high-priesthood and appointed Elionaios the son of Kithairos. This seems to have been one of the last acts of Agrippa. The death of Agrippa was followed by a dispute between Fadus and the Jews about the custody of the high-priestly vestments, and presumably the appointment of the high priest. The Jews appealed to Rome, and finally Claudius made Herod of Chalcis the custodian of the vestments. Then, in *Antiq.* xx. 1. 3, Josephus says that Herod of Chalcis removed the high priest, but the name he gives is not—as we should have expected—Elionaios, the last high priest mentioned, but 'him who was surnamed Kantheras.' Who was he ? It is quite possible that Kantheras was the surname of Elionaios, but this would leave no room for the Ishmael of the famine. It is therefore more likely that Kantheras is the surname of Ishmael, and that Josephus forgot to mention his appointment in place of Elionaios.[1]

*marginal note: The high priest Ishmael.*

## III. *The Proconsulship of Sergius Paulus*

Sergius Paulus, if the name be reported correctly, must have been Proconsul of Cyprus between the years 40 and 50, and probably within a year or two, one way or the other, of A.D. 45. The question is whether there is more to say about him on the basis of inscriptions or literature. Unfortunately there proves to be rather less than has often been supposed.

*marginal note: Sergius Paulus.*

The most striking piece of evidence, which has often seemed to confirm the statement of Acts without any doubt, proves in reality to have no bearing on it. This is the famous inscription from Soli in Cyprus, first published by General de Cesnola, and made famous by Lightfoot, which refers to a Proconsul Paulus. It was natural to suppose that this was the Proconsul Paulus mentioned in Acts, and that Sergius was accidentally

*marginal note: The inscription at Soli.*

---

[1] It is of course also possible that Ishmael is distinct from Kantheras, and that his time of office should be inserted between that of Elionaios and of Kantheras.

omitted. But the full text of the inscription, published in 1889 by D. G. Hogarth in *Devia Cypria*, p. 114, refutes the supposition.[1] It reads thus :

ΑΠΟΛΛωΝΙΟC Τω ΠΑΤΡΙ . . .
ΚΑΙ ΤΗ ΜΗΤΡΙ ΑΡΤ . . . *καθιερωσε*
ΤΟΝ ΠΕΡΙΒΟΛΟΝ ΚΑΙ ΤΗΝ . . . ΤΑC
ΥΜωΝ ΑΥΤωΝ ΕΝΤΟΛΑC
ΕΑΥΤΟΥ ΤΗC Σολιων ΠΟΛΕωC *αγορα*Ν*Ομησας,* ε
ΠΑΡΧΗCΑC; ΓΡΑ(μ)ΜΑΤΕΥCΑC ΑΡΧΙ*Ερασαμενος, επι του*
ΒΙΒΛΙΟΦΥΛΑΚΙΟΥ ΓΕΝΟΜΕΝΟC L ΙΓ · *μηνος δημαρχε*
Ζογcιογ ΚΕ ΤΙΜΗΤΕΥCΑC ΤΗΝ Βογλην δι
α ΕΖΕΤΑCΤωΝ ΕΠΙ Παγλογ *ανθυ*
ΠΑΤΟΥ·

According to Hogarth the two last lines ($\tau\iota\mu\eta\tau\epsilon\acute{\upsilon}\sigma\alpha\varsigma$ $\tau\grave{\eta}\nu$ $\beta o\upsilon\lambda\grave{\eta}\nu$ $\delta\iota\grave{\alpha}$ $\grave{\epsilon}\xi\epsilon\tau\alpha\sigma\tau\hat{\omega}\nu$ $\grave{\epsilon}\pi\grave{\iota}$ $\Pi\alpha\acute{\upsilon}\lambda o\upsilon$ $\grave{\alpha}\nu\theta\upsilon\pi\acute{\alpha}\tau o\upsilon$) are later than the rest. His explanation is that the mention of this reform of the Senate carried out by Apollonius was added later. There is a difference in the lettering which points to this, as well as the faulty alignment.

The natural explanation is that the mention of the reform was added later, because the reform itself was later. If so it follows that Paulus was proconsul after the date of the body of the inscription, but within the limits of one man's official career.

**The date of the inscription.** The date of the body of the inscription is given as 'the year 13.'

This can be explained in two ways :

(a) It is possible that the number refers to the year of the reign (or, more accurately, to the tribunicial appointment) of the emperor. If the emperor were Claudius, the thirteenth year would be A.D. 53, and Paulus must have been proconsul after this—an impossibly late date for Paul's visit to Cyprus.

(b) Inscriptions in the provinces generally date from the foundation of the province; Cyprus was annexed by Rome in 55 B.C., and Hogarth suggests that that is the Cyprian epoch. But (see note on xiii. 4) Cyprus did not become a province until 27 B.C., when it was made an imperial province, being changed to senatorial rank, with a proconsul, in 22 B.C. I have not found any definite evidence, but I doubt whether Cyprus can be said to have been a province before 27 B.C., and therefore imagine that the Cyprian epoch began in that year. In this case the thirteenth year was 14 B.C., or if, following Hogarth, we date from 55 B.C., it was 42 B.C. Paulus cannot have been Proconsul before 22 B.C. when the province became senatorial ; but 42 is not impossible, for Apollonius may have been in office in 42 B.C. and have 'revised' the senate twenty years

[1] It is important to notice that Cagnat, *Inscr. Gr.* vol. iii. No. 930, copies the older and less reliable transcript of General de Cesnola. Cagnat introduces some variations, and it is not clear whether these are emendations or errors, and—most remarkable of all—omits the date. There is no reason to doubt the accuracy of Hogarth's observation, especially since on this point he is in agreement with General de Cesnola.

or a little more later in the proconsulship of Paulus, if we suppose that
Paulus was one of the first proconsuls.    But of course neither 14 B.C. nor
42 B.C. leaves the faintest possibility that this Paulus was the Sergius
Paulus of Acts.   It is far more likely that he was Paullus Fabius Maximus,
who was consul in 11 B.C., as Mommsen suggested in his famous article
on 'Die Rechtsverhältnisse des Apostels Paulus' (*ZNTW*. ii. (1901)
pp. 81 ff.).   It is an interesting suggestion that this Paullus Fabius
Maximus may be referred to in *CIG*. 2629

> ΜΑΡΚΙΑΙ ΦΙΛΙΠΠΟΥ ΘΥΓΑΤΡΙ ΑΝΕΨΙΑΙ
> ΚΑΙϹΑΡΟϹ ΘΕΟΥ ϹΕΒΑϹΤΟΥ ΓΥΝΑΙΚΙ
> ΠΑΥΛΟΥ ΦΑΒΙΟΥ ΜΑΖΙΜΟΥ ϹΕΒΑϹΤΗϹ
> ΠΑΦΟΥ Η ΒΟΥΛΗ ΚΑΙ Ο ΔΗΜΟϹ

but it is noticeable that this inscription says nothing about the official
position of Fabius, and the Senate of Paphos would surely have mentioned
the fact that he was proconsul.

Hogarth, it is true, argued in *Devia Cypria*, pp. 113 ff., that the Paulus  Hogarth's
of the inscription might be Sergius Paulus, but he has to make two supposi-  arguments.
tions : (i.) that a ρ ( = 100) is missing from the date, (ii.) that the added lines
containing the reference to Paulus mean that the reform of the Senate
had taken place some time previously, and been forgotten in the original
inscription.   Then, dating from 55 B.C., he gives the inscription to A.D. 55
(113 years later) and supposes that Paulus had been proconsul about A.D. 45.

The first supposition is not impossible.   It appears that there is room
for a letter at the point marked with a dot in the transcription given
above,[1] and, though $\overline{\rho\iota\gamma}$ or $\overline{\gamma\iota\rho}$ are more probable arrangements, $\overline{\iota\gamma\rho}$ is
not impossible for 113.   But this would make Paulus proconsul in A.D. 87
if the Cyprian era began in 27 B.C. and in 59 if (as Hogarth thinks) it
began in 55 B.C.   In either case this Paulus cannot have been proconsul
in Paul's time.

The second supposition is extremely improbable.   The theory that a
postscript to the inscription (as the reference to Paulus admittedly was)
can refer, not to something which happened later, but to something which
had been done more than ten years previously and omitted by accident,
is a suggestion which would never occur to anyone who had not already
decided that Paulus was proconsul in 45.   Clearly this is a case in which,
if Acts be regarded as evidence that a Sergius Paulus was proconsul of
Cyprus in A.D. 45, the inscription of Soli may conceivably though very
improbably be interpreted so as to refer to this Paulus,   But if Acts is
under discussion the inscription adds nothing to our knowledge and
certainly does nothing to fix the chronology of Paul's journey.

Another supposed reference to Sergius Paulus, popularized by Light-  Pliny's
foot, has also been eliminated by better knowledge of the texts.   The  evidence.

---

[1] Of course this does not mean that there is a space left in the inscription.
Everything after $\overline{\iota\tau}$ is conjecture.   But there would be room for one more
letter as well as for the certain reconstruction [μηνὸς δημαρχε].   There is no
positive probability that the numeral was actually there.

edition of Pliny by Hardouin, used by Lightfoot, quoted in the list of
sources which Pliny says in book i. of his *Naturalis Historia* that he had
used in book ii., gives the name of Sergius Paulus, and the same name recurs
in the sources of book xviii. But the critical edition of Detlefsen shows that
the ms. tradition of Pliny in the list of authorities for book ii. gives *Sergius
Plautus*, conjectured with some probability to be the Stoic philosopher
mentioned by Quintilian (see *Prosopographia Imperii Romani*, s.v. *Sergius
Plautus*), and in the list of authorities for book xviii. is divided between
*Sergius Paulus* and *Sergius Plautus*.

Sergius Paulus the Curator of the Tiber.

There remains one possible reference to Sergius Paulus, which is un-
impeachable, but unfortunately does not relate him to Cyprus. In the
*Corpus Inscriptionum Latinarum*, vi. 4, ii. p. 3116, Inscription No. 31545
runs as follows :

PAULLUS · FABIUS · PERSICUS

C · EGGIUS · MARULLUS

L · SERGIUS · PAULLUS

C · OBELLIUS · RUfus

L · SCRIBONIUS LIBO

CURATORES riparum

ET · ALVei tiberis

EX · AUCTORITate

TI · CLAUDI · CAESARIS

AUG · GERMANICi

PRINCIPIS · S · ?

RIPAM CIPPIS · POSitis

TERMINAVERUNT · A · TRig ARio

AD · PONTEM · AGRIPPAe

Paullus Fabius Persicus was one of the *Fratres Arvales*, and probably
*Magister* in A.D. 35. He was also pontifex and *sodalis Augustalis* (*CIL.* iii.
6073). He was the friend of the Emperor Claudius and is spoken of by
Seneca, *De benef.* iv. 30. Waddington conjectures with probability that
he was proconsul of Asia, since the Ephesians put up an inscription to him.
(See H. W. Henzen, *Acta Fratrum Arvalium*, p. 186, and Waddington,
*Fastes*, p. 125.)

We know nothing of any of the others, but the name of L. Sergius
Paullus suggests that he may be the Sergius Paulus of Acts. The date
would fit admirably if he went to Cyprus soon after being one of the
Curators of the Tiber.

[For the literature on the subject see *Prosopographia imperii Romani*,
Cesnola, *Cypre*, p. 425, and *Salamina*, pp. 108 f. ; D. G. Hogarth, *Devia
Cypria*, pp. 113 ff. ; J. B. Lightfoot, *Contemporary Review*, vol. xxxii.
(1878), pp. 288 ff. (reprinted in *Essays on Supernatural Religion*, pp.
291 ff.) ; Th. Mommsen, ' Die Rechtsverhältnisse des Apostels Paulus,'
*ZNTW*. ii. (1901), pp. 81 ff. ; and for marvellously ingenious, but not
very convincing combinations, tending to connect the family of Sergius
Paulus with Cyprus, and to show that he was really converted by Paul,
see Ramsay in *The Bearing of Recent Research on the Trustworthiness*

*of the New Testament*, and in the *Expository Times*, April 1918, pp. 324 ff.]

### IV. *The Edict of Claudius banishing the Jews from Rome*

According to Acts xviii. 1 f., Aquila and Priscilla came to Corinth because Claudius had expelled all the Jews from Rome. Suetonius in his Life of Claudius chapter xxv. also mentions this expulsion, and he attributes it to the incessant disorder of the Jews, who were led on by 'Chrestus.' This may throw extremely important light on the origin of Christianity in Rome (see Vol. IV. on xviii. 1 f.), but unfortunately it tells us nothing precise about the date. Dio Cassius [1] confirms the evidence of Suetonius, but adds that the difficulty of expelling so many persons led to a revision of the decree, in which Claudius contented himself with forbidding Jewish assemblies. He relates this in conjunction with events that belong to the year A.D. 41. It is apparently a general remark which is not intended to apply especially to any one year, so that the date is not defined, but it must be admitted that if there were no reason to the contrary it would probably be put down to A.D. 41. Acts, however, distinctly says that Aquila and Priscilla had ' recently ' (προσφάτως) arrived from Italy, and 41 is far too early to be a conceivable date for Paul in Corinth.

The only author who gives a definite date is Orosius, a writer of ' history with a purpose' in the early fifth century, who as a rule did little more than repeat the statements of Eusebius, with some references to other sources, among which he may sometimes have made use of Julius Africanus. He says in his *Historia contra Paganos*, vii. 6. 15, " Anno eiusdem (*sc.* Claudii) nono expulsos per Claudium urbe Iudaeos Iosephus refert, sed me magis Suetonius movet qui ait hoc modo : Claudius Iudaeos impulsore Chresto assidue tumultuantes Roma expulit." Unfortunately Josephus nowhere mentions this fact in his extant writings, and either Orosius knew of other writings of Josephus (which is unlikely), or he quoted someone else and mistook his authority. The ninth year of Claudius is Jan. 25, A.D. 49 to Jan. 24, A.D. 50, and would fit in very well with Acts xviii. 1 and the general chronology of Paul. Ramsay,[2] it is true, considers that Orosius is often [3] a year wrong in his dates for Claudius, owing to confusion between ' calendar years' and ' years of reign,' and if so 50 rather than 49 is the real year of the edict, but because Orosius once made this error it does not follow that he always did so.

The edict of Claudius.

Orosius.

---

[1] Dio Cassius lx. 6. 6 τούς τε 'Ιουδαίους πλεονάσαντας αὖθις ὥστε χαλεπῶς ἂν ἄνευ ταραχῆς ὑπὸ τοῦ ὄχλου σφῶν τῆς πόλεως εἰρχθῆναι, οὐκ ἐξήλασε μέν, τῷ δὲ δὴ πατρίῳ βίῳ χρωμένους ἐκέλευσε μὴ συναθροίζεσθαι. It should be noted that Ewald, rather arbitrarily, inserted an οὐ before χρωμένους, thus gaining valuable evidence about Christianity. The text is sometimes so quoted, but in this form the evidence is Ewald's, not that of Dio.

[2] *St. Paul the Traveller and Roman Citizen*, p. 68.

[3] He dates the famine in Rome in the tenth year of Claudius (Jan. 50-Jan. 51), though Tacitus puts it 51.

It will be seen below (p. 464) that 49-50 is the probable date for Paul's arrival at Corinth, and so far as it goes this confirms Orosius, but Orosius unsupported by any other evidence is not a firm basis for any chronological statement.

The anti-oriental policy of Claudius.

It is sometimes thought that the action of Claudius was part of a general 'anti-oriental' policy. This view is supported by the evidence in Tacitus, *Ann.* xi. and xii., that in the second half of his reign Claudius endeavoured long and assiduously to conserve and perpetuate the old Roman religion and to suppress foreign superstitions. Thus in A.D. 47 he restored the college of Haruspices (*Ann.* xi. 15). In A.D. 48 he elevated several illustrious men to the patriciate (*ibid.* xi. 25. 3), doubtless in order to provide the priestly colleges with the required number of patrician members, as Augustus had done before him. In A.D. 49 he reintroduced the *Salutis Augurium* (*ibid.* xii. 23. 3), and enlarged the *Pomerium* (*ibid.* xii. 23. 4). This last measure made necessary the removal of whatever shrine or meeting-house of a *deus peregrinus* might have been previously in the area involved. About the same time several men and women were prosecuted for consulting astrologers—Lollia Paulina in A.D. 49 (*ibid.* xii. 22. 1-2), Furius Scribonianus in A.D. 52 (*ibid.* xii. 52. 1), and Statilius Taurus in A.D. 53 (*ibid.* xii. 59. 1-2). In A.D. 52 he caused the senate to order the banishment of astrologers from Italy (*ibid.* xii. 52. 3. Cf. Dio lxi. 33. 3b = Zon. xi. 10). Lastly, Jerome Carcopino (*La Basilique Pythagoricienne de la Porte Majeure*, Paris, 1926, pp. 62, 74, and *passim*), followed by Rostovtzeff (*Mystic Italy*, New York, 1927, pp. 130-132), has suggested that in A.D. 53 or 54 Claudius ordered the closing of the beautiful underground temple near the Porta Maggiore because it was dedicated to a foreign cult. On the other hand some modern historians believe that Claudius favoured the cult of Magna Mater and Attis (F. Cumont, *Religions orientales dans l'Empire romain*, and R. Pettazzoni, *I misteri*, Bologna, 1923, p. 126). But it would appear that he did so only after he purified its original Phrygian coarseness (Carcopino, *op. cit.* pp. 49-51), and made it acceptable to the Greco-Roman palate by mellowing it, as Suetonius seems to imply (*Claud.* 25), with Eleusinian flavour.[1]

All this is doubtless true, but it should be noted that the evidence of Suetonius is explicit that the Jews were expelled not on grounds of general policy but because of disorder due to a special cause. [See also Mommsen, *Röm. Ges.* v. p. 523.]

## V. *The Proconsulship of Gallio*

The Delphi inscription.

The date of Gallio is fixed with considerable exactness by an inscription[2] at Delphi. The text of this inscription is as follows :

---

[1] I am indebted to Prof. Scramuzza for this paragraph.

[2] This was first published by A. Nikitsky in *Epigraphical Studies at Delphi*. It has since often been republished, as, for instance, in Deissmann's *Paulus*.

Τιβερ[ιος Κλαυδιος Κ]αισ[αρ Σεβαστ]ος Γ[ερμανικος,
αρχιερευς μεγιστος, δημαρχικης εξου-]
σιας [το ιβ', αυτοκρατωρ τ]ο κϛ, π[ατηρ πα]τριδ[ος,
υπατος το ε', τιμητης, Δελφων τη πολει χαιρειν.]
παλ[αι μεν] τη π[ολει τ]ων Δελφ[ων προθ]υμο[ς
εγενομην και ευνους εξ αρ]
χης, αει [δ'] ετηρη[σα τη]ν θρησκει[αν τ]ου Απο[λλωνος
του Πυθιου· οσα δε]
νυν λεγεται και [πολ]ειτων ερι[δες ε]κειναι, ω[ν
μνημην πεποιηται Λευκιος Ιου]
νιος Γαλλιων, ο φ[ιλος] μου κα[ι ανθυ]πατος [της
Αχαιας],
. . . ετι εξειν τον πρ[οτερ]ο[ν ορισμον] . . . ιιε[ . . . των αλ]
λων πολεων κα . . .
αυτοις επτρε[π . . . Δελ
φων ως πολε[μιων οντων
ται μετωκι[ς . . .
[το]υτου . . .

This inscription is found on four fragments (Delphi 2178, 2271, 3883, and 4001). No one who has seen them appears to doubt that they are all part of the same original.

There are also three other fragments (Delphi 500, 2311, and 728), **Three doubtful fragments.** which apparently belong together, and according to Bourguet and Plooij are part of the same original as the other fragment. The reconstruction of the text in these three fragments, as given by Plooij, is

. . . ι μεν γαρε . . .
. . . τοπους κ[αι . . .
. . . ν παντως εν παντω σε[μνοτατω]
. . . θη οιτινε[ς]
. . . ι και το συνα . . .
. . . επι τω . . . ν . . .
[εν τοις ωρις] με[ν]οις μεν[ειν] . . .
. . . λαξε εντελλομαι γ . . .
ων εν αυτω γεγραμ[μενων]

It is, however, doubtful whether these three fragments really belong to the same inscription as the others, and in any case they make no intelligible addition to its meaning.

The translation of the certain portion would be "Tiberius Claudius **The mean-** Caesar Augustus Germanicus, Pontifex maximus, in the 12th year of his **ing of the inscription.** tribunicial power, acclaimed Emperor for the 26th time, father of his country, consul for the 5th time, Censor, sends greeting to the city of Delphi. I have for long been zealous for the city of Delphi and favourable to it from the beginning, and I have always observed the cult of the Pythian Apollo, but with regard to the present stories, and those quarrels of the citizens of which a report has been made by Lucius Junius Gallio, my friend, and proconsul of Achaia . . . will still hold the previous settlement. . . ."

There is fortunately no serious doubt about the supplements in the important parts of this inscription. Nearly all the phrases which are supplied belong to the conventional language of inscriptions. The most important, of course, are :

(a) The supplement of Ἀχαίας in line 6 ; but the previous word can only be [ἀνθύ]πατος, and in an inscription at Delphi Achaea is clearly the province intended. It is, of course, just possible to argue that the inscription might mean that Gallio had been proconsul, but the nature of the inscription renders this very unlikely, and the title 'friend of the Emperor' was particularly used of proconsuls in office.

(b) The supplement of the number 12 in connexion with the tribunicial power of the emperor ; but this is fixed with relative certainty by the fortunate preservation of the number 26 in line 2, which must refer to the imperial acclamation. Though in practice the emperors reigned for their life, they were acclaimed *imperator* at frequent but irregular intervals. The tribunicial power of the emperors, on the other hand, corresponded exactly with the actual years of their reign, which in the case of Claudius

The acclamation of Claudius. began on the 25th of January. The 11th year of Claudius (January 25, 51– January 24, 52) overlaps his 24th acclamation (*CIL.* iii. 1977) :

```
[ti · ] CLAUDIO · DRUS[i · f · ] CAESARI
AUG · [g]ERM · PONTIF · MAX
TRIB · [p] · XI IMP · X[x]IIII · COS · V
CENSORI · P · P · P · ANTEIO ¹ · LEG
             PRO · PR ·
```

His 25th is mentioned in *CIL.* xi. 824, but nothing more is legible. It may have been in his 11th year, but as in that year he was certainly acclaimed for the 22nd time (*CIL.* iii. 476), and presumably for the 23rd time as well as for the 24th, it is somewhat more probable that the 25th acclamation came in his 12th year. During that year he was certainly acclaimed for the 27th time (*CIL.* vi. 1256) :

```
TI · CLAUDIUS · DRUSI · F · CAISAR · AUGUSTUS · GERMANICUS · PONTIF ·
   MAXIM
TRIBUNICIA · POTESTATE · XII · COS · V IMPERATOR XXVII · PATER ·
   PATRIAE
AQUAS · CLAUDIAM · EX FONTIBUS · QUI · VOCABUNTUR · CAERULEUS ·
   ET · CURTIUS · A MILLIARIO · XXXXV
ITEM · ANIENEM · NOVAM A MILLIARIO · LXII · SUA · IMPENSA · IN URBEM ·
   PERDUCENDAS · CURAVIT
```

Moreover this acclamation must have been before August 1, as Frontinus xiii. 14 states : " C. Caesar . . . altero imperii sui anno M. Aquila Iuliano, P. Novio Asprenate coss. (A.D. 38) . . . duos ductus inchoavit. Quod opus Claudius magnificentissime consummavit dedicavitque Sulla et Titiano coss. (A.D. 52) Kalendis Augustis." This appears to have been his last acclamation, as an inscription of his 13th year (*CIL.* ii. 1953) gives that

¹ According to Tacitus, *Ann.* xiii. 22, P. Anteius was appointed *legatus* of Syria in A.D. 55.

number, and we have not yet any acclamation noted for his 14th year.

> TI · CLAUDIO · CAESARI · AUGUSTO
> PONTIFICI · MAXIMO · TRIB
> POTEST · XIII · IMP · XXVII · CONS
> V · P · P · CEN · VESTINUS · RUSTICI · F · X
> VIR · ET · RUSTICUS · F · D · S · P · D · D · CUIUS
> BASIS · CUM · VETUSTATE · CORRUPTA
> ESSET · INVICE · EIUS · VIBIA · RUS ·
> TICANA · NURUS · NOVAM · RESTITUIT

He died on October 12, 54. Moreover, there is definite evidence that his 26th acclamation overlapped his 12th year in a Greek inscription [1] from Caria which begins as follows :

> ΤιΒεριον ΚλαγΔιον Καιϲαρα Γερμανικον, Αγτο
> κρατορα, Θεον, Σεβαϲτον, αρχιερεα μεγιϲτον,
> Δημαρχικηϲ εϲογϲιαϲ το ΔωΔεκατον, γπατον το πεν
> πτον αγτοκρατορα το εικοϲτον και εκτον πατερα πατρι
> Δοϲ, Ερατοφανηϲ Χαρεινογ ΡοΔιοϲ κτλ.

Thus it is extremely probable that his 26th acclamation came in his 12th year, that is, between the 25th of January 52 and the 24th of January 53, though it is just possible that he was acclaimed both for the 25th and 26th times during his 11th year. But this would mean that he was acclaimed five times in one year, and it does not appear clear that in any other year he was ever acclaimed more than three times. We may take it, therefore, as almost certain that Gallio was proconsul of Achaia in the 12th year of Claudius, January 25, 52–January 24, 53.  *The date of Gallio.*

It is, however, important to notice the points which are not established by the Delphi inscription.  *Doubtful points.*

(i.) We do not know how long Gallio was proconsul. The normal length of office appears to have been one year, but two years was not unprecedented. Usually a proconsul entered on office in the beginning of summer (see Mommsen, *Röm. Staatsrecht*, ed. 3, vol. ii. p. 256). Thus, with the most probable interpretation of the Delphi inscription, we can fix the proconsulate of Gallio as including the year 52, but we do not know whether he became proconsul in that year or in the year previous (51), nor do we know when he retired. If he was proconsul for two years the year 50 is possible for the beginning and 54 for the end of his proconsulship. And if we accept an extremely improbable but not at present provably impossible crowding of acclamations early in the 11th year of Claudius, it would perhaps be possible to put these dates one year earlier. But this is so improbable as not to be worth considering unless other evidence should be found to point in that direction.

---

[1] An inscription put up to the gods and the people of Kys by Eratophanes of Rhodes. Kys is a small town in Caria. (See G. Cousin and G. Deschamps, 'Emplacement des ruines de la ville de Kûs en Carie,' in the *Bulletin de Correspondance hellénique*, xi. (1887), pp. 305 ff.)

(ii.) We do not know whether the episode which brought Paul before Gallio came at the beginning of his proconsulate, though this is often assumed ; we merely know from Acts that Gallio was proconsul (ἀνθυπάτου ὄντος). It is hazardous to argue that this means anything more than 'while Gallio was proconsul.' It is the context, not the grammar, which suggests that Gallio had just arrived when Paul was brought before him, though—to me at least—the suggestion is very plain.

(iii.) We do not know whether the Gallio episode came at the beginning, at the end, or in the middle of Paul's stay in Corinth. We know from Acts xviii. 11 that he stayed for a year and six months in Corinth, and the trial before Gallio is mentioned immediately after this chronological statement. At the end it states in verse 18 that Paul stayed some days longer. This arrangement of facts makes it probable, but does not wholly prove, that in the opinion of the author Paul was brought before Gallio towards the end of his stay in Corinth. It remains possible, considering Luke's methods, that he merely inserts the story of Gallio at the end of his account of Paul's activities in Corinth, and that this arrangement is not decisive as to the date.

Putting aside this possibility and assuming (a) that Gallio was proconsul for only one year, and (b) that he came to Achaia in the summer of 51 or of 52 and stayed until 52 or 53, Paul's trial before Gallio must have been somewhere in the twenty-four months (or a little more) between the summers of 51 and 53, and his arrival in Corinth must have been eighteen months earlier, that is, probably in the spring of 49 or 50.

## VI. *The Procuratorship of Porcius Festus*

The evidence of Josephus.

According to Josephus the sequence of events leading to the appointment of Festus was the following :

Cumanus succeeded Tiberius Alexander, and Herod of Chalcis died in the eighth year of Claudius (A.D. 48). The government of Cumanus was unsatisfactory, and as the result of an inquiry held by Ummidius Quadratus he was sent back to Rome. Claudius, on the advice of Jonathan the high priest, appointed Felix to succeed him. Apparently Felix was sent to Palestine before Agrippa was given Batanaea and Trachonitis, and Agrippa's promotion came after the completion of the twelfth year of Claudius (after Jan. 24, A.D. 53) so that Felix probably was sent to Palestine in 52 or possibly in 53.

Tacitus.

Such is the account given by Josephus, but the parallel narrative by Tacitus (*Ann.* xii. 54) is so different and so important that the text must be quoted. After describing the honours paid to Pallas, the brother of Felix, and how he had refused a vote of money from the senate, he ends with a characteristic sentence, "fixum est in aere publico senatus consultum, quo libertinus sestertii ter miliens possessor antiquae parsimoniae laudibus cumulabatur." He then goes on " At non frater eius, cognomento Felix, pari moderatione agebat, iam pridem Iudaeae inpositus et cuncta malefacta sibi inpune ratus tanta potentia subnixo. Sane praebuerant Iudaei speciem motus orta seditione, postquam ⟨a C. Caesare iussi erant effigiem eius in templo locare, et quamquam⟩ cognita caede eius haud obtemperatum esset, manebat metus ne quis principum eadem inperitaret. Atque interim Felix intempestivis remediis delicta accendebat, aemulo ad deterrima Ventidio ⟨Cumano⟩ cui pars provinciae habebatur, ita divisis ut huic Galilaeorum natio, Felici Samaritae parerent, discordes olim et tum contemptu regentium minus coercitis odiis. Igitur raptare inter se, inmittere latronum globos, conponere insidias et aliquando proeliis congredi, spoliaque et praedas ad procuratores referre, hique primo laetari, mox gliscente pernicie cum arma militum interiecissent, caesi milites; arsissetque bello provincia, ni Quadratus Suriae rector subvenisset. Nec diu adversus Iudaeos qui in necem militum proruperant, dubitatum quin capite poenas luerent: Cumanus et Felix cunctationem adferebant quia Claudius causis rebellionis auditis ius statuendi etiam de procuratoribus dederat. Sed Quadratus Felicem inter iudices ostentavit, receptum inter tribunal, quo studia accusantium deterrerentur; damnatusque flagitiorum quae duo deliquerant Cumanus et quies provinciae reddita."

Thus, according to him, Felix had been a colleague of Cumanus, and had been responsible for Samaria, while Cumanus looked after Galilee and presumably Judaea. Apparently each had the title of Procurator. Both should have been tried by Quadratus, but Felix was put on the bench instead of in the dock.

Speaking generally Josephus may be supposed to have had more accurate knowledge of Palestinian affairs than Tacitus. But two facts support the view that Josephus may have unduly compressed the statement of the facts. (a) Josephus himself states that Jonathan the high priest asked for the appointment of Felix as procurator (ἐπίτροπον) of Judaea. (b) In Acts xxiv. 10 Paul says that Felix had been ' a judge of this nation ' for many years. *[margin: Comparison of Josephus and Tacitus.]*

Both these facts suggest that Felix must have had a longer acquaintance with Palestine than his appointment as the successor to Cumanus would indicate. It is, however, very hard to form any theory which is more than plausible. Possibly Felix had held some military office in Samaria. Possibly there is some missing link in the story of the administration of Palestine; it is not inconceivable that the Legate of Syria was, at least after the withdrawal of Pilate, in control of the Roman interests in Judaea, Samaria, and Galilee. During the reign of Agrippa I. this control would be in abeyance; afterwards the succession of Tiberius Alexander, Cumanus and Felix may have been officially under the Legate of Syria, though the actual administration of Judaea may have been so completely in the hands of Cumanus and Felix that the statements of Josephus are practically correct. It is, however, desirable not to guess on this point but to recognize that there is a lacuna in our information which only fresh archaeological evidence can fill up.

Felix was in any case in control of Palestine when Paul was arrested in Jerusalem, and Acts xxiv. 27 goes on to say διετίας δὲ πληρωθείσης ἔλαβεν διάδοχον ὁ Φῆλιξ Πόρκιον Φῆστον. The meaning of this verse is wholly ambiguous. There is nothing in the structure of the sentence or in the context to decide whether it means that Felix was procurator for two years, and was then succeeded by Festus, or that he was replaced after Paul had been in prison for two years. (See further on p. 471, note 1.)

The year of the recall of Felix.

The year in which Felix was recalled seems at first to be clearly established by other evidence, but this clearness is completely obscured by a study of the data.

(a) Josephus (*Antiq.* xx. 8. 1 ff.) discusses in order the death of Claudius, the accession of Nero, and details as to the events in the procuratorship of Felix. The natural conclusion, drawn also by Eusebius, is that Felix was recalled by Nero, not by Claudius.

(b) Josephus (*Antiq.* xx. 8. 9) says that after Felix was recalled his brother Pallas saved him from complete disaster. Pallas was chief of the Treasury under Ummidius; he had contrived the Emperor's marriage with Agrippina and Nero's adoption; Nero, who was thus indebted to Pallas for the throne, naturally disliked him, and soon dismissed him. Moreover, according to Tacitus, the poisoning of Britannicus followed soon after the fall of Pallas, and Britannicus was then nearly fourteen years old. This would seem to fix the date of the fall of Pallas fairly well, as Suetonius states that the birthday of Britannicus was the twentieth of the reign of Claudius, that is, February 13. But unfortunately Tacitus says that Nero was two years older than Britannicus, which, as Nero was born on Dec. 15, A.D. 37, would mean that Britannicus was born on February 13, A.D. 40. But this would put his fourteenth birthday on Feb. 13, A.D. 54 when Nero was not yet emperor as he certainly was when Britannicus was poisoned.[1] Moreover Suetonius (*Claudius*, 27) says that Britannicus was born ' in secundo consulatu ' of Claudius, that is, in A.D. 42, which would bring his fourteenth year to 56. Obviously these data cannot be reconciled, and historians have to choose between them, but Suetonius is probably right, for certainly Britannicus was not killed in the reign of Claudius.

The most probable conclusion from these confused data is that Pallas fell late in A.D. 55, so that if Felix were recalled in the early spring of 55, Pallas would just have had time to protect him. In this case the summer of 55 is the most probable year for the entry of Festus into office [2] and should be regarded as the year in the autumn of which Paul left Caesarea for Rome, which he reached in the spring of 56. But it is possible that Festus did not reach his province until the year after the

---

[1] Harnack in his *Chronologie* emends Tacitus so as to make Britannicus die just before his fifteenth birthday.

[2] The mention of Drusilla in Acts xxiv. 22 ff. gives no help. Drusilla was the daughter of Agrippa. According to Josephus, when her father died in A.D. 44, she was six years old, so that she was born in A.D. 38. In 53 she married Azizus of Emesa, but she soon left him and married Felix. This indicates that the trial of Paul before Felix was not earlier than late in 53, and if the two years mentioned in Acts xxiv. 27 refer to Paul's imprisonment, 55 is the earliest possible as well as the most intrinsically probable date for the arrival of Festus. But 53 is far too early a date for Paul's last arrival in Jerusalem.

recall of Felix, so that Paul may have left Caesarea in 56 and reached Rome in 57.

### Conclusions

Such are the direct data on which we have to rely for any reconstruction of the chronology of Acts. To them the events described must be related by a kind of 'dead-reckoning' of time.

For the early period the most important help can be found not in Acts itself but in the Gospels and in Galatians. Obviously Acts begins immediately after the crucifixion of Jesus; if that date were certain it would supply a fixed point from which the dead-reckoning could begin. This is unfortunately not the case. A full discussion of the problem of the date of the crucifixion falls outside the province of this book, but the following points may be noted. Luke says that John the Baptist began to preach in the fourteenth year of Tiberius (A.D. 14–37). This marks A.D. 27 as the *terminus post quem* of the ministry of Jesus, but it is entirely uncertain whether an interval of weeks, months, or years intervened between the coming of John and the baptism of Jesus. Critics have next to decide whether the Synoptic tradition implies that Jesus had a ministry of more than one year, a subject which the paucity of evidence admirably fits for the long dissertations which have been devoted to it. Next they have to settle whether they will follow the Marcan tradition, which puts the crucifixion on the 15th of Nisan, or the Lucan-Johannine, which puts it on the 14th. Finally they have the double task of deciding in what years the 14th or 15th of Nisan fell on a Friday, as the one really certain fact is that Jesus was crucified on the day before the Sabbath. This task is complicated by doubts as to the method employed by the Jews to fix the day of the new moon.

It is extremely unlikely that we shall ever gain certainty on these points, but, partly, it is true, influenced by the necessity of finding room for the chronology implied by Acts and Galatians, modern scholars generally accept 29 or 30 as the date of the crucifixion. Turner's arguments for 29 seem the most convincing.

If, then, Acts xii. (the death of Herod) be fixed as referring to events in A.D. 44 and the first chapter belong to A.D. 29, the first part of Acts covers a period of fifteen years. This agrees quite well with Galatians, which says (or may say) that Paul's second visit to Jerusalem was fourteen years after his conversion. But the exact date of the conversion, and the general chronology of Acts i.-xv., depend not only on the date of the death of Herod and the Judaean famine but on the analysis of the sources of Acts.

The chronological importance of the death of Herod and of the famine in Judaea is intimately associated with the analysis of the sources of Acts.

Taking Acts as it stands the obvious meaning of the text is: (i.) Peter's imprisonment and release were just before the Passover (cf. xii. 3 f.); (ii.) Herod was in Jerusalem during the Passover, and immediately after it went to Caesarea, where he died (cf. xii. 19 and 21-23).

*[marginal notes:]* The date of the crucifixion. — Acts i.-xv. — The death of Herod and the analysis of Acts.

If the chronology given in Josephus be followed without regarding the possible identification of the day of Herod's death with the four-yearly feast in honour of the emperor, Herod's death was during his seventh year, i.e. not later than the spring of 44. Thus Peter's imprisonment must have been in the spring of 43 or 44. It is interesting to note that Eusebius, apparently in order to accommodate the facts to the belief that Peter was bishop of Rome for twenty-five years, puts the foundation of the church of Antioch and the departure of Peter for Rome in the year A.D. 42, though he puts the death of Herod Agrippa in 45, almost correctly.

The famine in Acts.

It is also clear that the text of Acts, as it now stands, places the famine in Judaea before the death of Herod. Acts xi. 27-30 cannot well mean anything except that the Christians in Antioch were warned by Agabus that there would be a famine in Judaea, and immediately sent help to Jerusalem. Of course it does not follow that when they did so famine was already raging; but it was in sight, and the announcement in xii. 25 of the completion of the relief work—if that be the meaning of the verse—seems to indicate that the editor—not necessarily his source—placed the famine before Herod's death and its relief in the same year.

In Josephus.

The evidence of Josephus, on the other hand is very clear, that the famine was not before but after the death of Herod, in the time of Tiberius Alexander, between whom and Herod intervened the procuratorship of Cuspius Fadus. Thus the famine was at least not earlier than 46.

The analysis of sources.

There is no possibility of reconciling Acts with Josephus if it be taken as a continuous and chronological narrative. If, however, we accept the analysis of sources suggested in Vol. II. pp. 156 f., a relatively easy solution is possible. According to it the story of Herod's death and of the departure of Peter from Jerusalem is not placed with chronological correctness. It ought to come before Acts xi. 27-30 instead of after it. In dealing with his sources the writer of Acts has missed the true chronological order. The question which is bound to rise in the mind of the investigator is whether there is not a further dislocation, so that Acts ix. 32-xi. 18 should come after rather than before the departure of Peter from Jerusalem. If this were so the chronological order would be: (i.) the death of Herod and Peter's departure from Jerusalem; (ii.) Peter's journey through Palestine to Caesarea; (iii.) the famine in Palestine, Peter's return to Jerusalem, and the Apostolic Council related from the Antiochian point of view in Acts xi. and Galatians ii., and from the point of view of Jerusalem in Acts xv.

E. Schwartz

This combination, which is certainly attractive though incapable of demonstration, brings out the strength of E. Schwartz's belief that Acts xiii. and xiv. and Acts xv. 40-xvi. 6 are fragments of two accounts of one journey which began after the Apostolic Council, and has been divided by the writer of Acts into two in the same way as he has duplicated the meeting of the Apostles in Jerusalem. Although Schwartz's view seems at first sight unduly revolutionary, its attractiveness increases when it is realized that any other system calls for a still further dislocation of the narrative in order to make Acts xiii. and xiv. come before the end of chapter xi. For if xi. 30 (= xii. 25) really refers to the same events as chap. xv., either it is necessary to put the journey described in xiii.-xiv. before xi. 27—and there appears to be no room for it ; or, if we say that Luke was right in putting this journey immediately after the famine-relief visit—which is really identical with xv.—we are driven to say that xiii.-xiv. correspond to xvi. 6 ff., and this is exactly Schwartz's hypothesis.

It should also be noted that this theory explains the text of xii. 25, which is now seen to be merely a duplicate of xi. 30. As it stands it ought to say that Paul and Barnabas returned *from* Jerusalem, but it betrays its real origin and nature by saying that they returned *to* Jerusalem.

Finally, it is noticeable how the whole problem revolves round the comparison of Acts xi., Acts xv., and Galatians ii. If we had not Galatians the problem would be simpler, though it would exist, for the difference in chronology between Acts and Josephus would remain. But as it is, possessing Galatians as we fortunately do, the solutions suggested here and in Additional Note 16 have to be considered. It is moreover a point of great significance that the source-analysis advocated here and in Vol. II. provides a solution not only of the difference between Acts and Galatians, but also of that between Acts and Josephus.

On this theory, then, we should have the following chronology for the Results. period of the famine :

1. Peter's imprisonment and escape from Jerusalem, March–April 44, or possibly August 43.
2. Herod's death in Caesarea, Spring 44.
3. Peter's Palestinian journey and the conversion of Cornelius, 44–46.
4. Barnabas, Paul, Agabus, etc., at Antioch, 45.
5. The famine and the relief-mission to Jerusalem, Peter's return, and the Apostolic Council, 46.
6. Peter's visit to Antioch, and the mission to the Gentiles of Barnabas and Paul, 47.

It is then easy to fit in the data in Galatians. Paul's conversion was probably fourteen years before the council, and in 32, or, allowing for the ancient method of reckoning, perhaps in 33. It would even be possible to adopt the other interpretation of Galatians which makes the fourteen years of ii. 1 exclude rather than include the three years of i. 18. This would put the conversion in 29 or 31 at the latest. 31 is possible, but 29 is improbable if the crucifixion was in that year.

If, however, these theories be rejected, and Acts be accepted in its Alterna-statement that Paul went to Jerusalem in the time of the famine and tives. again in the time of the Apostolic council, a different scheme must be adopted.

There are two possibilities : (i.) The famine corresponds to Paul's (i.). second visit described in Galatians ii. 1 ff. If so, this second visit was in 46, and the first missionary journey followed. This cannot have taken less than one season from spring to autumn (about thirty-two weeks) ; it need not but may have taken more. Thus the Apostolic council would probably have been in 48 or possibly in 47. Then followed the second journey, beginning in the spring of 49 ; it would take most of the season to reach Troas and Neapolis, and perhaps Philippi, Thessalonica and

Athens cover the winter of 49–50.   If he were in Beroea in February it would explain why he went to Athens by land, assuming that this view of his movements, taken in the commentary, be correct.   This would bring Paul to Corinth in the spring or summer of 50 and when he left it eighteen months later Gallio was certainly Proconsul.   Allowing for the flying visit to Palestine which makes the division between the 'second' and 'third' journeys, Paul may have reached Ephesus on his return in the late autumn of 51, but more probably in the summer of 52.   Thus he must have left Ephesus in 55 and probably arrived in Jerusalem in 56. This is hard to reconcile with the fact that Felix was procurator when Paul reached Jerusalem.   Festus must already have been in office in 56.

(iii.).   (ii.) The second visit of Galatians may be equated with Acts xv., as Lightfoot and others maintain.   If so, the chronology advocated above, on the theory that the visit in the time of the famine and the council are identical, holds good for all events after the council, but everything before it must be made at least one year earlier.   This is not impossible.

The period after the Council.   For the period after the apostolic council the next fixed point for dead-reckoning is Gallio's proconsulate, which (see pp. 460 ff.) can be fixed as including A.D. 52, and probably began in 50 or 51.   Paul according to Acts xviii. 11 was eighteen months in Corinth, so that he must have arrived in Corinth not earlier than 49, and possibly in 50.   Thus we have from 46 to 49 or 50 for the events between the Apostolic council and Paul's arrival at Corinth.   The events described in Acts xv.-xviii. fit excellently :

1. The Apostolic Council, 46.
2. Paul's departure for Antioch, spring of 47.
3. Journey across Asia Minor, 47–48.
4. Arrival at Neapolis, summer of 48.
5. Philippi—Thessalonica—Beroea—Athens, 48–49.
6. Arrival at Corinth, 49 (or possibly early in 50).
7. Appearance before Gallio, 51 (or perhaps 52).

The remaining point for dead-reckoning is the arrival of Festus in 55 or 56.   Once more it is easy enough to fit in the events :

1. Paul's departure from Corinth, summer of 51.
2. Visit to Antioch, winter of 51–52.
3. Return to Ephesus for three years, 52–54.
4. Visit to Corinth, early in 55.
5. Departure from Corinth, March 55.
6. Arrival in Jerusalem, Pentecost 55.[1]

[1] A further attempt to define the year of Paul's arrival in Jerusalem has sometimes, notably by Plooij, been based on Acts xx. 6 ff.   The theory is that Paul started from Philippi on the 22nd of Nisan (the day after the 'Days of unleavened bread'), and that since he reached Troas five days later, and after staying there seven days left on a Monday, he must have originally started from Philippi on a Friday.   Therefore in that year the 22nd of Nisan was a Friday, and astronomical tables show that this was so in 57—the year

7. Festus in Judaea, summer of 55 or 56.[1]
8. Paul's voyage to Rome, 55–56 or 56–57.

Before discussing the general nature of this scheme, it is desirable at this point to compare it with the dates given by Eusebius. The evidence is given in his two closely-connected works, the *Historia Ecclesiastica* and the *Chronicon*. There is considerable need for a really thorough treatise on the relation between these works. The *Chronicon* was written first, and is presumably the chronological basis on which Eusebius built up the narrative of the *Historia*. The two works do not always agree, though they usually do, and there is the added complication that the original text of the *Chronicon* is no longer extant. The introductory part is preserved in Armenian, and the chronological tables are extant in two corrupt forms: in Latin, in an edition made by Jerome,[2] and in Armenian.[3]

*The chronology of Eusebius.*

---

which Plooij regards as that of Paul's arrival in Jerusalem—or in 54. The weak spot in this ingenious argument, originally suggested by Ramsay, is the first and most important. It is quite likely that Paul left Philippi on a Friday; but Luke does not say that this was 'the 22nd of Nisan,' as Plooij does. He merely says that it was μετὰ τὰς ἡμέρας τῶν ἀζύμων. The obvious meaning is that Paul waited in Philippi until the Passover week was finished: it does not say whether he went away one or more days after this date. The exact day would depend then, as it would now, on when a boat was sailing. (See D. Plooij, *De Chronologie van het leven van Paulus*, Leiden, 1918, and W. M. Ramsay, 'A Second Fixed Point in the Pauline Chronology,' *Expositor*, 1900, pp. 81 ff.)

[1] It will be observed that this time-table is only possible if διετίας in xxiv. 27 refers to Felix rather than to Paul. That it refers to Paul is the more generally accepted view, but the opinion advocated above has the support of Petavius, *De doctrina temporum*, vol. ii. book 11, chap. 12, in the Venetian edition of 1757, p. 176, and in modern times of J. Wellhausen, 'Kritische Analyse der Apostelgeschichte' (*Gött. Abh.* xv. 2, 1914), p. 50, and E. Schwartz 'Zur Chronologie des Paulus' (*Gött. Nachr.*, 1907), p. 294.

[2] There are a fair number of MSS. of Jerome's version, but two stand out as pre-eminent. (1) O, a fifth-century MS. in the Bodleian Library at Oxford, and (2) S, fragments of a fifth-century MS. at Florence and elsewhere. The opinion of experts is divided as to the relative merits of their codices. (See the editions of J. K. Fotheringham (1923) and R. Helm in the Berlin Academy's edition of Eusebius, vol. vii. (1913–1926).)

[3] There are only two MSS. of the Armenian version, one in the Armenian Patriarchate in Constantinople (G), the other at Etschmiadzin (E). They are closely related to a common original which had already suffered much corruption. The earlier editions (Aucher in 1818, Zohrab in 1818, Petermann in Schoene's Eusebius in 1875) have been superseded by J. Karst's in the Berlin Academy's *Griechische christliche Schriftsteller d. ersten drei Jahrh.*, *Eusebius*, v., 1911. It has been disputed whether the Armenian was a direct translation from the Greek, or from an intermediate Syriac form. At present Karst's arguments have turned the scale in favour of direct translation from the Greek, but the question is scarcely closed.

The relative value of these versions is still, and perhaps always will be, an unsettled question.  Possibly Jerome's version is more accurate, but contains more editorial additions, and the Armenian may be less edited but more corrupt.

Latin and Armenian.    For the period covered by Acts the evidence of the *Chronicon* in the Latin and Armenian is as follows :

|  | Jerome | Armenian |
|---|---|---|
| The Crucifixion . . . | 31 | 31 |
| Death of Agrippa . . . | 44 | 44 |
| The Famine . . . . | 44 | 42 |
| Felix . . . . . | 51 | 51 |
| Paul before Felix . . . | 53 [1] | 51 |
| Festus . . . . . | 56 | 54 |

It is obvious that the two versions differ considerably.  In the date of the Famine and in that of Festus the Armenian is clearly wrong, and most writers prefer to follow Jerome.

Plooij and Erbes.    Plooij, however, basing his arguments on Erbes, *Die Todestage der Ap. Paulus und Petrus*, in discussing the date of Festus, contends that the Armenian is preferable to the Latin, and that Eusebius has been confused by following a Jewish source, perhaps Justus of Tiberias, which reckoned the years of Agrippa II. not, as Eusebius did, from the death of Agrippa I. in 44 but from the year when he actually was given the title of king in succession to Herod of Chalcis in A.D. 50.  Plooij thinks that all the Agrippa dates are therefore five years too early, and that Festus was appointed in 59.

This conclusion seems to me to fail for several reasons.  (*a*) It is not proved, and is in itself unlikely, that Eusebius was using Justus of Tiberias as his main guide.  (*b*) He certainly used Josephus largely ; and Josephus clearly indicates that Festus came in the reign of Nero, before Pallas was discredited.  (*c*) Conclusive against Plooij's theory is the fact that, if it be true, it ought to apply to Felix as well as to Festus ; if so, Felix was appointed in 56—an impossibly late date.

It is in just such points as these that the numerals in the Armenian are doubtful guides, and Jerome's figure is undoubtedly to be followed, especially since in the *Church History* Eusebius puts the arrival of Festus in the reign of Nero, where it clearly ought to be.

It will be seen that the Eusebian figures differ very little from those obtained from the earlier evidence.  This, however, merely means that Eusebius reached his results in much the same way as we do ; he had no other important evidence, and, for this period, his testimony has little

---

[1] The evidence is somewhat confused.  Jerome gives 51 for the arrival of Felix, and adds "aput quem Paulus apostolus accusatus in defensionem sui perorat," but as he places the episode of the Egyptian two years later, and connects it with Paul's arrest, he probably places Paul's arrest at least as late as 53.  Apparently the Armenian ascribes 'the Egyptian' to the same year as the arrival of Felix.

value.  For us, as for him, the chief sources of information must be Acts itself, Josephus, and Tacitus.

It is obvious that this chronological scheme, or any variation of it, General derived, as it must be, from such imperfect data, is merely an approxi- tions. mation, which can never be made accurate, and may be amended by months or at some points even by years without becoming seriously improbable.  As in all similar problems, the most plausible solution is that which gives the best answer to most difficulties.  In this case the points which will always cause perplexity are :

(i.) The exact fixing of the few definite data which we possess.  None (i.) Paucity can be established quite exactly, and only in the case of the death of of data. Herod, the proconsulate of Gallio, and—I should be inclined to add—the appointment of Festus, can it be said that the margin of possible errror is not great.  This is not very much to work upon ; there is consequently considerable strain on the dead-reckoning from event to event, and different investigators estimate differently the probable lapse of time. That this difference is, after all, not extreme may be shown by the following selection of typical results in tabular form.

| | Petavius | Wieseler | Harnack | Turner | Zahn | Lightfoot | Weber [1] | Plooij | Lake |
|---|---|---|---|---|---|---|---|---|---|
| The Crucifixion | 31 | 30 | 29 or 30 | 29 | 30 | (30) | — | 29 | 29-30 |
| Paul's Conversion | 33 | 40 | 30 | 35 | 35 | 34 | 31 | 30-1 | 32 |
| Famine Relief | 41 | 45 | (44) | 46 | 44 | 45 | 46-7 | 45-6 | }46 |
| Apostolic Council | 49 | 50 | 47 | 49 | 52 | 51 | 50 | 48 | }46 |
| Corinth | 50 | 52 | 48 | 50 | 52 | 52 | 50 | 50 | 49 |
| Last visit to Jerusalem | 53 | 58 | 54 | 56 | 58 | 58 | 55 | 57 | 55 |
| Appointment of Festus | 56 | 60 | 56 | 56 | 60 | 60 | 55 | 59 | 55 |

(ii.) The exact exegesis of the text is not always as clear as might (ii.) Doubt- have been hoped.  Much, for instance, depends on Gal. i. 18 ff., but few ful exegesis. more obscure passages can be found in Greek literature.  Similarly, the exact interpretations of Acts xviii. 12 [2] and of xxiv. 27 [3] are essential to the chronographer, and impossible to the exegete.

(iii.) The source criticism of Acts introduces complications which (iii.) Source cannot be ignored, even though it be impossible to simplify them. criticism. Especially is this true of Paul's first and second journeys, and the relation of the 'famine-relief visit' to the Apostolic council.  It is impossible to prove the truth of Ed. Schwartz's theory that the two journeys are merely two parts of one journey, but it will always remain

[1] The similarity of my results to Weber's is the more curious as I had finished this article before I had seen his book.

[2] Γαλλίωνος δὲ ἀνθυπάτου ὄντος κτλ.

[3] διετίας δὲ πληρωθείσης ἔλαβε διάδοχον ὁ Φῆλιξ Πόρκιον Φῆστον.

a possibility, and it obviously complicates [1] the work of the chronographer. Assuming that the famine-relief visit is the same as the Apostolic council, and that it was followed by one long journey through Asia Minor, Macedonia, and Achaia unbroken by any return to Antioch, the amount of time required for Paul's ministry is clearly shorter than it would otherwise be, and it is not difficult to suppose that he reached Jerusalem in 55.

The 'patchiness' of Acts.    (iv.) Finally, it cannot escape the attention of any who study the chronology of Acts, how vividly it illustrates the 'patchy' nature of the book. Chapters i.-ix. cover not more than three years, but chapters x.-xi. 25 cover fourteen, and the rest of the book (fourteen chapters) covers only nine. The same disproportion could be observed if a closer analysis were made of the relation between the passage of time and the length of the narrative. For the historian the importance of this observation is clear : we are dealing with selected episodes, not with a continuous history. For the chronographer its importance is somewhat different : it is a warning that the shortness of the description of any given event is no certain criterion of its duration. If, for instance, it were not for the casual reference to 'three years' in xx. 31, no one would have guessed from Acts that Paul had been so long in Ephesus.

[Among the many books on this subject the most valuable for the modern reader are A. von Harnack, *Chronologie der altchristliche Literatur*, i. pp. 236 ff. ; C. H. Turner, 'Chronology,' in Hastings' *Dictionary of the Bible*, but the works of Lightfoot, *Biblical Essays*, 1893, Zahn, *Einleitung in das N.T.* and detached notes in his commentary, and V. Weber, *Die antiochenische Kollekte*, are extremely instructive, and for those who read Dutch there is no more useful compendium of facts and theories than D. Plooij's *De Chronologie van het leven van Paulus*.]

## Note XXXV. Localities in and near Jerusalem mentioned in Acts

### By Kirsopp Lake

Palestinian localities in Acts.    It is remarkable how little definite mention is made in Acts of localities in Palestine, smaller than towns or villages, which can be identified, except in the neighbourhood of Jerusalem. Nor do those which are mentioned give rise to any topographical problems. Caesarea, Ptolemais, Lydda, etc., are all quite well known, and Acts neither solves nor complicates any question concerning them.

Jerusalem.    The case of Jerusalem is different. In its immediate neighbourhood or within its walls are the following [2] places mentioned in Acts :

[1] Though ultimately I think that it leads to a more satisfactory result than any other theory.

[2] The order is that which has proved most convenient for treatment in this note.

(1) The Mount of Olives and the village of Bethany.
(2) The Upper Room and the Tomb of David.
(3) The Court-room of the Sanhedrin.
(4) Three prisons.
(5) The Roman barracks.
(6) The Beautiful Gate of the Temple and Solomon's Porch.

### 1. *The Mount of Olives and Bethany*

The Mount of Olives is of course well known. It is the hill which overlooks the east side of the city. It is separated from Jerusalem by the rather deep valley of the Kedron, and from Scopus by a shallow depression. The only question relating to it is whether it should in the New Testament be called Mount Olivet, or the Olive Orchard (ἐλαιών = *olivetum*), or the Mount of Olives (ἐλαιῶν). Both names are found in the Bible and in Josephus. Probably both were always in use.

The situation of Bethany is a more difficult question. Since the Middle Ages and earlier it has been identified with the village now called El Azarijeh—an obvious Arab corruption of Lazarus, who lived in Bethany according to the gospel of John. This village is on the north side of the road which skirts the south end of the Mount of Olives, and goes down to Jericho. It is, however, not an ancient road. The old road to Jericho went over the Mount of Olives somewhat on its north side near Scopus. Moreover the gospels suggest that Bethany was on the road from Jericho to Jerusalem, or close to it.[1]

Luke seems to treat ' Mount of Olives ' and Bethany as interchangeable. In Luke xxiv. 50 he says that Jesus led the disciples out ἕως πρὸς Βηθανίαν, leading up to the Ascension ; and in the parallel account in Acts i. 12 it is said that the disciples returned, after the Ascension, from Mount Olivet. It would seem from this that Bethany was on the Mount of Olives (see also p. 21).

This conclusion is probably confirmed by Mark xi. From this it appears that Jesus was coming up from Jericho. That is a very hard walk, rising from below sea-level to more than 2000 feet above it. One of the worst parts on the old road is the last steep rise over the Mount of Olives. Apparently when Jesus reached this point he felt tired out, and sent his disciples into the village ' opposite ' to fetch an ass. Mark says that this was " when they approached Jerusalem, to Bethany, by the Mount of Olives." [2] ' Opposite them ' ought to mean ' ahead of,' but if the village was

*The Mount of Olives.*

*Bethany.*

*Bethany in Mark xi.*

---

[1] In Palestine, as in the hill country of Italy, villages are usually on a hill to the side of the road. But of course this does not apply so much when the road is actually going over a hill. It is obvious that when roads were used mostly for flocks, and village streets were about ten feet wide, the main road passes by a village, not through it.

[2] The text is not quite clear. The Western text (D lat) has only Bethany, Ψ sah only Bethphage. The Neutral text found also in Syr sin looks like a conflation, and the Western text is confirmed by the definite statement of Origen that Matthew says Bethphage only, Mark Bethany only, and Luke both Bethany and Bethphage (Orig. iii. 743).

off the road it may mean to one side of them. In any case the suggestion is that the disciples went on to a village higher up the eastern side of the Mount of Olives. The disciples found the ass, and, promising to return it, took it back to Jesus. The later gospels [1] represent Jesus as riding on it into Jerusalem, and mediaeval tradition said that he came in through the Shushan gate of the Temple (see below, pp. 479 f.). But Mark seems more probably to mean that Jesus rode into the village, welcomed by the villagers, and then went on, apparently next day,[2] into Jerusalem. In any case it is clear that Bethany was the headquarters of Jesus and the disciples during the Passover week and after the Crucifixion (see also pp. 15 f.). Luke at any rate is quite sure that Jesus came by the path over the top, or almost the top of the Mount of Olives, for he pictures Jesus as descending the Mount of Olives, and looking down on the city and weeping over it.[3] But he could not have done this had he gone through the modern Bethany, for that is almost in the valley south of the Mount of Olives, and no one wishing to enter Jerusalem would have climbed up the hill in order to walk down again. For anyone who had gone so far away from the road as to reach El Azarijeh the natural path would be more or less the present carriage road, below, not above, the level of the Temple, though it would probably have crossed the valley of the Kedron sooner than the present road does.

The identification of Bethany with El Azarijeh is therefore doubtful, and I believe that Bethany must have been a village farther north, on the eastern slope of the Mount of Olives, and probably rather high up.

## 2. *The Upper Room and the Tomb of David*

Sion.

The hill at the south-west corner of the present wall of Jerusalem is now called Sion, but there is no doubt that the ancient Sion, the city of David, was really the other hill, outside the south-east corner of the present wall, but inside that of Herod's time. Thus two changes have to be reckoned with. The present wall runs much to the north of the Herodian wall, and the name Sion has been moved across from the south-east to the south-west hill.

'En-nebi David.'

On the modern Sion is a complex of mediaeval buildings, shown to

[1] It seems worth pointing out that only the fourth gospel says that the branches which the villagers cut down were palms. Palm-trees do not grow wild in the country round Jerusalem, nor do they do so in Ephesus. But they are common in Alexandria. Have critics of the fourth gospel paid enough attention to this point?

[2] Mark says that they returned to Bethany after they 'looked at everything' in the Temple. That would take all day, and is inconceivable at the end of a walk from Jericho, even if that walk were spread over two days.

[3] Luke xix. 41. The story seems somewhat dislocated : Luke seems to think of Jesus as seeing the city after he had descended the Mount of Olives. Yet no one who has been in Palestine can doubt that the point where Jesus wept was on the top of the hill when the whole magnificent city lies at one's feet, suddenly and without warning.

visitors as covering the tomb of David,[1] and as the upper room (*coenaculum*) where the Eucharist was instituted, where the Holy Spirit descended on the Apostles, where John Mark and his mother lived, and where the Virgin passed to rest (the κοίμησις or *dormitio*).

So far as the tomb of David is concerned this identification is manifestly wrong, for it is clear from the Old Testament that David's tomb was near the Temple. It is tolerably certain that the modern story is a precarious inference from Acts ii. 29, " His tomb remains with us to this day." The argument is that Peter was speaking in the upper room, so that the tomb must have been in that locality, and the whole tradition that Sion and the tomb of David were on the south-west hill seems to depend on the identification of the upper room. *The tomb of David.*

So far as the upper room is concerned the present building is of course quite late ; probably nothing visible is older than a Franciscan foundation of the fourteenth century. It is, however, almost certain that this was the site of the Byzantine Church of the Apostles, and it is possible that this in turn represents a third-century tradition that here was (or, rather, had been) the upper room of Pentecost. The Byzantine church appears to have been founded by Maximus, bishop of Jerusalem between 331 and 349. Before this there may have been an earlier church on the same spot, but the evidence is not quite satisfactory. Epiphanius (*De mensuris et ponderibus*, xiv., Migne, *P.G.* xliii. 260 f.) says that when Hadrian visited Jerusalem he found it desolate except for a single synagogue and a church which had been built on the spot where the Apostles had lived in the upper room. Unfortunately those who use Epiphanius most trust him least. It is ominous that neither Eusebius nor the Pilgrim of Bordeaux say anything about this church, and it is to be feared that the tradition, like the church, is not older than the foundation of Maximus in the fourth century. *The upper room.*

That this was also the house of John Mark seems not to be part of the oldest tradition, and Acts xii. suggests that this house was not the same as that in which James was living. If either of these houses contained the upper room, it is perhaps more likely that it was the house of James.

[For a discussion of the *coenaculum* see especially Vincent et Abel, *Jerusalem*, ii. pp. 441 ff., and cf. Th. Zahn, ' Die Dormitio Sanctae Virginis und das Haus des Johannes Marcus,' *NKZ.* x. p. 408, and Lagrange, *Évangile selon S. Marc*, pp. 370 ff.]

### 3. *The Court-room of the Sanhedrin*

According to Josephus [2] the hall in which the Sanhedrin met was at the east end of the first, that is the oldest, wall, immediately west of the Temple, and between it and the Xystus, a large paved area west of the Temple. But according to the Talmud it was a room in the Temple at *Josephus.* *The Talmud.*

---

[1] For this reason the whole building is known as *En-nebi David*.

[2] *B.J.* v. 4. 2. Cf. ἀρχόμενον [τὸ ἀρχαῖον τεῖχος] δὲ κατὰ βορρᾶν ἀπὸ τοῦ Ἱππικοῦ καλουμένου πύργου καὶ διατεῖνον ἐπὶ τὸν ξυστόν, ἔπειτα τῇ βουλῇ συνάπτον, ἐπὶ τὴν ἑσπέριον τοῦ ἱεροῦ στοὰν ἀπηρτίζετο. This leaves it ambiguous whether

the south side of the fore-court, and it was called the Gazith, which might mean ' the room of squared stones.' Jewish authorities generally follow the Talmud, but Josephus is the earlier authority and must have had an intimate knowledge of the Temple and its surroundings. Possibly the Talmud is right in saying that the hall was called Gazith, and E. Schürer (*GJV*. ed. 4, ii. pp. 243 ff.) makes the attractive guess that ' Gazith ' covers an obscure allusion to the Xystus.

There is also a tradition that in the third century Rabbi Jose ben Halafta said that forty years before the fall of the Temple the Sanhedrin moved from the Gazith to a shop or market. Possibly this may have been at the spot indicated by Josephus; but the tradition is not corroborated and Jewish authorities attach little importance to it.

In support of Josephus it should be noted that the trial of Jesus was at night, and is therefore unlikely to have been in the Temple which was closed at sunset.

[See also the article in the *Jewish Encyclopaedia*, xi. 72.]

### 4. *The Prisons mentioned in Acts*

The prisons.    There are three prisons in Jerusalem mentioned in Acts: (i.) of the Sanhedrin; (ii.) of Herod; (iii.) of the Roman garrison. There is no tradition of any value concerning these, but their general situation may be guessed with some probability. (i.) The prison of the Sanhedrin is likely to have been either in the Temple, or in, probably below, the Gazith. (ii.) The prison of Herod was probably in the Praetorium, or Palace, on the west side of the city. This was built by Herod the Great, and used by the ruler of Jerusalem, whether king or procurator. (iii.) From the context in Acts xx. the prison of the Roman garrison is almost certain to have been in the barracks, that is in the tower Antonia.

### 5. *The Roman Barracks*

The Antonia.    According to Josephus the barracks of the Roman garrison were in the tower Antonia, the site of which is still visible. It was the old ' Baris,' the Hasmonean fortress rebuilt by Herod the Great,[1] and called Antonia by him in honour of Mark Antony. It was on the north-west of the Temple connected by steps with the Temple area, and Luke alludes to these steps in Acts xxi. 40. It was the traditional place in which the high-priestly robes were kept before the Roman occupation.[2]

---

the βουλή was inside or outside the Temple, but *B.J.* vi. 6. 3 seems to show that it was outside. Here Josephus says that the Romans τότε ἀρχεῖον . . . καὶ τὸ βουλευτήριον καὶ τὸν Ὀφλᾶν καλούμενον ὑφῆψαν, and since at the time which he is describing the Temple had not fallen it is clear that the ' council-room ' was outside the Temple wall. The βουλευτήριον of the second passage must be the same as the βουλή of the first.

[1] *Antiq.* xiii. 11. 2.

[2] For a summary of the history of the custody of the robes see Josephus, *Antiq.* xv. 11. 4.

The whole description of the tower is given by Josephus in *B.J.* v. 5. 8:
ἡ δ' Ἀντωνία κατὰ γωνίαν μὲν δύο στοῶν ἔκειτο τοῦ πρώτου ἱεροῦ,
τῆς τε πρὸς ἑσπέραν καὶ τῆς πρὸς ἄρκτον, δεδόμητο δ' ὑπὲρ πέτρας
πεντηκονταπήχους μὲν ὕψος, περικρήμνου δὲ πάσης· ἔργον δ' ἦν
Ἡρώδου τοῦ βασιλέως, ἐν ᾧ μάλιστα τὸ φύσει μεγαλόνουν ἐπεδείξατο.
πρῶτον μὲν γὰρ ἐκ ῥίζης ἡ πέτρα πλαξὶ κεκάλυπτο λείαις λίθων, εἴς
τε κάλλος καὶ ὡς ἀπολισθάνοι πᾶς ὁ προσβαίνειν ἢ κατιέναι πειρώμενος.
ἔπειτα πρὸ τῆς τοῦ πύργου δομήσεως τριῶν πηχῶν τεῖχος ἦν,
ἐνδοτέρω δὲ τούτου τὸ πᾶν ἀνάστημα τῆς Ἀντωνίας ἐπὶ τεσσαράκοντα
πήχεις ἠγείρετο. τὸ δ' ἔνδον βασιλείων εἶχε χώραν καὶ διάθεσιν·
μεμέριστο γὰρ εἰς πᾶσαν οἴκων ἰδέαν τε καὶ χρῆσιν περίστοά τε καὶ
βαλανεῖα καὶ στρατοπέδων αὐλαῖς πλατείαις, ὡς τῷ μὲν πάντ' ἔχειν
τὰ χρειώδη πόλις εἶναι δοκεῖν, τῇ πολυτελείᾳ δὲ βασίλειον. πυργοειδὴς
δὲ οὖσα τὸ πᾶν σχῆμα κατὰ γωνίαν τέσσαρσιν ἑτέροις διείληπτο
πύργοις, ὧν οἱ μὲν ἄλλοι πεντήκοντα τὸ ὕψος, ὁ δ' ἐπὶ τῇ μεσημβρινῇ
καὶ κατὰ ἀνατολὴν γωνίᾳ κείμενος ἑβδομήκοντα πηχῶν ἦν, ὡς καθορᾶν
ὅλον ἀπ' αὐτοῦ τὸ ἱερόν. καθὰ δὲ συνῆπτε ταῖς τοῦ ἱεροῦ στοαῖς εἰς
ἀμφοτέρας [1] εἶχε καταβάσεις, δι' ὧν κατῄεσαν οἱ φρουροί· καθῆστο
γὰρ ἀεὶ ἐπ' αὐτῆς τάγμα Ῥωμαίων, καὶ διιστάμενοι περὶ τὰς στοὰς
μετὰ τῶν ὅπλων ἐν ταῖς ἑορταῖς τὸν δῆμον, ὡς μή τι νεωτερισθείη,
παρεφύλαττον· φρούριον γὰρ ἐπέκειτο τῇ πόλει μὲν τὸ ἱερόν, τῷ ἱερῷ
δ' ἡ Ἀντωνία, κατὰ δὲ ταύτην οἱ τῶν τριῶν φύλακες ἦσαν· καὶ τῆς
ἄνω δὲ πόλεως ἴδιον φρούριον ἦν τὰ Ἡρώδου βασίλεια.

## 6. *The Beautiful Gate*

It has become an established part of Christian tradition that the
Beautiful Gate was on the eastern side of the Temple. With this
most recent commentators agree, but they differ as to which of the
eastern gates is intended, and of these two sets come into consideration.

(a) *The Exterior Gates.*—These led through the great wall surrounding The exterior
the whole Temple area. Of these walls we have two accounts. Accord- gates.
ing to Middoth i. 3 there were two gates on the south (the Huldah gates),
one on the west (Qiponos), one unused gate on the north (Tadi), and
the gate of Shushan on the east. According to Josephus, *Antiq.* xv. 11. 5,
there were four gates on the west, and more than one [2] on the south.
He does not mention any gate on the north or on the east. But Josephus
mentions that Herod joined up the tower of Antonia (the 'barracks' of
Acts xxi. 37) to the Temple area by a bridge, or bridges, and perhaps this
accounts for the absence of other gates on the north.

The Shushan gate is a more curious problem. Josephus does not The Shu-
mention it at all, but it is impossible to suppose that there was no gate on shan gate.
the side of the Temple opposite the Mount of Olives, or that the allusions

---

[1] This ἀμφοτέρας is hard to visualize. Does it mean that there was one flight
of steps at the juncture of the two colonnades ?

[2] If the text be right, he merely says πύλας.

to it in the Mishna are fiction.  The name Shushan is also a mystery ;
written in full it is שושן הבירה ‘ Shushan the Palace,’ and the favourite
explanation is that Cyrus insisted on some representation of Susa being
placed at the eastern gate.  This seems an explanation invented after the
real meaning was forgotten.  The most attractive suggestion seems to be
that of Prof. Julius Morgenstern who thinks that שוש may be a substitute for שש, and collects much interesting evidence to show that the
eastern gate of the Temple was once associated with the worship of the
Sun.  Especially noticeable is the custom at the Simḥat Bet Hašo’ebah ;
at the feast of Sukkot two priests went down to the eastern gate, turned
to the west and said, “ Our fathers who were in this place had their backs
to the Temple and their faces to the East, and prostrated themselves
towards the East, toward the Sun, but as for us, our eyes are toward
the Lord.” [1]

Aurea =
ὡραία.

Tradition, for what it is worth, has always identified the Shushan Gate
with the Beautiful Gate mentioned in Acts.  The tradition is, however,
worth very little.  The first suggestion that this eastern gate is the
Beautiful Gate seems to be Prudentius [2] in the fifth century, and in
crusading times this identification is probably intended by the term
Porta aurea which is clearly a misunderstanding of the Greek ὡραία,
actually transliterated horrea in the African Latin of Acts.  Thus there is
no really early evidence that the earliest Christians in Jerusalem held that
the Shushan Gate was the ‘ Beautiful ’ Gate.  But neither is there evidence
to the contrary, and so far as it goes the Shushan Gate may claim to be the
‘ Beautiful ’ Gate according to Christian tradition.  The absence of interest
in the book of Acts, so characteristic of the early Church, partly accounts
for the paucity of evidence.

Even more serious than the defect of Christian evidence is the lack of
Jewish testimony.  ‘ Beautiful ’ is not the name of any gate of the Temple
in any Jewish source.[3]  Thus the tradition cannot be recommended for
its antiquity.  It is, moreover, only partially supported by some degree
of intrinsic probability.  Not only the eastern gate, but the eastern front
of the Temple in general was especially decorated ; but, on the other
hand, the eastern side of the Temple must have been almost precipitous,
and it is hard to imagine that anyone ever used the Shushan Gate
unless he was coming from the Mount of Olives, or the villages in its
neighbourhood.  It is therefore unlikely to have been a customary place
for a beggar.

The interior
gates.

(b) The Interior Gates.—The evidence of Josephus as to the interior
gates of the Temple is found in Bellum Judaicum, v. 5. 2 f.  After describing

---

[1] ‘The Gates of Righteousness,’ Hebrew Union College Annual, vi. (1929)
p. 30.

[2] Diptychon, xliv.

[3] Prof. Morgenstern in the article quoted above tries to prove that the name
‘ Golden ’ is older than the crusading period ; if so this would be important,
but his arguments on this point seem less convincing than those connecting the
Shushan Gate with Sun-worship.

the second (or inner) temple, and its elevation by fourteen steps above
the level of the general area, he says [1] :

μετὰ δὲ τοὺς δεκατέσσαρας βαθμοὺς τὸ μέχρι τοῦ τείχους διάστημα Josephus.
πηχῶν ἦν δέκα, πᾶν ἰσόπεδον. ἔνθεν ἄλλοι πάλιν πεντέβαθμοι
κλίμακες ἀνῆγον ἐπὶ τὰς πύλας, αἳ ἀπὸ μὲν ἄρκτου καὶ μεσημβρίας
ὀκτώ, καθ᾽ ἑκάτερον τέσσαρες, δύο δ᾽ ἦσαν ἐξ ἀνατολῆς κατ᾽ ἀνάγκην·
διατετειχισμένου γὰρ κατὰ τοῦτο τὸ κλίμα ταῖς γυναιξὶν ἰδίου πρὸς
θρησκείαν χώρου ἔδει δευτέραν εἶναι πύλην· τέτμητο δ᾽ αὕτη τῆς πρώτης ἄντικρυς. κἀκ τῶν ἄλλων δὲ κλιμάτων μία μεσημβρινὴ πύλη
καὶ μία βόρειος, δι᾽ ἧς εἰς τὴν γυναικωνῖτιν εἰσῆγον· κατὰ γὰρ τὰς
ἄλλας οὐκ ἐξῆν παρελθεῖν γυναιξίν, ἀλλ᾽ οὐδὲ κατὰ τὴν σφετέραν
ὑπερβῆναι τὸ διατείχισμα. ἀνεῖτό γε μὴν ταῖς τ᾽ ἐπιχωρίοις καὶ ταῖς
ἔξωθεν ὁμοφύλοις ἐν ἴσῳ πρὸς θρησκείαν ὁ χῶρος. τὸ δὲ πρὸς δύσιν
μέρος οὐκ εἶχε πύλην, ἀλλὰ διηνεκὲς ἐδεδόμητο ταύτῃ τὸ τεῖχος. αἱ
στοαὶ δὲ μεταξὺ τῶν πυλῶν ἀπὸ τοῦ τείχους ἔνδον ἐστραμμέναι πρὸ τῶν
γαζοφυλακίων σφόδρα μὲν καλοῖς καὶ μεγάλοις ἀνείχοντο κίοσιν, ἦσαν
δ᾽ ἁπλαῖ, καὶ πλὴν τοῦ μεγέθους τῶν κάτω κατ᾽ οὐδὲν ἀπελείποντο.
3. Τῶν δὲ πυλῶν αἱ μὲν ἐννέα χρυσῷ καὶ ἀργύρῳ κεκαλυμμέναι
πανταχόθεν ἦσαν, ὁμοίως τε αἵ τε παραστάδες καὶ τὰ ὑπέρθυρα, μία δ᾽
ἡ ἔξωθεν τοῦ νεὼ Κορινθίου χαλκοῦ, πολὺ τῇ τιμῇ τὰς καταργύρους
καὶ περιχρύσους ὑπεράγουσα. καὶ δύο μὲν ἑκάστου πυλῶνος θύραι,
τριάκοντα δὲ πηχῶν τὸ ὕψος ἑκάστης καὶ τὸ πλάτος ἦν πεντεκαίδεκα.
μετὰ μέντοι τὰς εἰσόδους ἐνδοτέρω πλατυνόμενοι παρ᾽ ἑκάτερον τρια-
κονταπήχεις ἐξέδρας εἶχον εὖρός τε καὶ μῆκος πυργοειδεῖς, ὑψηλὰς δ᾽
ὑπὲρ τεσσαράκοντα πήχεις· δύο δ᾽ ἀνεῖχον ἑκάστην κίονες, δώδεκα πηχῶν
τὴν περιοχὴν ἔχοντες. καὶ τῶν μὲν ἄλλων ἴσον ἦν τὸ μέγεθος, ἡ δ᾽

---

[1] "Beyond the fourteen steps up to the wall there was a space of ten cubits
which was level. From this other stairs, of five steps each, led to the gates of
which there were eight on the north and south sides, on each side four, and of
necessity two on the east. For since a place had been walled off on that side
specially for the women to worship, there had to be a second gate, and it was
cut in line with the first. And on the other sides there was one gate on the
south and one on the north through which they went into the court of the
women ; for at the other gates, women were not allowed to pass ; nor at their
own gate could they go beyond the partition. This place was allotted on equal
terms to the women of the country, and of other countries of the same race.
The western side had no gate, but the wall was built without a break on that
side. Now the cloisters which were between the gates extended from the wall
inward, before the treasure rooms, and were supported by very fine and great
pillars. They were single, and except in size were no way inferior to those below.
"3. Of the gates nine were covered all over with gold and silver, as were the
door-posts and the lintels ; but there was one gate, that outside the shrine,
of Corinthian brass, greatly excelling in value those that were plated with silver
and gold. Each porch had two doors, and the height of each door was thirty
cubits, and the breadth fifteen. Moreover, after the entrance on the inside
they broadened and had on each side halls of thirty cubits built both in breadth
and in length like towers, and above forty cubits high. Two pillars twelve
cubits round also supported each. Now the size of the others was equal ; but

ὑπὲρ τὴν Κορινθίαν ἀπὸ τῆς γυναικωνίτιδος ἐξ ἀνατολῆς ἀνοιγομένη
τῆς τοῦ ναοῦ πύλης ἀντικρὺ πολὺ μείζων· πεντήκοντα γὰρ πηχῶν
οὖσα τὴν ἀνάστασιν τεσσαρακονταπήχεις τὰς θύρας εἶχε καὶ τὸν
κόσμον πολυτελέστερον ἐπὶ δαψιλὲς πάχος ἀργύρου τε καὶ χρυσοῦ.
τοῦτον δὲ ταῖς ἐννέα πύλαις ἐπέχεεν ὁ Τιβερίου πατὴρ Ἀλέξανδρος.
βαθμοὶ δὲ δεκαπέντε πρὸς τὴν μείζονα πύλην ἀπὸ τοῦ τῶν γυναικῶν
διατειχίσματος ἀνῆγον· τῶν γὰρ κατὰ τὰς ἄλλας πέντε βαθμῶν ἦσαν
βραχύτεροι.
4. Αὐτὸς δ ὁ ναὸς κατὰ μέσον κείμενος, τὸ ἅγιον ἱερόν, δώδεκα
βαθμοῖς ἦν ἀναβατός, καὶ τὸ μὲν κατὰ πρόσωπον ὕψος τε καὶ εὖρος
ἴσον ἀνὰ πήχεις ἑκατόν, κατόπιν δὲ τεσσαράκοντα πήχεσι στενότερος·
ἔμπροσθεν γὰρ ὥσπερ ὦμοι παρ ἑκάτερον εἰκοσαπήχεις διέβαινον. ἡ
πρώτη δ αὐτοῦ πύλη, πηχῶν ἑβδομήκοντα τὸ ὕψος οὖσα καὶ εὖρος
εἴκοσι καὶ πέντε, θύρας οὐκ εἶχε· τοῦ γὰρ οὐρανοῦ τὸ ἀφανὲς καὶ
ἀδιάκλειστον ἐνέφαινε· κεχρύσωτο δὲ τὰ μέτωπα πάντα, καὶ δι αὐτῆς
ὅ τε πρῶτος οἶκος ἔξωθεν πᾶς κατεφαίνετο μέγιστος ὤν, καὶ τὰ περὶ
τὴν εἴσω πύλην πάντα λαμπόμενα χρυσῷ τοῖς ὁρῶσιν ὑπέπιπτεν. τοῦ
ναοῦ δὲ ὄντος εἴσω διστέγου μόνος ὁ πρῶτος οἶκος προύκειτο καὶ διηνεκὲς
εἰς τὸ ὕψος ἀνατεινόμενος μὲν ἐπ ἐνενήκοντα πήχεις, μηκυνόμενος δὲ
ἐπὶ πεντήκοντα καὶ διαβαίνων ἐπ εἴκοσιν. ἡ δὲ διὰ τοῦ οἴκου πύλη
κεχρύσωτο μέν, ὡς ἔφην, πᾶσα καὶ ὅλος ὁ περὶ αὐτὴν τοῖχος, εἶχε δὲ
καὶ τὰς χρυσᾶς ὑπὲρ ἑαυτῆς ἀμπέλους, ἀφ ὧν βότρυες ἀνδρομήκεις
κατεκρέμαντο. ὄντος δὲ ἤδη τοῦ ναοῦ διστέγου, ταπεινοτέρα τῆς
ἔξωθεν ὄψεως ἡ ἔνδον ἦν καὶ θύρας εἶχε χρυσᾶς πεντηκονταπέντε
πήχεων τὸ ὕψος, εὖρος δ ἑκκαίδεκα.

that which was over the Corinthian gate and opened from the court of the
women on the east in line with the gate of the shrine was much larger ; for its
height was fifty cubits, and it had doors of forty cubits, and its ornamentation
was more costly as having much richer and thicker plates of silver and gold.
This ornamentation Alexander, the father of Tiberius, had put on the nine doors.
And there were fifteen steps, which led up from the wall of the court of the
women to the greater gate ; for they were shorter than the five steps at the others.
"4. Now the shrine itself, which was placed in the midst, the 'Holy' temple,
was approached by twelve steps ; and in front its height and its breadth were
equal, a hundred cubits each, but behind it was forty cubits narrower ; for in
front it had as if shoulders that projected twenty cubits further on each side.
Its first gate was seventy cubits high, and twenty-five broad, but it had no
doors ; for it represented the universal visibility of heaven, and it cannot be
excluded from any place. Its whole front was covered with gold, and through
it all the first room was visible from without in its greatness, and all the parts
about the inner gate, shining with gold, were presented to those who looked.
But as the shrine was of two stories within it was only the first house that was
continually open to our view in its height, for it extended to ninety cubits, and
it was fifty cubits long, and twenty across. But the gate through the house was,
as I said, covered all over with gold, as was all the wall about it ; it had also
golden vines above it, from which clusters of grapes hung, as big as a man. But
as the shrine was two-storied, the interior gate was lower than it appeared from
the outside, and it had golden doors fifty-five cubits high and sixteen broad."

This can hardly be described as lucid, but the general meaning is sufficiently plain.  On the west side of the Temple proper—not the Temple area—there was no door ; on the north and south sides there were four doors, and in each case the most easterly of the four opened into the ' court of women '—the extreme eastern end of the temple, divided by a wall from the court of men.  On the eastern side there was one gate opening into the court of the women, and there was there a line of entrances through the centre of the temple—(i.) through the wall dividing the court of the women from the court of the men (the second eastern gate) ; (ii.) through the wall dividing the court of the men from the Holy Place ; this how-ever had no door, but was permanently open ; (iii.) the door into the Holy of Holies, covered by a Babylonian curtain.  The outermost [1] of these was made of Corinthian bronze, and the one next to it was of unusual size.  Adding to these the first gate, entering from the temple area into the court of the women we get four entrances in a straight line east to west.

These gates are all mentioned with more or less clearness in the Mishna (tractate *Middoth*), and the Corinthian gate is obviously the same as that which the Mishna calls the Nicanor gate.  Nothing is known of this Nicanor, and the tradition that he brought this gate from Alexandria, that it was shipwrecked, swallowed by a whale and vomited on to the breakwater of Acco, cannot be wholly historical.  But that the name ' Nicanor ' refers to a man and is not a corruption of an adjective is proved by the recent discovery of the family tomb of Nicanor in Jerusalem.[2]

Commentators, as distinct from tradition, have fastened on the mag- nificence of the Nicanor gate as described both in the Mishna and in Josephus, and have, at least in recent times, agreed that this must be the Beautiful Gate of the Temple.  The difficulty is that this identification makes unintelligible the story in Acts in the Neutral text, which practically all commentators nevertheless accept.  According to it the episode of the beggar at the Beautiful Gate falls into three parts : (i.) Peter and John came to the Beautiful Gate and there healed the lame man.  (ii.) They went into the Temple (τὸ ἱερόν, iii. 8).  (iii.) They became the centre of a crowd which ran together to them in Solomon's Porch.  From this it is clear that (i.) Solomon's Porch was inside the ἱερόν, and therefore ἱερόν is used in the general sense of the Temple area, not of the Temple buildings in the narrower sense.  (ii.) The Beautiful door must have been on the outside of Solomon's Porch.  This story is intelligible only if the

---

[1] It is not quite clear whether Josephus means the gate between the court of the Gentiles and the court of the women, or between the court of the women and the court of the men.  Personally I think the former is his meaning, but the point is open to discussion.  In any case there seems no justification for E. Schürer's and O. Holtzmann's attempts to emend ἡ ἔξωθεν τοῦ νεώ into ἡ ἔξωθεν τῶν ἐώων, ἡ ἔξωθεν τῶν ἐν ἔῳ, or ἡ ἔωθεν τοῦ νεώ (see E. Schürer in Riehm's *Wörterbuch*, ed. 1884, ii. p. 1640, and *ZNTW*. vii. pp. 51 ff., and O. Holtzmann in *ZNTW*. ix. pp. 71 ff.).

[2] R. A. S. Macalister, *P.E.F.*, *Quart. Statement* xxxvii. (1905) pp. 353 f.

Beautiful Gate was one of the entrances to the Temple area, such as the Shushan Gate, not to the Temple proper.  Modern critics who favour the door of Nicanor suppose that Luke forgot to mention that after the apostles entered the Temple they came out again, and only then became the centre of the crowd in Solomon's Porch.  This is obviously a counsel of despair.

The Western text.

Few commentators, however, seem to have noticed that the Western text, on the other hand, exactly fits their views.  It runs : " He entered with them into the Temple and all the people saw him . . . and when Peter and John went out he went with them, holding on to them, and (the people) stood in amazement in the Porch called Solomon's."  This makes it clear that τὸ ἱερόν means the Temple buildings, not the Temple area, and that the Beautiful door was farther in than the Porch of Solomon. It would support admirably the identification of the Beautiful door with the door of Nicanor.

Thus, assuming always that the Beautiful Gate is one of the eastern gates—either the Nicanor gate as the Western text and modern commentators agree, or the Shushan gate as the Neutral text and Christian tradition agree—which is the more probable ?

The intrinsic superiority of the Western text.

On the whole it is far easier to see how the Shushan gate tradition arose as an emendation of the Nicanor tradition, rather than the other way. The Shushan gate is in itself intrinsically much less probable.  It is hard to imagine that anyone ever used the Shushan gate unless he was coming from the Mount of Olives or the villages in its neighbourhood.  It is therefore unlikely to have been used by a beggar who would naturally choose the most frequented place.  Moreover, unless we suppose that the Apostles were living at Bethany and not in the city of Jerusalem, the Eastern gate is extraordinarily unlikely to have been chosen by them as an entrance. On the eastern side the exterior wall of the Temple was also the wall of the city ; to enter by it it would be necessary to go out by one of the other gates, go down a steep valley and then up it again.  Except for those living on the other side of the Kedron the natural way into the Temple area would be one of the gates on the south or on the west.

This last argument is open to qualification because one of the points which is most seriously doubtful in the early history of the Church is how long the disciples made Bethany their headquarters (see pp. 15 f.). But the argument about the beggar seems strong, and turns the scale in favour of the Nicanor gate.  This is corroborated by the fact that both in Josephus and the Mishna the beauty of the Nicanor gate seems to be emphasized.

Thus the Nicanor gate seems to be the more probable identification for the Beautiful Gate ; but this necessitates our accepting the Western as the original text.  The Neutral text cannot be brought into agreement with it except by the most illegitimate contortion.

The origin of the 'Shushan theory.'

Nor is a convincing explanation hard to find for the origin of the Shushan identification.  At the time when the Christian Church began to ' identify ' sacred sites the Temple had been destroyed.  No one living remembered it.  There were no Jews in Jerusalem who could have given the tradition preserved in the Mishna. Probably no Christian in Jerusalem had ever heard of the Nicanor gate. But the Shushan gate was still there. It played a prominent part in the dramatic services of Palm Sunday and of the celebration of the Exaltation of the Cross on September 14. It was the most natural place possible to point out as the Beautiful Gate to those pious visitors who wished to see with their own eyes the places which they read about in the Scriptures.

It is thus quite easy to see how the 'Shushan' tradition arose to supplant the 'Nicanor' tradition. The reverse is quite impossible ; and the extremely important corollary is that the Western text which fits the Nicanor tradition and not the Shushan tradition must be original, and the Neutral which fits the Shushan and not the Nicanor tradition must be an emendation made after the beginning of the 'tradition of sacred sites,' which probably means in the third century.

One point remains. The question may well be asked why should it be assumed that the Beautiful Gate was on the eastern side at all ? May it not have been, for instance, on the south ? To this the answer is that there is no very strong evidence, but that two probabilities point to the eastern gates. *The eastern position of the Beautiful Gate.*

(i.) Both Josephus and Mishna agree that the eastern front of the Temple was the most gorgeous.

(ii.) The Porch of Solomon is more likely to have been on the east than anywhere else, though the usual statement that it certainly was there is unwarranted. The fact is that Josephus in *B.J.* v. 5. 1 says : *The Porch of Solomon.*

Τὸ δ' ἱερὸν ἵδρυτο μέν, ὥσπερ ἔφην, ἐπὶ λόφου καρτεροῦ, κατ' ἀρχὰς δὲ μόλις ἐξήρκει τὸ ἀνωτάτω χθαμαλὸν αὐτοῦ τῷ τε ναῷ καὶ τῷ βωμῷ· τὰ γὰρ πέριξ ἀπόκρημνος ἦν καὶ κατάντης. τοῦ δὲ βασιλέως Σολομῶνος, ὃς δὴ καὶ τὸν ναὸν ἔκτισεν, τὸ κατ' ἀνατολὰς μέρος ἐκτει- χίσαντος, ἐπετέθη μία στοὰ τῷ χώματι· καὶ κατά γε τὰ λοιπὰ μέρη γυμνὸς ὁ ναὸς ἦν.[1]

Plainly this does not say anything at all about the names given to parts of the second, still less of the Herodian temple ; but if Solomon built a colonnade on the east side of the Temple, and this was older than the other colonnades, it is possible that the name of Solomon was always attached to the eastern colonnade, or 'Porch.'

Now it is clear in Acts iii. that the scene of the whole episode was close to the Porch of Solomon, and that the Beautiful Gate led into or out of this Porch. If therefore this Porch was on the eastern side of the Temple, the Beautiful Gate was also on that side.

It is obvious that these arguments do not amount to demonstration, but they may at least be taken to show that the east is the most probable

---

[1] "Now the temple, as I have said, was built upon a steep hill. At first the level at the top was hardly enough for the shrine and the altar, for the ground about it was precipitous, and fell suddenly ; but when King Solomon, who also built the shrine, walled it in on its east side, there was added one cloister founded on the mound. On the other side the shrine stood uncovered."

side of the Temple both for ' Solomon's Porch ' and for the ' Beautiful Gate.'

Conclusion.    From this discussion it will be seen that of the places in Jerusalem mentioned in Acts none can be identified with certainty with any existing buildings, though the position of the tower of Antonia, and possibly some of its remains, can be fixed definitely. Not much aid can be expected from archaeological research in the immediate future. Jerusalem cannot be excavated partly because it is an inhabited city, but chiefly because ecclesiastical jealousy, national rivalry, and political expediency combine to support the claims of the Mohammedan Church to the exclusive control of Jewish and Christian sites such as the Temple, the Tomb of David, and the Upper Chamber where the Eucharist was instituted, and prevent any archaeological research.

Nor does tradition give much help. The local guides are indeed able to point out every spot mentioned in the Old or New Testaments, but investigation shows that very few indeed of their identifications were known before the third century. This is not really surprising. In A.D. 70, and again fifty years later, Jerusalem was very thoroughly destroyed. In 137 its ruins were partly rebuilt as the Greco-Roman city of Aelia Capitolina from which Jews were excluded. The Christian Church which grew up in this city was essentially Greek, and there is no trace in its history of Jewish influence or of any knowledge of the Jewish tradition. There was not only a complete destruction of buildings, but an absolute dislocation of tradition in Jerusalem.

In the third century Origen began a renewed interest in ' Sacred Sites.' Probably he asked questions of Palestinian Christians : Where was this house ? Where did such and such happen ? And the Palestinian Christians, like their successors, felt that it would be degrading to themselves and discourteous to a visitor not to supply definite if recent information.

The work of Origen which embodied the results of his inquiries is not extant ; but it was known to Eusebius and Jerome. Thus the earliest written accounts which we possess are that of Eusebius and the remarkable narrative of the Pilgrim of Bordeaux, which may be as early as 333. Both Eusebius and the Pilgrim were eager to learn everything possible, and when they fail to mention a ' traditional ' site, there is always a suspicion that the tradition is not as old as their time.

After the fourth century identifications grew apace, and by the eighth century most of the present tradition was established. Its growth and value are admirably criticized and discussed in the magistral work of Fathers Vincent and Abel of the Dominican House of St. Stephen in Jerusalem (the *École biblique*). The present note cannot deal with anything except quite the earliest period.

NOTE XXXVI. THE FAMILY TREE OF THE HERODS

By HENRY J. CADBURY

For our knowledge of the Herod family we are primarily dependent Josephus. upon the two overlapping historical works of Josephus, *The Jewish War*, written about A.D. 75–79, and the *Antiquities of the Jews*, completed in A.D. 93–94. The scope of these works was such that any historian dealing with the same subjects at length would necessarily refer often and fully to Herod the Great and his descendants. In the case of Josephus both his sources and his own interests further guaranteed attention to the Herods. For the reign of Herod the Great he used probably in addition to other sources the extensive work of Nicolaus of Damascus. That historian and the king were in the position to each other of counsellor and patron respectively, and there can be little doubt that the richness of detail in *Antiquities* xv.-xvii., if not the viewpoint of Josephus, is due to the work of Nicolaus.

One motive of Josephus in narrating so much about the descendants of Herod the Great he expresses in these words with which he introduces the pedigree :

" I desire therefore to speak at some length about Herod and his family as it was, partly because the account about them is relevant to the history, partly because it provides a proof of divine providence. It shows that without reverence for deity neither numbers nor any other form of superiority in the things aimed at by men are of any advantage, since it came to pass that within the course of a hundred years the descendants of Herod (and they were many) were, except for a few, destroyed." [1]

With Agrippa II. (died A.D. 100) Josephus claims to have had personal correspondence, in which the Jewish king testified in sixty-two letters to the truth of what Josephus had written in *The Jewish War* and offered to give him oral information about much that was not generally known (ὅταν μέντοι συντύχῃς μοι, καὶ αὐτός σε πολλὰ κατηχήσω τῶν ἀγνοουμένων).[2] There is no evidence, however, of more direct contact of the historian with the Herodian family.

The Roman historians, like Suetonius, Tacitus, and Dio Cassius, make Roman occasional references to the participation of the Herods in the affairs of historians wider history. Their information is, however, very slight and incomplete.[3] Similar in character are the references to the Herods in Luke-Acts. With that author, however, they are incidental not to Roman but to Christian history. They are perhaps more numerous in this work than in any extant writer except Josephus. It has been thought that they betray a special interest in the Herods on the part of ' Luke ' or of his sources of information. That they are more numerous in his gospel than in the others may be due in part to the fact that he is simply more inclined throughout to bring his account into touch with its secular background. I have summarized this material elsewhere as follows :

---

[1] *Antiq.* xviii. 5. 3, §§ 127 f.          [2] *Vita* 65, §§ 364, 366.
[3] Coins and inscriptions give some further data.

Luke's
position.
" He is aware of the friction between Jews and Romans and of the difficult and delicate middle position of the Herods.  He notes the hostility between Herod Antipas and Pontius Pilate and the courtesy of a visit of welcome paid by another Herod (Agrippa II.) to an incoming procurator, Porcius Festus.  He describes the political and economic relations of a third Herod (Agrippa I.) with his Phoenician neighbours.   On one occasion Luke undertakes to enumerate the contemporary rulers of four tetrarchies which at one time or another belonged to the Herodian domain.  He calls the praetorium at Caesarea the praetorium of Herod.

" There are other allusions to the Herodian *ménage* of a quite casual nature—to a business manager of Herod named Chuzas, one of ' The Prince's Playmates ' of Herod named Manaen, and a chamberlain of Herod named Blastus.  Women of the family are mentioned—Herodias, Drusilla, and Bernice.  They were all infamous in their marital relations, but Luke does not dwell on the scandals (he omits the story of the royal *danseuse* at Herod's birthday dinner and her gruesome prize), though he hints that they and their paramours were ' reproved ' ' with words of truth and temperance' dealing with ' justice and self-control and judgement to come.'   It is Luke alone who mentions that Herod Antipas both threatened Jesus and desired to see him and took a part in his trial. It is quite casually that he mentions the presence first of this prince and then of another Herod in Jerusalem at ' the days of unleavened bread.'  Luke's story of a certain man of noble family who went to get a kingdom and to return, only to be followed by an embassy of his own citizens trying to prevent his coronation, sounds like a chapter out of Herodian history." [1]

The genea-
logical tree
of ten
Herods.
The accompanying chart is taken with the permission of the publishers from H. St. John Thackeray's *Josephus*, vol. ii., in the Loeb Classical Library.  It gives as accurately and completely as our sources permit the persons named by Josephus.  If we had more independent sources we should have more difficulties.  The repetition of the same names in different generations and branches of the family, and the frequency of marriage within the family, of polygamy and of divorce, complicate the problem. Furthermore, the same individual is sometimes differently named in the sources.  Thus of the persons named in the New Testament (indicated in the chart by capitals) the first husband of Herodias is called Herod in Josephus, but Philip in the New Testament.[2]  Conversely the ' Herod ' of Acts xii. is regularly called Agrippa both in Josephus and everywhere else. As a matter of fact he, like his children and perhaps like earlier members of the family, had a regular Roman name, being possessed of citizenship

---

[1] *The Making of Luke-Acts*, pp. 240 f.

[2] The discrepancy is quite likely more than a mere difference in name. Variants in the text make it uncertain whether at Matt. xiv. 3 and Luke iii. 19 Philip should be named at all, while variants in the text at Mark vi. 22 suggest that the younger woman was Herodias, daughter of Antipas (instead of Salome, daughter of Herodias).  But these problems need not be discussed here.

# THE HERODIAN FAMILY

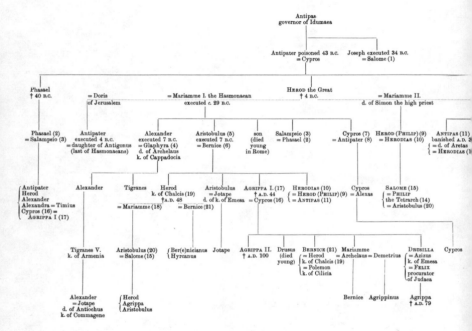

The names of persons mentioned more than once on this page are followed by figures in brackets for cross-reference.

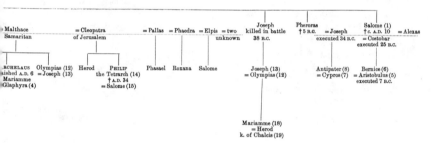

Malthace = Cleopatra = Pallas = Phaedra = Elpis = two Joseph Pheroras Salome (1)
Samaritan of Jerusalem unknown killed in battle † 5 B.C. = Joseph † c. A.D. 10 = Alexas
38 B.C. executed 34 B.C. = Costobar
executed 25 B.C.

RCHELAUS Olympias (12) Herod PHILIP Phasael Roxana Salome Joseph (13) Antipater (8) Bernice (6)
aished A.D. 6 = Joseph (13) the Tetrarch (14) = Olympias (12) = Cypros (7) = Aristobulus (5)
Mariamme † A.D. 34 executed 7 B.C.
Glaphyra (4) = Salome (15)

Mariamme (18)
= Herod
k. of Chalcis (19)

in the *gens Iulia*.[1] His son, Agrippa II. ('King Agrippa' of Acts xxvi.),
is named on coins and inscriptions Marcus Julius Agrippa.

Among modern studies on the Herodian family may be recommended
the work of W. Otto, published as articles in Pauly-Wissowa-Kroll, *R.E.*
Supplementband, ii., 1913, coll. 1 ff., and also in a separate volume with
introduction and index (*Herodes : Beiträge zur Geschichte des letzten
jüdischen Königshauses*, Stuttgart, 1913); the article by W. J. Wood-
house in *Ency. Biblica*, ii., 1901, coll. 2023 ff. (on whose chart that of
Thackeray appears to have been based), and E. Schürer's account in
the latest edition of his *Geschichte des jüdischen Volkes im Zeitalter Jesu
Christi.* A brief modern essay is Hugo Willrich's *Das Haus des Herodes :
zwischen Jerusalem und Rom*, 1929.

## Note XXXVII. Lucius of Cyrene

### By Henry J. Cadbury

There are two kinds of omission in the records of Paul's career that Omissions
tempt the reader to combination and conjecture. i. The lists of Hellenistic in Acts.
Christian leaders in Acts, other than the greatest of them who is the author's
hero, have a verisimilitude in their definiteness in name combined with an
absence of further record that is most tantalizing. Among the committee
of seven appointed for charitable relief in Jerusalem (Acts vi. 5) we hear
something more of the first two, Stephen and Philip, but nothing of
" Prochorus and Nicanor and Timon and Parmenas and Nicolas a proselyte
of Antioch." At Antioch we meet two other groups, one entirely anonymous consisting of men of Cyprus and Cyrene who spoke the word not to
the Jews merely but to the Hellenists (xi. 20), the other containing five
names : Barnabas, and Simeon called Niger, and Lucius of Cyrene, and
Manaen the 'foster brother' of Herod the Tetrarch, and Saul (xiii. 1).
Of these the first and last, here named each in one word, are of course
otherwise known, but of the other three, though each receives here an
additional characterization of different kinds, none is further mentioned.

ii. On the other hand the letters of Paul mention many of his own as- The Pauline
sociates. Some of these, like Barnabas and Timothy, are no less prominent Epistles.
in Acts and are certainly the same persons. Others, though named slightly
differently in the two sources, can be plausibly identified.[2] For still others,
though there is exact identity of name, some doubt exists whether they
may not be different persons. The more usual the name they bear the less
certain the identity. Among these are Aristarchus, Sosthenes, Erastus and
Gaius. These phenomena are such as one would expect with genuine records
of the kind that Acts and the epistles of Paul purport to be. But there are

---

[1] As the gentilic name suggests, the citizenship doubtless goes back to the
gift by Julius Caesar to Antipater, father of Herod the Great (Josephus, *B.J.* i.
9. 5, § 194=*Antiq.* xiv. 8. 3, § 137 ; cf. xvi. 2. 4, § 53).

[2] See note on Priscilla, Vol. IV. p. 221.

two of Paul's associates whose absence from the pages of Acts is striking, Titus and Lucas or Luke—Titus because of his prominence in Paul's activities, and Luke because of his presumed authorship of Acts. Of course for some readers this authorship is in itself a complete explanation of the absence of Luke's name. Pseudonymous writings say, " Now I, James " or " I, Simon Peter," [1] but even in the ' we ' passages Luke does not introduce his own name.[2] Such omission is natural. It may, however, be modesty, and on the theory that " the brother whose praise in the gospel is through all the churches " (2 Cor. viii. 18) is Luke, as a literal brother of Titus (see vs. 16),[3] this modesty has been made to extend so as to include the silence of Acts on Titus. The author suppresses not only his own name but that of his brother also.

Possible identification.

But for these as for other persons we ask : Cannot some further identifications be suggested ? To bring together two isolated data not only provides an economy of items to deal with, but helps satisfy the curiosity which an incompleter theory arouses. Thus of the Antiochian prophets and teachers in Acts xiii. 1 Barnabas the Cypriote (iv. 36) and Lucius of Cyrene may well be conjectured as two of the unnamed men of Cyprus and Cyrene in Acts xi. 20.[4] Titus and Lucius, like Marcus and Gaius, are mere Roman *praenomina*.[5] For Roman citizens all such names must have been very common and they occur often among others than citizens, sometimes with the further useful appendage of a differentiating name as in the case of Titus (or Titius) Justus (Acts xviii. 7) or—in reverse order—John, surnamed Mark (xii. 12, 25).

[1] *Protev. Jacobi*, xxv. 1 ; *Ev. Petri*, xii. 60.
[2] See, however, the characteristic " I, Luke " of the Armenian commentary of Ephrem mentioned below, p. 492.
[3] This theory has been revived of late years in England. See the articles in the *Expository Times*, xviii., 1907, pp. 285 (A. Souter), 335 f. (A. Souter), 380 f. (E. P. Boys-Smith) and in the *Expositor*, March 1917, pp. 218 ff. (E. F. Brown), with objections by V. Bartlet (*ibid.*, May 1917, pp. 367 ff.). Souter would extend this usage of ὁ ἀδελφός = ' his brother ' to 2 Cor. xii. 18 (of Titus as Luke's brother) and to Romans xvi. 23 (of Quartus as brother of Erastus), but obviously at 1 Cor. i. 1 Sosthenes and at 2 Cor. i. 1 Timothy are not the blood brothers of Paul.
[4] Cf. p. 400 and Vol. IV. p. 128.
[5] That all N.T. Marci are the same person is a large assumption. In the N.T. we have a Gaius each of Derbe (Acts xx. 4, but see note), of Macedonia (xix. 29, but see note), of Corinth (1 Cor. i. 14 ; cf. Rom. xvi. 23) and elsewhere (3 John 1). For patricians *praenomina* were at one time reduced to eighteen in number, each with its abbreviation, of which Publius (Acts xxviii. 7) is another N.T. example. Sextus and Quintus belong to this list but are not in the New Testament, though Quartus (Rom. xvi. 23), Tertius (xvi. 22) and Secundus (Acts xx. 4) all appear there. By Greeks Romans were often spoken of by a single name. This was usually the *cognomen*, but not infrequently the mere *praenomen* was used instead. Grants of Roman citizenship in large numbers made certain gentilic *nomina* almost as common as *praenomina*, e.g. Cornelius (Acts x. 1, see note), Julius (xxvii. 1) Claudius (xxiii. 26, see note).

With names like these nothing prevents our supposing that our records use sometimes the common and sometimes the less common name, without our realizing the identity. It is only frequency of occurrence and circumstantial evidence that has prevented our confusion about Simeon = Simon = Simon Peter = Peter = Cephas, or in Acts alone John = John Mark = Mark. It is not, then, the mere curiosity of the hagiographer's imagination that bids us ask : What other name had Titus ? Had the men named Lucius no *cognomina* also, if Romans, or no other name if they were mere *peregrini* ? In Latin circles Gaius was no more distinctive than an initial letter would be in modern names. Could not Gaius of Macedonia mentioned in Acts be, for example, the same person as Epaphroditus of Philippians ? There is an inscription to a Thessalonian Γαίῳ Κλωδίῳ ᾿Επαφροδείτῳ.[1]

In some cases the alias for a formal name would be its hypocoristic or abbreviated form. This is doubtless the relation of Priscilla (Acts) and Prisca (Paul), of Silvanus (Paul) and Silas (Acts). It may be that Epaphras (Colossians) is merely a shortened form of Epaphroditus (Philippians), though both occur in Paul's letters. The name Luke (Λουκᾶς) is certainly of similar formation. Like other hypocoristics, e.g. Apollos for Apollonius, Apollodorus etc., Theudas for Theodoros or Theodotus, Hermas for Hermogenes etc., Demas for Demetrius etc., Lucas could stand for one of several longer names. The usual suggestion has been that Λουκᾶς was for Λουκανός [2] but the possibility that it was sometimes interchangeable with Λούκιος has been confirmed by inscriptions from the sanctuary of Men Ascaenus at Antioch of Pisidia. In one of these occurs Λουκᾶς Τίλλιος Κρίτων where the triple name and the position of Λουκᾶς suggests that we have a substitute for the Latin *praenomen* Lucius. In two other inscriptions giving members of an identical family what is evidently the same individual is called in one case Λουκᾶς, in the other Λούκιος. Two full accounts of these finds are available to English readers and need not be here repeated.[3] It is possible that our Luke was also called Lucius.[4] Abbreviated names.

Now Deissmann proceeds to suggest that we identify Λουκᾶς of the other epistles and the evangelist with Λούκιος of Romans xvi. 21. This identification was made by Origen long ago, but it may be supported to-day by new arguments based on critical theories. Romans xvi. was written shortly before the journey described in Acts xx. 4. The latter lists among Paul's travelling companions Sopater and Timothy and (if the ' we ' is so correctly understood) Luke. Romans xvi. 21 sends greetings from Timothy, Lucius . . . and Sosipater. Moreover, Romans xvi. is often believed to have been written to Ephesus, and the letters in which Luke sends Luke and Lucius.

---

[1] *C.I.G.* 1987, cf. Lightfoot, *Biblical Essays*, pp. 246 f.

[2] In Latin the evangelist's name was *Lucanus* (*J.Th.S.* vi. pp. 255, 435).

[3] W. M. Ramsay, *The Bearing of Recent Discoveries on the Trustworthiness of the N.T.*, 1915, pp. 370-384; A. Deissmann, *Light from the Ancient East*[4], Appendix iv. (Eng. trans. 1927, pp. 435-438). Ramsay published a brief notice earlier in the *Athenaeum* for July 13, 1912.

[4] Zahn, *Kommentar zum N.T.* iii. pp. 735-738, Excurs I ' Der Name Lucas,' argues against the identification either of the names or of the persons. Was ὁ ἰατρός (Col. iv. 14) added to distinguish from other Lucii ?

greeting (Colossians and Philemon) are now thought by many to have been written somewhat earlier than Romans xvi., when both Luke and Paul were at Ephesus. It is easy to suppose that Luke was with Paul at Ephesus during his imprisonment—perhaps at one time his only companion (2 Tim. iv. 11). On a later occasion with Timothy and So(si)pater he is in Paul's company and sends greetings back to Ephesus. He himself as author records a journey in which all four of the persons mentioned are themselves part of a large company travelling not long afterward towards Ephesus on their way to Jerusalem.

*Lucius of Cyrene.*

But the other Lucius of the New Testament—the Cyrenian Christian prophet and teacher at Antioch (Acts xiii. 1)—has *a priori* as much right to be considered identical with Luke as has his namesake in the Epistle to Romans. No evidence of patristic conjecture to this effect is commonly quoted. Perhaps the Fathers felt that the 'we' passages could be more consistently understood if the author's own name was regularly suppressed in the book. This would be important, of course, where the 'we' is not used, but even in the 'we' passages and their context it was probably assumed that the author would not use his own name. At one 'we' passage it is true that the two forms of Armenian evidence that we have for Ephrem's commentary imply that Ephrem's paraphrase and perhaps the Syriac text of Acts read "But I, Luke, and those with me." [1] It is possible that to one who read with the Western text of the prophecy of Agabus to the Christians at Antioch in xi. 27 ff— "When *we* were gathered together," etc., Acts xiii. 1 would seem to be a continuation of the 'we' passage. At any rate, an early witness to the Western reading of xi. 27 does offer a little evidence that at xiii. 1 Lucius of Cyrene was understood as Luke.

*Prophetiae ex omnibus libris.*

This witness is what Theodore Zahn describes as "ein Kompendium der biblischen Prophetie aus der afrikanischen Kirche um 305-325." [2] It is known to us from a Latin MS. of the Ninth Century (Codex 133) in the library of St. Gall. Its Latin title was apparently *Prophetiae ex omnibus libris collectae*. It was first published by A. Amelli in 1897,[3] but Zahn in the essay just referred to supplies a more accurate text of the MS. and a tentative date for the original writing.

The relevant section reads as follows (lines 49 ff.) : *Et in actibus Apostolorum sic legimus : Erant etiam in eclesia prophetae et doctores Barnabas et Saulus, quibus imposuerunt manus prophetae : Symeon qui appellatus est Niger, et Lucius Cirenensis, qui manet usque adhuc et Ticius conlactaneus, qui acceperant responsum ab spiritum sanctum.* The substantial differences of this from other texts are, first, the omission of the names of Manaen and Herod, and, second, the addition of the name Ticius and of the words that precede it. The former may well be an accidental omission. Zahn supposes that by a sort of haplography a scribe's eye skipped after *Ticius* the equivalent of a στίχος, reading : *Antiocensis Manaenque Herodis*

[1] Vol. III. pp. 442 f., especially the note on pp. 443 f.

[2] See the essay so entitled in *Geschichtliche Studien Albert Hauck zum 70. Geburtstage dargebracht*, 1916, pp. 52-63.

[3] *Miscellanea Cassinese*, Heft 6, pp. 17 ff.

*tetrarchae.* To insert this probable omission restores the list to its usual contents except for the addition to the name of Lucius, *qui manet usque adhuc* and the insertion of *Titius [Antiocensis].* The former phrase is without doubt modelled on 1 Cor. xv. 6, where the Vulgate reads *ex quibus multi manent usque adhuc.* It is reasonable to suppose that, appended to the name of Lucius of Cyrene, it is an indication of the author's own identity.[1] Zahn, it is true, does not so understand it.[2] He thinks the original author would not have introduced himself as a prophet and teacher in Antioch " in dieser plumpen Weise." Besides, he does not accept Ramsay's equation of Lucas = Lucius.[3] But he believes the reading indicates an originality of text possible only in the first century when a writer can say that, though Paul and Barnabas and others are dead, one of their former associates at Antioch is still alive. For Zahn this writer can scarcely be any other writer than the author of Acts himself. He claims the reading here of this Latin work as the purest form of the Western Text and so finds a strong argument for the Western Text as representing the superior form of the text of Acts. Zahn's inferences in his repeated discussions of the passage I do not agree with. His arguments must be read elsewhere.[4] He has, however, called attention to what is rather, in my opinion, an interesting early Christian conjecture on the authorship of Luke-Acts.

If we take the passage as an early Christian conjecture, it is not difficult to see how it arose. It presupposes the tradition of Lucan authorship of Luke-Acts. It assumes that Luke and Lucius are variants of the same name. It may have assumed, either from the Western Text of Acts xi. 27 ff. or independently, that Luke had Antiochian connexions, but it cannot have gone so far as did the tradition that made him an Antiochian native,[5] since it is able to identify him with Lucius of Cyrene. And it doubtless assumed, and quite correctly, that a historian usually does not mention himself in the third person by name, without at the same time suggesting his authorship. I suspect that the authors of this conjecture also knew the tradition that Luke was connected with Titus, for Zahn may well be right in regarding *Ticius* (i.e. Titius) as a variant for Titus.[6] Of course the name of Titus may have been added to this list of Christians at Antioch quite independently. Gal. ii. 1 implies that Titus had been at Antioch with Paul and Barnabas. But all these data could come to a second or third century writer from traditions which we have knowledge of from other sources, without necessarily having any real historical facts behind them.

Another instance of the same identification may be added to that of the anonymous Latin *Prophetiae ex omnibus libris collectae.* This is Ephrem Ephrem.

---

[1] In like manner the sentence in John xxi. 24, " This is the disciple that bears witness of these things and wrote these things," may be an interpretation of authorship based on the suggestion " If I will that he tarry (μένειν, *manere*) till I come."

[2] *Kommentar zum N.T.* iii.³ 735 f., v.² 400 f. *note.*

[3] *Ibid.* iii.³ 736 ff.

[4] See especially his *Urausgabe der Apostelgeschichte des Lucas* ( = *Forschungen zur Geschichte des N.T. Kanons*, ix. Teil), 1916, pp. 145-149, 250, 386 f.

[5] See Vol. II. pp. 247 f.          [6] Cf. the variants at Acts xviii. 7.

Syrus in the fourth century. The Armenian text of his Commentary on Acts, published in 1921, was not known to me when I wrote in Vol. II. p. 247, that except for the *Prophetiae* " there seems to be no early example of identification of Luke with Lucius of Cyrene," nor has Zahn apparently brought Ephrem yet into connexion with his favourite argument. Ephrem evidently makes the following comment on the successive verses Acts xii. 25, xiii. 1 [1]: " But Saul and Barnabas, who carried food for the saints in Jerusalem, returned with John who was called Mark and so did Luke of Cyrene. But both these are evangelists and wrote before the discipleship of Paul, and therefore he used to repeat everywhere from their gospel." The relation of this comment to the text of Acts is, as often in Ephrem, somewhat confused. Mark and Lucius of Cyrene are not really connected in the narrative. But, finding them close together, Ephrem evidently thought of them as the two evangelists Mark and Luke. In other words, for him Lucius of Cyrene is Lucas the author not only of the gospel but of the Acts as well.[2] I see no reason to suppose that Ephrem had any different text from the ordinary one in this passage. His identification of Luke with the Cyrenian is made on the basis of tradition or else independently.

Criticism of the identification.    The conjecture has not more to commend it than have most such conjectures. A Lucius born at Cyrene, who may subsequently have been included among the men of Cyrene that were scattered from Jerusalem and preached at Antioch, and who was to be found there before Paul and Barnabas started with John Mark for their journey to Cyprus and the cities in the interior of Asia Minor, might have written Luke and Acts. The author of Acts has a good deal of information about early Christians at both Jerusalem and Antioch, and mentions Cyrenians in the Levant.[3] Lucius of Cyrene might have been called alternatively by the shorter Lucas. He might even have been a doctor. There was a school of medicine at Cyrene. He could have been a Gentile or he could have been a Jew who read, spoke and wrote Greek.[4] Jews were abundant at Cyrene [5] and Cyrenians were to be found in Jerusalem. But there is no certainty that the name Lucas of Paul's beloved physician stands in this instance for Lucius, or that the author of Luke-Acts bore either name, or that either of them had had personal connexions with Cyrene, Jerusalem or Antioch.

[1] See Conybeare's translation, Vol. III. p. 416.
[2] *Ibid.* p. 380.
[3] Luke xxiii. 26 ; Acts ii. 10 ; vi. 9 ; xi. 20.
[4] It is sometimes argued that the author of Acts was a Gentile and not a Jew, that Luke as listed in Col. iv. 14 is not a Jew, while both Lucius of Romans xvi. 21 (cf. Deissmann, *loc. cit.* p. 438) and Lucius of Cyrene were Jews (Zahn, *Kommentar*, iii.[3] 735 f.). But the evidence in none of the four cases is decisive.
[5] See Schürer, *GJV.*[4]iii. pp. 52 f. ; Juster, *Les Juifs*, i. p. 207 ; 1 Macc. xv. 23; Josephus, *C. Apion.* ii. 4 ; *Antiq.* xiv. 7. 2. Simon of Cyrene, the father of Alexander and Rufus (Mark xv. 21) was doubtless a Jew of the diaspora. His sons' names are brought together in the examples of substitutions to which the rabbis objected (see Vol. IV. p. 14). The patriarchs in Egypt " did not call Reuben Rufus nor Benjamin Alexander." See Eb. Nestle, *Expos. Times*, x., 1899, p. 527.

One other name or spelling should be mentioned in this connexion—
Λεύκιος. Though it occurs nowhere in the Greek New Testament, it
alternates with Λούκιος as a representative of the Latin *Lucius*. Moulton
and Milligan [1] give examples from as early as the second century B.C.,
and mention Nachmanson's supposition that it comes from a genuine
Greek name Λεύκιος (from λευκός). In early Christianity the name is
associated with the author of the oldest of the apocryphal Acts. Photius
(*Bibl.* cod. 114) read a work called the "itineraries of the Apostles in which
were included acts of Peter, John, Andrew, Thomas, Paul. The writer
of them, as the same book declares, is Leucius Charinus." The extant
texts of apocryphal Acts do not include the author's name, but the reference
to such Acts (especially those of John and Andrew) as written by Leucius
is as old as the fifth century.[2] The Fathers do not suggest that Leucius
is identical with Luke ; on the contrary they regarded him and his writings
as heretical. He is mentioned here because, whether a real person or imaginary, his name's resemblance to that of the canonical author may have been
influential in giving these apocrypha at one time the respect they enjoyed.
Is it possible that the name was invented or guessed on the assumption
of Lucan authorship ? The Canon of Muratori may well have meant to
attribute to Luke not only the canonical Acts, but also, in separate writing,
the apocryphal records of the death of Peter and the departure of Paul for
Spain. This suggestion was not only made by Pfister, in a study of the
end of Acts to which I have referred elsewhere,[3] but earlier by M. R.
James, whose words I shall quote. After discussing other evidence for
knowledge of the Leucian Acta by the author of the canon of Muratori
he says [4] :

"In the obscure and difficult passage which deals with the Acts of the
Apostles these words occur : 'sicuti et semote passionem Petri evidenter
declarat, sed et profectionem Pauli ab urbe ad Spaniam proficiscentis.'
Now the undoubtedly Leucian *Actus Petri cum Simone* (called, from the
unique MS. which contains them, the *Actus Petri Vercellensis*) begin, in
the form in which we have them, with the *profectio Pauli ab urbe in Spaniam*
and end with the *passio Petri*. It seems as if the author of the Muratorian
Fragment must have had the Acts of Peter in his mind. How then does
he apparently come to attribute to St. Luke a narrative which Luke did
not write ? Can it be that there was in his mind a confusion between Lucas
and Leucius ? Or is it possible that the person whom we know as Leucius
intended his readers to understand that Lucas was the writer of the
romances to which the name of Leucius is attached ? "

---

[1] *Vocabulary of the Greek N.T.* p. 381; cf. Moulton, *Grammar of N.T.
Greek*, ii. p. 88.

[2] Augustine, *Contra Felicem*, ii. 6, and other passages quoted by Lake and de
Zwaan in Hastings, *D.A.C.* i. 29 ff.

[3] See above in Addit. Note 26, pp. 336 ff.

[4] *Apocrypha Anecdota. Second Series* ( = *Texts and Studies*, v. 1), 1897, pp. x f.

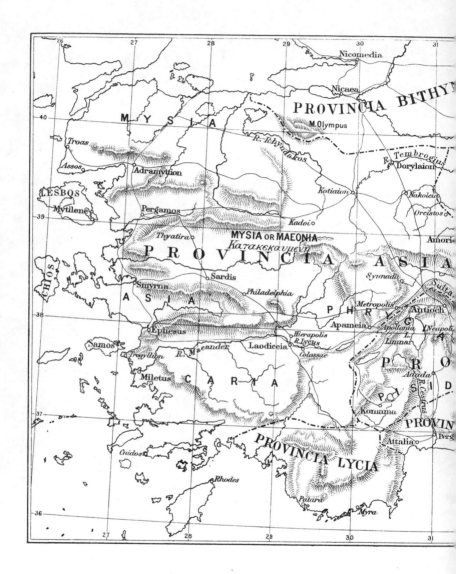

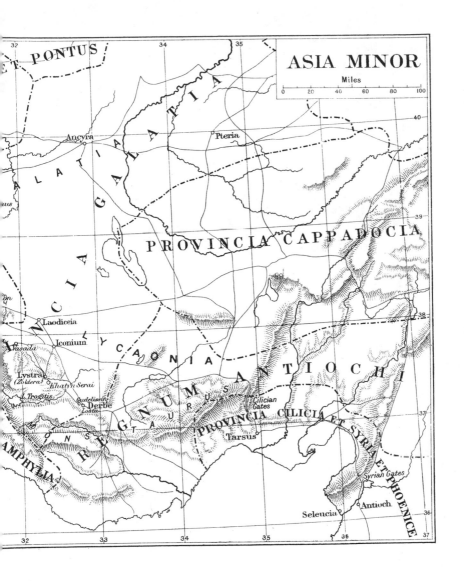

ASIA MINOR

Miles

0    20    40    60    80    100

PONTUS

GALATIA

Ancyra

Pteria

PROVINCIA CAPPADOCIA

Laodiceia

Iconium

LYCAONIA

Vasada

Lystra
(Zoldera)

Khatyn Serai

L. Trogitis

Gudelissin
Lostra

Derbe

TAURUS

ANTIOCHI

Cilician
Gates

REGNUM

TAURUS

PROVINCIA CILICIA ET SYRIA ET PHOENICE

Tarsus

AMPHYLIA

Syrian Gates

Seleucia

Antioch

# INDICES

# INDEX I

## PLACES, NAMES, AND SUBJECTS

# INDEX II

## QUOTATIONS

### (a) Old and New Testaments

2 M 2

## (b) Apocrypha and Pseudepigrapha of the Old Testament

## (c) Rabbinic Writings

M. = Mishna, T. = Tosefta, Bab. = Babylonian Talmud, Jer. = Jerusalem Talmud.

## (d) Classical and Early Christian Writers

# INDEX III

## PALAEOGRAPHICAL AND EPIGRAPHICAL

### (a) INSCRIPTIONS

## (b) Papyri

(For abbreviations see Vol. IV. Index III. (b))

## (c) Biblical Apparatus Criticus

# INDEX IV

## GREEK WORDS

545

# INDEX V

## SEMITIC WORDS AND TERMS

# Date Due

DEMCO NO. 25-370